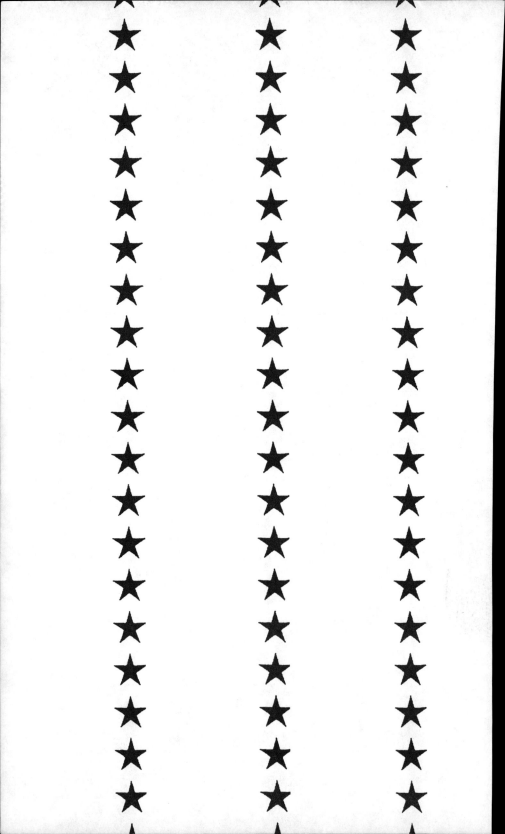

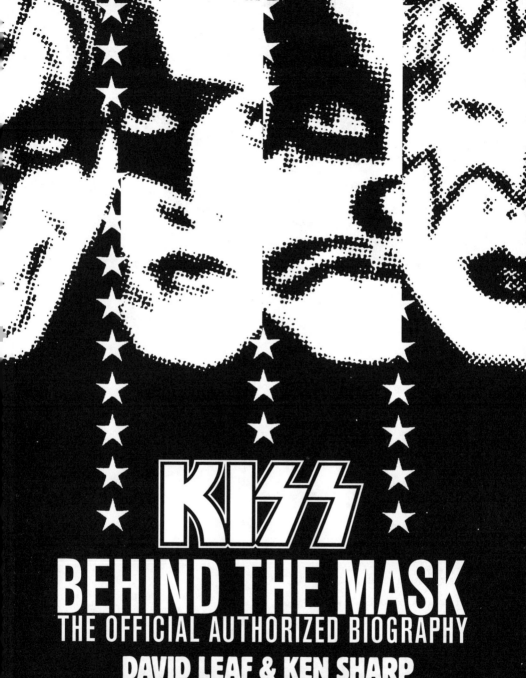

KISS

BEHIND THE MASK
THE OFFICIAL AUTHORIZED BIOGRAPHY

DAVID LEAF & KEN SHARP

WARNER BOOKS

An AOL Time Warner Company

ALL RIGHTS RESERVED.
WARNER BOOKS, INC., 1271 AVENUE OF THE AMERICAS, NEW YORK, NY 10020
VISIT OUR WEB SITE AT WWW.TWBOOKMARK.COM.

 AN AOL TIME WARNER COMPANY
PRINTED IN THE UNITED STATES OF AMERICA
FIRST PRINTING: OCTOBER 2003

10 9 8 7 6 5 4 3 2 1
THE LIBRARY OF CONGRESS CATALOGING-IN-PUBLICATION DATA
Leaf, David.
    Kiss : behind the mask : the official authorized biography / David Leaf
and Ken Sharp.
        p. cm.
    Includes index
    ISBN 0-446-53073-5
    1. Kiss (Musical group) 2. Rock musicians—United States—Biography.
I. Sharp, Ken. II. Title.

ML421.K57L43 2003
782.42166'092'2—dc21
    [B]   2003049694

UNDER LICENSE BY
SIGNATURES
NETWORK

DAVID WOULD LIKE TO DEDICATE
THIS BOOK TO A TRUE ROCK 'N' ROLLER,
MICHELE MYER, AND TO KEN SHARP,
WITHOUT WHOM THIS BOOK WOULD
STILL BE JUST AN UNPUBLISHED
MANUSCRIPT.

KEN WOULD LIKE TO DEDICATE THIS
BOOK TO HIS MOM FOR ALWAYS
BELIEVING…

CONTENTS

IF YOU ARE NOT A KISS FAN, PUT THIS BOOK DOWN. NOW

PREFACE

GOOD. ARE THEY ALL GONE? JUST CHECKING TO MAKE SURE WE'VE GOTTEN RID OF THE NONBELIEVERS. THIS BOOK ISN'T FOR THEM.

So, as you clearly are a KISS fan, take this book home, put a CD (*Dressed to Kill* or *Alive!* or *Destroyer* or *Love Gun*—pick your favorite) in your CD player, press Play, and sit back and read the most detailed, comprehensive biography ever written on your favorite band.

Now, as you're about to find out, this book is a collaboration presented in two parts, sort of like the DVD of a movie with lots of stuff added to the original release. Except this book never came out when it was supposed to back in 1980.

The narrative text that I wrote in 1979 (the first third of this book) was the result of KISS literally letting their hair down for what was supposed to be their authorized biography—their personal story of how they became KISS. The rest of the book is drawn from Ken Sharp's one-of-a-kind compendium of information about their music and career, gathered from hundreds of exclusive interviews Ken has conducted over the years.

The truth is, this book is essentially in your hands because of the passion KISS inspires in Ken. I'll get to that story in a second, but first, let me tell you about my own close encounter with the band and what it meant to me.

While my time alone with KISS would ultimately be relatively brief, it was certainly memorable. At that time—when I first met them—I probably appeared to be yet another smart-ass New York rock writer. (I was/am a smart-ass, but despite having previously written biographies of Brian Wilson and the Bee Gees, I really never considered myself to be a rock writer.) Was I somebody who respected what they had accomplished? They needn't have been concerned. My background is in journalism, and I knew that theirs would be a great tale. I didn't have an agenda. As a reporter, I was ready to hear their stories; I was fascinated to learn, from their point-of-view, about KISS's birth and their journey to iconic status.

My journey to the center of America began with my flight from New York to meet the band in Des Moines, Iowa. At the time I remember thinking about the odd intersection of my trip's itinerary with the Pope's American tour. Here I was, writing a story about a group who were considered by fanatical critics to be "Knights In Satan's Service," and it seemed that at just about every airport I flew into or out of (Chicago's O'Hare, Des Moines, et al.), my flight was delayed by the papal plane.

Now, in the midst of all of these papal goings on, when it came to KISS I must admit I was an agnostic. Didn't believe in 'em, but didn't think there was anything wrong with those who did. Actually, what I did know about KISS was mainly gleaned from one of my first jobs in Los Angeles: a short stint in the Casablanca Records mailroom, where I packed envelopes for the KISS Army. So I knew KISS had a large and loyal following, but other than that, when I headed out on the road to work with them on their authorized biography, I really didn't know what to expect. What I found were four very different men inside the very strange bubble of rock 'n' roll stardom.

It was the early fall of 1979 when I hit the road. Arriving in Des Moines, I took a taxi from the airport to the Holiday Inn, checked in, and went up to my room to wait for KISS to arrive so I could get to work. I learned very quickly that being on the road can be really boring. Believe me, there is nothing glamorous about waiting for a phone call from the road manager in a hotel room at two in the afternoon.

I hadn't been in my room for fifteen minutes before I began to feel the intense claustrophobia of being in the middle of nowhere. In that pre-cable universe, the TV in my room got only the three local channels and they were all tuned to the Pope saying mass. Considering the typical rock 'n' roll circus I was about to join, I probably should have been asking for absolution in advance. But listening to the mass, which was in Latin, really wasn't the kind of diversion I was looking for. And even though I had studied the language for three years in high school, I didn't remember much more than *Veni, vidi, vici. Porto, portare,* ad nauseam.

The walls of the Holiday Inn room closing in on me, I headed down to the lobby, hoping that the group had arrived so I could introduce myself to the road manager and meet the guys. Sitting in the entranceway with me were several KISS fans. They were hoping to get an autograph and a glimpse of Gene, Paul, Ace, and Peter without their makeup.

For the moment, I was happy to just observe. I watched as first Gene, then Paul, Ace, and Peter came in, greeted the fans, and signed as many albums as the fans had with them. I was curious and surprised. I had thought, incorrectly of course, that nobody knew what they looked like without their makeup, but these fans not only knew, but were thrilled to meet their heroes. As for KISS, sure, they looked and carried themselves like rock 'n' roll stars, but they clearly were also people who appreciated their fans.

Not too long after they checked in, I began doing interviews. As I explained to the band, my job was to be a recorder—I would totally put aside my musical tastes, essentially stay out of the way and let KISS talk directly to their fans, and reveal from the band's point of view the tale of how these four boys from New York had created this incredible rock 'n' roll institution.

The guys had every reason to be wary of me. I anticipated that they might be tired of explaining themselves. That turned out to be another miscalculation on my part. They couldn't have been more open or more gracious. They had already had so much experience with "outsiders" that they had apparently learned to size people up instantly, to decide right away whether or not a newcomer could be trusted. With me, it was less of an issue because I was on their team. I had been sent to help them tell their story, not my version of their story. This book was to be in their words. But still, when you're telling people your dreams and secrets, at some point, you make the decision to trust them. And I can tell you that without hesitation, the four members of KISS really couldn't have been more open to my questions.

I think I interviewed Peter first. He breezily told me his New York story, although we were frequently interrupted by the baseball playoff game that was on in the background. His beautiful then-girlfriend and soon-to-be-wife (now his ex-wife) was from Southern California, and she was anxiously rooting the Angels on, hoping they would make their first World Series. (They finally did last year.)

After a couple of hours with Peter, it was on to Paul, who couldn't have been friendlier or more accommodating. I don't think I interviewed Gene until after the Des Moines show. I'm not sure. What I am sure of is that my favorite memory of Gene was the amazing stack of photo albums he showed me. In the midst of his first "adult" romance (with Cher), those photos were his constant companions on tour. That notorious three-foot-high collection of souvenirs was a rock 'n' roll fantasy anybody could relate to.

Having met the guys, it was time to head out to the arena. I went with them backstage, spent the pre-show meal hanging around observing the routine, and stayed with them until just before they headed off for makeup. While they prepared for the show, I wandered the floor of the arena, trying to get a sense of the excitement that was building. Finally, as the lights dimmed, the screams of delight (*Our heroes are here! In Des Moines!*) made it very clear that what was about to happen was vitally important for the ten thousand fans gathered here. A major life's moment.

In memory, the show is a blur. I know I saw all the legendary signature moments, from Peter's levitating drum riser to Gene's fire-breathing and amazing tongue displays, to Ace's smoking guitar, and Paul's death-defying leaps. Other than that, I don't remember much. Except for the party after the concert.

Actually, before there could be a party, I had a lot more work to do. I needed to talk to Ace. And for him, the hotel bar was the obvious place. So as he held court, and as I politely downed what was for me a lot of alcohol (three glasses of wine), Ace told me his story. When the bar closed, Ace informed me (and everybody else within earshot) that while the interview was over, it was time for the party to move upstairs. All were invited, but what happened at the party was definitely off the record.

The party bled into the wee hours, and just as quickly as my time with KISS had begun, it was over. I said goodbye the next day, and I was on a plane back home to start writing. Truth is, I think I got more out of my brief tenure with KISS than I had expected. I believe it was through KISS that I finally came to understand the visceral pull of rock music—why KISS wasn't about critics and awards but about young people (mostly pre-teen and teenage boys) for whom KISS was the ultimate dream.

In rock-critic bullshit, I might have written that "in pre–World War II America, kids in small towns used to dream about running away from home and joining the circus. During the past forty years, that dream was replaced by the goal to escape the traditional workaday world by joining a rock 'n' roll band. For kids everywhere, going to see KISS fulfilled both those dreams." Maybe that's true. I don't really know. But I do know that for me, the dream that KISS fulfilled, however briefly, was my fantasy of being on the road with a rock 'n' roll band.

I had enjoyed my audience with the group, gathered their stories, and now it was time to retreat to my Southern California apartment and spin their anecdotes into a book that was going to be called *KISS: Behind the Mask*. And so I got to work. The idea of the title was that what they said in the interviews would reveal the people underneath the makeup. It wouldn't be a book about their music so much as it would be about how the four of them came together to embark upon this incredible journey.

In early 1980, after submitting the manuscript, I heard that the biography you're about to read would not be coming out. I was never told exactly what the problem was. I consigned the pile of pages to storage in a box that over the years was shoved further and further to the back of my life. And that's where it remained for a long, long time.

Then, about a decade ago, fate intervened. One day, while Ken Sharp was visiting Los Angeles, Elliot Kendall, a musician and mutual friend, introduced us over lunch. That day, talking about rock 'n' roll experiences, I mentioned that I had once written a book about KISS. Ken said, "No, you didn't." I said, "Yes, I did." Ken said, "It's impossible. I've read everything ever written about the group."

When I informed him that this was an unpublished manuscript, it was if I had just thrown a giant electrical switch. Ken's eyes lit up with excitement, the zeal of a true believer. He told me how big a fan he was of KISS, and that he had to read the book. I told him it was buried in storage, but if he would help me look for it, he could read it. Ken didn't hesitate, and he insisted on spending the afternoon digging through a huge pile of boxes to find it. He couldn't wait. He had to have it. Now.

After a brief excavation, we found the wrinkled pages, which we took to a nearby copy store. Ken took the manuscript back to Philadelphia, and called me the next day, brimming with enthusiasm. He said, "We have to get this out." And so began our odyssey toward the book you're holding, and that's really where this greatly expanded book begins.

Ken persuaded me that every KISS fan would love to read what I'd done because "There's nothing like this about KISS. They've never spoken publicly about their past in so much detail. Nothing like it had ever been written about them." I asked what he meant, and Ken explained that everything else written about KISS had focused on the music or the circus or the behind-the-scenes business machinations. But nowhere, Ken preached to me, not in any interview or any book, had the members of KISS spoken at such length about their roots, their personal lives, their dreams, how they met each other . . . the story of how they became KISS.

More than anything, it was Ken's determination that rescued the manuscript from the scrap heap, so you have him to thank. Personally, I'm indebted to him for helping me save a fascinating part of my life. A short while ago, as I was retyping it, I read my manuscript for the first time in twenty years. And I had the fun of reliving an experience that now feels like ten lifetimes ago.

But you should know that even as all these memories came rushing back to me, the one thing I did not do was rewrite the original manuscript. I took the advice of Ken (who is my KISS guru) that because what I had worked on in 1979 was a unique time capsule in KISStory, it should be printed as is. Yeah, I fixed up the grammar a bit, and I checked the spelling. Made a few things that I wrote clearer (I hope). And Ken (and several very devoted KISStorians) helped me correct some misinformation. After all, there's no real virtue in being purposely stupid. But the manuscript as published in this book is virtually unchanged. Uncensored. Unaltered from what would have come out in the year 1980.

What you're about to read is KISS's story, as they told it to me over twenty years ago. I hope you enjoy it as much as Ken did. But before you get there, it's Ken's turn. As Paul Harvey would say, "Here's the rest of the story...."

—DAVID LEAF

Introduced to KISS in the fall of 1975 by Dennis Martin, a long-haired, guitar-playing neighbor, I was magically transported by the raw, primal sounds of their music and a stage show that would rival the Ringling Bros. and Barnum & Bailey Circus.

My real baptism by fire into the KISS world came on March 24, 1976—the day I attended my first KISS concert, held at the Civic Center in Philadelphia. It was the *Alive!* tour. Mr. Ackler, my Three Tuns Junior High School teacher, took me and several friends to the concert. He was a brave man.

Intermingling with thousands of beer-swilling rock 'n' roll hellcats, and with the sweet smell of marijuana wafting through the arena, Mr. Ackler was clearly out of his element and this was his night in hell. He sat stonefaced in his chair for the entire show, almost like he was Krazy-Glued into his seat. Wearing a helpless look on his face, a little like a hostage in an insane asylum, or someone who spent a month at the Bates Motel, Mr. Ackler was spooked, seemingly immobilized by the madness and decibel-shattering volume of this rock 'n' roll party. One thing's for certain, Mr. Ackler couldn't wait for the final chords of the set closer, "Let Me Go, Rock 'n' Roll" to dissipate so he could vacate the arena and return as quickly as possible to the warm bosom of suburbia. But I was having the time of my life.

I remember being mesmerized when the arena finally went dark and a cascading rainbow of flickering lights covered the entire venue, reflected off a giant mirror ball hanging from the ceiling. As dense clouds of fog began to engulf the stage, a deafening explosion of flashpots and bombs signaled the appearance of KISS. An impressionable thirteen-year-old kid, I was awestruck in the presence of these larger-than-life superheroes, who wielded their instruments like alien gunslingers. Temporarily blinded by the flashing lights of the huge KISS sign, my eardrums felt like they were ready to burst—and I liked it. Screaming my lungs out while playing a mean air guitar, this symphony of rawness and rebellion was all I needed and ignited my enduring passion for the band. I would never be the same.

Forget school. What did algebra, science, and U.S. history have to do with the fire-breathing antics of KISS? I religiously read all the rock magazines—*Creem, Circus, Circus Raves, Hit Parader,* and *Rock Scene*—scouring them for the latest kernels of information about my favorite group. As a loyal, card-carrying member of their fan club I also regularly kept up with the activities of the band through my KISS Army newsletters and *Flash,* perhaps the earliest KISS fanzine. There were also several quickie KISS books published back in the '70s. The most impressive was *KISS* by Robert Duncan, which chronicled the band's career with equal doses of irreverent humor and solid historical information. But I, like many other KISS fans, hungered for the real story, a book that would draw me that much closer to the hottest band in the world.

Fast-forward to the early '90s. Little did I know that I'd have to wait that long until I found *that* book. But I have to admit that from the moment I began to read the book I literally couldn't put it down. And, as the book was written in 1979, fading memories and a temptation on the part of the band members to rewrite their KISStory wasn't an issue. After all, only six years had passed since these four struggling musicians were rehearsing in a freezing loft on 10 East 23rd Street, eating turkey sandwiches on Thanksgiving.

Around the same time as my first meeting with David, I had embarked on my own project, endeavoring to assemble a KISS oral history book. The project would comprise extensive interviews with the band, their inner circle, and their musical contemporaries ranging from Pete Townshend to Alice Cooper. Shortly after beginning my research, a lightbulb went on in my head, burning incandescently like the one stuck in Uncle Fester's mouth. Why didn't David and I join forces and compile our own KISS book? Thirteen years of exhaustive research ensued, and with it the accumulation of over fifteen hundred pages of original interviews with KISS and members of their inner sanctum.

Now in 2003, here are the fruits of our labor: David's original unchanged manuscript as first written in 1979 supplemented by my vast archive of original interviews. We hope you'll agree with us that this intimate oral history, as told by KISS, has been worth the wait. Dig in and enjoy.

—KEN SHARP

THE RISE TO THE TOP

★ ★ ★ ★ ★

BY DAVID LEAF

SECTION

01

This never-before-published manuscript was completed in 1979, and it has not been rewritten for this book. Featuring exclusive interviews with KISS, it is, in retrospect, a snapshot of KISS at the moment in the fall of 1979 when I spent a few days on the road with them. Had the interviews taken place in 1976 or 1982 or 1989 or '99, this book would undoubtedly have unfolded from a very different perspective. I believe that what makes this version of the KISS story so unique is that it's how they felt and what was on their minds at a time when they were still riding their first wave of success . . . before the first split. The nature of memory being what it is, if Gene, Paul, Peter, and Ace were to read this in 2003, I'm sure that some of the things they've said would make them laugh and some would make them shake their heads in disbelief. There will undoubtedly be some things they've completely forgotten, and there may even be a few things they wish they'd never said. I hope that, like me, they'll find the charm of this original manuscript is in the relative innocence we all were experiencing when it was created.

Since 1979, as you'll read in sections TWO and THREE, the four original members of KISS have survived some serious bumps in the road, some ups and downs. But in 1979, when I had the pleasure to help them tell their story in their own words, this is how it came out. As fans of the group, I only hope that you'll find special insight and inspiration in what they've said, and that what you read will only enhance your love of and devotion to your favorite group.

★ INTRODUCTION: 1979 ★★★★★★

The lights are extinguished to the roar of an impatient crowd. A powerful chord echoes throughout the arena as clouds of smoke fill the stage. Out of the mist, KISS appears, striking superhero poses as they are elevated to the top of the set. Their arrival is greeted with messianic fervor. *They* are *here!*

Then, the first note is struck, and for the next ninety minutes, nobody is still. The three front men are in perpetual motion, teasing their fans, whipping up the audience into a frenzy, playing with and off each other, performing incredible stunts amidst the rock 'n' roll. Gene, the blood-spitting, fire-breathing Demon, stalking the stage with lizard tongue in thigh-high boots . . . Paul, alternately leaping about or strutting the stage, the androgynous-sexual Starchild, the love object of all, the focus of all the sexual tension that the others create . . . Ace, the man from space, in silver mask and boots, shooting off raucous guitar licks into the stratosphere like a rock 'n' roll Flash Gordon . . . and in the back, Peter, perched on his levitating drums, surrounded by his giant cats, sitting bewhiskered and powerful, the Catman drummer, pounding out the beat to the heat.

Of course, it can't be taken in all at once. The first thing that catches your eye is the huge, winking electric logo: KISS. In big, bright bold neon, the name leaps at you, strong and sexy, like a Times Square marquee. The bombs explode, the lights flash, the fireworks shoot into the sky. To the uninitiated, a KISS concert is an assault on the senses, a decibel blitz and a visual invasion. To their fans, a KISS show is a high mass and most anybody attending their first KISS concert is converted. The lure of the carnival is irresistible. A KISS concert is a combination of Halloween, the Fourth of July, and a trip to the circus, and it's as full of wonderful surprises as Christmas morning.

Long before the faithful would have it, the evening is ending as the band (and the crowd) sings the first national anthem of KISS, the song that sums up their philosophy and appeal: "Rock and Roll All Nite."

Then, suddenly, it's over, and Gene, Paul, Peter, and Ace dash offstage, leaving behind thousands of satisfied fans.

When I first began this project, I had never seen KISS in concert, and their music was not part of my record collection. My images of KISS were the stereotypical ones—I thought they were a loud, unsubtle, obnoxious, antiquated rock group that wore hideous makeup and did all sorts of outrageous things onstage. From what little I knew, they were certainly not cut from the same cloth as my '60s heroes like the Beatles and Muhammad Ali. What I soon found out, though, was that KISS is a religion for millions of fans.

So I felt that I had been entrusted with a difficult task. Gene, Paul, Peter, and Ace were heroes to millions of kids who knew them only with their makeup on. My job was to get beyond the makeup, to go beneath the surface, to find out what they're really like.

But was that a good idea?

As I watched my first KISS concert, I began to feel a bit like Toto in *The Wizard of Oz*. Do you remember the scene near the end of the movie when the Wizard's wrath is being visited upon Dorothy, the Scarecrow, the Tin Woodsman, and the Cowardly Lion? While the Wizard is berating the heroic foursome, the little dog Toto spots a curtain off to the side, scurries over, and pulls it back, revealing an elderly gentleman manipulating some complicated machinery. And we all soon find out that *this* ordinary-looking man is masquerading as the great and powerful Oz.

When I first met KISS without their elaborate costumes and bizarre makeup, I wondered whether they too would be unexceptional. After all, onstage, they are so much larger than life. Would it be like meeting Clark Kent but not Superman?

The answer was quickly forthcoming. There was *nothing* about these men that was average, and as it turns out, like their stage personae, offstage they were as unlike each other as was imaginable. But similar to their characters, the members of KISS were four distinct and powerful people, different from one another even as they shared the common and unique bond of KISS.

What put these men onstage as KISS is a tale of remarkable drive, determination, and ambition. Separately, they struggled, but when they found one another, their talents blended to create KISS. This, then, is the personal KISStory of one of the most popular bands in rock 'n' roll history.

For some reason, I find myself writing about dogs a lot in this introduction. On *Rocky and His Friends*, a TV cartoon show that was popular when I was a kid, there was a clever dog named Mr. Peabody who spent his days "time traveling." I can hear him now. Listen. "Into the Wayback Machine, Sherman," he's saying to his faithful human companion. "Set the dials for 1950. New York City. We're going to meet four kids who will eventually become world-famous. Their names are Chaim Witz, Stanley Eisen, Peter Criscuola, and Paul Frehley. Collectively, their name is KISS."

—DAVID LEAF, LOS ANGELES, 1979

TONGUE TIED:
THE BAT LIZARD

Chapter **01**

The magic is done. The Wayback Machine has deposited us along the banks of the Mediterranean Sea, thousands of miles from the New York origins of KISS. Chaim Witz, later to become Gene Simmons, details his heritage. "My parents were born in Jand, Hungary, a small town on the Danube River. During World War II, my mother was in a concentration camp, and her mother, her brother, her grandmother, and most of her family were killed. After the war, my parents met in a way station, got married, and snuck into Israel. They didn't return to Hungary because Hungary, like a lot of countries, wasn't interested in taking back the Jews that were still alive. I was born August 25, 1949, in the port city of Haifa."

"When I was very young, we moved to the village of Carmel, where the Scrolls of Carmel were discovered. As a small child, I remember playing on a hill that had these little caves. There was always lots of stuff around, but I never gave it much thought. It turns out that some of the oldest specimens of human beings were discovered there. Everybody in America has the impression of Israel being the land of kibbutzes, but it's not. Israel is the most modern country in the Middle East. It's very Americanized. I remember in 1955 and '56, watching Jeff Chandler movies where he played Cochise. My first exposure to American culture was seeing the Indians in those movies. The language sounded very alien, like gibberish, and the Indians looked like they were from another planet."

In Israel, Gene was "a marbles champ. Marbles was the national pastime, and I was *it*. I was pretty good at tops, but marbles is where I killed everybody." Gene doesn't have any musical memories from those days, but he does recall "one thing that made me start wearing all the spider jewelry. It begins with the fact that in Israel, when you go into a public place, you wear your yarmulke. One day, I tried to put mine on before I left home, and for some reason, I just couldn't get it on my head. So I took it off, and the biggest daddy longlegs crawled out of the hat. Without exaggeration, it must have been two inches long. I was scared to death and it gave me nightmares. When I came to America, I suddenly realized that one of the ways to overcome fear is to confront it. So I started wearing spider jewelry. Now, I wear all kinds of this stuff that are gifts from fans. At my home, I've got an amazing collection of spiders."

In 1955, Gene's parents were divorced, and Gene and his mother, who had two brothers living in the U.S., emigrated to America in June of 1958. It was in America that Chaim became known as Gene Klein. "We first lived in the Williamsburg section of Brooklyn. It was a ghetto right across the border from Bedford Stuyvesant, which is now all black, but at that point it was turning into a Latino neighborhood. Our rent was $36 a month, and my mother went to work picking lint off clothes for $24 a week in the Bronx, a long subway ride from home. So I was alone most of the day."

American culture was so strange that almost everything Gene saw seemed bizarre. "There were some posters left over from Christmas, a Coca-Cola advertisement with Santa Claus drinking a Coke. I couldn't believe my eyes. First of all, I never heard of Santa Claus, and I thought he was a rabbi, because he had a beard. To me, the world was filled with Jews and Arabs, and that was it. In Israel, we never heard of Catholics or Christians. Never heard of Jesus Christ *at all*."

Gene's days in this new and foreign land were basically divided into two parts. Every day, for ten hours, he attended a yeshiva, a Jewish private school. In every other free moment, Gene's attention was focused on his two new loves—television and monsters. Making friends had never been easy for Gene, and the language barrier made it even more troublesome. Gene: "My difficulty in learning English definitely had an effect on me. I had trouble fitting in with the kids in the neighborhood. I was a loner for a while, partly because I was always out to prove that I was better than everyone I met. Since I couldn't speak a word of English at first, every time I opened my mouth, the kids would start laughing. So we played marbles. Laugh they did, but in the end, I walked away clutching tons of marbles. I still have them."

Those early years in America were a solitary time for Gene. "From the time I was nine till I was eleven, I was too busy watching TV to make friends. That was the only way I could learn the language. Because of the strong New York accents, I couldn't understand anything people said to me. The good diction I have now is a result of imitating what I heard on television."

A magazine called *Famous Monsters of Filmland* and superhero comic books (like *Superman*) became Gene's passion, partly because they were visual media, something that could be understood without knowing too much English. "The concept of anybody dressing up in outlandish outfits just attracted me. I guess what I really wanted was to have people look at me. Everything was so foreign and strange to me, and I wanted to overcome the language difficulty. I wanted to fit in."

One of Gene's most unusual memories is "the sound of American coins. Very strange to me. It sounded fake, like iron. I couldn't figure out why the coins made so much noise when people would jingle them around in their pockets. I thought it was a custom."

According to Gene, his days at the yeshiva "fulfilled everything that my mother thought I should be getting in terms of history and culture. But [after school] I'd get as much TV as I could, from *The Mickey Mouse Club* to *Yancy Derringer* and other great [now] obscure shows that I loved. What attracted me to shows like *Superman* was that these people were superhuman. The only place I'd heard about superhuman beings and people who could do things I couldn't was in religious books. But these guys on television were super and neat, and they weren't telling anybody what to do or think. Superman never told you what to do. He just flew around and did all this stuff that these religious guys were doing, without being a pain in the ass about it.

"This was my first connection with the anti-establishment. Guys like Tarzan and Yancy Derringer didn't have superpowers, but they were able to do things that I couldn't do. And they weren't boring about it. They were just themselves, didn't tell anybody how to dress or think. And they always looked completely different from everybody else. When Superman walked into a room, you noticed him. Nobody else dressed like that. I believe that this relates very strongly to what KISS does today."

In 1961, Gene and his mother moved to the Jackson Heights section of Queens, in New York City, and Gene transferred to public school. This less demanding school atmosphere gave Gene more time for his hobbies, including his first ventures into the world of fantasy. "As soon as I learned how to type, when I was thirteen, I started writing my own stories. I created a prehistoric character, Omar: The Cliff Dweller, and wrote stories about him. I would mimeograph them and hand them out in school. One of them was a composition that I got an A+ on.

"As far back as the fifth grade, I remember thinking that dinosaurs were very special. There was a science fair where I won second prize for making clay dinosaurs demonstrating the eating chain. It's interesting that Paul started drawing dinosaurs when he was five years old. Sometimes on tour, Paul and I will test each other about dinosaurs. One of my favorites was the pterodactyl. It has this bony structure at the end of its head that it used to whack its victims into unconsciousness. In terms of my stage image with the long tongue and the bun on top of my head, I think there's an interesting similarity."

Gene's interests in science fact and fiction date back to his earliest TV-viewing days. "I was very bored by *The Hardy Boys Go Eat Lunch*. So what? *I* was doing more exciting things than that. What *was* exciting to me was Superman going to Planet X to fight some evil character."

In his early teens, Gene's fascination with superheroes led him into publishing "amateur science fiction publications called fanzines which dealt with horror movies, comic books, as well as science fiction. These magazines would have reviews and short stories and small comic strips. I'd write most of the articles, and there were a few contributions from others. Some of my pen pal friends from those days have become editors at Marvel Comics and professional writers." For Gene, "the fanzines were giving me a sort of intellectual satiation. Also, I made a little money with which I bought a used mimeograph machine for $35."

Making money has always been important to Gene, and from his early teens through the early days of KISS, he has always had several jobs. It was his very industriousness that provided him with a firsthand sexual education. "In seventh grade, I delivered newspapers. A girl on my route's parents were away for vacation. She was in the eighth grade. Once a week, I'd go there to collect. One week, she paid me. She seduced me. I lost my virginity on Christmas Eve of 1963.

"It was around that time when my tongue just started to pop out of my mouth. At a party in early '64, I was slow-dancing with Irene Wouters. Some prankster turned off the lights, and Irene and I started necking and she stuck her tongue in my mouth. I almost threw up. But then, I started to do it to girls. At first, they'd say, 'Yucch.' Then, we'd compare tongues." Gene notes, tongue-in-cheek, "I never really had to hang around street corners for any of that stuff."

In analyzing his personality, Gene thinks that the fact he's "never been afraid of failure" is the key to his makeup. "It's okay for me to fail. I've never been afraid of asking people something, because even if they say no, there's always somebody who'll say yes.

"In my late teens, I weighed 220 pounds. I actually went and fitted myself for a training bra. I had a paunch, a beard that stretched under my chin, and a mustache. I was pretty hideous, but it never seemed to bother me. The big problem with fat people is what it does to their minds. Not me. I was fat for my first two years of college. When I was twenty, I lived with a girl for a short time, and she treated me like King Tut, which meant cakes every day. I would eat all of them. The point is, the biggest thing about being shy or being fat is that people are afraid of rejection. As soon as people understand that it's okay not to be liked by some people, they're better off."

Gene's career as a performer is a direct outgrowth of his philosophy. As he puts it, "'Go ahead, don't be afraid to take the first step, thinking you're going to fail, because then you're going to be standing still.' I was always interested in being in front of people. I guess it's called having a large ego. I was always in school plays through junior high, high school, and college. In fifth grade, I was Little John in *Robin Hood*. I played Curly in *Oklahoma!* In college, I was in James Thurber's *The Stork Who Married a Dumb Wife*. I played the French doctor who operated on women."

Gene feels that if he hadn't been able to perform, "if I had never gotten ego gratification, I would probably have had to do something very extreme to get it. I started getting into rock 'n' roll because I noticed that you got instant gratification from seeing people in the audience getting off on you."

Gene's introduction to rock 'n' roll came in 1962. "I became a big Chubby Checker fan, and learned how to twist. [Checker's "The Twist" was a number one record in 1960 *and* 1961 and launched a huge social phenomenon.] I was the twist champ of P.S. 145, Joseph Pulitzer Junior High School, two years in a row. It was a social tool, a way to meet girls." At a typical dance, Gene recalls, "the boys were on one side of the room, the girls on the other, and nobody would cross the floor. So I used to walk over and ask the black girls, 'cause they were the ones who knew how to twist. The white girls didn't know how. But I never wanted to *be* Chubby Checker, 'cause I could do it by being on the dance floor.

"Then, I saw that one show that everybody saw that changed all of our lives, the Beatles on *The Ed Sullivan Show* in February of '64. The thing that struck me was that they were like four Chubby Checkers, four guys who were being front men and each important to the band. Also, the four of them looked as if they belonged to the same band. They certainly looked different from everybody walking the street. Nobody looked like them, and because of that, people ridiculed them. At first, I couldn't make too much out of it. I just thought they were kind of weird. Meanwhile, my mom was watching with me, and she kept harping about how terrible it was. I didn't think it was bad or good. I asked my mother, 'Why would anybody want to look like that? Isn't that silly-looking?' And she said, 'They look like apes. Look at their hair. They look like gorillas.'"

In millions of homes across America, that parental reaction, that *scorn*, helped make the Beatles heroes for the '60s children. Gene was no different. "For some reason, I liked the fact that my mother didn't like them. So right after the show was over, I went to the bathroom and combed my hair to the front. I distinctly remember that my mother reacted badly to it. And I said, 'Gee, I like that.' All of a sudden, ears looked very strange. Mine stuck out a mile; if the wind came along, I would just take off."

Frank Sinatra. Elvis Presley. The Beatles. These three cultural and musical phenomena had one thing in common when they first hit. They belonged to *kids*. The screaming that their music inspired was a cacophony that adults couldn't tolerate, and they became heroes partly because of the reaction they caused in adults. Each "new" thing was outrageous to parents who had "outraged" their parents with the previous decade's teen idol. When the adults yelled, "Stop! Enough of that noise!" the kids would clutch harder and say, "That's mine!"

Gene believes that parental disapproval was instrumental in KISS's early success through excess. "Parents are always warning kids about staying away from bad influences and bad people. But kids don't want to listen. Rock 'n' roll is that pursuit of the wrong side of the tracks."

For Gene, rock 'n' roll was still something to watch. Although he sang in the school choir, he didn't play an instrument. In 1965, Gene began his rock 'n' roll career when he appeared at a junior high school assembly with his first group, the Missing Links. "After the speeches," Gene explains, "people would get up and sing. The Links was a trio. One guy played his Silvertone guitar, the other guy played his Mustang, and I sang. We did 'There's a Place' by the Beatles and 'Do You Love Me' by the Contours. Afterward, walking down the hall, I noticed that everybody talked to me. 'Hey, man. You a jive muth'fuck.' Those were the black guys. The white guys would say, 'Very nice.' And the girls all wanted to get close, like bees to honey. In fact, one of the new tunes I'm writing is called 'Girls Love Money.' Girls want to be looked at, and they're attracted to anything that glitters, fame or money. They want to be around a star, grab a little reflected spotlight."

That first show also gave Gene a hint that he was meant to be in the spotlight. "I looked to my left and my right, and those guys were sweating and perspiring and shaking. Not me. I guess I came off like Sergio Franchi. I'd cock one eyebrow a little bit higher than the other, that kind of stuff. At the time, I must have looked completely ridiculous. But I *knew* it was for me. I wanted to be looked at."

Gene's first real band, the Long Island Sounds, included "Steve Coronel, Seth Dogramajian, and Alan Graph on guitars, and Stan Singer on drums. I was the lead singer. At the time, I had a much higher voice and sounded like Paul McCartney. In those days, everybody became nasal and developed an English accent. The Beatles were by far my favorite group; I've always liked the same things the masses do.

"In 1967, I bought a $50 Segova bass, a Japanese model of McCartney's bass. And my mother bought me my first guitar, a Kent. I learned to play because the group I was in needed a bass player and we didn't want to get another guy. The first song I learned how to play was 'Hang on Sloopy,' the hit by the McCoys. I also learned a couple of chords at the same time, because bass and guitar are very similar. I would just watch the guitarist's hands and then go home and do it. Obviously, the first few times you look like a fool because your fingers don't do the right things. But I got better."

Gene had spent some time in groups like the Missing Links and the Rising Suns, but for most of the '60s, he played in the Long Island Sounds (who eventually shortened their name to Sounds). It was a typical bar band, singing the Top 40 hits of the day. Pay was about $150 a night, Gene recalls, "so each of us would make about $30 a weekend, which meant a week of going to movies, taking girls out, or whatever. Usually, when I took a girl out, I made sure she paid for herself." It was Gene's personal brand of women's liberation. "I'd be damned if I was going to spend my hard-earned money on girls, just to get a kiss at the end of the evening. If they wanted to be with me, they paid their own way."

In various incarnations, Sounds stayed together for four years. Then, in the fall of 1968, Gene left home for college, enrolling at Sullivan County Community College in New York's Catskill Mountains. Gene is very proud of the fact that he paid his tuition himself. "At the time, it was $3,000 a year, which was a lot of money. When I was eleven or twelve, I worked as a delivery boy and in a butcher shop. When I learned how to type, I would make as many pennies as I could typing everybody's school reports. By the time I was sixteen, I was working for the Kelly Girls typing agency. And I got a lot of work because every female executive wanted a male secretary. With that money, I was able to pay for my education as well as buy some Marshall amplifiers. That gave me real *power*. Because I had the best equipment, every band wanted me to join. *Every* band."

At college, Gene formed a new band which he christened Bullfrog Bheer. In addition to Top 40 material, this band played some of Gene's originals. "I was writing strange stuff then, some of which showed up on my solo albums. Ballady kind of things similar to 'Please Please Me,' that Beatle-esque kind of up and down strumming, lots of A minor and B minor and E chords. Some of those songs were on the early KISS albums.

"We'd play the beer bashes, doing things like [Procol Harum's] 'Whiter Shade of Pale,' [Joe Cocker's] 'Hitchcock Railway,' and 'If 6 Was 9,' the Jimi Hendrix song. Toward the end of the night, when everybody was blitzed, I could sneak in my originals. And if a song worked, somebody would come over and say, 'Do that song again.' I'd keep that one in the set and forget about the others. It was that kind of weeding-out process." Because Bullfrog Bheer was "playing original material, people would come from all over the Catskills to hear us. I'd have little concerts every weekend. We didn't really mean much, although we did get a little attention from a local radio station."

To Gene, writing songs was *his* unique skill. "At this point, I had never met anybody else who wrote songs. You never really think about the music stars, so I thought I was the only one who could write. I had a swelled head from thinking, 'God. I'm the only one who can do this stuff.'"

By the fall of 1970, Bullfrog Bheer was making regular appearances. The band was a moneymaking attraction, so when their lead guitarist got sick, Gene needed a fast fill-in, a replacement. "I got in touch with my old lead player from the Long Island Sounds, Steve Coronel. When I went to see Steve, there was this guy at his house." Back then, that guy was known as Stanley Eisen. But nowadays his name is Paul Stanley.

ALL-AMERICAN MAN:
THE STARCHILD

Chapter **02**

Like the other members of KISS, Paul Stanley came from humble beginnings and grew up with a resolve to prove to the world that he was something extraordinary.

"I grew up in upper Manhattan, 211th Street and Broadway. It was a mixed neighborhood," Paul recalls, "but we were the only Jewish family. There were a lot of immigrants from Germany and Hungary, but the majority of the people were Irish. My mother's German; my father was born here but his parents were Russian-Hungarian-Polish."

The Eisens' first child was a daughter, Julia, who is two years older than Paul. Paul was born on January 20, 1952. "I don't remember a lot from those days, because I was only eight when we moved. My family wasn't that well off. When I was six, my father bought me a bike, which was the only thing that I was given of any value. We weren't affluent, but we survived. There were times when money was very tight. In Manhattan, the four of us lived in a one-bedroom apartment; my parents slept in the living room and my sister and I shared the bedroom. My father worked as a furniture salesman, and my mother was a teacher. Originally, she was a registered nurse, and then she taught retarded kids. Ultimately, she became a full-time housewife."

Growing up in a tough Manhattan neighborhood, "my mother taught me that it's real important that you let everybody know not to mess with you. You don't let anyone take advantage of you. Because I was Jewish, I got into a lot of fights, and I would *maul* somebody to get the point across. I was a sturdy little kid, and nobody could really hurt me."

In 1960, the Eisen family moved to Kew Gardens in Queens, not too far away from where the Klein family was living. To Paul, Queens "was like the country to me, because there were trees outside the house. It was culture shock, because I had never seen grass growing in front of a house. I'd ride my bike around the block, and I couldn't get over how many trees there were. And the houses were only two stories high!"

It's interesting to note that like Gene, Paul was a loner in his youth. "I was a quiet kid. I don't know exactly why. When I was in kindergarten, I decided to become leader of the class. And I *was* the leader. Outside of that, I tended to be quiet and go off on my own. I wasn't the most sociable. Still, I always knew I'd be someone special."

For Paul, "grammar school was unpleasant. I tended to rebel, and I kind of fought my way through school. That's why *now* I understand what a lot of kids are going through. I was unhappy just because I didn't want the same things anyone else did. And their parents really pressured them into conforming, where mine really didn't. My parents let me do what I wanted. I had an upbringing where my parents cared a lot, but I wasn't brought up strictly. They may have left too much up to me. I don't know if that's the greatest way. I didn't get into a lot of trouble, but that was part of the responsibility that was put on my shoulders. It was understood that I was a smart guy and knew how to take care of myself and don't get into trouble. But if I really got out of line, they were there.

"For example, one afternoon, around fourth grade, I went to a friend's house and coaxed him out to play even though he said he had to do his homework. Went flying my kite and wound up falling in a swamp up to our waists. We got home really late, covered with muck, and after that, I wasn't supposed to see him. I called him up a few years ago, and he's an optometrist now. Almost all of the kids from my neighborhood in Queens grew up and became what their parents wanted them to be, mostly doctors and lawyers.

"I was a bad influence, and in a small neighborhood, things like that spread quickly. I was the wild one, and the other parents felt it was better to keep their kids away from me. So I had to have fun by myself. Sometimes, I'd have a partner in crime, but I got used to doing things by myself. And I got good at it, and became better at dealing with myself than I was with other people. At any rate, I never did anything that could have gotten me in a lot of trouble. But I just didn't fit it in. I didn't go to Hebrew school. I wasn't bar mitzvahed. I was the 'different' kid."

In school, even though he wasn't typical, Paul was usually "the teacher's pet. They knew I was bright, even though I didn't get good grades. I just didn't feel like doing the work, competing for grades. I think that it was the parents who were competing through their kids. In my class, the guy that got a 93 wasn't as good as the guy who got a 95, and the parents of the guy who got the 95 were much better than the parents of the kid who got the 93.

"When I tried, I did really well. Most of the time, I didn't try. My grades ranged from a 35 in Spanish to 99 in Art. I hated the competition for grades, and although I couldn't articulate it back then, I knew it was wrong to compete just to be part of the crowd. It's an unusual attitude for a child, but I knew most of those kids weren't happy, and I didn't want any part of it. I thought most of those parents were creeps, and I still do. I was always in the smart classes, but at the bottom of the smart class.

"My parents wanted me to do better. They'd come home from the parent-teacher meetings and say, 'The teacher says you're so bright, and you're not using your mind.' And I would say, 'Tomorrow, I'm going to start using it.' And that would last a day. Guilt is used a great deal in Jewish neighborhoods, but it didn't work with me."

Despite Paul's disinterest in school, it was the artistic talent he developed in school that rescued him from the problem of being the "odd one." Paul feels that "going to the High School of Music and Art was a blessing. Without that, I probably wouldn't have made it through school. When you have a talent, people give you a little more license to be crazy, so we were allowed to be different. When I went to Music and Art, my hair was past my shoulders and I wore a motorcycle jacket, but that was perfectly acceptable *because* I was an excellent artist. It's unfortunate that you need an excuse to be different. Being crazy is fine only if you have a talent. There's no reason why you can't be crazy anyway. It's just freedom. Anyway, I was much happier when I went to Music and Art."

Although Paul studied art at the legendary New York high school, it was music that had become his real joy. Paul: "I was glued to the radio and television, watching *American Bandstand* and a show that Alan Freed had in New York. My earliest memory, when I was five or six, is watching *Bandstand* and dreaming of being sixteen so I could go to Philadelphia and dance on *Bandstand*. And from back when I first saw that show, I wanted to be a rock star. Always.

"I started singing with my sister and her girlfriend when I was six. We'd do a cappella stuff. Everybody in my family has a good voice, and we all used to sing together, which is where I learned harmony."

Curiously, despite his early interest in music, Paul didn't have any rock 'n' roll heroes. "I was an imagination freak, and I always had this vision of myself on a white horse, doing battle. Like Zorro. When I was little, I always wanted to be a superhero. I saw myself as an Errol Flynn–type swashbuckler, in white flowing shirts and tight pants and boots turned over the cuff. I wanted long hair and eyes that would stare people down. I liked the idea of saving maidens in distress and wearing beautiful clothes. That's something I always thought of, and it's no longer a fantasy. I can do that now. Of course, I never discussed these dreams with my parents. They just saw me as a little kid with a big temper.

"The older I got, the more interested I became in music. I thought Eddie Cochran was cool. I liked Dion, the Drifters. And then the Beatles and Stones came along, and they were my heroes. My parents bought me my first guitar when I was seven, a little $15 wood guitar. I didn't know how to play it when I got it, but I thought I did because I was so into rock 'n' roll. While other kids were out playing in the empty lot next door, I was watching *American Bandstand.*

"My whole awareness of music came from my parents, who listened to classical music and light opera. Even today, I still like what they used to play. Beethoven is my favorite music. I don't get much chance to listen to it these days, but the fact that I liked the classics was another thing that set me aside from the rest of the kids."

More than anything, though, it was Paul's artistic ability that set him apart. "I was very, very good in art, and I could never understand why other kids couldn't look at something and then draw it without looking at the paper. It was this gift that I had, which I first discovered when I was five. I started drawing dinosaurs. It just seemed natural. I'd look at something and draw it."

Paul's parents recognized his talent, but "at first, they preferred the thought of my being a doctor. It's funny because when my parents finally got used to the idea of my becoming an artist instead of a doctor, I pulled a switch and said, 'I'm not going to be an artist. I'm going to be a rock star.'"

His decision to give up art for rock 'n' roll was based on his desire to avoid competition. "I was always very gifted in art. In elementary school, I was *the* artist in school. In junior high, I was one of the two artists in the school. I realized that the further I went, the more people there were to compete with. By the time I got to Music and Art, there was a school full of those people who had been the best in their schools. I began to realize that I stood a better chance with rock. Even before I could play, I would watch *The Ed Sullivan Show* and say, 'They're great, but I could do that. It's not beyond me.' The older I got, I saw less people who could do the rock thing and more people that could create good art."

More than anything, it might have been his formal art education that destroyed Paul's artistic urges. "It's possible that school really ruined it for me. Just like the parents in my neighborhood, the teachers in Music and Art were trying to live their lives through the students. All the mistakes or things they didn't get to do, they wanted you to do for them. And that's not fair. I found most of my art teachers telling me about the great potential I had and what they wanted me to do. If they were that great, why were they art teachers?

"When it turned into 'You need this piece in by next Wednesday,' art was ruined for me because it was no longer self-motivated. I don't think having deadlines is any way to create." Paul sums it up perfectly when he explains, "The reason I got involved with music is that nobody told me what to do."

On February 9, 1964, the Beatles were on *The Ed Sullivan Show*. Like Gene, Paul watched, transfixed. "That was the clincher," Paul exults. "I was amazed by how good they were on television. And by the magnetism they had. Back then, I was fighting my parents about the length of my hair. If I was lucky, it covered my ears, and if my parents were lucky, my ear lobes were showing. I would watch the Beatles with them and I would say, 'Don't you understand? I can't get my hair cut.'"

His parents must have understood, because on Paul's thirteenth birthday in 1965, his parents gave him his first real guitar, "although," Paul reluctantly reveals, "it was a cheapie Japanese folk guitar, when I really wanted an electric guitar. I put it under my bed for a few days; I didn't like it at all. Then I decided that *any* guitar was better than no guitar, so I took a couple of lessons."

Paul's parents enrolled him with a classical guitar teacher. "I didn't know there were different styles of playing. This guy had my leg on a stool, and my posture just so. It didn't look like George Harrison, and it certainly didn't sound like Bob Dylan. I couldn't figure out when he was gonna get to chords, and, of course, he had no intention of teaching me chords. So I dropped out of that and went to another teacher to learn chords. Right away, I started going beyond the teacher. They wanted to teach me at a certain speed, and I wanted to learn quicker than that. Once I had a basis, I started teaching myself.

"I was always coming out of my bedroom with the guitar and showing everybody what I could play. I had a harmonica around my neck too." Playing at being a Dylanesque folkie, Paul began to create. "The whole idea of learning the guitar was to write music. No sooner did I learn [the folk standard] 'Down in the Valley' than I decided to make it into a protest song. I can't remember the words, but it was ambitious. My parents didn't discourage me at all, but then again, they didn't realize how deeply I would get into it. Later on, they got a little worried when everyone else was going to college, and I was in my room with a Gibson guitar and an amplifier."

Paul faithfully followed the trends in those days, so in 1965, "I was heavy into the Byrds. I used to do a lot of picking, twelve-string kind of stuff. My first group was with a friend, Harold Shiff. He ultimately had to stop because his mother made him do his homework. He's [also] an optometrist now.

"Some of the guys in the band stayed with it. We played songs by the Lovin' Spoonful, the Yardbirds, the Kinks, and the Outsiders. We did a rock 'n' roll version of 'The Ballad of the Green Berets.' That was pretty punk. The group went through a million names, one of which was Incubus [a spirit that "screws" you in the night]. We played for friends at parties. I was the lead singer and rhythm guitarist, and I controlled the direction of the band. I usually knew what I wanted, even back then." There were no groupies yet, as Paul laughingly recalls. "There weren't any girls for us.

Especially me. I was just a little fat guy that played guitar and wanted to be skinny. I did get skinny when I was eighteen."

Before Stanley Eisen graduated from high school, he had a brief brush with the world of professional music. Paul: "It was around Jefferson Airplane time. I was fifteen and most of the people in this band were eighteen or nineteen. Even though I was the youngest, it was through me that the band got into the studio in the first place. These guys just wanted to sit around and play music in the basement. But I pushed. 'C'mon. Let's make a record.' Somehow, I got a producer interested in us. He was with Columbia Records."

The band was called the Post War Baby Boom, and they never released a record, a story that makes Paul laugh to this day. "Mind you, this was that Haight-Ashbury love period. The [lead] singer took acid and jumped into a fountain and caught a bad cold and [couldn't sing, so] we couldn't put vocals on the track. The song was 'Never Loving, Never Living.' One of mine."

Although Paul graduated from the High School of Music and Art in 1970, he had just about lost all interest in academia by that point. As he puts it, his two best subjects back then were "lunch and creative subway rides." In September 1970, Paul went to Bronx Community College "for about a week, only long enough to get a student loan. I took my loan, bought a car, and left school. There was no way that I could be in school and spend twenty-five hours a day dreaming about how I was going to be a rock star."

After leaving school, Paul concentrated his energies on his band, Uncle Joe, a three-piece outfit that compensated for its lack of a bass player by playing very, very loud. Paul and the other guitar player clashed because "I wanted to play rock 'n' roll, and he wanted to play blues. So he quit the band. The drummer knew another guitarist, and he joined for a little while. His name was Steve Coronel."

Like most of Paul's bands this one never got past a few rehearsals before it broke up. "It wasn't going anywhere," Paul remembers. "One day, after that group broke up, I was at Steve's house, and this fat guy with a beard came in. He needed Steve to go upstate and play with him 'cause his lead player was sick. And Steve said to this guy, 'This [referring to Paul] is my friend Stanley. He writes songs too.' As it turns out, this other guy writes songs, but he was a creep. He said, 'Oh yeah? You write songs? Let me hear some of them.' Me, being a nice guy, I sat down and played a couple. This guy used to think that only he and Lennon and McCartney wrote songs. After I played a few, he went, 'Hmmm. Not bad.' He was impressed because now he knew that he wasn't alone in the world. Now, [he knew] there were four of us who wrote songs. And that guy was Gene. And I hated him."

KINGS OF THE NIGHT TIME WORLD:
THE QUEST

Chapter **03**

Eventually, Gene and Paul would grow to respect and like each other, but that first day, Paul felt nothing but contempt for Gene. Actually, the feeling wasn't mutual, as Gene recalls.

"The first song he reeled off was called 'Sunday Driver,' which became 'Let Me Know' on the first KISS album. I was really impressed, although I must have come off very pompous and self-righteous. 'That's almost as good as my stuff,' I told him. And I said, 'That's very good.' And he was *real* pissed, as if to say, 'Who are you to tell me this is very good? This is great!'"

What Paul couldn't know was that for Gene "to tell somebody else they were good was the highest compliment I ever paid anybody. To him, of course, it was like, 'Hey, who are *you*, bozo?'"

Gene and Paul's relationship began and ended that day. Steve Coronel went upstate with Gene to join Bullfrog Bheer, but remained with Gene's band for only a few weeks. Steve soon returned to New York to form a band with Paul.

As 1970 became 1971, Steve and Paul continued to struggle, and their new group never actually coalesced. Steve suggested they invite Gene to join. At that point, Paul remembers saying, "It's Gene or me. You get one or the other."

Meanwhile, Gene had left Sullivan Community College for Richmond College on Staten Island in New York City. Before he formed a new group, Gene took out an advertisement in *The Village Voice* [the famous New York alternative weekly] in which he offered his equipment for rent. Again and again, it would be classified ads that would bring KISS together.

The first band that rented Gene's equipment included Brooke Ostrander, a keyboard player who was also a music teacher in New Jersey. Around Christmastime of 1971, Gene remembers, they began working together "on a demo tape. Brooke and I did it on a very old Sound tape recorder. One of the songs later became 'Nothin' to Lose' on the first KISS album. After we finished the tape, I wanted to put a band together. In early '72, I started hitting the record companies, making the rounds. From reading the music trade magazines, I didn't want to approach CBS or Warner Brothers or any of the biggies. I knew about this little label, Janus Records, and they only had two acts, and one of them was Lenny Bruce, who was dead. But Janus was distributed by Columbia. I figured that here was this real closet operation, and I knew even back then that you needed a small label with big distribution so they would pay attention to you.

"Janus Records bit. They said, 'Put a band together, and you've got yourself a deal.' So we had to put a band together very quickly. I placed an ad for a guitar player, and as it turned out, one of the first guys that called was Paul. But he didn't want to come all the way to New Jersey just to try out. So I called my old guitar player, Steve Coronel." Coronel agreed to give it another shot with Gene, and then he asked, "What about Paul?"

Gene continues the story. "I said, 'Sure. Bring him along. We'll need a rhythm player. I'll play bass.' So Paul played rhythm, Steve was on lead, Brooke was on keyboards, and Tony Zarrella was on drums." That band was first called Rainbow because they played all different kinds of music. Later, they changed their name to Wicked Lester.

Despite a bad beginning, Gene and Paul quickly became partners in music. "After the initial reaction," Paul notes, "we realized that we were an asset to each other. I think it was that more than anything else. Back then, you didn't often meet people who were writing songs and who could sing well.

"I think I stopped hating Gene when I realized he was good. Despite what I thought of him or the way he was with people, little by little, he began being different with me because he respected me. I began to see he was a talented guy and knew we had to work together. Possibly, Gene was still trying to prove who he was, but I knew we had to work things out because there was a chemistry between us. I knew that teams tend to make each other strong, balance each other out.

"Gene basically had the same drive I did. He was in college and had that same ambition to be somebody. He had a huge ego, which is great. He just had to learn to tame it a little and harness it. Put it to good advantage. He thought he was somebody special, and he began to see that I was somebody special. That's part of what makes the band work, even today. After disliking each other intensely, Gene and I became a team within Wicked Lester, its unofficial leaders."

In early '72, Wicked Lester practiced frequently and played an occasional club gig. Gene continued to pursue a recording contract. The first decision he made was to forget about Janus Records, because he didn't think they could handle a rock 'n' roll group. The band was also offered a contract by Buddah Records, but "Paul and I said no. We didn't want to sign with Buddah. The other guys wanted to sign with them, but since we were the writers, we said, 'You guys want to do it. That's okay. We'll take our material elsewhere.' We were gonna break the band up right there because Buddah had no rock 'n' roll acts; we didn't want to sign with a company that had all bubblegum acts." The head of Buddah Records at that time was a man named Neil Bogart. Eventually, after this near-miss, he will become a big part of the KISS story.

In the meantime, Wicked Lester's lack of success was causing Paul a great deal of difficulty at home. "My parents were asking, 'What are you doing with your life?' I didn't have any answers for that. The fact that I was making $30 every other month playing music didn't help. It was the first time I ever got paid for playing, but we weren't going anywhere. But you've got to follow your heart, do what you believe in. So Wicked Lester kept pounding away."

Finally, fate intervened. Paul recalls, he was hanging out in a clothing store when he met a guy who said to him, "You look like a guy in a band." When Paul replied in the affirmative, the guy said, "My name's Ron. I work for Electric Lady Studios. If you ever have a tape, call me up." As Gene remembers, "The next time Wicked Lester rehearsed, Paul was very excited, telling everybody that we had to call this guy." Paul did call and asked to speak to Ron. He was put through to a guy named Ron Johnsen, an engineer at the studio, who didn't know anything about Paul or his band. It turned out that the guy Paul had met was *the cleaning man* at the studio.

Anxiously seizing the opportunity, Paul proceeded to badger Ron Johnsen. Paul: "I must have called him fifteen times a day, over and over. I would speak to his secretary and try to get him to come hear us. When you're hungry and desperate, you have no pride. I would call this guy up constantly. Finally, Ron Johnsen got on the phone, and I said, 'It's because of people like you that my band's gonna break up. Nobody's willing to come see us. When you call a record company, they tell you that you need a manager. Call a manager and they want you to have a record contract. We're gonna break up if you don't come and see us.' "

Wicked Lester had rented a loft near Mott and Canal Streets in Chinatown for $40 a month. The space used to be a rehearsal hall, and it was to this hole in the wall that Ron Johnsen finally came. Gene remembers the promises. "This guy said we were as good as any band he'd ever heard. 'As good as Three Dog Night' was his comment. We're talkin' 'bout dinosaurs now. And so he said, 'We'll make a tape down at Electric Lady, for free, and if we sell it, I'll be your producer.'"

At first, as Paul recalls, nothing happened. "He said, 'We're gonna go in and do it. Start work.' But months passed, and the band broke up because we just couldn't wait. Then, Ron Johnsen called me up and said, 'I'm ready to go into the studio with you guys.' So I had to call up a bunch of guys with hurt feelings, guys who weren't even talking to each other. And I'd say, 'Look. This is our opportunity.' And we got back together and started recording. It took us almost a year to make an album, and it was the worst. Now, it's really funny . . . but it's embarrassing."

Paul remembers the record as being a trendsetter's nightmare. "If wah-wahs were big, we put it on the album. If ukuleles were big, we had a ukulele track. You name it, it was on that record. It was mostly terrible, but it did have two songs, 'She' and 'Love Her All I Can,' that did make it onto KISS albums."

The finished Wicked Lester album was purchased by CBS, but to this day, that album has never been released. Gene tells this story with great relish. After they made it as KISS, Gene explains, "we didn't want it to come out, so we bought it back from CBS." If CBS had realized that they had the record in their vaults, it is almost a certainty that they would have released it to capitalize on KISS's success. Gene laughs, "They never knew it was us. In 1979, we used the cover from the Wicked Lester LP on the *Laughing Dogs* cover."

It gave Gene and Paul great pleasure to pull a fast one on CBS. Gene: "Don Ellis, the A&R man at CBS, passed on KISS. He came and saw the band and said, 'Nah. That's not it.' That's Ellis," Gene spells. "E-L-L-I-S."

"Gene and I were unhappy with the direction of Wicked Lester," Paul notes. "There *was* no direction. We looked like people waiting for a bus. We wanted to do something original, and we came up with the idea of taking on new characters. In the original concept, I was going to look like a gunslinger, and Gene was going to look like a caveman. Actually, that was the beginning of the idea for KISS, but it wasn't working out with Wicked Lester."

According to Gene, the demise of Wicked Lester was inevitable. "We got hooked up with Alan Miller, who later worked for Bill Aucoin [KISS's manager]. At the time, Alan introduced us to Lew Linet, who was managing J.F. Murphy and Salt, who was being produced by Eddie Kramer. Eddie was enthusiastic about the Wicked Lester record and the group, but we soon realized that it wasn't going to work. There was a tall guy and a short guy, a fat guy and a thin guy. We sat down and confronted ourselves. 'What do we want to do?' Besides wanting to be rich and famous like everyone else, we knew we had to look like we belonged in the same band. Everybody had to be the same thing. We said, 'If we're gonna do it, it's gotta be the right way.' So we decided to break the band up."

When Epic (a CBS-affiliated label) decided not to release the Wicked Lester album, the five guys got to keep their advance money. Gene and Paul used their share to buy new equipment. As Paul remembers, "I bought my mother a washing machine and an amplifier for myself." Gene and Paul also rented a new rehearsal loft, this one located at Fifth Avenue and 23rd Street. It cost $200 a month, a considerable step up. The only problem was, the two songwriters didn't have a band.

Paul and Gene were "two of a kind" at that point, and together they began to search for the necessary pieces, the missing links that would make them a group. "We fired the other guys," Paul explains, "and we were thinking of replacing everyone. But in the interim, we came up with a much stronger concept."

Gene recalls what happened next. "The first thing I saw was an ad in *Rolling Stone*. 'Drummer, 11 years experience, willing to do anything.' I called him up. That drummer was Peter."

FELINE FURY: THE CATMAN

Chapter 04

Peter Criss was born in the Williamsburg section of Brooklyn, New York, on December 20, 1945, the oldest child of Loretta and Joseph Criscuola. He has a younger brother (Joey), and three sisters (Nancy, Donna, and Joanne), all of whom are younger. As Peter explains, "I'm the oldest, although I'm treated the youngest. I'll always be the baby of the family. It's the same way with the group. I'm the oldest, but I'm the baby of the group.

"I grew up in a rough neighborhood," Peter recalls, "and my parents weren't all that wealthy. Financially, we were lower-class, and all of us lived in a four-room apartment. We didn't have a lot, but there was always food on the table. I always had clean sheets and clean clothes, always had a starched shirt. It was the same shirt every day, but my mom washed it every night and ironed it before I went to school. My parents were really keeping it together."

Peter describes his neighborhood as "very Italian, Polish, and Irish. Very poor. No one could afford air-conditioning, so on hot summer nights, people would go outside and sit on the front stoop with iced tea and beer. And my swimming pool was an open fire hydrant. It was great."

Peter is a man who had a hard youth, and the scars sometimes show. "I went to a Catholic school called Transfiguration. They called it a school, but it was more like a concentration camp. The nuns who ran the school were really cruel, and I was always being disciplined. And that would kill me. So I started playing all these games to stay home from school. I'd play sick, 'cause I didn't want to get tortured. I'd tell my mom that the nuns would beat your knuckles with a ruler or lock you in a dark closet for hours or make you sit in the wastepaper basket as punishment. She wouldn't believe me. She'd say, 'How could a nun do that?'

"They'd do awful things. If I had to go the bathroom, they wouldn't let me go, so I'd pee in my pants. I'd have to sit there all day in class like that with people laughing at me. I just couldn't handle it, and I developed a mental block toward school. I did all sorts of things to avoid going to school, but by doing that, I only got dumber.

"My mother didn't understand why I was sick all the time, but finally, she realized what was going on, and she put me into a public school. I started passing my courses, and then my grades shot into the 80s and 90s. My mother said, 'Why wasn't this happening before?' I answered, 'Do you understand *now* what I've been telling you about the nuns?'"

Just like today in ghettos across the country, for teenagers growing up in the tough New York City neighborhoods of the late '50s and early '60s, it was challenging experience, truly the human equivalent of the "survival of the fittest" theory. For Peter, survival meant belonging to a gang. "In eighth grade, the neighborhood I lived in got worse and gangs became the big thing. The only way to exist after a while was to join a gang; otherwise, you would get beaten up every day. I didn't want to join, but I had no choice. If you didn't have a bunch of guys with you, you would get the shit kicked out of you."

Joining a gang included a frightening initiation rite. Peter: "To join, you had to do a thing we called 'rumbling.' It was a gang brawl, but to prove yourself, you had to be the first to charge the other gang, who were running at you with baseball bats and garbage can lids and car aerials. I got quite a few cuts from knives and razors. Up front, you were the first to get hit, and if you had enough guts to do that, you were in. And I did it. It was crazy, but if you had the guts, you could be one of the guys.

"Our gang was called the Phantom Lords. We rented a store as a clubhouse, put some red lights in, painted the windows black, and got a jukebox. There were two or three hundred guys in the gang. It was a famous gang, one of the biggest in Brooklyn. I worked my way up from being just a member to being vice president. Even at that time, I wasn't happy just being a member of something.

"The big TV show at the time was *The Untouchables*. So everybody dressed up like gangsters and carried zip guns. We even had uniforms. Everybody wore these white hats and pinstripe suits with suspenders. On the weekends, we'd have socials, blast the jukebox, and have lots of girls. It was a very decadent scene, actually. Pretty classy, but also pretty sick.

"On another level, though, it was exciting because it was *belonging*. And it was the in thing. You could make more girls if you were in a gang. Not only that, but being in a gang gives you a reputation of being tougher and you got respect in the neighborhood. When they knew you were in the Phantom Lords, people left you alone. So I got beaten up a lot less.

"Our gang got in a lot of trouble. Some of us were arrested for shooting and killing, and a lot of the members went to jail. It's weird to look back at the whole thing, because at the time, it seemed exciting. But there are a lot of really nice guys who became junkies and died of drug overdoses. It was a violent scene. It was insanity.

"Whenever we had a rumble, there was shooting and stabbing all over the place. I never stabbed anybody, but I hit a few people with bats and bricks. It was pretty scary, and I'm lucky I survived. I was only thirteen or fourteen, and I was running around with a zip gun in my pocket. I'd come home all bloody, and my folks would be very upset. My dad would tell me, 'We've got to move out of here,' but we never had enough bucks to get us out of the neighborhood."

Peter's survival instincts, like his cat personality, were very sharp, even as a teenager. But, Peter explains, he never had a killer instinct. "My father was rough on me sometimes, because I was the type of kid who would get in a fight, pin the guy down, and then let him up. When people got me down, they never let me up. So my old man used to tell me, 'There's only one way to fight, whether you're using your fists or a club. You've got to fight to win.'

"My mom and dad are great, even though I'm still the renegade of the family, the outlaw. One rule we always had was 'You don't lie. You don't steal.' My father's very Italian, and my mother's very Irish. And that's a weird combination. My dad was stern with me. He didn't like cursing in the house. If I swore at the table, my father would slap me across the mouth with a strap or something.

"I thought I was tough, 'cause I was in a gang. After a rumble, I'd come home all scratched up, and when he'd ask me where I'd been, I'd say, "I was in a friggin' rumble.' He'd slap the hell out of me and say, 'I don't care what you do outside, but you don't bring it into the house.' Even though he hit me a lot, he was extremely warm and lovable. He smacked me because I deserved it, and I realized that.

"I never hid anything from my father. He would rather I did it in front of him, whatever it might be. My mom and dad are really hip. I used to bring all these crazy musicians home when I was in bands, and we'd be starving and my mom would feed 'em. After a while, they'd even go over to my house without me. Just to hang out there, 'cause my folks were so hip. My mother's my biggest fan. She loves me to tell her the stories from when I'm on the road."

From the time he was ten until he was married, Peter spent a great deal of time living with his grandmother. "My parents lived a block away from my [maternal] grandmother. Her husband left her when they were fairly young, and I don't know why, but I just took to her. And she took me under her wing. She was a great lady. She had two jobs, and she'd still go to bars on the weekends. That was the kind of person she was.

"I didn't have the things that other kids on the block had because my parents were so poor. If one kid got a Schwinn bike, I didn't. But my grandmother would work overtime to make sure I got that Schwinn bike. She made sure I got what every other kid got. I really loved her a lot. When she died, we couldn't afford to have her name put on the stone. The first big money I ever made, I bought her a big head-stone. I took my mother there on Christmas Eve and said, 'Ma, Happy Birthday.' It was a little gift for my grandmother. That's one of the nice things about success. It was something I felt I owed her, because she hated my long practices at the drums. She was very old-fashioned; she wanted me to get a regular job. And I did. I worked as a dental mechanic, building teeth. I always had jobs. But I really started working because I wanted drums."

Unlike the other members of KISS, Peter's musical ambitions began long before the Beatles came along. "I remember seeing Elvis on *The Jackie Gleason Show* [Jackie's summer replacement, the Dorsey Brothers, had Elvis on six times], and I was blown away. I went out and bought a little plastic guitar, and I'd stand in front of the mirror, put water in my hair, give it a little brush, and sing 'Hound Dog.' My mother bought the record, and she used to make me do it for relatives. I'd come out and imitate Elvis for my family. Even then, I was entertaining. Even then, I was carrying on about rock 'n' roll.

"Elvis was one of my first heroes. I also loved Hopalong Cassidy and the Lone Ranger. As a kid, I had a whole Hopalong Cassidy suit, two six-guns and all. I loved all the cowboy shows like *Maverick, Have Gun Will Travel, Cheyenne, Sugarfoot,* and *Gunsmoke.* I'd wait up with potato chips and popcorn for *Sea Hunt.*

"But I never wanted to be a cowboy. From the first day I can remember, I was a drummer. When I was a kid, I started beating pots and pans, picking out ones with different sounds. My father had this old set of brushes, because he used to play a little drums. I drove my parents whacko beating on the pots, but they put up with it."

Peter's first exposure to music came from the radio. "All day long, my folks played the radio. Nothing but swing music. I grew up on Benny Goodman, Tommy Dorsey, and Glenn Miller. And I loved it. I would play along with it and dream of someday being a drummer, a singer, and a songwriter."

One of Peter's earliest memories is the Christmas when "my parents bought me a set of Rootie Kazootie [a TV character] drums. It was the first thing I went for that morning. There were other toys, but I went right for the drums. First time I hit 'em, I broke 'em. Went right through the skin. That was the first time I had sticks in my hand.

"When I was thirteen, I wrote my first song. It was like, 'Oh, honey. You know I love you baby.' Around then, I joined a doo-wop group, singing in subways and hallways. This guy in the group gave me an old army snare drum. I went home, and my dad built me a wooden box, put glitter on it. And it read, 'Stars.' That was the name of my band. And we took two paint cans and garbage can covers, and we put holes in them and put screws through the holes. So they had a sizzle sound. That was my first set of drums. And I would use them to back the group at social clubs. I was the only instrument. There were no guitars. They sang stuff by Frankie Lymon and the Teenagers. I wasn't getting paid. I just did it."

Peter's makeshift drum set was all he had, until "I was going to high school. I worked weekends as a delivery boy in a butcher shop. One of the butchers had a set of drums that were white mother-of-pearl, an exact duplicate of [drumming legend] Gene Krupa's set. And he said, 'I'll sell them to you for $200.' It took me a lot of months of deliveries and tips, of working and saving, but one day, I had enough to buy them. I took them home, and I would play along with the records. And when guys would come by to say, 'Come on out and play baseball' or 'Let's go to a rumble,' I'd say, 'No. I gotta practice. I gotta practice.' That's all I did. I'd go to school. I'd work. And I'd practice.

"One day, when I was sixteen, I passed by this basement, and there were these guys playing electric guitars. It flipped me out. I stood outside watching, and then, one of the guys came outside. I asked him if I could come in and watch. It just so happened that they were firing their drummer, and I tried out. I had never been in a band with real instruments, so I never knew how to play with guys with amplifiers. But they liked me, 'cause I really wanted to play. And I sang too.

"I joined them. They called themselves the Barracudas, and it was two guitars and me on drums. We played little clubs on the weekends and got paid about $10 or $15 a night doing six shows."

Peter was eighteen and a senior in high school when he and fate met head-on, and he became a professional musician. Peter: "I'll never forget that night. I was with some friends, and we went into the Metropole Café [a legendary club on Broadway near Times Square] for a drink, 'cause I knew one of the guys in the band [Joey Greco and the In Crowd]. Their drummer was sick, and they were playing without one. When they took a break, Joey, the guy I knew, came over and said, 'Peter, would you like to sit in?'

"There were a hundred people in there and go-go girls. In those days, the Metropole was a happening place. And I said, 'I'm afraid.' My friends with me said, 'Go ahead. Sit in!' So I played with them, and I did all right. It was my first shot at being on the bandstand with a whole lot of people watching. I was real scared and real excited."

After the show that night, Peter was invited to join the band. "By that time, I had actually become a butcher. I was finishing up school and still playing in the Barracudas. But they told me I would make $125 a week. I freaked out. The drummer in their band had broken his leg, so I knew it wasn't going to be forever. But it didn't matter. It was a *gig*. And it was the Metropole, a place where Gene Krupa had played, and that fascinated me. So I went home and I quit it all—the job, the band, and school—and I joined this group."

Although Peter's family was upset that he wasn't going to finish school, $125 a week was hard to argue with. "I told 'em I could always get the diploma, but I never went back. I've learned a lot by myself because traveling gives you a lot of time. I've educated myself."

If those days at the Metropole have taken on a romantic and legendary perspective to Peter, it's no surprise. It was not only his first real job as a musician, but more important than that, it was at the Metropole where Peter met Gene Krupa. When Joey Greco's drummer returned to action, Peter joined a new band, although Peter understandably can't remember that group's name. "I played in about eighty bands all together. Anyway, Krupa would play at the Metropole all day long, and sometimes on the weekends. I would get up early just to go there and watch him play every day. One day, he came over to me and said, 'You're here every day. How come?' And I said, 'I'm your biggest fan. You're the greatest drummer in the world.' And he said, 'You work here, don't you?' I said, 'Yeah, I'm a drummer. If I could only be like you, play like you, I'd give my right arm.' And he said, 'Come on and sit in with me.' And I flipped out. And I sat in. *Gene Krupa* gave me lessons every day. For free. It was the great moment of my life, up until then.

"When I told my father that I was getting lessons from Gene Krupa, he didn't believe me. But when he came to the club, I introduced him to Gene. It flipped my dad out." Peter took lessons from the legendary drummer until Krupa quit working at the Metropole.

From that point on, Peter's life was filled with the search for the right band. It was a long and difficult time for him. "From the time I was eighteen until I was twenty-four, I was really pushing hard to make it. That's when I changed my name [to Criss]. At first, I had to have phony ID cards and phony union cards, 'cause I was getting my first paychecks at sixteen with the Barracudas. Gene and Paul and Ace were still in school when I was on the road with Joey Dee." In 1962, Dee had a number one hit, "The Peppermint Twist," named after the Peppermint Lounge, a very in spot in the early '60s. Dee, who also scored a Top 10 hit in '62 with "Shout," had a band called the Starliters. Peter was a member for two months.

"I wanted to make it," Peter explains, "and I would do anything. In and out of groups all the time. Any chance with a name, I'd go with it, hoping I might make a connection." Peter knew and was friends with the other young musicians of the day, guys who would later end up in groups like the Lovin' Spoonful or the Blues Magoos. "So," Peter remembers, "if the Spoonful's drummer got sick, I'd instantly drop the band I was in, just to sit in for a week with them." Band-hopping, Peter played all of New York's great clubs, spots like Trude Heller's, the Electric Circus, and the Eighth Wonder. But it was a hard time for Peter. He'd be making money one week, and then the next, he'd be out of work.

Peter recalls those days. "In the '60s, I traveled with an Oldies But Goodies band. I'll never forget the first tour with Johnny Maestro and Cannibal and the Headhunters. That was really weird, eight guys living in a U-Haul, with the heater not working and blankets in the windows. Those tours were an interesting education. I learned by doing that stuff for a while, but I still wasn't happy. I wasn't playing my stuff. I was still being told what to play. After that, I was the only white guy in a fifteen-piece soul band. It was great, singing Otis Redding, Sam & Dave, and Wilson Pickett. I love R&B music, so I dug it."

Peter continued to search for the right band, but one problem he encountered was his insistence upon performing original material. Peter: "I had this thing about doing originals. [At a show], I'd tell the guys, 'Let's do one of my tunes.' And we'd do it and get fired. Simple as that. One time, the owner came up to me, one of these fat guys with a cigar, and he said, 'What the hell is that shit you're playing?' And I said, 'It's one of my songs.' He said, 'Play it again and you're fired.' When he walked away, I turned to the band. 'Do the other song I wrote.' I was always the leader of my groups, so they would listen to me. And we got fired. We kept losing gigs because of that, but we would always get a better one.

"Finally, I got a group, Brotherhood, where they let us do some original stuff, which wasn't too bad. We played a place called Arthur's for $200 a week, which was really big money. And the [Young] Rascals were up the block at the Phone Booth. Another spot we played at was the Action House. We'd open up for the Vagrants and the Rich Kids. That's when I met Leslie West, Corky Laing, and all those guys. Brotherhood was really dynamite. At the end of the show, I'd wreck my drums and the organ player would tip his organ over. The whole bit. It was a pretty good time in my life.

"After Brotherhood broke up, I practiced with Leslie before he formed Mountain. I quit because he put me on salary. I said, 'Fuck you. I'm gonna be *in* Mountain. I wanna be *hot*. I wanna be part of the band.' And I quit, and Leslie put Mountain together and they made it. I didn't.

"I kept struggling, and then I joined a band called Chelsea. It was an excellent group, real musicians, who could play everything from jazz to hard rock to soul. Our problem was variety. You couldn't pin a sound on us; we had all kinds of sounds. We made an album that came out on Decca, but the guy who managed us was a real rich little bastard. This kid wanted to be the manager of a rock band, so his father got us. And when things got tough, he dropped us. Out of the whole deal, all I got was a free bass drum. And Decca dropped us.

"Besides our musical diversity, the other problem with Chelsea was our image. We didn't have one. Everybody wore jeans, beards, and long hair. We played underground joints like the Village Gate, and the people loved the music. We came onstage in T-shirts and jeans, but no one cared.

"We were all kinda stoned from a little wine or smoking a joint, and we'd just jam and play. It was so good. I was *so* up. I had my hopes so high on it. But it failed, and when it did, I had a nervous breakdown. I would just sit in the house and do nothing. Just kept listening to the album, saying, 'I don't believe this didn't make it.' I was shocked that the public wouldn't accept this music. It wasn't crap. Larry Fallon, who did Van Morrison's *Astral Weeks*, arranged the horns and strings. I was so happy to finally be doing all original stuff and to be playing with real musicians. It was the biggest shock of my life, and I felt that I had to make it. When I didn't, I was so shocked. I was like a baby."

By this time, Peter had married Lydia, who watched helplessly as Peter suffered through a long depression. Gradually, he remembers, "I started picking up and playing and writing again. Then, I went to England looking for a group. No luck. My money ran out before I found anything. The one really interesting thing that happened over there was that I used to go to this club called Speakeasy and listen to a guy called Elton John. Every night. And he was nobody then."

Returning to New York, Lydia continued to support them, but times were so rough that Peter joined another club band, cranking out the hits. Peter: "This was the worst. This band had guys who were forty years old, and we'd play four nights a week at these real Mafia clubs. These guys had suits and accordions, and I would come in with velvet pants, a pink shirt, a satin scarf, round glasses, and hair down to my shoulders. They didn't like me too much. But I kept doing it, even though I couldn't really handle it. I needed the money."

One day, in 1972, Peter placed an ad in the musician's free classified section of *Rolling Stone*. The ad read: "Drummer, 11 years experience, willing to do anything." It brought quick results, as Peter recalls.

"We were having a party at home, and I got this call. We were all smashed on wine, and I pick up the phone and hear this very intellectual-sounding 'hello.' It was Gene, and we kid each other about it now, but I didn't know who it was then. He said, 'I saw your ad here. By the way, are you good-looking?' And I said, 'Wait a minute.' I yelled to everybody at the party, 'Hey, am I good looking?' And they all screamed, 'Yeaaaaah.' Then he asked me if had long hair. Did the same thing. More questions.

'Are you thin?' 'What are you?' 'Can you sing?' The answers were '140 pounds,' 'Italian,' and 'not only can I sing, but I write too.'"

Gene remembers what the conversation sounded like from his end. "When I called him up, I said, 'Hi, I'm Gene Klein, and I've got some money together. I've got a partner who writes songs. We both write. We both sing. We want to put together the next superband.' And Peter must have thought I was in the loony bin. And I said, 'Are you interested in joining a band like this?' He said, 'Sure.' Of course, I had never heard him play. I said, 'Before we try each other out musically, see if we fit, there's some other stuff that's real important. If it doesn't work, it doesn't matter what kind of musical taste we've got. 'Are you fat?' He was in the middle of a party, and he yelled to everybody, 'This guy wants to know if I'm fat.' Everybody went 'No!' I asked him if he had a mustache or a beard and if he had blond hair, would he be willing to dye it. [I asked] 'Are you ugly?' It was real important to Paul and I that we get the *look*."

Peter apparently gave the right answers, and he agreed to meet Gene and Paul the next day at Electric Ladyland. "I got all spiffed up in my pink satin pants and black velvet jacket and scarf," Peter remembers. "I was dressed to kill. And I went down to the Lady, and there were two guys outside in flowered shirts and jeans. They looked like nothin', and I passed 'em up and went inside. I asked the receptionist, 'Is there a Gene Klein and Paul Stanley here?' And the guy told me that they were downstairs. And I looked out the window and laughed to myself, *He* asked *me*, 'Do I dress up and look rock 'n' roll?'

"So I went back down and said, 'I'm Peter.' Gene said, 'You're hired.' It was great. I said, 'You haven't heard me play.' He said, 'It doesn't matter. You look it. You're a star.' At the time, I was dressing to be noticed, because I wanted to be a star, even though I used to get whistled at and called 'fag' and beaten up on the subway. Gene was very impressed."

Gene remembers two coincidences that made him feel that Peter's arrival "was meant to be. Peter once had been in a band called Lips, which is almost KISS. And Ron Johnsen, the guy who worked with me and Paul with Wicked Lester, turned out to have been the engineer of Peter's album with Chelsea. Definitely felt there was something there."

Whatever was there didn't click musically, as Peter recalls. "We had our first rehearsal, and it was a disaster. Terrible. I had to play somebody else's drums, and our musical tastes really clashed. They were into Zeppelin, and I was into the Stones. So they'd be doing Zeppelin things, and I'm in back doing a Charlie Watts thing. And it ain't working. So I said, 'Look, man. We can't cut it.' They agreed. But I said, 'Let's have another rehearsal anyway. Try it again.' And Gene said, 'I really don't want to lose you. All I want you to do is cut it.' I'll never forget him saying that. And I said,

'Someday, I'm gonna ram those words down your mouth. I'm gonna do more than cut it.' And the next rehearsal, we were great."

The difference, Peter points out, was in the material. "The first night, the first song they hit me with was a bitch. It was the hardest song they knew, the most technical. They did that just to bust my balls. So the next day, I said, 'Don't you guys have anything a little more rock 'n' roll? Something like Chuck Berry?' They did 'Strutter,' and I opened up with the drum. And it was great. We were really getting off. And I said, 'Now, that's cool.' And they said, 'You're hired.' And I said, 'Great.' And we became a trio."

NOTHIN' TO LOSE:
THE ROAD TO STARDOM

Chapter **05**

Gene, Peter, and Paul practiced every chance they could, but they knew that they were only at the beginning of a very long road. At the time, Gene was teaching elementary school, Paul was driving a cab part-time, and Peter was still making ends meet with his four nights a week in, as he calls it, "that Mafia-type band. Gene and Paul would come down weekends to watch, and it was weird. Their hair was down to their shoulders. One time, this really menacing-looking guy said to Gene, 'You wanna drink?' And Gene said, 'I don't drink.' So this guy said, 'You'll have a drink.' Gene said, 'I'll have a drink.' When the guy left, I said to Gene, 'Thank God you took the drink. We could get killed in here.' He said, 'What do you mean?' I said, 'Don't be naive, man. Look around you—mink coats, diamonds. What do you think's going on here?'"

Paul remembers going to see Peter play at those clubs and feeling that Peter "had star qualities. It looked like it was his band, and he was only the drummer. Yet he was the only person who made an impression, singing Wilson Pickett songs."

The club owners were always telling Peter to play softer, but one night, Peter recalls, "I said to myself, 'I don't care anymore.' And I just played with all my might. And I walked over to Gene and Paul and said, 'You got a full-time drummer. I just got fired.'"

Throughout the fall of 1972, the trio rehearsed in the loft that Gene and Paul had rented. Gene notes that "Paul and I bought an $1,800 sound system, which at the time was unheard of. No matter what else we did, we were going to be the *loudest* band that ever played. We had three stacks of Marshall amps.

"At first," Gene points out, "we looked just like another average rock 'n' roll band. But Paul and I realized early on that we had to look a little bit different. We took some real chances in the loft; we went off the deep end and tried to see what we were capable of with the makeup. I don't think there's anything terribly original about what we do, and I think that anybody who says that what they're doing is totally original is just blowing it out their asses in the grand manner.

"Before us, there was Alice Cooper and David Bowie, and before them, the Crazy World of Arthur Brown in the '60s. In the '50s, there was Screamin' Jay Hawkins, who used to climb out of a coffin carrying a human skull on a stick. People thought that was too much, but there have always been people willing to stick their necks out. Then, after a while, audiences aren't satisfied with what's already out there and things keep moving forward. We realized that to create our own situation, we would have to take the stuff that had gone before us one step further."

At the time, the New York Dolls were at the forefront of a growing New York scene. While KISS was influenced toward theatricality by the Dolls, Paul points out that "we definitely didn't want to be part of the Dolls' scene. There's only room for one at the top, and you can't out-Doll the Dolls. We knew that if we went in their direction, we would be compared to them. Besides, they were these little skinny guys in flashy clothes. They looked great. We weren't dressed like those guys, nor did we have that kind of image. We had to find our own image."

What Gene and Paul did admire about the Dolls was "that they all looked like they belonged to the same band. It was a real concise concept. They played one kind of music, and it worked." As Gene notes, "in late '72, we were rehearsing with makeup and looked like the Hello People [an early '70s band]. We used mime makeup. And I wore a sailor's outfit, and Paul wore his mom's glitter jacket. We couldn't really figure out where we were going, but we did know we didn't want it to look like a regular band." Then, one night, as Paul recalls, "Gene and I went to see the Dolls and afterward, we said, 'We've gotta drop the color and go in the opposite direction.'"

By this time, Paul feels that he and Gene had "really clicked as far as that we both knew what we wanted. And we complemented each other. I might come up with an idea, and Gene would say, 'No, we can't do that because of this,' and vice versa. There was a great give-and-take between us, especially in the beginning, when we needed direction and planning. More than the others, Gene and I have always been more businesslike, more involved in the shaping of the band, where we were gonna go and how we were gonna approach it."

Another consideration that was important to the trio was that, according to Paul, "we didn't want to make it or break it on the New York scene. Too many bands died because they were part of the New York glitter. So we tried to steer as far away from that as possible. Everybody, except us, was hanging out at [the legendary club] Max's Kansas City. They were all busy *looking* like stars. We were busy *becoming* stars."

"As a trio," Paul remembers, "we practiced about thirteen hours a day, every day. We really meant it. We had this dream of mixing theatrics with rock. When I used to go to the Fillmore East, I'd see these guys onstage wearing jeans, and I would think, 'That's wrong. He should look bigger-than-life. He should look like a star.' When you see the guy, you should feel, 'Wow! Look at that!' He should blow your mind. When I first saw David Bowie, I thought it was the greatest thing in the world.

"Gene and Paul wanted the same thing I did. It was amazing how the three of us and then the four of us had nothing in common socially, but we all wanted to create a group that meshed perfectly."

Paul agrees, adding, "Right from the start, it was understood that we were gonna wear makeup. Even when we were rehearsing as a trio, Peter wore cat makeup, Gene was wearing something weird, and I wore whiteface with lipstick and eye shadow. We tried all kinds of stuff."

Although the trio practiced religiously for months without ever playing a show, Paul fondly recalls those days "as some of the best memories I have. We didn't see it as total hardship. It was the road to stardom, almost like playing Monopoly. You gotta start at Go, not in the middle of the game. I always saw the hardest times, and there were no really bad times, as something that I would look back on one day, and I used to think it was gonna be a nice thing to look back on. The fun days. I remember Peter used to come to rehearsal at the loft with a bottle of cheap wine. It was *cold* [the temperature, not the wine], and he and I would drink Gallo sherry or port to keep warm, so we could rehearse." Paul explains that for the trio, there were no holidays. "On Thanksgiving Day in '72, Peter's mother made us turkey sandwiches. Those are great memories, and I knew even then that they would be great memories today. I knew that those things were as important as the music. It was all part of a situation that was priceless, something you could never buy."

By the end of 1972 the trio had several months of solid rehearsal behind them, and, as Gene notes, "we really had the music down. We were singing three-part harmony, and it was great. We never wanted to play in front of people where it was a situation of 'They're okay, 'cause they're just starting out.' Before anyone could see us, we had to be good. We spent a very cold New Year's Eve in the loft rehearsing. We invited a few friends to see what we were doing. They couldn't believe their eyes when they saw the makeup and the primitive costumes."

In December, 1972, the trio decided they needed a fourth member to complete the group . . . a lead guitarist to round out the sound. Paul recalls taking out "an ad in *The Village Voice*. It said, 'Hard rock group seeking guitarist with balls and flash,' except *The Village Voice* wouldn't print the word 'balls.' If you can believe that."

Guitarists responded by the dozen, Peter remembers. "You wouldn't believe what walked into that loft. Guys who knew one chord and couldn't play at all. After a while, I was going crazy." Paul: "All kinds of weirdos came down. One guy was Italian, just off the boat, and his wife was the interpreter. He didn't even bother to tune his guitar; he just took it out of the case and started playing."

"At one point," Gene remembers, "Bob Kulick, who [later] toured with Meat Loaf, was going to be the guitarist. But he didn't have the look; he had a beard, and he was a little chubbier back then. We were talking about him joining one day, when this guy walked in. With one orange sneaker and a red sneaker and a little orangey mustache. He looked like a mixture of Oriental and Norwegian.

"There were two parallel walls, and as he was walking through them, he just kind of veered off and walked into one of the walls. He was real rude, walking around and ignoring everybody. And I thought he was being rude on purpose. The guy was so flaky, up in the air, in his own world. I said, 'Would you please sit down. We're in the middle of talking to this guy. Wait your turn.' He answered, 'Hey. Wow, man. I've got . . .' I heard this voice come out of him and it was, 'Whoa.' I thought he was being a real wise guy. And I said, 'I'm gonna throw you on your ass if you don't sit down.' Again, he answered in his strange voice. 'Come on, guy. I just came in here to play guitar, don't you wanna rock 'n' roll?'"

Peter interjects. "I thought he was plastered out of his mind. I didn't believe what had come through the door. And I said, 'Either this guy's great or he's crazy, but you gotta let him play.' Gene was furious. I said, 'Wait a minute. Let him play.'"

Gene picks up the story. "We finally came to his turn, and I remember to this day, I said to him, 'You better play well or I'm gonna kick your ass.' Something like that. Or 'You're going out on your ass.'

"I said, 'Listen to the first two verses and the first two choruses. When the solo comes up, it's just gonna be the chorus section, so watch as the changes go by. And when the solo comes up, you'll know exactly where it is.' When the solo came up, he just wailed away. It was wonderful. It fit. It made sense. *And* he was tall enough.

"At the end of the song, I walked over to him. I shook his hand and said, 'I'm sorry I said anything to you. You be exactly the way you are. But the first thing you gotta do is shave off that mustache.' It was one of those stop-and-go growths. He said, 'What do you mean? This is the best-looking thing. The girls love it.' But still, he shaved it off."

Peter didn't care about the guy's mustache. "When he plugged in and played, he was great." And *he* was *Ace*.

EARTH TO JENDELL:
THE SPACE ACE

Chapter **06**

To his family, he's Paul. To the fans, he's "Ace from Space." To Gene Simmons, he's "a marshmallow." To Peter Criss, he's "the Dean Martin of the group." Paul Stanley feels that "Ace is very bright, much smarter than he wants anybody to know. Underneath his image is a good, sensitive, caring person."

Paul David Frehley, the last man to join KISS, is a New Yorker with an interesting heritage. "My father's Pennsylvania Dutch and German, and my mother's a farm girl from North Carolina. She's German and Indian. Her mother was a full-blooded Cherokee. I'm one-quarter Indian."

Born April 27, 1950, to Carl and Esther Frehley, Ace is the youngest of three children. His sister, Nancy, Ace is proud to say, "got her master's degree in chemistry and was a teacher before she got married. My brother, Charles, graduated tenth in his class from New York University. *I* was the black sheep of the family."

Ace grew up in the Mosholu Parkway section of the Bronx. "My dad's an electrical engineer, and my mother's a housewife." Just like Paul, before Ace turned to music, art was his number one passion. "I started drawing even before I went to school. My father used to bring home big boxes of paper, and I would just draw for hours."

Up until ninth grade, Ace was a star athlete, although he modestly claims that "the competition wasn't that fantastic at the parochial school I went to. I was the fastest kid in school, won all the races and medals for track. I was captain of the basketball team in eighth grade. On the softball team, I played shortstop. I was always at the toughest position," Ace points out, and then jokingly adds, "I was a star."

It is part of Ace's personality that sober self-analysis is nearly impossible, and he refuses to remain serious for any length of time, especially when talking about himself. As he recounts his personal history, he is full of jokes and put-downs of himself. But through it all, a pride in his accomplishments shines through, especially when it comes to his music.

Remembering how determined he was, Ace abandoned his athletic career when he saw it interfered with his guitar playing. "Lots of times, playing basketball, I'd get a sprained finger catching a pass, and I wouldn't be able to play guitar for a few days. I also played football for a year, but I got hit so hard once that I did a complete flip in the air and fell down. So I said to myself, 'This is bullshit. My hands are too important. The guitar comes first.'"

Ace's preoccupation with music began, naturally enough, at home. "There was always music in the house; I was surrounded by music. Everybody in my family plays piano except me. My father's an excellent pianist, and my brother's a classical guitarist.

"My brother started playing acoustic guitar when I was about twelve or thirteen. I fooled around with it, but acoustic guitar didn't excite me. A friend of mine had an electric guitar that I would play over at his house. At Christmas in '64, my parents got me an electric guitar. I just started practicing it. The first song I learned was [Herman's Hermits' 1965 number one hit] 'Mrs. Brown You've Got a Lovely Daughter.'"

Music, the central focus of Ace's teenage years, proved to be a lifesaver in his neighborhood, as Ace explains. "I was never a belligerent guy; I was always easygoing. But the reality of my situation was that where I lived, you were either a collegiate type or in a gang, a greaser. And I saw all the greasers getting all the chicks. Hanging out in a wild crowd was a much more appealing sort of lifestyle to me.

"As we got older, we started doing crazier things, and it got pretty heavy. Music took me away from that whole scene. Instead of hanging out at the corner candy store, looking for trouble, I was rehearsing with my band. Saved me. Of my friends from those days, a couple of 'em straightened out, but a lot of them are dead now. Wild people. If it wasn't for music, it's a pretty good chance that something bad would have happened to me."

Ace once summed up his youth very simply, although with slight exaggeration. "Everyone I grew up with is either dead or in jail." Where Ace's family lived wasn't nearly as bad as Peter's neighborhood, but it wasn't easy. There was all sorts of peer pressure to resist, and Ace was able to sidestep most of it because of his music. "Where I grew up, everyone my age experimented with drugs. I was never heavily into that kind of thing. Everyone tried marijuana and pills, but I shied away from that stuff because I thought it would hold me back from my creativity. From the time I started playing, all I could think about was my career."

A career in rock 'n' roll became Ace's overriding desire when he was sixteen. "I'll never forget the first live concert I ever went to. It was a [New York DJ] Murray the K show at an RKO theater in Manhattan. Mitch Ryder was the headliner. Opening up for them were The Who and Cream. I went insane. The Who really inspired me toward theatrical rock. When I saw them, it totally blew me away. I'd never seen anything like that. It was a big turning point.

"After the concert, I decided I wanted to be a professional rock musician, and nothing was gonna stop me. That show was kind of responsible for my wanting to be a rock 'n' roller. And I didn't care what anybody said. When I put my mind to something, I usually do it. It's gratifying to me to know that you can set a goal for yourself and achieve it, especially when it's a goal that's very hard to achieve.

"My parents always say that ever since I started playing guitar seriously, I used to say, 'I'm going to be a rock star. I know I can do it.' I used to look at guys on album covers and tell myself I would be on one someday. My parents always said, 'There's too much competition. You'll never make it.' But I stuck with it, and they really respect me now for not giving up."

Starting in 1965, Ace always had a group, although "in some of the early ones, I'd have to show the bass guitarist how to play because he couldn't figure it out. My first band was called The Exterminators. Our repertoire was very limited. We did 'Wipe Out' [by the Surfaris] and a couple of Beatles songs and a few others. A very limited repertoire," Ace laughs, "but my ability was very limited at the time."

As a teenager, Ace's idols were rock musicians. People like Jimi Hendrix, Pete Townshend, Eric Clapton, and Jimmy Page. "Those English guitar players were all great. Jeff Beck, [joking] Ed McMahon. Pete was one of my biggest idols. A lot of times, I was the only guitar player in the group, and I had to play a lot of chords to fill out the sound, and that's what Pete did in The Who."

In his late-teens, Ace started making money playing dances with his group. "I had so many groups—the Magic People, King Kong, Cathedral. My groups always did a lot of stuff by The Who, Cream, and Hendrix. In fact, some places wouldn't hire us because we didn't do enough Top 40 stuff.

"As I got older, we played a lot of bars and clubs. There was one placed called the Stumble Inn in Port Chester, New York. [joking] I used to stumble in and stumble out. We'd go down to the basement and steal the beer. That was a fun place."

One story that Ace does like to tell is the origin of his nickname. "I always had a lot of girlfriends. When I was in a group called King Kong, a power trio like Cream, I always used to set the drummer up with girls. When he would score, he would say, 'Wow. You're really an ace.' So he started calling me Ace all the time. And it stuck. When I joined KISS, there was already a Paul in the group, and every time somebody would say, 'Hey, Paul,' we would both turn around. So I said, 'Why don't you call me by my nickname. It's Ace.' It was the press that added 'Space' onto it."

In high school, one of his groups was "Cathedral, which consisted of Larry Kelly as lead singer, a guy named Gene on bass, and Chris Camiolo on drums." Ace interjects this aside: "Chris is a Port Authority cop at La Guardia Airport now, and the last time we landed there with KISS, he made sure the limousines were on the runway waiting for us. Larry co-wrote a song with me on my solo album.

"Anyway, one time Cathedral played at a high school dance in a big auditorium, and there were about a thousand people there. To me, at that time in my life, it was like playing Madison Square Garden. And I got this weird feeling that I was going to do this for my living, that I was going to be good and make it big. So once my band was working every weekend, I quit school."

Ace had never been an enthusiastic student. "I liked science and math was all right, but I didn't like English or history. I doubled up in art. I always took two art classes, and I was always the teacher's pet because I was the best artist in the school. They'd give me phony late passes for my other classes when I'd cut. Art teachers are usually the coolest teachers in the school.

"I consider myself to be a very intelligent guy, but I was a C student. I remember bringing home my report card the last year I was in high school, and my father said to me, 'Why can't you be like your sister and get good grades?' I said, 'Dad, it's not

MAGIC PEOPLE. STONE FOX, NEW JERSEY, NOVEMBER 23, 1968. LEFT TO RIGHT: LARRY KELLY, LEAD VOCALS, TOM STELLA, BASS, CHRIS CAMIOLO, DRUMS, ACE FREHLEY, LEAD GUITAR
(courtesy Chris Camiolo)

MAGIC PEOPLE. STONE FOX, NEW JERSEY, NOVEMBER 23, 1968, ACE FREHLEY, LEAD GUITAR, CHRIS CAMIOLO, DRUMS
(courtesy Chris Camiolo)

that I can't get straight A's. It's just that I'm bored with it. I want to play music, draw, go out with my friends and party.'

"He didn't believe that I could get good grades, so I said, 'I'll prove it to you.' For one semester, I got straight 90s. My average was around 95. I said, 'You see, Dad.' He said, 'Why can't you do this all the time?' But that wasn't my bag.

"I went to three different high schools. First, I went to a Lutheran school for a year, but I was too wild, so they kicked me out. Then I went to De Witt Clinton, a large boys school in the Bronx. It was a progressive place, but I was one of the first guys with long hair. It was me and one other guy, and they suspended me so many times and finally transferred me out because I refused to cut it.

"I wound up in Theodore Roosevelt High, and I lasted there about a year and a half. Things went well for a while. I was taking double art courses and painting a lot. I used to hang out with the head of the Art Department. But I got bored with school and dropped out in my last year. I wanted to devote more time to the group I was playing in. When that group broke up, I felt it was the right time to go back to school. At the time, I was seeing Jeanette Trerotola [Ace's wife-to-be], and she wanted me to get my diploma because she cared about me. My parents wanted me to get my diploma too. I knew that if I ever decided to go to college, I'd need a diploma. Also, I evaluated my credits and saw that it would take only about six months, so I went back.

"After I graduated, I was a mailman for a while, stationed at the Times Square Station, right across from the Port Authority Bus Terminal where all the weirdos hang out. I had my hat on and my bags, and I'd walk around delivering mail. I lasted about six months, which was the average time I held a job. I delivered furniture in the Bronx, worked as a messenger and as a delivery boy in a liquor store. I also drove a cab part-time when KISS was first getting started. I'd drive during the day and play at night."

Directionless, unwilling to settle for menial work or go to college, unable to find a band that he liked, Ace feels he "was at the most unstable point in my life when the draft [for the Vietnam War] came along. This was in 1970. I remember that I had to go to Fort Hamilton for an army physical, and I was just really crazy at the time. When I went down there, there were guys dressed as girls and trying all sorts of things to get out of the service. I talked to an army psychiatrist for about half an hour, and they finally gave me a 1-Y classification, which meant it was unlikely I would be called up."

Freed from his military obligations, Ace spent "the early '70s bouncing from band to band. I was always looking for a group that had everything, but it was hard to find the right people. I always wanted a group in which everybody was good-looking and had long hair and had their act together. But you'd always wind up with one guy who held the group back. It's very hard to find four or five people and make it happen.

"Six months before I joined KISS, I remember sitting with Jeanette in her car, drinking beer. She had to chauffeur me around because I didn't have a car. She said, 'How can you do this?' I said, 'I know I'm going to be a famous rock star, a millionaire.' She said, 'You're crazy.' To this day, she can't believe it, even when I tell her we're millionaires.

"I was the loser, the black sheep of the family, until I joined KISS. Now, I'm the big winner. But back in '72, I had nothing, zero. I had played with a lot of bands, but they never got anywhere. I even played in the Catskill Mountains in a lounge, playing cocktail music wearing a tuxedo." And then, Paul Frehley saw the ad that changed his name and his life.

"At the time, I was just breaking out of one band, and I was in limbo. I was looking for another group. That's why I answered the ad. And I remember it like it was yesterday, 'cause I had this gut reaction. When I saw that this group was looking for a guitar player, I knew it was going to be special.

"When I spoke to them on the phone, they asked me what I looked like. I'm thin now, but at the time I was thirty pounds lighter. I was really skinny, about six foot one, 130 pounds. They said, 'What do you look like?' I said that I look a little like Keith Richards, because I had his haircut at the time."

Ace was invited to the loft for an audition, but he had a financial problem. "I didn't have much money at the time. I couldn't take my equipment on the subway, and I certainly couldn't afford cab fare. So I had to con my mom into driving me there with my amplifier. I remember telling her, 'Mom, you gotta give me a ride. I really feel something special about this.' I just had weird vibes.

"I was always a sharp dresser. I'm the kind of guy who if I like the style, likes to buy the same thing in different colors. I used to walk into a shoe store, and if I found some slip-on shoes that I liked, I would buy four pair—one in orange, one in green, one in yellow, and one in white. I always wanted to be different, and that's one of the reasons I became so successful. I wasn't your average, run-of-the-mill kid from the Bronx. I used to dress wilder than most of the people in my neighborhood." Ace considers himself to be "a forerunner in style. I was the first one of my friends to get bell-bottoms. They all laughed, but six months later, they were all wearing them. That's the kind of person I was and will always be.

"I had bought some sneakers in red and orange, and I wore one of each to the audition. I don't remember if I did it as a goof, or if I wasn't looking when I got dressed, but I thought they kind of looked cute together. Gene and Paul didn't think it looked so cute. In fact, they thought it was pretty stupid.

"Anyway, when I got to the loft, what they did was simple. They said, 'We're gonna play a song for you. Listen to it once and then play along with us.' They played 'Deuce.' I fell in love with the song. I said, 'Wow. This sounds good.' I got up and jammed along. The song was in A, and I just soloed through the whole song. They all smiled. We jammed for a few more songs, and then they said, 'We like the way you play a lot. We'll call you.'

"I really wanted to be in the band. From the time I walked into the loft, I wanted them to call me. I remember coming home from the audition, walking into my house and telling my parents, 'I think I found a good band. I think this is it.' I just had a feeling that this was gonna be my long-awaited chance. And it was.

"Two weeks later, they brought me down again. They had their girlfriends there. I guess they wanted to get feedback, to know if I was made of the right stuff. I guess I was because that was the time we tied the knot, so to speak." Finally, Gene and Paul and Peter and Ace had what they all been searching for—a perfectly balanced group. They looked like a group, they played well together, and they all were willing to do whatever it would take to make it. They even had a game plan. Now, all they needed was a name.

FIRST KISS:
ROCK BOTTOM

Chapter **07**

With the addition of Ace, the still unnamed group became a foursome . . . four young musicians committed to creating a different kind of musical sensation.

By mid-January of 1973, it had already been decided that they would wear makeup, that the group's image would be dark and exciting and larger-than-life. To create the desired look, black and silver costumes were created. The specifics of the stage show hadn't been worked out yet, but the first pieces were beginning to fall into place.

"Paul was driving his Mustang, and I was in the back seat," Gene recalls, "and Peter was in front, 'cause I'm deathly afraid of cars. Ace wasn't there. We were trying to think of a name, and Paul, joking, said, 'How about Crimson Harpoon?' We all started laughing, and then he said, 'How about KISS?' And nobody laughed. It just fit."

"The week we decided to call ourselves KISS, I went home and made a button," Ace remembers. "I created a logo on it, and the only difference between that button and the logo as it is today is that I had a dot on the 'i' like a diamond. Despite what people say, I wasn't thinking of the [Nazi] SS when I designed it. I was thinking more of lightning bolts. In fact, my first boots had lightning bolts down the side."

The costumes at that time were very primitive, according to Paul. "Our outfits were predominantly black. I wore real high heels, skintight Lurex pants, black knee socks, and a black T-shirt that said 'KISS.' The costume cost about $45.

"I made the pants myself because I couldn't afford to buy them. So instead, I bought a couple of yards of Lurex material, and my mother said, 'What are you doing?' I said, 'I'm gonna make myself a pair of pants.' She said, 'You can't make pants.' I said, 'I'm gonna do it.' 'Can't' is the wrong thing to say to me. I took my favorite jeans apart to use as a pattern, and my mother showed me how to work the sewing machine. My father said, 'I really admire your perseverance. I'll buy you the pants.' At this point, there was no way I was gonna buy pants.

"So I made them, except for the zipper. And my mother said, 'You did a great job, but you can't put the zipper in.' But I did. And the pants were great, skintight, almost like knickers. When Gene saw them, he liked them, and I made him a pair. In all fairness, I didn't put anywhere near the work into his pair that I did into mine. I think I just wanted to show myself that I could do it. And yet, for the first tour, even after we had real costumes made, Gene still carried those pants in his suitcase in case he ever needed a backup. For years, you could look in Gene's suitcase and he had the pants. Mine were so tight they ultimately split right up the crotch when we were onstage one night. I was the hit of the evening that time."

KISS's first appearance was scheduled for a place called Popcorn. Gene remembers how "we started handing out these little leaflets. 'Come see KISS on January 30.' We also had this picture of us in which we looked like the Sons of the Dolls. One of Peter's friends blew it up into a big five-foot picture. We wanted to put it in the window at Popcorn, but I said to Ace, 'We can't do that. Nobody will know what it is. They'll think it's a drag show. Put the name of the group on it and make it look fancy.' And Ace did it, just created our logo."

By the time January 30 arrived, Popcorn, located at the northeast corner of Queens Boulevard and 47th Street in Queens, had changed its name to Coventry. "Needless to say," Gene admits, "there was nobody there."

That first show, though, proved that KISS was a new band with a knockout rock 'n' roll punch. "There was no compromise," Gene points out. "Our set was about fifteen songs, and they were all originals. Those songs wound up on the first two KISS albums, with one notable exception. 'Life in the Woods' was one of the all-time bombs. Paul wrote it."

Life in the woods would be easy
Make a house of flowers and trees
Keepin' in tune with the city
Singing along with the breeze.

Gene dryly suggests that "those words obviously didn't make it."

"Our show had no talking," Gene remembers. "Just bang-bang-bang, song-song-song and off the stage. We didn't have any effects at the time. We just did a lot of ménage à trois kind of stuff. I'd put one leg out, and Ace (who barely knew the changes) would kind of wrap around my leg and Paul would get in back of Ace, and we'd all move around, back and forth. And remember, this was in the days when nobody except Alice Cooper moved. All rock bands stood still."

The first special effect KISS developed was a joke, basically borrowed from the Harlem Globetrotters. Gene: "When we did the song 'Firehouse,' Paul had a bucket full of confetti that said, 'Water—In Case Of Fire.' And at the end of the song, he took the bucket and threw it into the audience and everyone went, 'OOOOO.' But there was no fire-breathing or any pyrotechnics. Just a lot of gyrating, a lot of jumping up and down. We'd tune offstage, walk through the crowd wearing these high heels, and go right up there and play.

"We must have looked like dinosaurs," Gene recalls. "By 1973, everybody had stopped wearing high heels. We had these six-inch boots with studs on them. It looked like an S&M thing, and if you didn't know what the studs were, they were the strangest things you ever saw. They looked like they weighed a ton. But the show itself was straight-ahead. Real raw, real short, real good rock 'n' roll."

According to Gene, "that night at Coventry, I put on whiteface, put my hair up, kind of had that batlike thing, but no black lipstick. I had the design. Paul put on rouge and that was it. Ace had his little design, but no whiteface. And Peter had only rouge on his cheeks and red lipstick."

Ace, the newest member of the group, had no qualms about putting on makeup. "It didn't bother me at all. I was always into wild things. The first night, I painted my face silver. The second night, I thought, 'That's boring. I'll have to think up something more imaginative.' I started painting stars on my eyes."

Paul remembers "playing with all different kinds of designs. The makeup was always basically the same, but what was on my eye kept changing. Ace thought of the star, and it fit, because when I was a kid, I loved drawing stars."

KISS played Coventry for three nights, and as Gene remembers, "the only people who showed up were Peter's wife, Lydia, and Jan Walsh, my girlfriend at the time. Jan was always very supportive. The girl that had the car and was always there for us. It was never a situation between she and I of an exclusive relationship. There were always lots of real good-looking girls around, so I was with whomever I wanted to be. But when I wanted to go out on a Friday or Saturday night, Jan would be the girl. She was fancier-looking, knew how to dress and all that stuff."

After the unsuccessful shows at Coventry, KISS returned to the loft for three weeks of rehearsals to try, in Gene's words, "to figure out what went wrong." All during that period, Gene was "paying the bills 'cause I was the only one working. Paul and I shared the rent at the loft, but I paid for everything else. All along, I kept little notes of what everybody owed me. Peter—$7.50. Ace—$14."

Ace recalls the poverty of that time. "I was broke before I joined KISS, and I was broke after I joined KISS. At one point, Gene was the only guy working, and I'd have to ask him to lend me money for the subway so I could get home. I didn't have a job, and my mom said, 'Son, you can't keep hitting me up for money so you can go drinking beer with your friends.' So I started driving a cab part-time."

To Gene, "it was an amazing situation where sometimes, I'd lend so much money to everybody that all I had left was about 50 cents, enough to get a doughnut and a cup of coffee and to work the next day."

Throughout the early '70s, right up until the week before KISS went on its first tour, Gene held a succession of jobs, ranging from assistant director of the Puerto Rican Interagency Council to a man Friday at *Vogue* magazine. Gene: "The point was, if the band didn't work out, I would always have enough money to get by. I'd work during the day, rehearse in the evening, and live in the loft. I had my bed and TV set up there."

Perhaps more than anything else, it is Gene's ambition that fueled KISS's rise to the top. "In most cases, if I didn't care, there wouldn't have been a band, but I was determined to keep it together. I wanted to be a millionaire before I was thirty. But I was going to make sure I had alternatives. After I graduated from Richmond College in '72, I became an apprentice teacher in the sixth grade at this very progressive public school. I only stayed for six months. I understood that I became a teacher because I wanted to get up onstage and have people notice me. I didn't last in a classroom because thirty people wasn't a big enough audience. I wanted forty thousand. Besides, those kids were devils, and I was ready to kill them."

Paul remembers that by 1973, "my parents were very worried. They wanted me to leave home unless I chipped in. I was eating like a man and taking up space, and I needed clothes and stuff, and yet I wasn't contributing any money. So there was a lot of pressure on me. But I wasn't going to move out until I was ready. I felt like they were trying to kick me out of the nest, and I was clutching on. That was a shock for me. All of a sudden, my parents were telling me I was a big boy. So I drove a cab part-time, pleaded poverty, and they hung in there with me. They were always with me. I didn't leave home until *after* the first KISS album."

Lew Linet, who was Wicked Lester's manager, would have become KISS's manager too, but, according to Paul, "he hated us. He thought we were much too loud and didn't know why we wanted to dress so crazy. He wanted us to look like the Beatles." Still, Linet was all KISS had, and it was up to him to find work for the group. Unable to book the band in New York City, Linet found KISS a job playing a small club called The Daisy, located in Amityville on the south shore of Long Island.

Paul describes the scene. "It was a tiny place. Actually, it was a store. It had a pool table, a bar, and a tiny stage. To go with our image, we set up our equipment onstage to make us look big. We used a lot of dummy amps, just boxes without speakers in them. And we told the lighting man to make sure the lights don't hit the amps because they'll shine right through.

"When we went onstage, we figured people would kill us for the way we looked if they knew this was one of our first gigs. So we took the bull by the horns and said, 'The reason we haven't played here before is that we've been so busy playing New York City.'"

The ploy didn't really work, Gene points out. "That night, about eighty people showed up. And when we came onstage and started playing, everybody was stunned. And they stopped drinking. That got the owner of the club real angry. When we had done the afternoon sound check, we were fairly normal, long-haired guys doing loud rock 'n' roll. So this guy Sid [Benjamin], who owned The Daisy, didn't know what we were about to unleash."

Gene continues the story. "By this time, Peter's wife, Lydia, and his little sister, and Paul and Paul's mother had put together black and silver outfits. I had a T-shirt with a skull and crossbones. And when we came out for the show in makeup, we scared the living daylights out of everybody. Nobody knew what the hell was going on. And we were playing real, real loud."

KISS had been booked for the weekend at The Daisy, but it looked like Friday might be opening and closing night. Gene: "Sid got very mad. He screamed, 'You guys are never coming back here again. Look at my bar. Everybody's stopped drinking.' That was his main concern, of course. Rock 'n' roll's supposed to make you thirsty. In fact, in the middle of 'Life in the Woods,' Peter would go into a repetitive drum kick and Paul and I would run out into the audience, take the drinks out of people's hands, slam the drinks on the table, and force the people to clap their hands along. Sid couldn't believe it. 'What are you doing?' he shouted. 'My customers aren't drinking.'

"The next night, there were 150 people there. We doubled Sid's audience in one night. And he said, 'You guys are the best band I ever saw.' And we went back there in March for two weekends in a row, and it was packed every night. Everybody wanted to come and see this new band.

"Of course, we would help it along. We used Sid's office as a dressing room, and there were always people calling on the phone asking, 'Who's playing tonight?' And I'd get on the phone and say, 'The most amazing band you've ever seen! For one night only! Tonight! Just back from their cross-country tour! KISS! Yes, the amazing band you can't live without!' Or I'd say, 'Live sacrifice onstage.' Anything. And the people would come. We built up a following.

"In fact, there was one couple in their late fifties. The guy was bald, but that didn't prevent he and his wife from getting up and dancing their butts off. Everybody was fascinated by us, and this was really only the third gig we'd ever played."

In December, KISS returned to Coventry for a weekend engagement. The headlining act was Isis, who, Gene recalls, "was a dyke band, so they wanted to prove to us that they were strong. And we had a big fight downstairs. Isis had just signed with Neil Bogart and Buddah Records."

It was around this time that KISS and Lew Linet parted company. Paul explains that, from the very beginning, "Lew wanted us to turn down the volume. He used to come to rehearsals and say, 'If you don't turn down, I'm walking out.' Obviously, he wasn't the guy for us, but we parted on good terms."

One thing that disappointed KISS was that when they played places like The Daisy, after the manager's share and expenses, the salary might be only $5 a man. Still, other than misfiring with Linet, KISS made no major mistakes during their rise to the top. Paul points out that "if there were lessons to be learned from other bands' mistakes, we tried to learn them." Paul feels KISS was ultimately successful because "we devoted twenty-five hours a day to the group. And it was meant to be. I think it's important for people to know that what makes success is the effort and time you spend on it. Nothing comes free. It's not luck. It's believing in yourself and really, *really* giving it your all. From the time that the group became a foursome, there was something very special about what we were doing. It was all really magical. It wasn't something that you could create artificially or buy. It was *there.*"

The magic, though, was still something that, except on a few occasions, hadn't been communicated to an audience. That didn't shake the group's belief in what they were doing. So when Lew Linet failed to share their vision, they didn't change. Lew left the team.

KISS decided that the only way to make a splash was to keep trying, and they tried everything imaginable. Probably the biggest difference between KISS and every other group in the world was their self-promotion effort. While KISS rehearsed by night, Gene sold the band by day.

Gene: "I was working at *Vogue* (as assistant to the editor) and had access to the mail room, paste-up department, and the Xerox machines. We took some pictures and wrote a little bio kit, and I put together a mailing list. From the trade magazines, I compiled a list of every record company. Then, I included every rock 'n' roll magazine and every daily newspaper in New York. Each time we played a show, I'd do a mass mailing. I printed complimentary tickets and invited everybody to come and see us the first time we played New York City."

That gig took place on May 4, 1973. Gene: "It was at a loft at 52 Bleecker Street [in Greenwich Village]. We agreed to play for free, and we supplied the sound system. About three hundred people showed up at $3 a head to see KISS open the show, then the Brats and Wayne County was the headliner. A couple of people came to see us, including [producer] Felix Pappalardi's wife, Gail, and Eddie Kramer, who was still working as an engineer at Electric Lady. We *died* when we found out he was in the audience. Ron Johnsen was there too. Actually, everybody that was in any band was there, including Debbie Harry, who was in the Stilettos then. This was before she formed Blondie. Teenage Lust was there, the Movies, Eric Emerson and the Tramps, and Harlots of 42nd Street, a popular band that never got a contract.

"And the [New York] Dolls. They all wanted to see what this new group KISS was about. They thought we were shit, but we knew, of course, that we could blow them off the stage. I met them in the bathroom that night when I was taking my makeup off. That was the night Paul had his first guitar stolen, one of his hand-made guitars."

KISS's New York premiere did not lead to instant stardom. Gene: "Nothing happened from that night. We now knew, though, from playing and seeing how we went over, that we were the best of the local bands. We were better than all those groups that had come to see us."

Gene's self-confidence has always been one of the key elements that propelled KISS to success. According to Gene, it comes from "early in life when I learned it was okay to fail at something. All you gotta do is get up and try again. And the next time, you do it better. Most people don't get to the first step. But I knew it was gonna take time. I didn't give up."

For Gene, the source of his drive is "ego, of course. Ego satiation. I want the pat on the back. I no longer care if I get respect 'cause I've got self-respect. I know exactly who I am. That's all I *need*." But, Gene admits, "I *want* notoriety. And I don't want just rock 'n' roll notoriety. I want, fifty years from now, to be the musical group of the '70s, just like the Beatles are the '60s and Elvis is the '50s. And I don't care if people don't remember a single song. I don't have any hang-ups about musicianship. By its very nature, rock 'n' roll is not complex music. It's throwaway art. The only thing I hope is that I entertain the people in my audience."

While today everybody leaves a KISS concert satisfied, back in June of 1973, their audience was almost nonexistent. They decided that the only way to get significant exposure was to put on their own shows. Paul explains, "Nobody in New York would hire us, but we were determined to make it. And the one who wins the race is the one who runs the fastest. And we were going to run faster than anybody else. I don't think half the bands back then knew *why* the audience liked them. They didn't think about that or what they could do to further their career. We spent a lot of time thinking about what we were doing, why we were doing it, and how it was gonna help us. Most other bands come and go, and once it's over, they don't know why. We weren't going to let that happen."

In their career push, Paul recalls that the next step was when "we started renting the ballroom of the Diplomat Hotel, a sleazy place on 43rd Street and Sixth Avenue in Manhattan. I would draw posters, and we would go around New York at night and put them up. The posters advertised a dance. In *The Village Voice*, we put an ad for a concert."

Gene continues the story. "If a band wasn't famous, I knew that you needed an event to draw a crowd. We used Friday the 13th. So on July 13, we played New York City for the second time. It cost us $650 to rent the Crystal Room at the Diplomat, which was an accomplishment because no other group had that kind of money. And besides, we had a great, state-of-the-art sound system.

"We charged $3.50, which was competitive prices for a rock show at that time. There were three bands on the bill. Opening the show were the Planets, always a favorite group of mine that never made it. Then came KISS, and headlining the show were the Brats. We agreed to pay the Brats a certain amount, and we would keep any amount over that. Even though we weren't headlining the show, it was us hiring the Brats. The whole show cost us about $1,000; we drew about five hundred people and made out like bandits.

"All kinds of people came down that night . . . Felix Pappalardi, other record industry people that we invited. The talk was spreading real fast."

Gene admits to an extra bit of promotion. "On the invitations, I played a dirty trick. You know, you play to win. I changed the names around so that it looked like KISS was headlining the show. And I put the show time as the time *we* went on, so that whoever came to see us would come when we were on. I knew that when our set was over, there would be forty minutes of people milling around, so [the guests] would think it was over and go home. I wanted them to look around and think something was happening for *KISS*. We gave out KISS T-shirts with the logo done in sparkles, and people were wearing them. So anybody who came would see KISS all over the place. And it worked. Everybody in town started talking about us."

The July show was a success. However, it was their next self-promoted concert, on August 10, that would prove to be the turning point in the group's career.

THE ELDERS:
BILL AUCOIN AND NEIL BOGART

Chapter **08**

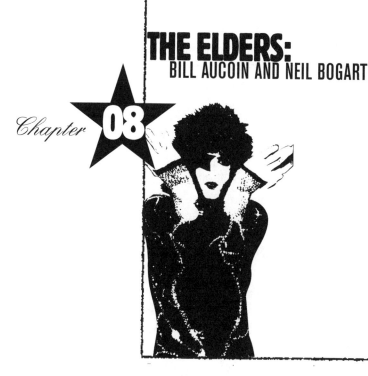

"At our next show," Gene recalls, "Luger was the opening act. They had Ivan Kral on guitar, and he's in the Patti Smith Group now. Also on the bill was Street Punk, a great little band. We always tried to help them out, but they killed themselves. They were their own worst enemy. Anyway, about five or six hundred people showed up, and Bill Aucoin was in the audience."

The arrival of Bill Aucoin has had an inestimable impact on KISS's career, and it is not an exaggeration to say that without Bill Aucoin, KISS might never have become a superstar attraction.

Paul remembers when he first saw Bill. "While we were playing, I saw these two straight-looking guys in the audience. They were wearing suits and had short hair, and in the crowd that we were drawing, they looked weird. I couldn't figure out what they were doing there."

Peter laughs when he recounts how his "sister Donna sold Bill on us. She was wearing a KISS T-shirt, and she was sitting next to Bill. Half of my family was there cheering. And Donna was screaming, 'They're great! They're Great! THEY'RE GREAT! Aren't they?' And Bill said, 'Yeah, I guess they are.'"

Gene details the tactics that attracted Bill Aucoin to that concert. "He was one of the people on our mailing list. All along, he was getting our bio kits that said things like, 'A band you cannot miss.' 'The band that will rule the earth.' Paul and I wrote it.

These were nice packages with posters and tickets, and everything was concise. We obviously knew what we were doing.

"Bill came to the show with an ad executive that he was working with. At the time, Bill's company, Direction Plus, was making rock 'n' roll commercials for television. His main client was Neil Bogart at Buddah Records. Anyway, at the end of the show, Bill approached me. I was still in makeup, and I was at a table with a photographer whose face I was sitting on every once in a while. Real big girl. *Mammaries.* Because he was a short-haired guy with a mustache and a suit and tie, I knew he was in the industry, but I didn't know who he was. He introduced himself and started talking to me, but I was playing these games with him. This girl kept sticking my face in her breasts or whatever. It was all very exotic. So while Bill was talking, I ignored him. It's an old trick, like a carrot in front of a mule. I was making a point with him. Still, I agreed to meet him the next day. Then, I told Paul about it."

"Frankly," Paul continues, "at first, I wasn't even interested in meeting him. Being in the rock 'n' roll world, you get jaded very quickly. There are so many people telling you, 'I'm gonna make you a star . . . You're the greatest thing I've ever seen . . . Baby, it's you and me.' These people are full of shit, and if you sign the wrong piece of paper, you wind up being owned by somebody. You can get screwed royally in this business.

"Even so, I went with Gene to see him. And it was the same that happened when Peter joined or when Ace joined. It was the next step. He became another member in the family. The chemistry was perfect.

"He said, 'I'm gonna get you a record contract within two weeks. I don't want to handle you unless I can make you the biggest band in the country.' We had heard that before, but somehow, it was totally different coming from him."

Gene explains why he felt that Bill Aucoin was the right man. "I knew he'd never managed a group before, but I also knew that he had produced a *television* show. Back then, I knew that the manager of KISS would have to be a multimedia person. KISS was never meant to be just another rock 'n' roll band; we were gonna fast outgrow the guitars. It was going to be a multimedia group; the group that can do everything.

"Paul and I used to talk about that. KISS was a real concept. I kept talking about Superman and the Incredible Hulk, and that KISS could be like that. Paul never understood why I read the superhero magazines, and he never believed we would be a comic book. But he did know for sure that we'd get on TV, or at the least, we'd get lots of pictures in magazines because we were interesting to look at. So Bill's television and film background was crucial.

"The first day we met Bill, he told us about a friend of his who was going to be starting his own record company. Bill thought we would be perfect as the label's first act. We didn't sign anything with Bill then; it was a verbal agreement. I remember the first thing I asked him was, 'Why do you want to do this? What's in it for you?' He said, 'I've never done this before, and I want to put together the kind of band that's gonna be the biggest band in the world.' One of those kind of raps. And it just so happened that's what we wanted too . . . to be the band that *can* do it all."

"After the meeting," Paul recalls, "we were walking in the Village, and we called Peter. And he said, 'Yeah, I've heard that before.' And we were saying, 'No. You don't understand. This time, it's different.'"

Peter's cynicism was well earned. His early experiences with the music business were more than just unpleasant; they were almost artistically destructive. Peter had played in Brotherhood, "and we won a contest at the Academy of Music. The prize was a contract to make a single for RCA Records. We recorded a song of mine called 'Gypsy,' but they never released it. So we forgot about it. Months and months later, I heard it on the radio. except the lyrics were changed, and it had a different title. I went crazy.

"Also, I went through bad times with Chelsea when [our manager] dropped us. That's what made me not trust managers. I was very skeptical about Bill. He really had to prove his shit to me." Ironically, despite his concerns, Peter and Bill hit it off immediately. "I liked him right away. When I met him, I was impressed. I felt he was honest. He's one of the most honest men I've ever met in my life. He's helped us a lot. He is 'the fifth KISS.'"

In the early '70s, Bill Aucoin was producing a television show, *Flipside*, which was about the record business. In 1973, he started getting "weekly bulletins from this group, KISS. My only thought about it, from looking at the pictures, was that they'd be a terrific performing band. At the time, the New York Dolls were receiving a tremendous amount of publicity even though they weren't selling records.

"When I decided to go into the music industry, I decided to go and take a look at KISS because of what they sent me, because of their determination and persistence. That first night, they were still in pretty rough form in the sense that they certainly didn't have what the show is today. The makeup wasn't all uniform, but it was there. One thing that impressed me was the fact that they really wanted to perform. They weren't sidestepping it at all. That made me decide to give it a chance.

"When I met Gene and Paul, I said, 'If we're going to do it, if you're interested in working hard and making this a major, major group, then I'd be willing to put as much as I can behind it.' I can remember them saying, 'Boy, if we could just be as big as the New York Dolls.' I kept saying to them, 'I hope you're going to be a lot bigger.' I saw flaws in the Dolls' situation."

In a sense, KISS chose Aucoin and vice versa. "I had been approached by other bands, but KISS were the ones that were probably the most conscious of where I was. A lot of potentially successful bands will call or send something once and then give up. They [KISS] called and wrote to me week after week. And I was just one of hundreds of people they were contacting regularly. That showed a determination to succeed.

Those mailings and calls take a lot, especially if you haven't had any success and people aren't coming to see you. It can be tough to keep going, to keep saying, 'Let's try again.'

"When I first saw their show, I didn't know whether they had talent, but I saw in them the desire to turn on an audience. I knew that was an essential ingredient, that will to please. So I told the guys, 'I'll back the group, and I will make it happen. We'll start a management company, and we'll get the whole thing together in about two weeks.' I told them there was no obligation, and that we would not sign any papers until we were satisfied that we were happy with one another.

"I don't think they expected I would move so quickly. I first met them in August, got them a record deal in September, signed with them in October, they recorded an album in November, and by December, the first KISS album was finished, and we had begun working on the show."

Earlier in 1973, Eddie Kramer at Electric Lady Studios had repaid an old debt to Gene and Paul with studio time. Kramer, who would later produce several KISS albums, had gone into the studio with KISS to produce a five-song demo tape— "Strutter," "Deuce," "Cold Gin," "Watchin' You," and "Black Diamond." It was that tape Bill Aucoin used to sell KISS.

"Neil Bogart had been a guest on *Flipside,* and I had produced a number of commercials for him for Buddah Records. I sent him the tape, and after he listened to it, he played it for his young, hot production team, Kenny Kerner and Richie Wise. They told Neil how terrific KISS was, and Neil in turned asked them if they would like to produce KISS. When they said they would love the opportunity, Neil said, 'Let's try it.'

"This," Bill explains, "was in August of '73, long before Neil had ever seen the group. The day after he got the tape, I called him and said, 'I believe in this group. One, I think the demo is good. Two, I think they've got a tremendous and very positive energy. Three, I don't think their egos are going to get in the way of their career.'

"One of KISS's selling points was their ability to get along with each other. Record companies were leery of backing groups because sometimes just as a group would be making it, their egos would get in the way and the group would break up. It was a gamble that record companies didn't like to take, especially with an untried group like KISS."

Gene recalls that after Kerner and Wise "convinced Neil Bogart to sign us, Neil flew to New York to meet his new group. It was a difficult time for him. He was going through all kinds of stuff. Still at Buddah, he was planning on forming his own record company by the end of the year. We met him at the end of August."

Having given Bill Aucoin two weeks to get KISS a record deal, the band, Gene remembers, "went to see him, saying, 'A couple of weeks have gone by. Are we gonna do it?' And Bill said, 'I'd like you to meet somebody.' In walks Neil with film clips, the TV commercials that he and Bill had done. And Neil said, 'I want to put together the kind of group that is going to do all the things . . .'

"He was talking right up our alley. Same stuff we wanted. Except at this point, Neil doesn't know anything about our makeup or our logo. All he knew was that we were a hard rock band whose music fit his concept. Still, we were really impressed. Everybody spoke the same language. We all wanted to do the same thing. It made a lot of sense. It was gonna be Bill's first band, our first album, and it was going to be the first release for Emerald City Records. Before the first KISS album came out, Neil Bogart had changed the name of his label. Also a tribute to a classic film, the name he chose was Casablanca.

In September of 1973, Bill Aucoin put the four members of KISS on a $75 a week salary so they could concentrate on developing their music and show. As Gene recalls, "This was amazing to us. Everybody except me quit his job. Ace stopped delivering liquor, and Paul stopped driving a cab. Seventy-five dollars was very easy to live on."

In late August, KISS returned to The Daisy for the last time, and in early October, they played their first show for Neil Bogart. The place was Le Tang Ballet Studios, directly across from Bell Sound, where KISS would record their first album. The reaction they got that day is etched in Gene's memory.

"Neil wanted to introduce us to the press and get some of his friends interested. People like Richard Robinson, Lisa Robinson, [writers for *Rock Scene* and *Creem*] and Alison Steele, a disc jockey in New York. Neil came and sat down front with Richie Wise and Kenny Kerner. Sean Delaney was there. At the time, he was a creative person hanging out with Bill. He would later prove to be a real asset to the band.

"We came out and did our five songs. Neil Bogart's mouth is *hanging* open. He has no idea what's going on. During 'Life in the Woods,' we put down our guitars and ran into the audience. I grabbed Neil's hands and was clapping them for him. Literally, his mouth is wide open. At the end of the last song, 'Firehouse,' we threw the confetti in his face. And then we ran out of the room while the equipment was still feeding back.

"Finally, somebody unplugged the equipment, and for a long time, there was a lot of silence. Nobody knew what to say. Neil wasn't sure if it was gonna happen or not. But Sean Delaney was jumping up and down. 'Wow! I never saw anything like it! Great band! Wow!' Neil didn't quite know what to make of it."

Shortly after that show, KISS signed a management agreement with Bill Aucoin. As Gene puts it, "We knew it felt right." In November, KISS began recording their first album and finished mixing it by the end of November.

The formation of Bill Aucoin's Rock Steady management company was the final step in formalizing the relationship between KISS and Bill Aucoin. Aucoin also made a suggestion to the band that was revolutionary for the music business. Bill felt that KISS should be set up as a *financial* democracy, and he explains the reasoning behind the idea. "When we began, I knew that some of the members of the group were stronger onstage than the others, and that it would take time for everyone to gain equal strength musically as well as in performing. I knew that a flaw could destroy the group, and I was determined that there wouldn't be a flaw. If somebody reaps too much of the rewards of success, then you don't have a group, you have four musicians, which doesn't work for long. It has to be a unit. I knew the group had a chance to go far and wanted to avoid any possibility that the group would destroy itself.

"I approached the guys and said, 'We all agree that we're going to be a major act, and that means a lot of money. In the long run, the difference between one person making a few thousand or even a few hundred thousand dollars is not going to mean anything. I don't want you to break up over money. It's going to be hard if some of you are only making a salary and just surviving, and the others are getting extra money from songwriting. Let's make our arrangements so unified that nothing can destroy it and certainly not money.'"

Paul feels that "Bill's suggestions were important because Gene and I had been writing almost all of the material. And if we had hits, sooner or later, somebody would feel left out. We knew you're better off taking a smaller piece of something huge, than taking a bigger piece of something small. Also, I didn't want to be faced with someone saying, 'I have to have my songs on the album because I want the publishing money.' So the way we've always worked it is that whoever has the best material, we use it. And split the money four ways. As long as everybody does their share of work, then nobody feels cheated. You can't put a price tag on somebody's contribution."

Given the ambition for KISS that everybody harbored, it was an unprecedented experiment, especially for an industry as cutthroat as the record business. As Bill explains, "we set KISS up as an equal partnership. Share and share alike."

In addition to his business sense, Gene also credits Bill Aucoin with the imagination that helped make KISS larger-than-life. "To put it bluntly, the four of us created the makeup, the logo, the tunes, and the look and feel of KISS. But it was Bill who took it all the way. It was Bill who said, 'Let's take this to the nth degree. Let's breathe fire. Let's have explosions and all sorts of things.' We didn't have the technical expertise and/or the money to do any of that. But Bill and Neil did. They bought us new amplifiers, new equipment, new guitars and drums. They spent thousands of dollars."

On December 21 and 22, KISS returned to the Coventry for a pair of farewell shows. "Before we played Coventry," Gene recalls, "Bill had brought a magician to one of our rehearsals. Bill said, 'If we're gonna do it, let's take it all the way.' And the magician taught me how to breathe fire.

"That show at Coventry was incredible. Everybody was on their feet, screaming their heads off. Nobody could believe it. The club only held three hundred people and anybody who was anybody in the New York scene came down. That gig was preparation for our New Year's Eve show, which was to be our first official unveiling. We played the Academy of Music, December 31, 1973, and we were paid $250." But KISS didn't earn their place on the stage that night, according to Gene. "As a favor, we were tacked onto a bill that included Iggy & the Stooges, Teenage Lust, with Blue Öyster Cult headlining. We were fourth on the bill.

"Before we came out, before the first note was hit, the announcer screamed: 'All right! You wanted them. You've got them. The hottest band in the world! Here they are—KISS!' And a flash pot went off, and everybody grabbed their heart. It was New Year's Eve, and those people were there for a good time, drinking and smoking. Nobody knew what was going on. By the fourth song, I was [literally] smoking. During 'Firehouse,' when I did the fire-breathing, my hair caught on fire, the left side of my head was in flames. I didn't know what was going on except all of a sudden, the *entire* audience was on its feet. Sean Delaney put out the fire, and we continued the show. And it really was a show.

"We had this huge logo, the biggest thing you ever saw. It was this six-foot thing that flashed on and off. Nobody else had a logo. And then the drum platform levitated at the end, and the people were pulling their hair out. They didn't know what the hell happened. All together, we did thirty minutes, got off, and we were not allowed an encore.

"A week later, the first issue of *Sounds* magazine came out, and that was the first time we were ever written up. The article mentioned KISS all through the review, and they used three pictures from the concert—one of Iggy, one of Teenage Lust, and the biggest picture was of me! We [also] got our first real review from Fred Kirby in *Variety*. He reviewed all four groups in one article. The entire first paragraph, which was half the review, was about KISS, this 'ghoulish rock 'n' roll band that was a combination of . . .' Needless to say, people hated us or loved us. But right from the beginning, they couldn't stop talking about us."

KISS's name and image were making an immediate impact, and it wasn't totally positive. Bill Aucoin: "Neil was bombarded by his friends in the industry who thought he had made a mistake. He was rapped for signing us as his first group and because we wore makeup and played hard-core rock 'n' roll, which wasn't popular at the time. Neil really went out on a limb, and he took the brunt of it because at the time, no one knew who I was."

On January 8, KISS was scheduled to play a press party/showcase at the Fillmore East. Bill remembers that right before the event, "Neil called me from California and said, 'Bill. I'm getting beaten to death with this makeup. Are you really sure you want to do the makeup.' And I said, 'This is what KISS is about, a part of everything they're doing.' Neil asked me to ask them if they would consider taking it off if they have to.

But when I asked them, they just looked at me kind of funny. I said, 'Okay. You don't have to say any more.'

"Despite the flak, we went straight ahead with the makeup. For a while, we did change Paul's, because Neil thought the star was too feminine, too much like the Dolls, and that could be confusing. The Dolls had already started downhill at that point, and Neil didn't want any association between the groups. He feared that might bring KISS down to the Dolls' level. So we changed Paul's star to a raccoon-type mask, which he hated. That lasted about two weeks before we went back to the star.

"It's important," Bill explains, "to remember that the original idea behind the makeup was so that people would notice them, so they'd be of the same caliber as their idols, the New York Dolls. But they wanted to look even more extreme. The makeup KISS wears isn't at all feminine. It's a lot closer to the actors in Japanese Kabuki theater than the Dolls' drag queen look. [The makeup] coupled with their theatrics did make people sit up and take notice. In spite of the abuse Neil took from the music industry, he never wavered outwardly in his support of us. He might have had some second thoughts, but he never said so."

And really, by the time of the Fillmore East press party on January 8, it was too late to turn back. Gene remembers that day spotting "the old Alice Cooper set from his *Billion Dollar Babies* tour in the back of the Fillmore. It was almost like, 'Here it is. Carry on.'"

It has been suggested that the KISS-Aucoin-Bogart team designed their show to fill the void that Alice Cooper had left when he retired from touring. Gene agrees with that assessment. "There's no hiding that," he admits. "But isn't it wonderful that when a big band decides to take a vacation, there's somebody new. The Stones didn't come out for two years, and they begat Aerosmith. Bad Company went off the road, and it begat Foreigner. That's great."

Gene recounts that memorable, but not happy, day at the Fillmore. "Neil came out and said something like, 'Here's a new group, KISS.' And we played a twenty-minute set. The show was really only to introduce KISS to the industry, but it wasn't a pleasant introduction. We got reviews that went something like, 'New label. Casablanca. Not yet out. The first act is gonna be KISS. They sounded like a dinosaur in heat.' I thought, 'Wow! Look at that.'"

The one moment from the showcase worth remembering was when Gene's mother proved how effective the makeup was. Gene: "After the performance, we came back out onstage to greet people. My mother walked up to Paul and said how proud she was of him. I was on the other side of the stage. She thought Paul was me."

After that show, Gene notes, "We did nothing, just talked about the shows. We couldn't really figure out if it was good or bad, but we knew there was a lot of energy. I remember that Paul and I were excited because we played on the same stage that

PAUL IN BANDIT MAKEUP, ACADEMY OF MUSIC, NEW YORK CITY, JANUARY 28, 1974

(© KISS Catalog Ltd.)

Slade had played on. That was a big deal." KISS were still big rock 'n' roll fans. It wouldn't be too long before they were rock 'n' roll stars.

On January 26, 1974, KISS returned to the Academy of Music (their fee had escalated to $750), third on the bill behind Silverhead and a pre-*Rumours* incarnation of Fleetwood Mac. In early February, the Mike Quatro Band canceled out of their upcoming Canadian tour. KISS took their place. Without a record in the stores, without any fanfare, KISS left New York for their first concert appearances away from the security of their home. At the time, they couldn't know that it was the beginning of a tour that would last for virtually the rest of the decade.

Chapter **09**

"Without exaggeration," Gene feels, "it's been almost one long tour for KISS, one year blending into the next—for four years straight, on the road, then off the road and into the studio and then back on the road."

On February 5, 1974, KISS made their out-of-town debut. Gene: "Nobody knew what was going on. The Canadian announcer came out and very sedately said, 'Ladies and gentlemen, here they are, a very nice warm welcome, for KISS.' And there was the crash and the explosion, and everybody went, 'Oooo.' They didn't know what to expect; they were used to the Guess Who." After that show, "I sent a postcard to one of the girls back home, the first letter that I ever wrote anybody from the road. And it said, 'We are a household word.' For the rest of the tour, everybody kept bugging me about that, but in my mind, we made it long before we ever 'Made it.'

"We got paid $750 a night for five days," Gene recalls, "but we were losing money. We had a big road crew and the levitating drum set and all that." As Paul notes, "When we first hit the road, it cost us about $7,000 a week, and we were making nowhere near that, so we put ourselves in a deep hole. But our philosophy was that you get out what you put in. Bill and Neil invested in our shows even when they couldn't afford it. We felt that sooner or later, it would pay off, or we were all going to be in *a lot* of financial trouble. We starved for a long time because of it, but it paid off."

Some of the group's earliest tours were financed on nothing more than Bill Aucoin's credit cards. Nobody else had any money.

After the brief Canadian tour ended, KISS headed for California for the official launching of Casablanca Records at a party at Los Angeles's Century Plaza Hotel. "That was the first real impact," Gene believes, "because everybody was there. [Actor] David Janssen and Alice Cooper and Iggy Pop and Michael Des Barres. And the press. It was the introduction of Casablanca Records to the industry, and we did a very loud, twenty-minute set. Everybody was cupping their ears. Needless to say, we did not get an encore from the industry. Everybody said that we would last six months.

"After the show, we met Alice Cooper, and he was wonderful. He has a great sense of humor. He had two comments: 'Some people will do anything to make it,' 'What you guys need is a gimmick.' Obviously, he was kidding. Also, I finally met somebody other than myself who was into horror movies, and Alice and I talked about that stuff for a while. Three days later, we did Dick Clark's [late-night, ABC-TV music show] *In Concert*, and all of a sudden, people just knew who we were."

KISS went back on the road, where they were still a supporting act. Among the groups they opened for were the New York Dolls, Nazareth, Golden Earring, Climax Blues Band, Argent, Redbone, and Aerosmith. KISS would open for anybody who would have them, but after a while, as Bill Aucoin points out, "nobody wanted to take us on tour with them." Why? Very simply, KISS was blowing the headliners off the stage.

Meanwhile, both Bill Aucoin and Neil Bogart watched the slow growth of KISS. They'd invested their faith, their careers, and all their money in the band, but as Bill notes, "I always knew KISS was going to be a success. It's hard to say why, but there was never a doubt in my mind. My only desire was to have them put on a bigger-than-life show, to make them characters that were larger-than-life. Some of this came from the costumes and the platform shoes. Then, slowly, we expanded the show with the special effects, giving each character as much as they could handle. We found out that they were capable of doing a much more dramatic show than even *they* thought they could do. Paul learned how to capture an audience with his prancing and strutting . . . Gene electrified them with his grotesque gestures . . . Ace and Peter commanded attention with their dynamic playing. We took what they had and magnified it."

Recalling those early days, Bill explains that "they all took time to develop. Paul did very little talking at the beginning until he felt comfortable controlling an audience. Now, of course, he does most of it. Peter's levitating drum riser seemed crazy at the time, but Peter handled it very well. So we added drumsticks that would shoot fire. All sorts of crazy things to make it bigger-than-life, to make it much more exciting.

"Because of my television background, I worked on the visual aspects of performing. Fans pay to see a show, and we were all tired of groups just standing still. My idea was to stage a spectacle, which was just the opposite of the prevailing ideas in the music business at the time. From the very beginning, they were very excited about it all. A big factor in all of this was Sean Delaney. When he'd seen them at Le Tang Studios, he said, 'I was prepared to hate this, but it could be really good.' Sean got involved, helped develop the show. Sean is a very strong-willed and strong creative person, and he would correct any weak points in the show. He went on tour with them and was a very strong part of making sure it all happened, even if they didn't understand or were a little afraid. He wouldn't even allow them to think there were weaknesses. He'd just say, 'Let's do it.' His attitude was, 'We're going to do it no matter what.' And it worked."

Along with determined management and their circuslike rock show, there was one other important ingredient that made it all possible. Money. Bill Aucoin: "I invested somewhere between $250,000 to $300,000 of my own money into KISS for costumes, effects, and touring expenses. That was my whole roll, every cent I had. Neil Bogart was in the same boat."

When Casablanca Records was first formed, the label was affiliated with and distributed by Warner Brothers Records. Bill: "Warners was flabbergasted that Neil was putting that much money behind one group. They thought he should spread it out among a lot of artists who would have a better chance to break into the charts. What Neil was doing was just unheard of, and all along the word from Warners was 'No. No. No.' My accountants were no different. They were freaking out on a day-to-day basis. I'm sure they wrote me off."

According to Bill, "the industry couldn't understand how we could travel with such a big show. Major acts weren't doing it, never mind opening acts. Nobody could figure out how we could make it work night after night. Very simply, we had a bright young road crew with us from the beginning. They would kill for KISS."

Bill Aucoin isn't exaggerating, as Gene explains. "We had a big road manager, Junior, who thought nothing of pulling knives. Everybody in the road crew wore leather. They were a killer crew and very proud. They spray-painted the KISS logo on their jackets. And they would kill for us. Literally."

Gene remembers one concert in Chicago when KISS was second on a bill between opening act Man and headliners Argent. "After we went onstage, the place went bonkers. They called us back for an encore, but Argent's road manager pulled the plug on us. Junior picked this guy up and put him into one of the big road cases and locked it. And plugged us back in. Argent's roadies were looking for this guy, wondering whether they should let us take an encore. And Junior says, 'He's fine. He told us to go back on.' After our encore, Junior let him out of the box.

"Another time, this same guy pulled a knife on Junior. Junior bent his knife back at him, and the guy said, 'I think it's time for your encore.' So we always got at least one encore; we were never, ever booed off the stage. The reception was always good."

In concert, the still relatively unknown KISS was getting standing ovations, but that hadn't yet translated into big record sales. The first album, released in February 1974, sold around 75,000 copies, which, considering that they hadn't scored a hit single, wasn't too bad. And it certainly was good enough to warrant a return trip to the studio.

Bill Aucoin remembers that the group was "touring as hard as they could, playing as many concerts as possible. They worked their way across the country to Los Angeles and recorded *Hotter Than Hell* that August at Village Recorders in L.A.

"That was a little crazy," Bill says, "because it was the first time the guys had been away from home and lived in a new place for a long period of time. L.A. drove them nuts, they didn't know anybody there and they weren't accepted. It was uncomfortable for them and totally different from what they were used to."

Hotter Than Hell, released in October '74, sold around 125,000 copies, a major improvement, and quite remarkable because you basically couldn't hear KISS on the radio. Bill: "We were all anxious to go back to New York, but we knew that we would have to tour. It was our only way of reaching the public because KISS didn't get any airplay. The DJs complained about our image and didn't take us seriously. We were hard-core rock 'n' roll at a time when the talk was about the death of rock.

"That was only one of the problems we faced. We couldn't get decent bookings. Every time we played with an act for the first time, they would watch from the side of the stage, half laughing and half not believing. Then, they saw the audience go nuts for KISS and be far less enthusiastic for the group that followed. So the headlining acts became less willing to let KISS open. It got worse and worse. It took six months after starting the second major tour before we finally broke into headlining." KISS's first bill-topping show was in St. Louis, a prelude to what they would find when they returned to New York.

After returning to New York, KISS recorded *Dressed to Kill*, their third LP. This time, Neil Bogart produced them, in the midst of the confusion surrounding a major move by Casablanca. Originally funded by Warner Brothers, Neil, according to Bill Aucoin, "decided that he wanted to do it on his own. His ideas didn't fit into a large corporate structure. When he went on his own, he didn't have the money Warners did. Consequently, he couldn't give sufficient promotional support to our third album." It was released in March and, given the Warners-Casablanca situation, it remarkably sold 200,000 copies. Substantial growth. But not stardom. Not yet.

It would be another year before the mass market would catch up with KISS, but as a live act. Nineteen seventy-five was the year KISS became a major attraction. Bill Aucoin: "A whole generation that missed the rock of the '60s and wanted to see it were coming to see us. When we finally returned to New York, I talked promoter Ron Delsener into booking us into the Beacon Theater. It holds three thousand people, and we sold out so quickly that Ron had to book a second show that night."

March 1975 at the Beacon was the night Peter remembers as "the moment that I thought we'd made it. The lights were out, and we were backstage, just ready to go on, and I heard, from a distance, 'KISS! KISS! KISS!' That's all I heard. As we went down the stairs to the stage, it got louder and louder, till it was like thunder. 'KISS! KISS! KISS!' And when we hit the stage, the kids were going crazy, rushing the stage, jumping up on the seats. That's when I said, 'This is it. We made it. We did it! There's something about us that's different.'"

 PETER CRISS ON THE THUNDER DRUMS, PARAMOUNT THEATRE, PORTLAND, OREGON, MAY 24, 1975
(photo by Steve Frame)

To put this show in perspective, Peter explains that "at our first gigs, everybody just sat there in total shock. It wasn't until the middle of the show that they started getting into it and really believing that we meant it. Gene would go out and look in their faces like, 'We're not kidding. We want to rock.' Finally, they'd realize we were okay, that we weren't put-ons and we weren't gay and we weren't from another planet." Gene adds, "although we'd gotten good responses everywhere else, the show at the Beacon was one of the first shows we ever did where nobody sat down, from beginning to end. We knew we made it that night because the month before, we had opened up for Jo Jo Gunne in California. At the Beacon, they opened up for us. Coming back to New York, all the media attention caught up with us."

According to Bill, "After the Beacon they started selling out everywhere. KISS [had already] broken big in Detroit. Their first major concert [after the Beacon] was in May at Cobo Hall in Detroit. The enthusiasm there was incredible. In Cadillac, Michigan, an entire high school turned out in KISS makeup. There was an entire campaign in Cadillac to build the KISS spirit in the town, and the whole town went along with the idea. Everyone—the mayor, the local politicians—wore KISS makeup. It was amazingly successful. When we returned to Detroit in 1979, Cobo Hall couldn't hold all the fans, and we played to 34,000 at the Silverdome stadium."

In the spring of '75, the studio version of "Rock and Roll All Nite" had been a minor hit, but as Gene admits, "we were still 'the live concert band.' Radio stations were starting to play our records, because they saw that our shows had become the rage. But it was still, 'You gotta go see this band.'"

By then, it had already been decided that the next record would be a live album. According to Bill, this was "based on the fact that KISS's live performance was so strong and the audience reaction was so positive. I thought, 'if anything could kick the group off, it's a live album.'"

However, before that record was released, Casablanca and KISS had to settle what Bill calls a "topsy-turvy situation. Collecting our royalties from Casablanca had become a problem, and we considered going to another label. I think that was the lowest point we ever reached, although I never felt that it wasn't going to work out eventually. Still, it was an awkward situation because Neil had given us our first break, but because of his difficulties, KISS wasn't getting paid. I was caught in the middle of a painful dilemma, although as the group's manager, I had to go against Neil."

The conflict between KISS and Casablanca was resolved with the release of the live album, Bill recalls. "I had a gut feeling that it would work, and Neil went along with us, as he always has. His support at the time closed the gap that had come between us and marked the turning point for the group."

At the time, a live album was completely contrary to the trends in the record industry. This was before *Frampton Comes Alive!* was such a tremendous success. In

1975, a live album, Bill Aucoin was told, "would be the death of the group. People said that the first three albums hadn't sold well, and there is no reason to think that a live album of the same material will sell. I had only my own belief and Neil's support. We plowed ahead."

Recorded on tour in Davenport, Iowa; New Jersey; and Cleveland, Ohio; but mostly at the Cobo Arena concert, *Alive!* spawned the hit version of "Rock and Roll All Nite" and put both Casablanca and KISS on the charts and into the black financially.

Peter explains that "all along, we tried to capture our live sound in the studios, which is impossible. We kept saying, 'What's wrong with our records?' When we did the live album, we realized the secret was that we're great live. In those days, we didn't think of ourselves as a good studio band." The excitement of a KISS concert, captured on vinyl, turned radio stations and rock fans all over American on to the KISS phenomenon.

Alive!, Gene points out, "was in the charts for over sixty weeks. On New Year's Eve '75/'76, we got a Gold album, and within another month, sales doubled and it became a Platinum album. Two months later, it was double Platinum." To Paul, that first Gold record "brought tears. I shed tears of joy when *Alive!* went Gold." It also brought tears of relief to Neil Bogart and Casablanca Records. Gene: "Casablanca was literally going broke until the album happened."

Paul feels that *Alive!* was such a big hit because "it captured what we were doing. It had taken us a while to know what the audience wanted. After we began to pack them in night after night, we became even more determined to give them what they came to see. We could see the difference in audience response.

"We understood the audience because, in a sense, we are the audience. We know what looks good, and we do it. I know that I would enjoy seeing us if I were sitting down with the crowd. I may be onstage and say to myself, 'Why don't you shake your ass?' And then I shake it and say, 'That was great!' So I'm having a great time onstage. I never see it as work. Even if I don't sleep the night before, when I get on that stage, I come alive. No matter what kind of hassles I'm having, when I hit the stage, I blow them from my mind. For an hour and a half, while I'm on stage with KISS, I'm escaping from myself. It does the same thing for the audience. It's fantasy and escape and power, and it's no different for them than for me."

To Gene, "the basic premise behind KISS is that we are there to give people a couple of hours of pure escapism. We are there to entertain. At the end of a KISS concert, you don't walk out of there troubled with the times. We're not here to tell you how bad things are. Everybody's aware of that. We want to make you forget, give you a good time."

The feeling in that fun-filled nonmessage, something that the group had trouble creating in the studio, was perfectly expressed on *Alive!* The excitement of their concerts combined with the simple fun of their music made the lyrics of their first hit an emblematic anthem:

I Wanna Rock and Roll All Nite
And Party Every Day!

That sentiment propelled *Alive!* into the charts. The two-record set eventually sold almost three million copies, and it cemented both Casablanca's and KISS's future.

"From that point on," Bill Aucoin recalls, "we got enough airplay to help KISS's career. Actually, we knew about six months before *Alive!* was released that we were destined for success based on the growth of the recognition and airplay the group was getting. I also think that not getting overexposed by the mass media during the first two years allowed KISS to grow slowly and achieve success at their own pace. If they had gotten too much attention at first, they could have been destroyed." By the end of 1975, KISS was so big that groups like Blue Öyster Cult, groups that had allowed KISS to open for them, found themselves in the position of opening for KISS. For KISS, it was a satisfying twist.

In the fall of '75, KISS went into the studio to make their next album, and they were determined to create something more advanced than their previous studio efforts. With Alice Cooper's ex-producer Bob Ezrin in charge, KISS recorded *Destroyer*, a significant departure for them. It's filled with studio tricks and sound effects that KISS fans weren't accustomed to. It also contained the group's first ballad, "Beth."

It is ironic that as a rock 'n' roll band, no song they've ever recorded has created the stir that "Beth" did. And it almost didn't make it onto the record, as Peter, the chief composer of the song, recalls. "I used to come in with tons of material, and Gene and Paul were always turning it down, saying 'That's not our style.' They were doing most of the writing, and I felt like I wasn't contributing. When I came in with 'Beth,' the reaction was, 'What the hell is this? We don't do ballads.' And I kept insisting, 'This is really good, and I'd like to do it.' And Bob Ezrin said, 'Let's do it. Let's try something new.' Gene was for it, and all the guys said, 'Okay.' 'Beth' was about my ex-wife, Lydia, but it's really about any Lydia who was ever married to an artist who leaves home and travels."

Back on the road with their new and elaborate *Destroyer* stage set, KISS journeyed to England and Europe for a mildly received tour. When they came back, "Beth" was on its way to the top of the charts.

During the summer of 1976, "Beth" was released on the flip side of "Detroit Rock City," the third single from *Destroyer*. Obviously, nobody had a lot of confidence in its potential, but it became the biggest hit the group has ever had. Peter: "When 'Beth' hit, I felt like I had done something. I won the People's Choice Award for it, and the guys were really happy for me."

GENE ACTING BULLISH, RICHFIELD COLISEUM, CLEVELAND, OHIO, SEPTEMBER 3, 1976
(photo: www.janetmacoska.com)

Destroyer, the group's second Gold album, generated "a lot of bad fan mail," according to Ace. "People thought it was more of a Bob Ezrin album than a KISS album. The production of the music called for me to play in a more restrained way, but I learned a lot from Ezrin. I didn't feel restrained at all doing that record, and I think it was some of the best playing I've ever done."

Musical improvements aside, Bill Aucoin feels that "'Beth' was so much of a departure that the fans didn't quite know what to make of it. They were shocked. For us, that was an experimental period, and it was an odd situation at first. We had to let the fans know that everything was all right, that we were just trying some new things."

Returning to an old formula, KISS recorded another live album, although this time there was no audience. *Rock and Roll Over* was recorded live in September 1976 at the Nanuet Star Theatre in upstate New York. That fall, KISS made their first prime-time television appearance on *The Paul Lynde Halloween Special.* According to Bill Aucoin, "the producers asked us to appear, and at first I said no. When they explained how we fit into the concept for the show, I knew it was right. The appearance was well received and pushed their career up a bit more. Mass exposure helps in small doses."

Indeed it does. *Destroyer* had been certified Platinum in September, and *Rock and Roll Over*, released shortly after the Paul Lynde special, became the first KISS album to ship Gold. Every record the group has released since *Alive!* has sold at least one million copies.

For KISS, the breakthrough was national. They were headlining major arenas all over the country. But there remained one place left to conquer: their hometown, New York.

On February 18, 1977 . . . three years to the day of their Casablanca launching . . . KISS played an SRO show at Madison Square Garden. Peter explains the significance of that show. "To me, when we played The Daisy or any other club, it was the Garden. I was always saying to the guys in the dressing room, and [remember], this was when the dressing room was the size of a bathroom, 'When we go out, it's the Garden. I don't care if there are five people. Let's play like we're playing the Garden.' And we did. We killed every night.

"In those early days, the Garden was my dream. I remember passing the old Garden [located on Eighth Avenue between 49th and 50th streets] when I was ten years old. I was with my mom, and I said, 'Ma. I'm gonna play that place someday for you.' And I did. It was the biggest moment of my life."

To Paul, that concert was proof of KISS's success. "We broke around the country before we hit in New York, and I can remember coming off tour, and I would meet friends of mine and they'd say, 'How's your band doing?' At that point, we already had two or three albums out. And I said, 'Good. We did a show with J. Geils Band and the James Gang.' And they were surprised and impressed. 'You opened for them?' I said, 'We were headlining.'

"So it was important for us to go home to New York and let everybody know what had gone down. That's our hometown, and we've always thought of ourselves as New York boys and a New York band. It was a big deal to play for our families and friends . . . nerve-wracking to say the least. We were beside ourselves backstage, sweating and very, very nervous. And before we went on, all of us shook hands and said, 'Well, we're here. We're really at the Garden.'"

Ace also feels that it "was the Garden that cinched it for me. It was incredible playing Madison Square Garden for the first time, and it sold out. That was the greatest feeling." With Ace, though, there is always a punch line. "They gave us a nice, warm welcome, and I was really happy. On the opening note, I got hit with an egg and a big can of beer bounced off my guitar neck." New Yorkers have a unique way of saying "Welcome home and congratulations."

Nineteen seventy-seven, like every year before it, was filled with hard work, but finally, after a hugely successful tour of Japan, KISS took a vacation in April, their first real rest since 1973. However, it was a short-lived break because KISS was back in the studio that May. With Eddie Kramer again producing, KISS recorded *Love Gun* at New York's Record Plant studio. Released in late June, it became the first KISS LP to *ship* Platinum. In the fall of 1977, *Alive II* was released, and it too shipped over one million copies.

Through all of this, KISS remained, above all, a rock 'n' roll band on the road. If they weren't in the studio, they were playing a concert somewhere in the world. To rock fans everywhere, "the road" is an exciting concept. It conjures up images of wild parties and drugs and booze and groupies. Like any other group, KISS has indulged in the excesses of life on the road, but as they explain, it's all part of surviving the most rigorous and demanding part of a musical career.

"The road," Paul notes, "takes a lot of getting used to. When we first went out on tour, one of us was sick every week. It's exhausting."

For Peter, the moodiest of the foursome, the constant travel is "monotonous and lonely. Sure, it can be glamorous and it does have its moments. Some nights, we'll have pie or orange fights or wreck a room or have a great card game, but usually, it's just tiring. Touring is spending most of your time waiting for that hour and a half on stage, so you can forget about the hassles of touring. [Peter's ex-wife] Lydia used to travel with me sometimes, but usually I'm alone. And I tend to get very lonely. It's tough for a married guy on the road. I don't like sleeping in a different bed every night, but it's part of the job. Now, [model] Debbie [Svensk, Peter's steady girlfriend] will join me when she can."

According to Peter, being KISS's road manager is one of the most thankless jobs in the world. "We're on our twelfth one now, and prospective road managers aren't exactly knocking down our door for the job. It's not easy dealing with four different people. I wouldn't want the job myself.

"One road manager really did a dumb thing. We were doing a very heavy tour, six days a week. I was using extra-heavy drumsticks. During one show, I tore the ligaments in my arm. Afterward I told the road manager about it. But I kept playing, and to compensate, I started putting weight on my other arm. The pain was so bad that I started getting morphine shots. So I said to this road manager, 'I'm really hurting. Did you call Bill and tell him what's wrong with me?' And he said, 'Yeah. I called him. Leave it up to me. I'll take care of it.'

EARTH TO JENDELL, RICHFIELD COLISEUM, CLEVELAND, OHIO, SEPTEMBER 3, 1976
(photo: www.janetmacoska.com)

"So, I kept going, and after a while, it got to the point where I was taking two shots of morphine each night. One night, on my way to a show, I started crying. I couldn't handle the pain anymore. I couldn't handle the needles. Paul went berserk, and then *he* called Bill. He said to Bill, 'Do you know what's going on with Peter? He's ruining his career. He can't lift his arms. He's dependent on morphine now.' Bill didn't know anything about it; no one had called him. The road manager had never reported back to Bill, so we fired him and canceled the rest of the tour."

Fortunately, Peter recovered, something that he was used to doing. "Ever since I was a kid," he explains, "I've had accidents. I fell out of a tree, and I was sick a lot." Being accident-prone is one thing; being a target is another. "We were in Memphis, and one minute I'm playing and the next thing I know, I'm in an ambulance. Some kid threw a huge firecracker, an M-80, onstage and blew me right off the drums. I woke up in an ambulance and couldn't hear for six months.

"I was really pissed; it could have blown my head off. Actually, I was more angry about the fact that I was up there to give this kid a good time, and he was tryin' to hurt me. And I got so angry after I woke up in the ambulance that I made them take me back to the hall. I went back to the drums, back into the show, and they gave me a standing ovation."

Because KISS has been accused, particularly in the South and the Southwest, of playing the "Devil's Music," touring can be very scary. Peter: "Sometimes, these religious weirdos will get outside the hall with signs that say we're from hell. Once, this cop, a real Southern guy with a .357 Magnum . . . he must have weighed about eighty thousand pounds—said to me, 'Are you really from hell?' I said, 'Look. I've got a cross on. I believe in God.' Sometimes, I'm scared thinkin' there's some nut in the audience with a rifle thinkin' he's gonna pop one of us off. So we have bodyguards and people watching out for us."

On occasion, the protests against the group become absurd. Gene: "There's a religious group down South that has been saying for years that KISS stands for 'Knights In Satan's Service.' We kept writing them letters saying, 'That's not true. It's 'Keep It Simple, Stupid.' Eventually, they printed a retraction when this church started getting letters from kids and parents.

"Some people just don't understand what KISS is about. We don't tell people what to do or think or smoke or drink. We don't offer comments on the present world situation, political or otherwise. *That's* dangerous. We are a pretty shallow band, but I don't mean that negatively. We're a hedonistic band, and our lyrics are concerned with the senses . . . rock 'n' roll and having a good time."

For Gene, having a good time on the road usually means girls. For years, his hobby was collecting Polaroid snapshots of every girl he's had the pleasure to have known. "I've got 1,500 pictures of girls in various stages of undress. And some terrific movies. But everybody's got their relief to the boredom of the road. Lots of rock 'n' roll people like drugs. With me, it's girls."

Paul also has a reputation as a ladies' man. "Being on the road is Disneyland at times, a real fantasy. Things that get taken for normal on the road would appear, to the average person, to be totally absurd. My outlet, my means of survival on the road, is the hope of meeting some incredible girl. I'm always chasing that oasis, that mirage. The real knockouts, somebody that I can relate to, somebody I might fly to a show, are few and far between.

"I have a hard time," Paul admits, "keeping it together on the road. The fact that I could have girls all day is old news. I'm past quantity. It's quality or nothing. That's not always the best way to go, but I have a pretty high opinion of myself. It's not a matter of somebody being good enough for me, but if there's no spark, I'd rather be alone. My idea of being with somebody means giving them my energy, my concern, my all. People are too important to play with."

Paul continues: "When I go over the edge on the road, I call up friends, and I get very quiet." Ace, whose humor can turn Peter's deepest depressions into laugh riots, can't work his magic on Paul. "When I clam up," Paul explains, "the guys in the band leave me to work it out myself. They pretend everything is all right. When you go crazy on the road, there's not much you *can* do. Unfortunately, you're out there. Usually, after a few days of being down, I'll be okay, and then Peter or Ace will say, 'I knew something was bothering you.' Sometimes, Peter will ask me if I'm okay, and I'll say I'm all right even when I'm not. There's nothing anyone can really do. The moments of insanity pass. You just have to hang in there. The one saving factor is that I can get a lot of it out onstage. I know that if I'm really down or frustrated, I can do a great show. I'll vent all my frustration and just beat myself to death onstage."

Ace, the irrepressible member of the foursome, tends to be the most unmanageable on the road. He tells one story that sums up a hundred other nights. "In Arkansas once, I met a friend of mine from New York, and after the show, we got really bombed. When the hotel bar closed, we went to my room, which was on the top floor, facing the main street. Me, my friend, and another guy threw every piece of furniture out the window and watched it explode. I'm glad we didn't kill anybody. My friend and his friend split, and that's when the cops came."

At first, the police knocked on the wrong door. They went to Paul's room and caused Paul serious discomfort, because at the time, he was entertaining an underage lady who was working her way through the hotel. Envisioning nights in jail, Paul hustled her into her clothes. But when he answered the door, the police saw they were at the wrong place. Paul's room still had its furniture. So they went to the next door. Ace picks up the story.

"Our road manager, Frankie Scinlaro, ran in and told me, 'Get under the covers, put the pillow over your head, and I'll take care of everything.' Two minutes later, two state troopers walk into the room. Now, Frankie was the best bullshit artist I ever met in my life. He said to the cops, 'Look at my poor boy here. You won't believe what happened, officers. He had all these people here, gave 'em free food, free drinks. He passed out on his bed hours ago, and they wrecked his room. He doesn't know anything about this. I can't wake him. I'm afraid to.' And the cops bought the story."

Frankie Scinlaro was also Peter's "favorite road manager. He was just as crazy as we were, so we couldn't put anything over on him. I loved that guy. He was the only person who could put Gene in his place. Gene would say, 'Frankie, you're really immature.' And Frank would say, 'Gee, you're really smart. I wish I was a teacher like you.' He treated Gene like an asshole. He was great."

Ace, who established a wild reputation by pitching several television sets through open windows, has continued to use the tube for survival on the road but in a much more sedate manner. "I have a videodisc and a Betamax recorder, and I bring movies on the road with me. I try to keep myself occupied." It's important that he does, because Ace's idle hands are the devil's tools. He proved that one night: "I Krazy-Glued all my furniture to the ceiling. When Frankie came in, he thought he was on acid or something."

In spring of 1977, the road warriors returned to Japan, but fortunately for everybody's sanity, by February of 1978, KISS was not on tour. For the moment, the long and winding road was behind them.

LARGER THAN LIFE

Chapter **10**

In May of 1978, KISS began work on their first movie, a television film called *KISS Meets the Phantom of the Park*.

According to Peter, "Bill thought it was time for us to disappear, to take a rest and then come back and be more in demand. The rest was long overdue, but the film knocked the hell out of us. While we were making it, I thought of leaving the band. That's how crazy the movie made me. I've always wanted to be a serious actor, like Al Pacino or Robert DeNiro." Peter, who is almost a character right out of *Mean Streets*, didn't like "the slapstick. It was the Marx Brothers/*A Hard Day's Night* type of movie. Still, it was a hell of an experience, and I learned a lot."

For Paul, making the movie was "interesting more than it was fun. During it, everybody's telling you how great it's going to be. That's what keeps you going. And then you see it, and it's awful. So I wouldn't want to make another movie without total creative control."

Ace found the work "hard, a lot of fun, and interesting, although it got boring having to wait around in makeup for hours. It could have been better; it could have been worse. But after all, we're not actors. We're rock musicians."

Gene gets the last word on the movie. "It was wonderfully exciting to make, and the next one will be that much better."

The six weeks of filming were followed by the group's most ambitious project to date—the recording of four solo albums. Bill Aucoin explains that "the idea we have about KISS is to develop their characters and to make the characters as strong as their music and vice versa. I always wanted to make them superheroes and make them strong individually as well as part of the group. Using the visual media, like with *KISS Meets the Phantom*, is one way to do that. Another is through their music, and that's why we did the solo albums. After a certain number of group records, you need a departure. We knew that the group was still strong and wanted to stay together. We also felt we were ready to go to the next level and at that point, it meant letting them expand on their own. All the ideas that each one of them wanted to do but weren't right for KISS as a group could be done on the solo albums." The records were also a chance for KISS to showcase their growing musical skills.

"On my album," Ace points out, "I played lead, rhythm and acoustic guitar, some bass, synthesizer, and sang the lead and background vocals. Basically, I did the whole album with just Anton Fig on percussion and producer Eddie Kramer. Eddie and I worked together more closely than we ever did on the KISS albums because he didn't have to deal with the rest of the group. It was just me. I think I surprised a lot of people with that album. I'm very happy with it. I'm proud of every song. I never worked harder in my life, and I think it's a fantastic record. It did the best of the four."

Peter used his solo album to "understand all the instruments. I used horns and a full orchestra. Vini Poncia, who also produced *Dynasty*, did my record, and he taught me how to sing like I'd never sung before. I learned more about music because I was surrounded with the best musicians. The album has a lot of good music, and it definitely wasn't teenybopper stuff. I'm not a kid anymore; I want to progress and play to an older audience."

For Gene, his solo album was a chance to be someone other than "the Gene Simmons onstage, the guy with the tongue and the blood. I wanted to bring out other sides of me, like the Beatle-esque ballads on that record. In fact, Gene Simmons was singing for the first time on the solo album. I think I turned some heads."

Paul, the last to finish his record, feels that "my solo album is a bit different from KISS, but it wouldn't be fair to go too far from KISS. As an individual artist, each one of us is much more open to do things their own way without compromising and stretching the identity. It's not like my solo album is an operetta or anything drastically different. But yeah, in its own way it's got a very strong identity of its own. There's a good deal of acoustic guitar on it. There's one track called 'Hold Me, Touch Me' that's got a full orchestra on it."

Never before had an ongoing group recorded solo albums by each of its members at the same time. And the simultaneous release of the records was an unprecedented move in the industry. It also frightened a lot of Casablanca executives. Still, Bill

Aucoin relates, "it was one of those gut reactions again. I said, 'We're putting four albums out at once, and I want each one of them to turn Platinum. We're going to ship four million albums in one day.' Everybody just wiped their brow and told me that nobody would buy them. But it worked because the energy and excitement was there plus *KISS Meets the Phantom* came out at the same time. Distributors who would never buy a large quantity of records all of a sudden bought them. One distributor bought one million albums, 250,000 of each. It was a scary day when we shipped four million solo albums; it was incredible."

Besides the "incredible" sales, Ace thinks "the solo albums brought out sides of each of us we didn't know we had, and as a result, made us stronger as a unit. A lot of times when we play live, we have to sacrifice our musicianship to jump in the air or whatever. I'm sure we could play more proficiently if we stood still, but it's a give-and-take situation. We sacrifice the music a little for the show."

More than anything else, it is this aspect of KISS that comes in for the most critical abuse. Even when Ace says, "I laugh at the critics. Nothing gets under my skin," his pride as a musician is still wounded. Peter explains that "we get defensive about our music because we've gotten some disastrous write-ups. They call us loud and lousy, but the writer never says, 'It was sold out, and the kids had a great time.' And that's sad. I took up music because I love playin' and makin' people happy. I thank God that I can give that to the kids, but they never write about that."

Gene is the most analytical and disgusted when it comes to the press. "Among the so-called rock critics, there's a lot of jealousy. They're upset because they realize there's nothing they can do about our popularity. Also, they suffer from peer group pressure. A lot of it. To be a critic, you must be cool. You can't be a critic and say, 'I love Olivia Newton-John and Led Zeppelin' in the same breath. It's sad that they don't realize that people don't really care what they say. Ultimately, though, you do want everybody to like you, but we know that not everybody will like KISS. But just once, I'd like to see somebody write, 'I hate KISS. They're the worst trash that's ever existed. I went to their concert and twenty thousand people went nuts.'"

"Self-respect," Paul feels, "is what's really important. No matter what anybody else thinks of what I do, in the end, it's what *I* think. I don't ever want to feel, 'Maybe those critics are right.' I know they're all wrong, and I don't even give 'em the time of day. I am the ultimate at what I do, and as long as I can think that, I'm fine."

"A lot of times," Peter notes, "people will ask, 'Why the makeup?' It's just part of show business. Al Jolson did it. We're just giving people a show. One writer asked me, 'What are you trying to say?' We're not saying anything deeper than 'Rock and Roll All Night and Party Every Day.' It's just good rock 'n' roll. People used to say about us, 'You play three-chord jerk-off music.' Chuck Berry is famous for playing three chords. There's nothing wrong with it as long as it's done well. And we do that.

There's no bullshit. That's what KISS is about. And that's why we have one of the best and most loyal audiences."

All their protestations aside, KISS does want to be respected musically, although Gene thinks it's a pointless pursuit. "We could do things in 7/8 time, but that would be self-defeating in the end. I think people want to enjoy music, not study it. The hardest thing to do is write memorable songs. Hopefully, we write songs people want to hear. Otherwise, they wouldn't buy our records. We've won all kinds of 'Best Group' awards from all kinds of magazines. KISS was voted one of the Top 10 groups in *Playboy*'s music poll, and we weren't even listed in the nominations. It was a write-in. That means a lot more than fifteen people sitting in Beverly Hills deciding who gets the Grammys."

In the past, KISS used to think of themselves as a band that you had to see live to appreciate. "Now," Peter exclaims, "we don't think that at all. We're way better musicians than we were. Our music's changed. Doing the four separate albums was great, and we all learned a lot."

Paul points out that the group "takes a tremendous amount of pride in what we do because we get so much flak about the makeup. I think all of that stuff is great as long as we're good musically. I wouldn't want to look the way we look onstage if we weren't good. I would feel that it wasn't justified."

Making *KISS Meets the Phantom of the Park* and the four solo albums were the first steps in the group's "master plan" to, in Gene's words "become a rock 'n' roll superhero band." From the very beginning, the four members of KISS have grown into different stage personae, and over the years, these differences have evolved into elaborate creatures.

What is important to understand, according to Gene, is that "these are not characters. We're not acting. I think of it as the portion of our personality that comes out onstage, things we wouldn't normally do on the street."

For example, Gene's demonic characteristics have emerged from his love of horror movies. "It's probably a combination of Lon Chaney in an old silent movie, *London After Midnight*, and Bela Lugosi's hand gestures. Then, throw in the bulkiness of the monster lizards like Godzilla, the special way they walk, pulling the body forward." That is a very subdued way to describe a man who eats fire, spits blood, uses his tongue as a knife, and prowls the stage like an angry predator.

Paul thinks that their onstage characters are so real because they have roots in each man's childhood. "What makes KISS credible is that what we're doing is really inside of us. It's not an act. It's something that's very comfortable. I look in the mirror when I have the makeup on, and it's me. It's not me wearing makeup. It's another part of me.

"In the beginning, I think it was something that I wanted to be more than something that I was. Now, it is something that I am. I think all of us feel that way. When

I was a kid, I wanted to be sexy, wanted to be wanted. I wanted to be a ladies' man. And I was a fat little kid. Of course, I wouldn't want to live like the star-lover all the time. It would kill me. But it's definitely a side of me I enjoy letting out."

"Each one of us has a mirror," Peter explains, "and we sit next to each other putting on the makeup. Everyone's nervous before a show, and we each show it differently. Gene hollers, dictates, and yells at everybody. Paul prances around a bit, runs around the room. Gene may pick on people for the dumbest things, but that's Gene. He's just nervous. Ace will have a beer and tell jokes, but he's nervous too. I walk around a lot, pacing in and out of the room.

"About five minutes before we go on, we throw everybody out of the room and just sit around quietly, the four of us, and we'll rap a little, talk about anything but the show. It's just nervous talk, but it's kind of like therapy. By the time the makeup is done, it's time to go on, and you don't have a chance to think about being nervous.

"One night, it hit me. I saw this face with a silver nose. My eyes started to turn green, and all of a sudden, I was in my outfit, clipping my belt on. There *was* a transformation. It wasn't Peter. It wasn't me. It was a cat, and I was hot. My adrenaline was going. But my character is me. The weirdest thing is, I don't even know how to control it when it hits the stage. And it takes a while to get back to me after the show, to get myself together again. I'm like a madman after a show, so everybody leaves me alone."

Ace is the only one of the group that thinks his onstage character isn't "really me. The kids are in love with a character I portray. Some of the characteristics are part of me offstage, but they don't idolize me the way I really am." Almost instantly, Ace contradicts himself. "It's almost an alter ego. Actually, I'm pretty spaced out onstage, and I guess I'm pretty spaced out offstage."

The attempts to "unmask" KISS are endless, and Paul "isn't bothered by it anymore. I think we've established a mystique, and our fans don't want to see us without the makeup. And if they do, it really doesn't mean anything because what's important is what we are in KISS, not physically what we are offstage. What's in our hearts doesn't change with the makeup."

Ace recalls the time "in 1978 when a photographer saw Michael Corby of the Babys in Studio 54 and thought it was Paul Stanley. The New York *Daily News* printed the photo. They had to correct themselves a few days later, although I'm sure a lot of people still think it's a picture of Paul. But the point is, fans wrote in and said, 'Please don't print pictures of Paul like that.' Even the fans want the mystique preserved. Our fans are into us as superheroes. Who wants to see Batman dressed in jeans and a T-shirt? Everybody asks us if we'll unmask ourselves before we quit. I guess it's inevitably going to happen, but it's hard to say when. I'm surprised we've kept it going this long. Once we do it, it's going to damage the myth."

Paul laughs at the "talk that KISS wears makeup to cover bad skin. That's not true at all. Once, I used to drink a lot of carrot juice, but I was getting too much Vitamin A and my skin broke out. When I switched to apple juice and Perrier water, my skin cleared up."

Paul insists, "There's no need for anybody to see our faces. We've reached the point where as members of KISS, we are a household word. I saw a political cartoon about wall posters in China and right in the middle of it was a poster of KISS. We're much bigger than a rock band; we're celebrities to the masses. I know that when a maître d' of the Palm restaurant asks if he can put my face on the wall. My picture, in makeup, is on the wall, but when they asked me if they could do it I wasn't wearing makeup. So people are beginning to know us as members of KISS without the paint."

There was *one* occasion when KISS played for an audience without their makeup. Paul: "At Ace's wedding in 1976, there was a band playing, but it was understood before we got there that we were gonna wind up playing. We had to. And we got up and played 'Strutter,' 'Rock And Roll All Nite,' and "Nothin' to Lose.' It was pretty funny, and it must have been weird with us in these white suits. Those memories are the best."

Peter loves "the game of Dodge the Photographer," but feels that the unmasking of KISS isn't a good idea. "I don't want to see the Lone Ranger without his mask. Still, someday, I'd like to come out from behind the mask. I'd like my mother to see my face on magazine covers so she can say, 'That's my son!'"

BEHIND THE MASK

Chapter  **11**

What are they *really* like? Probably no other group has been the target of that question more often because not only has KISS never been photographed without their makeup, but until this book, they have never publicly examined their private lives and the impact of their success with any significant depth.

Obviously, they are all millionaires, but Paul explains, "none of us really talk about money. We don't let it become that important because we are musicians, and we are a band. Personally, I don't live extravagantly; I wear jeans, I own a car, and I live in an apartment. I'm still a city boy. If money is good for anything, it's peace of mind. You don't have to worry about not having it. What did give me a great deal of satisfaction was buying my parents a car. But I live like a rock 'n' roller, not a Rockefeller.

"What means the most to me is that I was right. I knew that I was capable of doing something, and even when everybody told me I was wrong, I went against the rules and discovered I was right. When you take gambles, it gets scary. There were many nights of self-doubt when I wondered if I was right. It would have been a lot safer to have become a lawyer than to think you're going to become a big rock star. And it was only after my dream became a reality that I was satisfied. Really, it was simple ego gratification. It proved to me that if you follow your intuition and believe in yourself, you can do anything you want."

Paul, the principal sex symbol of the group, is a bachelor and admits that "falling in love is something that doesn't happen too often. When I was about fourteen, I fell in love. This girl was wonderful. I could be rowdy or very obnoxious and yet she loved me. As young as she was, she found and loved something deep inside of me. It bothered me so much that I did everything I could to make her not love me. I'd spray her living room with the garden hose, all sorts of mean things, but it didn't matter. I wrestled with her love for years because she really cared a lot. That was hard for me to deal with, because I was too young to understand. Now she's married and I still talk to her. She and her husband came to one of our concerts. They're good people. And she still loves me, which is very nice. I always thought it was romantic to have a girlfriend, even when I was a kid. Everybody else thought it was silly, especially the girls. I don't ever remember disliking girls. As a teenager, I always thought they were hot, in their place."

When Paul "finally moved out of my parents' home, I moved in with this girl. I went from being the kid in the house to having someone depending upon me. Sometimes, I think the best way to learn something is to be pushed into it. You grow up very fast when you don't have a choice. Nowadays, I'm usually easily bored with women, but back then, it was nice to be with somebody that you felt comfortable with. I lived with her for two years, and after we broke up, I swore that I would never live with anybody again. There aren't any accepted rules in living together, and it can be harder than being married. It's so vague. Are you their roommate and exclusive lover? Do you support them?"

Recalling a more troubling relationship, Paul tells of "another girl when I was growing up who had two separate personalities. I thought at first that she was putting me on, but she wasn't. It was like *Sybil*. She was very lovely and beautiful, and on the other hand, she was this creepy, macho chick. It was so strange. When she was seventeen, she would do things like lock herself in her room for three or four days at a time or paint her walls black. I wasn't in love with her, though. She was very, very interesting, not your average run-of-the-mill person, but there's a big difference between being infatuated and intrigued with someone and being in love.

"Love is great until you hate the person, and there is a very fine line between love and hate. I've seen people happily married for years and then, all of a sudden, it's all over. When I marry, I want to know it will last. For me, getting married and having children is part of a dream, but I can't do it now. I see too many girls I want to be with, sleep with, take to dinner, and spend a few days with. It's very hard to be in love with somebody and do that other stuff."

When Paul is ready to settle down, "I'll be a great father. I'm fascinated by the idea of kids, because to me, they're like a blackboard, a clean slate. Basically, you do the writing on it; what you write is the foundation of their lives."

Paul knows that with KISS's mass popularity, he could influence thousands of young people, "which is partially why I don't like to talk about what I may have done with drugs or liquor. People have to find those things out for themselves. Nobody needs me to tell them that there are drugs that can hurt you. Everybody knows that. It would be big-headed for me to start telling people how to live.

"Sometimes, though, I'm not sure that we shouldn't take a stand on an issue. The problem with that is that what you say is given extra weight because you're a celebrity. That's wrong. But if you feel strongly about something, maybe you should use your influence."

In the distant future, when Paul is no longer an active, touring member of KISS, he wants to continue his musical career producing other groups. Already, he's made an album with the group New England, and Paul feels he will make a great studio producer. Most of Paul's friends are in the music business, because "that is what I have in common with them. They are the people I feel comfortable with. The guys in the band are my friends.

"I value my friends at this point, and I do know who they are. If there is anything that all this has taught me it is to have insight and learn who is for real and who is not. With fame, you develop a sixth sense about who is genuine. I have some friends that go back as far as the late '60s, but the guys I went to school with have gone a different way. Once in a while, I hear from someone that I once hung out with, and they are awestruck. That makes me very uncomfortable. It's a shame that there has to be this wall between people."

Away from KISS, Paul lives a quiet life. "I like my own company, and I like time to think by myself. People have told me that I'm close-mouthed, but I just don't need to hear myself. I like to be alone and listen to music. Depending upon my mood, it can range from Beethoven to Fleetwood Mac. And when I'm in a wild mood, I listen to heavy rock 'n' roll, and I listen to it very loud. That's the only way to hear it. I enjoy going out with friends too. My idea of a great night is to stay out dancing until five in the morning and come home all tired and sweaty.

"After being on the road, being home takes some getting used to. When I'm on the road, I know that at any time I can ring one of fifteen rooms and have company. When I'm home, I'm not with people that are salaried. On the road, I can get yeses from everybody, but when you're home, you get nos."

When KISS's days on the road end, Paul feels he'll be happy with "some good company and my house. But there is a side of me that always wants to perform." In that vein, Paul says he'll "go back into art. I don't know how or when, but I will. As you get older, you change the way you relate to things. It's the same with my parents. They used to have one of my paintings on the wall, but when I went to see them recently, they had replaced it with my first Gold album for *Alive!* and they had put my painting behind a door. At first, I was disturbed, but then I realized that they had totally accepted me for what I am and had put everything in the right perspective.

"My parents are right up there with me on Cloud Nine. I'm not from a wealthy family, but now, because of me, they have nice things they dreamed of having. Throughout the hard days, they never really gave me a bad time, and now they can laugh with me. They'll say, 'Who would know that when you said you were gonna do it that you would really do it.'"

Despite his spaced-out, Dean Martin image, Ace may well be the smartest member of KISS. "I had an argument with Gene and Paul, who said that because they write most of the material that I was not very bright. So I said, 'You'd be surprised how bright I am.' I bought these IQ tests, and Paul and I took them. There was no fooling around; we timed it and went by the rules. Paul's IQ is 140, which is very good, near genius. Mine is 164, which *is* genius. I always knew I was brighter than the next kid; I was just bored."

Ace doesn't have time to be bored anymore. His life is filled with the demands of his career, which leaves little time for his outside interests. "I have sixty-five guitars I want to play. I've got my own recording studio. I'd like to study micro-organisms. I'd like to start making movies." Ace believes that he's "the kind of person who could have been an inventor. I'm a lot like my father. That's why I've always loved science and magic and electronics. When I was twelve or thirteen, I could take anything apart and fix it."

Ace explains that "it was my idea to make the guitar explode. Obviously, I needed help to build it, but it was my concept. All the special effects I do are my idea initially. I'm an electronics buff. I recently spent $5,000 on a laserium for my home. I saw it, and I said, 'I've gotta have it.' Mark my words. I'm going to invent something revolutionary someday.

"Computers fascinate me too. I play chess against a computer. I know I don't come across like the kind of guy who is interested in such things, but that's because I have a reputation of being someone who drinks too much . . . of being spaced out . . . a guy who tells a lot of jokes. That's almost a facade I put up sometimes.

"On second thought," Ace reveals, "maybe it's not a facade. It's really a big part of me. Laughing and telling jokes is a lot more exciting than talking bullshit. What I enjoy is making people laugh. I know I'm my own best audience, and I even laugh at my own jokes. I used to tell a lot more jokes than I do now. To be honest, I don't remember 'em anymore. Maybe I've been on the road too long. Or I'm burnt out. I used to be able to sit at a party and rattle off forty jokes, one after the other." Here's a sample of Ace's humor from the man himself: "I went to the dentist the other day, and I said, 'Doc, my teeth are really yellow. What can you do for me?' He said, 'Wear a brown tie.'" Rim shot.

This rock 'n' roll Henny Youngman may not tell the best jokes, but the joke-telling is followed by Ace's laugh. And it is the funniest cackle you've ever heard. Ace: "At one point in my life, I thought I'd try stand-up comedy, but now it would be a total disaster 'cause I'd forget the jokes." Ace adds, half seriously, "Like Marlon Brando. He can't remember his lines, and I can't remember mine." Continuing to joke, "Thank God I can remember my licks on the guitar."

For Ace, "the best thing money has done for me is that I was able to buy a beautiful home and build a twenty-four-track recording studio underground. It's one thing when somebody tells you that you're rich, but it's very special to look at your own house and five acres of land and know that it's yours." Away from the road, Ace is content to spend time at his country estate. "I like being home. After being adored and treated special for months on the road, I like to get away from all that, just be with my friends, put on my dirty jeans and a T-shirt and go to the old bars I used to hang out in before I became famous. When I can relax with my buddies, it makes me feel like a regular person again. Most of my friends are still struggling musicians, but they never ask me for help. They have more pride than that."

Ace's need for privacy is ensured by the anonymity the makeup gives the members of KISS, and he enjoys "walking down the street and not being recognized. I wouldn't want to give that up. If I couldn't go someplace without being recognized, I think it would drive me crazy. We've always had trouble maintaining our privacy. Kids find out where we live, and then we have to move. I hate to say it, because of that, I'm not friendly with the people in my neighborhood."

Ace's family and friends come first and last. "I married into a large Italian family, and I love them all. Jeanette and I met at a birthday party in the Bronx. I knew her cousin, and Jeanette came to this party with her and another girl. This other girl [Diane] and I went out for about a year, and I ended up leaving Diane for Jeanette. We went together for about five years before we got married on May 1, 1976. I didn't want to get married until I could give her a nice home and a car. She came from a well-to-do family, and I didn't want to lower her lifestyle. When I was a bum, they didn't like me, and when I became a success, they liked me. But that's normal. That's the way parents are.

"Jeanette's grandfather is the third vice president of the Teamsters Union. In fact, when the Teamsters had their convention in Las Vegas, we went out there. They're good people. You hear all these things about how the Teamsters are mobsters, but I haven't seen anything like that from my relationship with Jeanette's grandfather. He's a real nice gentleman." Ace adds his usual punch line. "Print that. Please."

Of all the members of KISS, Ace has always been the most reluctant to open up in interviews. He explains that he's been deliberately uncooperative because "I like my image. It's mysterious. When the press writes about the group, they usually say that 'Ace Frehley's the most mysterious and is elusive.' I like that."

"Basically," Ace declares, "I'm a pretty happy guy. I'm pretty well off financially and could quit the band tomorrow and never have to work again. But I'd probably go crazy. Invariably, I will do what makes me happiest. Right now, I'm happier playing rock 'n' roll than anything else. Five or ten years from now, I don't know what I'll be doing except that it will be whatever makes me happy. I've always lived my life that way.

"I'm only twenty-eight, and I can't be a rock star for thirty more years, so I have to plan my life a little. If I could be a successful record producer, I think that would make me happy. And I'll get back to my art. The only thing I hated putting aside for my music was my painting and drawing. I'm going to get back into it when I retire from the music business many years from now.

"What's important to me now is my home, my wife, and maybe raising a family. But I won't have kids until I can spend time with them. Basically, I'm a very private person. I bought my dream house because it's secluded, and when I come off the road, I don't want to be bothered by anyone. I enjoy being on my own, taking it easy. I like my quiet moments, and I need the time to just sit and think.

"In thinking ahead, I've found that once you've achieved something, you've got to set different sights. I've never taken advantage of the people that worship me, but there is one bit of advice I'd like to give: 'Never set your sights low. Set 'em high, so that if you get halfway there, you've still done a lot.' I think people limit themselves, and I believe people can do anything they want. You have to have self-confidence to succeed in life. And keep setting your sights on something. You may achieve it. Otherwise, you're just going to stagnate, and I'm not going to do that.

"When I said I was going to be a rock 'n' roll star, everybody told me there was too much competition. It's funny, but all my old friends call me up to say the same thing to me, like a broken record . . . "Wow, Ace. You said you were gonna do it, and you did it. I can't believe it. It's incredible.' A lot of people talk. Talk is cheap."

Deep down, Ace Frehley considers himself "a romantic at heart. I don't show it a lot, but I cry at movies." Of the foursome's offstage lives, nothing is harder than trying to reconcile the image of Ace from Space crying at the end of a movie.

For Gene, private romantic notions are almost impossible because he is involved in one of the most publicized of Hollywood relationships. "I don't know if I'm capable of a lasting relationship with one woman," Gene honestly admits, "because I know I'm a snake. But I happen to be nuts about Cher. She knows that if the impulse hits me, I'll go out with whichever girl catches my fancy. Still, Cher's the first real relationship I've had."

In 1965, Sonny & Cher were the anti-establishment couple of the pop music world, but in 1980, Gene explains, "the kids don't like my association with her. But that's tough. To them, Cher's real Hollywood, but the truth is, she's got nothing to do with that scene. She is as different from the onstage Cher as I am from the onstage Gene Simmons. In fact, she's straighter than me, if you can believe that.

"If I was thinking about career moves or anything like that, I certainly could have made a better choice. But I am crazy about her. Cher doesn't have anything to do with KISS. She's part of my private life. In other words, there probably won't be a Cher-Gene album. I don't really like the kind of music Cher does, and she's not a particularly big fan of KISS."

Cher and Gene met at a party Neil Bogart gave for California governor Jerry Brown on February 18, 1978. Neil had asked Cher if she wanted to be on Gene's solo album, "and he shouldn't have done that," Gene insists. "She had just signed with Casablanca Records, and of course the industry thought our working together was a publicity stunt. I apologized to her at the end of the evening for that, but I thought she was an asshole and she thought I was a super-asshole."

That instant dislike also sparked intense interest, and Gene and Cher spent the early morning hours after the party at Cher's house talking about "all sorts of things. I left at 5:30 in the morning just wondering, 'What's going on here?' The next day, I asked her out, and we ended up aimlessly driving around, just talking. We're so different, and we don't like the same things at all, but we did like each other. And I've never liked kids, but I'm a slave to her son, Elijah.

"That night, we went to see the Tubes, and that's how they wound up on her TV special. She wanted KISS to be on the show singing 'God of Thunder,' and I was supposed to rip her clothes off at the end. We decided that wasn't such a good idea. Two days [after we met], I had to leave for business in New York. As soon as I landed, I sent her a telegram that said, 'I had a nice flight. I thought of you. I miss you.' That night she called, and for the entire week I was in New York, we talked an average of eight hours a day on the telephone. It was crazy for me. During the first telephone conversation, we told each other, 'I love you.' I'd never said that to anybody. At that time, we had never kissed or even held hands. She wasn't my type of girl, too thin, no substance. I always thought I liked girls who were big and chunky.

"When I got back to L.A., Cher and I lived together for a week, and then I had to leave for a short Japanese tour. While I was in Japan, my phone bill was $2,500 and hers was at least that much. When I returned to L.A. to make *KISS Meets the Phantom*, the press really latched on to our relationship. A *People* magazine reporter came to interview Cher at her house and saw me scurrying around. But so far, it's been quiet and calm and nobody's really bothered us."

Gene, a "victim" of "first love," has enjoyed lavishing Cher with attention. "I threw a surprise birthday party for Cher that must have cost $10,000. That morning, at 10:00 A.M., when Cher answered her door, a thirty-piece choir sang 'Happy Birthday.' After breakfast, around noon, a thirty-piece band marched up to the hotel we were staying at. They were in full regalia, playing 'Happy Birthday.' Between one and three that afternoon, there was a plane circling the hotel carrying a banner that said, 'Cher—Happy Birthday.' That afternoon, an army tank arrived at the hotel, and we got in and drove to her surprise birthday party."

When Cher and Gene go out together, dozens of photographers try to get a photo of the unmasked Gene. How does he avoid the flashing lightbulbs? "It's simple," Gene jokes. "I disguise myself as Sonny Bono."

To Paul, Gene's relationship with Cher "is almost like a [second] childhood for him. He's going through a lot of eye-opening things. Being in love is so new for him. When it first happened, he didn't call anybody. I guess he didn't know how to deal with it. When I finally spoke with him, we had a real nice, heart-to-heart, brother-chum kind of talk." As for the notoriety the relationship attracts, Paul feels that "each one of us gives so much to the band, so much to the public, that what we choose to do with our own time is totally without explanation or any kind of apologies. What we do out of the public eye is really nobody's business, but it's obviously not easy for Gene with Cher."

But just because he's a man in love doesn't mean that he still isn't wildly ambitious. Gene's greatest desire is to have a career like "my greatest idol, Lon Chaney. 'Man of 1,000 Faces' on my solo album is about him. I've always thought the man was way ahead of his time. In silent movies, when people were wearing only powder on their faces, this man was contorting his body and putting on elaborate makeup and becoming all kinds of different people. The thing that fascinated me about him was that he could be the Phantom of the Opera or the Hunchback of Notre Dame and still be the same person underneath. I'm very serious about pursuing an acting career, and I'd love to be a character actor doing horror films. My face has never been seen, so I'd love to play parts where I look different in every movie."

In Gene's mind, there is no doubt that he is "going to be a horror movie actor à la Boris Karloff or Bela Lugosi. But unlike them, I'd be proud to be stereotyped. I want to be typecast as Gene Simmons, something I will create. I would like to see myself as Gene Simmons, someone bigger than Dracula." Like the members of the KISS Army, Gene was once a rabid fan. "I used to be in the original Count Dracula Society in L.A., but I've since become a personality on my own. I can take my place alongside Dracula. You don't have time to think somebody else is great when you have to support yourself ego-wise. Still, Dracula influences my performance, but not in the conscious sense that I imitate him. I use what I've absorbed from *Dracula* and a lot of the early German expressionist films, the ones with a lot of shadowy black and white. That influences me, but it's not a case of saying, 'I've got to *be* Dracula.' I've never wanted to be Dracula. I just wanted to be somebody big and powerful and awesome, and Dracula seemed to embody those qualities. There are two big differences between Dracula and what I do. First, he drank blood, and I spit it. Also, to Dracula, people were slaves. When I'm up there onstage, KISS are slaves to the audience."

Absorbing the adulation of millions is very much like a religion, but Gene isn't very religious. "Growing up in Israel, we were nationalistic, not religious. When I came to America and went to yeshiva, I was very religious, to a point where the tradition reinforced the religious belief. As I started to ask questions, I slowly got out of it. So if I am religious, it certainly is not with man's conception of God. More than anything else, I think God is probably in man's image rather than the other way around. And I can't love anybody that thinks they're more important than anyone else. I don't care what anybody says.

"On a very innocent level, the worship the fans have for KISS is a religion. There is a kind of KISS nation, and if you're a KISS freak, if you believe in KISS, what you do is *enjoy* yourself. But there's no doctrine. We don't teach you anything. So if it is a religion, it's [one of] fun . . . the religion of having a good time. And that may be the most profound religion of all.

"Established religion serves a very real purpose for the elderly, the sick, the lonely, and the poor. It gives them hope and some people need a name for hope, be it Moses or Jesus or Buddha or whoever. That's wonderful. But the concept of crusades killing in the name of a deity that is against killing is repulsive to me. Through history, religion has been so misshapen, but KISS doesn't do that. We're not missionaries trying to convert anybody to believe anything."

Gene is determined to keep KISS apolitical, and he thinks that "when the current generation gets into political power, Republicans and Democrats will be obsolete. People will support a candidate because of his stands on the issues, not because of his party affiliation. Politics is very interesting, but politicians themselves are tremendously boring. They have no pizzazz, no style. President Kennedy had a lot of style."

Gene's career ambition centers on the movies and the music business, and like his fellow KISSmen, he is determined to forge new careers for himself. Gene is always in pursuit of the magic of rock 'n' roll and has become somewhat of a patron saint to new groups that are just getting started in the business. In 1977, he saw a band in a club, liked them, and financed a demo recording. The band used that tape to get a recording deal. But there were no strings attached. Gene did it because he believed in the group. The band, Van Halen, is now one of Warner Brothers' biggest acts and their first two albums are million sellers.

From that and other similar experiences, Gene feels "that in the future, if I want to become a manager, I'll be able to do it. I love to go see new bands, having never heard their songs, because I love *seeing* stuff before I've heard it. I'm never going to give up my music, but I would like to expand into producing other groups. And I'll do it, when it's the right time.

For now, Gene "needs twenty-four hours of life all the time, the hustle of big cities. When someone asks me what my astrological sign is, I answer, 'The dollar sign.'

Of course, I'm being humorous 'cause I'm not really a materialistic person. A person can only eat one meal at a time, wear one set of clothes. There are only so many hours in a day to enjoy things. People misunderstand wealth. Boring people use wealth in a boring way. If you're inventive, money can make life really interesting. But *ego*, not money, has been the guiding force in my career."

Still, Gene believes, "rich or poor, man is the master of his own destiny. And no matter what, you have to keep trying to make things better. The very least you can do is go down fighting. I believe in living, in accepting existence for what it is. Maybe that's the goal of religion—to make sure we live out our whole life, to make sure we don't commit suicide."

Gene is not a solitary man, but "to this day, I have a problem with most people. This is going to sound unfriendly but it's not. It takes a lot to keep me interested and most people are dreadfully boring." For Gene, life is a challenge, and he's got a huge backlog of goals, from his movie career to the next attractive girl. And even though it may seem that he has an oversized ego, it only serves to help him get maximum enjoyment from life and KISS's success. After all, it was Gene's childhood love of comics and monsters that provided the original impetus behind KISS, so if he brags a lot, he's earned that right.

For Peter, the success that KISS has achieved means everything. Like Gene, Paul, and Ace, Peter always knew he was special and different, but he struggled professionally for over ten years before joining KISS. Those years have left their mark, but fame and fortune have allowed Peter to gradually accept his stardom and himself.

"My brother used to give me a hard time," Peter recalls. "He used to say, 'You'll never amount to anything.' It gave me a great deal of satisfaction when he apologized, because I knew I'd make it one day." Family love is important to Peter. "My father and I are extremely close; he's my buddy and my pal. I'll come off the road and stop by to have a beer with him. He knows a lot, and it's only since I've grown up that I realize how much he knew. My father's very intelligent even though he doesn't have a college degree.

"I always wanted to do things for my mother," Peter explains, "but for a long time, she wouldn't let me. Now, she wants it. I got my parents out of the slums, and I got my dad a little antique store. I got my mom's teeth fixed. Diabetes runs in our family; my grandmother died of it. My mother recently became a diabetic, and," Peter happily confesses, "I could afford to send her to a specialist."

One of the most difficult aspects of success for Peter is that his old friends have trouble relating to him. "When I see my friends now," Peter notes, "they're scared of me. And it makes me feel terrible. I am really interested in them, but they think that because I'm a big star that I wouldn't care about their lives. I've lost them, and it makes me feel sad. They don't want to be with me because they say they feel small or inadequate. I haven't changed except in the respect that I've set a goal and achieved it. But I'll still go to McDonald's or to a bar or to shoot pool.

"Sometimes, I ask myself, 'How come a kid from Brooklyn, out of the millions of drummers in the world, made it to the top?' It's amazing, but I believe that I was born to bust away from it, and that made me different. When I was young, I started getting gray hair. People thought I'd dyed it and called me gay. And we'd fight. I bought Beatle boots and grew my hair long. More fights. I was always kind of an outcast, even though I belonged to a gang. Being separate made me take a chance. I could've failed, but you gotta try. That's what separates me from my old friends. They never tried, and we're not friends anymore, so you can see that success has its price.

"Of course, there are plenty of rewards as well. Years ago, we wrote to all the drum companies, asking for free drums in exchange for an endorsement. They all refused except for Pearl. Now, I get all sorts of letters begging me to drop Pearl, but I wouldn't leave them for anything. They've treated me like God, and now I'm gonna design my own set of wood drums, and they're gonna make 'em for me. That's a big thrill, 'cause I'm gonna design the drums not knowing whether they're gonna work or not, but no one in the world will have them but me."

In 1978, Peter saw a therapist and one of the results is that in conversation he has become extremely candid. "I do what you don't think I'm gonna do. I'm really off the wall at times, but I find that best. I love to do things on the spur of the moment. I'm a very sensitive person, I'm honest and I have a bad temper. When I lose it, you'll be talking to a whole different person. But I am very young at heart. I'm still like a kid in that I love buying toys, things that make me comfortable in my own world. A lot of people think of me as 'drummer macho,' a real bastard, but I'm not. Sometimes, I'm quiet, and other times, I can be nuts. I'm a manic-depressive, so I'm either up or down, which is a terrible way to be. When I do interviews, sometimes I'm too honest, and I'll say things that I know will get me in trouble. This will really flip the reporter out. But it's like Frank Sinatra and the press. By the way, he's my idol. He is God to me."

Like the cat he is onstage, Peter has nine lives, but he admits that "they're all used up, finished, gone. I'm very, very lucky. I've been through some close calls, wrecking cars and such. I love to race. Now, I go to the Malibu Grand Prix to get it out of my system. Later on, I'll probably get into racing, but on a real track."

Peter's future plans also include a strong desire to do "serious acting. That will have to wait until we stop touring in a few years. I've also invented a board game about the rock 'n' roll business called Make It to the Top. I even wrote a song by the same name that Cher is going to record."

The success of KISS, for Peter, has been mixed with the bittersweet taste of a failed marriage followed by new love. "When Lydia and I got married, I was too young. She's a great lady and all, but it didn't last. She wasn't for me. She didn't give me a feeling of security. People grow and she wasn't growing with me, and it was holding me back. More than that, because I am so sensitive, I need a lot of affection. I need to be hugged and loved, and I wasn't getting that for a lot of years in my marriage. I don't think anyone ever saw Lydia and me kiss in public. We weren't a very warm couple, and I need that to progress. I guess Lydia couldn't really understand my crazy musician friends and my lifestyle. Above all, our marriage wasn't really love. Everything was calculated; she was working and I was gigging. And it didn't work out."

Their 1979 divorce cost Peter his Connecticut dream house, "but I wanted the divorce and I was willing to pay for it. I want to marry Deborah." Talking about his lady, "when I first met Deborah, she didn't know who I was, which was great. I met her at a party that Rod Stewart gave, and the funny thing is, I didn't even want to go to the party. Ace and Paul actually came to my room and dressed me, forced me to go.

"Deborah was on the dance floor, and she was winking at me. I put my drink down and grabbed her off the floor. She flipped out because nobody had ever done that to her before. I thought I was Mr. Cool. I said, 'Hey, baby. Do you want to get in my limo and go for a ride?' The limo took us back to my hotel and then I said, 'Let's go back to the party. I've got my Porsche in the garage downstairs.' All this time, I think that I'm impressing her, and she just thinks I'm some little rich spoiled brat.

"There was almost no conversation between us, but finally I said, 'You know who I am, of course.' She didn't, so I said, 'I'm Peter Criss.' And she said, 'So. I'm Deborah Svensk.' I said, 'Who's that?' She said, 'I'm a model, and I've been in *Vogue* and *Playboy*.'

"So I told her I was in KISS, and she said that the last time she'd heard about KISS was from her brother, who was screaming about how great KISS was. She thought KISS was shit. She told me, 'I hate them. They wear makeup and look like maniacs.' Meanwhile, I'm sitting there thinking, 'There goes my chance of making it with her. She hates my band.' Still, there must have been some attraction because we had dinner that night. She said, 'I never thought your band was any good.' And I asked her, 'Why were you winking at me?' She said, 'I thought you were good-looking.'

"The next day, we had lunch and dinner, and then we went to the beach for a long walk. That's where it started. It was just like in a movie, walking along the ocean. I kissed her. It was incredible. I felt like a little kid. Holding hands was great, just looking at her face and drinking it in. I had never met anybody like her in my life, and I never thought I would. I've never been so happy as I am with Deborah. I'm really in love; I'm the happiest guy in the world."

For Peter, since meeting Deborah, it's been "the first time I really felt love. My whole life, I was never in love, so I didn't know how to handle the feeling. I figured that Deborah couldn't love me because she's so gorgeous. But she did. We lived together the whole time I was working on my solo album. She stuck through the whole record with me. She's a good lady, and that's important. You've gotta have somebody who takes care of you."

Peter explains that because Deborah had dated some musicians, she knew the life of being on the road. If I'm up all night recording and I bring home tapes, she'll get up, have a cup of coffee, and listen to them. You need somebody to listen to your music and tell you, 'That's good.'

"Sometimes," Peter admits, "you look at *Playboy* and think they're all dumb blondes, but Deborah is extremely bright. She went to college, and her father's an engineer. He's from Sweden. She's also part Indian, so with me being Irish and Italian, our fights are heavy."

Peter feels that marriage and children are in his future. "People think that rock stars don't want the American dream, but I do. I want apple pie. I want to come home and have my kid run up to the car and say, 'Hi, Dad.' I want a dog. The whole bit. I had a great mansion, but the house had no love in it. Now, Deborah gives me all the affection I can handle, and I dig it. There are a lot of things we share that I never shared with anyone. She respects me as a man and as a person and thinks I'm the greatest. It's nice to hear that now and then. When I'm with this girl, I'm thinking how lucky I am. 'Is this me?' We root for each other. She changed my life so much that I don't need to be destructive. Deborah has made me very happy.

"I didn't think I'd ever make it this big," Peter explains, "but there's a loneliness to it." Don't get him wrong. Peter's "happy I made it. [But] my dad used to say, 'It's lonely at the top.' I said, 'Bull. I'll be surrounded by people.' After a while, I found out that a lot of people were just leeches for my money and my stardom. Soon, you find yourself with just your lady, which is okay. Deborah and I don't need to go out to have a good time. We're happy to stay home and watch TV and eat popcorn and play Rummy 500 all night.

"Sure, the money's great 'cause you can buy toys to make you happy—a house, a boat, a car—and you need that for your sanity. The glamour and money is nice, and I think we deserve it. We worked for it. The one thing I've gotta say is that I really like the guys [Ace, Gene, and Paul] and I admire them."

For Ace, fame and fortune are fun but he doesn't seem to worry at all about the future. "The band could break up tomorrow or I could be broke, and it wouldn't bother me. I'd just go on." The success of KISS, according to Ace, has been a wonderful dream come true except that "being with the group makes it hard to branch out. I have to check with everybody before I go somewhere or make a big decision. I just can't go off by myself like I could before. Success is not what I thought it would be, but nothing ever really is. I didn't realize how much I'd have to give up in my personal life."

Gene finds that he has "the unique opportunity not to have to be Mick Jagger twenty-four hours a day. I can go buy a pizza or go to the movies with everybody. I'm not afraid of being recognized, and I'm not disturbed because I'm not recognized. Either way, I already get more attention than I could ever want. If I need any more than I get, I think you would have to take me away in a straitjacket.

"Success has meant to me everything I've ever heard from anybody who has become famous. You can buy your parents everything you've always wanted to buy them. I bought my parents a home in the suburbs and one in a foreign country too. My mother's my biggest fan. She collects everything about me and KISS, reads all the rock magazines. In fact, that's her biggest pleasure."

KISS's success has satisfied Gene's ego, although there is a side of him that wants to come out from behind the mask. "I was thinking of doing one of those 'You don't know me but . . .' American Express advertisements on TV. But I don't think there's any reason to unmask. I know who I am."

To Paul, stardom is "totally different than I thought it would be. When I was younger, and this may sound redundant, but 'you can only conceive what you can fathom.' Fame is only what you can understand fame to be, in your current world. So six years ago, my idea of fame was living in a garden apartment, but everybody knew who I was. And having money.

"Obviously, that's not fame, but how would anybody know what they would have five years later? Fame makes you a man, makes you grow up. You're exposed to a lot of things. You meet people that in your wildest dreams you wouldn't be around, and you're with celebrities on an equal basis.

"I think the danger of fame is that you become so wrapped up in yourself that you really do think the world revolves around you. That's ridiculous, and I really learned my lesson about four years ago when I almost drowned. I was in Hawaii, swimming off a catamaran about a mile and a half from shore. I got swept away in the heavy current and couldn't get back to shore. A man in a motorboat saw me and rescued me, but at one point, I was as good as dead.

"While I was floating in the water and thinking that I was about to die, my life passed in front of me. Everybody thinks they're so important, but when I was being swallowed up by the ocean, I realized how unimportant we all are. When you're fighting for your life, just to stay afloat and the waves won't let you, you discover that you're not so strong and powerful.

"What I've discovered is that life itself is a challenge. While there are few challenges left in my career with KISS, I feel that growing as a person is the biggest job of all."

To Bill Aucoin, the four men have handled their enormous success well, even though, as Bill explains, "it came quickly. They had the street smarts to pull them through. The only big change is that they are now millionaires and can do pretty much what they want. But it wasn't always that way.

"In the beginning," Bill remembers, looking back, "they were so broke. One time, Paul came into my office to borrow $5. He didn't have any money at all. When he sat down across the desk from me, I sat back and put my foot on the chair, and he saw little holes in the soles of my shoes. He knew it was rough, but he had no idea how rough. Paul started looking me over and saw a hole in my sweater. So he said, 'Just came in to see you,' and walked out. He *never* asked me for the $5.

"There was another time when I had run out of money, and Neil couldn't give us any more. I went to Gene and said, 'How much can you lend me?' Gene said, 'I have $1,000 saved.' I knew we would be getting some income in the near future, so I said, 'Can I have it for the group? I'll give it back to you in two weeks.' He blinked a couple of times, but I don't think he ever had any doubts. The next day, he brought me a cashier's check for $1,000."

Bill points out that "those kinds of things happened all the time in the early days. We've always been close and that's helped tremendously. There's no ego-fighting. The difference between them then and now is that they're more sensitive. They've been around the world and met more people, so they understand more about people. Their view of the world is more sophisticated."

The long-term future of KISS, to both Bill Aucoin and the group, is a straight-ahead road to superhero stardom. But as KISS was built on their in-concert appearances, 1979 saw their return to the stage. Gene: "We're not the type of band that takes a year off to do nothing. We didn't tour for a year, didn't play one date, but we worked harder in that year than we ever did before. We were about to start another movie, but we decided that we'd better go out and do the 1979 tour or people would forget that we're a real rock 'n' roll band. It was a reaffirmation of the audience's belief in us, showing them that we're real and not just four actors or faces on a lunchbox. We have to keep going out there and showing people we can still kick it out."

Peter explains that "we had to go back out to prove that we hadn't broken up. There were rumors around that I was leaving the band. I love the guys, and I don't wanna split. There's still a lot of music to be played. But the year off screwed us up a lot. I almost got killed in a car accident, and I got divorced. Gene met Cher. We were away from one another, and that was weird. It took us a while and a lot of work to get back to our peak.

"The only way," Peter insists, "to touch people is to play to them. And on that tour, we had a lot of fun, more fun playing than ever before. I'm having a good time; so is the audience. And that's the main thing. All four of us really believe in what we're doing to the hilt. I'm not claiming to be Keith Moon, but I do what I do best. It's not a complicated trip. There was no legendary American rock 'n' roll band before, and I feel KISS is it. And I'm proud of it. The band has been extremely close lately, getting along better than we ever did. We've all mellowed, and we've gotten into doing things together. We're a lot more mature and more complimentary to one another."

Ace points out that "after being together this long, a lot of groups have ego problems and friction, but we're all good friends. I think a lot of the reason for that is that we're all different personalities, so we don't hang around with each other off the road. So when we're on the road, we get along better. Also, we respect each other as stars in our own right. There's a mutual respect. Third, KISS is a very democratic group. I think that's why it has lasted, and it will continue as long as we want it to."

One of Paul's best friends said to him about four years ago, "'You know you're at your peak now. It's downhill from here.' But I know that's ridiculous. We're all committed to KISS. There's something that binds us together that will never change. We're four guys from New York who owe each other everything."

Nineteen seventy-nine's American tour was KISS's proof that they're the best rock 'n' roll band around, and their 1979 album, *Dynasty*, was evidence of their musical growth. "It's more sophisticated and musical," Peter notes, "but we didn't lose any of our younger fans because of the difference in style. A kid who was thirteen when he bought his first KISS albums was twenty when *Dynasty* came out. We've always wanted to keep our fans and progress along with them."

"In terms of longevity," Gene explains, "we know exactly what we're doing. We're very conscious of not moving too fast for our audience. Why should we? A new KISS album should not be completely different because that would be disturbing."

Paul would "prefer to see KISS change at this point musically than see us start copying ourselves. The worst thing is to became a parody of what you are. But you can't lose your musical identity. You can broaden your horizons, go a little further, but KISS can't be hard rock one day and a swing band the next. You can alter your approach slowly."

The first significant change in the group's music was their huge hit single from *Dynasty*, "I Was Made for Lovin' You." According to Paul, "I wrote that because I thought, 'Let's have a big hit.'" With a danceable beat and a catchy tune, it was one of the group's biggest American hits, as well as their first major hit in Europe.

In 1976, KISS had done a small tour of Europe and England and it was not a major success. It was also the time, Gene remembers, "when the first strains of people calling us Nazis began. It was the most ridiculous thing. KISS is 50 percent Jewish." But when they went to Germany, KISS had to cover up the logo because of the resemblance of the lightning bolts to Germany's notorious SS. This year, Gene claims, "When we go to Europe, we'll show 'em what it's all about."

What it's all about is an incredibly ambitious group that is never satisfied. "Once we've conquered the world," Ace proclaims, "we'll go to the moon for a concert." While that's not likely to happen in the foreseeable future, KISS does have plans for expanding the group's audience. "There's so much stuff I want to do," Gene admits. "I'm working on a traveling amusement park based on KISS. And we're going to have our own comic book company and our own book publishing company. The KISS concept will continue beyond its members. *Beatlemania* has got nothing on us. A KISS Broadway *show* would be the best. We are going to be launched as characters; we'll become the modern-day Bowery Boys. And other actors will portray us. There's no reason why we can't continue as superheroes long after we put down the guitars. KISS is going to continue past the life of the rock 'n' roll band. KISS will outlive itself.

"Already, all over the world," Gene points out, "imitation groups are springing up. Of course, they can't re-create our show. Minute for minute, thrill for thrill, it's the greatest show on earth. I don't think there's anything that compares with it. And after the show, kids live the KISS lifestyle, play the records, put our pictures on the wall. If they go out and buy KISS costumes and makeup, they can become us. The last band you could do that with was the Beatles. People bought Beatle wigs and that transcended the music. Don't misunderstand where I'm coming from," Gene cautions. "The Who used flash pots long before us and wrote probably the ultimate in anthems, 'My Generation.' But what I'm talking about is the impact on society. KISS has become rock 'n' roll circus entertainment for the whole family. Rock 'n' roll tried to create a generation gap, and KISS is bridging it. If the parents can swallow KISS, every other rock 'n' roll band will be much more palatable." Gene believes that "the rules of rock 'n' roll no longer work with us. We are a band unto itself."

Bill Aucoin has no doubts. "KISS can last forever. They are superheroes, like Superman or Spider-Man, and they will continue as long as they can physically and emotionally withstand the type of pressure that is required to keep up the image that they have created. It's really up to them. What they do is tremendously difficult, and when the day comes that they decide they can't do it any longer, they will leave a legacy to the '80s the way the Beatles did for the '70s."

Bill Aucoin gets the final word. "My whole life has changed as a result of my love for the four of them. When I'm around the kind of love and energy that they generate, I know that I've made the right decisions. I am not only their manager, but I am one of their biggest fans, and I share the hopes with their millions of fans around the world that they will go on forever."

SPEAKING IN TONGUES

★★★★★

BY KEN SHARP

SECTION

02

The first installment of section Two offers an overview of KISS's nonmakeup years leading to 1996's reunion of the original band. Next are candid interviews conducted with KISS between 1996 and 2000. Closing out this section, the "speaking in tongues" chapter draws together firsthand commentary from the band and members of their inner circle chronicling significant touchstones and quintessential events in KISStory.

CREATURES OF THE NIGHT:
THE AFTERMATH

Chapter **12**

In 1978, KISS were arguably the most popular band in the world. A year later, their golden empire began to slowly crumble. On the surface, KISS appeared to be infallible, but upon closer inspection, cracks were beginning to surface and the machine was close to breaking down completely. While KISS's new studio recording, *Dynasty,* soared to number nine on the *Billboard* chart and their single, "I Was Made for Lovin' You" was a smash hit, the team had clearly splintered, its members mired in petty jealousy, substance abuse, and festering conflict.

In September of 1978, the release of the KISS solo albums served as a harbinger that all was not well in KISS land; competition among the members as to whose record would sell the best intensified their already out-of-control egos. Fanning the flames of discontent further was the grim reality that KISS had begun to lose many of their older fans. Once every parent's worst nightmare, KISS had lost that crucial element of danger, and in the process were transformed into a kiddie band embraced by the ten-and-under crowd, an audience enamored more with the group's cartoon-ish image and merchandise than their music. The single, "I Was Made for Lovin' You," further alienated their hard-core fan base, whose clear disdain for disco-rock severely eroded their once inviolable code of KISS fanaticism.

Nineteen seventy-nine signaled the death knell for the original KISS lineup. The rot had truly set in. Paul and Gene's relationship with Peter Criss, in particular, had reached an all-time low. Plagued by a debilitating dependence on drugs and alcohol, Criss was by now totally out of control. Once able to bluff his way through a show, despite being high or strung-out on pills, on the *Dynasty* tour, Criss's grave substance abuse problem began to noticeably impair his skills as a drummer. Throughout the tour, Criss was a musical liability. In order for KISS to survive, something had to be done—and quick. Things finally came to a dramatic head at the conclusion of the *Dynasty* tour, which claimed the band's first casualty. Peter Criss was no longer a member of KISS.

Keeping silent on Criss's departure from the group, KISS recorded their next album, *Unmasked*, under a tight veil of secrecy. Utilizing session drummer Anton Fig (who also played on most of the cuts on *Dynasty*), the album found the band pursuing an even poppier direction than *Dynasty*, which further perplexed their rapidly shrinking fan base. Harboring a crisp, power pop sound akin to that of Raspberries, *Unmasked* ultimately suffered from its lightweight musical approach. Gone was the primal musical ferocity characterizing vintage KISS. Clearly, KISS's mistaken foray into melodic pop coupled with the band's image problems further confounded their card-carrying legion of KISS Army acolytes and the album sank without a trace in America. Although still superstars in Europe and especially Australia, *Unmasked* reached only a disappointing number thirty-five in America. This was a miserable showing for a group that had been selected by the Gallup Poll three years earlier as the most popular rock band, topping such legends as the Beatles and Led Zeppelin.

KISS were DOA in the States. A year earlier, the big picture was infinitely rosier, KISS had played two dates at New York's Madison Square Garden. Now the band's lone U.S. *Unmasked* date was held at a much smaller New York City venue, the Palladium. It was a far cry from past Kabuki glories.

PETE TOWNSHEND, THE WHO:

KISS are straight out of *Creem* magazine meets Las Vegas or New Orleans. KISS is a very American kind of Mardi Gras thing. They couldn't have happened in England. Maybe they could have happened in Berlin, in which case their music wouldn't have been like their music. They would have looked like they look but they would have made a different kind of music. KISS are a very American phenomenon. As a result of that, I haven't really sat and listened to their music but maybe I should.

Announcing the departure of Peter Criss, the band held auditions for a new drummer and selected Paul Caravello, later renamed Eric Carr. Carr's drumming style aligned itself more comfortably with the band's hard rock roots—Led Zeppelin, Slade, and Humble Pie—than his predecessor's swing/big band style. Coupled with his drumming prowess, Carr was also a talented songwriter and vocalist too.

Before deciding upon the makeup persona of Fox, Carr underwent a number of botched makeup and costume designs, including one blunder that reportedly made him look like Big Bird from the popular children's TV show *Sesame Street*. Once his makeup design was finalized, Carr was thrust into the unforgiving glare of fame's white-hot spotlight.

Less than a month after joining KISS, Carr's first performance with the band (at the above-mentioned Palladium show) went off without a hitch. Following this one-off concert, KISS embarked on a six-week tour of Europe before scurrying Down Under to the friendlier frontiers of Australia, where they were greeted with Beatlemania-like intensity. Thanks to the overwhelming success of the *Unmasked* album and number one single, "Shandi," the group performed a series of sold-out shows in such locales as Sydney, Adelaide, Perth, and Melbourne. To this day, KISS's 1980 tour of Australia is fondly remembered among the band as a career milestone. Yet one thing was soberingly clear: While KISS were still tremendously popular overseas, in America their star had clearly fallen.

In a last-ditch effort to regain their popularity and break new artistic ground, KISS reunited with *Destroyer* producer Bob Ezrin for 1981's *Music from "The Elder."* The concept, initiated by Gene Simmons, centered upon a young boy's rite of passage, a heroic life's journey through personal discovery, doubt, and ultimate self-realization. Months of recording ensued, with the end result sounding unlike anything in the KISS pantheon. Indeed, after the album's release, some pundits described the album as bearing the trippy prog rock hallmarks of vintage Genesis, Pink Floyd, and Jethro Tull.

Frehley, in particular, voiced his dissatisfaction with the new, more "mature" direction and viciously locked horns with producer Bob Ezrin. A traditional rock 'n' roll drummer, Eric Carr also found it difficult working under the creative and stylistic constraints set forth on *Music from "The Elder."* In fact on one track, "I," Carr was unable to provide Ezrin with the desired percussive rigidity and was replaced by studio drummer Allan Schwartzberg, who previously played on Gene Simmons's solo album.

Despite its share of ambitious tracks like "A World Without Heroes" (co-written by Lou Reed), "Just a Boy," and "Under the Rose," *Music from "The Elder"* was a shocking departure from KISS's Sturm und Drang metallic sound, and not surprisingly sank like a stone, barely eking its way to a dismal number seventy-five, KISS's worst LP showing in years. A misguided attempt to elicit critical respectability (*Rolling Stone* magazine gave it a positive review), *Music from "The Elder"* was a flop of major proportions, an incalculable disaster. Ironically, despite its decidedly cool response from the KISS Army, years after its release *Music from "The Elder"* now commands its share of newfound respect and belated praise from the band's legion of followers.

By the time KISS had finished recording *Music from "The Elder,"* Ace Frehley knew that his days in the band were numbered. Exceedingly disenchanted by the group's schizophrenic musical direction and feeling increasingly stifled and bored by their cartoon rock image, the band's resident Spaceman decided to leave KISS. Ace's sudden departure, marking the second original member to exit the band in only two years, leveled a devastating blow to KISS's downward-spiraling fortunes and couldn't have happened at a more inopportune time.

Still smarting from the trainwreck that was *Music from "The Elder,"* the band were vitally concerned about the rapidly dwindling numbers in the KISS Army. Screw critical respectability and pretentious concept rock, KISS needed a molten metal makeover and fast. The solution was simple. Before they wound up "Where Are They Now" fodder, KISS needed to crank their amplifiers to 10, and reemerge with a hard rock album.

Nineteen eighty-two's *Creatures of the Night* fit the bill perfectly. Sonically, the record boldly captured the group's full-bodied hard rock sound. Eric Carr's drumming, in particular, never sounded better, boasting a larger-than-life sound that would have made Led Zeppelin drummer John Bonham's hair stand on end. Dedicated to Neil Bogart, the crafty Casablanca Records ringmaster who had recently died of cancer, the *Creatures of the Night* album resounded with the earthquake force and lyrical firepower that KISS fans craved and expected. Two of the best songs on the album, "War Machine" and "Rock and Roll Hell," were co-written by then unknown and future rock star Bryan Adams.

But now it was on to the matter of the missing Ace. And it's here where KISS can be accused of willful subterfuge. Fans were clearly left in the dark, was Ace still in the band or was he out? Despite Frehley's painted Spaceman visage gracing the album cover, he did not play on the record, replaced by a variety of session guitarists including future Mr. Mister guitarist Steve Farris and jazz-rock great Robben Ford. Bridgeport, Connecticut–born guitarist Vincent Cusano (later renamed Vinnie Vincent), who also played on the album and co-wrote most of the tracks, was officially brought into the fold as new lead guitarist. Vincent assumed a new spooky makeup design, his face adorned with a golden Egyptian ankh symbol.

Creatures of the Night succeeded in reestablishing KISS as a hard rock outfit but suffered from disappointingly lukewarm sales. The accompanying U.S. tour was also a bust, finding the band playing to half-empty arenas. Making matters worse, while on the *Creatures* tour, the band were plagued by throngs of angry religious protesters who charged that KISS were evil messengers of Satan. They would claim that KISS's name stood for "Knights In Satan's Service." Dumbfounded by such ludicrous accusations, Simmons and Stanley took to the media in full force, appearing on various national television news programs and print media to vigorously refute such outrageous claims. Yet despite the controversy surrounding their *Creatures* tour dates, the resultant hype didn't help matters. Code blue had been sounded, and KISS was on life support.

How could they stop the bleeding? Unbeknownst to their fans, KISS's June 1983 shows at Maracana Stadium in Rio de Janeiro, Brazil, were their last shows with makeup. Performing in front of 137,000 fans, KISS closed their makeup era with aplomb as conquering heroes. Fans knew that major changes were afoot after picking up the group's latest album, *Lick It Up*, which was issued on September 23, 1983. The unthinkable had occurred, akin to Superman being revealed as mild-mannered reporter Clark Kent. *Lick It Up*'s simple white cover unveiled a photograph of Paul, Gene, Eric, and Vinnie sans makeup. Not surprisingly, this move inflamed some critics, who charged that KISS's unmasking was a calculated last-ditch marketing attempt from a group sinking faster than the *Titanic*.

Produced by Michael James Jackson, *Lick It Up* exhibited a heavy, metallic sound, distinguished by the rock/rap stylings of "All Hell's Breakin' Loose," Stanley's epic ballad, "A Million to One," and the lascivious title track. The album was a surprise hit, restoring KISS to Platinum status. Even more importantly, *Lick It Up* attracted scores of new fans that were unfamiliar with the band's storied makeup past.

Performing their first show without makeup on October 11, 1983, in Lisbon, Portugal, KISS proved that with or without the greasepaint and seven-inch leather heels, they were still an unstoppable rock 'n' roll force. The addition of new member, lead guitarist Vinnie Vincent, a gifted songwriter and musician, also pumped fresh blood into the KISS songwriting and touring machine. However, Vincent didn't last long in the KISS fold. Personal and creative friction between Vincent and founders Stanley and Simmons led to the Egyptian wizard being unceremoniously booted after completion of the U.S. leg of the band's *Lick It Up* tour.

ROGER DALTREY, THE WHO:

I say this with regret, I never actually saw any of KISS's live shows. But I loved them. I thought that KISS really had the right attitude. They never ever took themselves too seriously and they made some fucking good music.

JOHN ENTWISTLE, THE WHO:

I like KISS. They were so over the top. They took the theatrical stuff a little further than The Who and they wore more makeup than us [laughs].

Rejuvenated by the success of the *Lick It Up* album and tour, KISS began the search for lead guitarist number three. Enter Mark Norton, later renamed Mark St. John, who lent his lightning-fast guitar acrobatics to the outfit's next studio album, *Animalize*. Around this time, a major obstacle derailed the band. The culprit was Gene Simmons, whose once rock-solid commitment to KISS was seriously wavering. Seduced by the lure of Hollywood, Simmons aggressively pursued an acting career, eventually appearing in such films as *Runaway* (with Tom Selleck), *Trick or Treat, Never Too Young to Die, Wanted: Dead or Alive,* and *Red Surf.*

For the recording of *Animalize,* an album produced by Paul Stanley, Simmons's silver screen flirtation seriously handicapped his creative contributions to the record. Ex-Plasmatics bassist Jean Beauvoir, a friend of Stanley's, handled some of the four-finger work. The fans, unaware of Simmons's declining creative involvement, seemingly couldn't have cared less as *Animalize* vaulted to Platinum status. "Heaven's on Fire," the album's lead-off single, remains one of KISS's most popular nonmakeup tracks (the song was one of only three nonmakeup cuts performed on the group's 2000–2001 Farewell Tour).

As KISS began to prepare for yet another touring juggernaut, their new guitarist, Mark St. John, battled with his own precarious medical predicament. His hands swelling and unable to play, St. John was diagnosed with Reiter's syndrome, a rare disease of the joints. On KISS's European trek, St. John forlornly watched from the side of the stage as temporary replacement Bruce Kulick blazed up and down the fretboard. Recommended to the band by older brother Bob Kulick, a longtime friend of KISS's (Bob contributed lead guitar work on *Alive II, Killers,* and Paul Stanley's 1978 solo album), the new hired hand settled in quite comfortably. Frustrated by St. John's continued medical problems and energized by the smooth transition of their interim guitarist for hire, KISS welcomed Bruce Kulick into the fold as guitarist number four. Clearly, by this time, KISS's revolving lead guitar slot had taken on an almost hilarious Spinal Tap–like familiarity; you needed a scorecard to keep up with who was KISS's latest axe slinger of preference.

Yet unlike past guitarists Vincent and St. John, whose time in KISS was fleeting, Kulick would remain in the band for over ten years. Kulick's incendiary guitar stylings fired the recording of the KISS's next studio album, 1985's *Asylum.* Cut from the same stylistic swath as *Animalize,* the album, co-produced by Stanley and Simmons, yielded another Platinum award. Three singles were issued from the record, including the hit "Tears Are Falling" and "Who Wants to Be Lonely" and "Uh! All Night."

Aside from his extracurricular thespian pursuits, Simmons also kept busy carving out a career as a producer, working with the likes of Plasmatics vocalist Wendy O. Williams, House of Lords, Doro Pesch, E-Z-O, Black 'n Blue, and Keel. His bandmate, Paul Stanley, kept his priorities closer to home, devoting all of his creative energies to KISS. Besides a co-production credit on New England's debut LP and mooted production work with Guns N' Roses, Poison, and Cher, Stanley was KISS's go-to member in the '80s: ever reliable, ever creative, he was a model team player.

Nineteen eighty-seven was also the year that KISS first opened up their vaults. *Exposed,* the group's first video documentary, was issued in May of 1987, a compendium of rare concert clips and tongue-in-cheek interviews. Over the years, the

KISS Army's thirst for compelling visual material would be satisfied with a succession of best-selling home video releases.

For KISS's fourteenth studio album, the group enlisted the expertise of producer Ron Nevison, who had recently produced mega-Platinum albums for Heart and Ozzy Osbourne. With Nevison on board, the band felt confident that his involvement would help fuel a new commercial upswing for the seasoned metal warriors. Released in September of 1987, *Crazy Nights* was a slick and well-crafted effort, wrapped in velvety keyboards, lush harmonies, and swirling guitars. The anthemic title track and radio-friendly power ballad, "Reason to Live," helped *Crazy Nights* land a respectable number eighteen placing on the U.S. charts but the album fell far short of being the seismic commercial hit they envisioned. Overseas, the story was considerably more upbeat. The single, "Crazy Crazy Nights," with its fist-waving Slade-sounding chorus, was a smash number four hit in Britain. Galvanized by their U.K. success, the group participated in a massive outdoor *Monsters of Rock* show at Castle Donnington in England, performing alongside such heavy rock stalwarts as Guns N' Roses, ex–Van Halen lead singer David Lee Roth, Iron Maiden, and Megadeth.

Celebrating KISSmas 1988 in grand style came a new greatest hits compilation, *Smashes, Thrashes and Hits*. With songs spanning the group's entire career, the record also featured two new studio cuts, "Let's Put the X in Sex" and "(You Make Me) Rock Hard" plus a version of "Beth" featuring newly recorded vocals by drummer Eric Carr.

Upon the conclusion of KISS's *Crazy Nights* world tour, Paul Stanley wasn't ready to hang up his rock 'n' roll shoes and go on holiday. In February 1989, Stanley embarked on a short U.S. club tour, performing vintage KISS classics, songs from his 1978 solo album, along with a cover of Led Zeppelin's "Communication Breakdown." The tour was a resounding success, priming Stanley's creative juices for KISS's next studio album.

Hot in the Shade was the result, landing in record shops in October 1989. The leadoff single, "Hide Your Heart," a song Stanley premiered on his 1989 solo tour, was a modest number twenty-two hit. Recognizing that his outside pursuits had damaged the creative core of KISS, Simmons reemerged on *Hot in the Shade* with renewed dedication and focus. Not surprisingly, now that Simmons was fully recommitted to KISS, the album would go on to yield the band's biggest hit in fourteen years. Penned by Paul Stanley and Michael Bolton, the power ballad "Forever" rocketed to a number six chart placing. Promoting the follow-up single, "Rise to It," the band had another trick up their collective sleeve. In the video, Paul and Gene are filmed putting on the makeup again in a fantasy backstage scenario prefacing the actual performance of the track. This unexpected stunt added fuel to the impending rumors of a KISS reunion tour.

BRIAN WILSON, THE BEACH BOYS:

KISS is an interesting band indeed. I like their energy.

Yet in the face of the group's commercial renaissance, unspeakable tragedy was right around the corner . . . In 1991, KISS received the heartbreaking news that Eric Carr was stricken with cancer. After a successful operation in April of 1991, Carr rejoined his bandmates in the studio to add background vocals to a reworked version of Argent's early '70s hit "God Gave Rock and Roll to You." Recorded for the *Bill and Ted's Bogus Journey* soundtrack album, the track, renamed "God Gave Rock and Roll to You II," bore new lyrics and a baroque-sounding bridge showcasing Carr's counterharmony vocals. Carr wasn't in any condition to play drums on the track so the band tapped Eric Singer, who previously performed on Paul Stanley's solo tour, to take his place. Despite the prayers of the entire KISS community, Carr eventually succumbed to the disease on November 24, 1991. Since his death, Carr's musical legacy has grown immeasurably with the release of *Rockology*, a solo CD of previously unreleased music, and the *Inside the Tale of the Fox* documentary.

Shaken by the passing of their longtime friend and drummer, KISS soldiered on. In May of 1992, KISS released *Revenge*, their first long-player to showcase new recruit, drummer Eric Singer. Reuniting with producer Bob Ezrin of *Destroyer* and *Music from "The Elder"* fame, *Revenge* harked back to the group's archetypal '70s sound, an uncompromising declaration of everything that KISS believed in, ranking among their most accomplished records to date.

Breaking into the *Billboard* album charts at number six, KISS once again took to the road, treating their loyal fans to a two-and-a-half-hour show packed with KISS favorites, old and new. Also released that year was *X-Treme Closeup*, a home video chronicling the group's colorful history via vintage live clips from the mid-'70s plus footage culled from their *Revenge* tour.

Fifteen years since the release of their last live album, KISS answered the persistent demands of their fan base with *Alive III*, issued in May of 1993. Recorded in Indianapolis, Cleveland, and Detroit, the record was produced by Eddie Kramer, who twirled the dials for *Alive!* and *Alive II*. Peaking at number nine, *Alive III* was an explosive reminder that KISS hadn't lost their prowess as a dynamic live attraction. Live footage culled from the *Revenge* national trek coupled with candid interview clips made their home video *KISS Konfidential* a best-seller. And to top off a productive year, KISS was inducted into the Hollywood Walk of Fame, joining such luminaries as Van Halen, Aerosmith, Little Richard, and Ozzy Osbourne.

Nineteen ninety-four brought more good tidings for KISS fans with the June release of *KISS My A**: Classic KISS Regrooved*, a tribute album comprising KISS covers interpreted by the likes of Garth Brooks (he performed a cover of "Hard Luck

Woman" with backing by KISS), Lenny Kravitz with Stevie Wonder, and the Gin Blossoms. Now once again considered hip, *KISS My A*** further illustrated KISS's incredibly broad fan base. In July, KISS performed "Hard Luck Woman" with Garth Brooks and "Christine Sixteen" with the Gin Blossoms on *The Tonight Show with Jay Leno* and *Late Night with David Letterman*. Two months after the release of their tribute album came the *KISS My A*** home video, another best-selling compilation of live clips and TV commercials.

Nineteen ninety-five was truly a banner year for KISS. After a short Japanese tour and the reissue of the KISS Marvel comic book, the band published *KISStory,* a beautifully designed 440-page tome profusely illustrated with hundreds of photographs, scores of rare memorabilia, and incisive text. Then in lieu of a proper concert tour, the band held their own officially sanctioned KISS conventions in America and Australia. Displays of vintage costumes and memorabilia, a video show, dealer's room, and a question-and-answer session were among the festivities. Most importantly, these conventions served as a joyous celebration of KISS's heritage for both their fans and the band themselves. The intimate nature of the conventions afforded the group the opportunity to get up close and personal with their fans. Topping off each convention, the band performed acoustic sets comprising seldom—if ever—played live KISS jewels like "Room Service," "Mr. Speed," "Plaster Caster," and "Larger Than Life." The first U.S. KISS con kicked off on June 17 in Los Angeles and featured a surprise appearance by former KISS drummer Peter Criss, who sang several songs onstage with the band, including "Hard Luck Woman."

The all-acoustic format of these convention shows was such a major hit with the fans that it led directly to the band's appearance on MTV's highly rated *Unplugged* program. Closing one chapter of KISStory while opening a new one at the same time, the vital importance of the group's appearance on *Unplugged* cannot be underestimated. It clearly served as the prime catalyst for the most exciting and at one time most unthinkable event of all, a reunion of the original members.

ALIVE AGAIN:
THE REUNION TOUR INTERVIEW

Chapter **13**

"You wanted the best and you got it, the hottest band in the land . . . KISS!" Those immortal words were loudly and proudly bellowed out immediately prior to KISS's impressive entrance at concerts, often accompanied by huge fiery flames that singed the ceilings of that lucky town's arena. Now the original lineup of KISS was back, adorned in Kabuki makeup and wearing their classic *Love Gun*–era costumes.

A surprise appearance at 1996's Grammy Awards in Los Angeles triumphantly signaled the return of KISS. This was followed in April with the reunion press conference held on the USS *Intrepid* aircraft carrier in New York City. For many in the audience, it was the first time they'd seen KISS wearing makeup. Frehley opened up the festivities by admitting, "We look as silly as we did fifteen years ago."

Q How did the KISS *Unplugged* show lead to a reunion of the original band?

GENE SIMMONS: It started with Peter, who called me at home when I was putting together the KISS conventions. We wanted a one-of-a-kind event that combined *Star Trek* meets Disneyland. Peter himself had appeared at fan conventions. His daughter started talking about the KISS thing because it had been growing and growing with a brand-new generation who'd never seen the original band. He called and said, "I want to come down and bring my daughter. Is that okay?" And I said, "Sure, absolutely." Eric Singer said, "You invited Peter but you didn't invite him to sing a song with us?" It didn't even dawn on me because Eric is the drummer in KISS and Peter was the drummer in KISS. Out of respect to Eric, I didn't want to fuel rumors. Eric said it was cool. Peter came down and we started playing around and it sounded terrific. When we played two songs with Peter at the convention it was such a rush—for the fans, for myself, and for Paul. It was bizarre. Whatever problems we had in the past with Peter you just sort of forget about it, you're just glad to see each other. We were coming to the East Coast and we didn't want to insult Ace after Peter appeared at a convention on the West Coast. As it happens, they were both playing clubs together so they couldn't make it to the New York convention. But as the *Unplugged* MTV thing was coming up, the irony of it was the planets lined up and we all decided to do it. And to Eric and Bruce's [Kulick] credit, both of them said, don't worry about us, this'll be great for the fans. It just happened naturally. After the KISS *Unplugged* show it was a very bizarre time for us. It was kind of a realization on Paul and my part that, number one, there's definitely a chemistry that you just can't put a want ad out and find. The magic could have been gone. It's all about that sparkle. If it's there, it's there. If it's not, it's not. It's nothing you can buy in a grocery store on the top shelf marked for sale today. And the other element is as people. Are you full of shit or are you not? Are your defense mechanisms working or not? So what happened was we went to dinner a couple of times and just hung. It seemed obvious that the specter of the makeup tour was coming up. It was sort of possessing all of us at the same time. We were all getting the same fever at the same time. Before we could go forward there had to be a clearing of the air. Ace and Peter had to come clean. I may be a workaholic, stubborn, hard-nosed, but there's no question that I work my butt off for the band. It was never a question of if Ace and Peter were good or bad guys. It was always a matter of substances, whether it was booze or drugs. And KISS have absolutely no tolerance for that kind of stuff. So they had to come clean. Before we could even talk about the future, How are you doing? How's your health? How's your mind? Have you looked in the mirror and been honest with yourself? They came clean. They said they fucked up and you can't blame anyone else. It's hard enough to get along with people straight much less high. You may be able to have a civil conversation with Dr. Jekyll but forget Mr. Hyde. You just can't even get to first base. Then we had to see if there was dedication. The second time around is twice as hard as the first time. We have the biggest competition: ourselves twenty years ago.

 Where were you and what was it like when you first put the makeup and costumes back on?

PAUL STANLEY: It was a bit bizarre. It was kind of like going through a door and then time-traveling. It's very bizarre to see the band and to have it be so unchanged. What makes it even more odd is to look at everybody and go, "Wow, we all look the same."

PETER CRISS: Major emotional and major trippy. For a second I got freaked out and I thought [laughing] that I was losing my mind and was caught up in a bad acid reversal.

What can I say? It was like looking in the mirror after seventeen years and seeing the same faces and it was frightening.

ALICE COOPER:

I had no problem with KISS for one reason, it never touched on what Alice did. I always said that KISS were comic book heroes where Alice was much more Phantom of the Opera. KISS was another band that had a couple of good special effects. I thought the breathing of fire was a very good idea and some of the costumes were over-the-top. And I liked their music. I thought the music was pretty good. But they didn't get involved in the actual psycho sickness that made Alice a dangerous character. KISS was never nearly as dangerous as Alice. KISS were great merchandisers. They knew exactly how to merchandise themselves. They were smart.

 What was the vibe like at KISS's reunion press conference?

PAUL STANLEY: The cool thing about KISS at this point is so many people have memories and events in their lives that are tied into KISS and to see the band in the flesh just transports those people. When we walked out at the Grammys most of the audience's eyes lit up and their jaws dropped. Not because of anything else except it pushes buttons in them. You know the first time you got laid or the first time you drove your parents' car or the first time you took off work to go to a show. It's about a lot of firsts and a lot of the bands remember that. It touches buttons and then for the people who never saw KISS in those days, the stories are so legendary that it does the same thing to them.

 Do you ever wake up and say, "Wow, I'm back in KISS again"?

PETER CRISS: You know what, I'm waiting for that, and I know it's gonna come. When we got back from New York, Gene and I flew back together and I was jet-lagged. He called me at six in the morning and said, "Peter, we just sold out Tiger Stadium in forty-seven minutes." And I went, "Gene, I'm exhausted, it's six in the morning." And then I hung up the phone and I jumped out of the bed and went, "Holy Shit!" No one will break that record ever. One day I'm gonna wake up and go "Holy Shit!" I didn't think the reunion was gonna happen but I wanted it to happen.

 Tell me about the stage show.

PAUL STANLEY: What we wanted to do was look at the '77 show in a sense as a pinnacle. This is what we will build on but not copy. Sure, there are elements of it that are in this. But there are elements from other shows in the sense that there's bombs and the flying rig and the breaking of the guitars. Ace's smoking guitars and things like that. It's really the ultimate KISS show in the sense that we looked at the show which we thought was our best and said, "Top this."

WELCOME TO THE SHOW:
YOU'RE IN THE PSYCHO CIRCUS

Chapter **14**

Prior to KISS's landmark reunion tour in 1996, there existed a frosty, cold war between two factions of the original band. In one corner stood founding members Gene Simmons and Paul Stanley, both dedicated to moving forward with its current incarnation of the group. In another corner stood the outcasts, ex-members Ace Frehley and Peter Criss, wizened warriors of the musical circle. The stage was all but set for a bloody WWF Death Match. Yet much to the profound appreciation of the KISS Army, relations among the original band members warmed considerably, leading to the group's reunion on MTV's *Unplugged.*

Now that the brass knuckles were put away and the band had kissed and made up, the unthinkable was now a possibility. KISS would reunite and boldly reclaim their enduring legacy as one of rock's most influential and exciting groups. Max Factor was smiling; the pancake makeup was back, the black leather, sequins, and dragon boots were dusted off and pulled out of the catacombs. KISS were reborn, both musically and spiritually.

Taking their reunion to another level, KISS regrouped and entered the studio with producer Bruce Fairbairn to craft *Psycho Circus*, the original band's first studio recording in almost twenty years. Not surprisingly, the *Psycho Circus* tour was an eye-popping, larger-than-life spectacle, utilizing the latest cutting-edge 3-D technology.

Bring us back to the band's first full reunion show in 1996 at Detroit's Tiger Stadium.

PETER CRISS: I broke down and cried, I got so overwhelmed. It almost seemed like some sort of dream I was in. We were working so hard for that night, hours and hours of vigorous training. It was like boot camp. I had to look at thousands of hours of KISS on video. I had to go back to being the Catman, this alter ego that I really put out of my life and then I had to deal with him again. It was a stone reality to me every night when I was sitting home alone in my apartment watching myself when I was twenty-five years old, I was flipping out. And I knew I had to be that again so the pressure was enormous. But yet KISS had so much pressure in those days that it was almost like "Here comes the pressure again, we've got to prove we're the baddest band, the greatest band on earth. We're the American Beatles." All that shit we used to tell each other. One minute I'm sitting and talking to Gene and the next minute we're on a golf cart, the two of us, going up a ramp in a stadium, and it was like, "Holy shit! Either I'm dreamin' this and there is a time warp or there is a time machine. And maybe it was all a bad dream and this was the way it was goin'." All that shit ran through my head. And when I got behind the drums and started the show I was in shock. I think I was in shock throughout the whole show actually [laughs]. I broke down during "Beth." It just flipped me out, even when we got into when the guys were movin' back and forth, moments like that I'd fill up. Watchin' Ace take a solo and watchin' Paul dance across the stage, it was the most poetic thing. It was just "Wow!"

 It must have been surreal looking to your left and right seeing Ace and Gene in full makeup.

PAUL STANLEY: Oh yeah, but that didn't stop opening night. There were many many nights when I was looking around the stage and going, "This is magic." This is beyond anybody's wildest fantasies. What was important about these shows is we had a much bigger task than people understood. We didn't have to be as good as we used to be. We had to be as good as people thought we were. The show wasn't to be a replica of what we've done, it was to be what people imagined we had done. Our biggest competition was our history. The only competition we had was the shadow that our past casts on us. We had to be totally committed and also totally sure that we could not only live up to the legend but also surpass it. People wanted this so badly that we weren't going to do it unless everybody was thrilled at the end of the show. There's nothing worse than asking for something and then being disappointed. There's nothing worse than having the memory of something tainted and marred by the reality of the present.

 # JOHN PAUL JONES, LED ZEPPELIN:

I thought that KISS did a great show with the makeup. It's an event, it's a show, people go for a good time.

Q **Discuss working with the original band again.**

GENE SIMMONS: The original lineup is really the most bizarre mixture of guys you'd ever want to meet because we each have nothing in common. Even Paul and I. On the surface it looks like Paul and I are like brothers attached at the hip but we have almost nothing in common. When it comes to food Peter and I are closer. We sort of like the same foods. Ace is like no human being that walked the planet. One-of-a-kind. People think he's always bombed. Now he is not. His memory is selective at best. Ace can be very incisive. Among all of us he's probably the one most based in fantasy. He believes in UFOs, he believes in conspiracy theories. Parrots love Ace 'cause when he talks they all pick up "one of us" [imitates Ace speaking in high-pitched voice]. I guess I'm the most dry guy, black is black and white is white. Paul's much more romantic, a "Why can't it be better?" kind of a guy. Peter's a street guy, and is much more volatile emotionally. He's completely different now, now that Peter and Ace are straight, it's like that Clark Kent and Superman thing or perhaps Jekyll and Hyde.

Q **When you sat down to write for _Psycho Circus_, did you specifically try to tailor your writing to the band's vintage sound?**

GENE SIMMONS: Yes. Also it has to do with Ace and Peter being in the band. If Bruce and Eric tried to play this stuff it would sound different. It would sound too good because literally Bruce and Eric are actually more proficient on their instruments. But Ace and Peter have a point of view and style, which is quintessential KISS. And nobody's been able to do that. I've heard tribute bands and it sounds close, but it's never the same. There's a way that Ace and Peter play that is just what KISS is. Every other version of the band that we've had that tried to do those songs winds up being too good. It's almost like one of the best things in life is a good, sloppy burger. And if you do it too well it doesn't have that flavor, it doesn't taste good.

PAUL STANLEY: I wrote specifically to capture the essence of what we had done. Not re-creating or making a retro album, not trying to make an album that sounded like it was recorded twenty years ago. It was more about capturing and rekindling the spirit of the band. The thing I always loved about _Destroyer_ is it pushed the envelope and pushed the parameters of what we could do. It pushed us to the limit and yet everything stayed true to us because it was all comfortable, there was nothing forced or contrived. The idea with this album at least from my point of view is to make sure that we weren't restricted with what we could be but were open to do anything as long as it was comfortable.

ACE FREHLEY: I just write what's on my mind, I don't really think about it. If you pulled my song "Into the Void," my style hasn't really changed that much. I think I've just improved as a songwriter and improved as a guitarist. My singing's gotten better. Your voice is like a muscle, the more you use it, the stronger it gets. It's amazing. The more you practice, the better you play.

 Tell us about the 3-D stage show.

GENE SIMMONS: The *Psycho Circus* tour is going to be like nothing anybody's ever seen literally and figuratively because if you've ever been to an IMAX movie and put on your glasses, that's what's going to happen. We've got the biggest screens you can imagine. The technology is cutting-edge. Nobody's got this, it's live 3-D. You can watch it without your glasses and you'll see something going on, it'll play with your senses. But when you put your glasses on, which you'll get with your tickets, KISS glasses, when you put them on, anything that's 2-D, like if I look at you with my glasses on you look the same. But when I look at the screen and you see me spitting blood and the blood is dripping around, you'll see the tongue come right in front of your face and you'll actually feel moisture on you because we're going to throw water into the audience. You'll smell it, see it, feel it, hear it.

 Were you surprised at how successful KISS's reunion tour was?

PETER CRISS: Yeah, I was surprised [laughs]. I remember one night we were on the jet and I'm sitting next to Ace and Gene was sitting there. It's really late and we were tired. By now we had played like 168 shows. We're sitting there and I went, "God, this is blowing my mind." We all just knew that it ain't never been like that.

 One band rarely cited by the group as a pivotal influence is Slade. Listening to Slade's back catalogue, you can hear how they infiltrated KISS's sound.

PAUL STANLEY: Slade was awesome. In many ways Slade was the English counterpart to us. Slade wrote these great anthems. Live, they were simple, but boy did they put their boot up your ass. They did some shows with us too. Noddy [Holder] is a great singer. The whole band almost looked like some sort of cartoon come to life. They were like a steamroller. They weren't a profound influence but I understood their point of reference. It was similar to where we were coming from. I think at some point they rewrote their songs too often. But when they did it right there were some great songs and live, they were just great. My mirror Iceman guitar was actually not a unique or original idea. Noddy had a top hat with mirrors on it so when they hit his hat with a spotlight, he had these huge circle mirrors on his hat. So when they hit his hat, these beams of light came out of his head. And it was such a cool idea that that's where the idea for the mirrored guitar came from.

PAUL RODGERS, BAD COMPANY:

I think KISS is absolutely amazing. They're very unique. KISS reminds me a little of the early Mott the Hoople, especially the bass player with his outrageous silver high heel boots that came up real high. All without a hint of embarrassment [laughs]. KISS is totally full-on. Full marks for being full-on. They just took it to the max, you couldn't go beyond that.

GENE SIMMONS: "Deuce" sounds more like Slade. "Let Me Know" also could have been a Slade song with the structure of the chords [sings "Gudbuy T' Jane"]. And also pieces of "Rock and Roll All Nite," the chordal patterns. The part "you drive us wild, we'll drive you crazy" [sings a line from Slade's "Mama Weer All Crazee Now":] "Ma, ma, mama we're all crazy now." They were a big influence on me but not until I saw them. My girlfriend at the time, Jan Walsh, had Slade records [*Slayed,* and *Sladest*] in her basement and I put them on and I was floored. The stuff just floored me with its simplicity and guitars. Ironically enough it was the bass player, Jim Lea, who did most of the songwriting. So when I finally saw them with Paul, it was Frampton's Camel, Slade, and the J. Geils Band. Slade did not actually go over well but they floored me. I went "Wow!"

 Is the *Psycho Circus* trek KISS's farewell tour?

ACE FREHLEY: I think this can go on for as long as all four of us can look at each other and say we're still having fun. And if the kids are still saying we want another tour and we're all enjoying ourselves. I think we're gonna stop when we're not having fun with it anymore.

FANFARE: THE FINAL FAREWELL

Chapter 15

Flash-forward to a date still to be announced . . . Somewhere in America, KISS are onstage performing their national anthem, "Rock and Roll All Nite," the final song capping their blockbuster farewell tour. A torrential rainstorm of multicolored confetti falls furiously upon the ravenous crowd of fervent KISS acolytes. It looks like World World III onstage; bombs are detonating, towering walls of flames are engulfing both sides of the stage, and there's enough fireworks to level a small country. Upon the conclusion of "Rock and Roll All Nite," Paul Stanley, aping his hero, Pete Townshend, violently smashes his guitar, in a time-tested ritual that signals the end of this pinnacle performance . . . and KISS's career as one of rock's most spectacular and groundbreaking live acts. Hand in hand, Paul, Gene, Ace, and Peter take their last bows to a deafening roar of the KISS Army. Then it's all over. The lights go up and the audience slowly departs from the venue, witnessing firsthand KISS taking a giant step into mythology, a magical land where superheroes never die and never grow old.

With four grown men wearing Kabuki makeup and prancing around the stage in seven-inch leather heels, it comes as no surprise that KISS were misunderstood from the beginning. Critics routinely dismissed them as a "flash in the pan," musical misanthropes pandering to the lowest common denominator. They said KISS wouldn't last.

Long after the Starchild, the Demon, the Space Ace, and the Cat hang up their black leather, studs, and sequins and take off the greasepaint for good, the memories will remain unburnished, charged into the psyche of KISS fans everywhere.

JOE PERRY, AEROSMITH:

I can remember hearing KISS's first record before they opened for us. I remember hearing a few songs on there that were pretty cool. They fit in with the type of rock 'n' roll that I liked. I didn't realize at that point that it was just a background for the bigger spectacle. Then we played with them and the audience loved them. This was back before they had all the fancy suits; it was before they really had the money to do the whole costumes. They put on a good show. I remember the drum riser breaking a lot. It would stop and start. At that point they were still trying to do their show on a shoestring. They obviously had a vision for where they were going and what they wanted. I remember the road crews were at each other's throats. KISS opened for us and they had so much production and it made us adjust. I remember the show at the Michigan Palace and there were some weapons pulled. The vibes between the road crews weren't too good. The only time I saw them play in the '70s was at the first gig we did with them, it was at the Painter's Mill Music Fair in 1974. They played the songs from the record, they rocked out and they were good. The audience loved them. It was entertaining. We were trying to beat our heads against the wall and be a good band and we were kind of going, "What do we have to do, put makeup on?" As for Ace's guitar playing? As long as someone entertains an audience I think they're good. I can say that he's not Jimmy Page but neither am I. He played what needed to be played and filled the niche. He played KISS songs great. Ace does his whole thing. He had rockets shooting out of his guitar, teetering along on his seven-inch platforms. I don't think there was rivalry between KISS and Aerosmith. We were so different. They were on lunchboxes; it was a whole different thing. We were a little bit more elitist about the music. So it wasn't like we saw us as competing for the same audience. We saw a lot of the same people at the same shows for both bands. I don't know if we ever felt this competition. Steven [Tyler] did feel a little bit more of a competition with them. Anyone that would like them more than us he saw as a threat. Steven feels that way about anybody. Whether it's KISS, Ted Nugent, or Robert Plant, I know he always wants to stay at least one step ahead. KISS certainly became more of a household word than Aerosmith because of the across-the-board merchandising. They even had a pinball machine. They had merchandising that we never would have gone near. They were cartoon characters. It's pretty amazing. They were truly a unique act. Everybody else was out there trying to play music and write great songs but they didn't really care that much. They were writing their own brand of music and it was the soundtrack to their show. They had some great rock 'n' roll songs like "Strutter." Some of the other stuff worked great for their visuals but I wouldn't put on a KISS record from front to back. Back in the '70s, I remember Peter and Paul coming by the studio and rubbing elbows. There was more of camaraderie than a competition. The first gig was probably when they were the closest to being an ordinary rock band with a little bit of makeup thrown in. Within months they did something that was totally unique. They were an amazing piece of entertainment. They were so unique. Little kids wanted to dress up like them. They were more across-the-board than we were. We were picking up the mantle of what bands before us did, people like the Yardbirds and the Stones and Zeppelin. We saw ourselves as the American version of that. KISS was unique, there weren't any other bands doing what they did. They had the whole package. The whole band and my family went to see KISS on their comeback tour in Boston. I thought it was great. It was great to see them back. We saw them right before they went on backstage. They came over and they were bigger than life. It was really a lot of fun. They had all the modern production, everything they did in the '70s plus. KISS made a lot of kids happy and they influenced a lot of the young bands that are out now. A part of it is their music was so accessible and easy to play. That's part of rock 'n' roll where you see someone like KISS and say, "I can do that too." And even if you don't end up doing it past playing in the garage with your friends you've lived the dream a little bit for yourself.

PAUL STANLEY

 How do you think you'll be feeling during the last KISS live show ever?

PAUL STANLEY: In my life so many of my dreams have come true that I can only look at it as a huge accomplishment. I don't look at anything I do with a lot of sadness because then you're not really appreciating what it is. You should look at the positive side, that you actually did it.

 If you put KISS's sound under a microscope and had to select one or two bands that were the primary elements for your sound, who would you choose?

PAUL STANLEY: I think the initial foundation was Humble Pie. The idea of two guitars was really best typified by Humble Pie because a lot of your classic loud British bands only had one guitar. Then there was The Who. We also sometimes made an attempt to be Stonesy or Beatle-esque and trying to add in some Led Zeppelin.

 Hypothetically, if you had to be another member of KISS for one show, what member would you like to be and why?

PAUL STANLEY: [long pause] I think I'd like to be Peter because it's so easy to think about the challenge of playing chords and notes. Everybody wants to be where they're not. So of course Peter wants to be in the front. It's a nice place to visit but I wouldn't want to live there. But yeah, I'd like to be behind the drums for a day.

 How would you describe yourself growing up, what were you like?

PAUL STANLEY: Unhappy [laughs]. Unhappy is the best word that comes to mind.

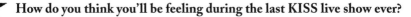 **What were you unhappy about?**

PAUL STANLEY: Just who I was and problems I had and difficulties because of my ear, all kinds of things. Whenever you have difficulties, they manifest themselves in all different ways. And you wind up doing all kinds of things to protect yourself, which cause even more problems. Being different and being a kid is something all parents should do their best to help.

 You mentioned having problems with your ear, can you hear out of both ears?

PAUL STANLEY: No, I can't hear at all in my right ear. I have bone conduction. In other words, if you press something against the side of my head I can hear. You don't miss anything that you don't really comprehend. If I press something against the side of my head I can kind of hear stereo but that doesn't sound real to me. That's not how I hear music. For me it's just confusing. It throws me off.

 Discuss how your singing style changed in the late '70s taking on a more operatic quality.

PAUL STANLEY: I think my real early stuff is a little narrow in vocal range. At that time I was trying to find my footing. I'm real comfortable with my vocal sound around *Dressed to Kill*. I was singing so much that I was either gonna destroy myself or learn to sing a little differently. I needed to change the way I sang because I wanted to be able to expand what I sang. I was limited by my range and I wanted to be able to sing more. I was also intrigued by how other singers were hitting notes that I couldn't hit. In the '80s, sometimes what I was attempting to do got ridiculous. It's like when you get a car with a lot of horsepower; you floor it a bunch until you realize that it ain't always about flooring it. I was in awe of some of the notes that I can hit. The beauty of having a career that lasts a long time is everybody sees your baby pictures. By the time *Creatures* happened, I was feeling pretty good as a vocalist. Afterward, it got a little out of hand. I think I do my best singing live. I think I went through a period of singing live where there was a whole lot of unnecessary vocal gymnastics.

 ## BRAD WHITFORD, AEROSMITH:

Aerosmith and KISS played on the same bill back in the early days. I knew nothing about KISS then and they blew me away. They were playing my favorite kind of music, which is guitar hard rock, really simple. It was a really powerful show. I remember their crew and our crew having this enormous fight because they were making ridiculous demands and I'm sure we were too. One of my first feelings about KISS was like "Wait a minute, unfair advantage here!" They had taken all these other elements and thrown it into the mix. It was totally unique. We seemed like two different types of bands. I don't think we ever felt a rivalry at all with KISS. We're all friends, we get along fine with those guys. Like Aerosmith, KISS has an incredibly loyal fan base, which makes us each unique.

You have spoken about being at odds with producer Bruce Fairbairn during the recording of the reunion CD, *Psycho Circus*.

PAUL STANLEY: This is a delicate subject because we're talking about somebody who is no longer with us. It's certainly not bashing somebody who isn't here to defend himself. I would say the same thing if he were. I think working with Bruce was a major disappointment. His first choice of songs was so bizarre. If he could have done an album of songs like "Within," that was what Bruce thought we should be doing. It was astonishing to me because he didn't have a clue as to what the essence and balance of KISS is about. He didn't understand the dynamics of an album, maybe he understood a Loverboy album or a Bon Jovi album. Clearly he was completely lost. It's essential for somebody that comes in to bring in an extra ingredient. It's not essential for somebody to come in and reinvent the wheel. Ultimately what happened is I told Bruce I had enough. I said, "This is your first KISS album, it's not mine." I thought at times Bruce's nose was so far up Gene's ass that he could barely breathe. It's maddening to be in a situation where you see somebody leading something you've spent thirty years working on into a ditch. He'd done some really great work with other acts. But quite honestly I don't know what his contribution was and what theirs were.

 Are there plans for KISS to continue musically?

PAUL STANLEY: We're open to anything. We're open to see where this leads. It's never over. We'd be deluding ourselves even if we wanted to that we could end this. It's completely out of our hands. The only thing is how much do we want to participate because KISS will continue regardless. I enjoy it. It's been a part of most of my life.

GENE SIMMONS

 Unlike boxers that come back beyond their prime, KISS has chosen not to do that. KISS is going out on top with a Farewell Tour.

GENE SIMMONS: We started as four guys off the streets of New York City. We had done everything there was to do. We did a 3-D tour, we were given a Hollywood Star on the Walk of Fame and the *Detroit Rock City* movie came out. We basically decided, why not hang up the boot heels and say thank you very much even though it was sooner than the five-year plan we had. We simply decided we hadn't done it the right way, which was to get up onstage and say thank you to the people who put us here. It was the ethical way of closing the final chapter of the *live* band.

Q **Hypothetically, if you had to be another member of KISS for one day, onstage in makeup and costume, who would you choose and why?**

GENE SIMMONS: Peter. You can get your aggression out on the drums. I can't be Ace because I'd be nullified. And Paul's very comfortable with a sort of androgyny on stage. He's clearly heterosexual, yet has no problem with sort of vamping it up. At least consciously I'd have difficulty with it.

Q **You spoke once about feeling that the first three or four KISS albums were not musically innovative and were derivative of the band's influences. Why do you think fans, old and new, select those albums as among the band's best?**

GENE SIMMONS: When the Beatles first came out they sort of did a hybrid of Motown and Chuck Berry. They mixed it up and came up with their own thing. So even though what we did might seem a retread of everything that we liked, English and American, it still came out of our mouths and minds. So there was something decidedly different about it. There was a celebratory sense to it. They were uplifting. To put those records on they sort of bounce with life. When English bands like Genesis and Jethro Tull started veering away from the meat and potatoes of rock 'n' roll, and with Black Sabbath talking about the darkness, we centered right into the stuff that made rock 'n' roll great for us, which was the uplifting qualities. The *us* . . . the "you and I against the world" sense.

PETER CRISS

Q Are you sad that this is the last KISS tour?

PETER CRISS: There's a side of me that goes, "Aw man, where did the thirty years go?" Like when you're sitting in a train and watching all the stations go by, that's how it's been for me. It seems like that's how it's been for me in the last thirty years. It's been like a roller coaster. Am I sad? Yeah, I'm sad for the fact that we've done so much, we've accomplished so much I think in the history of rock 'n' roll for a band coming out of New York City. We really stuck to our guns, we never went where the fashion is, we were more passionate. And I love that about the band. But in a way I'm glad too because I'd rather leave the party early. Everybody hates someone who stays at the party too long and you've gotta throw them out. I'd hate to see a star of mine who was aging and had a big belly [laughs] and had tits and had a problem making it up on the stage. It would break my heart. And I don't want to see anybody go out like that so this is the best way to go out while we're still strong and we look good and we feel good.

Q **Last song, last show, what emotions are going to be running through your mind?**

PETER CRISS: I don't know if I'll be able to finish the song because I'm a pretty emotional guy. More than all of us, I think Gene, who lives, shits, and breathes KISS, will really feel it. I think I'll cry, I don't think I'll make it through. I'll be thinking so much, where did it go and why is it over and now how do I get this adrenaline that I used to get, where do I channel that?

 Q **One of the best things about the KISS reunion is you were given a second chance to shine once more with the band.**

PETER CRISS: It was tough. A falling star is not a great thing to be. When I fell from grace, I didn't appreciate what I was given. I was saying, "Big deal, another house, another mansion, another tour." I did not appreciate what was given to me. I grew up very poor and I should have appreciated it. When it was taken from me, I knew it. I prayed and prayed. And then I met Gigi, who's a Christian and who doesn't do drugs or anything, helped straighten my life out. God answered my prayers and I got a second chance. And no one gets a second chance. I'm financially set forever. I've got a beautiful home, I've got my health.

 # BOB SEGER:

I'll never forget playing with KISS in Philadelphia. We used to start with two, three songs in a row and try to get the crowd on our side by really hitting them hard with some good stuff. After the third song, instead of [imitates loud cheering] "Yay!!," it was more of, "KISS, KISS, KISS!!" [laughs] There was some cheering but it was also, "Let's get to the other guys." [laughs] They had some really avid fans. The big thing we had to worry about was losing our hearing. We'd go watch KISS do the first couple of songs and we had to find out where the explosions and pyrotechnics were [laughs] so we weren't damaged [laughs]. I was very fearful of losing my hearing. Playing with KISS was very helpful to us. We were able to get in front of huge audiences. When people ask me "What was it like opening for KISS?" I always tell them that they were the nicest guys. They were fair. Even if they were running behind, they made sure we got a sound check, which was unusual. They were really, really good to us. I thought the KISS show was really strong. I'm always still cheering for them, I'm happy they're still doing well. I've always told anybody who will listen, from Kid Rock to the Eagles, you take care of your audience by showing up and you continually show up. And KISS does that really well. They keep going out and people wanna see you and if you show up they are so grateful. If you care about your fans and you show up, you're gonna be beloved. I think that's the way it is with KISS. They've had that army since '75 and they have treated them well. It's a great lesson. A lot of people get big and don't want to tour. That's the wrong way to do it. Serve your audience. They can tell when you care about them. KISS were like me, they weren't a super-gifted musician like John Lennon. They worked hard to come up with their hooks and they deserve all the success they got. KISS knows what their audience wants, and they deliver it. If it was easy everybody would do it. Anybody who slams them has never done it. I totally respect them. They're the best at what they do, history has proven that.

What will you miss most about being in KISS?

PETER CRISS: There's something about us, I don't know what the hell it is [laughs]. I sit in bed some nights and go, "Would I go fishing with Gene?" "No." "Would I go to a baseball game and have a beer and a hot dog with Paul?" And I go, "No." "Would I go out with Ace jogging?" I don't think so. So what do I have in common with these guys? It's gotta be magic. It's always been magic. When I first got together with Gene and Paul and we were a trio, I felt it then. There's something that when the four of us put that face paint on and we walk up those stairs, I've never had that feeling with anybody else on this planet. And I'll miss that. And the laughing and the goofing with each other I'll really miss, the putting each other down the way we do [laughs]. Nobody can put me down like those guys can and I like it because we're like brothers. And there's times I wanna kick the shit out of them and there's times I wanna love them to death. It's a real love-hate relationship with KISS. It's always been.

If you could take a time machine back to when you were a teenager, what type of person was Peter Criss the fifteen-year-old?

PETER CRISS: You'd see this little Italian kid who lived in four rooms with seven people. I had one brother, three sisters, Mom and Dad. My dad did not go to school, he wasn't educated, so he worked his ass off day in and day out. My mom, God bless her, was amazing for me. From day one when I was beating on her pots and pans, breaking and busting them, she never complained once. They were all for me. I was always banging around the house on stuff and driving my dad to drink, well he didn't but . . . My mom was always, "Keep it up, keep it up." You'd see a guy up in a tenement building playing a set of 1935 Slingerland drums instead of playing stickball. Living in Brooklyn, you had to be in a gang to survive. And I was a Catholic kid and I went to Catholic school but hey, I didn't want to get beat up either [laughs] every day so it was either you join 'em or you get beat up by them. I kinda was into the gangs but I didn't favor it and I was against beating people up. I didn't think that was so cool. I was a young rebel in a tough neighborhood and I was a tough guy, and I got my ass kicked enough too. I always felt part of something. I guess that was always sort of important in a poor neighborhood to be part of something because you don't want to be on your own. They seem to always pick out like sharks, there's the kid who's not like one of us, kick his ass.

How close did you come to becoming a real criminal?

PETER CRISS: Oh God, I was making my own guns at fourteen. I was selling guns to gangs, zip guns [laughs]. So I was getting close. I could have been in jail by fifteen, sixteen. I could have been in jail for shooting someone or getting arrested for stuff like that. In rumbles, I got into some really bad fights.

 What was the worst trouble you ever got yourself in?

PETER CRISS: I stabbed a guy [laughs] in a gang war way back in Brooklyn. And I came home and there was blood on my shirt and I was beat. My mom asked, "What happened to you?" I said, "Ma, this guy hit me with a garbage can cover and he kept hitting me and hitting me so I pulled my knife out and stabbed him." And she was like [incredulously], "Did you kill him?" And I said, "No, I didn't kill him, I just stabbed him in the arm." I'll never forget that because that was a really traumatizing thing for me and I would never dream of it but I had to survive also.

 What do you feel was the biggest disappointment in the band's career?

PETER CRISS: We didn't have many disappointments, we were so blessed. I think a mistake, not a disappointment, was making four solo albums. I think we all went crazy and got egotistically insane. Everybody got to be, "I'm so great I can do my own stuff and I don't need you guys because I wrote 'Beth' and I can just go out on that." It caused a cancer in the band. That's when I really started feeling the decline.

ACE FREHLEY

 KISS is on their Farewell Tour, share your feelings.

ACE FREHLEY: I have mixed emotions about it. Everybody knows that I've gone through ups and downs with Paul and Gene but there's something about KISS, it's hard to put my finger on it. Even if we're arguing big-time before a show and we're putting on the makeup, all of a sudden when we get announced and we jump up onstage, the chemistry takes over. For two hours we're mesmerized by the audience and the audience is mesmerized by us. I think I'll miss it. You can't do it forever.

 What KISS song would you like to re-record?

ACE FREHLEY: When I think back and I listen to the original recording of "Cold Gin" it's so slow and so dry, there's no ambience to it. I would like to re-record "Cold Gin" with today's equipment.

Hypothetically, if you had to wear the makeup and costume of another band member for one concert, which member would you choose to be and why?

ACE FREHLEY: None of them [laughs]. I wouldn't do it. I am Ace. I am the Spaceman. I created that character because it's an extension of my personality. I couldn't do any of the other three. No way. I would look like a fuckin' idiot [laughs].

 You had your fair share of scrapes with the law. How many times have you been in jail?

ACE FREHLEY: [laughs] I've been in jail several times. Drunk driving, yadda yadda yadda. By the time I was eighteen I was probably arrested a dozen times. I was a wild kid. The only thing that saved my ass was rock 'n' roll. When my friends started calling me up on weekends, "Hey, we're going to go out and rob cars tonight," I'd say, "I can't, I have a gig." [laughs] Eventually my band became real popular. We were working five nights a week, I dropped out of school. One of the bands was the Magic People. One was Honey. Then I had a three-piece, the Muff Divers [laughs], that used to play up in the Catskills at Kutsher's ski resort.

 Do you have a message for the fans?

ACE FREHLEY: All I can say is without the fans I wouldn't be here. The bottom line is KISS fans are the most dedicated fans that I've ever come across. I'd just like to say thank you because without you guys I wouldn't be here doing what I'm doing.

SPEAKING IN TONGUES

Chapter **16**

MUSICAL BEGINNINGS

GENE SIMMONS: The first song I ever learned to play was "Hang on Sloopy" by the McCoys. When the *Meet the Beatles* album first came out, that changed my life. You had four guys that played their own instruments. They weren't dancing onstage, and they weren't doing steps. It was like white noise and jangly guitars. It was jarring and yet it was pop. They looked weird but everybody looked like they belonged in the same band. When I was fifteen, I saw Tommy James and the Shondells, Al Kooper, and the 4 Seasons. After the concert I went home and said to my friends, "Wow, I just came from a rock 'n' roll concert. It was great, I was right up front. In fact, I can still hear it." And everybody said, "What are you talking about?" What I heard was the buzz that you get from hearing too much loud music.

PAUL STANLEY: I was shy and very introverted. I spent a lot of time on my own, playing the guitar. There was a music store in New York called Manny's and I used to hang out there and wait to see what rock 'n' roll stars would come in. I always knew I was special. There are all different words you can say. I was weird. Special was weird. Somebody will look at you and say, "Gee, you're special," and somebody else won't understand what you're doing, they'll say, "You're crazy." So I was both. I always wanted to do music but at some point you get brainwashed or talked into doing something more practical. And art seemed to be more practical even though for most people anything outside of the norm would seem pretty risky. In terms of what I wanted to do, art seemed the lesser of the two evils. I didn't give myself a real chance at art. I probably could have been successful, but it's a lot more gratifying to play for twenty thousand people a night than it is to paint. No one ever applauded when they saw my paintings. But ultimately I had to really give in to my urges. I don't think I ever doubted that I was going to succeed. Maybe the best way to succeed is to never doubt it. You may fail but I think the most important thing is having that determination and belief in yourself.

PAUL STANLEY: One of the reasons I wanted to be a rock star was to have girls at my beck and call. I think if you talk to anybody in rock music, they'll tell you the same thing. How else could I get girls? I wasn't on the football team. I did play some football when I was a kid. The first time somebody tackled me, I landed on my stomach and had the air knocked out of me. I was the kind of guy that would play until I got hurt so that was the only time I played tackle football. I used to wrestle a lot. Once when I was around seventeen I was hanging out in Central Park with a friend of mine. We were wrestling and he broke my arm. Last time I wrestled.

ERIC CARMEN, RASPBERRIES:

The weirdest date the Raspberries ever played was opening for KISS. The bill originally was KISS and Iggy Pop on New Year's Eve. Iggy Pop had been billed and advertised for three weeks and at the last moment, like a week before the show, the chamber of commerce refused to let him in the city. So they just stuck us on the bill. This was just when KISS was starting to catch fire and we walked in and there was an audience full of screaming doped-up maniacs waiting to see Iggy Pop walk out of that stage and we walked out and it was like Vietnam. It was a real serious disaster. People were throwing things. Beer cans, cherry bombs, missiles, and projectiles of all sorts coming on that stage. At one point I walked up to the mike and respectfully said, "We don't want to be in here any more than you want us here, but if anything else comes out of that audience, we're out of here. I don't want to be a moving target." And then somebody threw something at our drummer. The barrage stopped and then Wally [Bryson] went up and rather tersely gave them a quick view what was on his mind with four letters or less. They calmed down after that. Then KISS came out after us, with nine-inch platform boots and black leather and smoke bombs. I remember seeing Gene Simmons swigging down a little Dixie cup full of Scope and kerosene, before he breathed fire. I remember walking backstage and saying to my manager, "If this is what I have to do to make it in rock 'n' roll, I quit."

PAUL STANLEY: As I grew up, I realized that my parents were really down-to-earth people who are hip on the inside, not superficially, and I respect them for that. My father never grew big muttonchop sideburns or wore Nehru jackets. He never made a fool of himself or embarrassed me. He was always cool. Like all parents, mine worried about their only son. In the beginning, Gene and my parents showed up at some of our club dates. After all, when your son wears high heels, tight pants, and makeup, you want to see what he's doing on the weekends.

PAUL STANLEY: I had a couple of jobs. Once I worked in a factory that was owned by my friend's father. Also I drove a cab. The worst was in a grocery store where the manager was telling me, "You've got a great future here. You could be the next manager of the store. You're gonna get to lock the door at night." That wasn't exactly what I wanted out of life. Besides, I was wearing a wig to cover all my hair, so I was afraid to smile 'cause I thought the wig would r-r-r-rip and pop off the top of my head.

PAUL STANLEY: I think that what I identified in bands like the Beatles and the Byrds besides the visual of seeing a band that looked like a unit was the melodic sense that those early bands had. I heard the same thing in the early Who stuff. There were great harmonies, great melodies over a lot of power, and that's what's always appealed to me about what I've wanted us to do. I always wanted to have a vehicle to sing my ass off and have choruses that were memorable and have something underneath it that was driving it like a locomotive.

ACE FREHLEY: I grew up in the Bronx around Bedford Park Boulevard, Fordham Road. When I was young it wasn't that bad an area but I always looked for the worst people to hang out with [laughs]. I always wanted to be with the gang leaders. My favorite classes in school were art, science, and music, that's what I excelled in. I wasn't too hip on English or math, but geometry was fun. My first guitar was a Japanese Zimgar. It cost $23 and I got it on my thirteenth birthday for Christmas. One of the first songs I learned to play on guitar was "I Want to Hold Your Hand." The Beatles had a big influence on me when I was very young. But as I matured as a teenager, I started leaning toward the Rolling Stones. I identified with them more, because they were more of a rebel group. Those guys were getting busted. They were just outcasts and basically I was the same way when I was a teenager. I was more into the bad-boy image. I was the Fonzie of my neighborhood. I remember learning the lick in "The Last Time" by the Rolling Stones. I had just bought a new Ampeg amp with reverb and I reproduced it. It sounded just like the record. In my senior year in high school, I was in a very popular local band and I met a lot of girls because of that. I used to set up a lot of my friends with different girls. That's how I got my nickname Ace, because I always used to set up my friends with beautiful girls, and they go, "Wow, you're such an Ace for doing this."

ACE FREHLEY: My first live show was at a synagogue in Riverdale with a group called the Four Roses. I was about fourteen years old and my knees were shaking even though there was only about twenty-five people in the audience. I wasn't singing lead vocals then. It took me a long time to get around to singing lead. I grew up in a religious family and I used to sing in the choir. I always had a voice. It was just a matter of getting over the shyness of being a singer.

PETER CRISS: My dad was a real big-band fanatic. He loved Gene Krupa, Benny Goodman, loved that big swing sound. He told me, "You'll never be like Gene Krupa." I'd say, "Yeah Dad, we'll see." And I never will, I think Gene Krupa is the greatest drummer on this planet. I tried to get close to him and as I grew older, I bought all his albums and knew how famous he was. I'd go to the Metropole and see Krupa there or Dizzy Gillespie, Max Roach. I'd hang around Gene's dressing room and knock and go "Mr. Krupa, can I come in?" And he'd say, "Yeah, come on in," and I'd say, "How did you do this or that? Maybe you could show me." After a while, I was such a pain in the ass that he had no choice but to show me things. He gave me his time, one of the nicest guys on the planet. That's where I got my drum boogie. See, I played jazz before I ever played rock. That's what I first liked and I still do. Rock came to me in the early '60s.

JOEY RAMONE, THE RAMONES:

KISS and the Ramones both grew up in Queens. I was at their first show ever. I was also at the show where they first got signed to Casablanca Records at Coventry. At the time I think they were the loudest band I ever heard. I liked a lot of their stuff. They were fun and had great songs. I saw them when they first started out and they just had dry ice; Gene had a skull-and-crossbones T-shirt. This was way before their image and show thing came together. KISS were fans of the Ramones too. I remember KISS hanging at CBGB and them coming to see us. As a matter of a fact, they used one of our songs for their film, *Detroit Rock City.* Later, I saw them on the *Destroyer* tour. It was like a big freak show; everybody was dressed up like them. I always really liked *Destroyer*. It was big-sounding and had a lot of great songs. I loved the song "Detroit Rock City." The production on the album is great too. I was always a big fan of the early Alice Cooper stuff so I was a fan of the producer Bob Ezrin as well.

PETER CRISS: I wasn't good at football, I was too skinny. I was too short for basketball. I was fairly decent in baseball but I was a very good swimmer. I used to compete at the YMCA and I won a lot of trophies and medals. What's ironic about that is although I'm an excellent swimmer, I almost drowned once and Gene saved me.

JOHNNY RAMONE, THE RAMONES:

KISS is one of the most exciting and entertaining rock bands of the past thirty years.

DREAMS

PAUL STANLEY: I always kept in my head that I would be somebody. When I was a little kid before I even thought about what I would do. You know they always ask kids, "What are you going to do when you grow up?" Before people would ask that, I never felt like everybody else. You are fueled by your belief that you can do it. I don't think that anybody can put aside totally the thought of it not working. Usually that's a little too frightening to deal with. When you are committing your time to something, it's kind of hard to sit back and think about the consequences of it not working out. So you don't dwell on that.

DEE DEE RAMONE, THE RAMONES:

The first time I saw KISS was at a loft with Wayne County. Everybody was sort of afraid of them. KISS acted like a tough band that had already been touring for a while. I saw them again at the Academy of Music, they were opening for Iggy & the Stooges, Blue Öyster Cult, and Teenage Lust. Everybody there must have been a Stooges fan and KISS took over the whole night. Nobody could believe what they were seeing. They had ten Marshall stacks on each side; it was a real show. Gene Simmons's hair caught on fire that night. What I liked most about KISS was their success. Right away I loved that they could withstand the bitching in a band and they persevered and came out standing tall. They had a lot of success. I liked Ace Frehley the best in the band 'cause his sound was great. Their songwriting was also good. If they want to know the opinion of the members of the Ramones what KISS song we liked best . . . it was their disco song, "I Was Made for Lovin' You." It's great.

GENE SIMMONS: I knew in the earlier bands that it wasn't going to happen. I didn't know with KISS if it was going to happen because it was out there at the time. But secretly down inside you know when you haven't got the goods. You can bullshit all you want. You can fool yourself all you want in public but then when you go to sleep at night and you're hoping "Dear God, oh please make it work," the fact that you're doing that means you don't have the goods. The idea of not listening to anybody else is if you fail, then at least you fail on your own terms. And if you win, then you have nobody to thank but yourself and that's the only way I prefer winning. I don't want to win and turn around to somebody and say thank you. Listen to no one.

ACE FREHLEY: I always knew I was going to be famous. I used to tell people 'cause I grew up without having a lot of money. I couldn't even afford a car. Luckily I had girlfriends with cars. But I always knew I'd make it. It's funny the first car I bought when we started making money in KISS was a Cadillac Eldorado. I forgot to put oil in it though so I had a melted-down engine after four months.

LENNY KRAVITZ:

I grew up on all kinds of music, soul, R&B, blues. But it was KISS who were the first group which made me think I want to be onstage doing this. They were so larger than life and so underrated and just got shit on because of their whole theatrical thing. Ace Frehley is a great guitar player.

PAUL MEETS GENE

STEVE CORONEL: In 1970, I got together with Gene at Brooke Ostrander's apartment in New Jersey and we were talking about putting a band together. I was trying to think of somebody who could complete the circle. We needed a lead singer, a guy who can sing and play. I thought of Stanley. I said, "What if I hook you up with this guy Stanley?" I called him and said, "Gene and I want to meet with you." I arranged for the meeting one evening at my apartment in Washington Heights. The meeting was in my living room, which I had painted gloss black; it all looked kind of funky for 1970. I remember Stanley played a red guitar. Gene was leaning against the bed, which I had elevated three and a half feet off the floor because I had put it on top of two Marshall cabinets. I remember Gene had his finger up to his lip [laughs] as he often does when he's considering things. Stanley was playing one of his songs, "Sunday Driver," which was Move-influenced and it sounded pretty darn good. He and Gene took turns playing songs. Gene played "Stanley the Parrot" and whatever else he had at the time, which wasn't all that great. I think Stanley's stuff sounded a lot better. Same with the singing. So when Stanley was done playing [nonchalantly] Gene said, "Yeah, that was good." He was pissed off so he could barely muster that. He also begrudgingly admired Stan because he was good. The culmination of the meeting was good, everybody was happy and positive about starting up this new band. Paul and Gene spoke to each other a few days later and they decided that there was room for both of them in the group.

PAUL STANLEY: With friendships that last for a long time, initially you may have a real strong aversion to somebody. I met Gene at Steve Coronel's house. We just didn't hit it off, but it didn't matter that much to me. I didn't lose sleep over it. I told Steve I wasn't interested in playing with him. But at some point we started putting our stuff aside and with time you see. If two stones rub against each other long enough, they smooth out and all the sharp edges disappear. That's kind of what you do. You also start to figure out what you don't say to each other and what makes the other guy angry. I know that Gene is very aware of certain things that drive me nuts. I'm not saying that what he does drives me nuts. There are just certain things he knows don't work for me. So, he doesn't do them. Likewise there are times where I just stay out of the way rather than getting on his case about something. Some stuff is not that important. To work with somebody and have an ongoing relationship, like with your brother, you've got to know where to draw the line.

GENE SIMMONS: I was not aware of another human being on the face of the planet. I was so wrapped up in Gene Simmons that I thought I was the messiah, Jesus Christ notwithstanding or whoever else thinks he's God. I thought I was it, the living, breathing God that walks. I couldn't believe that anybody else would have the balls to say "Oh I write songs too." I wasn't really being impertinent or unfriendly or anything. But I had so much confidence in myself at that point, in a very real way, it numbed me to other people. I had come from the mountains. I lived in South Fallsburg. I was huge, massive. I had a beard, wore overalls, and at that point I weighed 225 pounds. I was massive. It wasn't so much fat as much it was just big all over. I was so impressed with the fact that I taught myself how to play guitar and bass and learned how to write songs that I thought it was the first time that any human being had ever done it. Somehow when you thought about the Beatles and all the rest of them you just never thought that they were human beings. They just always were, it was like the sun and the moon, they were always there.

PETER'S EARLY PRE-KISS BANDS

PETER CRISS: The Barracudas were a New York cellar band, basement cellar band. Three-piece: sax, guitar, and drums. We did all cover shit, we did "Tequila" and "Sleepwalk" and "La Bamba." I used to sing all the John Lennon songs. I used to sing "In My Life." I used to wait to sing that all night. We were a great little band, we played all the Brooklyn clubs. Brotherhood was another great band. We worked with the Hassles—Billy Joel's band at the time—the Vagrants, the Rich Kids, Mountain. We were a really hot band, we were like the Rascals, we were like a white black band. We did originals and cover tunes. We had a Hammond B-3 organ, lead guitar, bass guitar, drums. We would kick ass, we were a really kick-ass band for the New York circuit. I was in Chelsea, we put out one album on Decca. Lips was Stan Penridge and this guy named Mike Benvenga who's since passed on. Lips was another badass trio. We would do Cream and Jimi Hendrix, all this speed metal trio shit. I thought I was Mitch Mitchell. Lips was really out there.

INCUBUS/UNCLE JOE/TREE

PAUL STANLEY: Incubus was another name for my band Uncle Joe. It was me, Matt Rael, and a drummer named Neil Teeman, who I went to school with. We never had a bass player. We just played real loud. We were doing covers by Zeppelin, Mountain, and Free. When I was with the Post War Baby Boom, Matt's older brother Jon was in that group and I was suddenly taken into the older brother's band. I moved up in the world. Incubus didn't do many live shows. We were kids. The most we could hope for is have some friends come over in the basement. I don't think we were doing originals then, just covers. I have a tape of Uncle Joe. We're doing this song we made up in the studio called "Stop, Look to Listen." I sing lead on it. That must have been done in '66. It's just three fourteen-year-old guys, two guys with loud amplifiers and a drummer. It's kinda heavy-ish. Steve Coronel was in a band called Tree, which was the band that I was in when I met Gene. That was me, Steve, a bass player named Marty Cohen, and Stan Singer on drums. Stan had played with Gene in another band.

MILLEMO

ACE FREHLEY: The first band I did serious recording with was called Millemo. It stood for "Music of the Forest." It's a Portuguese word. We cut a demo on RCA at RCA Studios. We had a producer and we were gonna get a deal with RCA. I did it when I was about nineteen or twenty. It was never released. It sounded like an East Coast version of Jefferson Airplane. It was a girl and a guy singer up front, I think his name was Tom Lewis. We had a keyboard player, another guitarist, me, a bass player named Barry Dempsey, and a drummer named Dave. I have the tape somewhere. It's pretty funny stuff. I did very little writing with them. They had most of the songs already written. I was the last one to join the group. We played the Village Gate a couple of times and we played the Fillmore East before it closed.

EARLY DAYS

PETER CRISS: We were a trio for a good year, but it was good because it got us tight. After the first meeting at Electric Lady we decided to meet at the loft to try things out. When I got there they had the other drummer's drums [Tony Zarrella from Wicked Lester] set up. Now, anybody's who's a drummer knows that you don't play well on another drummer's drums because it's such a personal thing; equipment an inch away from where you're used to can mean life and death to a drummer. Anyway, I played lousy and we were all sad about it because we wanted it to work out. So I suggested we try it again but that I bring my drums . . . and that was it. We played great. Paul and I were really buddies, we really hung out. We would talk on the phone like girls for hours. I mean five, six, seven hours on the phone. Paulie and I had an unbeliev-able relationship.

RON JOHNSEN (WICKED LESTER PRODUCER): I saw KISS at their loft and they were just outra-geous, a lot of high energy, a lot of wild playing. They were just hitting the walls. They were a very physical act, rough and rowdy. A lot of their vision came from groups like the New York Dolls and the Brats.

LEW LINET (EARLY KISS MANAGER): Every time I'd come by to rehearsals I began to notice little compacts of makeup. First thing I noticed was that they were wearing eyeliner, then a little bit of rouge, then a little bit of an eyebrow pencil and it took off from there. Every rehearsal became a little bit louder and the band wore a bit more makeup. They were putting together what their dream was, a loud, old-fashioned hard rock band, kind of a Rolling Stones, David Bowie, Alice Cooper amalgamation.

PAUL STANLEY: The loft on 10 East 23rd Street was a little room on the fourth floor. We put egg crates on the walls to absorb the sound but that didn't work. We rehearsed constantly because we didn't want people to say "They're awful" and then later say, "Oh, they've gotten better." We wanted to have a certain level of proficiency before we played for a paying audience. On New Year's Eve, 1973, we invited our friends to the loft to see what we were doing. When they saw us in makeup, they thought we were all crazy, so we played and got drunk. At that point, we were still perfecting what we were doing and inviting our friends was part of our plan. We didn't want to play for people until we thought we were ready.

KISS IMAGE

PETER CRISS: We copied a lot of things. A lot of our ideas, the art of what we did came from the Beatles, Alice Cooper, the New York Dolls. We sat down and said, "What if all that was rolled into one? Four Alice Coopers, the Beatles, what would that be like?" And it worked, it was brilliant. We went to see an Alice Cooper concert and I'll never forget it. Gene and I sat in our chairs in the back and Paul and Ace literally ran all the way down the stairs to be right up in front of the stage. That's how impressed they were. Gene and I kind of looked at one another and said, "Wow, this guy is really good!" We got back to our loft that night and we played and we said, "Wait a minute, what if there was four Alice Coopers?" Nobody else wore makeup but him. We did some soul searching and became the characters we are today. We looked at our personalities and drew from it. Gene was always into monsters. Paul was the true rock star and Ace was definitely from another planet. And I was the total cat.

ACE FREHLEY: I designed Paul's makeup. Paul's original makeup was a circle around his eye like the fuckin' dog, Pete the Pup, in *Our Gang* [laughs]. I said, "Why don't you do a star instead of that? That looks retarded."

BOB GRUEN (PHOTOGRAPHER): KISS told me that they were very much influenced by the Dolls. In fact one night after KISS was rehearsing they went to see the Dolls at the Diplomat Hotel. The Dolls were a great-looking band. KISS decided that they couldn't compete with the Dolls in the sense of being better looking. So they did something completely opposite, which was to be monsters instead of trying to be attractive. The Dolls were very rhythm-and-blues-oriented where KISS was much more of a metal, hard rock sound.

PAUL STANLEY: You couldn't be from New York and not be aware of the New York Dolls. If you were in a rock band, just because of where you were from, there had to be some attention given to the Dolls. I remember going to see them at the Hotel Diplomat. Once you saw them you realized that you couldn't beat them at their own game so you had to find another way to look.

BILL AUCOIN (KISS MANAGER): When they went from Wicked Lester, they were in drag. Then because of the success of the New York Dolls they changed their image because they didn't want to be a copy. They wanted to be different so they started playing off what they loved in their own life. Ace loved space, Gene loved horror movies. Paul always wanted to be a rock 'n' roll star and Peter loved cats. That's basically how it began. We just embellished as much as we could. You see, my idea of management is you don't try and get an act to do what you want. What you do is you get to know an act. You see what's inside of them and you take out something special and embellish it and give it back to the act. So the act never feels it is being told everything that's not theirs. It should be theirs or everything will fall apart.

FIRST KISS PROMO PHOTO, 1973
(© KISS Catalog Ltd.)

KEVIN BACON:

My son became a huge fan about two years ago. We went to Jones Beach and saw them. One of my favorite things about KISS is their attitude, just not taking it too seriously. You hear Gene and Paul talk and the way they discuss it is great. "We set out to have as much fun as we possibly can and we're still having fun." It's great, I love that.

SEAN DELANEY (CREATIVE CONSULTANT/CHOREOGRAPHER): When all the makeup got on their faces, the only one that looked closest to human was Paul Stanley. He had the star on his face, but everything else was the Demon . . . Do demons talk to you? No, they growl but they don't talk. Ace would have opened his mouth and went, "Ha! How you doing?" Peter was way back at the drums, cats don't talk to you. Paul had to learn exact lines. I used to work with him on "How 'ya doin'?" What would happen is that Paul would get excited and do things like this [gestures] . . . this is what you call a "He She." One of the first reviews was "Paul Stanley bi-modulates, bi-sexually across the stage" . . . Paul died! They just called him a queer in public! Oh no! Paul had the ability to be very masculine onstage and, at the same time, very feminine. Paul would go to stick his leg out and everybody would grab it. Not just the girls, but the guys too! He got to the point where he became sort of scared of the audience. The four guys had a way to aggravate each other. "He She" is all you had to call Paul to get him pissed. Gene was "Mr. Marvello" because he knew everything about everything. So when he'd start telling the band what it was they'd all go, "Shhh! Marvello speaks!"

GENE SIMMONS: Even in the early club days, I was doing the tongue thing. It just somehow stuck out . . .

JOYCE BOGART (KISS CO-MANAGER): Neil [Bogart] and I and Bill were very involved in putting together what today PR people would call their "branding." We worked with them to develop their makeup, which was not the same as it is now. We worked on their costumes as well; hiring a designer, going over sketches. Neil and I even went to a shop near my house in the West Village called the Pleasure Chest and bought the spiked dog collars that KISS wore. We looked for ways to develop their act . . . we went to magic stores—the one on Broadway that all the pros went to—and bought them the drum riser, flash paper, and flash pots. We brought back the disco ball. Bill and Neil and I hired a magician named Presto who came to my freshly painted white office to teach one of the band members to spit fire. Gene was the only one brave enough to volunteer. The first time Gene breathed fire he blew so hard that he scorched all my white walls black and I had to call the painter back in.

JOYCE BOGART: KISS had worked out their initial concept, their logo, their sound, and even some of their merchandising with the KISS T-shirts. The ultimate KISS T-shirt was the first one we made with the rhinestones. They knew where they wanted to go from the beginning with us. They wanted to take it as big as it could go but we really enhanced all the details. We grounded the concept, gave some backstory to their concept. Because of our film backgrounds we had them write their stories. Who were each of these characters? What was the Cat? Where was he from? Why was Peter the Cat and Ace the Spaceman? (The latter was easy.) We incorporated this into their PR kits and their interview stories in magazines. It gave them a mysterious aura—a larger-than-life essence—and a kind of comic-book quality. We gave them the resources and added our ideas to theirs to make the possibilities larger than life, never been done before and more professional. We worked together as a team on every aspect of their careers. One idea would lead to another and Neil was game enough to pay for it and make it happen. And we had a great time doing it. We loved working with each other. It was an amazing time and when KISS finally made it big . . . when the twenty thousand screaming fans at Cobo Hall in Detroit held those lighters high, we enjoyed that success together—Bill, Neil, and I.

 ## TED NUGENT:

As a rock 'n' roll force to reckon with, you've got to absolutely cheer KISS. If that's not rock 'n' roll, the Rolling Stones aren't rock 'n' roll. And quite honestly in its own way, the people that think Bruce Springsteen is some purist, he goes through as much manipulation in imagery control as KISS does with makeup. I mean, gimme a break! Somebody recommended to Bruce Springsteen that he has a baseball cap hanging out of his back pocket of just perfectly abused dungarees in front of an American flag singing "Born in the U.S.A." Give me a fuckin' break, that's as manipulative as the fuckin' cat makeup on Peter Criss. Don't get me wrong, I think Bruce is fun but I think KISS is more fun because they're over-the-top. And over-the-top is where I like to spend most of my time.

EARLY KISS SHOWS

GENE SIMMONS: I originally made a deal with a club in Queens called Popcorn, later changed to Coventry. It was owned by the boys [imitates tough guy accent] "who kind of talked like this." We played a Wednesday, Thursday, Friday and were paid $30. The club held maybe three to four hundred people. That first night we changed the name of the band from Wicked Lester to KISS.

STEPHANIE TUDOR (AUCOIN MANAGEMENT ASSISTANT DIRECTOR OF PRODUCTION): Coventry was like a low-class Max's Kansas City but it was a great place to find new bands. The New York Dolls played there once a month, bands like Teenage Lust, Luger, and Street Punk. A lot of great bands that made it later on played there, like Aerosmith.

LEW LINET: Coventry was a toilet. Those gigs were awful. Nobody liked them, nobody clapped. The makeup was in its infancy stage, they were wearing a kind of effeminate

makeup at that point. In that period I had to make a decision, I just didn't care for that genre of music. I told them, "With all due respect, I think you need a manager who is committed to what you do." They would tell me, "Lew, mark our words, we are going to be the biggest band in America." I said that I hoped it was true but I didn't think they'd become that big because what they did was derivative of bands like The Who. But they did it. Gene and Stanley are the epitome of American entrepreneurial spirit, they are the epitome of drive, commitment, and persistence.

PETER CRISS: I think three people showed up for our first gig at Coventry, Gene's girlfriend and a couple of our friends. My mom made up the T-shirts. But we still put on the makeup, went onstage, and played. We kicked ass for nobody, and that's what I respected about them guys from day one. We always stuck to what we practiced and what we worked on no matter what was out there. We still gave it our all. When we got to The Daisy [a club in Amityville, Long Island] my conception was that it's a bar but that we should look at it as the [Madison Square] Garden. And I remember when we finally got to play the Garden, Gene says, "You little son of a bitch, now we're really playing there!"

LEW LINET: KISS was a tremendously loud raunchy band and I couldn't get them any gigs in the city so I had to go to other places like Long Island. I managed a band called J.F. Murphy and Salt, who played a place in Amityville called The Daisy. It was run by a nice guy named Sid Benjamin. So I went to Sid and he booked them at The Daisy. The club was a casual teenage, early twenties joint. It was in a nice area, it was clean. It was just a bar with a little bandstand at one end of the place. I wasn't into KISS's hard rock music, but I think Sid liked them.

PAUL STANLEY: The guy at The Daisy gave us a gig as a favor to our old manager. We wore makeup then, but it was not as sophisticated as it is now. The rest of the band pretty much looked the same, but I didn't. I wore just eye makeup and rouge. It was the same idea but different makeup. Our outfits were predominately black. I was wearing real high heels, skintight Lurex pants, black knee socks, and a black T-shirt that said "KISS." The costume cost about $45 for the shoes, $3 for the T-shirt, and about $5 worth of Lurex. I made the pants myself because I couldn't afford to buy them. Instead I went out and bought the material and then my father said, "Well, nice try but I'll buy you the pants . . . I admire you for wanting to make the pants but you can't, you've never done it before." I said, "Oh yeah?" So I took my best pair of jeans apart, cut the Lurex like the jeans, asked my mother to show me how the sewing machine worked, and made myself a pair of pants. I wore them at The Daisy and they were so tight they ultimately tore on stage, right up the crotch from stem to stem. I was the hit of the evening. I made Gene a pair of pants too and he still has them. The Daisy was a really cheap place, drinks were 35 cents. Most bands that played there did four sets a night and we came in like big stars and told them we'd play twice a night for a weekend's worth of work. They gave us $100 for two nights. After expenses I think the four of us walked away with $3.50 per man. We played The Daisy about five times, five weekend gigs. That was the plan, to play The Daisy until we were ready.

RON JOHNSEN: I was living in a neighborhood in Rockland County that sponsored a charity for a local library. It was in the Palisades, New York, right across the river from Dobbs Ferry where my wife and I were living. The entertainment chairman asked me if I could get them some entertainment for the party. I was working with a bunch of groups and one of them was KISS. On party night [May 26, 1973] I had three bands. And KISS was one of those. They hung out in my house and we helped them put on their makeup. They went onstage and they were just outrageous. There were a bunch of older, middle-aged people there and it was shock to their system to hear KISS.

GENE SIMMONS: I knew that KISS would become successful but when it did, I couldn't believe it. I certainly had confidence in us otherwise I wouldn't have been able to put makeup and high heels after it stopped being fashionable. KISS is its own fashion.

PAUL STANLEY: I was not satisfied with myself and my friends until KISS came along and turned my life around. This was the first band I'd ever been in where people lived in different sections of New York. That was interesting for me, because my world, which had been very limited, was beginning to spread out a little.

EDDIE KRAMER (PRODUCER): I saw them on Friday, July 13, of '73 at the Hotel Diplomat. Rich Totoian of Windfall Records [Mountain's record label], Bill Aucoin, and I were invited to that show. It was very off-the-wall stuff. For some people it was revolting, but to me it was very interesting because nobody was doing the full makeup trip. They had a lot to learn. They weren't great musicians. However, they did have a great stage act and they were very organized.

BILL AUCOIN: When I first saw KISS at the Hotel Diplomat in 1973 they didn't have much of a show. They had the red beacons, a couple of amps. They were wearing black jeans. No one could afford leather. The show was just a regular rock 'n' roll show except they had spontaneity. They wanted to do something different and they wanted it very badly. That kind of devotion is worth more than anything. It's so special and you start picking up on it. I saw that magic in them.

BOB GRUEN: Working for KISS as a photographer was somewhat difficult. I did a lot of work for Buddah Records so I knew Neil [Bogart]. I'd done a number of jobs for Labelle and Sha Na Na. When KISS came to the Casablanca label, I was already the Buddah photographer and that's how I started working with KISS. I took pictures of KISS and Neil, who was also wearing makeup. He was handcuffed to their record contract. It was done during sound check at their New Year's Eve show at the

HOTEL DIPLOMAT POSTER, AUGUST 10, 1973
(© KISS Catalog Ltd.)

Academy of Music. That's the first time I saw them play, they were opening for Iggy & the Stooges. Gene went to throw a fireball and his hair caught on fire. At the same time I remember that Peter Criss had these drumsticks that he would throw up in the air and they would explode. But one of them exploded in his hand.

KISS LOGO

ACE FREHLEY: I've always been a graphic artist. When I was sixteen years old, my guidance counselor said, "You have no business being in this school. You belong in an art school developing your talents." My specialty is logos. I designed the KISS logo in about three minutes. I do my best stuff quickly.

BILL AUCOIN: When we played at the Academy of Music, that was the first time we had the KISS logo in the background. They let us get away with it because they didn't know what this damn opening act was gonna do. Everyone who walked into the theater saw the KISS logo already set up. So the hour before the show all you saw was the KISS logo. From there we learned a lot of lessons that we got away with all the way through their career.

OZZY OSBOURNE:

It wasn't all that many years ago, that you couldn't walk around anywhere without getting KISSed off. Everybody was KISS crazy in 1976. They were mega. They were one of the most original bands to have major pyro shows. They had everything from KISS makeup, KISS dolls, KISS games, KISS everything.

FIRST KISS DEMO

RON JOHNSEN (PRODUCER): I called Eddie Kramer and told him that I had this wild, almost heavy metal type of act. I told him I had lost this deal with CBS and I needed to find them a new record deal and that he was the strongest hard rock engineer/producer that I knew that could do this. Eddie came with me and my then wife, Joyce, to see them play. They all ended up having to put cotton in their ears because it was so intensely loud. At one point, I turned around and my wife collapsed, she had fainted. Eddie and I had to drag her downstairs to get her some air. Eddie said that he'd be willing to go into the studio and cut some demos for me.

PAUL STANLEY: The demo is great. The studio owed us some money and we said, "Give us some time in the studio and get Eddie Kramer to produce our demo."

GENE SIMMONS: We did the tracks in one day and the vocals the next. In a day it was mixed. Paul and I had done some background vocal session work for Ron Johnsen on an artist named Lyn Christopher, another called Mr. Gee Whiz, and one or two other artists. So the studio owed us about a thousand dollars each. They said, "You can either have it in cash or you can come in and use it in studio time." And we wisely said, "We'll use it in studio time but only if we can get Eddie Kramer to produce it." The Eddie Kramer demos of those songs are better than what turned up on the first KISS album. With all due respect, our producer, Richie Wise, who I thought was terrific, tried to calm it down a little bit. They'd come from producing Stories, Gladys Knight & the Pips. Some of the tempos were brought a down little bit. We were told the energy was a little too high for a record. Maybe that's why the demos have more energy. We just sort of went, "This is who we are."

ACE FREHLEY: I was very nervous recording our first album. The original demo is much more relaxed than the actual album. I had just joined the group and we'd been rehearsing on a regular basis. We went in to cut five songs. Ron Johnsen was producing and then Eddie Kramer took over the board and we started rockin'. In those days, working with Eddie Kramer was a big deal to us 'cause we were just kids and he had worked with Jimi Hendrix and Led Zeppelin.

EDDIE KRAMER: Paul and Gene were hanging around the studio. I always saw them there because they were working with Ron Johnsen doing the Wicked Lester thing. And then one day Ron called me and said, "Look, Gene and Paul want to form a new band, it's gonna be a rock 'n' roll band. I'm not really into it but could you do it for me because it's more your speed?" And I said, "Sure, I'll have a go." The studio [Electric Lady] was pretty new at the time and I said to Dave Wittman, who was my assistant at that point, "We're gonna do a demo for a new band Gene and Paul have got called KISS." We recorded it in Studio B. It's a very small studio. I said, "We'll do it the original way that we used to record four-track." So we lined up the old four-track machine. I remember Ace was very skinny. God, he was so skinny in those days. He was driving a cab in the Bronx and he was all excited, like a kid in a candy store making his first demo. Everybody played at once and it was great. To this day Gene and Paul and Ace think it's one of the best things they've ever done. It's got "Deuce," "Cold Gin," "Strutter," "Watchin' You," and "Black Diamond." Five songs. I didn't hear the material until we walked into the studio and did it. I saw them perform live at one of their very first shows at the Hotel Diplomat when they first started wearing makeup. In the studio I remember Gene showing me this spiral notebook which had all these drawings of various members of the band and what they would look like with the makeup on. He had it all planned out. I thought Gene and Paul were well organized. In those days they weren't great musicians. They had a lot to learn. However, they did have a very unique stage act. Nobody else was doing it. It was very off-the-wall stuff, wearing makeup and high boots and calling the band KISS. For some people it was revolting, but to me it was very interesting because nobody had done that before. Obviously it captured the imagination of the kids.

KISS LANDS MANAGEMENT

JOYCE BOGART (KISS CO-MANAGER): In 1972, I met Bill Aucoin when he was directing the feature film based on the play *Oh, Calcutta!* It was a play done in the nude by an ensemble of actors. I signed on as Bill's assistant. It was the first videotape feature film ever done and the crew were all Korean War veterans who learned electronics in the army. This was as far from the glamour of the film business as could be. There was a lot of diplomacy to be done between them and the all-nude cast, shooting on location in upstate New York, who loved to tease the conservative crew. Bill and I formed a TV and film production company, Direction Plus, and eventually we formed our management company, Rock Steady. It was named after the Aretha Franklin song of the same name. Bill asked me to come up with a name that the banks would appreciate if we wanted to get a loan. Direction Plus produced a syndicated half-hour show called *Flipside*, which aired thirteen episodes. With a record company president or famous producer as the host of each show, rock groups assumed that we had the ear of these presidents. We started to receive tapes and be hounded by rock bands. KISS was the loudest and eventually Bill and then both of us went to see them. Bill and I came from theater, film, TV, and advertising—the best possible synthesis of background talents to support a group like KISS. We both loved music and had done a lot with it in our productions. We shot the first promotional films for record companies. Neil [Bogart] was one of the first. We were the first to tape MTV-like video promos with the groups in costumes. This was way before MTV—1973—only *In Concert* and *Flipside* were on TV. You couldn't get your act on anywhere else so we proposed that the companies make commercial TV spots to go with those shows and use the longer footage in Europe where there were shows you could place these three- to ten-minute segments. We learned a lot about how the record industry promoted its acts from selling these pieces. I also wrote them so I spent time with the marketing people and the artists. I was a producer at a major advertising agency and would hire Bill at Teletape to direct commercials for our clients. I had worked in advertising for years assisting creative directors and producers so I was very marketing-oriented. The visual was big for both of us, which really enabled us to assist KISS to create the ultimate act and to promote it with cutting-edge techniques. When we booked *Flipside* we had contact with the top people of each record company. It was great promotion for them. They could bring on and get exposure for any beginning act they were pushing . . . if they brought on a big-name talent to headline, so to speak.

KISS SIGNS WITH CASABLANCA RECORDS

JOYCE BOGART: Bill and I decided to give KISS's tape to Neil Bogart when he was still the president of Buddah Records. He was knocked out and loved the music. I think we told him about their act but he really thought they were a group he wanted to sign based on the music alone. As he was planning on leaving and forming his own label, he asked if we would bring them to him when he started Casablanca. True to his word, he came to see the group as soon as he put his deal together. The room was small, the music of course was beyond loud, and Neil was in the first row. Gene came down into the audience and took Neil's hands and made him clap along. After the show, the group, Bill, Neil, and I met in a tiny room, maybe a supply closet. We stood in a small circle, the group in full costume and makeup as Neil told KISS he wanted them to be his first signing for Casablanca. When he finished his speech outlining their future and telling them how excited he was, that he thought they were stars, Peter Criss fell down. He just fell off his high heels and landed with great force on his rear. We all roared, including Peter. You might say it sealed the deal.

NODDY HOLDER, SLADE:

To me, they were the perfect American band because they took what was best about British music and Americanized it. And they certainly took the image of the glam rock thing that was happening in England. I knew KISS were very influenced by Slade. It was a great compliment for a band like KISS to mention us as an influence. They took everything that was good about Slade and took it to the farthest extreme. Like Slade, KISS did anthem songs but in an American way.

KENNY KERNER (KISS PRODUCER): I used to walk to Neil's [Bogart] office every week or two and I'd pick up a box of all of the tapes that came in the mail and I'd take them home. In one of the boxes of tapes that I brought home one blisteringly cold winter afternoon was a demo reel-to-reel tape from KISS with a black and white photo. I looked at the photo and by no means was it the makeup or the definition that they have now. It looked like some kind of Kabuki act in makeup. I got the idea instantly of what they were trying to do. So I put the tape on and it was great. It was real raw. It had "Deuce" and "Strutter" on it and some other real good songs. This was on a Friday. I didn't even listen to the rest of the stuff. On Monday morning I took the tape and picture back to Neil at Buddah. I said, "Neil, this is a great tape, I think we should sign these guys." And he said, "I can't sign them to Buddah but I'm starting a brand-new label called Casablanca." And he said, "Let me listen to the tape." The next day he said, "You're right. We're going to sign them as the first act to Casablanca." Neil was always into hype. If you could hype it, it was perfect for Neil. So he immediately saw that. I said, "Who's managing the band?" And he said they're working with a guy who runs a production company called Direction Plus. His name is Bill Aucoin. He directed some off-Broadway plays and runs a production company and his partner is Joyce Biawitz [the future Joyce Bogart]. So we came down on one night, Bill, myself, Joyce, Richie [Wise], Neil, the Kama Sutra/Casablanca promotion staff (because he took the same people with him when he left the label), and we went into this little rehearsal studio called Le Tang's Studios. The room was as big as a shoe box, literally from the back of the stage to the front door when you came in couldn't have been more than thirty feet. So it was real small. The group came in and the first thing that I remember is that they were huge, they looked twelve feet tall. They had platform shoes that had to be a foot high and the stage was about a foot off the ground. So they looked like skyscrapers. They all wore black outfits, their faces were painted. Gene had his tongue going. It was raw but I was scared shitless. The band was ecstatic to be signed because it was with a new label. Whenever you're with a new label you know you're going to get a push. They trusted us because we were real hot producers at the time. They were ecstatic all the way around.

SEAN DELANEY: It was so unlike anything that it had to be incredible. It was new, it was something that wasn't being done . . . So try to imagine, in a small rehearsal studio, four guys are up there playing. In front of them are Bill Aucoin, Neil Bogart, Joyce Biawitz [co-manager of KISS], and myself. They finished the first song and no applause. Gene walks down to Neil Bogart, grabs both of his hands, and makes him applaud . . . and Neil started applauding because he was scared to death. And I said to myself at that moment, "I wanna be involved in this" because that's the kind of balls you have to have to do anything.

PAUL STANLEY: When we signed with Casablanca, it felt really good and new. There was the feeling back then that they needed us because KISS *was* Casablanca. I think a lot of creativity comes from when you want something very badly. Neil wanted his record company to be great and he needed to devote everything to whomever he signed to the label. That fit in with all of our plans.

LARRY HARRIS (CASABLANCA RECORDS SENIOR VICE PRESIDENT): Casablanca was a true '70s record label. It was all of the things people associate with the music business in the '70s, the drugs, the sex. There was sex going on in the office during business hours. There was drug taking going in the office too. You could smell marijuana in the halls. There were heavier drugs too, cocaine and our drug of choice, Quaaludes.

STAN CORNYN (WARNER BROTHERS EXECUTIVE VICE PRESIDENT): Neil Bogart was fairly well known as a wonderful hustler. "Hustler" is a complimentary word. Warner Brothers was very interested in getting into the company someone who had done bubblegum and all kinds of stuff that we didn't do. Between Mo Ostin and Joe Smith at Warner Brothers, we made a distributed label deal with Casablanca. That entailed money for Casablanca in exchange for the distribution rights, manufacturing, and marketing. We didn't have anything to do with the talent. Neil would deliver the masters and packages to us and we would take it into the commercial world. As typical of these deals we would split the profits 50-50.

BUCK DHARMA, BLUE ÖYSTER CULT:

KISS opened for us at the Academy of Music, that legendary show where Gene's hair caught fire. KISS actually toured with us for a few months. It's funny, we weren't that big ourselves. Blue Öyster Cult was headlining small places. The funny thing is KISS would open the show and they would show up with a semi and a crew of about ten guys. And we had a little box truck and three roadies [laughs]. So we were kind of scratching our heads. And also they're big guys and we're short guys. They were wearing these platform boots and they looked like Godzilla. We were pretty much awed by the whole KISS experience. They were certainly well funded right from the beginning, even when they weren't making money. They had elaborate pyro shows and gags. I think there was some jealousy on our part over the years. Oddly enough, KISS and Blue Öyster Cult have always respected each other to this day. It was less of any real enmity, it was more like kidding around. I admire what Gene and Paul have done. I don't think I could do it. I just don't have that kind of personality. We had some great parties together when we were touring with KISS. One of the few trashings that I've done was a hotel room in Tampa, Florida, where KISS and Blue Öyster Cult threw all of the furniture into the pool about five stories down [laughs].

KISS LIVE IN 1974
(© KISS Catalog Ltd.)

ACADEMY OF MUSIC NEW YEAR'S EVE 1973–1974

PETER CRISS: The first time I really felt like a star was at that show. Gene and Paul gave me that feeling. I was going, "I don't know if we're gonna make it. We ain't going nowhere" and all that bullshit. And they sent a limo for me and I go "Wow, this is cool! [laughs] This is what the big guys must feel like."

MANAGER, BILL AUCOIN

PETER CRISS: Bill was the Brian Epstein of KISS. He was brilliant. I knew this guy was going to be like our "fifth" member of KISS. Bill was a visionary. He had the belief that we could do it and that nothing could stop us. He took our self-esteem as high as it could go. He took time out for each individual to tell their deepest sorrows and heartaches and love. Each one of us would go to his room and tell him how bad or good we were feeling. He was a father, an uncle, a mother, a brother, and a sister. I love him.

PAUL STANLEY: At his best Bill was the greatest manager we could have hoped for. He shared our vision and was a calming force and also a teacher. He was unique in that his background was not management but his connection to us was so complete and multileveled.

PAUL WESTERBERG, THE REPLACEMENTS:

They were the band that I was ashamed to like but I would go in my room and play 'em and love 'em. *Destroyer* had some great stuff on it.

GENE SIMMONS: Bill was terrific. He was a showman, a guy who believed in doing it all. I was the one who sent him the promo package with the bio and invitation to the Hotel Diplomat show. I wanted somebody who wasn't just going to manage the band but somebody who had a point of view who understood visuals and television and promotion. He came to the Hotel Diplomat and he was the one who pitched to manage us. Eddie Kramer came down, Ron Johnsen, CBS Records, Rich Totoian from Windfall Records, who had Mountain. When we came off the stage after our Diplomat performance, he cornered me and brought me over to the side. I still had my makeup on. As soon as I saw him sit me down I motioned for a girl that I had just seen with a capital S the night before. She was dressed very sexy and she came and sat on my lap. While he was talking to me I was bouncing her up on my leg for effect so that he thought, "My God, something's going on!" He was very enticed by the whole notion, it happened very fast. Bill was very, very important to the band. He introduced us to his live-in relationship with Sean Delaney, who we didn't know about it that way and didn't really care. It never mattered. Sean Delaney played a very important part in the beginning of the band as well. He was a road manager, he would suggest moves. He co-wrote songs with the band. He was more of an idea guy.

NEIL BOGART

JOYCE BOGART: Neil was a man who lived to invent the next trend. He was fiercely loyal to the artists he chose, making them family, as he did his staff, many of whom traveled with him from Cameo/Parkway to Buddah to Casablanca and then Boardwalk afterward. He was responsible for the genre called bubblegum music and even invented the term. The story goes that he was watching a kid chewing gum at the bus stop and wanted to create that happy-go-lucky type of attitude in music. He was the first to create a twelve-inch—ever—with Donna Summer's "Love to Love You Baby" and the first to do disco promotion, to have a promo department to sell records through club play as an alternative to radio. Most of the great disco music came from Casablanca. He was a master promoter and the king of the art of independent promotion and distribution. So many of his acts are still around today as is the music his companies recorded. Neil got the KISS concept right away. It was a match made in heaven . . . a natural . . . as KISS was a high concept act and he was a promoter. I don't think any other music executive then or today would have had seen all the possibilities for promotion and merchandising so clearly. Neil loved fun and he loved nothing more than creating something that was fun for other people to enjoy. He saw this possibility in KISS immediately. He had been a singer, a musician, an actor, and a producer. KISS provided him with a matrix to play; to use the synthesis of all his talent and experience. And the fact that everyone else thought he was crazy for signing them only made it more of a delicious challenge. When the world told Neil it would never work, he knew he was on the right track. He was looking to create something new, not to follow trends. He was willing to stick his neck out and put his money and all his contacts and influence behind making the band a success. He was responsible for getting the band booked on tours, which was no small feat. No one wanted to tour with them. All the agents told us to leave the equipment home as it was too expensive to tour. They didn't get it. He insisted with his friends at [the talent agency] ATI that they book the band. Jeff Franklin was very important here and was Neil's very good friend. He would loan us money we needed to stay on the road. We couldn't have had that if it wasn't for Neil. He used his long-term friendships to get KISS television exposure on every show that featured music from Dick Clark's specials to *The Mike Douglas Show.*

GENE SIMMONS: Neil was the last of his kind. He was a showman. He's the bubblegum king, he created that sound. He created disco in America. He created a long-playing record, the EP. Here's a guy who was all about singles and yet the first band he signs to Casablanca Records doesn't have any singles. He was all about very stylized, kind of beat music and we had nothing to do with it. He was very much a guy who wanted to be in charge, "do it my way or the highway." And yet he met a group of guys who basically said the same thing. He wanted to sign us and didn't believe in the makeup. We said, "All or nothing. You get the makeup and the band or you get nothing." What he was best at was believing in something if *you* believed in it. He was able to put his own beliefs aside if he saw passion. And when he did it he did it with all his heart. He was the very first person who ever sat me down at his house and said, "Gene, don't think of yourself as a guy in a band. You should have your own record company, you should manage other artists, you should do other things." It opened my eyes.

PAUL STANLEY: When I think of Neil, I think of P. T. Barnum because Neil was the circus barker. You know, "Hurry, hurry see the bearded lady." He was Colonel Tom Parker selling dancing chickens. He put a hot plate under a piece of tile and had chickens dancing on top of it because their feet were getting hot. He was very much into salesmanship. When he believed in something he sold it. However the downside of that was I don't think Neil was very concerned with the long-term success. He would do anything to have a hit with something regardless of what impact it might have on a career. Neil wasn't used to long-term because I think Neil was used to careers not lasting. So the name of the game was have a hit.

ACE FREHLEY: Neil was a visionary. Neil had the guts to push us when a lot of people didn't believe in us. I respect him very much for that. I thought he was a genius and an innovator in the music business. He was not afraid to take chances. He rolled the dice with us. A lot of other companies didn't want to touch us. We made him a multi-millionaire but unfortunately God decided to take him at an early age. But I had the utmost respect for him. God rest his soul.

PETER CRISS: Neil was to me the last Barnum & Bailey of rock 'n' roll. He would put up a million to make a hundred, but if it made the audience wild that was his statement. There's no one around anymore like that.

BILL AUCOIN: The greatest thing about Neil was you could have a handshake with Neil and that was as good as anything. You never had to go to paper. When he made a commitment to you, you didn't have to have lawyers all around, he would stick by his word.

LARRY HARRIS (CASABLANCA RECORDS SENIOR VICE PRESIDENT): Neil was a very big gambler. Neil gambled on everything in life. He gambled on a cockroach running across the table before another cockroach. It was in his makeup that he was going to roll the dice. Neil is probably one of the only guys in music who could do everything. Neil could do production, Neil could do publishing, Neil could put together an international deal. The lawyers would come in and Neil would tell the right things to put in the contracts. Neil could go in a studio and cut a record, he did it with KISS. Plus he knew promotion. He was the ultimate when it came to being a promotion guy. Nothing was too low on the totem pole for Neil to do. He was like Ray Kroc at McDonald's who would sweep the floor at a McDonald's and then oversee a board meeting.

JOYCE BOGART: Neil was involved in every aspect of their career. He worked with myself, Bill, and the group to choose the artwork for their covers, the photographs, to design the radio promotional campaign, to create a PR campaign with both an outside and internal PR dept. And everything was the best he could afford to provide. They worked with all the best—from photographers to producers. And when we were all out of money, he advanced us the money to continue when any other label would say that we had already used up our advance.

LARRY HARRIS: Neil believed in KISS like I believed in the band, especially when we saw what they could do to an audience. Not so much how good their music was on record, it was always the live performance. What we learned even before we had KISS is that if you have a band with a live performance that's incredible, no matter how good or bad they are on vinyl you can sell some product. We did it with Sha Na Na at Buddah Records. They were a wonderful band live and we were still able to sell a decent amount of product on a group that was doing twenty-year-old cover songs.

STAN CORNYN (WARNER BROTHERS EXECUTIVE VICE PRESIDENT): Neil was an unrelenting, won't-take-no-for-an-answer type of guy. We were used to a certain kind of behavior where people would ask for things and we would explain to them why we couldn't do it, and that would be the dialogue. Neil didn't know how to say, "Oh, too bad." He knew how to say, "Dammit, we must do it!" He was very good at that. He would not even take maybe for an answer. From our standpoint at the label, this got to be really expensive. If the record went Top 10, Neil would say, "Time for a new campaign!" [laughs] He wanted it to be number one. There never was a diminution of his demands upon us. We expected some of that, but when we determined a record wasn't making it, we would say, "Next." The first two KISS albums were not major successes but they got major promotion and a certain attention for the visuals of the act. But they didn't really click on radio and therefore didn't sell very well.

SEAN DELANEY

PAUL STANLEY: Sean was a creative dynamo who was an important part of the early team. He was responsible single-handedly for taking a move that we did and by repeating it in the show, it became the signature classic KISS side-to-side movement. That was something we did on our own but he said, "You should make more of it and do it as a choreographed part," which we never would have thought of. Sean was a great sounding board, and in different ways than Bill, just on a creative level, another point of view.

BILL AUCOIN: Sean was the resident genius. He is the most creative person I ever met in my life. When I started with KISS, I asked him to get involved. Sean had a great theatrical sense. He could always tell when something wasn't right.

ACE FREHLEY: Sean Delaney did so much for the band. When you listen to Paul and Gene talk these days they try to come off as they were the fuckin' brains behind KISS, whereas in the early days Sean Delaney had more input on the choreography than Paul and Gene. Sean played a major part in getting our show together. I don't think he ever got the credit that was due him as a songwriter or what he added to the shows, the costumes, the choreography. He was a major, major contributor to all that shit.

PETER CRISS: Sean was very influential. He was a very very bright man. He was Bill's partner so to say and he was incredibly the whip thrower on the band. He would stay on our ass morning, noon, and night at rehearsals until we really got it right. He had four videos running on us all of the time getting our moves together, getting our choreography together. It was his idea how we were to do "Beth" live. He wanted me to come up and sit on a stool in front of everybody all alone with a microphone. And that was his idea. I said, "Aw fuck, I can't do this, I'm protected behind my drums." Sean said, "Trust me, it'll be huge!" And he was right. Then when I went out and did it and got the response then you couldn't get me out of it. Then I was hooked.

JIM LEA, SLADE:

Gene said that Slade were the first band that showed an audience how to riot. KISS grasped what was going on so they said, "Okay, we'll have their idea and we'll just Americanize it." And that's what they did. Where we might have had a confetti machine, they just made everything James Bond.

BLOOD-SPITTING

GENE SIMMONS: I remember seeing Christopher Lee as Dracula in one of the Hammer films, *Blood of Dracula* or *Horror of Dracula*. I'll never forget when he bit into something and his mouth was covered with blood. I thought, that's cool, I should do that onstage. Why? Why do little boys stick frogs up girls' skirts? Because they squeal and that's fun.

KISS AND *CREEM*

JAAN UHELSZKI (*CREEM* JOURNALIST): I actually inherited the KISS beat at *Creem*, because no one else really wanted it. For me, nothing is more compelling than an idea whose time has come. KISS's had. They first came into my life when their promotion man at Casablanca Records called and asked if we would do a *Creem* profile—the fake ad we used to have in the magazine based on the Dewar's Scotch ad. So, without any hesitation, Larry Harris brought them to our office, a rather casual suite of offices in suburban Detroit above a movie theater. They walked in without their trademark makeup, looking like four rather normal rock types. Very politely they asked if they could take over the women's bathroom to suit up. The transformation was incredible. When they had their makeup on they became towering giants and they took up more

psychic space than they did without the makeup on. It was pure bedlam, with the staff secretaries fighting to sit on Gene Simmons's lap and the dentists across the hall from us popping in to see what all the commotion was. And there was a lot of commotion, it was strange what havoc a few jars of clown makeup, red lipstick, and eyeliner could wreak. Charlie Auringer, *Creem's* art director, took the shot with them in full regalia and that was it. Or so we thought. They retired to the bathroom again, removed the makeup, and were about to pop back into their waiting cars, but Charlie convinced them to pose for one picture without their makeup. I think it was so early in the game that they just agreed. Just one of those split-second things. That was the beginning of our relationship with the band. After that anything we asked their management for, they always complied. We gave them a lot of coverage when everybody else was treating them like a joke. To me it was a campy, bizarre, death-of-art, Warholian kind of thing. Why would you ruin their superhero kind of appeal by printing that photo of them without makeup? It never really entered our minds to do that. Okay, maybe it entered our minds, but . . .

PAUL STANLEY: We got duped into doing that photo for *Creem* without makeup. We were doing a photo shoot at their offices and they said, "We just spoke to your management and they said we could take pictures of the band without your makeup." And being green, we said, "Really?" And they said, "Yes, really." And we said, "Okay." It's a cool picture in terms of marking a certain period where most people never got a chance to see what we looked like.

LARRY HARRIS (CASABLANCA RECORDS SENIOR VICE PRESIDENT): *Rolling Stone* magazine wouldn't do anything about KISS. Neil [Bogart] and the magazine's publisher, Jann Wenner, always disliked each other. The two music magazines that I felt would work with KISS were *Creem* and *Circus.* I met Barry Kramer, the publisher and owner of *Creem,* and worked out a deal with them where we would purchase on a long-term basis the inside front cover for advertising KISS. We also supplied *Creem* with thousands of free KISS albums to give away to people who subscribed to the magazine. So *Creem* was more amenable to covering the band on a regular basis. In every *Circus* magazine there was a readers' poll. The label purchased about three or four hundred copies of the magazine and stuffed the ballot box. Me, and my secretaries at Casablanca filled out the polls with votes for the members of KISS. I made a similar deal with *Circus's* publisher Gerald Rothberg, where I purchased the back cover of the magazine for a long period of time. This gave *Circus* an incentive to cover KISS as much as possible.

CADILLAC HIGH SCHOOL KISS DAY

CAROL ROSS (KISS PUBLICIST): There was a football coach from Cadillac High who wrote a letter to Bill [Aucoin] saying he was having problems with his football team. They were losing games and he was going to have them practice to KISS music. He told

 BOY HOWDY! MADNESS—KISS GET *CREEMED*, 1974
(Photo by Charlie Auringer)

 KISS SANS MAKEUP, *CREEM* PHOTO SHOOT, 1974
(Photo by Charlie Auringer)

Bill once he had them practice to KISS music they started winning football games. Bill showed me the letter and I thought, "What if we bring KISS to Cadillac, Michigan, to do a surprise concert for the school and the football team?" We called the coach and he freaked out. He spoke to the mayor, the school officials and they were all excited. They were going to have a parade. They were naming the main street "KISS Boulevard." The football team all wore KISS makeup. They made it a two-day event. We flew in and we were marching on the football field with the school band. We had a press conference with the mayor and they all wore makeup [laughs]. They went to the fire departments. It was amazing. I had gotten every magazine and newspaper to cover it. It became an international event.

PETER CRISS: That was so cool. They had a big marching band. We left in a helicopter and dropped tons of flyers that said, "KISS Loves You."

ACE FREHLEY: We had those outfits on and it was really cold. I remember we did a parade through the main street on a float. It was pretty bizarre. I have fond memories of the people all wearing KISS makeup, they were really gracious and hospitable.

DEVELOPING THE SMOKING GUITAR

ACE FREHLEY: I like special effects. I always think if you can do something interesting on stage, the more you can get the audience off. In the mid-'70s, one day in Canada on one of our very first tours I went to a magic shop, a novelty place, and got some of those smoke bombs. I put the smoke bomb inside the compartment where the volume and tone controls are on the Les Paul, and I just left a little hole with the fuse coming out that I could light with a cigarette lighter. And the smoke would go through the canals where the wires are and would come out through the pickups. It worked. Of course it ended up fucking up all the volume controls and gummed it up with gook and stuff. Then eventually I revamped a guitar with a special pickup with a movie light built in and a whole electronic system that would trigger a smoke bomb and trigger movie lights. That was the first effect of mine. Then I came up with the rocket idea and most recently the pinwheel idea.

NEAR ELECTROCUTION IN LAKELAND, FLORIDA, 1976

ACE FREHLEY: My guitar wasn't grounded to the railing and we weren't using wireless guitars then. I could have easily died that night. It wasn't my time. I was out for a while and then they revived me. I had no feeling in my fingers. They had to carry me down the back steps. When I came to I said, "What happened?" And they said, "You were electrocuted!" I had no feeling in my left hand. The audience started to chant my name and my adrenaline started pumping and I said that I'd go back out and finish the show but I didn't know how long I could play. I remember playing but it was sloppy because I had burns on my hands. Right after that tour we researched who was making the best wireless units and they were really expensive. But we got them.

EMPIRE STATE BUILDING PHOTO SHOOT

PETER CRISS: I got so drunk with Ace. We drank so much champagne and I was loaded on that shoot. I was feeling great as we all do on champagne. Ace and I were loaded. We had a ball. I was hanging off the fucking edge of the damn thing [laughs]. Gene was having a heart attack about it.

ACE FREHLEY: I remember crawling [laughs] through this elevator room to get to the edge of where we were gonna do the photo session. It was pretty bizarre seeing the motors for the elevators and the cables. I don't have a fear of heights so I thought it was cool. There was a kind of safety thing there so I don't think we were in any real danger.

PAUL STANLEY: We were all scared shitless. You could see one arm and one hand of each guy and the other hand was holding on for dear life. It's pretty awesome to be up there and look and see three states. We climbed the ladder in those boots. It was a pretty interesting time.

GENE SIMMONS: We were nuts! We would do anything you would imagine. Let's go on top of the Empire State Building and hang over the side, for a photo. That'll look cool. Let's go?

MERCHANDISING

RON BOUTWELL (KISS MERCHANDISING HEAD): I had several meetings with Neil Bogart regarding merchandising and asked him if I paid for all the inserts would he put them in their albums, which he did. I had to fight, kick, and scream to get an Elton John fan club started in '74. I had no problem with KISS. They said, "Yeah, we've got to have a fan club!" We formed the KISS Army, put the insert in for people to join, and included a list of merchandise. We started doing two, three, four, five thousand dollars a day and the fan club was near a hundred thousand members. Gene was the most interested in merchandising. He sat down with me developing the concepts. It was big business. There was an article that came out in 1978, which said KISS had generated over $111 million in the retail sale of KISS merchandise in 1978 alone. Probably the most popular item that people bought was the Donruss chewing gum cards. We got incredible royalties on that. I also did a pinball machine with Bally. It was the most popular pinball machine at the time.

AL ROSS (EXECUTIVE VICE PRESIDENT OF AUCOIN MANAGEMENT): Ron was really a pioneer in merchandising. He was the first one to ever sell a T-shirt at a concert, a Bobby Sherman show. He was an ex-carny, a very clever guy. He was a real huckster but he had a feeling for what the business was all about.

BILL AUCOIN: I always knew that KISS were merchandisable. Plus the fact that real fans, real strong fans always want some form of memorabilia. It was kind of obvious. I always told my staff that anything that's possible, let us see it. We almost made the Fortune 500 in the sense of the company. KISS had grossed $111 million that year, which was a huge amount for any company and that was gross. That wasn't in their pockets. But $55 million of it was merchandising. Boutwell was the company that we initially started and then I bought Boutwell and changed it to Niocua, which is Aucoin backward. My ego went crazy, I guess.

ROY WOOD, THE MOVE:

When we toured with Wizzard in America, we did a few gigs supporting KISS. Gene Simmons and I did this radio interview in Detroit. Gene actually admitted on the air that KISS had been influenced by my makeup, which I thought was nice of him to say in public.

RON BOUTWELL: The per capita gross that KISS fans would spend at each show was the highest in the world for any recording artist. It ranged between $2 and $4 per person. And this was in the '70s.

AL ROSS: It was no-holds-barred in terms of the merchandising. We would tell people wanting a license for a product, "Money is not our problem here, we just want a very big royalty." We didn't ask for money up front because we knew the products were going to be very successful. KISS was involved in every piece of merchandise, nothing was done without their approval. We did an enormous amount of licensing. At one point we must have had 150 to 200 separate licenses.

RON BOUTWELL: KISS was one of the only bands that I ever worked with that felt merchandising was an integral part of the success and future stability of the band. Also the income that had been derived from it was becoming a major portion of the group's income.

PETER CRISS: One night I got home around seven in the morning, really bombed, and because I have insomnia I put the TV on. There were these little dolls on TV flying around and they looked like us. I thought I was hallucinating and I said to myself, "I'm never getting high again." Later I found out that it was a commercial for the KISS dolls.

RON BOUTWELL: There was really only one licensing deal that I turned down. Somebody wanted to do KISS prophylactics. And everybody laughed when I told them about it except Gene. Gene became very very angry with me and said, "How dare you turn down that possibility! That's tremendous, we should have licensed it. We would have got incredible press!"

BILL AUCOIN: Around 1979, the band began to think it was getting too kiddie-like. The fans became younger and younger. The generation that initially loved them were getting older and they were going on to other music. I kept saying, "You can't let the merchandising go, it's way too important. You developed this, we protected it for years." I spent five years getting their faces copyrighted by the Library of Congress. And now they're telling me they don't want to do merchandise. Ace felt the merchandise was taking over. Ace always wanted to be known as a good musician. They said, "You want to keep the merchandise happening because you own the merchandising company!" The reason I owned the merchandising company was to have as much control over what we did.

MARVEL COMIC

STAN LEE (MARVEL COMICS CHIEF): Gene Simmons is one of the biggest comic fans. He contacted us and we decided to do a comic book KISS. Me and the guys from KISS had to drive to Buffalo, because we were doing some sort of publicity stunt there where the band poured their own blood into the printer's ink. So we landed in Buffalo and there was a police escort to take us to a printing plant. I couldn't get over this because there were two motorcycle policemen and these nuts in costume in the back seat of the limousine and the cops were stopping traffic at every intersection, so that we could go for our publicity gig. All I could think about was there are probably doctors riding somewhere to an emergency operation or people with important business things and they're stopping at the intersection so that KISS can do their publicity. I thought, this really says something about the human condition in America. Every minute Gene Simmons would say, "Stan, do you remember that story you did in 1964? Do you remember what you wrote on page 12, panel 3, and . . ."

STEVE GERBER (MARVEL COMICS WRITER AND EDITOR): It was really the first comic book of its kind. The difference in those earlier comic books is that they were all aimed at children. The KISS comic was aimed at the real audience of the band. It was a leap for comic books at the time. The first rock 'n' roll comic that Marvel ever did was the KISS book. In fact it established a whole line of similar comics. It was the first magazine-sized comic book done in color, and it was a real fight to get it done that way. It had to be approached like we were publishing a rock 'n' roll magazine because it was going to be out there on the stands with all these other rock magazines. There was no reason for anyone to buy this if it didn't look as good as any of the music magazines. In that sense, it had to be something spectacular. It had to be something to just leap off the stands at you. That's why I used the metallic ink and we did the red hellish cover [laughs]. This is going to sound unbelievable to any comic book fan but they didn't want to do that because they told me, "Nobody's going to pay $1.50 for a comic book." We used metallic ink on the cover for the KISS logo, I think it was the first time that had been done. It was the first time that I had ever written a comic book on living human beings [laughs]. That was different.

SEAN DELANEY: I had come back off the road and I walked into our office. There was never a closed door between Bill and I, I was always part of whatever was going on. I walked in and there a hippie-looking guy with long hair, Steve Gerber, and this older gentleman with a goatee, Stan Lee. And on the table were these storyboards. I picked this thing up and I'm looking at it and there's sort of weird drawings of the guys in KISS. Gene is saying, "We have to go to Mexico City because Necros has caused air pollution. We have to do a free concert and raise money in support for clean air!" I picked this stuff up and I ripped it in half. And I said, [loudly] "What the fuck is this? This isn't about my babies! If you're gonna be doing a story, they're not musicians, they're superheroes!" The person that I am in that comic is the guy who says, "Play hard, play fair, nobody hurt," 'cause that was one of my sayings with the band and with the road crew. Then Stan Lee says, "How would they become superheroes?" And I said, "Because I gave them their talisman." The talisman idea was the box of "KHYSCZ." The guy with the ponytail and the "play hard, play fair, nobody hurt" gives the four boys this box and in the box are four talismen. The cat, the demon, the lightning, and the star. I came up with the idea of what each one's powers were. Then I sat there and wrote with Steve Gerber.

GENE SIMMONS: Sean Delaney had a lot to do with that comic. He wrote some of the story. There was a trial run. Sean wrote a two-page comic strip for *Creem* magazine where we were semi-super-heroic kind of guys. Marvel Comics put us in a *Howard the Duck* comic where Howard the Duck was possessed by KISS. It also happened to be a very big seller for them so they thought, "We've got something here." I insisted that we don't do just a comic book. I told everyone it's got to be a $1.50 comic book. I'd rather do it in magazine style so you don't have to go to the comic book section because lots of fans don't want to read comic books. I'd rather be next to *Time* magazine. So reluctantly Marvel went along with it. Those two KISS Marvel comic books were their biggest sellers for twenty years.

STEVE GERBER: Certain things seemed apparent right from the very beginning. The superpowers of the characters were just obvious. Paul had the star coming from the star eye and the cat powers for Peter Criss and Ace was just warping everywhere [laughs]. I think that was Ace's power where he could warp time and space. Gene breathed fire where today I would probably have done something a lot nastier with the tongue [laughs]. Amazingly it was one of the easier stories that I had written in a lot of ways again because I knew the guys. Ace really talks like that [laughs] and Gene was an interesting character to write because it was like doing this very literate articulate devil kind of character, which is exactly what he is. Peter was the most difficult one to write because basically he was a very quiet guy anyway. But again with the cat persona that wasn't a big problem and Paul's personality was maybe the most show-bizzy of any of them in, say, the Las Vegas spectacle of the term.

STEVE GERBER: Gene was probably the one who had the most input into the comic book because he had been a big comic book fan for years. Sean Delaney contributed a great deal as did Bill Aucoin and some of the other people who worked at Aucoin Management. The project itself probably took about two, three months.

PAUL STANLEY: I thought it was great regardless of whether I was a fan of comics. Just the idea. Any time your face is on something or there's a story about you it's very exciting. It's thrilling when you see a comic written about you. It's a hell of a lot more thrilling than seeing a Superman comic.

GENE SIMMONS: How often can you read Shakespeare? I'd rather read KISS comics.

PETER CRISS: I was into a lot of the same comics that Gene was, things like *Creepy* and *Eerie* and *Weird* [laughs]. He couldn't believe the collection I had. I had a major collection and that's what we had in common when we finally started talking to each other. I told him, "Oh God, I got that *Creepy*, I got that *Eerie*, and I got that *Weird.*" And he was like, "Holy shit!" So we got along because that was one of the things we had in common. Those KISS comics were great, the artwork was brilliant! We gave our own blood to be used in the printing of it [laughs].

CAROL ROSS (PUBLICIST): Alan Miller came up to our office and we were trying to come up with something that would be of interest for our announcement about the KISS comic book. So we went up to where they make the comic books and we had them cut KISS's fingers and pour the blood into the red ink which was used in the comic book. See, that makes the announcement of this more interesting because it was KISS's own blood flowing through the comic. The fans went crazy.

JAPAN TOUR 1977

PETER CRISS: We went over on our 747, it was beautiful. We started getting close to Japan and put our costumes and makeup on. We got there and there were thousands and thousands of kids at the airport. But customs looked at the passports and said, "Well you may not be the right guys." Bill [Aucoin] begged them, "Please don't make them take it off." We were pissed and tired. We went into this little room, took it all off, the customs guy came in and we had to put it all back on again. Then we were chased like the Beatles in *Hard Day's Night.* It was great.

ACE FREHLEY: The nice thing about being in Japan with platform shoes on is you're already tall and you never get lost.

GENE SIMMONS: Clearly when we went to Japan it felt like another planet because from a Westerner's view, everybody looked the same. There was a height and color of hair. There were no blondes whatsoever. Everybody was five foot two. If at any time we felt like strangers in a strange land, that was it. We towered above them. We always wore our heels. We were close to seven feet tall. When we got off the plane we looked around and thought, "What planet is this?" The food was bizarre. People are eating suction cups and raw fish. The fans were a combination of the most well behaved and the most psychotic fans you've ever seen. They would stay seated because it was a rule with the cops there. If you rush the stage they get in there with the billy clubs and the dogs and that's it. So they would remain seated while we played. At the end of the song the only thing that was missing was a Buddhist setting himself on fire. Then they'd sit back down.

PAUL STANLEY: Nothing could prepare you for it because when people are telling you how big you are, you're big compared to what? Until you're faced with mass hysteria [laughs] it doesn't really sink in. What happens and it happened in Australia too, by virtue of you not being there, the anticipation that builds up is enormous. For you not having been in a certain country makes them that much more rabid for you to go.

JOHN FANNON, NEW ENGLAND:

New England opened thirty or forty shows for KISS on their *Dynasty* tour and that was great. Everyone would probably agree that KISS's place in rock 'n' roll history has been paved by their concept and their big theatrical show. But to me if their music didn't impact people they wouldn't still be playing in arenas. If you don't have good music and you're not a great band, you're not going to last as long as they did. Only the great bands can have the success that they've had for so long. It was classic, entertaining arena rock.

BOB GRUEN (PHOTOGRAPHER): I was the official photographer on their tour of Japan. The fans were great to them in Japan. It was like KISSmania. The idea of their act has a lot of influence from the Japanese Kabuki in Japanese theater. I felt like I was a general in the KISS Army when we were in Kyoto, the ancient capital of Japan. The first place KISS went to was a giant Buddha, which I didn't know was a very sacred shrine to the dead. I was in the cab and the bus with KISS was following the cab. I was showing the Polaroids to the cab driver and he would start driving and the bus would follow and we would go to that place. As we were coming up to the hill to the first shrine, I saw Mr. Udo [tour promoter] hustling down the hill. I didn't know that he tried to tell the monks that ran the place that we were coming. They objected strenuously. And rather than deal with a fight he just kind of split [laughs]. I didn't have any idea what was up so we just all showed up and KISS started piling off the bus. I start telling them to get up in front of the statue like it's a state park or something. There was some kind of discussion going in the corner with the Japanese people talking to the translators. I said to the translators, "Just keep 'em busy for a few minutes." I sent the band up, we took a bunch of pictures. A bunch of kids ran over and got in the pictures. Then we figured out we were being thrown out and we left. So I showed the cab driver the next picture and everybody got back in the bus and they followed the cab to the next shrine. All the people who had been at the shrine were so freaked out that KISS were there that they followed us to the next place. So we had these huge crowds following us. By the time we left there and went to the third place, the Golden Pagoda, we had a huge line of thirty or forty cars following the KISS bus. So it was this giant parade through Kyoto. After the third place it was such a big mob scene that we had to beat it back to the hotel.

BILLY MILLER (KISS ROAD MANAGER): We were in Japan and everyone suggested that the last person the press should talk to is Ace. *Playboy* had waited for days and days to talk to Ace and everyone kept making excuses for him. He waited until the very end of the trip before he gave this guy an interview. We were upstairs at the top of the Okura Hotel. So they bring over Ace for the interview and they promised he would be sober. He comes upstairs and the writer asks Ace, "What does it feel like to have all this attention paid to you? Look what you've accomplished." And Ace goes, "Ack!" And the guy goes "What about all the things you've done?" He goes, "Ack!" The writer says, "Wait a minute, are you going to answer this?" And Ace goes, "Ack! What do you mean, Curly?" He called everyone Curly. So he says, "All right, Curly, it's great. Ack!," gets up and leaves the interview and everybody is looking at each other and doesn't have a clue to what has just gone on.

JOHN HARTE (TOUR SECURITY): The first time we played at the Budokan before anything happened you heard this high shrill. And it was all these Japanese girls in the front rows screaming. They were so young and their voices were so high-pitched that it was a really weird sound.

PAUL CHAVARRIA (KISS ROADIE, 1974–1979): We were the kings of the party in Japan. One of our crew members, Ron Cameron, was with this girl the entire time we were in Japan. She said something to him one day [imitates Japanese woman], "You may only be loadie but you lock star to me." [laughs] And I thought that was just a classic line.

BILLY MILLER: There was a big fight in their dressing room. Peter was unhappy. Ace was unhappy. Paul was unhappy. There was tension and it just got angry. Peter was acting like an asshole. He didn't want to play certain songs. It got to a point where it was Peter and Ace against Gene and Paul and they just started throwing things at each other and screaming and yelling.

AL ROSS (EXECUTIVE VICE PRESIDENT OF AUCOIN MANAGEMENT): It started as a shouting argument. They were all screaming at each other. This happened in the dressing room on our second visit to Japan in 1978. Then they closed the door and we couldn't get in. The next thing you knew is that there was glass flying and bottles flying. It took the road manager and the security people to break this door down to get in there and just hold these guys apart. Ace totally destroyed the dressing room. Then they went on and did a two-hour show but they never talked to each other again the time they were there. The problem is the conflict was always between Gene and Paul on one side and Ace and Peter on the other. It was always like that.

BRIAN MAY, QUEEN:

I like KISS a lot. Queen were often compared to KISS at the time. We were sort of counterparts. They were the American version and we were the English version. I think we went into it with slightly different ideas. KISS came more from a presentation view to begin with and moved more toward the musical. I think we probably started in the musical and worked more toward the presentation. I have a great regard for KISS 'cause it's all-out. They just had their vision, they had their dream, and they damn well went for it.

KISS MEETS THE PHANTOM OF THE PARK

PAUL STANLEY: How do I view the film? As infrequently as possible [laughs]. Due to a lot of circumstances out of our control, I thought it turned out kind of distorted and embarrassing because it really wasn't supposed to be the way it turned out but television censorship is such that they seem to have a hard time with certain things. The film just kept going off on tangents and by the time it was done I really didn't have much desire to see it.

GENE SIMMONS: I have nothing to say about that movie except that it was interesting to make. Also, it was a learning experience. It taught me that the next time somebody says, "Don't worry, it'll be fine," that you should still roll up your sleeves and stick your nose into it just to make sure. Because when the movie or anything comes out with your name on it ultimately you're responsible for it. So, it was interesting to do, but I don't think it's a very good movie.

ACE FREHLEY: My stuntman was black, putting white makeup on him did the trick, but they had to put flesh makeup on his hands! He was a great guy. There was one scene in the haunted place and I had an argument with the director. I just hopped in my Mercedes and took off. There was one scene where they needed me and my stuntman was my stand-in. There was a close-up shot and you can definitely tell that it's not me. When he gets knocked against the wall by Dracula or somebody, if you freeze-frame it, it's very obvious that it's not me.

PETER CRISS: At that time, '78, I was doing cocaine and drinking and getting crazy. I remember how hard it was getting up at six in the morning and being in makeup at eight and they would cake it on, putting on three or more layers, so if you wanted to rest you couldn't. If you moved your head you'd mess it all up again. And I didn't like the waiting. We were so used to getting onstage and going at it. No one told us we were going to be sitting for a long time. For me, I'm such a hyper guy, I'd go in and the minute the makeup was on, I'd break open a beer and I'd start partying.

NIKKI SIXX, MÖTLEY CRÜE:

I was always more influenced by KISS's music and songwriting than by their performance. Their songs are chock-full of hooks and great arrangements. It was the soundtrack for my generation.

ACE FREHLEY: That was a good comedy [laughs]. One funny part in that film was the scene at the pool where the actor walks up with a cop while we were sitting on those big chairs. I wish I had the outtakes because he fell when he was walking toward us and cut his hand. We had to take a ten-minute break. When somebody falls I have this imagery in my mind [laughs]. He fell, they patched his hand up, and he came over and I'm supposed to do my line. And every time I'm supposed to do my line in my mind I would imagine him falling and I'd fuck it up. We had to do twenty-five takes until I got it right [laughs]. I mean it became contagious, even Paul and Gene were fuckin' losing it.

ACE FREHLEY: Believe it or not, when I got the original script I didn't have one line except for "Ack!" That was the only thing I would say. When I was drunk and if I didn't want to be bothered by people I would just go "Ack!" [laughs] I guess they didn't think I was capable of saying any lines at the time. I was drinking a lot. I thought I pulled off my lines okay. Peter didn't even talk in the film [laughs]. Usually when you do a film you have to go and redo some of the dialogue, you have to do looping. He never made it, so they had another actor speak his lines.

PETER CRISS: I wanted to go into acting and when I did I hated it [laughs] because it wasn't the acting that I wanted. I wanted to be Al Pacino [laughs]. Here's the separation, the Cat is not an actor. He's a rock star. And so are those guys, they aren't actors. I hated doing the film. They didn't use my voice probably because I read the dialogue so bad. I just hated every minute of it. When I look at it now I love it. My daughter just thinks it's the greatest movie she's ever seen. But it wasn't a great time for me. I just met Deborah. I was still married and I was having an affair with her and Jesus Christ I had all my energies into this beautiful centerfolder. The fucking solo albums was the worst of it. We should never have done that. I'll be the first member to admit that. And Ace will agree, we've talked about this. It was the biggest mistake we ever did because we all went our own ways. We all went into this fucking musical thing that I thought could probably be a whole career for me. I didn't need these guys anymore. I had "Beth," it won the People's Choice Award. Fuck this, I'm doing my own music! I freaked out. So did everyone else. I think all of us should have taken the solo album music and all of us should have played on that together and that would have been KISS. So if I had to redo things I would never have done the solo albums and I would have put my brain in a different place for that movie.

ACE FREHLEY: The hurry-up-and-wait stuff drove me crazy. I'm used to touring and everything's boom, boom, boom! But when you make a movie, you've got to wait around sometimes for hours. You get to the set real early and sometimes they make you wait four or five hours until they get to a scene. Then there's lighting. They'll do a scene and you'll think you did it great and then they'll say the lighting was wrong or the sound guy screwed up. Some days we'd get there at 8:00 A.M. There were some fifteen-hour days. In the original script, I didn't have one line, so I said "You better put in some lines for me or I'm not gonna do this film." [laughs] So they wrote in some lines for me. It was a good learning experience.

ANGUS YOUNG, AC/DC:

Early in our career, we were having a lot of trouble at the time getting on tours because our band was real good. The headliners would be like, "Get rid of them!" KISS asked for us, they weren't afraid. Gene Simmons came and saw us play at the Whisky in L.A. I remember that he got us on some of their bigger dates so that was real good for us.

PAUL STANLEY: We initially were going to write all new songs for *KISS Meets the Phantom.* That was the original idea. But it became impossible as we were doing the film. The "Rip and Destroy" song came about when one key song was needed at the end of the film where the evil KISS is trying to get everybody to riot. So I went into a trailer, took "Hotter Than Hell," and wrote new lyrics [laughs]. There was only one verse.

ACE FREHLEY: We were constantly together and we were getting on each other's nerves. Me and Peter are party animals and Paul and Gene weren't. It got to the point where there was friction. We just needed a break. The solo albums for a while helped keep the group together. At the same token, the success of my solo album opened my eyes and made me a little more cocky. It made me realize that I had the ability to do it on my own. That planted the seed for me that eventually I was gonna do my own thing.

JOSEPH BARBERA (HANNA-BARBERA PRODUCER): It was a heck of a picture. *KISS Meets the Phantom of the Park* was really another version of *The Phantom of the Opera.* We had this demented genius living down in the bowels of the amusement park and he created all these animatronics. When KISS set up to do a concert there he saw it as a distinct threat to him. So he wanted to destroy them and that's how the story went.

Gordon Hessler directed the film, he used to do a lot of pictures for AIP, pretty scary horror films. It was a heck of a show and KISS were terrific people to work with. We went out to film the concert at Magic Mountain amusement park and there were thirty thousand people there. They had their set, which was worth a million dollars. When they did their songs, it was incredible. Another part of the film I loved was when those white monkeys started climbing up the roller coaster. They were wonderful people to work with. There was a budget you had to stay with because it was a "Movie of the Week," a television movie. I think the movie cost $2 million, $3 million dollars. It was a hell of a production. The KISS people were way ahead of their time. The film is a real classic, very original.

AL ROSS (EXECUTIVE VICE PRESIDENT OF AUCOIN MANAGEMENT): Anthony Zerbe is a marvelous actor but the casting of the guy and girl was less than spectacular, they were just stiffs.

PETER CRISS: Paul didn't really play [the acoustic guitar in the scene where "Beth" is played in the film], it was done by a studio musician. I was supposed to fake playing the guitar but I was so sloppy with the fingerwork that Paul jumped right in and said, "I'll do it," where Ace really should have done it. That's when we really started battling each other. On that movie we were battling already. I don't remember going back into the studio singing it. [Why his speaking voice is not used in film] I'll never know. They said that my voice stunk. Hey man, I could pick up the phone and call somebody for something and they could pick up the phone and know it's me right away. I know no one has a voice like mine. You know Ace the minute you pick up the phone [imitates Ace's voice]. I can imitate him so well I can almost fool people that I'm Ace at times. You know Paul immediately and you know Gene immediately. I thought I had a real unique voice. [response to band saying he did not show up for looping, which is why his voice is not in film] That's bullshit. I went to all the looping. I went to all the fucking shit I had to go to. Yes, I was stoned all the time. So was Ace. We were both party animals at that point in our career. We had broads in our trailer, six, seven broads at a time in our trailer. I mean every fucking day, with the makeup on! [laughs] The refrigerator loaded with beer. We were then into coke. We were just animals. We made Tommy Lee [Mötley Crüe] look like a child. We were fucking them in the back, the front, the bathrooms. We were just crazy. So I was exhausted half the time because we would shoot at six in the morning, sometimes until three in the morning. So maybe my voice did sound like shit. I think whoever they got to replace me just blew it. They could have done much better than that. At least they could have gotten a guy who sounds closer to me than that. I got so many letters from KISS fans saying, "What the fuck is this! How dare this guy use someone else's voice!" So there was a lot of controversy about that.

BILLY SQUIER:

My band Piper opened for KISS in the '70s and I learned a lot from that experience. I thought the KISS show was amazing. I think the fact that their show was so spectacular often caused you to overlook how good Paul's voice was or the fact that Ace could really play guitar. The point when I started telling people that they had KISS pegged all wrong was with the *Destroyer* album. I started hearing songs that made me go, "These guys have got a fucking handle on this, they really know what they're trying to do and they're articulating it."

PAUL CHAVARRIA (KISS ROADIE, 1974–1979): We were out at the bottom of the roller coaster at Magic Mountain. It was the day we were shooting the live concert. We had this huge tarp across the back of the stage. These winds came out of nowhere and started pushing the scaffolding, almost getting ready to rip the roof down. Every one of the roadies took a utility knife, raced up to this thing, and started cutting all of these bungee cables that were holding the tarp down. This tarp went flying off into the wind, it was gone. Had we not done that it probably would have forced the roof down on the production, which might have killed the band. And no one was gonna let that happen.

BILL AUCOIN: It wasn't a very good film. Don't forget that I'm a director/producer. Hanna-Barbera didn't want to spend that much money on it. It was a television film and they thought they could get away with it for a lot less money. And they had hired a pretty good director. But when the director tried to get great scenes out of Gene and Paul, and Ace and Peter, it took twice as long because they had never done it before. It wasn't their fault. So Hanna-Barbera came in and they fired the director and got someone else who did it. "Okay, that's the line, Peter. Go on, goodbye," and that was it. It could have been a lot better than it was. But the fact that we did it was great. Sometimes you have to think creatively that it's better that you do something and make it happen because you keep growing from it and whatever. They could have done a lot more if it all stayed together.

CAROL KAYE (PUBLICIST, THE PRESS OFFICE LTD.): We had a screening of *KISS Meets the Phantom* with maybe thirty people in the room. We're all watching the movie and it was very quiet. It was kind of surreal [laughs]. At certain moments in the film I remember Ace cackling in the back of the room. Ace's laugh made everybody else laugh. The film didn't turn out the way they hoped it would [laughs]. Unfortunately it wasn't another *Hard Day's Night*.

AL ROSS: The film was originally going to be shown in theaters, then it turned into a TV movie. In the very beginning it was looked upon as a low-budget job and that's not what it was supposed to be. There was a lot of tension on the set, it was very stressful for the band. There was conflict on every day of the film shoot. For Gene and Paul this was the ultimate, to be on the big screen. But Ace and Peter, psychologically or subconsciously, looked at this as saying all this is going to do is keep this KISS thing going. I think it was time for them to get out. The fact that "Beth" was such a big hit inflamed Peter's ego. From that point on all he wanted to do was put a tuxedo on and go play Las Vegas like Frank Sinatra.

THE *TOMORROW* SHOW TV APPEARANCE

GENE SIMMONS: The Tom Snyder show experience was horrific. Ace was bombed and Peter was in his "I'm Italian and I love guns" mood. I was trying very desperately to keep it together. Tom Snyder kept going to Ace, the guy who was cracking up and having a good time. Ace and Peter would play off of each other. As soon as Peter saw that Ace was having a good time, it was almost license for him to say, "Oh yeah, I like guns and I'm in gangs." You're rich and you're in a rock 'n' roll band. He was never in a gang. They both loved the idea that they were bad boys. They're not bad boys. If these guys were in gangs they would have wound up being dog food.

PETER CRISS: We took over the show. Ace was drinking champagne, he was shit-faced. I think he passed out in the dressing room afterward. Gene was steaming because Ace took over on the show and he was so funny. I thought it was terrific, I was Ace's biggest fan that night.

ACE FREHLEY: I was totally totally nervous. This was the first time I was ever going to do a major network show where I knew millions of people would be watching. At that point I was still having stage fright. I was definitely afraid to be in front of a camera. So on the way down I drank a half a bottle of Stolie. I usually don't drink vodka, I'm usually just a beer drinker. All it did was basically make me normal and relaxed because I was so terrified. I remember the producer called me up. They called me on an off-day where I wasn't really into a talkative mood. Even Tom mentions it in the interview saying, "My producer told me that Ace probably won't talk at all." It was just one of those spontaneous things that worked out. I have no idea where I came up with those jokes, the one about the cows in Bombay, the plumber. It just came off the top of my head.

BILL AUCOIN: My favorite TV appearance was the *Tomorrow* show. What happened was when Ace was interviewed for the show he was drunk so he didn't do the initial interview before the show. So they tell Snyder that "Gene and Paul are your main people. Peter is pretty good and Ace isn't gonna do anything. He'll probably sit there like a bump on a log." I shared a bottle of champagne with Ace in the dressing room and he was ready! And Snyder couldn't believe it, he thought his people had set him up. Every time Ace said something Snyder went to pieces. He was laughing and screaming. It was a turn of events that worked brilliantly. Gene was upset because Ace took over the show.

CAROL KAYE (PUBLICIST, THE PRESS OFFICE LTD.): We booked the band on the Tom Snyder show. It wasn't an everyday occurrence back then to see a rock band on a late-night interview program. This was a major coup to have KISS on the Tom Snyder show. Tom had this little stuffed animal that he kept next to his seat. Ace kept picking up this stuffed animal and playing with it [laughs]. He called it a "Space Bear." Ace was very drunk and I was very scared the show wouldn't come off well. But Ace came off as lovable. He's not a mean drunk, he's just a lovable drunk. He kept playing with this stuffed bear. Even though Tom was desperately trying to conduct a normal interview, you can see his eye keep going to the bear. I remember when we broke to go to commercial, Tom Snyder, who's about six foot five, gets up and says, "Gimme back my bear!" [laughs] I'll never forget that. Here are these guys that are eight feet tall in their costumes and here's Tom Snyder fighting over this little stuffed bear. That's hilarious to me.

"SHANDI" VIDEO

PETER CRISS: I'll never forget it. I remember when we were shooting the video, there was a sadness you could feel through the place. When we finished doing the "Shandi" video we all came back into the dressing room, you could just feel it, man. You could feel that the vibes were totally uncomfortable for everybody. I knew I was taking my makeup off for the last time and that I was leaving the band. They couldn't get theirs off quick enough to get out of there because they couldn't even be near me because they were so uncomfortable about it. And before I knew it I was sitting in this room all by myself [laughs] and they were gone and I was taking my makeup off and I just started crying and crying and crying. I just couldn't stop crying. I was all alone. I finally took off all my makeup, put my street clothes on, and I looked at my outfit for the last time and I said, "Wow, I guess this is it." It was a really hard time for me.

GEDDY LEE, RUSH:

I think KISS brought a sense of entertainment to rock 'n' roll. KISS worked hard to put on a great show every night. From Rush's point of view, we learned the importance of adding entertainment to a musical scenario from watching them.

PETER LEAVES KISS

BILL AUCOIN: Peter didn't want to leave the band. Peter got very emotional and he was having problems. And Gene and Paul said, "Look, we gotta ask him to leave." I didn't really want him to leave and Ace didn't want him to leave. We had meetings with lawyers and business managers and the inevitable happened. Peter wasn't strong enough to fight on his own, unfortunately. That was the beginning of money being more important to the band, unfortunately.

AUSTRALIA TOUR 1980

PAUL STANLEY: Australia was amazing. We were big beyond any comprehension. Much the same as Japan but different in the sense that we were in an English-speaking country. It was pretty staggering. We couldn't leave the hotels. "Shandi" had already been a hit there. We were the front headline of the papers for virtually three or four weeks. It reached the point where I was asking that we not have any more parties because literally every night the promoter threw a party for us. And each party they rounded up all the celebs, actresses, models in each city and the parties were for us and all the women they could find. They would take over a club. Men were not allowed. So it was a very interesting time. Then if we got bored in Sydney when we were there, they would rent these big boats for us and just cater them and we would spend the day going around Sydney harbor with whatever company we felt like having.

BILL AUCOIN: We took probably the biggest show ever to Australia. They'd never seen anything like us. Rupert Murdoch backed the show as the promoter. We had our own 727. We had our own helicopter and nine limousines so it was almost like anything we wanted went. And it really did. The whole country stopped for us.

GEORGE SEWITT (ROAD MANAGER): Australia was unbelievable. It was the same excitement and craziness that happened when the Beatles landed in America for the first time. There were thousands of kids at the airport and in the streets. People would disguise themselves as room-service waiters to try and meet the band. We had the top floor of the Hilton and there were kids literally climbing the side of the hotel and they made it. The guys would stay at the hotel under pseudonyms. Paul was Mike Riffone, like "microphone." Gene would be William Pratt, Boris Karloff's real name.

ACE FREHLEY: I remember a lot of girls, a lot of champagne [laughs]. Actually that was probably one of the most fun tours we ever did because we were there for six weeks and we only did eight or ten shows. The promoter was having as much fun as we were. He used to rent yachts, fill up the boat with lobster and champagne, and go out and circle around Sydney harbor. The boat would be filled with models. It was like a dream tour.

ACE FREHLEY: The dinner with Elton [John] on our tour of Australia was pretty funny because we were at one of those Japanese steak houses where the guys cook in front of you and I had a little too much to drink. I was drinking those sweet tropical drinks where you can't taste the alcohol [laughs]. So I probably had three or four. I ended up putting on one of those chef's caps and told Elton's chef to get lost. I started throwing the shrimp up and bouncing it off of Elton's and his manager's heads [laughs]. Finally Bill Aucoin came over and said, "Why don't you take a walk out in the rock garden?" [laughs] It was pretty funny. They had to take me away. Elton was pretty cool about it, he didn't freak out.

PETER FRAMPTON:

KISS is like the circus comes to town. They were the Cirque du Soleil of rock [laughs]. I applauded them for that.

KISS—BILL AUCOIN PARTING

BILL AUCOIN: It was obvious that it was coming because it wasn't fun for me anymore and I don't think it was fun for them to be around me because I wasn't as dedicated. It wasn't the same group. After ten years you get burned out. So one day they walked into the office and we discussed it and we wound up crying. I remember we were all crying our eyes out. Tears, and crying and hugging each other. It was very unusual for them. And that was it.

THE FILM *DETROIT ROCK CITY*

ADAM RIFKIN—director / TIM SULLIVAN—associate producer / CARL V. DUPRÉ—writer
GIUSEPPE ANDREWS—actor, Lex / SAM HUNTINGTON—actor, Jam / JAMES DeBELLO—actor, Trip
DIANE WARREN—songwriter

ADAM RIFKIN: For me, I fell in love with the idea of re-creating this period in time from my past. I have a real romance and nostalgia for those years. This movie gave me an opportunity to re-create that time, not necessarily the way it really was but the way I like to remember that it was. The archetype story is the quest. To me whether the quest is the Holy Grail or the Fountain of Youth, the quest for this movie is tickets to a KISS concert and that's pretty funny. I wanted the film to be enjoyable whether you liked KISS or hated them. If you like the characters, then you're vested with the quest, whatever that quest may be. I wanted *Detroit Rock City* to be today's *Rock 'n' Roll High School*. This movie is about being a teenager in the '70s. KISS is easily the most colorful and popular '70s pop culture icon band. That KISS is the driving force in the film gives it a certain timelessness that will always render it rediscoverable. Whether the film did well at the box office or not, I'm proud of the film. I'm thrilled that people are discovering it on video, DVD, and cable.

JOHN OATES, HALL & OATES:

Other than what David Bowie did with Ziggy Stardust, I think KISS set a standard for a certain kind of visual performance that defines glam rock.

TIM SULLIVAN: Quite frankly, as the KISS fan who grew up to be the associate producer of the KISS fan movie, it was the greatest experience of my life. Back in the day [I was thirteen when I saw then for the first time in 1977], KISS changed my life. They stood for rebellion. Rebellion against conformity and the mundane. That's kinda been my mantra in all my endeavors. "Don't let them tell you that there's too much noise."

Basically, don't listen to the people who say you can never do it. Follow your heart and make it happen. So in the summer of 1998, after having been friends with Gene ever since I first interviewed him for *Fangoria* magazine in 1982, I found myself working at New Line Cinema, and in a position to help grease the wheels of getting *Detroit Rock City* made. Working with the kick-ass cast and crew, and of course, Gene and KISS themselves, I fell into the role of "Keeper of the KISS Flame," making sure everything was true for the fans. After all, *Detroit Rock City* was intended to be a valentine to those fans. Along the way, there were many, many unforgettable moments. Just one of them would have been a dream come true for the thirteen-year-old-me daydreaming way back when. But I was blessed with an embarrassment of riches. Early on, Adam Rifkin and I wanted to make sure that Ace and Peter felt part of the project. The two of us took them out to dinner at a Japanese restaurant overlooking Hollywood after one of their *Psycho Circus* rehearsals. It was great getting to know them on their own. We discussed an initial concept of having KISS do out-of-makeup cameos. Ace was gonna play his own roadie, we talked about Peter playing the scalper, Paul as the strip club MC, and Gene as the priest! Unfortunately, it didn't work out, as the touring schedule just didn't allow them to come to Canada for more than one day. But we did have a great dinner!

IAN GILLAN, DEEP PURPLE:

KISS's very visual kind of thing was good. I thought their image was fun. You gotta run the full gamut. You can't just be too academic about music. The kind of bands I played with in the early days, the Kinks, Free, Zeppelin, Black Sabbath, T-Rex, they were all completely different. So you look at Arthur Brown and then you've got KISS.

CARL V. DUPRÉ: *Detroit Rock City* was a dream come true in every way imaginable for me, as a writer, movie buff, and of course as a huge KISS fan. My main influence was *I Wanna Hold Your Hand*, an early Bob Zemeckis comedy about several young girls trying to see the Beatles' first Ed Sullivan appearance in New York. I was trading crazy concert stories with a good friend of mine, who also happened to be a big KISS fan as well. I told him about a couple of childhood buddies who got into a Who concert by beating each other up and pretending they were mugged out of their tickets. This guy almost died laughing. Finally I said, "Someone should make a movie like *I Wanna Hold Your Hand* . . . only with a KISS concert as the Holy Grail." This friend of mine said, "Carl, you have to write that." An early version of *Detroit Rock City* started with our four heroes camped out in sleeping bags waiting to buy tickets, then slowly built up to the actual day of the concert. Another was told in an anthology manner, each of the four kids' stories start to finish, overlapping and intersecting at certain points with the others, much like *Pulp Fiction* or *Go*. But none of it was working so I gave up on *Detroit Rock City*. Oh well, I thought, I tried. Then I went to lunch with that friend of mine and another buddy of his, a movie director. My friend told the director, "Carl's working on a '70s script about a bunch of kids going to a KISS concert." I hadn't mentioned to my friend that I'd ditched the idea wholesale. This director's eyes lit up. "I'd love to read it," he said. "When will you be finished?" Before I could answer, my friend said, "He's been working on it for about three months now." The director looked at me, "What do you figure, another three months?" I nodded, sure. And went into panic mode when I got home. I knew I had to relaunch *Detroit Rock City* from square one. This time I focused on the day of the concert. The electricity that hangs in the air, the tickets burning in your pocket, the day you've waited so long for finally arrived! For some weird reason I knew there were three segments to this new take on *Detroit Rock City*. The first was showing how dedicated these kids were to KISS and to one another, their tickets are destroyed, they win them back, they bust [their buddy] Jam out of Catholic school. The second was the road trip, the battle with the "guidos," the arrival in Detroit only to find they *didn't* win the tickets, the car getting stolen. The third was the "every man for himself" section—where each kid goes on his own quest to get a ticket. I finished the first draft of that script in three months just in time to give it to this director who'd wanted to read it. He thought it was great. He had only one question: "How are you gonna get it to KISS?" With no connection to the band, I realized I had just made an egregious error. I vowed never, ever, ever to write another script that prominently featured a known entity. It wasn't all for nothing, though. The script did help me to get my first writing gig, on a TV show. The executive producer, another friend of mine, hired me on the basis of two spec screenplays I'd done, one being *Detroit Rock City*. But basically *Detroit Rock City* sat in my desk for about a year. Then one day I struck up a conversation with another struggling filmmaker. The two of us compared notes and his jaw dropped when I told him I'd written a script about KISS. He knew an actor who was a big KISS fan too and was always looking for scripts. I sent it to this actor and a chain reaction began. That weekend, I heard KISS announce they were getting back into makeup and doing a reunion tour. Meanwhile *Detroit Rock City* started getting passed from this actor, to his manager, to a casting agent who was looking to produce and was doing lunch that day with another burgeoning producer, Barry Levine, the guy who used to photograph KISS back in the '70s. He had just gotten a call from KISS's management to come out of retirement and shoot their reunion kickoff. Thinking the KISS connection was a funny coincidence, the casting agent handed the photographer *Detroit Rock City*. He read it and then gave it to KISS's manager. So basically by the next Monday, about ten days after I had given it to the actor, I get this call. "Gene read the script, he's given it his blessing." I'm thinking, Gene? "That's right, Gene Simmons." And that was just the beginning. From there on out *Detroit Rock City* seemed to have a life of its own, generating all sorts of happy coincidences (one of the producers called what was going on "KISSmet"). Less than two years after that phone call, I was on the set of *Detroit Rock City* in Toronto. Kevin Corrigan, the actor who was the big fan, wound up getting a role in it. The friend of mine who kept pushing me to write it? That was Peter Schink, the man who wound up editing the movie. And the executive producer of that TV show, the man who'd read *Detroit Rock City* and gave me my first writing gig, that was Adam Rifkin.

NANCY WILSON, HEART:

KISS had total savvy as far as publicity and, image-wise, they had it going on. I think it was a brilliant stroke to become cartoons. Marketing-wise they were completely brilliant in their strategies.

TIM SULLIVAN: It was imperative that all the KISS props and memorabilia be authentic. It would drive me crazy to show up on the set and see posters of Vinnie Vincent on the walls of Lex's basement. Jimmy and Eddie used to laugh when I tore them down, but I knew the fans would be watching. Gene certainly was. Most of the props came from his collection. One time he called me to say he thought Peter's hair should be longer and dyed gray. He's such an animal, he literally called me on his cell from a concert during Peter's drum solo! When we shot the big concert sequence, I remember Gene walking over to me and pointing to a kid in the rafters dressed in his *Dynasty* costume. He told me to make sure we never filmed the kid, as *Dynasty* was '79, and the movie took place in '77! Though most of the KISS props came from Gene's personal collection, many came from the fans themselves. Whenever we needed something Gene didn't have, I would call Mike Brandvold of KISSONLINE, and he would put the word out on the Web. That's how we got the *Love Gun* towel that Eddie uses to cover up his bong. The lady who sent it to us asked for no payment, only that Ace wiped his sweat in it before we sent it back! When Ace heard this, he insisted I take a picture of him wrapped up in the towel, which I did, and which was sent to one very surprised and happy fan!

TIM SULLIVAN: It was amazing to see the *Love Gun* stage completely re-created by our production designer, Steve Hardie. It was literally an exact replica. The feeling of déjà vu it gave me was unbelievable. I was not alone in feeling this way. The first time the band saw the stage was magical. It was set up at an arena in Hamilton, Canada. The guys showed up at 7:00 A.M., walked sleepily (and a bit grumpily) into the darkened arena. Just me and them in this huge space. I turned on the lights and Bam! there it was, the *Alive II/Love Gun* stage. The guys just couldn't believe it. Peter, particularly, got very emotional when he saw it, a flood of memories rushing over him. I think we all kinda thought it might have been a better choice than the *Psycho Circus* set they were touring with at the time.

GIUSEPPE ANDREWS: I loved what our director, Adam Rifkin, did with the film. Before the shoot, Adam conveyed what KISS fans were like in terms of their loyalty and fanaticism and that translated in our performance. The chemistry between the four guys, me, Eddie, Jimmy, and Sam, really came through, especially in the car scene. It was a great shoot. I didn't see it as a teen movie, it was much hipper than that. *Detroit Rock City* is definitely a cult classic. Thankfully the film's found a new audience with home video. It really didn't get the push it deserved from New Line, otherwise it would have been a smash.

SAM HUNTINGTON: It was a fun, feel-good, road trip film. When I first read the script, it felt more like it was a teen-driven movie. But as we worked on it, it was apparent that its appeal would be much broader, which worked to its advantage. The last scene in the film where I catch Peter's drumstick was cool because I was gonna have a moment with Peter Criss! Then after we shot it, I heard that Peter also felt that scene was special, saying, "We had a moment."

JAMES DEBELLO: People come up to me and talk about the film, saying, "Dude, that was me thirty years ago! KISS rules!" My favorite scene in the movie is when Eddie's in the strip bar and a girl buys him a glass of bourbon. He takes a sip and spits it out and says, "It's gone bad!" [laughs]

TIM SULLIVAN: A lot of people gave us flak that the new KISS song ["Nothing Can Keep Me from You"] used for the closing credits was a ballad rather than a rocker, but I know where Paul was coming from. At the time, Aerosmith had a huge hit with their *Armageddon* ballad, and the song's author, Diane Warren, was a good friend of Paul's. Paul was very proud of "Nothing Can Keep Me from You," and rightly so. I remember the first time he played it for us. All the producers sat in a darkened sound booth [Gene was there too], and Paul played the tune. I was struck by his amazing vocal performance. I told Paul that I always felt he was the heart and soul of KISS, and now he had provided just that, the heart and soul, for *Detroit Rock City*.

DIANE WARREN: I love "Nothing Can Keep Me from You." That song should have really been a huge hit. The record KISS did was fantastic. The emotion of that song is intense. When anybody does one of my songs, it's an honor, whether it's Aerosmith doing "I Don't Want to Miss a Thing" or KISS doing "Nothing Can Keep Me from You." Paul told me about the movie *Detroit Rock City* and said that he wanted a great big ballad. He'd come to me with a little lyric concept talking about what the movie was about, these kids would do anything to see KISS. I thought I could write a song that could tie in with that and yet stand on its own outside the movie and be relevant as a love song. It's like, nothing can keep me from seeing my favorite band or nothing can keep me from loving you. For me it was an easy song to write, I'm kind of like that in real life.

RICK NIELSEN, CHEAP TRICK:

KISS are the band that your parents love to hate. We did three months opening for KISS—June, July, and August of 1977. It was kind of funny opening for KISS because KISS never got a good review even though they went over great every night. It was embarrassing because we would get great reviews every night and they'd get slammed. We got along great. KISS sort of took us under their wing in a way. Gene and Paul saw us play in New York City at Max's Kansas City. There was hardly anybody there. But they were clapping and really enjoyed the band. I came out and started playing my guitar on Gene's table and he had a $20 bill there. I picked it up and I ate it in front of him. Then his story is it was a $50, he was too embarrassed it was a lousy $20. He never lets me forget that. KISS were way ahead of the game as far as being too loud, too fast, too over-the-top. They were right there. They did it all. KISS loved that we mentioned them in our song "Surrender." [recites lyrics] "Mommy and Daddy rolling on the couch, rolling numbers, got my KISS records out." We got some KISS flats, the covers of their albums, and we'd throw one out every night when we performed the song.

TIM SULLIVAN: So much shit has been said about the inner workings of the band, who gets along with whom, who played (or didn't play) on what songs and what albums. Yeah, I'll admit, sometimes those dynamics got a bit sticky during production. But I truly believe that at the end of the day, the purity of where it all started still burns deep within the original members of KISS. No one can ever tell me differently because I saw it with my own two eyes on the day Gene, Paul, Ace, and Peter strolled into the studio located above the Hollywood Athletic Club to record the new version of "Detroit Rock City" that was used in the movie [though sadly never released on the soundtrack album]. It was just the four of them and a sound engineer. Spirits were flying high. And so were the jokes and camaraderie. Rehearsals were going well, and the guys seemed hungry and eager to prove themselves to us film guys. Peter recorded his part first while Paul faced him from behind the sound booth and played a guide guitar track. Peter truly was the Catman, pounding those drums lean and mean. Then Gene came in and laid down the bass part, Paul continuing to guide the session. He was the demon, off in his own world as he performed, eyes closed, listening to the temp track on headphones. Then Ace entered and sat down shoulder to shoulder with Paul on the couch in the mixing console. It was dark, and all I could see was their silhouettes as they plowed through that famous guitar solo. Ace was pitch-perfect. Paul was the muse. Their guitars soared. With that done, Paul went into the recording booth and sung his heart out. Even though Paul has probably sung the song a million times, he sang it with a rawness and urgency that felt like it was the very first time. Within a mere four hours, the track was done. Perfect. Ready for playback for the climactic concert scene. And it was just the four of them, like it was in the beginning. And as time has proved, probably the end, for that was the last time to this date that Gene, Paul, Ace, and Peter have gone into a studio, just the four of them, and recorded a song together. People, let me tell you, they fucking rocked.

ROAD STORIES

SEAN DELANEY: On the first tour, we had two vehicles, a station wagon and a twenty-two-foot Hertz rental truck. We had two roadies driving that and I was with the band in the station wagon. In the beginning of the tour everything was fine. We're singing songs, "99 Bottles of Beer on the Wall" . . . and as the tour went on, the happiness sort of dropped because you're in a station wagon and you're driving six, seven hundred miles a day. You're tired, you're sick, you're getting paid nothing. People have never seen you, so when you first get up onstage the audience are throwing bottles and booing. So the tension is really heavy between the band. They would do things to me like they'd all sit in the back seat and take little pieces of cotton and stick them on top of my head. I'd be driving and I wouldn't even know . . . I'd end up with a Marie Antoinette thing and driving to some redneck gas station, "Hey, bud, fill it up." And they'd look at me and they'd [KISS] all laugh and hide in the back. So the tension got worse and worse. We all went to see *Deliverance*. We were down South and for these guys from New York, we're in hillbilly land. It was a real nice development with a house and eight acres of land, but to them it had to be hillbillies. I missed a turn and Ace starts poking me and telling me, "Remember where you're driving," and Peter starts poking me and I'm sitting there and all of the sudden I get an idea. I reached down and turned the ignition off, tapped the gas pedal to flood the engine and the car goes "Roomp, roomp" . . . I said, "Guys, oh my God, we're out of gas!" Here we are in a wooded area and they think *Deliverance*. They were scared to death! Here they are, four guys with tinted black hair and skulls all over, some casual daytime makeup, down in the South and they were panic-stricken! I tell them to get in the back of the station wagon and lay down. Then I cover them up with a blanket. So here's four sets of platform heels sticking straight up and a blanket. I get out and sit down and drink two or three beers. Twenty minutes later, I walk back over to the car and they're still lying under this blanket and I started to laugh hysterically. Peter would not speak to me for two solid weeks. Not a word! It's nice to get even.

SYLVAIN SYLVAIN, THE NEW YORK DOLLS:

The Dolls became popular really fast. We put on makeup to get girlfriends. KISS quickly found out that if you're a guy wearing makeup you get a lot of chicks. We used to play the Hotel Diplomat all the time, way before KISS. I remember the first time I saw KISS playing there, Peter Criss was sitting down with his mother in the back room and she was going, "Peter, why this! This is weird!" He was going, "No no, Ma, this is great! The New York Dolls did it. This is like the Dolls in a way. You saw how popular they got." We were in the fuckin' *Daily News* and KISS was asking how, "How did you guys get this press?" I've always said this over the years. There's no real comparison with KISS and the New York Dolls. If you're a schmuck sitting in Split Lip, Nevada, and you haven't been out of your cabin for a long fuckin' time, you would say, "Yeah, the New York Dolls and KISS, they both wear makeup." That's the only thing you could say. To me KISS always seemed like they were soul-searching. They really didn't know who the fuck they are. I thought their music was very very simple. The reason why I think they made it and we didn't is because it was an easier pill for America to fuckin' swallow. They didn't ask you to have sex with Frankenstein, the Dolls did. We went on tour with KISS. Some schmuck came up with the great idea of a "Glitter Rock" tour [laughs]. It was the New York Dolls as headliners, and the opening band would be either Aerosmith or Blue Öyster Cult. Then we started to add special guests, and KISS was one of our special guests. Here's a funny story that happened during the tour. We were really popular in the Midwest. Back in the very early '70s, if you were a rock band, no matter where you were people came up to you and asked you if you were Alice Cooper. They asked you for your Alice Cooper autograph, thinking any band with long hair and looks weird is Alice Cooper [laughs]. This is one of my lessons that I told Paul [Stanley]. I told him, "Paul, you're going to have to pay tribute to the king." And he said, "Sylvain, what the fuck are you talking about?" I said, "Alice Cooper is the king, no matter who you are, people are going to come up to you and ask you for your Alice Cooper autograph." So here we are in some airport lobby some-place and I'm hearing my name in the background, "Sylvain, Sylvain!" And it's Paul Stanley running to me, all out of breath, and I said, "What?! What happened?" And he said, "I signed my first Alice Cooper autograph!" [laughs] And I could have fuckin' peed my pants. The Dolls were an underground, subterranean, sleazoid rock band. America could bank on something like KISS but not on the Dolls. Every now and then one of them dies. To America, we were gay. We were drag queens. We were disgusting. We were diseased and drug addicts. Compared to KISS we were a lot more dangerous.

JOYCE BOGART: The group was playing the Midwest opening for Rory Gallagher, an artist they should not have been playing with but as I said we could not get them on tours. The club was enormous. It must have held three thousand kids and Neil had invited every DJ, promotion man, and distributor in the Midwest. It was the major promotion night of the tour. The group was intro'd as "From New York, KISS." The crowd booed (they don't like New York there), but by the second song the joint was rocking. They loved this group and all the Casablanca people were beaming at the reaction. They ended the set and the crowd thundered their need for an encore. A few minutes went by and nothing happened. Neil and I were getting nervous . . . a few more minutes the crowd is on the verge of taking the place apart as Neil screams to me over the din, "Where the hell is your group?" I fight my way through the beer-swilling, rowdy crowd to the backstage area and find the back doors open to the cold outside and Peter on the ground with the road manager trying to revive him. The ceiling in the club was very low. When the drum riser rose during "Black Diamond," all the smoke from the flash pots went to the top of the room causing Peter to fall in a dead faint backward ten feet down only to end up in the arms of a very alert and very strong road manager.

JOYCE BOGART: Neil and Larry Harris and I flew into St. Louis for a festival concert that KSHE, a radio station, was sponsoring. KISS had never played during the day outside in the sun and bright lights. As the day got hotter the makeup melted and the wind and sun obliterated the special fire effects and even made them dangerous to the band and the rest of us on the stage. But the worst thing was the way the stage was constructed. It seemed to be just boards over risers that were not tied down well and every time the group jumped [about every sixty seconds] the amps behind them would start to fall down. Neil and Larry Harris and I spent the whole concert holding up the amps. We couldn't hear for weeks. No more outdoor festivals.

ACE FREHLEY: I was sitting in my room at the Edgewater Hotel in Seattle with one of our road crew, John Harte. In the gift shop they sell these hooks, shrimp you can put on them, and fishing line. You can fish out your window. So I called up John Harte and said, "Do you want to watch the ball game together? Bring up a six-pack of beer." So he said, "All right, Curly." Right before we came I put three shrimp on this triple hook and threw it out about fifty feet. It was a hundred-foot line. I didn't want to hold it so I tied it on the chandelier above us where we were sitting. If the chandelier moved, we knew we had a bite. So me and John are having a beer and watching the ball game and the chandelier moved a little. I said, "Is that an earthquake or a bite?" [laughs] And he goes, "I think you're getting a bite." Then it fucking moved dramatically. So I quickly unhooked it and wrapped it around my hand three or four times and all of a sudden I was tugging on this fucking thing and it was beating me. So I said, "John, I can't handle this," and he grabbed it out of my hand. And John couldn't bring it in. Then we looked out the window and we saw like a fucking great white [laughs]. That thing must have been twelve, fifteen feet long. So we just let it go. There was no way we would be able to pull it up. Those fucking things weigh a ton. I thought I was gonna catch a twelve-inch fish and I end up catching a fucking great white [laughs].

DON BREWER, GRAND FUNK RAILROAD:

KISS brought the arena rock show to the max. KISS were big fans of Grand Funk because we were an arena rock band. As we went through the years, bands like KISS started refining the show. When KISS came along they would say, "It's not just about music, it's a show too."

PETER CRISS: I used to put eggs in Gene's boots and when he'd go put them on he'd look at me and say, "You son of a bitch, Peter!" We would make fun of each other, which was so healthy. Then the last five minutes before we went on, no one was allowed in the dressing room because that was our time for meditating. We'd all grab each other's hands and say, "Let's kick ass!"

EDDIE KRAMER: We were recording the *Alive!* album and the club owner was a real gonif, a real crook. We were in this fifteen-hundred-seat place right on the boardwalk and it was the middle of the afternoon and there was no fucking PA. I said, "Where's the PA?" They sent out two of their bodyguards and they stole scaffolding from a local building site and brought it in there to put the speaker monitors up. Then when we were all ready to go, and the crowd was going absolutely bananas, everyone was in the dressing room with Bill Aucoin and this owner. And Bill Aucoin would not let the band out onstage until this guy paid him in cash. He said, "Look, if you don't pay me in cash I'm gonna cancel the show and this whole hall will be torn down by the kids." And he paid him [laughs].

PAUL STANLEY: I remember coming into my room and the lights were off, which was really strange because I hadn't turned the lights off. I put the lights on when I first walked into the room. Then I went into the living room and turned on the light. I went into the bedroom and also turned on the light, which was also dark and there was some girl under the covers. It almost gave me a heart attack. Maybe under other circumstances I would have asked her to stay but it threw me so [laughs] I yelled, "Get Out!" There's also been girls getting in on food carts and stuff like that. Room service, that kind of thing.

JULIAN LENNON:

One of the first albums I ever bought in America was KISS *Alive!* I listened to that nonstop way back then. When you saw this whole act that was going on with the flames and the blood and the enormity of it, it was impressive.

BILLY MILLER (KISS ROAD MANAGER): KISS were amazing onstage. They could be literally fighting like cats and dogs, they could be ripping each other's fucking hair out and the time they were onstage they were the most professional, consummate in-sync band I've ever worked with. They were so concerned with the fans and the level of production, the idea of how to produce a better show and give everyone their money's worth. There wasn't a better show on earth.

ACE FREHLEY: Anaheim Stadium, 1976, was a real media event. When we walked down the stairs Gene fell down the stairs [laughs]. He couldn't help it, there was too much fog.

ROD ARGENT:

We [Argent] were playing in the States in the '70s and I was idling about onstage waiting for the opening act to appear. Suddenly these guys swept by who looked about twelve feet tall, on the highest platform heels I'd ever seen. A drum riser appeared being lifted by a forklift truck, and there was the sound of explosions as rockets were set off. And this was the opening act! I thought, how are we going to follow that? KISS were outrageous and effective and I knew something had to happen with them. Incidentally, I thought that years later they turned in a great version of Argent's "God Gave Rock and Roll to You."

PETER CRISS: I decked Ace once while we were on tour. The story is we played a hockey arena in Canada and it was so hot. It was so hot, hotter than hell, and Ace sat down on the stage because he was so exhausted. Now I didn't take that for granted at that point, today I would. But I took it like, "You lazy son of a bitch, how dare you sit down while I'm banging my brains out back here with two little fans on me. You're sitting down while Paul and Gene are running back and forth." So on the encore when we went back to the dressing room, Ace sat down and he was breathing hard. I was sweaty and I said, "You fucking lazy motherfucker, you better go out on this fucking encore and kick ass." And he grabbed a big bottle of orange juice and threw it at me and it smashed in the wall behind me. I went "Shit! You fuck!" And I got up and punched him and knocked him right out. They revived him, he got up and the fans were still screaming. I said, "I'm sorry, Ace," and he said [imitates Ace's voice], "No, I'm sorry too. You've got one fucking right, man! You almost broke my fucking jaw." I could have kicked all their asses, I was a badass. I was a real street fighter. We also had a lot of food fights too. Food fights were my favorites [laughs]. I would always be the first to throw the rolls. On that night of the fight, Ace put his arm around me and said, "Hey listen, man, let's ride back together in the limo to the Learjet. Let's party and make up." We drank four or five bottles of champagne and ever since then that made us the tightest it ever made us.

DAVE DAVIES, THE KINKS:

KISS were like the *Rocky Horror Picture Show* come to life.

BILL AUCOIN: "He She" was Ace and Peter's nickname for Paul. Paul used to love to get dressed in drag. He used to get the guys dressed in drag every once in a while. One day we're on tour in Kansas City and Grace Slick was on the road because she was gonna marry our lighting guy. And so they know I'm coming. I'm walking up to the arena and I see someone run in. And I'm saying, "He saw me run in. They're planning something. I can smell it a mile away." You have to imagine this. Paul went out and bought dresses for all the guys, stockings, high heels, the whole number. I walk in the door and they're all in drag with Grace Slick up front [laughs]. I was too shocked. I was on the floor. Then they started running after me because I know they wanted to get me in drag. I just flew but I couldn't believe it. You can't imagine seeing Grace Slick out there pretending to sing with KISS doing doo-wops in back of her. It was hysterical.

RAY MANZAREK, THE DOORS:

They're the rock/wrestling connection. If you like wrestling, you're gonna love KISS.

JAAN UHELSZKI (*CREEM* WRITER): Strangely enough, I was the only person to have played onstage with KISS. It started off as a joke. In 1975, I wrote a story on KISS for *Creem* called "I Dreamed I Was Onstage with KISS in My Maidenform Bra." One night I was sitting around with Connie Kramer, the associate publisher, and we ruminated about dressing up like KISS. "How funny it would be if I dressed up like KISS and no one would know the difference." I said, "You know what, I'm going to see if they'll go for it." I called Larry Harris, their record promotion guy who initially introduced us to them, and I told him I wanted to perform with them and write a story from the perspective as one of KISS. It was a George Plimpton kind of thing, participatory journalism. I was surprised when he agreed. The only stipulation was I couldn't call them a glam band. As if they were! After they agreed I had this sinking feeling—now I really had to go through with it. I'm not shy but I never had any desire or inclination to be a singer or a musician. Just to prove that all rock writers really aren't frustrated rock stars. For me, it was the thrill of the story. When the day finally arrived for me to do the story, I went down to KISS's sound check at Cobo Hall. Once I got there, I realized that the band had no idea that I was going to go onstage with them— their record company and management hadn't bothered to tell them. When I explained my intention to perform with them, they thought I was kidding. Finally we got it all straightened out, and I went home and packed a bag with six-inch-high platform heels, a pair of dancer's tights, a leotard, and some rather Gothic-looking jewelry, and met the band at the airport the next morning. Much to my dismay we took a small private plane with the band to Johnstown, Pennsylvania, where they were performing. It was incredibly bumpy and I spent the ride in a state of hysteria—but all that turbulence did manage to distract me. I hadn't even begun to worry about my performance at that point, although it was less than twelve hours away. Johnstown was a coal-mining city. There had been an awful flood there years and years ago, and the city was scarred by that. It had a rather dark, doomsday kind of vibe. But it didn't seem to bother the band, they were seasoned travelers by 1975, and the cities had begun to blur. Once we were checked in, they began giving me advice about being onstage—like a frustrated flock of stage mothers. "Don't look at the audience," Ace advised as we had lunch. "Remember, wear your guitar really low, it's sexier that way," Paul reminded me, as if I knew. And on and on, until it was too much to remember, and began making me more nervous instead of less. The oddest part of the entire experience was being made up. It was absolutely hilarious and strangely revealing to me. They had tacitly agreed that they didn't want just one of them making me up. I had to have a combination of each of their makeup insignias. I remember Paul hissing to Gene, "Don't make her up to look just like you." Ace didn't pull any punches, then or now, and blurted out, "God, Jaan, you don't know anything about makeup!" This was the '70s and nobody really wore makeup. It was a more, how you say, natural time, except for KISS of course. As a reporter, the good part for me was that KISS weren't inhibited about having someone there observing them. This seemed like some logical extension of the joke of their very existence, taking it one step further. By the time showtime came around I was almost paralyzed with fear. Their manager, Bill Aucoin, watched me like a hawk, so I wouldn't bolt, calmly attempting to talk me down. When the crucial moment came—at the first strains of "Rock and Roll All Nite"—he actually pushed me onstage. "Get out there." I think I just couldn't get over how absurd it all was, I remember thinking. "My God, I was dressed up like them," except I think I looked more like Cat Woman. It was bizarre. I sang on the choruses of "Rock and Roll All Nite," and as a result learned an important lesson about rock stars. Once you're out there you totally understand what it's all about. There's a surge of power and adrenaline that's intoxicating. When you're out there in front of a screaming crowd, there is no fear. All I remember thinking is I didn't want it to stop. I think that experience has impacted everything I've written afterward because I know what it's like to live, if only for five minutes, on the other side. It was an amazing thing for me. I definitely have much more empathy and much more of an understanding of musicians and that thrill, and how hard it is to give up that surge of power you get every night. You understand what it was like to stand in front of people. It was not a huge crowd that I played in front of, probably about six thousand people. But I felt a sense of raw power. It was a galvanizing, out-of-body force, making me become much more than myself.

JONATHAN CAIN, JOURNEY:

KISS had flair, it was almost Broadway rock. They brought a sense of party to the stage and theater and good time rock 'n' roll in a spectacle sort of way. Much like Journey was obsessed with giving the people the best show they could give 'em.

PAUL CHAVARRIA (KISS ROADIE, 1974–1979): There was a night Gene accidentally made me catch on fire. We were in Oklahoma City. Gene came over, took the liquid from me, and I gave him the torch so he could breathe fire. I always had more wet towels than you could ever imagine. I was so alert, always wanting to be there in case Gene caught himself on fire. That night was bad. He didn't spew everything out like he normally did. He goes and blows the fire and the flames just went all over him, his face and his hair. The flame backed up and started burning him. I went flying out and threw this towel over him to put the fire out. He spewed the rest of the stuff and it hit my jeans and they burst into flames immediately. I'm putting him out and I'm on fire [laughs]. There's these safety commercials that say, "When you're on fire, roll." When it's happening to you, you don't think about that, you're standing on a stage and you're burning. I put him out and I take off running and jump off the stage. And these two firemen, one pushes me down and the other fire-extinguishes the hell out of me. I run back to my side of the stage and Gene comes back at the end of the song and I go, "Are you okay?" And he goes, "No thanks to you, you asshole! Where the hell were you?" After the show, I go back in the dressing room and pull my jeans down and show him the burn marks right at the thigh where the rivets in the jeans had burned into my skin. I said to him, "See, see! I was there!" There are so many people in the music that went to universities and schools. With us, we basically learned everything at one of the greatest universities in the world. It was called KISS U. You went there and you learned everything about rock theater. You could learn about sound, lighting, staging, logistics.

FRANK DIMINO, ANGEL (KISS'S LABEL MATES ON CASABLANCA RECORDS):

KISS took visuals to a new dimension. People ultimately want to be entertained and KISS really delivered a great show. When Angel came up with the idea of wearing all white, I don't remember anyone saying, "Wow, that's a great idea, KISS is in black and you're in white." We were throwing ideas around, it was the band, our manager, David Joseph, and Neil [Bogart]. There was no conscious effort on our part to be the opposite of KISS.

GEORGE SEWITT (KISS ROAD MANAGER): We were playing on the grounds of the Vatican in Rome. We were doing this effect where Gene would fly through the air during the show. We had this guy whose sole job was to hook up this contraption and make Gene fly. We had rehearsals and ironed out all the bugs. When we got to Italy we didn't realize there was a difference in electricity. Because of the difference in electricity this guy had to give this knob to control Gene more power. Gene soared above the stage and was supposed to land gently on this platform by the lighting truss. Instead he went crashing into it. Gene was backstage going "You motherfucker!" Just screaming and going crazy because he almost got killed.

PETER CRISS: It's important to separate the onstage Peter from the person I am offstage. If I started believing I'm a legend I'll go nuts. Gene and Paul are very close and Ace and I hang out together. We both grew up on the streets and we both like to drink. In the early days Ace and I were always wrecking hotel rooms and throwing TV sets out the window. We'd buy BB guns and shoot up the rooms. We're both wacko, we're dangerous.

BILL AUCOIN: Once Ace was mad at Gene and Paul and pretended like he was drunk. And I get a call from Paul or Gene and they say, "You've got to come out here right away, Bill. Ace won't make the show tonight, he's drunk and we had to carry him into the hotel." So I get on the plane and I fly out somewhere in the Midwest. They showed up at the airport in a limousine saying, "What are we going to do? We're gonna lose all this money and we have to do this show tonight. He's never gonna get it together. He's out of his mind." I said, "Let me go out and see him." So I go up [laughs] and I knock on the door. [imitates Ace's voice] "Who is it?" "It's Bill." "Oh, Bill." He comes to the door and he says, "I got 'em today, Bill, I got 'em today." So I sat up there drinking some beers with Ace knowing that Ace had just done them in. So they come to the door and Ace says, "I'll show up for sound check but don't tell them." So they came to the door and Ace laid on the bed with his tongue sticking out and I said, "I think he might make it." They actually got me to fly out and Ace is up in his room having a couple of beers laughing his head off.

BILLY MILLER: There was a night when Gene's hair caught on fire. There was one night when he got scared and swallowed some of the stuff and we had to give him ipecac to help him vomit. He looked like the chick from *The Exorcist*. One night there was no ipecac and Gene went berserk. You had a guy that was playing for twenty thousand people, he goes back, gets the torch, gets set to blow fire and looks around and is thinking, "Where's the ipecac?" People tried to pull shit over on him and he knew. Those people weren't around too long.

BILLY MILLER: Ace would go to hobby shops and buy crossbows. He would shoot the fucking things and scare the piss out of people. He would shoot holes through all the artwork in the hotels. We were walking from the hotel lobby into a vestibule where Ace was and a fucking arrow came by. It missed my nose by three inches.

 ## LITTLE STEVEN:

I didn't take KISS particularly seriously when they started. It was sort of a cartoon. I saw them for the first time on their reunion tour and I was really really shocked. It was one great song after the next, nothing but terrific songs. It was a great, great show. It's funny how you get a different perspective through the years. Even though KISS's whole dressing-up thing was a gimmick, musically, they're just a terrific rock 'n' roll band.

PETER CRISS: We were doing this big show at this big hall and Paul said, "Hey, let's have some fun. Let's get out of the car in drag." And we did it. Paul went out with a bodyguard to a J.C. Penney's and he bought all the women's outfits [laughs]. He was very good at it by the way. He picked out matching outfits with hats, wigs, and dresses and bras and nylons and high heels and matching bags, earrings [laughs]. It was the whole fucking nine yards. We did it to surprise Bill and to freak out the press. Here we pulled in and the doors opened and Gene put his long leg out first with a high heel like a chick [laughing] and it was great, they were blown. I forgot about all that. That was actually very cool. Then we all started coming out shaking our asses and we all had tissue paper padded in our bras. It was a wonderful idea of Paul's.

 ACE IN THE OZONE, ARROWHEAD POND OF ANAHEIM, ANAHEIM,
CALIFORNIA, MARCH 18, 2000

(Photo by Terri Sharp)

PETER CRISS: I would wreck my room a lot on the road. It took a lot to calm me down. It was a bitch because I do suffer from hypertension ever since I was a kid. I've been on Valium all my life because of that. And with that and the adrenaline, Jesus Christ, I was a mental case. To get me in my room and close the door and all of a sudden it was quiet and I'm looking in the mirror and my makeup is kind of dripping off, I'm just ready to like eat the wall and bite the frigging TV. I got the makeup off and I would stay in the shower for like an hour to just try and calm down. I would come out and order up a couple of beers or so and then the chicks of course. There was always a room where we had all the girls waiting for us. So you bag a babe and you bring her back to your room and you ball her and then if you don't like her you get another one or take a bunch of them and ball them all. So that's what we kind of did. Whoever we were getting was getting great screws because we were really jacked up.

TONI TENNILLE, CAPTAIN & TENNILLE:

I loved KISS [laughs]. Neil Bogart invited us to one of their shows in L.A. and I just thought it was a hoot! The music was actually very good. It was beautifully produced, the sound was great, and I thought the guys were funny. I appreciated and understood what they were doing, it was theater.

JOHN HARTE (SECURITY): Once Peter showed up at the airport in his pajamas. That's because of George Sewitt and I. We said, "You're gonna make this plane or else!" So he left his pajamas on and we carried his big pillows and put him on the plane.

PETER CRISS: It was dirty of us but we just wanted to get Gene high [laughs] and so did the crew. It was the last show and it was my birthday. It was my twenty-ninth birthday, in Detroit at the Palace. Someone made hash brownies, and we said, "Fuck it, let him eat 'em." And he ate 'em. He called me up and the conversation on the phone was just, wow!

KIM FOWLEY (KISS COLLABORATOR):

KISS is as American as apple pie, Robin Hood, or any fable from a thousand years ago. It's mythology for teenagers.

SHOUT IT OUT LOUD

★★★★★

BY KEN SHARP

SECTION

03

From Gene's and Paul's formative years with Wicked Lester to 1998's reunion CD, *psycho circus,* the book's final section, "shout it out loud," provides an exhaustive examination of KISS's musical output. For the very first time, their musical saga is told exclusively through the eyes of the people that made it happen in the first place—KISS, their producers, engineers, songwriting collaborators, musical sidemen, management, record company personnel, and more.

SHOUT IT OUT LOUD:
ALBUM BY ALBUM, SONG BY SONG

Chapter **17**

WICKED LESTER

GENE SIMMONS–lead vocals, bass / PAUL STANLEY–lead vocals, rhythm guitar
BROOKE OSTRANDER–keyboards / TONY ZARRELLA–drums / STEVE CORONEL–lead guitar
RON JOHNSEN–producer / LEW LINET–manager / BARRY MANN–songwriter
TOM WERMAN–Epic Records A&R

RAINBOW/WICKED LESTER ORIGINS

BROOKE OSTRANDER: I met Gene through Larry DiMarzio. They went to school together in Staten Island. I was playing with Larry in Queens with a cover band, Gas, Food and Lodging. Larry told me that he was going to introduce me to this guy who had written a bunch of original material. So he brought Gene out to meet me. Gene and I very much connected in terms of what we wanted to do. That was our initial contact. Then a month later, I finished playing with the cover band. That ran its course for me. Gene was going to school at Staten Island Community College. This was in December 1969, January 1970. Gene had a bunch of songs that he wanted to record. I had figured out how to overdub back in those days, channeling back and forth from one tape machine to the next. Gene sang, played bass and some guitar. Paul McCartney was his hero. He loved the way Paul wrote and played bass. Mitchell Eisenberg, one

electric lady studios
52 west 8 street new york city ny 10011 212 777-0150

CLIENT: EPIC		REEL NO.		W.O.#			
ARTIST: WICKED LESTER		TAPE NO.		MASTER:		30 I.P.S.	NAB
PRODUCER: RON JOHNSEN		STUDIO A ☐ REMIX A ☐		COPY ☒		15 I.P.S.	IEC
ENGINEER: RALPH MOSS		STUDIO B ☒ REMIX B ☐		DOLBY:		7½ I.P.S. ☒	CCIR
DATE: OCT. 5, 1972							

24 TR ☐	16 TR ☐	12 TR ☐	8 TR ☐	4 TR ☐	2 TR ☒	MONO ☐

TAKE	START	STOP	TITLE	COMMENTS	EDITS
			"LOVE HER ALL I CAN"	PLAYED THROUGH DOLBY	
Gene Simmons - Bass			"SIMPLE TYPE"	IN RECORDING.	
Tony Zarrella - Drums			"SHE"	- STEREO -	
Paul Stanley - Rhythm			"TOO MANY MONDAYS" (BARRY MANN)		
Ron Leyend - Lead			"WHAT HAPPENS IN THE DARKNESS" (FAMOUS MUSIC INC)		
Brook Ostrender Keys			"KEEP ME WAITING"		
			"MOLLY"		
			"WHEN THE BELL RINGS" (FAMOUS MUSIC INC)		
			"SWEET OPHELIA" (BARRY MANN)		
			"WE WANT TO SHOUT IT OUT LOUD" HOLLYS		
			* PLEASE RETURN TO TAPE FILE AFTER USE.		

WICKED LESTER REEL-TO-REEL TAPE BOX
(courtesy of Tony Zarrella)

of my students, came in and played a few lead guitar parts. I played keyboards. Gene and I put together various songs that he wanted to record. One was a real up-tempo country song called "About Her." Another one was called "Amen Corner." We also recorded "Stanley the Parrot." That's Gene on lead guitar and Joe Davidson on drums. So for four or five months Gene and I made these tapes and Gene shopped them around. The labels recommended we come back when we got a band together. So Gene found Paul, who was Stan Eisen at that point. I brought in drummer Joe Davidson and then we were a foursome. Then Gene contacted his friend Steve Coronel, who played lead guitar, and we were now a five-piece. Then Joe left and I brought in Tony Zarrella as the drummer.

TONY ZARRELLA: I did the audition in a loft on Canal Street. The band liked my double-bass drum set. We hit it off well. We played a little of everything; we did original material and some cover tunes. Paul always liked "Locomotive Breath" by Jethro Tull so we played that. By the time the group played live we were pretty much doing all our own material. After the audition, I had planned to move to California. The trip was canceled and I called the group and asked them if they still needed a drummer. They said yes. I went back to play with them again and they decided to ask me to join.

STEVE CORONEL: The group was first called Rainbow, that lasted awhile and then we changed the name to Wicked Lester.

GENE SIMMONS: Paul came up with the name Wicked Lester.

BROOKE OSTRANDER: I think Steve came up with the Wicked Lester logo.

STEVE CORONEL: We used to rehearse on the corner of Mott and Canal streets, upstairs from the Norman Watch company. This sculptor had the place. He told us we could rehearse there in the evenings when he was done sculpting. The driving force behind Wicked Lester was to sound like a good, clean rock band. There was no complicated direction. The idea was to bring in all of our favorite influences, Free, Buffalo Springfield, the Move, and the Beatles and marry them all into a direction based on these new songs. It was a big mix. It needed more development, it needed more song-writing work. The problem with Wicked Lester was when you can't hear the band rehearsing, how can you work on a song and decide what direction it's going in? You can't hear any nuances if it's too loud. I always used to tell them, "Why don't you turn it down?" Stanley and I would drink a little bit. Gene would never drink. We used to get Boone's Farm apple wine, Ripple, and Night Train. We tried all the bum's stuff. We wanted to really be nitty-gritty. In the winter it was so cold up there, and we were experimenting with alcohol. We were eighteen, nineteen years old.

BROOKE OSTRANDER: We got our loft in New York in the summer of 1970. The loft was located in Chinatown on Canal Street. It was a fifth-floor walk-up. It was me, Gene, Stan, Steve, and Tony in the group at that point. Tony's a cousin of my best friend's girlfriend.

RAINBOW/WICKED LESTER LIVE SHOWS

BROOKE OSTRANDER: Rainbow's first gig was in Staten Island at Richmond College in May of '71. Gene managed to get the gig through somebody he knew at the college. They advertised us as the entertainment.

PAUL STANLEY: There was literally nobody at our first gig as Wicked Lester. The small armory we played may have held five hundred people, it doesn't mean they're going to show up. The place was literally empty. I don't know if there was ten people there. It was pouring out and the only thing that made that gig memorable for me was I caught the crabs in the bathroom. Safe to say, nobody ever came to see us [laughs]. The only time there was ever anybody to see Wicked Lester at a gig [laughs] was because there was something else going on. There was no buzz about us.

BROOKE OSTRANDER: We played three sets. We didn't do any covers that night. We had decided we were at a point where we wanted to see what people thought of our original material. I have a tape of that gig. [Author's note: According to Ostrander, the complete set list featured the following songs in order: "Goin' Blind," "About Her," "Love Her All I Can," "Keep Me Waiting," "Suitor," "First Time Around," "Eskimo Sun," "Stanley the Parrot," "It's a Wonder," "Movin' On," "Sweet Flora," "Sunday Driver," "When I Awoke," "Let's All Fly Away," "She," "Simple Type," "I Am a New Man," and "She Goes."] Paul spoke to the audience with a Cockney accent. I don't remember why [laughs]. As far as being a front man, Paul was the best suited for that out of the group.

GENE SIMMONS: The second gig we played was for a B'nai Brith event in Atlantic City. We did some cover songs because there were thirteen-year old girls who could care less about how creative we were. We did "Locomotive Breath," Rock Me Baby" by the Jeff Beck Group. We did "Jumpin' Jack Flash," which I didn't play well because I never bothered to learn it.

BROOKE OSTRANDER: Rainbow didn't do many gigs. We played the prom at McManus Junior High in Linden, New Jersey. I taught there. I was the band director. The gig went great. I told the kids who were getting the groups together that we did original material. It wasn't going to be a Top 40 band. In the summer of '71, we played a big youth convention down in Atlantic City. After playing at that convention, we decided we should start doing some cover tunes. We worked on a couple. We did some Jethro Tull tunes, a couple of Moody Blues tunes, a couple of Stones tunes. We ended up doing one set of cover tunes, which we interspersed throughout the night when people started bugging us, "Why don't you do something we know?" We got a dozen cover tunes together just to play for people when they wanted to hear something familiar.

STEVE CORONEL: We hardly played live at all. We were concentrating on writing songs and rehearsing. We wanted to get tight. None of us wanted to play out. We have to kill them when we play, we can't just be half-assed. We gotta be great. We did a couple of covers. We used to do "All Right Now" by Free. Stanley and I used to love that and we did "Rock and Roll Woman" by Buffalo Springfield.

PAUL STANLEY: I remember playing "When You Dance" by Neil Young live with Wicked Lester.

BROOKE OSTRANDER: We did another gig down the Jersey shore at the Osprey. It was this huge club in Manasquan, New Jersey, which was located on the boardwalk. The band was still called Rainbow at that time. It didn't become Wicked Lester until we were in the studio. Once we got into the studio, we started doing some research to find out if we could continue to use this name. And that's when we found out there was another band who had the name Rainbow.

WICKED LESTER LIVE, NEW YORK, 1971. LEFT TO RIGHT: PAUL STANLEY AND KEYBOARDIST BROOKE OSTRANDER
(© KISS Catalog Ltd.)

GENE SIMMONS: The third gig we played was in South Fallsburg, New York, at the Rivoli Theater. There was a bridge connecting one section to another and under the bridge were these falls and you could dive off into this little pool of water that became the river. There were these rocks under the bridge. While people were swimming we set up the amplifiers foolishly and started to play there outside. It didn't sound very good. Then I arranged for us to play at a movie theater right outside of South Fallsburg. People had come to see a movie but before they saw the movie they got to hear us. There are photos of that show in the *KISStory* book that were taken by my then girlfriend, Nancy.

PAUL STANLEY: We had all the amplifiers laying flat on the stage so people could watch the movie. Then at midnight when the movie was over we picked up all the amps and played for whoever was there. There may have been forty people there. I just remember I was real tired and ready to go to sleep.

TONY ZARRELLA: Wicked Lester toyed with "Firehouse," which later appeared on KISS's first album. It was written and developed during the Wicked Lester days. I remember playing songs live that were never recorded by the band like "Eskimo Sun," "About Her," and "Suitor."

WICKED LESTER RECORD DEAL

TONY ZARRELLA: It was still called Rainbow when we signed our artist management agreement on July 1, 1972. Stanley Snadowsky was our first manager and attorney. He owned a club and was dealing with us on a managerial/attorney level so there was a conflict of interest. That's when Lew Linet came into the picture.

LEW LINET: Ron Johnsen called and said that he had a group that sounded like Three Dog Night. He asked if I would be interested in hearing them. I listened to their tape and I didn't care for it. Three or four months later, Ron calls again and says the guys have somebody new in the band and asked if I would listen to some more material. So I listened again and I liked the material very much and I became their manager. Gene and Stanley stood out as leaders of the band. They were very young and were very eager to become stars. There was no real image. It was just a band with five different guys, a couple of them had long hair and long beards. Stanley and Gene were not like that; they had more of a British feel. The music was singer-songwriter, folk rock songs with a little bit of an edge.

RON JOHNSEN: Paul and Gene looked like they had a lot of potential magic between them. The other kids in the band were pretty naive although Brooke was an excellent musician.

BROOKE OSTRANDER: In the summer, Wicked Lester was splitting the bill at the Village Gate with Harry Chapin. We were showcasing for Elektra Records. Harry got the deal with Elektra and we didn't. We did a couple of auditions at Electric Lady. We later got a deal with Metromedia Records. We started recording an album for the label and then the deal fell through. Ron Johnsen said there was some kind of A&R squabble going on at the label and they ended up dumping whatever had been picked up in the previous two months. Shortly thereafter, Wicked Lester got a deal with Epic. Tom Werman took over as the liaison between the label and the studio. Ron [Johnsen] was independently producing us through the auspices of Electric Lady.

RON JOHNSEN: Mike Jeffries needed an act signed to Polydor to fulfill his contract. I had met Paul and Gene and heard Wicked Lester and got involved. I recorded a few songs with them at Electric Lady Studios, "When the Bell Rings" and "(What Happens) In the Darkness." I gave the tape to Jeffries, who ran up to Polydor to see if he could get them a deal. They said no. I went back into the studio with them and polished the songs up a bit more and recorded some new ones too. It came out good, they sounded pretty decent. Then I gave the tape to Billy Michelle at Famous Music and he took it over to Epic Records.

LEW LINET: Ron Johnsen had started negotiations with Don Ellis at Epic but the deal was not proceeding. There was a great deal of confusion because Ron was primarily into publishing and producing. So I took over at that point and got in touch with Don Ellis. I went in with some demo tapes and made the deal. The guys got paid a very nice advance of $20,000 and they got that cash up-front.

GENE SIMMONS: It was Epic who said they would like to buy the Wicked Lester record. We went into CBS Studios to showcase for the executives at CBS Studios, who said, "You have to get rid of your guitar player, Steven Coronel. You need another guitar player."

STEVE CORONEL: The record company didn't like me. I think it was that damn song, "Love Her All I Can." I couldn't play the lead break on that song because I never heard the song [laughs]. Now I'm playing it in the showcase and I think I fucked it up. We did the showcase in this really old, miserable-looking place. I think we played about four or five songs. Maybe the record company guys didn't like the way I looked. They figured this guy doesn't look right and these guys looked like they belonged together more. I don't look like Donny Osmond, let's face it. These guys were looking at us with a fine-tooth comb and they didn't like the way I looked, I can't fault them for that. I would have done the same thing. About three weeks after the showcase, Gene came over my apartment and said, "Look, I think we're gonna split up and go in different directions. We're gonna disband the band because it's not working, We're not getting any deals out of it." I was a bit hurt and shocked by it. But on the other hand, I was learning Yes songs and I loved the songs they were doing. So I figured this was fine, I'll start my own band and play what I wanna play. But they did stay together, unbeknownst to me.

RON JOHNSEN: Steve [Coronel] didn't have a lot of strong ideas for songs he didn't write. Ron Leejack was very good at cutting leads so we put him on as many songs as we could. I think we paid him as a session man, he was not officially a member. But he put the cherry on the whipped cream.

BROOKE OSTRANDER: I don't know what Epic found objectionable because I liked Steve [Coronel] a lot. I thought he was very unique. He had a definite style of his own. But we had to make a decision at that point whether or not we take the deal and get another guitar player or forget that deal and try and continue as the same group. We came to the conclusion that we'd rather take the deal. So at that point we had to come up with another guitar player and we found Ron Leejack.

RON LEEJACK: The A&R man for Epic, Tom Werman, came down to a showcase. I had my amp set up where I thought he'd be sitting. Luckily it was where he was sitting and we played for him. He went berserk. He loved it. As a guitar player, I'm not hot all the time but that day I was burning. Tom loved my playing and signed us to Epic.

TOM WERMAN: What attracted me to Wicked Lester was their harmonies. They were a straight pop group, a little lightweight. I liked the songs, some of the harmonies that KISS would later use showed up in Wicked Lester. "Sweet Ophelia" was great. I also liked "Too Many Mondays." I remember spending quite a few nights at Electric Lady when Wicked Lester were doing the record. That was my first real studio experience watching a record made.

RECORDING THE WICKED LESTER ALBUM

STEVE CORONEL: Neil Teeman was working part-time as an engineer at Electric Lady Studios and he knew Ron Johnsen. Ron was working there as an incumbent producer. So Neil hooked us up with Ron and we recorded an album. We had a great deal going there. They gave us spec time at Electric Lady. We were there for a period of months, whenever they'd have free studio time we'd get called in.

RON JOHNSEN: The album was done in the fall of 1971. I produced it and used two engineers, Ralph Moss and Bernie Kirsh. We struggled with each song. I would go into the studio with an idea and work from the bottom up. They had an idea of the chord structures and where the melodies were going and the overall arrangement. But I think Paul and Gene were as surprised as me by the final results. They had no idea of what I was gonna do. Paul was a solid rhythm guitarist, Gene played very good bass. Brooke was the real master musician. Tony was a decent drummer.

BROOKE OSTRANDER: The first demos were made to try and attract some attention. We recorded three songs live to a two-track, "Keep Me Waiting," "She," and "Simple Type." We ran back and did overdubs on vocals. We were all pretty much enamored by the way it sounded. We got about halfway through recording the album and the Metromedia deal fell through. Once we got the deal with Epic and had switched guitar players, Ron Johnsen started rerecording the lead guitar parts with Ronnie Leejack. He didn't like how Ron's guitar work sounded with the existing tracks so he decided he was going to scrap it and start all over again with Ronnie playing all the guitar stuff. We rerecorded a couple of the songs completely, "Love Her All I Can," "Keep Me Waiting," and "She."

BROOKE OSTRANDER: It was a fairly time-consuming project. We didn't go in on big blocks of time. There were times when we would be in the studio for four or five days in a row but mostly we would only be able to record for a couple of days, listen back, experiment, and remix. It was not a very streamlined process.

PAUL STANLEY: It took a year to record the Wicked Lester album. We were doing it all on spec time because nobody was paying for it. We were literally going into the studio when there was free time. Weeks could go by and then we might go in for two days or we might go in for thirty-six hours straight. Ron Johnsen brought in the outside material. I remember going to the Paramount building, which is now the Trump hotel on Columbus Circle. We went to Famous Music Publishing, Billy Michelle's office. Billy came up with songs that he wanted us to record and we would sit there and listen to things.

BROOKE OSTRANDER: Ron Johnsen had a friend named Billy Michelle at Famous Music, a publishing company. They sent Ron a bunch of demo records. Ron went through a bunch of them and picked out some. We had decided to do "Too Many Mondays" and "Sweet Ophelia." Barry Mann wrote "Too Many Mondays" and "Sweet Ophelia." And then he had these other songs that he wanted us to try. We ended up recording "(What Happens) In the Darkness," "When the Bell Rings" and "We Wanna Shout It Out Loud."

TONY ZARRELLA: Electric Lady was the premier studio where all the top stars wanted to record so therefore time was limited and it was only available sporadically, after hours, sometimes late in the evening. It was not unusual for us to walk out of the studio at five or six in the morning. We originally went into Electric Lady to rehearse prior to recording because we needed to get the songs into shape before laying them down. We'd do our basic tracks and a lot of overdubbing. It was very tedious because we didn't have that much blocked time. The song that stood out the most for me was "Long Road." It's a very interesting song. It had a little more depth and maturity than the other songs we recorded. Paul played harmonica, banjo, and guitar on that. Brooke played keyboards and tuba on it.

BROOKE OSTRANDER: While we were at Electric Lady, Stephen Stills was doing the *Manassas* album. Steve actually played a solo on "Sweet Ophelia." It didn't work out real great [laughs]. We kept it until Ron Leejack joined and then we compared Stills's solo with Ron's solo and we liked Ron's better. Jeff Beck was around. He was working with Stevie Wonder. Roberta Flack was around, John Mayall. We'd go in to watch their sessions and then they'd come in and watch our sessions.

TONY ZARRELLA: We used to hang outside the studio a lot and watch people. One day Gene coerced this girl who was always hanging around the studio and said, "Hey listen, we're a famous rock 'n' roll band, we're an up-and-coming group." She was very impressed and we invited her down to the studio. The next thing we know we're inside Studio A and she was sitting down in one of the large chairs and Gene was saying, "Well listen, what are you going to do for us?" She was in awe of everything. If you've ever been down in Electric Lady they had this big mural across the wall, three women sitting at the controls of a spaceship. It's very impressive. Gene said, "Why don't you take your clothes off?" And she said, "Oh, I'd love to." So she went into the vocal booth and everybody joined in. I was basically watching a lot. I think Gene was more vocal than anything else. I remember Ronnie Leejack coming out of the vocal booth going, "Gee, does anybody have a tape head cleaner or something?" [laughs] He was really concerned about catching a disease. Then Paul went in there with his vibrator doing his thing. It was a wild, fun experience.

WICKED LESTER ALBUM

Release date: canceled by Epic Records/three tracks released on *KISS: The Box Set*
PAUL STANLEY—lead vocals, rhythm guitar, banjo / GENE SIMMONS—lead vocals, bass
STEVE CORONEL—lead guitar / BROOKE OSTRANDER—keyboards, organ, flute, horns
RON LEEJACK—lead guitar / TONY ZARRELLA—drums
RON JOHNSEN—producer / BARRY MANN—songwriter

PAUL STANLEY: With Wicked Lester, we were at a point in our careers where we were happy to just go in and record. We were basically good boys. We did everything that the producer [Ron Johnsen] told us. The reason the record never came out is that Gene and I bought it back. It's pretty bad. It's not a good record by any stretch of the imagination plus it's bad for somebody to hear it and think that it's our ideas. I'd describe Wicked Lester as eclectic crap. "We Wanna Shout It Out Loud" was a Hollies tune, real English pop. "Too Many Mondays" was written by Barry Mann. Barry Mann wrote tons and tons of hits during the '60s. Carole King and Neil Sedaka and Barry Mann pretty much wrote everything that came out.

GENE SIMMONS: Eclectic is a fair description of the band because it's not just a collection of songs but whether the band has a real sense of who they are. It's almost like a fashion daisy, like one of these people that comes to clubs one day with green hair and one day with dreadlocks. Although it's interesting and creative, they lack an identity. The next day they show up with pancake makeup. Interesting is eclectic. It just doesn't have a backbone. Wicked Lester may be an interesting collection of songs but I don't get a backbone or identity from it.

PAUL STANLEY: When we were recording the Wicked Lester stuff, whatever was hip at the moment we put on. If a record came out with a wah-wah pedal, there was a wah-wah pedal. If somebody had a slide guitar, let's put a slide guitar. So some of those songs were unbelievable. There would be a horn part, then there's a slide guitar that comes in and banjos, some really weird stuff. I think it's pretty funny. It's not that I'm embarrassed by it. You let something pass for long enough and time goes by and you can kind of chuckle at it. I think it's kind of funny to hear an eighteen-year-old kid trying to sound like Tom Jones. I had a real smooth voice at that point and I wanted to sound real tough and husky. I mean, it's like a twelve-year old trying to sound like a blues singer. There is some pretty funny stuff on that record. You had to be there to really appreciate it. It was a period where we were happy to be in the recording studio and we would do anything anybody told us.

GENE SIMMONS: I'm embarrassed by that album. In fact, we bought that record after we finished it to prevent it from coming out because we just didn't think it was a very good record. From a KISS fan's point of view, it's, "Oh, it's obscure and vintage." But it didn't hold up to anything. It was as good as a Looking Glass LP but that's about it.

RON LEEJACK: I describe Wicked Lester as the Beach Boys on a bad acid trip. There was no real image to the band. I had a mustache and hair down to my waist. We all had long hair except for Brooke, I think he was going bald. He looked like a schoolteacher. Brooke was very talented, he could play every instrument. You hear the horns on there, the piano, flute, organ? That's him, very talented musically. He could write charts and read music, the other guys couldn't. Tony had a beard and looked like Yosemite Sam [laughs]. He looked like somebody you dug out of the ice.

GENE SIMMONS: Wicked Lester was a fine idea but it could just never go the distance. It looked like the U.N. You had one of everything, tall guys, short guys. It was a Mutt & Jeff kind of band.

BROOKE OSTRANDER: I thought there should have been more of our original material on the album than the cover tunes we did. I respected Ron Johnsen. He had an idea in his head how he thought this was going to work and be marketed. I kind of let go, thinking Ron's the producer and knows much more than we do about all of this. I do believe that the album was more musically sophisticated than the stuff KISS has done. We had the harmonies, we had the production. Some of that was Ron, some of that was us, and some of that was the material that we were using.

TONY ZARRELLA: Looking back, I have mixed feelings about the album. I felt the music was still in the developmental stages. I thought the songs were good but the band never reached its full potential. We didn't have enough time to develop our personality and style as a band.

★ "MOLLY" ★

PAUL STANLEY: I wanted to try writing one of those cutesy [Paul] McCartney songs where he's playing the guitar. "Molly" sounded like McCartney *Ram* era stuff. I played banjo on it, but the rest of the band wound up adding horns to it. I couldn't get those horns off my songs, they followed me like a shadow. We would basically do what we were told. There was an essence at the bottom of each of those songs that was where it started. What it grew into sometimes was not anybody's vision, certainly not mine. "Molly" having horns on it and answering background harmonies wasn't what the song was about.

RON JOHNSEN: "Molly" was a weird song, I don't know if anybody really wanted to do it. I added a giant horn section, some celeste, clavinet. I think the reason for some of the Beatle-esque influences is I'm a fan of the Beatles' producer, George Martin. I was inspired to create picturesque things with those songs. I think a lot of that came from listening to the Beatles.

BROOKE OSTRANDER: "Molly" was a song that Stanley wrote to bug Gene. Gene was trying to write something McCartneyish and Stan told him he could do it in a weekend and he wrote "Molly." It's a great little tune.

★ "KEEP ME WAITING" ★

PAUL STANLEY: "Keep Me Waiting" was a real cool song but I didn't think the band did a great version of it. But it was a good song when we played it live. "Keep Me Waiting" is closer to what I had in mind for Wicked Lester. Considering that there's nothing stellar in the batch of Wicked Lester songs and that I was seventeen years old, it's a lot to ask to have musical maturity. The Stevie Winwoods of the world don't come along very often [laughs]. When I write a song I have a pretty good idea of what I want it to sound like. Sometimes it gets way off track when everybody adds their two cents. You wind up with a lot of chiefs and no Indians. In Wicked Lester, we found horns on a lot of songs that I never quite understood. I never pictured "Keep Me Waiting" to have horns on it but there they were. I was not in a position to argue too much because quite honestly I was thankful to be in the studio. At that point, being in the studio was like kindergarten. There was so much to learn. I was more apt to listen and do what I was asked to do.

STEVE CORONEL: We used to play "Keep Me Waiting" live. That's a really nice song by Stanley. I even liked the way we played it. That was one of the few Wicked Lester songs that really had a good structure to it and you could hear it.

BROOKE OSTRANDER: That song and "Love Her All I Can" went over really well live.

RON JOHNSEN: On "Keep Me Waiting," there's a lot of experimentation in sounds, in the rhythms and certainly with the voices. I also threw in a gong in the middle section. We also used slide guitar on it. And on the ending of "Keep Me Waiting" Brooke played a flügelhorn.

★ "SWEET OPHELIA" ★

RON JOHNSEN: "Sweet Ophelia" was a study in something comical. I wanted it light and cute. It was a pretty funky track. Paul put a wah-wah guitar part on it. I think the song had a lot of visual appeal.

BARRY MANN: I wrote that with Gerry Goffin and recorded it on my album *Lay It Out,* which came out in the early '70s. When I heard the Wicked Lester version I thought it was very interesting, you would have no idea that this later became KISS. I think they gave the song a little bit more edge. There was less finesse, it was less manicured.

BROOKE OSTRANDER: Ron Johnsen was very tight with Barry Mann. Those songs made perfect sense plus Barry was one of the best songwriters in Tin Pan Alley at that point.

PAUL STANLEY: "Sweet Ophelia" was like a novelty track. I wasn't sold on every song on that album but when you're seventeen years old and you're dreaming of recording an album and you're doing it, you're happy for what you have.

STEVE CORONEL: "Sweet Ophelia" was a good song but not for us at all. We should have never been anywhere near it.

TONY ZARRELLA: I liked the rhythm section on that song. As a drummer, it was fun song to play.

★ "TOO MANY MONDAYS" ★

BROOKE OSTRANDER: I had more fun recording "Too Many Mondays" than any of the songs on the album. I just loved that song.

RON JOHNSEN: "Too Many Mondays" sounded like it could have been the single. It was one of my favorite songs because I always admired Barry Mann. I recorded all the demos he did for [Don] Kirshner, "Kicks," "We Gotta Get Out of This Place." Brooke played some really good piano in the break. Paul did all the lead work in that song with a slide. The ending has a bunch of countermelodies. And as the song was called "Too Many Mondays," I took the line from the Mamas and the Papas "Monday, Monday" and sort of went over and over on that on an instrumental basis.

BARRY MANN: I liked their version of "Too Many Mondays." It was less delicate than my approach. I wrote that with my wife, Cynthia [Weil], that song was on my *Lay It Out* album too. I've seen Paul Stanley since and I remember we talked about it, kind of laughed at it. He's a terrific guy, very together. I know Paul from way back.

PAUL STANLEY: About six months ago, Barry [Mann] and Cynthia [Weil] were over at my house for dinner and I sat down and played "Too Many Mondays" on an acoustic guitar. I said, "Remember this?"

★ "WHEN THE BELL RINGS" ★

BROOKE OSTRANDER: That song absolutely cooked when we had everything done but the vocals. Then we did the vocals and to me it was a letdown. I didn't like the lyrics because I thought they were too bubblegumish. But at the same time it was just one of those songs and it worked.

RON JOHNSEN: I did a lot of effect work on that. I may have gotten the switch off in vocals from Paul to Gene from the original demo [Author's note: written by Austin Roberts and Chris Welch]. When it came to the ending we modulated and it's a big kickoff, a real good fade ending.

STEVE CORONEL: I hated "When the Bell Rings." I hated all those songs that Ron Johnsen gave us, it was so off in the wrong direction that I couldn't believe it.

★ "SHE" ★

STEVE CORONEL: Ron Johnsen had to do something with his time. I take a very flippant look at people because you know what they are, "I've got to produce this thing, I've got to put horns on it, Jethro Tull's happening so let's make it sound like them with the flutes." Left to our own devices I don't think we would have ever done that. Also Brooke and the other guys had their own take on the music. When a band gets together, not everyone should be in the same band at the same time. Me being a guitar player, "She" would have turned out more the way that KISS wound up doing it. The Wicked Lester version of it is all lollipops and sugar, it didn't really sound like a heavy metal song.

BROOKE OSTRANDER: I had a really good time playing flute on "She." That's my Ian Anderson impersonation. But I wish that there had been a little more vocal variation on it.

RON JOHNSEN: "She" had a lot of dramatics to it. We kind of copied Jethro Tull with the flute. It was another weird song that had some complicated ideas for lyrics. Gene was trying to illustrate a girl running around who was a bad influence and she was no good. I told Gene that he ought to change the line from "She's no good" to "She's so good." And he said, "Wow, I never thought of that." I said, "You need to have a nice dirty sexy song." Gene had one of these juvenile little sexy minds, he got off on that.

★ "(WHAT HAPPENS) IN THE DARKNESS" ★

BROOKE OSTRANDER: It ended up sounding like a dance song. It ultimately preceded disco. Everything that we did was aimed at being danceable. We aimed at being a commercial Top 40 band, not an underground band.

STEVE CORONEL: Stanley came up with the slide guitar part for "(What Happens) In the Darkness." I was indignant. I said, "Hey, I'm the guitar player, I should be coming up with the part for this and you're already telling me what to play." The slide part did work and it sounded fine. So I begrudgingly learned the part.

RON JOHNSEN: Gene played an incredible bass line on that song. He did some very melodic patterns. It was a real tough song to record, we had a lot problems with it rhythmically. The playing was rushed. I had Paul play dobro on it, I sat it down in his lap and he played it bottleneck-style like a guitar. [Author's note: The song was written by Tamy Smith.]

★ "SIMPLE TYPE" ★

GENE SIMMONS: "Simple Type" started off as a song poem. It was written about guys who wanted to express their manhood through physicality, which is to say they were violent. I'd never physically been in a fight in my life and I never picked on anybody my size either. It always struck me as bizarre that usually the smaller guys barked loudest. The littlest dogs always go in packs. "Simple Type" addressed the issue of a guy, me in this case, [recites lyrics] "Walking down the street one day, celebrating Friday the 13th of May, then I met a simple type who wanted to fight . . ." I had these hippie-esque notions, "Can't you find a way, why do you have to keep on fighting this way?" It was first recorded by myself and Brooke Ostrander and then Wicked Lester recorded it. When KISS got together we played it at The Daisy. Then I forgot about the song, it just didn't feel right for KISS.

BROOKE OSTRANDER: "Simple Type" was one of the first songs we started working on. I got a kick out of that, I enjoyed it. It's very different. Gene was a very moody guy. On that song his dark-side philosophical moods came out. Gene and I had many discussions over the educated way versus the noneducated way in music. That was one of those songs where Gene did a bunch of things he wasn't supposed to do. That was one of the first times that I had to rethink my premise of music education.

STEVE CORONEL: [recites lyrics] "I was walking down the street one day . . ." What is that Israeli rock, Gene? Very early Gene, he was finding his direction.

RON JOHNSEN: We brought in Ronnie Leejack to do the leads and did a lot of vocal work on it.

★ "LOVE HER ALL I CAN" ★

BROOKE OSTRANDER: "Love Her All I Can" was Stan's. That was always our opener wherever we played live.

RON JOHNSEN: It was very danceable. The arrangement with the background vocals with Gene and Paul was basically a rhythmic idea with how the melody line was going. We did two- or three-part harmony. Every time we did a harmony we would double or triple it. It would end up with either six or nine voices on backgrounds.

STEVE CORONEL: That was a real good song. I had a real hard time playing the guitar break on it. There was a four-chord change there that I just couldn't figure out where to go with it. That was one of the reasons I wanted to play at a lower volume in the loft [laughs]. I don't think I had a tape of it that I could take home and practice on.

PAUL STANLEY: The way KISS recorded "Love Her All I Can" was the way it was written. What wound up on the Wicked Lester album was just weird. It sounded like the Swingle Singers. They did weird, jazzy tracks.

★ "WE WANNA SHOUT IT OUT LOUD" ★

GENE SIMMONS: It was a songwriting demo we heard that was written by Allan Clarke and Terry Sylvester of the Hollies. It was never released on a Hollies record.

TONY ZARRELLA: "We Wanna Shout It Out Loud" was similar to "Long Road" as far as style and content. It was a quality song, the production fit the track perfectly. It was our Beatles-sounding anthem.

RON JOHNSEN: I was very close to the people at Dick James Music because my attorney, Bob Casper, was representing that company. I got a copy of an album that had some songs on it that Dick James Music represented and I heard "We Wanna Shout It Out Loud." We had five copyrights of original Wicked Lester songs and the other five were a combination of Screen Gems, Famous Music, and Dick James Music. Our version of the song was very different from the Hollies' rendition, which was an acoustic folky type of version. Paul played some pseudo George Harrison sounding slide guitar at the end. The backgrounds were three different kinds of countermelodies. Brooke played two or three different horn parts. The fade ending was real cool, with a multiple of things adding and building.

★ "LONG ROAD" ★

PAUL STANLEY: "Long Road" was written by an English writing team. That's me playing harmonica. It was like, "What do you want? You want a wah-wah guitar? We'll bring one in. You want a banjo?"

WICKED LESTER ALBUM COVER

GENE SIMMONS: The album cover showed a New York street kid with a bazooka hat on and there's a dog taking a pee with his leg raised. The Wicked Lester album cover was later used in the late '70s for a group on Columbia Records called Laughing Dogs.

BROOKE OSTRANDER: The back cover photo was taken in this posh 79th Street apartment, near Riverside Drive. It was this huge apartment with a piano, and the urns and everything else.

TONY ZARRELLA: I remember the apartment had very high ceilings and a Victorian interior design.

BROOKE OSTRANDER: We were told to be dressed in a cool way. The photographer was there with all his stuff, umbrellas and lights. We did what he told us to do. He took a number of of Polaroid proofs and I think we all ended up with one of those.

PAUL STANLEY: The cover was done, it was my concept. It's a cool picture. The album was pretty much ready to go into production.

WICKED LESTER DISBAND

BROOKE OSTRANDER: Gene had a portfolio that he carried around and a journal. He had sketches of staging equipment. Gene became real fascinated with Alice Cooper and that's when he started getting into the makeup concept. He came back with sketch after sketch of this stuff. I loved the idea. I was sort of at odds with myself how to maintain my teaching status and become some kind of rock 'n' roll maniac. Gene came up with the idea of makeup and stage names. Stan wasn't initially too thrilled with that but he got into it fairly quickly. Ron didn't like it and Tony hated it. That was one of the contentions with the label because now Gene wanted to change the name of the band to KISS. The record company wasn't too thrilled with it.

BROOKE OSTRANDER: The Wicked Lester album wasn't released for a variety of reasons. One, we ended up coming back to practice at the loft one night—this was in the fall of 1972—and all of our equipment was stolen. They had emptied it out. Everything was stolen, guitars, bass, keyboards, amplifiers, drums, speaker cabinets, mixing cabinets. Somebody literally came in at night and loaded all that stuff out of there. So we had no equipment.

TONY ZARRELLA: I remember going up to the loft with Paul and he said, "Tony, all our equipment is gone!" I thought he was joking. So I walked into the room and the whole place was totally cleared out. All that was left was a cymbal stand with a cowbell on it. We were attempting to put together our act because the album was done and we were getting ready to tour.

BROOKE OSTRANDER: It was our impression that the record was going to come out in Thanksgiving of 1972. That was the original plan. Gene, Stan, and Tony went ahead and bought some instruments. I didn't have keyboards and they cost a whole lot of money that I didn't have. Somewhere in that time period, this is now going into October, we were told that now the album was going to come out at the first of the year because three major Epic artists, Edgar Winter, and the Hollies, and somebody else, were releasing albums at the same time. And Epic did not have the money to cover the advertising for all of them. So we ended up being put on the back burner. It came at exactly the worst possible time because we were in desperate need of exposure and money. Ultimately that was the last straw for me. I was just tapped out at that point in terms of money and patience. That's when I left and I sought my release from the record company. When I left, there was no Wicked Lester because they couldn't do it without me. Gene and Stanley decided that that was going to be the end of it. I'm not real clear exactly what happened with Ron Leejack and Tony but essentially the group just disbanded. It was the first of November or thereabouts of '72. I never understood why Epic never released the record.

TONY ZARRELLA: There were disagreements in the band as far as direction. I didn't really care, I liked hard rock, the conceptual stuff, and I liked the middle-of-the-road stuff too.

TOM WERMAN: Epic didn't really like the record. But I liked it a lot. It was Don's [Ellis] decision not to release the record. He just didn't get it. He also turned down Lynyrd Skynyrd and Rush.

SPACE ACE ON THE *ALIVE!* TOUR, 1975
(Photo by Fin Costello/© KISS Catalog Ltd.)

PAUL STRUTTING IT UP, 1976
(© KISS Catalog Ltd.)

LOVE GUN TOUR PHOTO SHOOT, 1977
(© KISS CATALOG LTD.)

STARCROSSED, 1976
(© KISS Catalog Ltd.)

ACE, *DESTROYER* TOUR, 1976
(© KISS Catalog Ltd.)

KISS LIVE, ACADEMY OF MUSIC, NEW YORK CITY, JANUARY 23, 1974
(© KISS Catalog Ltd.)

THE ELDER PHOTO SESSION, 1981
(© KISS Catalog Ltd.)

PAUL BRANDISHING CHERISHED
GIBSON FIREBIRD GUITAR, LIVE 1975
(Photo by Fin Costello/© KISS Catalog Ltd.)

ACE, EARLY 1974
(Photo by Fin Costello/© KISS Catalog Ltd.)

PAUL WEARING ALTERNATE
LOVE GUN COSTUME, JUNE 1978
(Photo by Barry Levine/© KISS Catalog Ltd.)

KISS ATOP NEW YORK'S EMPIRE STATE BUILDING, JUNE 1976
(Photo by Barry Levine/© KISS Catalog Ltd.)

KISS LIVE, 1975
(© KISS Catalog Ltd.)

ALTERNATE *ALIVE!* ALBUM COVER PHOTOGRAPH,
MICHIGAN PALACE, DETROIT, MICHIGAN, MAY 15, 1975
(Photo by Fin Costello/© KISS Catalog Ltd.)

ALTERNATE *ALIVE II* ALBUM INLAY CONCERT PHOTO, SAN DIEGO SPORTS ARENA,
SAN DIEGO, CALIFORNIA, AUGUST 1977

EARLY KISS PHOTO SESSION, 1974
(© KISS Catalog Ltd.)

PETER, *ALIVE!* PHOTO SHOOT, MICHIGAN PALACE,
DETROIT, MICHIGAN, MAY 15, 1975

(Photo by Fin Costello/© KISS Catalog Ltd.)

ACE, 1978
(© KISS Catalog Ltd.)

PAUL WEARING BANDIT MAKEUP DESIGN,
EARLY 1974
(© KISS Catalog Ltd.)

THE ARTIST FORMERLY KNOWN AS CHAIM WITZ, *DESTROYER* TOUR, 1976
(© KISS Catalog Ltd.)

ACE TUNING UP BACKSTAGE, 1975
(Photo by Fin Costello/© KISS Catalog Ltd.)

KISS *ALIVE!* TOUR, EARLY 1976
(©KISS Catalog Ltd.)

KISS REUNION PRESS CONFERENCE, USS *INTREPID* AIRCRAFT CARRIER,
NEW YORK CITY, APRIL 16, 1996
(Photo by Terri Sharp)

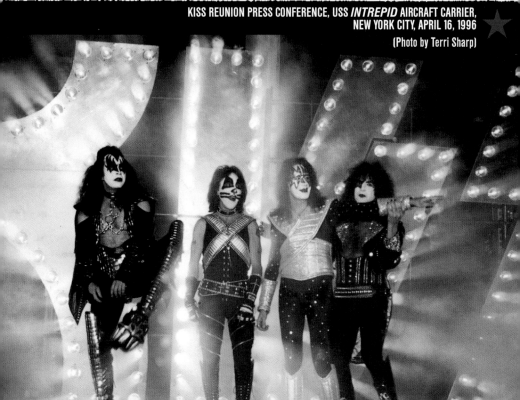

ALTERNATE IMAGE FOR KISS FIRST ALBUM PROMO POSTER, 1974
(© KISS Catalog Ltd.)

PAUL PLAYING A GIBSON
DOUBLE-NECK GUITAR, 1978

(© KISS Catalog Ltd.)

ACE KICKING OUT THE JAMS, *ALIVE!* PHOTO SHOOT,
MICHIGAN PALACE, DETROIT, MICHIGAN, MAY 15, 1975

(Photo by Fin Costello/© KISS Catalog Ltd.)

CO-AUTHOR KEN SHARP WITH KISS, USS *INTREPID*
AIRCRAFT CARRIER, NEW YORK CITY, APRIL 16, 1996

(Photo by Terri Sharp)

MAGIC PEOPLE, STONE FOX, NEW JERSEY, NOVEMBER 23,
1968, ACE FREHLEY, LEAD GUITAR, CHRIS CAMIOLO, DRUMS

(Courtesy Chris Camiolo)

PAUL IN BANDIT MAKEUP, 1974
(© KISS Catalog Ltd.)

WINDMILL CITY, SAN DIEGO SPORTS ARENA, SAN DIEGO, CALIFORNIA, MARCH 19, 2000

(Photo by Terri Sharp)

GENE, 1978

GENE, ARROWHEAD POND OF ANAHEIM, ANAHEIM, CALIFORNIA, MARCH 18, 2000

(Photo by Terri Sharp)

PAUL, 1974
(© KISS Catalog Ltd.)

LEW LINET: The next question was maybe Epic would sell me the tapes if I could find somebody to release the record. Stan and Gene came to my apartment and said they wanted to split from the others and form a high-powered hard rock band. They said they'd have to find some players and they were going to need a rehearsal space. I found them a little rehearsal room on 10 East 23rd Street. They started to work together and audition drummers and guitar players. The auditions were so loud that they used to keep a table of earplugs for anybody coming into that room. It was deafening.

GENE SIMMONS: Wicked Lester just wasn't working out. Paul and I decided, "We're going to redo this. We're gonna get different guys, this is not the band we want to do." When we got Peter [Criss] in the band and started wearing makeup we still had a record contract at Epic and said, "Do you want to buy this because we don't want to do Wicked Lester?" That's when we invited down Don Ellis, the A&R vice president for Epic. We thought we could just exchange KISS for Wicked Lester. But we quickly found out that it doesn't work that way.

TOM WERMAN: I saw them at a loft on 23rd Street. There were only three of us from Epic there, Don Ellis, myself, and Bill Walsh, who worked A&R at Epic for about a year. I couldn't really recognize Paul, Gene, and Peter because they were wearing whiteface makeup and some lipstick. They were definitely in costume, wearing black cloth tights. They looked pretty bizarre. The performance was wonderful. It was really good, really loud, and really hard-core compared to Wicked Lester. And the best part was the pail of confetti that Paul threw at us at the end. And we all ducked thinking it was water. It was fun and it kind of capped the performance and said, "This is our attitude. This is a show." Don and Bill didn't get it, plain and simple, and passed on signing them.

RON JOHNSEN: In 1977, I was called by CBS because they were planning to release the Wicked Lester album. They wanted me to remix the songs to make them sound more contemporary. So I went in and remixed the whole Wicked Lester album. Then Casablanca got word that CBS was going to release the tapes and everybody freaked out. Neil made arrangements to stop CBS from releasing it and bought the rights back.

PAUL STANLEY: We knew the record was in Epic's vaults but we thought we'd let sleeping dogs lie. But as soon as KISS started to make noise, the label was planning to release it. We thought it would confuse our fans and also diffuse and dilute our image. We said, "How much is it gonna cost us to not have it come out?"

BILL AUCOIN: I told Neil Bogart that we can't let it come out. So we agreed to buy the album back from CBS.

KISS
KISS

Release date: February 8, 1974
KISS / RICHIE WISE–producer / KENNY KERNER–producer / BILL AUCOIN–manager
JOYCE BOGART–co-manager / LARRY HARRIS–Casablanca Records senior vice president
STAN CORNYN–Warner Brothers executive vice president / JOEL BRODSKY–photographer
MARK HUDSON–Hudson Brothers (Casablanca Records label mates)
HARVEY KUBERNIK–media coordinator, Danny Goldberg Associates

PAUL STANLEY: Recording the first album was the culmination of everything I'd worked for up to that point. Looking back on it, some bands have had the good fortune of being in the studio with technicians and a creative team that could capture their sound. And I think unfortunately, starting with the first album, that was never achieved with KISS. Though it documents our songs, it doesn't in any way capture what the band was about live and sonically. But what came from inside us managed to transcend what is sorely lacking in terms of the scope of the recording. I'd give the first KISS album five stars, because that's the mother of all others. That was like our *Declaration of Independence*, and everything that came after that is based on that album.

GENE SIMMONS: The first album is the first time we all got pregnant. The baby came out and that's what it was. There wasn't a lot of foresight. It was all done in three weeks. Two weeks of recording and then mixing. We recorded the first KISS album at Bell Sound in New York. It was kind of an extension of the first demos we did. We were totally green, didn't have a clue to what was going on. I would give it three stars. Sonically it doesn't stand the test of time. It was produced pretty low-budget on sixteen-track. I quite like the album, I think the songs stand up. There's some interesting playing. The tempo of the songs is slower than I'm used to hearing. I like the first few records very much.

ACE FREHLEY: I'd give it five stars. It was one of our best records because it had that spontaneity and that tough kind of sound. We were all very hungry at that point in our lives. I think we put in 110 percent on that record. It was the first time I ever did a real album. In retrospect, Richie and Kenny weren't the greatest producers. They were as green as we were. When you listen to it, production-wise it's lacking a lot. I don't think Richie and Kenny had a great knowledge of getting great sounds. Eddie Kramer would work with me on sounds, like getting natural ambience and all sorts of shit like that. The songs on the first album are good. We knew those songs backward and forward.

PETER CRISS: I'd give it five stars because it was the first. The first album was my baby. I gave it my all. I loved all the songs on it like "Strutter," which is one of my favorite

KISS songs, "Deuce," and "Firehouse." I wanted it. I didn't want to have to go back to the bars. I put my whole heart and soul into it, which I didn't do with every one of them. I just was so amazed that we were in a studio and signed to a real record contract even though it was a nobody contract at the time. But we did it, we really did it. We made our dream come true.

KENNY KERNER: Richie [Wise] and I listened to what they did on their demo tape just to get a feeling for the songs and to determine what songs were good and what songs needed rearranging. After watching KISS play live at Le Tang's and Coventry in Queens, we decided that this had to be a real street album, a real raw album. Exactly the way they are live is the way they should sound like. Richie was really into the technical aspects of recording. He was concerned with "Give me ten more db" of this. Richie liked to turn the knobs. I found that really boring and besides I wasn't really qualified to do that. I would book all the musicians, book the studio time, work on which songs would be recorded. I was a fanatic about the lyrics. I would go over the lyrics to make sure the words weren't broken up improperly so they sounded stupid. Once we actually got into the studio, I'd be behind the board, with Richie doing what he did. If somebody fucked up, either one of us would press the button and go, "You messed up, do it again." After that I would continue on with the album credits, which photos to use, whereas Richie would start preproduction on the next thing. I was more concerned with the image of the band, the sequencing of songs, which songs should be singles as opposed to album tracks.

RICHIE WISE: We recorded the first KISS album at Bell Sound, which was owned by the company that owned Buddah Records. Buddah was the company where Neil Bogart came from. I remember the first KISS album taking six days to record and seven days to mix for a total of thirteen days. We would cut three songs or so in a day, three basic tracks, drums, bass, and two rhythm guitars. Ace would overdub his solos not long after we cut the tracks. Then we would spend the last three days of the recording doing the vocals. KISS was such an easy band to record, the songs fell together so quickly.

RICHIE WISE: As a producer, I was involved with every aspect of KISS's songs, starting with choosing the songs, the arrangements, and the recording. I don't think there were any major changes to any of the KISS songs. I did guide the group in rearranging the early songs from the original demos done by Eddie Kramer and getting them into tighter shape, more into three- or four-minute jobs. The group knew the songs pretty well and we would make the changes on the fly before we recorded them. They wanted to keep it raw.

KENNY KERNER: The band was totally together. Nothing was written in the studio with the exception of "Kissin' Time," which we rewrote. They played everything live. The guitar solos were overdubbed and the vocals were overdubbed. The whole rhythm section was live, bass, drums, rhythm guitars. We had a great studio rapport with the bands we produced. We'd go in there and have fun. We'd tell them, "The tape was always running and if you don't get it we'll do it again." There was no pressure on anybody.

RICHIE WISE: Paul was always very exciting, he had that Steve Marriott energy. Paul wanted to be the greatest rhythm player like Pete Townshend. He was a nice solid rhythm player. The person I thought that was the best in the band was Gene. Gene was an exceptional bass player, I found his lines to be very, very musical. He also really had that attitude with his singing. Ace was a very solid guitar player, didn't have a lot of tricks up his sleeve but what he did, he did extremely well. In hindsight, Peter Criss was pretty terrible. At the time I thought he was okay. He was not from the John Bonham, AC/DC school. Therefore the group didn't have that rock drum groove thing happening. Peter was a really good guy. I remember liking him a whole lot. In hindsight he was very lucky to have been in that band.

RICHIE WISE: If there's one thing that stands out in my mind about working with KISS on their first album is their absolute focus beyond any artist that I have ever worked with. They had blinders on. The desire to be huge, the desire to hit the grand slam right out of the box was the foundation that KISS was built on. Nothing was gonna stop them from becoming the biggest band in the world. I never sensed that KISS was about making musical magic, they wanted to make rock 'n' roll history.

RICHIE WISE: Gene was always money motivated, he wanted nothing less than for KISS to be the biggest group in the world. To me, putting on the best show possible was always what was most important to KISS, more so than trying to be the best songwriters or the best players or the best singers.

RICHIE WISE: The first KISS album is fabulous and really stands up. It has a timeless sound. But at the time I thought it sounded wimpy. I didn't think the guitars were distorted enough, I didn't think that the album was aggressive enough.

PETER CRISS: When they shot the front cover of the album, they got a makeup guy to come in. I was against it. He put all those dots on my stupid whiskers. The rest of the band did their own makeup. We wanted the cover to look like the *Meet the Beatles* album cover. We wore this huge black curtain draped over us. They cut holes in it and it weighed at least a million pounds. We stayed under it for hours, it was so hot.

JOEL BRODSKY: I shot between five hundred and a thousand album covers including the Doors' *Strange Days* and Van Morrison's *Astral Weeks*. I was given the assignment to shoot the KISS album cover by Casablanca. I had done a lot of stuff for Buddah Records with Neil Bogart. The shoot was done in New York City at my studio on

57th Street. They had a guy who helped them with their makeup, a painter named Mario Rivoli. The makeup was unique at the time, it was the beginning of glitter. It was a basic four heads on a square picture, a little like the *Meet the Beatles* cover. I've done that kind of cover a number of other times with other people, like Nazz, Todd Rundgren's band. My philosophy of album covers is if people knew the music, they were gonna buy it in a brown paper bag. If you were brand-new like KISS, and you needed to attract attention, the cover did it. And that's a cover that attracted attention. The photo session lasted a little less than an hour but the makeup session probably lasted three hours. They were draped in black velvet with a black background. It was really Simmons and Stanley who were most concerned with the visuals of the shoot. KISS were reasonably cooperative. I remember the other guys were all on the set and we were all waiting for Gene Simmons to come out. I couldn't get Simmons out of the dressing room, I was getting more and more aggravated. He wanted his makeup to be perfect. I told him, "If you're not out in fifteen minutes, there's not going to be anyone here to take this picture!" [laughs] The story about me wanting to put balloons behind them, thinking they were circus clowns, is not true. That's someone's imagination. Years later, I'm still proud of that KISS album cover.

STAN CORNYN: KISS performed a kickoff party for their first album at the Century Plaza Hotel. Bob Regehr at Warner Brothers had done a *Casablanca* theme to the room. There was a Humphrey Bogart look-alike wandering around in a white tux jacket. I think there was also a Maltese Falcon there and maybe a roulette table. This anonymous ballroom had a stage at one end. I was having cocktails and dinner with my fellow executives and then KISS came on to perform. Gene had the longest tongue I've ever seen. The band was an assault on your visual senses as well as your ears. I remember we all thought KISS was amusing, fun. Listen, we were people who had seen Jimi Hendrix in a boa lighting his guitar on fire in Monterey. So KISS seemed like a variation, not an epiphany. I don't mean to put it down. Those guys did a long-lasting good presentation and eventually the act became popular and went on.

JOYCE BOGART: The Century Plaza Casablanca party was the biggest party the town had seen. It was to introduce the record company, not the band, which was secondary, really. It was extremely successful on every level, except for the reaction to KISS. It was a theme party with look-alikes from the movie and *tout de Hollywood* in costumes of the era, but a disaster for the band. Neil had told them to play full throttle, to not hold back. But a hotel ballroom is no place for a rock band with a sound like KISS. Warner Brothers hated them immediately. Of all the guests that night, I think only Alice Cooper got it.

BILL AUCOIN: Warner Brothers told Neil [Bogart], "If you want to stay on the label, take off that makeup!" Neil called me and said, "Warner Brothers is driving me crazy.

Would you ask the group if they will take off the makeup?" I said, "Neil, this isn't going to happen." He said, "If they don't want to do it, I'll stand behind them but Warner Brothers just doesn't want to work with it."

HARVEY KUBERNIK: I remember photographer Richard Creamer beaming after their showcase. We both agreed, that as loud and calculated as KISS appeared, it was a relief from most of the lame, white, phony country rock singer-songwriters that local music press was drooling over, who were just as calculated, but no one wanted to admit it. Not long afterward, Creamer and I went to an *In Concert* TV taping and we heard KISS doing their sound check from outside. The rumble from the parking lot was louder than the 1971 L.A. earthquake!

STAN CORNYN: When you saw the drummer's drumsticks explode, not to mention Gene Simmons blowing fire, his lizard tongue, all the makeup, and the sort of drag king outfits they would wear, one of the perceptions at Warner Brothers was perhaps maybe there's not much music under it [laughs]. The image slapped you right in the stomach. I thought it was camp, I thought it was clever. I didn't want to live with it [laughs], but it was notable and we did our job. Warner Brothers is a company which had been the home to outrageous acts like Tiny Tim, Alice Cooper, the Fugs, and the Grateful Dead before they became respectable. All those acts out of New York. Frank Zappa with the Bizarre label, the GTO's, Wild Man Fischer. We were home to the outrageous. KISS was slicker in my perception. You never would think of the Fugs as having any Hollywood character, you thought of KISS as having a Hollywood design to it. I'm not saying that's bad because Hollywood design works well. But it wasn't like the Fugs or Alice Cooper, kinda funky and outrageous. We even thought Jethro Tull was a little weird because the flautist stood on one leg like a pelican. We were home to all of this and frankly kind of enjoyed it. There was only so much Vic Damone you can take in life [laughs]. We liked KISS, but we also were a business. When it went over-the-top from Neil's pressures, you finally just said, "Neil, stop already!" [laughs] But he didn't know how.

STAN CORNYN: Bob Merlis, a publicist in our New York office, was handling KISS's first New York show. Nobody wanted to show the gentlemen's real faces. He took them to Georgette Klinger, a woman's makeup salon. They were interviewed with steaming towels over their faces. It was quite an attention-getter.

STAN CORNYN: How the deal ended with Neil was he got deep into debt with us, the chances of recouping were very remote. In the meantime he was feeling like he wasn't getting a fair shake. Neil's brother-in-law, Bucky Rheingold, who worked for him, was in our offices. Bucky overheard the promotion weekly call, which would go out to thirty people on the line with our home office talking to them and setting priorities.

He found out that KISS records were not number one priority at Warner Brothers. KISS was a number one priority at Casablanca, but wasn't top priority at our label because we had thirty other records to promote and evaluate. I think maybe the promotion weekly phone call was taped because he had pretty good evidence. He played it for Neil and a charge was mounted against Warner Brothers Records. Warner Brothers was in a high-fatigue mode when it came to these charges coming at it. Mo [Ostin] heard his promotion people admit that KISS wasn't a top priority. He heard the whines from our executives, "Oh my God, what next!" and the pressure from Neil for other acts and decided that our deal with Casablanca didn't seem to be going anywhere. An accord was reached with Neil. Mo released Casablanca from the label with no penalty. He told him just pay us back when the numbers allow that. Casablanca's debt was sizable, about $750,000 dollars. I later asked Mo if Neil paid him back and he said yes [laughs].

LARRY HARRIS: We had no cash because at that point all the money was coming from Warner Brothers. We started to get some money from independent distributors but that was coming in slowly and there were bills to pay—salaries, electricity, and rent. One day Neil walked into my office and said, "Do you know anybody who has $10,000?" In those days $10,000 was a lot more than it is today. I said, "You can borrow it from my father." Neil said, "No, I don't want your father to be in a position like that." Instead he hopped on a plane and flew to Vegas, where he had a line of credit at Caesars. He went into the casino, drew out the money as if he was going to use it to gamble, and took the money and came back to L.A. Neil was a very big gambler. If you look at his whole life everything he did was a gamble.

LARRY HARRIS: When we left Warners, the only thing we had that was really selling at all was KISS. We were street-wise New Yorkers who went out to California and we were going to show the world how to sell records. "Fuck everybody else! We're gonna show all you laid-back California people how it's supposed to be done." KISS was getting very little respect critically. Very few of the radio people took them seriously because they wore makeup and looked weird. The cool stuff happening in those days was the Eagles and Led Zeppelin. We may have been guilty of overhyping KISS but we didn't see anything wrong with it. People look at the word "hype" and it seems like a negative. We never thought that the word hype was a negative. We thought the word hype was good. To us, hype meant that people were going to hear about what we were doing with KISS whether people liked it or not. As far as we were concerned, any press was good.

JOYCE BOGART: Neil believed in KISS and supported them with all his considerable creativity and his enormous talent for promotion and his quite formidable contacts in the industry. He backed them financially even when he couldn't afford it. Warner Brothers hated KISS and wouldn't promote them, so Neil bought himself out of his deal with Warners. We had called the Warner Brothers secret promotion phone line and heard their guys being told not to work the KISS record at all. KISS had the goods, the talent, and the desire, but would they have happened without Neil?

LARRY HARRIS: Casablanca paid all of the promoter's costs for advertising if they booked KISS. So there was minimal risk involved in booking KISS as a headliner because we were covering all the advertising costs and no label does that. People thought we were crazy because we weren't advertising an album, we were advertising a live show hoping that show would translate into album sales.

MARK HUDSON: Being on Casablanca Records was scary. The decor in the office was like the movie *Casablanca*. Fake palm trees, big '30s fans on the ceiling moving slowly, and a life-size stuffed camel. The day-to-day goings-on at the label were musical and also fanciful. There was enough blow to powder a hundred babies' butts. Yet the people working at Casablanca were like a family. Despite the overindulgence, everyone worked hard, day and night. KISS, Donna Summer, Parliament, and the Hudson Brothers were the first acts signed to Casablanca. I remember KISS coming into the Casablanca offices and meeting them. They were all really really nice. I hit it off with Paul and we immediately sat down in a room and played "I'll Feel a Whole Lot Better" by the Byrds on acoustic guitars. I'm thinking, KISS is a band and they're kind of Beatley. Next thing I know, I see their first album cover and I internally hemorrhaged. It's Satan in tights [laughs]. You mean this guy who I just played a Byrds song with is doing this? Neil told my brothers and I, "You just wait, these guys are going to be the biggest thing in rock 'n' roll!" Then Neil put the record on and we knew immediately that he was right because it was theatrical and it was dark, it was fun, and most of all, it kicked ass.

★ "STRUTTER" ★

PAUL STANLEY: "Strutter" was written when the band was a trio, Peter, Gene, and I. Gene and I used to show up before rehearsals and just write music for this new band we were forming called KISS. We knew what kind of music we wanted to write and we started playing what became "Strutter." Lyrically, "Strutter" was my ongoing fascination with women in the New York glitter scene. In some ways it was a sister song to "Black Diamond." I was a middle-class kid from the suburbs who was suddenly thrown into this rock world that was taking place in New York. This whole lifestyle, and sense of fashion. There's more of a tip of the hat to [Bob] Dylan in there than anything else. The Dylan song "Just Like a Woman," which says, [recites lyrics] "She makes love just like a woman, but she breaks just like a little girl." In "Strutter" you get [recites lyrics], "She gets her satins like a lady, she gets her way just like a child." Musically, the song came fairly quickly. It was based chordally on a song Gene had called

"Stanley the Parrot." We picked up the tempo and it started to feel Stonesy with that swagger and attitude. I said that the song strutted and from there we wound up with "Strutter."

GENE SIMMONS: Our music is very honest, gut-level, straight-ahead stuff. When you're talking about a strutter you're not talking about other levels of reality. I don't think we ever cared about that. In the late '60s, things got so pompous and good old rock 'n' roll became rock. Like it was the Rock of Gibraltar. Nonsense. Rock 'n' roll comes from an old black song. Rockin' 'n' rollin' meant fucking. I think rock 'n' roll suffers from the same thing that KISS suffers from, a lack of respect. But it doesn't matter because rock 'n' roll is the biggest form of music that ever was. Classical musicians will never like us. So KISS's problem is rock 'n' roll's problem.

HANDWRITTEN LYRICS FOR "STRUTTER" AND UNRELEASED SONG, "HIGH AND LOW"
(© KISS Catalog Ltd.)

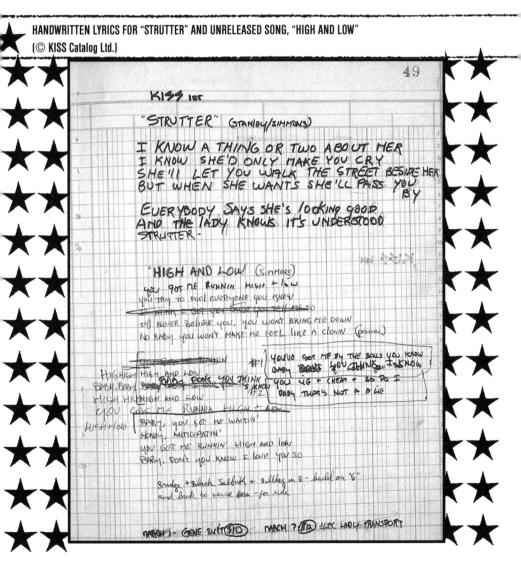

★ "NOTHIN' TO LOSE" ★

GENE SIMMONS: "Nothin' to Lose" came to me after hearing the line in two different songs. One was a Little Richard song. I saw Little Richard singing it, [sings in Little Richard style] "Before I had a baby . . ." Then there was another song called "Sea Cruise," which had the line 'you got nothin' to lose, won't you let me take you on a sea cruise."

PETER CRISS: I liked the song because I grew up on R&B music, Sam Cooke, Sam & Dave, Otis Redding, and Wilson Pickett. So my vocals added soul to Paul's and Gene's voices. Eddie Kramer always said he loved my voice.

GENE SIMMONS: Lyrically, "Nothin' to Lose" is about anal sex. The lyric goes, [recites lyrics], "I thought about the back door, I didn't know what to say. But once I had a baby, I tried every way. She didn't want to do it. But she did any way."

RICHIE WISE: I brought in Bruce Foster, a lifelong friend of mine, to play piano on "Nothin' to Lose." That's him in the chorus with a little Jerry Lee Lewis thing goin' on.

★ "FIREHOUSE" ★

PAUL STANLEY: I wrote "Firehouse" when I was high school. At that point, I had been writing songs for about five years. Back then I couldn't afford to buy old British albums and I was really into that kind of music. There was a band called the Move who had a song I liked called "Fire Brigade." So I stole it and rewrote it.

★ "COLD GIN" ★

ACE FREHLEY: I wrote "Cold Gin" in a subway in my head, lyrics, music [laughs]. I had a spiral notebook with me. I can write songs in my head and I know what the chords are. I never took a guitar lesson, nobody believes that. I didn't realize it was gonna become a KISS classic.

★ "LET ME KNOW" ★

PAUL STANLEY: "Let Me Know" started off as a song called "Sunday Driver" and it was the first song that I ever played for Gene when we first met. Steve Coronel, the guitar player that we both played with in separate bands, introduced us. He said, "Gene, this is my friend Stan. He plays and he writes." Gene said, "Oh, play me one of your songs," and I played him "Sunday Driver." For Gene it was a revelation because I don't think he realized that there were other people walking the streets as common people who could write songs besides him and Lennon and McCartney. "Let Me Know" later got a bridge in it and wound up on our first album.

★ "KISSIN' TIME" ★

KENNY KERNER: Neil Bogart was into gimmicks. He was looking for a way to get a song from the record onto Top 40 radio. The AOR [Album Oriented Rock] people were getting it onto FM radio because of the band's live show and the way they looked and all the controversy. But Neil wanted to break the band with a Top 40 single and he didn't think there was anything on the first record that could do that for the band. One of the promotion people came up with the idea of kissing contests all across the country and the people that kiss the longest get some kind of a prize. Neil said, "Yeah! You know what we could do? We can take that old Bobby Rydell song "Kissin' Time" and redo that and put it on the record and then release it as a single to coincide with this national kissing contest." When the band heard that, we all flipped out and it was everybody on one side against Neil on the other side. It was just the wrong call for a band already steeped in controversy. You don't add more to it. That just made it a bubblegum rock band. We sat there in the studio the same day we recorded the basic track and completely rewrote the lyrics. There was me, Richie, the guys in the band, Bill Aucoin, and Sean Delaney. We all had paper and pencils and we were going, "Okay, Detroit. We can leave Detroit in the lyrics because Detroit is a rock city. And we gotta mention New York because we're from New York." And we went through this whole geographical thing about which cities we have to mention and which cities we would rhyme. We rewrote the whole thing right there in the studio.

JOYCE BOGART: Neil conceived this to get attention for the band and it garnered enormous press everywhere. We did a kissing contest in the top ten markets where the finalists kissed in large venues while the judges (us in New York City) rolled around on roller skates looking for infractions. The band was a bit confused and I think uncomfortable with such a blatant promotion that seemed to have nothing to do with their music. In the Midwest, in the largest mall in the U.S.A., KISS was introduced with much fanfare, but the enormous crowd continued to watch the kissers. Neil went up to the top balcony and threw money down by the group causing everyone to be staring at them when all the photos were taken.

PAUL STANLEY: "Kissin' Time" was one of the Neil Bogart ruses. He told us that it was just being recorded for a commercial and that it'll never come out as a single. That was part of Neil's philosophy; Neil, bless his soul, if he could get you a hit today and ruin your career that was well worth it 'cause you'd have had a hit. So that's just a different way of looking at things. We were perfectly capable of writing our own material and at that point to have to record a Bobby Rydell song was unnecessary.

RICHIE WISE: You have to understand that Neil Bogart couldn't give a shit. For Neil, the artist was the fifth most important thing. The first was the song, the production, the promotion, and then the artist somewhere down the line [laughs]. Caring about the artist and the artist's vision didn't mean shit to him. The most important thing to him was marketing.

BILL AUCOIN: Everybody hated it. Neil was going to do this major promotion and he was going to spend a fortune on it. So I said "Guys, we have to do it." There are certain things in everyone's career where you know it's not what you want to do, but you know, if you don't do it, you're really stupid. With KISS we did a lot of crazy things and got away with them about 80 percent of the time. We were really lucky. We failed 20 percent of the time with real disasters, but no one knows about them.

★ "DEUCE" ★

GENE SIMMONS: "Deuce" was written in my head on a bus. I heard the lick, the riff, the melody, the whole thing. "Deuce" was written on bass. It was a very linear song. As soon as the riff came, the first verse came, then I wrote the bridge and then I wrote the chorus. We arranged it right on the spot and knew that it would be a staple for years. In fact, when we first went on tour with our first record, it was the opening song of the show and we would come back for encores and not have any songs left and do "Deuce" again. Then if we would get a second encore we would do "Deuce" again. Lyrically, I had no idea what I was talking about. Sometimes stuff means a lot, sometimes it means nothing.

PAUL STANLEY: The beginning of the song was me ripping off the Raspberries. The beginning of "Deuce," the thing that starts it off, is me bastardizing "Go All the Way."

ACE FREHLEY: It's my favorite KISS song. When I auditioned for KISS they said, "We're going to play you a song and for you to listen and then try playing along." The song was "Deuce" and they played it as a three-piece and the song was in the key of A. I thought, that's easy enough, so I got up and wailed for four minutes playing lead work over it.

★ "LOVE THEME FROM KISS" ★

GENE SIMMONS: "Love Theme from Kiss" was shortened way down. It was originally seven minutes long. It started off with an instrumental and then went into another section called "You're Much Too Young." "Acrobat" became "Love Theme from Kiss" and then it went off into a "Detroit Rock City" riff, which Paul ripped off but never gave me credit for it.

KENNY KERNER: As far as doing an instrumental, there obviously were no ballads on the album. Instead of just doing another rock song with another rock lyric they said, "Hey, how about this?" because it was different. I think just to be a little different and diverse they threw that in.

★ "100,000 YEARS" ★

GENE SIMMONS: I read a book called *100,000 Years* where 100,000 years ago we were visited by aliens, also Einstein's theory of relativity. I was reading all kinds of space and time continuance stuff, and it was all swirling around my head. And I started to think what happens if you're an astronaut and you leave, how long could you stay in love? I wrote it at the Puerto Rican Interagency Council while I was working there in the daytime as the assistant to the director. So I showed this stuff to Paul, and he's going, "Are you out of your mind? What's 100,000 years?" I said, "Let's just try it." And then Paul came up with some stuff, and I added the riff.

PAUL STANLEY: I came up with the entire lyric, the melody. My recollection is that I think the bass pattern was changed and what went on top of that was basically mine.

★ "BLACK DIAMOND" ★

PAUL STANLEY: "Black Diamond" was a song that I wrote about New York. Back then, all we could write about was what we knew. New York was very dear to us and life there was all we could write about. Seeing hookers on the street, whether we lived it, we saw it and it kind of gave us something to fantasize about. I never wrote with the intention of anyone else singing my songs. Peter wound up singing "Black Diamond" because we needed a song that he would sing on the album plus he was fairly insistent. We thought much as the Beatles did that we wanted to have different people singing different tracks. So "Black Diamond" became his song and luckily it did because it's a great song for him. Traditionally, every drummer we've had has had to have a raspy voice and be able to sing that song.

PETER CRISS: Eddie Kramer loved my screaming voice and said, "Peter's got to sing this."

RICHIE WISE: "Black Diamond" was Peter's Ringo cut. As a singer, Peter had pitch problems up the ass. But Peter had a real gravelly sound that was heartfelt. Gene and Paul were pretty much on the money with their vocals in the studio. I remember that Paul tried to hit some real high notes and harmonies. We probably slowed down the tapes a few times to make it easier for him to get those high notes.

HOTTER THAN HELL

Release date: October 22, 1974
KISS / BILL AUCOIN–manager / RICHIE WISE–producer / KENNY KERNER–producer
STEVE CORONEL–songwriter / PAUL CHAVARRIA–roadie (1974–1979)
NORMAN SEEFF–photographer

GENE SIMMONS: We'd been touring pretty nonstop from the time the first record came out, so by the time we got to L.A. to do *Hotter Than Hell*, we were actually right in the middle of a tour. We played Santa Monica Civic with Wishbone Ash and we were third on the bill. But those songs were pretty much written on the road and some of the songs were left over from the first KISS demo. I quite like *Hotter Than Hell*. I'd give the whole album three stars.

PAUL STANLEY: I'd give *Hotter Than Hell* three stars. There's some songs I really like. *Hotter Than Hell* was the first album where we couldn't rely on material we'd written in high school and forward. Although there were some leftover songs on the album from our club days, it really came down to writing a new batch of songs, which was daunting. We had years to sift through all our best material for the first album. For the second album it was instant rock. We hoped to remedy the sonic deficiencies we found in the first album. We were never as rock-'n'-rolly or good-timey as we sounded on that album. We were much heavier live. So we tried to capture sonically how we sounded live. Unfortunately, the people that we were working with might not have been the right people to be doing it with. It was our first extended trip to Los Angeles. We were living the rock 'n' roll lifestyle of an up-and-coming band at the Ramada on Sunset. We were listening to Mott the Hoople, just hanging out, and having a cool time. The party that went into the photo session for that album kind of summed up what life was like in L.A. at that time.

PETER CRISS: We were still green. We had one album and it didn't do well, so we were really hoping this would do better 'cause no one really took the first one to heart. It didn't go Gold or Platinum for a long time. But it was also done in California. Paul had his guitar stolen. There was a lot of bad vibes. That happened and we weren't used to California. We were New Yorkers, we were like, "Hey, fuck you, I'll kick your ass!" We weren't used to this California scene. We were kind of into the L.A. scene kind of. It was kind of decadent and it was really wild. It was the swinging '70s. They were just starting and they were just getting into the orgies and the coke and the wildness. We were getting wilder then. I'd give that album three stars because there was a lot of decadence going on.

ACE FREHLEY: *Hotter Than Hell* was a harder album to record than our first record because we had toured so extensively and then all of a sudden the record company wanted us to put out another album. You don't have ten songs you've been rehearsing for a year. We recorded it in L.A. at Village Recorders. That was a tougher record to do. But working in L.A. was fun. I'd give *Hotter Than Hell* three and a half stars.

GENE SIMMONS: When we were doing *Hotter Than Hell*, we had risen in salary to $85, from $75 a week. We couldn't afford room service because we were staying in hotels. We would literally go to the grocery store and buy beans and eggs and subsist as best we could. We didn't have this sense that we were going to scale the heights and yet we were happy. Even back then it was obvious that I had nothing in common with Ace and Peter socially. With Paul I could communicate because he was a straight guy and responsible. With Ace and Peter if I wanted to have a good time, for them it was spelled "b-o-m-b-e-d." The priorities were different. All those variables went into it as a record. Some of the small demons within the band started to raise their head. The difference in the personalities were starting to come into the band and between its members. Even though it was the same production team as the first album, we didn't have the temperament to stick it out and do a proper studio album. That takes time. We weren't experienced. Another thing was it was torture being with the same guys seven days a week. The production values of the record had more to do with "Gee, I like that song more than that song." It didn't have to do with real engineering styles. We were all like blind men walking through the dark.

KENNY KERNER: We just got on the phone and said to KISS, "Listen, we live here now, would you come out here to do the record? Casablanca's out here in Los Angeles, Richie and I are out here, our engineer, Warren Dewey, is out here." We went to

Village Recorders, and the first day we set up, Paul's guitar was stolen [a custom-made Flying V]. So it immediately got off to a bad start.

BILL AUCOIN: The band was homesick. They just didn't feel comfortable. They were from the streets of New York. KISS were afraid of this glamorous town and their look was a strictly New York street look. It was awkward for them.

PETER CRISS: I did miss New York. I'm from Brooklyn and I thought I was on another planet. It was tough on us. We were never away from home that long. But it was a great album. We had a lot of fun. I love "Mainline" and "Strange Ways." I loved singing them because I went in, there was nobody on my ass, they let me sing the way I wanted to sing and the proof is in the pudding.

KENNY KERNER: That album again was done basically live. It sounds a little heavier. We just doubled a lot more things. They hated it here [laughs]. They made no bones about it. We were used to it but they didn't want to leave New York. I love "Got to Choose" and "Goin' Blind." It's so eerie and it's so unlike anything else on that record. "Hotter Than Hell" is a great title song.

RICHIE WISE: I hated the sound of that album. I swear to God, every two days there would be new speakers in the room. They were changing them on us all the time because they were having problems. We couldn't get it to sound right, the vibes was really bad. It's the worst-sounding album I ever recorded. It was overly compressed and overdriven. We couldn't get a mix to sound right. I knew I was in trouble with that record after the mix. I would have loved to have remixed that whole album in a different studio but it was too late. So I spent every waking minute trying to master the record and get the bottom to sound better, the high end to sound better. But it was too late. I knew that there was a sonic problem. I think we came out with a very brittle-sounding album that was very unpleasant, very harsh and just disgusting. The intent was to make a Black Sabbath kind of sounding record, but it just didn't pan out sonically.

GENE SIMMONS: Kenny Kerner was not really producing, he was involved more with taking care of the business side of it. He was really the one who had the passion for the band. Richie Wise had been in the group Dust and was a songwriter himself and had never made it. In some ways we just sort of went along with his perception of what we should and what we shouldn't do. But in essence we recorded the songs as they were written.

RICHIE WISE: It was not a joyous time for the band. When you do a first album and it's not a huge success, you want to do a second album and solve the problem. But there really wasn't a problem on the first album. Nothing would have been better than to go in and emulate the first album but only with a new batch of songs and a little improvement here and there. Instead everybody said, "To hell with the first album, let's do a whole new thing." I'll take the blame for wanting to make it heavy and distorted and overdriven. It taught me a lot as a producer. Sometimes all you've got to do is move a foot, not a mile, to get where you gotta go.

KENNY KERNER: Paul really worked on being a real good singer and a good performer. Gene worked on his bass playing and was very conscious of what he played. Sometimes Peter had a timing problem. He worked on that and didn't do anything incredibly complex. He played for the song, not how many fills he could do. They all played for the song. Nobody did anything to show off in that band. Ace had no problems playing at all and had a great sense of humor. He probably was the most talented. Each member of KISS was more committed to the band than they were to their ego. They were a band. KISS were mediocre musicians, but to become successful you don't have to be an Eric Clapton on guitar or a Ginger Baker or a Jack Bruce. What made KISS great was their determination, their stick-to-it-iveness. They brought an excitement to rock that had never been here before. They were bigger than life, they were superheroes to kids. They gave the people something to believe in and they extended the myth of rock 'n' roll and that goes beyond talent.

KENNY KERNER: At one point, a couple years into the band, Paul started getting really pissed at Gene. He told Gene that he was hogging all his camera shots whenever they were filmed live. They had this big meeting with Bill about it and Gene looked at Paul and said, "Listen, if you want to get the cameras to shoot you you gotta do something to get them to notice you. Don't tell me to tone down what I'm doing so you can be photographed. You should tone up," because Gene had this big leg kick and the twirling of his hair and his tongue. Paul was just standing there looking nice and not even doing anything. So Gene was absolutely right. And that's what started to break Paul out of his shell. If you notice when he moved around more and stood across the stage and ran across to Gene that the camera followed him [laughs].

RICHIE WISE: We were fooling around one day in the studio. Ace and I tied Paul's hands up with tape. He was walking around the studio and couldn't move his hands. Then I said, "Let me take the tape off." I took a razor blade and I remember cutting through the tape and actually cutting Paul right on the wrist. He was pissed. I felt so bad. In my haste I wasn't as careful as I should have been.

RICHIE WISE: I'm very very proud that so many of those songs on *KISS* and *Hotter Than Hell* are *the* classics. When they play live and do "Firehouse" and "Strutter," those are fucking great. So for me, hey I'm the producer of "Strutter," I arranged that sonofabitch.

GENE SIMMONS: Even by the second record, Ace and Peter started to act up. Peter threatened to leave the band yet again if we didn't leave the seven-minute drum solo he insisted on recording in the middle of "Strange Ways." Ace got into one of his famous car wrecks that smashed up his face so we couldn't shoot the album cover. He came in late and put on half the makeup on his face, the other half was battered. The art department had to superimpose the makeup on the other side of his face.

ACE FREHLEY: For one photo session we did for the *Hotter Than Hell* album, this doctor told me I could only put makeup on half of my face. So all the shots were profiles [laughs]. I got into a car accident. Something pissed me off. I got drunk one night and I kept driving around the Hollywood Hills. I kept going around the same block faster and faster [laughs] until I lost control and hit a telephone pole. I think I was just testing destiny. I got out of the car and I had cut my head. I walked back down to the hotel and I knocked on my road manager's door and there's blood running all down my face. He said, "Oh God, what happened to you?" I go, "I wrecked a car." One of many [laughs], it was like the beginning of the saga.

GENE SIMMONS: We did a photo session with Norman Seeff in Los Angeles. Norman was a very bright but strange guy who believed that photo sessions should be this other thing. So he would create a climate and bring down everybody and anybody. Girls who would blow you, anything that would happen just to get a sense of something. That session was one of the few times that I've seen Paul drunk. He was blitzed. The only thing that was missing was Rod Serling going [imitates Serling's voice] "Witness Paul Stanley entering the Twilight Zone." There was a photo of him with a girl who had nothing on, sort of painted like *Goldfinger* with silver stuff. I don't even think Paul was aware that there were forces of gravity. So he reached over and in one shot you sort of see him nuzzling with this chickie and the next second he's over the bed. He'd fallen over. At the end of the photo session I had to carry him to the car and lock him in the back seat.

PETER CRISS: It was a wild photo session for the back cover. I was sitting in the armchair there with this broad giving me head with this mask on. It was really fucking wild. Paul was in bed with a bunch of broads and me in a robe over this big knight's table's chair. The photographer [Norman Seeff] got us all drunk. That was the idea. He got us all loaded. Everyone was drunk except Gene but Gene had to be drunk on the whole room being drunk. Even the models and the people in the room were drunk. No one was sober but Gene but he had to be intoxicated from just the intoxication of the whole vibe.

PAUL STANLEY: I don't know if anybody can make out the back cover of the album but we were having this wild, wild party with tons of people in weird outfits. Ten minutes after that picture was taken I passed out. I cut my hand, I don't know how I did it. It was pretty strange. I was so drunk that they locked me in a car and I couldn't find my way out. Like any of the Fellini films, *Satyricon*, it was bizarre but it was really great too. It was a party unlike most others that I've been to. A lot of the pictures taken for the back cover have never seen the light of day because some people didn't want to be incriminated by the pictures. Someone would go, "Oh, I can't let so-and-so see me at that party."

GENE SIMMONS: It was Norman Seeff's idea to put the Japanese lettering on the album cover. The result of that was the Japanese instantly took to the band. We started reading cover stories about the band. Some people suspected we were Japanese. The Japanese thought we had taken the makeup from Japanese Kabuki theater.

NORMAN SEEFF: The *Hotter Than Hell* photo shoot was done at the Raleigh stages in Hollywood. The front and back cover were shot on the same day. I had just come back from Japan and met one of the great Japanese artists, Tadanori Yokoo. He was a combination of Timothy Leary, Andy Warhol, and Picasso. I think the way KISS were dressed and who they were suggested to me that Yokoo's work would be an ideal direction for them. As we went further, I thought "Why not put the title in Japanese as well?" I called in a brilliant designer, John Van Hamersveld, to do the design. The album's title dictated the party shot, the *Satyricon* fantasy concept for the back cover. My whole approach is forging a creative partnership with people, it's very free-form. I made it clear that this is a stage for creative improvisation. KISS were doing a rock 'n' roll ballet for the shoot where each of the individuals were playing a part. It was incredibly exciting, they worked so well off of each other. They came in and they delivered.

★ "GOT TO CHOOSE" ★

PAUL STANLEY: "Got to Choose" is one of my favorite KISS songs. Wilson Pickett did a song called "Ninety-Nine and a Half (Won't Do)." There was a band called Boomerang, which featured some of the guys from Vanilla Fudge and they did a version of "Ninety-Nine and a Half (Won't Do)." I'm pretty sure that's the riff I used in "Got to Choose."

★ "PARASITE" ★

ACE FREHLEY: On the *Psycho Circus* tour we were thinking of doing "Parasite." I broke into it at sound check. I don't play it like Bruce Kulick played it, which was very precise. I play it sloppy. That's the way I wrote it. I forgot that KISS were doing "Parasite" with Bruce. Paul said, "You're not playing it right." And I go, "Bullshit [laughs], I wrote the fucking song!" [laughs] He said, "No, you have to play it more staccato." And I go, "No, that's not the way I wrote the fucking song, listen to the record."

★ "GOIN' BLIND" ★

STEVE CORONEL: I like "Goin' Blind." It was originally called "Little Lady." I wrote the chords for that at home. Gene and I both liked Mountain. I wanted to do something like "Theme for an Imaginary Western," that type of big rolling kind of chord progression and that's what I came up with. The chords for that are nice, it's got a nice melody. Gene came up with the words and the melody. I like the way KISS did it on *Unplugged*. To this day, it blows my mind that KISS became the biggest-selling group in the United States. Gene will be the first one to say it, there's no accounting for taste. He'd be the first one to say he's not the greatest singer or musician but he's been tremendously successful.

GENE SIMMONS: "Goin' Blind" dates back to '70. At that point I was listening a lot to Cream and Mountain. "Goin' Blind" happens to be one of my favorite songs. Even something about the recording of it seemed to work for me, the compression on the drums.

KISS GET DUPED INTO POSING FOR *CREEM* PHOTO SHOOT WITHOUT MAKEUP, 1974
(Photo by Charlie Auringer)

★ "HOTTER THAN HELL" ★

PAUL STANLEY: "Hotter Than Hell" was a real cool tune that was very much influenced by Free, the whole idea of sparse playing and storytelling. It had that simplicity, a framework to sing over and certain chord voicings that Free used in "All Right Now." Even thematically, "All Right Now" told the story of seeing a girl in the street and a guy trying to pick her up. "Hotter Than Hell" is about a guy seeing a girl and trying to pick her up and what she replies to him, which is basically the same thing that happens in "All Right Now." The song didn't have an end to it. It could have just gone out with the chorus but I had this guitar figure, which at the time I thought was more like "Iron Man" by Black Sabbath. It just became the tag that Ace soloed over and we went out on that.

PAUL CHAVARRIA: That was the first time we ever got to use a gong. We used to carry that on tour with us and Peter would play it. It got to the point where we had to find someone else to hit it so Peter could continue to play the tune himself.

★ "LET ME GO, ROCK 'N' ROLL" ★

GENE SIMMONS: "Let Me Go, Rock 'n' Roll" was written at the Puerto Rican Interagency Council. I wrote the lyric top to bottom and then Paul added the chordal pattern. And I took that riff from an old Paul thing that he wrote called, "Where There's Smoke There's Fire." Paul's original lyric was, "If you're gonna go to Puerto Rico . . ." I was going, "Paul, I don't think so."

★ "ALL THE WAY" ★

GENE SIMMONS: The idea behind "All the Way" was this girl always keeps talking about her mother or father, it's like, "Just shut up! Do you want to come out with me or not?" I actually ripped the lick off from a group that Mitch Ryder had called Detroit. They had one song out that sounded very much like Mountain. I remember the cowbell part in "All the Way" came from thinking about sticking in a bit of [Mountain's] "Mississippi Queen." Anytime you hear quarter notes on a cowbell you think of Mountain. But the truth was whoever would write the song would come in and play it for the band on guitar and everybody would listen to it and you would sort of play what you heard. And then the writer of the song would try and veer it back to the way it was. So everybody basically had a free hand with the arrangement.

★ "WATCHIN' YOU" ★

GENE SIMMONS: "Watchin' You" was kind of a rip of "Mississippi Queen." I wrote that song in the Wicked Lester days. The lyrical notion of "Watchin' You" came from an Alfred Hitchcock movie called *Rear Window.* The movie is about this guy watching an actual murder going down. James Stewart is in a wheelchair and sees it happening. Also the voyeuristic aspect of watching sexy women get undressed is a common occurrence in New York City because everybody lives in tall buildings and you have windows looking in other people's windows. It was very quick imagery. Some of the lyrics are more stream-of-consciousness. [recites lyrics] "Limpin' as you do, I'm watchin'you" doesn't make a whole lot of sense. It's just literally what came out.

GENE AND PETER, *MIDNIGHT SPECIAL* TV TAPING, APRIL 1, 1975, BURBANK, CALIFORNIA
(© KISS Catalog Ltd.)

★ "MAINLINE" ★

PAUL STANLEY: "Mainline" is a cool rock 'n' roll song. Peter said to Gene and I, "If I don't sing this song, I'll quit the band." If it means that much to you, fine, sing the song. I didn't write the song for someone else, I wrote the song for me. I'd rather somebody say to me, "This means a lot to me," than to start holding things over my head. When you call somebody's bluff on something, if it really matters to me, guess what pal, you lose. Don't dare me unless you're ready to pay the consequences. When I play, I play to win. It's funny, even Gene knows I don't make bets with anybody unless I'm going to win. When somebody sees that I'm going to bet them, it's pretty much time to take your money and go home. I play to win.

★ "COMIN' HOME" ★

PAUL STANLEY: We were stuck at a terrible hotel where we had these real little rooms and we were all homesick. I really missed New York. I know Ace and I wrote it, but I don't remember how or where. I don't remember writing it with Ace but I'm sure we did. Once in a while we would try different combinations of people writing.

ACE FREHLEY: I don't remember much about writing that song. I was drunk a whole lot in those early days [laughs]. If I had a part Paul would say, "Why don't you try putting this part with that part?" We never really spent a lot of time sitting together writing.

★ "STRANGE WAYS" ★

ACE FREHLEY: I love "Strange Ways." I just came up with the riff. It was one of those inspired, heavy tunes. I didn't feel comfortable as a singer at that point. Paul and Gene are very intimidating people. A lot of time they tend to make people feel inadequate. It took me a while to get over my feeling of inadequacy. I didn't think I was as good a singer as I am. It took me a while to come out of my shell. Whenever I wrote songs in the early days, I'd always ask Peter to sing lead so he would get some of the spotlight. I wasn't that secure with myself as a singer around Paul, Gene, and Peter. They were all confident lead singers and even though I knew I could sing, they didn't encourage it, so I kind of just laid back. "Strange Ways" was never performed live by KISS. I forgot how heavy it was. One of my favorite guitar solos is the one on "Strange Ways." It was done in one take. I just closed my eyes and that's what came out. Usually, I record in the control room, but for that solo I went out and stood in front of the amp and got that wild feedback bend at the beginning. It sounded like a dinosaur.

PETER CRISS: Ace wrote it and I sang it. It was really different for me, really heavy and new. I'd never sung anything like it, it wasn't exactly R&B. It was a great challenge to me and I loved it.

DRESSED TO KILL

Release date: March 19, 1975
KISS / STEVE CORONEL–songwriter / JOYCE BOGART–KISS co-manager
LARRY HARRIS–Casablanca Records senior vice president / DAVE WITTMAN–engineer
BOB GRUEN–photographer / CAROL ROSS–publicist
PAUL CHAVARRIA–roadie (1974–1979)

PAUL STANLEY: I'd give *Dressed to Kill* three and a half stars. A lot of people like that album. I like it. The first album was so important, because it was the first. The next two were us trying to build on that foundation. Those three records are the basis for everything, but I think the first one is really on target. We were so worried with *Dressed to Kill* that it was so short. We really felt like, here are the songs and that's enough. *Dressed to Kill* was interesting because we were doing a show in Los Angeles at Santa Monica Civic and basically Neil [Bogart] came backstage and said, "You've got to go back to New York and do an album. We need another album." We were short of material. In the beginning, we were releasing albums every six months and we were on tour with *Hotter Than Hell*. We were playing with Jo Jo Gunne. We were nowhere near ready to do an album. The next day we were on our way back to New York and a lot of those songs were written in the studio before the session. Every morning Gene and I would go to Electric Lady and write songs. Then Peter and Ace would show up and we'd say, "Okay, today's song is called 'Rock and Roll All Nite' or today's song is called 'Room Service.'"

GENE SIMMONS: We weren't selling records. We were barely getting by. I didn't get a chance to do much writing because we were constantly touring. Some of the songs that wound up on it were leftover songs, "She" and "Love Her All I Can" went back to the Wicked Lester days. *Dressed to Kill* was certainly the record where we flew by the seat of our pants. On the first two records, we basically reproduced what we did live.

GENE SIMMONS: Neil Bogart had come down and taken a personal interest in the band. He was probably our biggest supporter. He told us he wanted to produce the record. We convinced Neil that we should do it together because we were a little afraid that Neil would take us down to what he did best, which was disco. But the truth is in terms of producing, Neil was more of a cheerleader. He didn't give us parts or ask, "What's the point of view of this song?" But what he did know was that he wanted to capture more of what he saw live than what our records became in the studio. And again we didn't take a lot of time with sounds. Everything just went down fast. *Dressed to Kill* is okay, but I don't think the record quite has the songs the first two records had. Two and a half stars.

PETER CRISS: I'd give that one two stars. Neil Bogart wasn't a producer, so that's why I rate it that way. He was smoking a lot of pot in those days and I know when you smoke pot you can't hear things correctly. Everything sounds great. And then the next day you come in and go, "Holy shit, that's terrible!" because pot makes things sound good. I've experimented with it and I know about it. I know when I smoked pot and put headsets on, it was like, "Oh wow, man, that's so cool!" But I just don't think Neil went into it with a producer's attitude. Maybe I'd give it three stars actually because the band worked hard. We put a lot of guts into it to to get him through. We had fun and we were back home in Electric Lady so it's a three. We got a lot of offers [from record labels wanting to sign the band]. It was like, "Holy shit!" In the beginning, nobody wanted us and here's the same people calling back and saying, "We want you." So we figured we've got something here. Now we know we've got something, "So fuck you, let's stick with Casablanca since they're new and we're their first babies and we know they're going to bust their balls for us." So we stuck with them. We wouldn't have got as much attention from another label as Neil Bogart gave to us. Here, Neil was literally producing us himself and he was president of the company. You couldn't get more loyalty.

ACE FREHLEY: Neil let us do what we felt like doing and put in his two cents here or there. He had some good ideas. It was different working with Neil because he was the president of Casablanca and you couldn't be as outlandish and wild as you wanted to be. It was intimidating to an extent. I recently listened to that album again. I hadn't listened to it in a long time and I listened to the CD. There was a lot of energy in that record. I was real happy with a lot of the solos I did. It shows growth from the first record [laughs]. Probably a four.

PETER CRISS: Neil [Bogart] wanted to be a producer. He said, "Eddie [Kramer] and them guys are jerks, they don't know nothin' about what they're doing," but neither did he, really. I mean, let him run a record company and he'll run the world. But you couldn't put him behind a console 'cause he was really dangerous!

KISS LIVE AT THE TOWER THEATER, PHILADELPHIA, MAY 3, 1975
(PAUL IS WEARING SUNGLASSES DUE TO EYE INFECTION)
(© KISS Catalog Ltd.)

JOYCE BOGART: Neil [Bogart] understood the music and arranged for them to work with producers who would give them the best sound. He got involved in choosing the material and producing *Dressed to Kill* because he felt he knew what he could get played on radio. He was attempting to make them a little more commercial in that way and still keep their authenticity. And later on, he risked doing a huge live album at a time when no one but supergroups did live albums and they were not the big sellers of an artist's career.

BILL AUCOIN: Neil [Bogart] produced *Dressed to Kill* because we couldn't afford a producer. It was a way to cut costs. We had made a decision that the only way we could keep KISS records in the stores was to have them come out approximately every six months. That would tell the record stores that we had a new record coming out and they could keep the records they already had because it will always sell some catalogue. That was the ploy, to keep the records in the stores and not have them sent back.

LARRY HARRIS: KISS was losing money on every tour date they did. It was costing a lot more to run the company. Before we left Warner Brothers there were only four people at Casablanca. Now we had to hire a whole company and had a great deal more expenses. Every six months we had to have an album from KISS just to keep the cash flow going for us and for them. We insisted upon these albums constantly and sometimes the band wasn't ready or they'd be on the road and they hadn't written any songs.

BILL AUCOIN: The first KISS album sold about sixty thousand, the next sold about eighty to a hundred thousand. The *Dressed to Kill* album sold about 150,000 thousand units. From Neil's [Bogart] point of view it was building. But more importantly the buzz was really starting to happen. We were selling out halls even if we were special guests. The only reason we got to be special guests on any tour was we would sell tickets and would put the headliner into commissions. Most headliners didn't want us to be on the show because we wouldn't do the show unless we could do our pyrotechnics. No headliner really wanted that to happen. The agent would go to their manager and say, "Listen, KISS is gonna be the difference between you making a couple of thousand dollars and you making ten thousand."

PAUL STANLEY: On *Dressed to Kill* Ace was playing out of a cardboard box. He had this amp that he made that was in a cardboard box.

DAVE WITTMAN: We did the whole album at Electric Lady in Studio B. It was a funky little room. KISS did the rhythm tracks live. They would get the songs in like two or three takes. KISS were always well rehearsed, everything went real smoothly. Neil [Bogart] had a lot of strong ideas the way KISS should sound at that point. The amps they used for that album were these real little Fender Champ amps. Gene may have used an Ampeg B-15 amp. They played as loud as those little amps could get. I'd be surprised if they put out more than fifteen or twenty watts.

PAUL STANLEY: By *Dressed to Kill* we were ready to leave the label because we weren't getting our royalties. Around that time, we weren't exactly a hot item, but there were offers from other labels. The only thing that pulled everything together was *Alive!* in terms of us receiving our money and renegotiating our contract. There was a gray area because Joyce [Biawitz] was involved at that point with Neil and it's hard when that's also part of the management team. So at some point I think she realized that it was best for her to separate from Bill.

KENNY KERNER: Bill and Joyce were partners in the Direction Plus company and were also co-managing KISS. What happened was eventually Joyce started going out with Neil Bogart, which immediately made it a conflict of interest. There she was managing a band and supposedly looking out for the band's best interests and quite frankly going to bed with the president of the label, who has totally different interests from the band in certain areas. One incident stands out in particular. We had a meeting in my apartment here in Los Angeles with the whole band, Joyce, Bill [Aucoin], Richie [Wise] and I. We were discussing a substantial offer from Atlantic Records. They offered us a million-dollar deal to take the band, me and Richie as producers, Bill and Joyce as managers, the whole package. We wanted to take the band off Casablanca Records and go with a major label that could really make the band explode. We discussed all kind of possibilities, the meeting ended and everybody went home. Coincidentally, the next day Neil Bogart knew everything that happened at the meeting. He fired Richie and I and decided to produce the third album himself, which was his way of trying to gain control over the band. Neil figured if he was in the studio with the band for a month, he'd be able to win them over. He wanted to buy the management out from Bill. There was only one possible way for him to have found out about that meeting and that was through Joyce. She went home that night, got into bed with Neil, and went, "Oh honey, by the way . . ." And their relationship got stronger and stronger until they eventually married. It became clear that she couldn't be on the side of the group anymore, it was just a major conflict of interest. There was no resentment on Bill's part. He just went on as the sole manager of the band. He didn't hold a grudge and never tried to get even with Neil.

BOB GRUEN: The *Dressed to Kill* album cover shot came out of a shoot I did for a two-page photo comic for *Creem* magazine. The concept of the comic was KISS were on their way to work as average, normal-looking people. That's why they're wearing suits and ties. They're reading a newspaper and discover that there's going to be a John

Denver concert and they want to save the world from John Denver. So they run into a phone booth and pull off their suits and come running out of the phone booth as KISS. They go around putting up posters advertising a concert for John Denver. All the people show up and instead of John Denver they get KISS. The people get excited and KISS basically saves the world with rock 'n' roll. At the end they get a roomful of girls and they get medals pinned on their chests. It was a very funny little comic. So for that photo shoot KISS started out wearing suits. Some of the ties were mine. On the album cover you can see Gene wearing my ex-wife's clogs [laughs]. While we were together shooting, I had KISS stop for a minute at the southwest corner of 23rd Street and Eighth Avenue and took a group shot of them dressed in the suits. They liked the picture so much that they used it for the cover of *Dressed to Kill*. Later on, I remember shooting some photos of them in the suits and ties with Neil Bogart at Electric Lady, making it seem as if they always wore those suits and dressed like that.

CAROL ROSS: KISS was the first client I brought into Rogers & Cowan, one of the major international public relations agencies. During a creative staff meeting I showed pictures of KISS and everyone went into shock. I explained that this was not a gimmick, this was an imaginative concept. I had to lay out a campaign to get the press interested in KISS because at that point no one had taken them seriously. When I started calling the media, I had to hold the phone away from my ears because people were laughing hysterically. "KISS? Are you kidding?" They said they were a joke and couldn't play music. I went back to Bill Aucoin and said that we have to educate the media to what KISS is all about. I figured that I had to take all the negativity from the media and make it positive. One of the most important things is I knew I had a band who understood publicity, which helped to make a difficult task a little easier. They were willing to do anything that needed to be done to make people aware of them. A few close friends of mine within the press were nice enough to start doing little favors for me. I had given them breaks with other clients and sometimes in this business you have to do that. You say, "I'll arrange for you to speak to so-and-so but I want you to give some consideration to KISS." That's ultimately how we started to make the breakthrough. When things started to break for KISS, all of a sudden everyone was admitting they were a phenomenon. And everyone in the media wanted to take credit for breaking the band.

★ "ROOM SERVICE" ★

PAUL STANLEY: I love "Room Service." There's a good riff in it. "Room Service" was about touring. I lived on the road at that point. I was more in my element being in my hotel than being in my apartment and I was more in my element getting room service in any way, shape, or form it came.

65

KISS "DRESSED TO KILL"

FEB 6. 75

TWO TIMER c SIMMONS o

                    B tells me
My Baby SHE THINKS SHE'S HIGH FASHION
She says SHE THINKS SHE LOOKS DIVINE
About That's WHAT I KEEP TELLIN' HER
          E
I TELL HER ALL THE TIME   —A
                     B

you know SHE TELLS ME SHE LIKES FAST CARS
SHE SAYS SHE LIKES MINE THE BEST
AND JUST BECAUSE OF THAT BABY
YOU'D THINK SHE'LL FORGET THE REST   NO, NO, N

        C SHARP
       JUST CALL ME A THREE TIME LOSER
       THAT'S ALL I'LL EVER BE   A. B   B
 chorus 'CAUSE MY BABY'S A TWO TIMER
       YOU KNOW SHE'S TWO TIMIN' ME   C SHARP
                                 B
             F MY BABY'S A TWO TIMER C SHARP
             SHE'S NOTHING BUT A   "
             SHE MAKES ME CRAZY SHE'S - -

MY BABY'S A TWO TIMER
A TWO TIMER SHE'LL ALWAYS BE
BUT HER LOVE'S GOT SUCH A STRONG HOLD
IT'S GOT A HOLD ON ME

★ "TWO TIMER" ★

GENE SIMMONS: "Two Timer" came very fast, very natural. It was written on guitar. That was a demo I recorded in Minnesota. "Two Timer's" frame of reference is Humble Pie, although when I listen back to it there's not a riff or melody line that resembles the band. I know Paul heard "Two Timer" and liked the chord changes in the opening of the song. It's the exact same chords used in the opening of "Detroit Rock City."

★ "LADIES IN WAITING" ★

GENE SIMMONS: We were literally rehearsing at a rehearsal hall for our new record. This was in between tours and we just didn't have enough songs for the new album. We used some of the leftover songs from the demos and we tried to rework some of the Wicked Lester songs. "Ladies in Waiting" was a title that I had lying around. It came very fast, there wasn't a lot of thought to it. That song was pretty much done in the studio. I taught the band the song earlier in the afternoon and the lyrics were written pretty much on the spot. Again, in those days we really didn't have time to sit down and think about anything. It just happened fast.

★ "GETAWAY" ★

ACE FREHLEY: "Getaway" was just one of those forgotten tunes. Peter sang lead on that. I wasn't singing lead then, I was too afraid. I was too shy to sing. I didn't think I could do it. But once I got one under my belt with "Shock Me," I wanted more and more and more. Once I did my solo album, which became the most successful of the four, that's when I really realized that the band was holding me back. I wasn't blossoming.

PETER CRISS: I loved singing it. Great song too.

★ "ROCK BOTTOM" ★

PAUL STANLEY: "Rock Bottom" was a weird song because it was actually two different things. Ace wrote the intro and I wrote the actual song. Every once in a while I write a song in the key of A that has a certain sound to it. "Hotter Than Hell" was like that and "Rock Bottom" had that. There are all kinds of songs based in some way on "All Right Now" by Free.

ACE FREHLEY: I had an instrumental thing I was working on and Paul liked it. Paul started playing the counterpart to it and he said, "This might make a really good intro to a song I'm working on." So we tried it and we liked it and we recorded it and it made it onto the album. For the record, I used a Guild twelve-string guitar. The last time we played it was on the reunion tour. Did you see the double-neck guitar I was playing? That is the only cherry sunburst double-neck in the world.

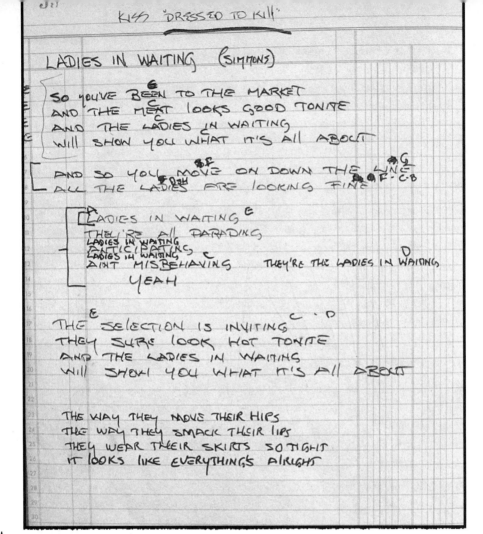

GENE SIMMONS HANDWRITTEN LYRICS, "LADIES IN WAITING"
(© KISS Catalog Ltd.)

★ "C'MON AND LOVE ME" ★

PAUL STANLEY: I love "C'mon and Love Me." I was talking to someone about how over the years you can become a better songwriter. But you can also lose the essence and purity of what made you in the beginning 'cause what you did early on was just based upon free association, just purging yourself and cool stuff would come out. "C'mon and Love Me" was written like that. It was very autobiographical and very much a point of view of a lifestyle that I was living but it wasn't a calculated study. It was basically just spitting out a song. I really liked it, still do, the verse, chorus, the whole thing. That's the first time I played lead guitar on a KISS song, that's me playing the lead at the beginning.

★ "ANYTHING FOR MY BABY" ★

PAUL STANLEY: There were elements of Bachman Turner Overdrive in "Anything for My Baby." I remember being in the studio and we were trying to make the guitars sound better. We were adding acoustic guitars to reinforce the electric guitars because BTO was doing it. Some people seem to like that song but I don't get it. It's one of those songs that I wrote that I'm not all that fond of.

★ "SHE" ★

STEVE CORONEL: The reason "She" was written because I went downtown with money in my pocket to 48th Street looking for a guitar. I bought a guitar that I fell in love with, this beautiful black guitar called "The Black Widow." I took it home, and sat in the bedroom in the back of my grandparents' apartment and I started strumming around with it and turning it up. I hit [imitates song's chordal opening and riffs]. It's a crappy little song [laughs]. You have an Indian war chant with the tanks rolling, the whole part [recites lyrics] "She walks by moonlight . . ." It's real dinosaur rock. It's fun, it has a lot of power to it. I like the way it starts out. It seemed like a good little idea. It was simple. The next day I brought what I had put together into the loft and said to Gene, "I've got a good piece here, do you want to try and write something?" And he said, "All right, play it for me." I remember he was standing up and I played the intro and went into the verse. He closed his eyes and he gets the feeling for it, shaking his head and in about four minutes he starting singing some of the lyrics. It must have taken a half-hour to get it all written.

GENE SIMMONS: Steve Coronel and I wrote that around the time when he and I were just sitting around writing songs. He had the riff. [hums the riff from "She"] I remember writing "See You Tonite" right around there and I'm going, "Gee, it's too bad we can't be in a band and play this." He kept saying, "That's my favorite song, let's play that song."

★ "LOVE HER ALL I CAN" ★

PAUL STANLEY: "Love Her All I Can" was a Wicked Lester song. When we were doing *Dressed to Kill* we were short of songs. [It was inspired by] The Who and the Nazz, Todd Rundgren's old band. They had a song called "Open My Eyes," it's basically the same intro. They copied The Who and we kind of copied them.

GENE SIMMONS: I think in horns when I do riffs. [imitates the opening part of song] The intro to that song was a horn line riff based on the Nazz's "Open My Eyes."

★ "ROCK AND ROLL ALL NITE" ★

PAUL STANLEY: "Rock and Roll All Nite" was written while we were in L.A. at the Continental Hyatt House. Neil [Bogart] said to us, "You guys need an anthem." At that time rock bands didn't have anthems. But Neil was real smart and really ahead of his time and he said, "Sly and the Family Stone had 'Stand' and 'I Want to Take You Higher.'" So he said, "You guys really should have an anthem." I wrote the chorus and Gene wrote the verses. We brought all our friends in the studio to sing backgrounds on it. Friends, girlfriends, sisters, brothers, anybody. It sounded like a perfectly good song. It's a track that the audience had to connect to, that's what made it what it is. It was released as a single and it tanked. It wasn't until the live version came out that it became a hit.

GENE SIMMONS: Originally, I had this song called "Drive Me Wild." It was the notion of a car as an analogy to a woman, twin orbs shining in the night, the obvious sexual references are there. The idea if I drive a car, "You drive me wild, I'll drive you crazy" idea. The idea of driving wild was the double entendre of the word "drive." I never really had the chorus. So, when Neil Bogart suggested that we write an anthem, Paul and I had never heard that word before except for the Ayn Rand novel *Anthem*. Neil said, "Write something that says something about how you feel. What is your philosophy?" We thought that was an interesting notion 'cause we always liked writing about how we feel and most importantly who we are. It came very fast. Paul just walked in and goes, "Look what I have." [sings] "I wanna rock and roll all nite . . ." That immediately hooked me because of course it's "I" not "we." That's probably the main difference between Queen and KISS. Queen was always about "We," "We Will Rock You." And we were always about "I." We've always thought one voice spoke louder, a personal point of view was much more important. One-notion-can-change-the-world kind of a thing. So, the pieces were basically stuck together. Take my verse and attach it to Paul's chorus and you've got a song. For the studio version, Neil Bogart was there and he went all the way back to the disco days with a group called Steam [sings the group's song, "Na Na Hey Hey Kiss Him Goodbye"]. In those days you'd have twenty people in the studio and everybody would be singing. Everybody was in there singing on the chorus of "Rock and Roll All Nite," including every studio musician, Lydia Criss, roadies, everybody.

ACE FREHLEY: "Rock and Roll All Nite" is a great song. After we recorded it in the studio, we knew it was gonna be an anthem. I knew it was gonna be something special. The song says it all. It's easy to play too. The good thing about that song is when you're playing it it's the end of the night and the show's almost over.

PAUL CHAVARRIA: We were in the studio for the recording of "Rock and Roll All Nite." All of the road crew wore black leather jackets with black T-shirts with rhinestones on the front that said KISS. One of the roadies, Moose [Peter Oreckinto], did this trick with a zipper [makes sound of zipper]. Then it got to be all the roadies doing this zipper trick. Gene or Paul decided they wanted to mike it and hear what it sounded like on the song. It made the track, you can hear the zipper in a couple of places on the song [imitates zipper sound], "zip, zip, zip." It's all of us doing this zipper move [laughs].

ALIVE!

Release date: September 10, 1975
KISS / EDDIE KRAMER–producer / BILL AUCOIN–manager
LARRY HARRIS–Casablanca Records senior vice president
FIN COSTELLO–photographer / DENNIS WOLOCH–album designer
LEE NEAVES and BRUCE REDOUTE–teenagers on back cover of album

PAUL STANLEY: *Alive!* gets double five stars! I think it was important because we wanted to put out a souvenir, almost like when you go to the circus. It was like a musical program. We were in a lot of trouble because we reached a point where a lot of other bands wouldn't let us open for them anymore. So, we literally were sitting around not touring. It was an album that put us in a position to headline. It wasn't a make-or-break record but it was a real important album.

GENE SIMMONS: Four stars. We were all so innocent in those days. Everything that happened was just bigger than life. We knew something was going on. We were selling out concerts. We couldn't find groups to play with. We were thrown off of an Argent tour, a Savoy Brown tour. Black Sabbath threw us off their tour. It was a live-or-die situation for Casablanca. They didn't have any hits. But we just did what we did. And we always went against the grain. Recording a live album when you really haven't even made it, we hadn't even had a Gold record. We just decided that we were gonna do a live album and we were gonna make it a double live album. I think that record sonically is what the band is about. Somehow taking an audience away from our songs makes it a lot more clinical or colder.

PAUL STANLEY: The great thing about *Alive!* is that it was a recording that featured and paid tribute to the audience as much as the band. I think that's what people respond to so well with *Alive!* It really captures the live experience in terms of what it felt like in the audience. It was real important to me that the audience not be background because at a KISS concert in some ways the audience is competing with the band [laughs]. It's a communal effort. It's like a church revival; it's trying to get everybody to peak together. *Alive!* really spotlights the experience not only in terms of what the band was doing but what the audience was doing.

EDDIE KRAMER: I was disappointed that I didn't get to produce KISS's first album since I did their demo, which got them their record deal. Politics prevailed. The first two albums were okay. I'm pretty sure the band wasn't totally happy with the sound of them. But when it came to the live album, it was a strange series of coincidences and circumstances. I got a phone call from Neil Bogart one night saying, "Look, KISS want to do a live album. Are you interested?" I said, "Well, let me think about it," because sitting on my desk I had a tape from Tom Scholz [leader of Boston]. I listened to this tape and said, "Gee, this is really fucking good." I was anguishing over the decision. "Should I do KISS or should I produce this band from Boston led by Tom Scholz?" In the end I called up Tom Scholz and said, "Look, what do you want me to do with this tape? It's really very good. I couldn't add anything to do it. I suggest you put it out like it is." I still think it's great. I decided to go for KISS because of the challenge of making those guys sound great. *Alive!* was recorded in various locations—Wildwood, New Jersey; Davenport, Iowa; Cleveland; and Detroit.

PETER CRISS: I give the album five stars. I loved it. It was exciting. We were finally doing a live album. For me, it's a five. Plus, I did one of my best drum solos I've ever done on "100,000 Years." Today, I still think that was one of my best drum solos ever. Fans still come up to me and say, "How do you do that '100,000 Years'?" To me, that was one of the first heavy metal drum solos. There really wasn't a heavy metal drum solo with an audience participating with the screaming and the phasing of the drums. I still use some of the solo in my updated solo. I still add little pieces of it and I swear to God, the minute I add those pieces, the audience goes crazy. We had to touch things up. A lot of people do that. A lot of things were touched up; a lot of vocals, harmonies, guitar parts, bass parts, definitely drum parts. Just little parts because when you play live you play faster because your adrenaline is pumped up. I worked with a click track in the studio, but you can't onstage and I'm so geared up that I'm a little quicker.

ACE FREHLEY: *Alive!* is a five. A lot of guitar players come up to me and say *Alive!* is their rock 'n' roll bible. That's how they learned how to play guitar, which I find flattering. If that album bombed we would have been dropped from the label. But I knew the record was gonna be great because I believe the only way to capture KISS is with a live record. At that point, our studio albums didn't capture us as well as the live album. I thought I played better live because the audience inspired me.

PAUL STANLEY: I really enjoy myself onstage, prancing around, shaking my ass, shaking my head, playing the guitar between my legs. I enjoy it as much as the audience. Basically I am entertaining myself up there. I have a great time, teasing and prancing. I love it. There are some nights when you just know that it's magic, the ultimate. We strive to create a certain standard of excellence. But you can never re-create spontaneity. That's where you can fall into trouble. You've got to increase your standards all the time and not copy yourself. If I do a show that I know isn't good, it's very embarrassing, not because of what other people think, but because I have to live with myself. I've seen the same reaction from Ace. Most of the time people don't know when we've had an off night, but we do and it makes us angry. It's very important for us to be proud of what we're doing. The image is only valid as long as we're good.

ACE FREHLEY: In the early days, I used to get so excited playing guitar that I might fall off the front of the stage. Gene and Paul would lean over me and pretend it was part of the show.

PETER CRISS: It's important that we have a good time 'cause if they see us havin' fun, they'll have a good time. I'm in the back drumming and it's a show to me. I get off on the three guys just as much as the audience. It's important to get really close with your audience.

ACE FREHLEY: When we started out, we always had the attitude even when we were third or fourth on the bill, that we were the headliners and it was our gig. We were out to blow everyone off the stage. But now that we're on top, we don't feel any pressure that younger bands will come along and try to outdo us.

PAUL STANLEY: KISS is loud, but that's part of what makes us larger than life. The band makes its own rules. We play louder than any band because that is the decibel level that we believe is right for our music. When we first played in Japan in 1977, health officials measured the decibel level to make sure we weren't going to damage anyone's ears. The decibel level was 136, the Concorde is 100. We don't believe in cutting corners and we don't. We've never been concerned with cost, but we have been with the quality of our performance. When money is made, we put it back in to make the show better.

GENE SIMMONS: I love the road. I can exist on the road forever. I think hotels are magical places. You pick up the phone and food appears in your room. You want to go out and the limousines pick you up out front.

PETER CRISS: The live version of "Rock and Roll All Nite" captures us for exactly for what we were. It captured the live insanity, adrenaline, audience vibes.

LARRY HARRIS: Compared to other singles on our label like "Y.M.C.A" or "Love to Love You Baby," "Rock and Roll All Nite" was not a big single. It was never a big Top 40 song, it was a much bigger FM rock song. But it's a wonderful song and to this day it's still on the radio constantly.

ACE FREHLEY: Some of it was [re-recorded in the studio]. I don't really remember to what extent but some of the stuff just had to be fixed.

PAUL STANLEY: Every album gets patched up a bit for all kinds of reasons. If you listen to "C'mon and Love Me" there's a bass mistake that goes throughout the whole song, every time we go into the chorus. It's by no means perfect. When I listen to it now, I know I could have fixed up the vocals and really done a much better job on the songs. But I think it's as honest as it needs to be. It's anything but flawless. If we wanted a really flawless record, we would have doctored it up, but it's as close to live as it needs to be. I have no qualms about that.

BILL AUCOIN: We were editing and re-recording some of the live tracks at Electric Lady for *Alive!* Most of the live album wasn't really live, but that's not unusual for live albums to be touched up.

GENE SIMMONS: It happened so long ago. I do remember going back in and redoing some of the vocal things, but I think by and large what you heard is what you got. There's certainly enough mistakes on there.

EDDIE KRAMER: As far as I'm concerned a lot more was re-recorded than what they remember. Quite frankly some of the songs we stripped back and just left the drums and re-recorded the bass, and Paul's rhythm guitar. Ace's guitar generally speaking was not too bad but even then we had to replace some stuff. Quite a few vocals. You know, with all that jumping around it was impossible to get an accurate performance. The re-recording was done at Electric Lady. The whole idea was you would listen to the audience reaction and listen to the delay of the vocal and synch it up exactly with the performance that was there. If there were repairs to be made, if it was like a bad note that was hit, you'd just do it in sync and then you'd fix the bad note. You'd disguise that there's a bad note there. The same with the guitars. You try to get them as accurately as possible and by the time you add the audience back in again it sounds fine. I mean it's done all the time. We're not the only people to have done it. I remember when we were mixing it back the second time, I was playing it back off two machines and I got the audience on the B or the C side, I can't remember, where the audience fades up and it's phasing because I was copying and it's kind of interesting so we left it in. It was a good live album for its day. It sold two, three million copies. It was somewhat re-created in the studio, but faithfully to the point where it sounded live. Nobody really knew for years. Five, ten years after the fact people were asking me how I did that album and when I told them that it was basically re-created in the studio including audience loops, they couldn't believe it. So hey, it was one of those things. You do what you do to make the record sound great. It enhanced their performances. I don't think that we were cheating. What we were doing was just fixing up a very, very tough live performance where the artists were not totally in control. I don't care how great you are, there is no way you can do the kind of stuff that KISS does onstage and come off sounding in tune and in time. It's impossible. So we didn't touch the drums, and we used the audiences that were there. We enhanced them and made them sound bigger and fatter and made the record sound good. Paul's voice was plopped in a few times to make it sound good, the same with the rhythm guitars, and the same with Ace's guitars. Most of his solos we kept intact. Peter's vocals were cool. We kept those. Paul's raps were just culled from various performances and edited together.

PAUL CHAVARRIA: Every guy on the road crew that worked for KISS in those days was a perfectionist. Everybody wanted everything to be right. When Peter's drum kit didn't rise at Cobo Hall, one of the shows taped for the *Alive!* album, we took it out on ourselves. The road crew would kill for KISS. We would die for those guys. We would dive in front of them if people got in their way. We would attack somebody if anybody tried to pick a fight with the boys. We were their security. Our leader was J. R. Smalling. We called him the "Black Oak" because he was so big. He could take on anybody and do anything he had to do. J.R. did the famous intro that's on the *Alive!* album. [recites intro] "You wanted the best and you got it, the hottest band in the land . . . KISS!"

ACE FREHLEY: That's when we started making money. I remember when we put out the live album it was basically something to put out until we did another studio album. We had no idea it was going to be as successful as it was.

EDDIE KRAMER: In retrospect, *Alive!* was fairly groundbreaking because no heavy metal band had done a record like this. The reason for the success of the record if I could analyze that would be the fact that they toured very heavily in the Midwest and the South for two years. And then by the time we came out with the live album they had registered fans that must have been in the 150,000 to 200,000 [range]. And we knew that they could sell 150,000, 200,000 copies. So we thought, okay, this record is gonna do 300,000, 350,000. Nobody thought in their wildest imagination that it would go Gold. When it went Gold, we went nuts. When it went Platinum, we went crazy and so on. And it was not expected.

BILL AUCOIN: We decided to do a live album because it was less expensive than recording a studio record. We had never gotten a royalty statement from Casablanca. Neil [Bogart] was going through all sorts of craziness with the company. They had left Warner Brothers. Neil mortgaged his house and asked independent distributors to put money into the company to keep it going. They did that based on the fact that Neil had success when he was at Buddah. Casablanca were really at the end of their rope. That's one of the reasons I used my American Express card to finance KISS on tour because the record label couldn't afford to give us any more money. When I challenged Casablanca over their nonpayment of royalties, the lawyers revealed that we were suing the label. It became a real war. Neil took offense to that because he had done a lot for us. I adored Neil and he took it very negatively. Neil felt I was going against him and Joyce [Biawitz] was caught in the middle. She was talking about getting married to Neil. We were just releasing *Alive!* and I said, "If we don't get things straightened out now we're dead." The word on the street in the record industry was that KISS was starting to break. They were listening to the kids who were saying, "KISS, KISS, KISS . . ." We finally worked it out but all the other record companies were rushing in saying, "Sign here, sign here." Doug Morris from Big Tree, which was part of Atlantic, wanted to sign KISS. But I really had no reason to leave Neil. I just had to straighten out this business end. Neil actually went to the guys and asked them to leave me. He told them that he would manage them and Casablanca would do everything. This was all because I was going against him. The guys made it clear to Neil that they wouldn't leave me. Basically we had Neil and Casablanca over the barrel. We signed a new deal with Casablanca, who paid us a lump sum of what we were owed, and we would go forward. We didn't have any money. In fact, I couldn't afford rent. Fortunately, I lived in a house where the landlady was a creative person and so she understood. So she just let it slide for a while. My friends said I was nuts because I managed a group wearing makeup. They said, "You better take Bill out tonight otherwise he is not going to eat." So they would take turns calling me and saying, "How about going out tonight?" That's how I ate. Ironically, that was when we went from literally having no money to getting a check for $2 million. This was back in '75 when $2 million was like $10 million. All I can remember is staring at those zeroes. I sat there and kept counting the zeros. I must have counted those zeros a thousand times.

LARRY HARRIS: *Alive!* surprised us too. The album came out in the fall of '75. At the same time, Parliament and Donna Summer had albums out. All of a sudden, those three albums started to sell. We had a big problem. We didn't have the money to press the product. We went so far in debt with the pressing plants already and owed them so much money that they didn't want to press any more records for us. Neil went to each pressing plant and begged and cajoled and made whatever deals he had to make to persuade them to press more records. All three of those albums exploded at one time and it almost put us out of business. It's one of those cases where success could put you out of business.

BILL AUCOIN: Joyce met Neil on *Flipside* and she fell in love with him. Neil said, "You come and live with me and I'll marry you." Neil told me, "Joyce is leaving the company. I want you to buy her out." And we came up with a figure. This happened during the making of the live album.

FIN COSTELLO: The cover was shot at the Michigan Palace in Detroit [now a parking lot], which had been the home of the Stooges, and MC5. It was being used by KISS for rehearsals for their Cobo Hall show, where they were recording the live album. We hung a backdrop in front of the drums and did some shots for the European and Japanese magazines and then went on to film and photograph a run-through of the show. I had just moved to the U.S. from London, where I had worked with bands like Deep Purple, Humble Pie, and Status Quo. Quo had a bit in their show where the three guitarists came close together and did a little dance kind of thing, which had impressed Gene. It became a sort of in joke during the shoot. I kept saying, "Let's do the Quo shot again," until eventually Paul said, "Hey man, we are KISS not Quo." As you can see from the high angle of the camera this could not have been taken at a live show, as I would have had to have been suspended above the stage to get that angle.

Technically, it's not very good as a photograph but really cuts it in terms of atmosphere. The album's back cover was the big surprise for me. I thought that a shot showing the size of the gig might work and went down to the front just before the show. As I was taking a shot, these two kids walked into frame with a poster they had made. They were pleased to have their picture taken but must have been as surprised as me when it made the back cover. A fan's dream come true.

BRUCE REDOUTE: The photo of Lee and I holding the KISS poster was taken at Cobo Hall in May of 1975. We were fifteen years old at the time. We brought the poster because we were hoping to get noticed. And we got noticed big-time! We were sitting in the sixteenth row and a lot of the photographers on the main floor just went wild shooting us holding the poster. Months went by and the *Alive!* album came out. When we saw that the entire back cover was the photo of Lee and I holding the poster, we were astounded. It was a dream come true for us. We still have the poster, we take turns guarding it! [laughs]

LEE NEAVES: Bruce said, "Why don't you make up a banner for the KISS concert?" It took me an hour or two to do the artwork, and then Bruce and Bob Bommarito helped color it. If I knew it was gonna be famous, I would have taken my time [laughs]. So we brought the poster to the show and unveiled it. Soon a huge crowd of people gathered around it. Evidently it caught the attention of someone backstage wondering what the commotion was. Then this photographer came up to us and asked us if he could take a photo. He posed me and asked me to put my arm up. When *Alive!* came out, I went to the department store Korvette's and saw it for the first time. I turned the album over and it was us! To this day, it's still amazing to me, I'm a part of KISStory!

DENNIS WOLOCH: Bill Aucoin shared space at Howard Marks Advertising. KISS had three albums out already. I had done a little bit of work for them before, a little mini-poster. Bill came to me and said, "They're coming out with a live album, do you want to design it?" I said, "Sure." So he supplied me with pictures and that was it. I had the idea for the little handwritten notes by the band that went inside the album. I told the guys to use different kinds of paper and different pens so it didn't look like they all sat down and did it at the same time. So, it had a little more of a personal touch.

DESTROYER

Release date: March 15, 1976

KISS / BOB EZRIN–producer/songwriter / JAY MESSINA–engineer / CORKY STASIAK–engineer
STAN PENRIDGE–songwriter / KIM FOWLEY–songwriter / MARK ANTHONY–songwriter
DICK WAGNER–session guitarist / BILL AUCOIN–manager
SEAN DELANEY–KISS creative consultant/choreographer/collaborator
DENNIS WOLOCH–album designer

GENE SIMMONS: It was a different world. We didn't know what we were getting ourselves into. *Alive!* was kind of a bookend of what we had done up until that time. We thought it was time to take a step forward. We didn't want to do it ourselves because we thought we were too close to it so that's why Bob Ezrin came in. And actually the combination worked really well because he has much more of a classical background than we do, so "Beth" kind of happened. He co-wrote that with Peter although Peter doesn't really play an instrument. He just had this melody in his mind. Ezrin absolutely had his own way of recording things. He half engineered that record anyway. I don't think we had a sense of anything [of how special the record was]. In fact we were scared some things sounded too different. We were very concerned about "Beth." I'd give *Destroyer* four and a half stars.

PETER CRISS: Oh fuck, *Destroyer* gets five stars! God, I worked so hard on it. At the time I actually went to a primal therapy institute where John Lennon went because I went so far into it that I totally lost all reality. Then I was getting introduced to coke and there was a lot of it. I got so engulfed in that shit on *Destroyer*, so into the songs. Of all the KISS albums that probably has my most brilliant drumming. It has my most unique drumming. I picked every part out. I planned every part, I wrote every part out. I never did this on any other album. "Do You Love Me?" is killer. *Destroyer* was a very difficult and hard album. "Beth" is on it. The album was failing. It was falling off the charts. It wasn't making it. As far as I know some DJ picked it up and started playing "Beth." And all of a sudden Neil Bogart starts going, "Wait a minute, they're really playing this a lot." All of a sudden, before you know it, he's putting a lot of money behind it and they're people out all over the field pushing "Beth." Next, all of a sudden it's number one and I'm winning a People's Choice Award and fuck, the album goes double Platinum [laughs]. It was like, what happened? We were really sweating it like crazy. We were going, "Is this going to work? Did we do the right thing?" We used Bob Ezrin and no one is better than that. We spent a fortune to do it and we were really sweating when we saw it going down in *Billboard*. We started going, "Oh no, Jesus Christ." After all the primal therapy I went through I said, "This can't happen." But one snowy night around the holidays, Bill Aucoin dropped by my

RECORD PLANT STUDIOS
321 WEST 44th STREET, NEW YORK, N.Y. 10036 • (212) 581-6505

RUFF MIXES

| ARTIST | PROD. | W.O. | ENG. | REEL |
| KISS | MR Bob EZRIN | | JAY CORK | 1 |

| CLIENT | DATE | MACH. # | TRKS. | IPS. | OF |
| Rock STEADY | 1-17-76 | A | 2 | 15 | 1 |

TAKE	TITLE	TIME	COMMENT
	SHOUT IT out loud		
	SWEET PAIN		
	DETROIT Rock City		
	King of the nigh time World		
	Do you love ME ?		
	TAILs		

406
AMPEX

DESTROYER REEL-TO-REEL TAPE BOX
(© KISS Catalog Ltd.)

brownstone apartment and we had a fire going. We all sat around the couch and Bill said, "Listen to this." And he put "Beth" on and it was real quiet. It was an incredible moment. We listened to it and all of a sudden we looked at each other and went, "Fuck, that's good. That's really magical." Then when it was done playing Bill said, "Guess what? The album's got a bullet again and it's doing great. This is going to be the hit off the album." We just all dropped dead. I remember it was such a beautiful moment. We had all these candles lit. It was just wild, I'll never forget it.

PAUL STANLEY: I like *Destroyer* a lot. I'd give that five stars. It's an ambitious album. Working with Bob Ezrin that first time was like boot camp. We went in there kind of green, and came out a lot smarter for it. It stands the test of time real well.

ACE FREHLEY: At that point in time, I was a party animal. I was hitting Studio 54 a lot. A lot of times I'd show up late or with a hangover. There's no secret about that. Bob Ezrin would crack the whip and a lot of times he didn't have patience. All the records he did with Alice Cooper he used studio guitar players. A lot of times for me to get a guitar solo right I've got to get the right mood and I don't like pressure. Sometimes Bob didn't have the patience that other producers that I've worked with in the past have had. I'm not a schooled musician, if I didn't have something pat, a lot of times Bob would fuckin' make me feel inadequate, which I didn't find too thrilling. That was one of the things about that record that I didn't like. But there were some times that Bob and I hit it off and we saw eye-to-eye. There were brilliant moments on that record.

ACE FREHLEY: I think that's a great record. The actual finished product was very innovative and it showed growth for us. He made us look at things in a different light.

PAUL STANLEY: The Alice Cooper stuff was so brilliant that we needed a producer. Even though we didn't know half of what we thought we knew, we weren't really ready to listen to anybody. But Ezrin's talent and track record was undeniable. It wasn't something that was left-field from what we were doing. It was very akin to what we had done. What Bob taught us was discipline in the studio. For that first project, *Destroyer*, he wore a whistle around his neck and would blow it and call us "campers." He was not above pointing a finger in your face and yelling at you. That's pretty funny when you're selling out arenas all over and you have somebody in the studio that's treating you like an imbecile. Really what it was, was musical boot camp. It was trying to get the best out of us and trying to get us to set a new standard for ourselves.

BILL AUCOIN: I got involved with Bob because he had done the [Alice] Cooper thing and he was also very excited. Bob had called me once because his son kept talking about the KISS group. He figured that if his son kept talking about the group something had to happen. So he called and I said, "Why don't you come down and let's talk about it?" Bob is very bright. He was into it because of his son. He got caught up in the excitement. Bob is very strong. I think Ace called him "The Dictator." But I loved him because he was bright and together and he really wanted to make a very successful record. And he was good for them I thought. It brought them to another level plus the fact that it was still a real rock 'n' roll record. I wanted to try to cut across a wider range and show people that they could really do something more significant.

BOB EZRIN: A kid in Toronto had my phone number. He used to call me all the time and tell me about all the hot new stuff. One day he called me and said, "There is a band that you have to produce and they're called KISS. These guys need you, they are the greatest band in the world, but there is something missing from their music." Then by coincidence, about two weeks later, I ran into them in the stairway of CTV in Toronto, where they were doing an interview. These monsters came down the stairs, seven and a half feet tall, absolutely dwarfed me as I was coming up the stairs. I felt like I was shaking hands with my father. It was just such a coincidence that I would run into these guys after that phone call. I told them that I had been told that I should produce them. I said we better get together and talk about this. We met in New York City in a restaurant and talked about what KISS stood for and who they were. Then it was arranged for me to come to Michigan to see them perform. They were playing a mid-sized arena. I remember from the time they hit the stage to the time they left the entire audience was on their feet. I was just blown away by the power of them and I also saw some areas which needed some improvement. So, we met immediately thereafter and talked about what they wanted to accomplish with their next record, to take them over the hump from being best of the B bands to top of the A group. I felt that specifically for the *Destroyer* record we had to build a little more humanity into the group. We had to expand the audience beyond fifteen-year-old boys and go after some girls too. We had to introduce a little pathos. The analogy I used was they reminded me a little bit of the Lee Marvin character in *The Wild One*. I wanted to change them into Marlon Brando. We aggressively went after finding a ballad and things like "Do You Love Me?"—songs that reached out to the girls in the audience.

CORKY STASIAK: I have diaries going back over twenty-five years. The sessions for *Destroyer* started on January 4, 1976, and we finished mixing the album on February 3. We did the binaural recording of the introduction of "Detroit Rock City" on February 4 and mixed that into the record. Then we mastered the album on February 5.

CORKY STASIAK: Before we started the *Destroyer* album Bob told me that we had to pump these guys up. They were down and out, they'd been kicked around. Their prior studio albums sounded like dog doody. They were getting screwed by their record label; Casablanca was a disco label. They're the only rock artist on the label. *Alive!* had just come out, they were just starting to sell records. Once *Alive!* started selling, they were so elated, the mood of the *Destroyer* album changed. They came in kind of dejected and now they were like the happiest guys in the world. I remember Gene saying, "We're backing into 400,000 records sold, this record might even go fucking Gold!" [laughs]

BOB EZRIN: KISS played everything very professionally and proficiently. It wasn't until we got to rehearsal and we started to mess around with ideas and I said, "Well, okay, why don't we try this in half-time?" Peter Criss looked at me like I just spoke Greek to him. I said, "Do you know what half-time is?" and he said, "Not really." I said,

"Well, that's okay. It's when we are playing in 4/4, do you know what 4/4 is?" And he said, "Well, not really." So I said, "Instruments down, we are going to school." I dragged a blackboard in and I started asking questions to find out what they did or didn't know. The reason for this is if you have a common language things go quicker. When you are building a house you should know the terminology, and when you are trying to build a song you should know the terminology of music. It's just easier to be able to say let's do this in E flat than to say let's do this on that first fret just below that little dot over there. We decided that it would be a worthwhile investment to take a few days and go through music basics, just to get the band to feel comfortable. Then when we got to things like time signatures the band said, "There is no way that we can do this," I said, "Sure we can," and we came up with that passage in "Flaming Youth" [imitates "Flaming Youth" guitar riff]. I just had Peter keep playing quarter-notes on the floor and the guys playing the 7/4 riff and the riff turned itself around and nobody had to do anything and they were just blown away that they could do this. It was like a kid driving a car for the first time.

PAUL STANLEY: Bob was very much into texture and depth and color. I think when we came into the studio we probably thought color was how much treble or bass you'd put on your Marshall amp. Bob was dealing with doubling guitars, with one guitar slightly VSO'd [vari-speeding] so they'd be slightly out of tune to each other to just make the guitar bigger. So what you would do is record one guitar and then you would slightly slow down the tape machine, almost imperceptibly. Then you would do another guitar part and you would just double your other part. The two of them together would sound great. We used it all the time. It was kind of like flanging and phasing. It gives the guitar a shimmer. On "Detroit Rock City" and "Shout It Out Loud," all the power chords are being doubled with a grand piano. It really gave it a unique sound that initially some people didn't like. Actually some people would hear that and go, "That's not heavy enough."

PETER CRISS: Ezrin truly knew how far to push us, he really had his thumb on it, especially with me at times 'cause I have a raging temper. He would really push me to that stage and then I would take it out on the drums. It would turn out great [laughs].

BOB EZRIN: We had a lot of fun doing that album. We spent so much time kidding around. There were so many moments of gaffer-taping someone from their neck to their ankles and dumping them into the garbage outside [laughs]. Or pie fights.

SEAN DELANEY: When we went into the studio the first time to meet him he [Bob Ezrin] was sitting there stark-assed naked! [with a bow tie]. That album had a lot of Bob Ezrin in it. He's probably one of the most amazing producers in my lifetime . . . because I produced *Double Platinum* with Mike Stone and we had to remix all of the tracks and Bob records with all of the special effects and everything on the tape. You cannot change anything Bob Ezrin has ever done—there it is, like it or not.

PETER CRISS: Bob Ezrin was like a boy genius. He just knew exactly what to do, even with the glass-breaking sound in "Detroit Rock City." I think he got a Ferrari and recorded the engine revved up. Then he recorded some real-live accident that happened somewhere and then he literally recorded the broom sweeping up the glass. The guy was really ahead of his time.

BOB EZRIN: When I'm producing an album I try and get into the act's head. I try to understand who they are. My function during the making of the album is to remain the conscience of the personality and try to hold the project to that while at the same time try to expand the horizons of the personality of the act I'm working with.

CORKY STASIAK: Bob used to wear a whistle around his neck. His big thing was saying, "C'mon campers, let's get going!" You had to round up rock musicians from roaming around, going into other studios and disappearing. And it wasn't Gene and Paul who he had to keep in check. Gene and Paul were there, they were the nucleus. Those guys were like Lennon and McCartney. Gene and Paul would sit down and do whatever it took to make it happen. Ace was a little bent out of shape that the music wasn't always taking a rock 'n' roll course. Ace was a rock 'n' roll guy. Ezrin came up with a lot of great ideas. They were ecstatic about doing that album. I mostly worked with Gene and Paul and Ace. Once the basic tracks were cut, Peter was out of there. You didn't see him much except for vocal overdubs and the "Beth" session. Ace hung in for a while but I think he felt browbeaten by Bob. You're gonna get a great performance from Ace every time but you've got to give him rope. It's like fishing, when a fish takes that bait, you've got to let that fish swim with it. You gotta let him go with the idea. Ace wanted to find that moment in time and burn that lead solo. Bob used to compile guitar leads. We used to do this a lot, a lead on track one, a lead on track two, a lead on track three, edit the best together on an open track. Once he got that he'd say, "Here's what I wanna hear, Ace, go out and do that on another track." Ace is not that kind of player. After Ace got browbeaten by Bob, he threw up his hands and said, "Just give me the tracks when you're finished with them, give me rough copies on cassettes and let me go home and write some leads," and he did just that. He came back with a lead but unfortunately Bob shot him down one too many times. Some producers leave their stamp on a production and that's Bob. Some producers like Eddie Kramer let the band happen. Neither method is wrong; it's subjective.

CORKY STASIAK: During the recording of *Destroyer,* Bob said to the band, "Do you wanna make a great album or a three-chord record?" And the guys said, "We want to make a great album." And Bob said, "That's why we're doing the record this way."

Ezrin's the type of producer who says, "Either you lead, you follow, or you get the fuck out of the way!"

JAY MESSINA: I remember once that somebody goofed and the band just stopped playing. And Bob, half jokingly, said, "Don't you ever stop a take unless I tell you!" I remember the look on Gene's face, like "Who is this guy, talking to us like that?" [laughs]

CORKY STASIAK: Bob was a taskmaster. He was a stickler in terms of drumming, going back to Neal Smith of the Alice Cooper band. Peter's time used to waver a bit. We tried using a click track with Peter, kind of like a metronome, to help him keep time. And it drove Peter crazy. So Bob came up with this idea of putting a little Shure 57 microphone in a hollowed-out tape box with foam around it. We strung that into the studio and into Peter's headphones. To keep Peter in time, Bob would sit there throughout every song and just bang on that box. The idea was later copied by Eddie Kramer.

CORKY STASIAK: Gene, Paul, Peter, and Ace are good musicians but not technically perfect; few are in rock 'n' roll. The thing about Ace is that he has got a brilliant spontaneity to his playing. The trick is to capture it when it happens and not to let it go. When Ace plays he comes from a "feel" kind of place. Bob went through take after take with Ace. I thought that a lot of the things that Ace had done were magic. Every now and then, I was surprised to hear that we were going for another take. But I put my trust in Bob because he had a vision in his mind of how it should sound, and he had made a lot of great records.

JAY MESSINA: In the back of Record Plant was a hallway that sounded great with drums. We had Gene and Peter out there playing and Ace and Paul in the studio. We couldn't see Gene and Peter. We were doing this track and all of a sudden Gene and Peter stopped playing. There was a few seconds of silence. Bob and I were looking at each other wondering what happened. We found out that a few janitors came in the room emptying the garbage. For a while Gene and Peter kept playing while they were watching these guys walk back and forth with the garbage but then they finally cracked and started laughing hysterically.

CORKY STASIAK: I was a singer and I got a job at a recording studio and worked my way up to engineer. At one point, I auditioned to be the lead singer for Steely Dan. There was a guy who came in with a little acoustic guitar. He had a red beard, long red hair, wore a buckskin fringe jacket, and said he was a teacher. Walter Becker and Donald Fagen were working with me and said, "Listen, we have to audition this one other guy." So he played and sang and they said, "Okay, thank you very much," and he left. Later on, I found out that was Gene Simmons.

CORKY STASIAK: We had almost finished *Destroyer.* We did a schmooze fest at the studio for Bill Aucoin, Neil Bogart, and some of the dignitaries over at Casablanca to demo the new album for them. We set up some microphones and did a guitar overdub in front of everyone to kind of get them involved. We wanted to make everyone think that they were there when we did it. I think it was on "Shout It Out Loud." After we did the guitar, Bob said let's set up for a vocal overdub. Now a little background. Five years before, my ex-girlfriend bought me a Firebird guitar at a pawn shop, the same model Paul had. The guitar is all one piece of wood, the headstock is inordinately heavy, and set at a forty-five-degree angle from the body. The body has an oblique shape to it: most guitars have a rounded, symmetrical body, but the Firebird does not: it's on an angle. One day I threw my guitar down on the bed in frustration when I couldn't get it in tune. It bounced off the bed, hit the floor headstock-first with a "Boiiing," and snapped the neck at the nut. I told the guys about this experience, and insisted that they buy guitar stands because they tended to set their guitars against anything handy, usually an Anvil case when not in use, and the guitars could easily fall over. Particularly the Firebird, with its asymmetrical shape. So they went out and spent $200 on guitar stands. Within a week, they were back to leaning their guitars against the Anvil cases, and not using the stands. So here we are in the control room playing the music back for Neil Bogart and company. Bob said, "Let's do a vocal over-dub, they need a pair of headphones." To keep the headphone wire away from your arm when you play, you have to put the headphones through the strap of the guitar. So not thinking, I grabbed the headphone wire and pulled it. Paul's headphones were still connected to the guitar strap, which was leaning against an Anvil case. When I yanked at the cord, the guitar started to fall. As it was falling, I leaped across the studio to save it, and just missed catching it. I heard a loud "Boiiing!" and knew exactly what had happened: the guitar had fallen over and the neck snapped in half at the nut. That was Paul's favorite guitar. I went into the control room and told him we had had a little accident, and your guitar fell. He said, "Well, just pick it up." I walked him out into to the studio. When he saw the guitar lying on the floor broken, he said, "Oh my God, my favorite guitar!" It killed me because I knew it couldn't be fixed. But Paul was very, very gracious about it. That guitar was the black Gibson Firebird, the one pictured on the cover of *Alive!* To this day I still feel miserable about it.

BILL AUCOIN: There was always some turmoil in the band. Probably the happiest they were was with the first two albums and the live album. On *Destroyer* the separation happened between the band. Ace and Peter didn't get along with [Bob] Ezrin. There was always that upheaval. Paul and Gene felt it the most. Ultimately, no matter what happened it always fell back on their hands to finish everything.

JAY MESSINA: The *Destroyer* album was fulfilling because we had a chance to experiment with a lot of sounds. We didn't have to rush through the recording. The record was sophisticated in one sense but it also had that raw, high-energy rock 'n' roll feel. I think Bob did a really good job of capturing what KISS was all about.

BOB EZRIN: With *Destroyer*, there was a major backlash from the hard-core fan base and particularly at the grassroots rock press level. There was a lot of confusion and maybe even resentment for what we had done. More because we had messed with something that these guys were comfortable with, and also because part of KISS's allure to them was that it was so antithetical to everything else that existed in the mainstream of show biz. It was like music with pimples, just like them. It had pimples and ragged clothes and it was weird and it broke a lot of rules. It was comic-book-like so it seemed to be aimed specifically at them. When we took it to yet another stage of comic-bookdom, I understand that at first glance *Destroyer* could have looked to the hard-core grassroots critic like KISS selling out, but more to the point it was KISS reaching out. I was surprised by the fact that the band themselves kind of lost faith in *Destroyer*—about six months after it was released they got really scared by it. They got scared because it didn't seem to be happening and that the grassroots press was relentless at tearing it apart. They called us every name under the sun. One guy threatened to come to Toronto and pop me on the nose on behalf of KISS fans everywhere.

PAUL STANLEY: Initially I think there was a quick 850,000 that had sold and then we kind of hit a wall. Coming on the heels of the live album people were expecting something that was more immediately obvious. And *Destroyer* was really an album that we hoped would grow on you, that it would last. It was easy and very dangerous to have an album as huge as *Alive!* because our albums before that sold fairly minimally and it was widely thought that the next album would do the same. We were very concerned that we not go back and do the same thing again.

GENE SIMMONS: The fans really hated it. We had to do the record because once you do a double live record you go, "Okay, that's the bookend to that part of our career." Either you become trapped by your own doing or your undoing in this case or you try to move on and evolve. We were writing these songs all along but we were editing ourselves a lot more 'cause I had always written Beatle-esque stuff. And Ezrin let some of that through. "Great Expectations" was really a song about the band. [sings] "You watch Paul playing guitar, you see what his hands can do, and you wish you were the one he was doing it to."

BOB EZRIN: "Ain't None of Your Business" was a song KISS recorded for the album but it was left off. It was written by Michael Des Barres during his days with the band Monarch. It's not as sophisticated as the other tracks; it didn't belong in the package.

BILL AUCOIN: We had some problems with the *Destroyer* album cover. Ironically, the first oil painting that was done wasn't exciting enough. We did that painting twice. The first one just wasn't dynamic enough. So we had the artist do another. There are two paintings of that cover.

DENNIS WOLOCH: Gene is a big comic book fan and he's very knowledgeable about science fiction. He mentioned getting Frank Frazetta to do the artwork on the cover. So I did a lot of work on the phone trying to get Frank and it was impossible. First of all, he wanted $15,000 and he wanted to keep the art and said that we could only use it one time. I said, "Not with KISS, KISS uses it for everything. Lunch boxes, T-shirts. And they also want to own it." So there was no deal. I went to the comic book store and I saw a *Creepy* comic book that had a robot on it. I loved the way the guy had painted it. And it was Ken Kelly. I met with Ken at the office and told him he was the guy. It turns out that Ken is Frank Frazetta's cousin. It was an unbelievable coincidence. As an art director I prided myself on using talent that wasn't used in the music business before so it would bring a fresh look to the thing. I mean, Ken Kelly never did an album cover until *Destroyer*, he just did *Creepy* comic book covers and he got paid $75 for them. We gave him $5,000 so he was pretty happy. Great cover.

★ "DETROIT ROCK CITY" ★

PAUL STANLEY: Bob Ezrin made a point of trying to get us to stop writing songs about getting laid, which was valid. But he needed to understand that's all we ever did [laughs]. We had a hard time writing about anything else because we barely had our pants on anytime. But he very much wanted us to broaden our writing. I had the basic riff of the song, the "Get up, get down," part but I didn't know what the song was about except it was about Detroit. And then I remembered on the previous tour, I think it was in Charlotte, somebody had gotten hit by a car and killed outside the arena. I remember thinking how weird it is that people's lives end so quickly. People can be on their way to something that's really a party and a celebration of being alive and die in the process of doing it. So that became the basis of the lyric. All the other stuff that got added to the beginning of the song and the end of the album was because we were afraid the album was too short. That intro of the album coupled with the end, "Do You Love Me?" played backward and the "rock and roll party" part taken from *Alive!*, was really Bob just trying to extend the album. People sometimes react strangely when they hear a word, like horns or piano. Everybody likes "Detroit Rock City" a lot. Well, what is making the guitar chords sound so cool is there is a piano playing along with it. Instead of being afraid of words, listen to it and see if you like it. I'm not one for selling out what we do. KISS is too important and we stay true to it.

BOB EZRIN: That was a technique we were using then, which was not having eight tracks of the same guitar. At that time, we double-tracked both guitars and rhythms with different sounds and then added a subliminal piano part where I would voice it pretty well the same as the guitars were playing and tucked it in underneath to give it some more balls.

BOB EZRIN: I wrote the guitar solo on "Detroit Rock City." "Detroit Rock City" was kind of like a mini-movie. We got to the point that we had seen the introduction and met the characters, and it was time to set up a little tension with a moment of high drama. I felt like this was the sequence where he was driving and this would be the music that would go underneath it. I wrote that in my head. I don't think I actually picked up an instrument. It's not exactly original. It is pretty well an old-fashioned flamenco theme adapted to hard rock music and it's not because I'm some kind of musicology major. It was my take on gladiator music. It was heroic and yet in a strange way because it was so balls-out heroic it was foreboding. I also worked on the lyrics, the melody, and the basic structure of the song. We created it as we went along. As the track was starting to take on epic proportions, the story was being written. As we were doing it, we realized that we had a certain responsibility to our audience and that we didn't want to glorify getting fucked up, especially since this was one band that overall is pretty straight. Some past members of KISS have had their well-publicized problems with alcohol and drugs, but Gene and Paul, the two key members and spokesmen of the band, had always been utterly straight. I have kids and I have always been very much aware of my responsibility as someone that makes records, and I've never wanted to glorify that.

PETER CRISS: A lot of the drumming on "Detroit Rock City" was my idea but a lot of it was Paul's and Bob Ezrin's. They constantly made me play what they wanted, but it was still my arms and my hands and my heart doing it. But it wasn't as much freedom as I usually had. Bob had a click track in my headphones, which I hated. I don't think any drummer likes that. It's good for your time and at that moment my time was wild. Bob had me playing drums in an empty elevator shaft, which I thought was brilliant.

GENE SIMMONS: The bass part is very nontypical of me. It's very R&B, almost like the song "Freddy's Dead" by Isaac Hayes. That's the bass line from "Shaft." The bass line from "Detroit Rock City " is similar, but not the same thing note for note. Bob [Ezrin] also came up with the guitar solo that Ace played. It's very flamenco. We thought he was on crack when he suggested it. We said, "What are you out of your mind? This sounds like we just came from Spain like we were Los Bravos or something." But as soon as we heard it put together with the drums, he knew more than we did. What can we say?

CORKY STASIAK: On February 4, 1976, we did a binaural recording of the opening introduction of "Detroit Rock City." Someone had devised these microphones years before implanted in a stethoscope that go in both of your ears. It picks up the sound bouncing off your ear canal, and you come up with a sound just like the human ear hears it. This was the first experiment of the stereo process. The sound of it isn't really obvious unless you put on headphones; when you do, you have this incredible stereo effect that will scare the shit out of you. If you close your eyes, you are there. I got Bob real interested in doing a binaural recording from an article I found in an old audio magazine. Just before we started mixing, Bob got a binaural microphone from Sony. Bob came up with this concept for the introduction of "Detroit Rock City" where a woman is washing dishes and listening to a radio describing a fatal car crash. It was real cold and snowing that day. I had my Toyota SR-5 outside. We ran some wires from Studio B all the way outside through the car window and out the car window and back. I put the binaural microphones in my ears. I walked outside, jingled the car keys, and opened the car door, closed it. Put the keys in and started the car, "Zoom, zoom . . ." [imitates car acceleration sounds] If you listen to me pretending to drive, that's me humming. I turned the radio on, I had a cassette player in my car, we had a cassette of the *Alive!* album and I cued it up to "Rock and Roll All Nite." Bob Ezrin did the voice of a news reporter. We put his voice through a little radio and recorded it off the radio. If you listen to this opening through headphones, you get this eerie feeling that this is all happening to you.

★ "KING OF THE NIGHT TIME WORLD" ★

PAUL STANLEY: The way "King of the Night Time World" came about is much the same as "Do You Love Me?" There were a few songs where Bob [Ezrin] had sent out the word for any bits and pieces or any songs that were floating around. And "King of the Night Time World" came in and it was perfect. It embodied so much the attitude of the band and was very much in keeping with "Detroit Rock City" and in keeping with my personality.

KIM FOWLEY: The late Mark Anthony was a really good songwriter and a member of a band called the Hollywood Stars. Bob Ezrin was asked to produce the original lineup. He called me up and said, "Look, I don't like the band, but I love that song 'King of the Night Time World.' There's something there, but it needs to be written. If the band ever breaks up, call me and I'll find a home for it." So after the Hollywood Stars broke up, I called Ezrin and he told me the song would be good for KISS. It was written in an alley behind a rehearsal room in North Hollywood. This nymphomaniac named Irene, who looked like a younger version of Pamela Anderson Lee, was giving head to the drummer of the Hollywood Stars. They thought they were in a dark alley and one of the roadies went in and turned the lights on them both. So when I looked up I saw the drummer's cock in her mouth in the silhouette of the headlight and that became "Headlight queen." I'm sitting there writing the lyrics and thought [laughing], "I'm going to put that in the song, 'You're my headlight queen.'" Mark was playing rhythm guitar and I was coming up with the lyric and this guy was getting head in the alley. Paul later added some new guitar parts and riffs, there were also some lyrical and melodic changes.

MARK ANTHONY: That was a song by my band the Hollywood Stars. I wrote all the music and Kim Fowley came up with the lyrical ideas. Bob Ezrin called us and said, "Whatever happened to that song 'King of the Night Time World'?" He gave a tape of it to Paul Stanley, who rewrote some of the lyrics and rearranged the song. I really like what KISS did on it.

BOB EZRIN: Kim [Fowley] knew that I was producing KISS and he sent me a bunch of stuff and I rejected most of it. But that one song really stood out. It was changed and altered to suit Paul's character.

PETER CRISS: I think "King of the Night Time World" was really great. I played the shit out of that. It was amazing if you listen to the drums, all the work in it is really brilliant. That was a lot of physical work and yet it was tasteful. The dynamics of that song were incredible. I felt like I was marching to a war and then all of a sudden I'm rockin' and rollin' [laughs].

★ "GOD OF THUNDER" ★

PAUL STANLEY: "God of Thunder" was originally written as my theme song. There's Apollo, there's Zeus, there's the God of the Sea, there's Neptune, there's all these icons. And then the God of Thunder is me, yours truly. I went in and did the demo of it and we started rehearsing it with Bob [Ezrin]. Bob wanted to slow it down and that was great, it sounded really heavy. And then Bob said, "And Gene's gonna sing it." I was devastated. Our rule was producer has final say because Gene and I could bat something back and forth so endlessly that we needed somebody else to come in to be able to put an end to that. If you're gonna play that game, it has to apply even when you don't want it to. So I was floored and completely incredulous that Bob wanted Gene to sing the song. But you know what? It's a perfect Gene song and I never could have done what Gene did with the song because it's really the embodiment of who he is. It's always interesting that Gene's signature song is mine [laughs]. So I get a certain amount of solace in that and clearly at this point it's impossible to separate him from that song.

BOB EZRIN: "God of Thunder" was a great song written by Paul. But the moment I heard it I felt that it made more sense for Gene's character. Somehow, it didn't fit with the more sensitive and vulnerable persona that we were developing for Paul, like "Do You Love Me?" We arranged it to be as heavy as we could make it and Gene was in full monster mode when he sang the vocals. In the middle of those sessions, my sons visited the studio. David was nine and Josh was four at the time. I had bought them a futuristic walkie-talkie set on a trip to Paris, which had a space helmet for one kid and a handset for the other. They were wearing this stuff when they came to the Record Plant to spend the afternoon. I had the idea that we would mike the helmet and get the kids to make monster noises into the handset and then we would effect these noises to make them lower and more ominous-sounding. The kids loved being a part of the recording. They were veterans by now, having already been on Lou Reed's *Berlin,* but that's another story. They started making monster sounds and wailed like little banshees and the effect was so weird that we decided to keep it the way it was without lowering their pitch. So, on the front of the record and throughout the song, we have the sounds of David and Josh making monster noises into a French walkie-talkie. Not exactly scary stuff but lots of fun.

★ "GREAT EXPECTATIONS" ★

GENE SIMMONS: "Great Expectations" was written on bass. I wrote the tune, but Ezrin kept changing and modulating the chords. It was probably the most sophisticated song on the album. I remember that took forever [to record]. It was an ode to groupie-dom, [recites some of song's lyrics] "You watch me singing the song. You see what my mouth can do and you wish you were the one I was doing it to." It's very romantic.

BOB EZRIN: "Great Expectations" was KISS's equivalent of the "Dance of the Hippos" in *Fantasia.* It presented a caricature of the already larger-than-life character that Gene played, wrapped in musical brocade and chintz as outlandish as any romantic opera. We cut the choir and orchestra at A&R Studios. We decided to make an event of the "sweetening" session since KISS had never done anything like this before. We invited the press to attend the session; I can't remember exactly what we

called it but it was something like "The Grand KISS Orchestration and Choral Session." The band attended in their new *Destroyer* costumes and full makeup. The orchestra was dressed in tuxedo T-shirts and the Brooklyn Boys Choir were in traditional African dashikis. I had my entire staff in tuxedos and I wore white tie and tails, top hat and a cape. It was a real spectacle. Imagine that picture and then superimpose it on the misogynistic lyrics, macho vocal performance, and the mock-classical arrangement of the song, which borrowed shamelessly from Beethoven's *Pathétique* Sonata by the way. I laugh every time I hear it. It was audacity elevated to an art form.

"GREAT EXPECTATIONS" RECORDING SESSION, KISS WITH BROOKLYN BOYS CHOIR, JANUARY 1976, A&R STUDIOS, NEW YORK CITY
(© KISS Catalog Ltd.)

★ "FLAMING YOUTH" ★

PAUL STANLEY: We played that on the *Destroyer* tour. There are elements of "Flaming Youth" that I really like and some that just really turn my stomach a bit, hearing a calliope I just don't get. That was Bob's [Ezrin] idea. It's a little too smart and too creative. Dick Wagner plays the guitar solo and sings background vocals on the song.

BOB EZRIN: We actually rented a calliope for that song and got it in there and it made the sound of [imitates calliope circuslike sound]. I loved it. I took a lot of heat for "Flaming Youth" from the band, especially the calliope part. I guess it was a little cartoonish. The arrangement on that song owed a great deal to the Beatles (obviously).

GENE SIMMONS: We were talking to Ezrin about a New York band called Flaming Youth. We opened for them on our first show at the New York Academy of Music. Ezrin just immediately went, "'Flaming Youth,' what a great title! We're gonna write a song called 'Flaming Youth.'" Then Ezrin said, "What have you got? Let's put some pieces together." Because usually when you write a song by yourself a verse could be good or a bridge could be good and the idea is to put together a Frankenstein of body parts of songs. I had a song called "Mad Dog" that went [hums part of "Flaming Youth"] and that's where the riff came from. Somehow the lyric was tossed around between all of us and Ezrin put all the parts together.

ACE FREHLEY: I think I came up with the lead riffs in the opening of the song and maybe something in the bridge. When I first joined KISS I really didn't consider myself a songwriter per se, even though I had written some songs. Paul and Gene, prior to joining KISS, had Wicked Lester and they had done most of the writing on that stuff. It took a couple of albums for me to really blossom as a writer. As the years progressed it was real obvious that I was growing as a writer and by the time I did my solo album, I really had gotten much better and felt more sure of myself.

PETER CRISS: Bob wanted drumming that I was not really accustomed to [imitates drumming]. It was really regimented, some of it was really hard. It was really powerful. When I would get done with Bob and I would hear it back, right down to "Flaming Youth" to all the stuff we did on that album, "Detroit Rock City," I loved it. Sometimes I'd have to play along with a click track, I still sometimes work with a click, I think there's nothing wrong with it. The greatest drummers in the world sometimes have trouble with time. But yeah, there were times I had to record on that album with a click track. I was always used to just playing from the fucking start, I was another Keith Moon when I was younger. But with Ezrin, I would sit back and go, "Wow, holy shit, I didn't think I could do that!"

DICK WAGNER: I played guitar on "Flaming Youth." I did all my guitar work on *Destroyer* in two days. I loved the direction of the album. I thought it was very good, fundamental, guitar-oriented stuff that really appealed to me. I was very happy to play on the album. As far as not being credited on the album, with KISS and Aerosmith, they wanted to make it seem like the group is playing everything. So at that particular point in their career they didn't really want to give credits. I'm sure today they'd feel differently. There's always a feeling of "It would be nice if they gave me credit." But to say that it made me crazy, no. I had a lot of fun. They're great guys, it was fun to hang out with them.

★ "SWEET PAIN" ★

GENE SIMMONS: "Sweet Pain" started off as a lick that I had for a song called "Rock and Rolls Royce." I've always been fascinated with the notion of cars and how much America is tied into cars more than any other culture on the face of the planet. The whole notion of cars, hot rods, girls in cars is clearly an American invention. In fact, cars were invented in America. So "Rock and Rolls Royce" sounded to me like another kind of phrase that ran right off your tongue like "Rock and Roll Over." The song wasn't up to snuff. Bob Ezrin stuck in the riff at the end of "Sweet Pain." The riff that's on the bottom of the solo is that riff from "Rock and Rolls Royce." And "Sweet Pain" ironically enough was influenced much more by "Wild Thing." Not lyrically but the tone of it with the vocal. Paul likes to sing an octave above where the chordal pattern is. The thing about "Wild Thing" that impressed me is the vocal didn't soar above it or didn't go underneath it. I tried to keep the vocals close to the chords. In those days, songwriting came very fast. Bob rearranged the song and Ace never showed up to play his parts so we brought in Dick Wagner to come in and play the solo. With songwriting there doesn't seem to be any process at all. You'll get as many different ways of writing songs as songwriters who you talk to. Some people really do have a formula. Some people start off with a melody and then they apply it to a chordal passage and then they will finally figure out what the lyrics are, and very last will probably come up with the title. For me, sometimes the title can be a thing that starts the entire process going. Sometimes it will be a riff. Some songs are written on bass and some are written on keyboards like "Christine Sixteen."

ACE FREHLEY: I had done a solo on "Sweet Pain" and it was okay. I said, "Maybe I'll come in tomorrow and take another shot at it." Dick Wagner, the guy who plays lead guitar on the Alice Cooper records, was in town. He stopped by the studio and I'm not sure exactly what went down, whether Gene or Paul said, "Why don't we let Dick Wagner take a shot at doing the solo?" Dick's a very good guitar player. He just knocked out a great solo. They decided to keep it but they didn't let me know about it. They didn't check with me or ask me if it was okay. When I first played the record back, I go, "That's not my fuckin' solo! What the fuck is this shit?" I called Gene and tore him a new asshole. He gave me some bullshit saying, "We tried to call you but we couldn't find you." One of many bull-shit stories, lies, lies, lies.

DICK WAGNER: Bob [Ezrin] and I worked together on a lot of projects including Alice Cooper. I was living in New York City and Bob would call me in to do sessions. He called me in to play on the *Destroyer* album. I played guitar on a few songs on the record: "Sweet Pain," "Flaming Youth," and "Beth." Bob likes my style. I guess I have a knack for finding the right solo to play. I wasn't given a whole direction of what to play, the direction was *where* to play. I loved playing on that album. Gene and Paul are great guys, I've gotten to be good friends with them over the years.

CORKY STASIAK: Dick Wagner is a fantastic muscle guitar player. Bob played him the whole album and said, "Do what you want, but stay in the mode of this style of music."

★ "SHOUT IT OUT LOUD" ★

PAUL STANLEY: We wrote "Shout It Out Loud" one morning before we went into the studio. That was when Gene lived across the street from me. So Gene came over and we went over to Bob's [Ezrin] house and Bob had a piano. Before we went in to do one of the *Destroyer* sessions, we went to Bob's house and played piano and we were writing the song. We were trying to cop some Motown kind of stuff, Four Tops kind of stuff with the answering background vocals.

GENE SIMMONS: I came in with the title because in Wicked Lester we used to do a Hollies song called "We Wanna Shout It Out Loud." I came up with [singing] "Shout it, shout it, shout it out loud." I always thought the idea was bigger than what they were trying to say with it, with the lyric implying "We have a secret, but don't tell people we have a relationship." I always thought just like that commercial on TV, that it was just "Shout It." When you've got something you want to shout it out to the world and it doesn't matter what it is. Bob and Paul kept saying, "Shout *what?*" I said, "Who cares!" Whether it's national fervor or my team's better . . . it's a team rally. And then Paul came up with the verse.

BOB EZRIN: "Shout It Out Loud" took shape at my piano in my apartment in New York City. Paul and Gene would come over and we'd write there together. I remember the breakthrough on the song being the descending bass line. Once I heard that, I knew exactly how I wanted to treat the song. I loved writing with those guys. It wasn't often that they would actually write together. Most often they would work at their individual apartments and record ideas to cassette that they would bring in and show me. But every once in a while we'd all get together and churn something out. It wasn't just the music that made those times work for me. I felt like I was hanging out with my cousins. I was so comfortable with them both and so enjoyed their company.

★ "BETH" ★

PETER CRISS: The melody for the song came to me on a train going to New York City and Stan [Penridge] and I worked on it to finish it. It was changed to "Beth" by Bob Ezrin. At one time we were going to play it together [live] but Bill [Aucoin] said, "The only way this is going to work is if Peter sings live with a tape." My biggest fear was what if the tape would slow down, would I have to sing slow with it? But that never really happened. Then to leave my drums and sing in front of the audience "naked," as I called it, I was so scared. But the first night I did it, I saw the response and it was the biggest rush for me. Then they couldn't get me off the stage!

STAN PENRIDGE: "Beth" originally was called "Beck." It was a song written when Peter and I were still in the band Chelsea. Two of the members [Mike Brand and Peter Shepley] had moved from Manhattan about seventy miles west into the hills of New Jersey. Rehearsals at that point were quite a commute. Mike Brand's wife, Becky, would constantly be calling and interrupting our rehearsals. It got to the point where I literally took Mike's replies and wrote them down in what was called my "Wizard book." Although Mike Benvenga, Peter, and myself hadn't officially quit and formed Lips yet we were meeting together at my place in Manhattan and recording improvisational pieces and various oldies. "Beck" came together at one of these get-togethers. There are a number of early versions of "Beck." It was basically written as a joke. If you take the lyric and imagine it as Mike Brand answering his badgering wife you should get the picture. "Beck" was a bright tempo in keeping with the light feel of the subject matter. The Bob Ezrin arrangement used the same melody. It became a ballad obviously. I think it's a classic recording. I loved it then, I love it now. It's a standard because it is truly a piece of music that reaches just about everyone and transcends the boundaries of its time.

GENE SIMMONS: I was crazy about it. I was the one who told Peter, he was singing the melody in the car. We would ride together, Peter and I, Ace and Paul. That's how usually we divided it up. He started singing the melody and I went, "What's that?" And he goes, "It's a song called 'Beck.'" And I go,

"'Beck?' What the fuck is that, is it about Jeff Beck?" "No, it's about a girl named Becky." I said, "You should change the title to 'Beth' and when you go back to New York you should play it for Bob Ezrin because that's a good melody." Ezrin rewrote the lyric for "Beth," "Me and the boys will be playing," that's all Ezrin and he wrote the middle section and arranged the entire thing.

BILL AUCOIN: Paul and Gene wanted to take "Beth" off the album. I said, "Look, I think it's a hit. I know it's not necessarily a KISS song but it does have a rock 'n' roll lyric to it. It's gonna stay on the album." And they didn't fight me after that. I always thought "Beth" was a major hit because no one else did. I remember I was sitting at Peter's little apartment and listening to the tape and I said, "Boy this is a hit, this is a hit!" And I'd see people's eyes roll. It was the biggest hit I think they ever had. Of course I didn't like it when I started hearing it in elevators. Oh boy, that was a tough one.

PETER CRISS: The day we recorded it, Bob Ezrin had everybody in tuxedos, the New York Philharmonic. When we went to the Record Plant to do the vocals Gene and Paul were in the console room. I'll never forget it, they were looking at me like it was one big fucking joke. And I couldn't get into it and Bob knew it and threw them out. They left, I did it in five takes and it was beautiful.

CORKY STASIAK: On January 13, 1976, the orchestral and choral sections were done for "Beth" at A&R Studios. KISS showed up in full makeup for a photo session in the studio. Bob, Jay, and I wore long-tailed tuxes and we wore white gloves [laughs]. Everyone in the orchestra were given tuxedo T-shirts to wear.

BOB EZRIN: There was a song and it may have been called "Beck" originally. In the nicest way possible, it was important that Peter had a song on the record, so we went digging through the archives of whatever Peter had. He had this song which was kind of countrified, and a little bit folky. It really didn't match what we were doing at all. But I heard something in it and I took it home and translated it to the piano. I rewrote it a bit and thought about a kind of orchestral approach to it. In fact, I rewrote it substantially and brought it back in and went, "You mean something like this, Peter?" [laughs] It was important that he felt that he was participating as much as possible. It was something that I heard in another form, but it didn't become the "Beth" you know and love until it went to my house for while. I thought it was kind of theater. We did it at the session where we had the whole orchestra in tuxedo T-shirts. All the staff was in tails and the band were in full costume and there were prop trees in the studio [laughs]. It was so high camp and fabulous. It was purposely in keeping with what KISS had become. It was kind of early days then and people weren't quite used to the theatricality going beyond the bodies of the members of the group themselves.

DICK WAGNER: I played acoustic guitar on "Beth." I love melodic songs so this was a natural song for me to play on. Bob [Ezrin] and I are very compatible in terms of styles, especially ballads, because we've done a lot of stuff over the years together. Before working on that album I'd done Alice Cooper's *Welcome to My Nightmare* record with Bob, doing the song "Only Women Bleed." During that era, Bob and I came up with a lot of very melodic songs. I wish I had written "Beth" because it's just a beautiful song. I thought it was a hit the first time I heard it.

CORKY STASIAK: On June 22, 1977, Sean Delaney and I mixed "Beth" without a lead vocal. It was done so they could play that on tour and Peter could sing it with the orchestral backing.

PETER CRISS: We thought about doing it live with the whole band at one point. Bill Aucoin, our original manager, who I still love very much, we thought that this is a great song, it was getting major airplay, we got a People's Choice Award for it, this song has to be played live. Bill said there's no way around it. And we're going, "Oh my God, there's not even drums in it!"

★ "DO YOU LOVE ME?" ★

PAUL STANLEY: Quite a bit of "Do You Love Me?" was written and was brought into us during *Destroyer*. Bob [Ezrin] had called Kim Fowley to see if there was anything around that might be of interest and then we finished it. I still think it's one of my favorite tracks. It's got great attitude. My favorite part of "Do You Love Me?" is the end. There are these orchestral bells because I love them. The middle section is really cool. To me it's closer to some of the Mott the Hoople stuff in its glorification of rock 'n' roll, celebrating being a rock star and that kind of life.

KIM FOWLEY: Bob Ezrin called me up and said I have the title of a song "Do You Love Me?" and some chords. He said, "Why don't you write me a lyric about a rock star who questions the motives of a groupie-type." He said, "In the world of pensions, the KISS catalogue will pay your bills as an old man." I was with Joan Jett at LAX airport waiting for some girl who didn't get in the Runaways. Joan asked me what I was doing. I said, [laughing] "I'm figuring out my pension, leave me alone." So I took a napkin and wrote the lyrics in twenty minutes as we were waiting for the plane to land. I went to Ezrin's rented house and he said, "Okay, you better have the same exact meter to these lyrics as I have the chords for." So he started playing the song with the lyrics and said, "You got lucky, you've got two songs on *Destroyer*. And I said "Pension!" And then the song went through some more co-writing. Paul changed some lyrics and musically added a lot. Both "Do You Love Me?" and "King of the Night Time World" went through the KISS treatment. Nirvana recorded "Do You Love Me?" on the KISS tribute album, *Hard to Believe*.

BOB EZRIN: We may have used a bit of Kim's [Fowley] lyrics. "Do You Love Me?" really came off a piano up around Benedict Canyon in a house right around the corner where the Sharon Tate murders happened. It was a kind of Gothic living room with high windows, piano right in the window. I was there by myself going [starts singing] "Do You Love Me?" I don't remember if I took that from something Paul fed me or not but I do remember the night that I spent sort of honing it into a piece of material.

ROCK AND ROLL OVER

Release date: November 1, 1976
KISS / EDDIE KRAMER–producer / CORKY STASIAK–engineer / BILL AUCOIN–manager
STAN PENRIDGE–songwriter / LARRY HARRIS–Casablanca Records senior vice president
BOB KULICK–demo session lead guitarist / BILL LETTANG–demo session drummer
DANNY GOLDBERG–Danny Goldberg, Inc. / DENNIS WOLOCH–album designer

PAUL STANLEY: I really like that one. We wanted to retain some of the stuff that Bob [Ezrin] taught us, but get a little more raw. We got scared after *Destroyer* and decided to go back to something that was more familiar and that was the *Rock and Roll Over* album. It worked fine. But quite honestly the sound of *Destroyer* next to *Rock and Roll Over* was like a step toward something that was more familiar and less adventurous. It's interesting, as we were doing *Destroyer* I remember being incredibly excited about the ground we were breaking and sonically what we were exploring and thematically what we were doing. It was really a step that I was excited to take. Once it was done we certainly had no intention of seeing our success wane. It was received well but in some ways tepidly compared to what we were expecting. At that point, to sell eight hundred and some odd thousand albums was a feat, but to us it was not what we had in mind. When *Destroyer* met with kind of quizzical response from people our first thought was, "Let's go back in on the next album to what's more familiar," which is chickenshit and a matter of self-preservation. I was happy to go back to that template but again I was constantly disappointed with what those albums ended up sounding like. I wanted them to sound as good as a Zeppelin album. There was no reason that sonically we shouldn't have sounded ballpark to the heaviest bands out there. It certainly doesn't fall on our shoulders because we were babes in the woods. When we decided to take a left turn after *Destroyer*, I still had hope beyond hope that we could capture what we were about in the studio. It wasn't like chasing the Holy Grail or the brass ring, it was done all the time. Unfortunately, some of the people we worked with didn't have the capacity to do that. I like *Rock and Roll Over* very much. It's a great album. I just think it's so unfortunate that the recordings are so marginal. I'd give *Rock and Roll Over* five stars.

GENE SIMMONS: We wouldn't have done another album like *Destroyer*. "Beth" was a massive hit. We were capable of doing that kind of stuff, but it was Bob [Ezrin] who kind of put the pieces together. We tried to work with him soon after *Destroyer*, but he'd moved on to something else. We had gone through our Bob Ezrin phase. Ace and Peter, in particular, kept saying that we shouldn't be doing that kind of music, we should be more of a rock 'n' roll band. Paul and I were both aware that *Destroyer* was the right way to go and we should have stayed with Ezrin for a few records and seen what the good ship KISS could do. But within the band there was too much turmoil. There was always a simpler KISS in the minds of Ace and Peter. We decided again to recapture some of the live feeling. We wanted to make sure the group didn't get starch in our collars, that it didn't get too stiff. *Destroyer* was very much a studio record. We didn't want the fans to get the sense that we were gonna do studio records from now on. You know, electronics improved but the songwriting pretty much went back to basics. The strain was getting to the band on that record. Three stars.

PETER CRISS: I'd give that a four. It was the first time they separated me from the boys. I played up in the bathrooms with a video camera and they played down in the theater.

It was my idea and Eddie Kramer's. I liked the idea. It was like, "A bathroom! Great! Do you know how fucking loud it will be?" I liked the idea because I could see the guys on the camera and I was in the bathroom all by myself and I'd play games on them. I would make funny pictures and I'd put them in front of the screen and they'd lose me. And they'd see these weird things like flying saucers from Mars and "Fuck you" or I'd draw a dick [laughs]. Eddie just couldn't handle it. He'd say "Stop this shit, we gotta get this done." [Response to Gene saying he had best voice in band] That was very nice of him. Eddie Kramer and Vini Poncia and Bob Ezrin all said the same thing, they all agreed with Gene.

ACE FREHLEY: In comparison to *Destroyer*, *Rock and Roll Over* was rawer, not as sophisticated. But that was Eddie's style of production. I think it was more KISS. *Destroyer* was more Bob Ezrin's influence. *Rock and Roll Over* was a lot of fun because we were working with Eddie Kramer, who I always got along with. We recorded the album about fifteen minutes from my house. I'd recently gotten married and I got a new car and it was nice. I was living in Tarrytown and we recorded it at a theater-in-the-round. Eddie Kramer just brought in all this stuff and actually built a recording studio. That album was a lot of fun. Bob [Ezrin] could do orchestration and scoring. Eddie and I were on the same page technically, he always liked to experiment with different guitar sounds and amps. We used to go to pawn shops and pick up Fender amps. Eddie was willing to put a little extra time in working with me and we'd come up with something special. That was something that Bob didn't come to realize until maybe later on listening to my guitar work. I'd give it four stars.

EDDIE KRAMER: *Destroyer* was a good record for a couple of tracks but it wasn't really KISS. And I think the fans really were a bit pissed off about that. So KISS wanted to get back to their roots, which is straight-ahead rock 'n' roll. That's basically what we did. Bob Ezrin took a lot of flak for the *Destroyer* album. Even though it was very successful, *Destroyer* as a rock 'n' roll album is not a good album. But as a commercial success because of the one single, no doubt about it. I think Ezrin came to them from a different point of view. But looking at it today from what he's done on *Revenge*, I think *Revenge* is probably one of their best albums. I absolutely commend him and KISS on that album, I think it's brilliant. He only has my utmost admiration. I think he's a very good producer. However, when you compare his style to my style, in those days I think my style of production probably suited the band better. We recorded the album at the Star Theatre in Nanuet, New York. I like to record bands in a live situation and use the acoustics of the room to create the sound and give the band a different edge. It was in the round. We put the vocals in the hallway. We'd put the drums in the middle of the stage. We would put the bass underneath the stage. We would put the guitars in a different room. We'd sometimes put the drums in a smaller room. We used the whole building. Basic tracks would go this way, we'd do drums and bass and acoustic guitar or drums and bass and a rhythm guitar and I would be the timekeeper. I'd go and keep the time in the room because Peter didn't want to use a click track and I'd have to beat on a big wooden box and he'd watch me. I'd destroy about twenty wooden boxes during the whole session. Peter had some timing problems but the thing is he wasn't used to working in the studio and I helped keep his time together and he respected me. I tried to help him lock up and it worked fine. I'd go for the big drum sound and the big guitar sound and once they'd hear the sounds coming through the speakers on the headphones their approach would be slightly different. But they wanted it to sound big and nasty and crunchy. In those days I didn't get demos. We ran the song down, I listened to it and I figured out where the song should go. When I hear a song for the first time I know what I'm going to do with it because I have this vision in my mind. The album didn't take that long to do, probably a couple of months.

EDDIE KRAMER: My approach is more "Show me what you've got and let's see if we can twist and turn it and make it better." Ace was definitely the person in the band who was the most underrated. He had a real grasp of what it would take to drive the album along. Paul had the ability to write great stuff. Gene was a genius in terms of concept stuff. By the time KISS came to record *Rock and Roll Over* they had really improved their playing skills. They'd done the live record and *Destroyer*. It was time for them to cut loose and show what they could do as players. That was my philosophy with the *Rock and Roll Over* album. This was KISS playing good, rootsy rock 'n' roll. They were not highly skilled players at that point. They were getting there. KISS wasn't really concentrating on their playing ability, they were concentrating on their abilities as performers and entertainers and something had to suffer.

CORKY STASIAK: KISS loved and admired Eddie Kramer. He'd done Zeppelin and Hendrix. Eddie was also the producer of their first album that went Gold, *Alive!* Eddie is the kind of producer who doesn't put his will on the band, he wants to draw the performance out of the artist. [Bob] Ezrin will do anything, edit, overdub, and use other musicians to get what he wants. He wants to make sure that the performance he gets from the artists is what he hears in his head. Neither way is wrong, but that's how they both worked.

CORKY STASIAK: We started recording *Rock and Roll Over* on September 30, 1976, and finished on October 16. We recorded the album at the Nanuet Star Theatre, an abandoned theater-in-the-round.

GENE SIMMONS: The theater was partly owned by Frank Sinatra.

CORKY STASIAK: We were working sixteen, seventeen hours a day. Only the basic tracks were recorded there. We arranged for a PA system to enhance the sound of the drums.

We had microphones all over the theater. Ace's, Paul's, and Gene's amplifiers were under the stage in dressing rooms so nothing bled into the drum mikes. When Peter played it sounded like thunder. We had microphones up on the thirtieth row, all the way around in a circle. When we came back to the Record Plant we had drums, bass, and some guitars locked in. We did all the overdubs quick at Record Plant. I love the sound of that album. Great acoustics! It's my favorite-sounding KISS album because of the sound we got at the Nanuet Star Theatre. It's raw and big, and for me, it ranks up with Led Zeppelin sound-wise.

PETER AND PAUL STANLEY AT SOUND CHECK, 1977
(© Snowsaw Archives)

EDDIE KRAMER: I'm used to recording in all kinds of weird places. I've recorded in mansions, I've recorded in virtually every space you could think of. We wanted a place where we would be secure and yet we could feel free to experiment and get different acoustic sounds. And also have a live sound. I specified we should go to record in some place open and big. We dragged the Record Plant truck up there and the rest is history.

EDDIE KRAMER: I remember Ace coming in and shooting out all the lights in the building with his nine-millimeter air gun. That was an amusing incident. The theater was in-the-round and the stage revolved. I remember there was always a thought, "Hey, let's get Peter playing drums and let's flip the whole stage around." [laughs] But I don't think that ever happened.

EDDIE KRAMER: You always had to beat cardboard boxes for Peter to keep time 'cause he had a problem with time. It was very tough for him. But once he got it, it was fine. He had a distinctive style. He played hard and once he got into the groove and watched what I was trying to get at, he got into it.

PETER CRISS: When we worked again with Eddie on *Rock and Roll Over* it was great. He was kind of free-going and he'd have his tea. He loved my drumming, called me a thunder drummer.

BILL AUCOIN: We were getting to the point where we were doing a lot of albums. And it was really Neil's [Bogart] idea at the beginning. This is really interesting. Neil's thing was "Gee, I'm not sure what I'm going to do here. I can't have albums come back." Because Casablanca was a small company, he couldn't afford to have returns because it would have killed the company. So we came up with the plan about doing an album every six months [laughs]. Because just when the record stores were going to send them back Neil would say, "A new one's coming." So they would say, "I've got to keep it for catalogue." When you send a new record the catalogue needs to be there. So anyway, that's what happened. Before the returns came back we'd put out a new record. But it had a real toll on the group.

CORKY STASIAK: Eddie had these special tube mikes, they don't make them anymore. He used these mikes on Led Zeppelin, Jimi Hendrix. He used them to mike the drums. It took us two days to set up this thunderous drum sound. The band loved the sound. We left everything set up and came back the next day to start recording the album. I grew up in L.A., I'm a surfer. Sean Delaney brought in a Hobie skateboard. I said, "Let me show you some tricks." I got on the skateboard and showed him how to do all of these spins and kicks. This was a theater in-the-round, like a bowl. When you come in off the street the theater has an arc to it, it was very steep. So Sean said to me, "Wouldn't it be neat if we could skateboard down the aisle?" I said, "I can do that." And he said, "You can? I'm afraid to do it." And I said, "I'll do it, fuck it, let me try it." I got on his Hobie skateboard and took off skating down the aisle and the seats are whizzing by, faster and faster. Halfway down I realize I'm going way too fast to jump off. If I jump off I'm gonna break my neck in the seats. So I thought, just before I hit the stage I'll jump off this thing and jump onto the stage. In theory that's a great idea. But when you're going that fast and inertia hits you it's real hard to jump. I got to the end of the aisle and I jumped off the skateboard as planned, but my toes just grazed the end of the stage and it straightened my body out. I dove headfirst into the drum set, knocking down every mike, every drum, every wire [laughs] that had taken us two days to set up. It fell down like timber. Luckily I didn't break anything, except two fingers on my right hand. I said, "Oh shit, we're gonna be recording in an hour, what am I gonna do now?" So I got up and with one hand reset all the drums and mikes back to where

I remembered them being. Just as soon as I was done in walks Eddie Kramer and the boys. I had taken gaffer tape and gaffer-taped my two fingers together. To this day, I haven't told anyone what had happened. Eddie asked if I made sure all the mikes were working. I said, "Yeah," and he said, "Get Peter out there and do one more run-through." Paul was sitting next to me at the recording console. Peter sits down, does a couple of drum rolls around the toms-toms, and Paul looks at me and says, "You know, Corky, it sounds better now than I remember it sounding last night." I never told the guys that story. That session lasted for fifteen and a half hours. When we were finished [laughing] I drove right to the emergency room, got my fingers X-rayed. I had fractured both of them. Next day I came in with my fingers in a cast [laughs].

CORKY STASIAK: My name was accidentally left off the *Rock and Roll Over* album. I think the first 250,000 copies came out without my name listed as engineer. Then it was later added to other pressings. To all those KISS collectors out there: Try to find a *Rock and Roll Over* album with, and without, my name on it to make your collection complete.

LARRY HARRIS: In those days there was something called payola. It could be cash, it could be women, or it could be drugs. Payola was used with KISS on Top 40 radio. Payola was widespread, it involved all the other big bands at the time too, not just KISS. KISS didn't know this nor should they have known this. They had nothing to do with the way we promoted the product. I think Casablanca participated in payola to a lesser degree than the other labels because we didn't have as much money. We hired the right people who could get our records on radio stations and keep them on for a certain period of time whether or not they were selling. This happened with almost all of KISS's singles. The reality of this is after a certain level if a record didn't start selling it wasn't going to. "Beth" was the one KISS single that happened very, very quickly. That's the single that was really legitimate without us pulling any fast moves. "Calling Dr. Love," "Hard Luck Woman," "Christine Sixteen" were not big records. They were singles that we manipulated to look big using various methods. One was using the charts, one was buying our way onto Top 40 radio through payola. A perfect example is one of the stations in Miami. We would consistently make deals with them. If they would play certain records we would get them groups to perform in concert for free. If they did us a favor on KISS or Donna Summer we would get them a band to perform in one of their shows.

BILL AUCOIN: They were never hits or anything close to it, they were all paid for, anything other than "I Was Made for Lovin' You" and "Beth." "New York Groove" kind of had a life of its own and, of course, we kept trying to make "Rock and Roll All Nite" a hit and that was semireal. We finally got some real action on it at radio. I'm not sure it ever translated into a hell of a lot of sales. But at least we got people who wanted to play it as opposed to people who were being paid to play it. In those days that was accepted practice. It wasn't only happening at Casablanca, it was widespread. You'd pay anyone you could to get records played. Casablanca was a free-flowing company [laughing] when it came to that. When the government starting looking at payola in the music industry, Neil was questioning it, saying, "What the hell can we do now?" I'll never forget the day when we came up with one of the solutions, which was to give key people in radio and independent promotion credit cards so there wasn't money changing hands. But you could call so-and-so and say, "Okay, you can spend $200 on your credit card this month," and the bill would go to Casablanca. I'm sure it still happens today in one form or another. KISS was working hard at what they needed to do, which was performing and building a fan base, they weren't aware of the day-to-day needs and practices of promoting their records.

DANNY GOLDBERG: In late '76 to '77 I had a PR firm, Danny Goldberg, Inc. KISS was a client. I worked their album *Rock and Roll Over*. KISS is a publicist's dream. Not only do they have the tremendous visual uniqueness with the makeup and the stage show but with Gene and Paul you had two of the most articulate people in rock as far as being able to talk about themselves and understanding how to give a writer a good story. Their manager, Bill Aucoin, was very PR-savvy also. Compared to rock bands where it was just about the music like Bad Company, who I'd worked for the year before, KISS was a pleasure. At that time, Gene and Paul were focusing on wanting more mainstream rock press coverage. They'd been in the ghetto of the equivalent of metal magazines. For example, *Rolling Stone* had never done a feature on them. I was able to persuade Chuck Young, who worked for *Rolling Stone*, to do a piece on them. Getting the feature was a big deal to Gene. The memory I have of that is when Chuck Young was interviewing him, Gene's mother unexpectedly came into his apartment on Central Park South. She had a key and walked in without knocking. He was quite embarrassed to have his mother interrupting a *Rolling Stone* interview, which for years he'd be coveting. She was jabbering on about the matzoh brei that she brought him and referring to him as Chaim, which is his given name. To my amazement, Chuck Young never referred to that incident. If I were a reporter I would have eaten it up because it was such a contrast between the public image of Gene and the relationship that he had with his mom. Chuck wrote a very cynical piece about them where he likened their music to "buffalo farts." I was mortified and disappointed when the article came out. I asked Gene what he thought of it and he said, "Better that they publish an article about us than if they didn't run an article at all." Gene's a great example of making the best out of every situation, taking your lumps and moving on.

DENNIS WOLOCH: Michael Doret did the cover for *Rock and Roll Over*. He was a great illustrator/designer working in New York City. I knew his style, that really flat style that he worked in. He had done *Time* magazine covers and was an award-winning designer. *Rock and Roll Over* turned out to be perhaps the most successful KISS album cover because it was used on more things than anything else. And it really works, it's so flat, and powerful, and graphic-looking. When Michael Doret did *Rock and Roll Over* I insisted—and this gets technical—but there's no real artwork for that job. It's all black ink on acetate. So he did printer's separation and we never did art.

★ "I WANT YOU" ★

PAUL STANLEY: I wrote "I Want You" at a sound check onstage in England when we were on our first tour there. There was something about being on some of those stages that just felt so magical because my heroes all played on them. We'd be on some stage and they'd say, "The Beatles were on this stage or Zeppelin was on this stage" and you kind of summon the spirits to enter your body. "I Want You" came at that point.

★ "TAKE ME" ★

PAUL STANLEY: "Take Me" had a great attitude. I was really in my glory at that point. I'm this big rock star, getting laid all the time, all this adulation. "Put your hand in my pocket, grab on to my rocket," it was just about the glory of being alive. All those songs were just about the lifestyle, whether it was cocksmanship, rock 'n' roll, and sex.

★ "CALLING DR. LOVE" ★

GENE SIMMONS: I cut the demo with me playing the guitars and Katey Sagal singing harmony. I found Katey in a trio, the Group with No Name. They recorded an album for Casablanca Records. Katey Sagal, and Fran Gold, who was one of the Harlots, and another girl. So it was Gene Simmons with three girls singing. That was the original idea behind "Calling Dr. Love." They were originally singing the chorus to "Dr. Love" but Paul and I sang it falsetto. I thought that the demo had more of the feel that I wanted. I didn't think we really captured it as a band.

ACE FREHLEY: I like the "Dr. Love" guitar solo. If I was doing a solo for a song that Gene wrote like "Dr. Love," a lot of times he would give me ideas or sing me a melody. He might say, "Why don't you try this idea?" or refer to a solo I had done on an earlier record. He'd give me ideas if I was stumped.

★ "LADIES ROOM" ★

GENE SIMMONS: "Ladies Room" was written in a rehearsal studio. It's about a girl that you meet in a restaurant and you have nowhere to go and I say, "Hey, I'll meet you in the ladies' room and we'll discuss our merger, the urge to merge."

PETER BEHIND THE SKINS, RICHFIELD COLISEUM, CLEVELAND, OHIO, SEPTEMBER 3, 1976
(Photo: www.janetmacoska.com)

★ "BABY DRIVER" ★

PETER CRISS: The band didn't play it the way it was written and that's what pissed me off about it. They had to do it their way and we got into major fights every night over it. I've got a cut of it the real way and it just wasn't done that way on the album. They did the same thing to "Dirty Livin'." The right way was slower [starts singing some of riff slower]. The riff was done with voices not guitars and that's what I wanted. It went to number one in Italy I found out because I got some royalties from it. "Hard Luck Woman" went number one in Tokyo. On "Dirty Livin'" they didn't get that vocal hum. So anyhow "Baby Driver" was more like [sings] "Go baby driver, just driving on down the road." It had much more soul to it and they made me cut it out and sing it more straight and that bothered me. I have a soul voice. That's my roots. The original demo of that is better than our recording. The band rearranged it. All of a sudden it had different harmonies and it lost its feel.

STAN PENRIDGE: "Baby Driver" and "Dirty Livin'" were written while Peter, Mike Benvenga, and I were in Lips. "Baby Driver" is about Mike. It was a joke song. "Baby Driver" was written specifically over the purchase of Mike Benvenga's Alfa Romeo Spyder. Lips were working at the St. James Infirmary up in Hunter Mountain, New York. Peter and I would usually take the bus. Mike got this Alfa, but never told us ahead of time. The three of us couldn't have all fit in it anyway. But one weekend we arrived and found Mike was already there [he wasn't on the bus] and we were pissed. Probably more jealous than pissed but Pete and I didn't play it like that. We all shared an eight-by-ten room, literally, above an antique shop. We didn't speak all weekend, just wrote little put-downs in the "Wizard book" that eventually became enough for a tune. I don't believe we ever told Mike about who "Baby Driver" was but he knew. It was a sore spot for years. Mike always thought Peter and I were ganging up on him in one way or another. Looking back on it, I think we did shut Mike out quite a bit. It was a money thing. His folks helped him out, he always had a few extra bucks to spend, and that was his way of rubbing it in, just a bunch of kids in their early twenties acting silly.

★ "LOVE 'EM AND LEAVE 'EM" ★

GENE SIMMONS: If you listen to the verse lick [imitates riff], it's the exact same lick that's stuck in the solo part of "Sweet Pain." And both of those songs came from "Rock and Rolls Royce." "Love 'Em and Leave 'Em" is my philosophy. The point of view is if a girl's got an opening, I've certainly got a stiff proposition. My point of view about sex has always been to never take it too seriously and always have a lot of fun with it. That's why the lyric is a bit embarrassing. Later on with a song like "Burn Bitch Burn," "I wanna put my log in your fireplace," it's so patently ridiculous, but hopefully people will understand that it's tongue-in-cheek, my tongue in her cheek.

★ "MR. SPEED" ★

PAUL STANLEY: I like "Mr. Speed." There's a whole plethora of songs that came during the time that were just about swagger, being a rock 'n' roller, living that life and having a great time. I became a better writer, but that doesn't necessarily mean the songs are better, and yet there are things in "Mr. Speed" that came naturally that I could never bring out of me today. The songs I wrote later are well-structured, smart songs. Songs like "I Stole Your Love" and "C'mon and Love Me" are much more honest and right to the point. I couldn't write those today if you put a gun to my head.

BOB KULICK: I played on the demo of that. I'd go in the studio with Paul and I'd play the solo. And then he'd go to the band and say, "Here's a song I'd like to do," and they'd wind up recutting it.

BILL LETTANG: "Mr. Speed" is the only demo I did with Paul. It's featured on the KISS box set. Paul was emphatic about me playing like Charlie Watts, the drummer in the Rolling Stones. The song had a Stones feel and swagger.

★ "SEE YOU IN YOUR DREAMS" ★

GENE SIMMONS: "See You in Your Dreams" was a funny song because the original demo had all kinds of people on it, Katey Sagal from *Married . . . with Children,* and Michael Des Barres. All kinds of friends would pop in and sing on the stuff.

★ "HARD LUCK WOMAN" ★

PAUL STANLEY: "Hard Luck Woman" was a song not meant for the band. It's one of those challenges that I like to give myself, whether it was writing "I Was Made for Lovin' You" or going "Let me see if I can write a song for Rod Stewart." When I wrote "I Was Made for Lovin' You" that was me going, "Let me see if I can write one of these dance songs." When I heard "Maggie May," "You Wear It Well," "Mandolin Wind," I said, "I think I can do this," so that's what "Hard Luck Woman" was. And once it was finished, it certainly wasn't going to be for KISS. But when everybody heard it and we had had a hit with "Beth," we didn't know where to go from there. The safest route was "Let's have Peter sing a song. And by the way, it sounds a lot like a Rod Stewart track." And we played it as such. There were a lot of acoustic guitars.

PETER CRISS: "Hard Luck Woman" pissed me off. Number one, Paul wrote it and said it was for Rod Stewart. He played it for me on acoustic guitar and I just loved it. I said, "Hey, fucko, how about me? Fuck Rod Stewart, I'll sing the shit out of it." Eddie heard it and said I had to sing this. He said I sounded better than Rod Stewart. Then when we got into it they really got on my case in the studio. They wanted it to sound as close to Rod Stewart. I said, "Let me do it my way. Let me sing it. You'll get your raspy shit when you want it but I've got to still sound like Peter. I'm not Rod Stewart, Paul. I know you wanted him to do it but I'm not going to mimic him."

EDDIE KRAMER: Paul was playing that song and I was fascinated by it. I thought, "Wow, this would be excellent for the record. We've gotta have that, that's a great, great song!" The song had a strong "Maggie May" content. And the fact that it would be so cool for KISS to do an acoustic song. Peter had the natural voice to sing it. I remember working very hard and diligently trying to get a good acoustic guitar sound and working on the structure of the song. "Hard Luck Woman" was great. Both Paul and Ace played acoustic on that. That was a big surprise actually. I like that track. I like the way Peter's voice sounds. He's got a great voice. The guy had a real emotional way of singing. There was a certain quality to his voice that none of the other guys had. It's maybe one of the reasons why "Beth" was so successful.

★ "MAKIN' LOVE" ★

PAUL STANLEY: It's a great song. I was such a huge Zeppelin fan. "Makin' Love" was a tip of the hat to "Whole Lotta Love." That's what I was striving for. Often I would write what would come to mind and then there were other times I would have a song in mind that I liked a lot. And I might be going for a style or a feel. I had to work within my own ability. At that point my vocal range was much more limited than it became with time. I have a feeling that if that song were done today [laughing] it would sound a whole lot more like Led Zeppelin than it sounded like then. There are a plethora of songs from that era that I would have to struggle to come close to the quality today. Spontaneity often comes from innocence and a naiveté where your writing is more free-form and free-association so what comes out is in some ways more profound and certainly more sponta-neous as opposed to worked over. I think that songs like "C'mon and Love Me," and "Got to Choose," the lyrics for a lot of those songs was written in a half-hour, if that. They were a sponta-neous reflection of what I was doing or thinking.

LOVE GUN

Release date: June 17, 1977
KISS / EDDIE KRAMER—producer / CORKY STASIAK—engineer / STAN PENRIDGE—songwriter
BILL AUCOIN—manager / LARRY HARRIS—Casablanca Records senior vice president
CAROL ROSS—president of the Press Office Ltd. (KISS publicity firm)
CAROL KAYE—publicist, the Press Office Ltd. / DENNIS WOLOCH—album designer
HARVEY KUBERNIK—media coordinator for Danny Goldberg, Inc.
CYNTHIA PLASTER CASTER—plaster caster

PAUL STANLEY: To me the highpoints of *Love Gun* were high enough to raise the low points like "Then She Kissed Me." Just for the songs "Christine Sixteen," "Love Gun," "I Stole Your Love," and "Shock Me" is enough to make any album great. I had fun making *Love Gun* because I was feeling my oats. I was going into Electric Lady Studios on my own and cutting tracks that we would ultimately go in and copy. By then I had a very clear vision of what I wanted to do and in some ways what KISS was going to do. I remember cutting the demo for "Love Gun," which is basically note for note the same as the master. "I Stole Your Love" is the same and "Tomorrow and Tonight." It was a great time for me. I really had free rein to book studio time and work out my songs. The songs [laughing] would never turn into Wicked Lester songs. For better or worse, I worked out all the parts. If I didn't play them I told someone else what to play. When KISS went in the studio we just re-created them because they were essentially tailor-made for KISS. I'd give that four and a half, five stars. It's a great album. I'm proud of the record.

PETER CRISS: I'd give that a four. I'd give it a four because they did do "Hooligan" the way I wanted it done and Eddie just loved me singing. Eddie wanted me to sing even more songs than that. And that was another controversy. He wanted me to do a couple of Paul's songs and Paul freaked out [laughs]. "Fuck that shit, he ain't singing one of my songs!" [laughs] Eddie told him to try it and Paul said, "If he tries it you'll like it and I won't sing it."

GENE SIMMONS: To satiate Ace and Peter, we stayed with Eddie Kramer. Eddie's a great guy, but in no way was the band challenged with Eddie because for one thing Eddie didn't write songs and Bob Ezrin did. Bob was also an arranger and a conceptualist. He was a guy with a vision who would say, "Okay, what does this mean?" He could take a song and really take it to the next step. Eddie was a terrific guy, but he was basically an engineer. We gave him producer credit because he was called a producer, but Eddie's an engineer. He would twiddle the knobs and watch over somebody who mixed it. Eddie helped mix it but that's it. The songs remained as they remained. [On *Love Gun* and *Rock and Roll Over* being almost companion albums in sound] We liked the whole process and the direction was very defined. We didn't want to stray too much from where we were because we were on to a good thing. It felt comfortable. We knew who we were and we knew what the music was. Certainly the band did what it did and you couldn't confuse what we did with other bands, so we liked the clear identity. I'd give it three stars. "Almost Human" is one of my favorite songs.

ACE FREHLEY: I thought *Love Gun* was a good record. Every album we did we learned more. Eddie Kramer taught me a lot. It was a four. I was real happy with the way "Shock Me" came out.

EDDIE KRAMER: Gene and Paul have always been the driving force behind the band. Ace would always be relied upon to get really cool solos. Gene's a great businessman and Paul is really the front man star. He really worked very hard at becoming a great guitar player. Paul's a damn good guitar player. Ace is a natural; Paul had to work at it.

EDDIE KRAMER: KISS had learned a lot by that point and wanted to express themselves even more, hence the co-production of *Love Gun*. We recorded at the Record Plant.

I remember cutting the drums for the *Love Gun* album in the hallway. Going back to the Record Plant, for me, was not the most pleasant experience because Electric Lady is the studio I built for Jimi [Hendrix] and the one I was most happy with. Getting the sounds on the *Love Gun* album was relatively easy. Getting Ace's sound was fairly straight-ahead. Getting cool sounds for Paul and Gene was sometimes a little tougher. Gene was easier once I established what to do. You have to differentiate between Paul's guitar sound and Ace's sound. It was tougher because you wanted to make sure that Paul's sound was distinctive away from Ace's sound. Getting the performances was a little bit tougher even though they were much more experienced by this point. I'm very honest with artists that I work with. I say, "I know you can do a better track" or "That's a great one, do not touch that one." At this point KISS were getting really good. Ace was remarkable. He was the most underrated guitar player. I could always count on him to come through. I could see there was a really distinctive ability with Ace, the ability to play blues and play various styles. He's a competent guitar player and inventive. I encouraged him to take chances. That was something I enjoyed bringing out of him. It takes time. You can't expect to have great solos twenty-four hours a day, that's not going to happen. You have to give the artist breathing room. I did that with all of them, particularly with Ace because I knew I could get some cool sounds out of him. The guy has a very unique take on things.

CORKY STASIAK: *Love Gun* was recorded from May 3, 1977, to May 28. We started recording the album on the 3rd and according to my diaries Ace finally came in on May 9. A lot of the basic tracks we did on *Love Gun* did not include Ace, it was just Paul, Gene, and Peter.

LARRY HARRIS: The object was always to make KISS look bigger than they were. As far as we were concerned, if we could make somebody perceive it, then it would be true. With my association with *Billboard*, I was able to get five KISS albums on the charts at one time; this was around '77, '78. I walked in and gave them inflated sales figures, which they could have easily checked if they chose to but they didn't. I helped manipulate the charts for all of our acts at Casablanca. This was happening all over the business. In the record industry, if you go top one hundred in *Billboard* with your product, the rack jobbers, the people who sell records in Wal-Mart and Kmart, those huge mass merchandisers, will take your record. If you're not top one hundred in *Billboard* they won't. So, the minute KISS's album hit the top one hundred, Handleman, one of the major rack jobbers, would purchase 100,000, 200,000 albums in one shot. If the records didn't sell we'd be taking them back. But Neil was a gambler and that was not a problem.

BILL AUCOIN: We had a lot of discussions with everyone about counterfeiting. Everyone was pressing up records and shipping them out the back door. I don't think an artist in those days ever knew what the real sales were because everyone was ripping everyone else off. Once everyone knew KISS was selling records they got counterfeited. One thing I thought they couldn't afford to do was the merchandising because it cost too much and it was too complicated to include the little giveaways that came up with the albums. By the time I got to *Love Gun* and the little "love gun" that came with the record, I was always challenged by "How the hell do we do this so people can't copy us?"

GENE SIMMONS: KISS found itself in a very strange position of appealing to a wide range of ages, where most heavy bands appeal to a teen male audience. We found that girls liked us as much as guys. All of a sudden we started to get really young fans. Early on, KISS basically agreed that credibility was an impediment. KISS is able to go where no band has gone before. And so KISS in a lot of ways reflected American pop culture. It's no secret that Fred Flintstone started out as a cartoon and eventually wound up being a multiple vitamin. When you bought your cereal box, you also got prizes in the middle besides the cereal that you love so much. It just makes life more fun. Maybe that's what it's really about. Marketing is a fancy word, but what it really means is there's no reason why you shouldn't have fun doing stuff. Our philosophy has always been to give the KISS fans more, in the shows and in the albums. Sort of a Crackerjack box approach. You can have the peanuts, the popcorn, and you also get a prize. So the notion of giving the fans something a little extra came into play where the albums came with things like posters, tattoos, stickers, and a miniature love gun. When you really look at it, these things are not all that valuable, it just says, "for the same price, here's something extra, thanks very much." I'm the one who kept pushing for it. All the rest of the guys disliked that whole part of it, they wanted to be thought of as serious musicians. I had no delusions about that.

CAROL KAYE: I started working with KISS in June of 1977. It was an amazing time in my life. KISS had just recorded *Love Gun*. I was working at Aucoin Management and I remember that Al Ross, the VP of publicity, started freaking out in the office because *Love Gun* went to number four. It was KISS's highest charting album at the time.

CAROL ROSS: From the very beginning, it was an incredible challenge doing KISS's publicity, the launching of a band that looked the way they did at a time when no one was prepared for that. The closest thing was David Bowie. The most important fact is that they were great guys as individuals and even greater guys as professionals. They were never late, they never made excuses, they did what they had to do. And that's a publicist's dream.

CAROL KAYE: Having worked with everyone from Queen to Aerosmith, with KISS, I had the greatest band to learn from. It was baptism by fire for me. What greater speakers are there in rock 'n' roll than Gene Simmons and Paul Stanley? KISS were the masters of publicity. I learned from them how to become a great publicist. Sitting in on interviews they did I was always amazed at the quotes they'd come up with. They controlled the interviews and made it work for them.

CAROL KAYE: Besides KISS, the Press Office handled many other acts, Billy Squier's band, Piper, Toby Beau, Starz, Blondie, and the Ramones. We also worked with Paul and Linda McCartney and their band, Wings. Paul McCartney was definitely aware of KISS. During this period I don't think there was a person on earth who didn't know who KISS was.

HARVEY KUBERNIK: Around 1978, I took a job with Danny Goldberg, Inc., a media and management company. I wrote a *Love Gun* media bio, and arranged interviews for Gene and Paul. To this day, I admire the drive and energy of Gene. Even if it was 7:00 A.M. on a Saturday morning, I'd pick him up in my yellow Ford Mustang and schlepp him off to appear on a radio show like *Earth News*. Paul was always very accessible and available to promote the record as well. Gene was also hip to the emerging music and punk independent fanzines like *Denim Delinquent*, and was once pen pals with Greg Shaw of *Bomp!* He knew the legacy and heritage of Hollywood, specifically the studios, the horror and sci-fi films. I remember that Gene really liked the Jeff Beck Group's *Truth* LP. Paul dug Dylan's *Highway 61*. We all worshipped the Pretty Things. I had a couple of Dave Clark Five albums so I was really cool to them. Not fashionable during a disco world. Gene asked me to set up a fanzine interview as well. He spoke about wanting to reach a wider demographic. So I invited Phast Phreddie of *Back Door Man* to Village Recorders in Westwood for an interview. Gene endeared himself forever to me when he uttered the response, "I'd rather fuck Joni Mitchell than listen to her music." This was before our PC society, and the mag ran the quip.

CAROL KAYE: When I started working with KISS they were the biggest band in the world. They were voted number one in the Gallup poll. They were on the cover of every music magazine, *Creem, Circus, Hit Parader, Rock Scene*. In promoting the *Love Gun* album I tried to broaden their horizons in the press. I thought it was important to maintain the loyal audience they had but to continually attract new fans. To me it was obvious, "Let's work with the teen magazines." *16* magazine were great to KISS. The editor, Hedy End, was very receptive. They were in *16* for three years straight. The guys didn't mind the coverage in the teen magazines. They did many, many interviews. They had exposure every month. When the solo records came out they even put the individual members on the cover. We ran contests with these magazines every month. We also worked a lot with *Super Teen*. It was important for KISS that every member have their share of the spotlight. KISS were a band, it wasn't the Gene and Paul show.

DENNIS WOLOCH: Ken Kelly did the *Love Gun* album cover. That same woman pictured over and over in the cover painting is his wife. Because he had no models and was working late at night he went, "Come here, honey, and sit down." I know the band liked Ken's two album covers because they're great big oil paintings and they're very impressive to look at in person.

★ "I STOLE YOUR LOVE" ★

PAUL STANLEY: "I Stole Your Love" came quickly. It was kind of like the sister song to "Love Gun." So it came around the same time. Again, swagger and attitude. That song was influenced in some ways by the Deep Purple song "Burn." There's an old standard called "Fascinating Rhythm," which is what "Burn" is based on. The songs I was writing at the time were a certain type. I was trying to get closer to the things I liked in the British bands that were my influences. And then interestingly, once you had KISS play it, the song took off in a different direction because of the perspective of the players in KISS. So, if I had done those songs a hundred percent my way they would have sounded more similar to those influences. That's the beauty of being in a band, each person brings their own perspective and takes it some place you might not.

★ "CHRISTINE SIXTEEN" ★

GENE SIMMONS: "Christine Sixteen" was written on keyboards. I've always been a fan of the original doo-wop records. Instead of having a solo, the guys would talk. Even Elvis did that. This was the day before saxophones and guitars would take solos in the middle of a song. The talking part in the song sounds to me like a dirty old man [recites some of talking lyrics], "When I see you coming out of school that day . . . " Sounds like a guy on the telephone. Ace hated it when he first heard it. He said, "That's not rock 'n' roll." And I'm going, "Well, guess what? It's gonna be on the record." Paul ripped off a few of my song titles. I told Paul I was writing a new song called "Black Diamond" and that I was gonna rip off the Rolling Stones song "Brown Sugar." And it would be like it sounds. They sound like they're sisters, "Brown Sugar," the younger sister of "Black Diamond," who is the experienced prostitute walking the streets. That was gonna be my story, she's out on the streets for a living, "Black Diamond." Next day Paul comes in and says, "Hey, I wrote a song called 'Black Diamond.' " And I said, "You're kidding me, I was gonna write one." Likewise with "Psycho Circus," I actually started writing a song called "Psycho Circus" first and Paul beat me to the punch. Paul and I always made fun of each other's songwriting styles because we hardly wrote songs in the same room. He said, "The only things you ever write about are silly ideas. You're always talking about monsters and stuff." "God of Thunder" is Paul's version of a song that I would have written. We were playing Japan in '77 and the title came about because of a conversation. The title immediately grabbed me, "Christine Sixteen" is a force dangerous, it's forbidden fruit.

PAUL STANLEY: I was writing a song called "Christine Sixteen" and Gene liked the title, so he stole it, which isn't unusual because I stole the title of "Black Diamond" from him. That's how that came about.

EDDIE KRAMER: I played piano on it. Gene was standing next to me but he didn't play it, I played it. He actually coached me on how to play like a Neanderthal person.

★ "GOT LOVE FOR SALE" ★

GENE SIMMONS: I wrote "Got Love for Sale" at the Sunset Marquis, when we got back from Japan, along with "Christine Sixteen." And then "Got Love for Sale," "Christine Sixteen," and "Tunnel of Love" were all recorded with the Van Halen brothers—Eddie, Alex—and myself.

★ "SHOCK ME" ★

ACE FREHLEY: I got electrocuted in Florida and I survived. The guys said, "Why don't you write a song about getting electrocuted?" And I came up with "Shock Me." I knew it was definitely a good riff. Paul and Gene pushed me to sing lead vocals on the song. They said, "It's time you should do a lead vocal." I was still nervous and I ended up singing it on my back. I had Eddie Kramer lower the lights in the studio. Then the first night I did it I was very nervous. After the first performance of "Shock Me" in front of ten, twenty thousand people, I was fine. I'd been doing backgrounds and they realized my voice was strong enough to carry a lead vocal.

EDDIE KRAMER: When we did the first solo album, I have very distinct memories of him lying on his back clutching a bottle of beer under his chest singing the vocal because he felt more in touch with the earth and more stable that way. But whether it was on "Shock Me" or not, I'm not sure. My recollection is that it was on the first solo album.

PAUL STANLEY: To me, "Shock Me" is arguably the best song Ace wrote by himself. It's by far and away in a class by itself.

CORKY STASIAK: Ace was a busy man on May 17. He cut the leads for "Christine Sixteen" and recorded the track "Shock Me." Peter's drumming was exceptional.

★ "TOMORROW AND TONIGHT" ★

PAUL STANLEY: There were elements in "Tomorrow and Tonight" that actually came from Mott the Hoople. There's a Mott the Hoople song called "Golden Age of Rock and Roll." I liked that so there was some of that song in it. And it was also one of those "Let me see if I can write another 'Rock and Roll All Nite.'" You usually can't write two of the same song and have them both be great.

CORKY STASIAK: The background vocalists that sang on "Tomorrow and Tonight" were Tasha Thomas, Raymond Simpson—Valerie Simpson's brother—and a woman named Hilda. They made up the KISSettes.

PAUL STANLEY: One of the background vocalists, Ray Simpson, later would replace the first cop in the Village People.

THE DEMON UNLEASHED, RICHFIELD COLISEUM, CLEVELAND, OHIO, JANUARY 8, 1978
(photo: www.janetmacoska.com)

★ "LOVE GUN" ★

PAUL STANLEY: I wrote "Love Gun" on the airplane to Japan. That was written in my head, the whole thing. And then when I landed I had to play it to make sure it worked and it was all there. I think most of the time when you write songs that are great, you know it. I always thought "Love Gun" was a great song, and today I still think it's a tremendous song. It's probably the song I enjoy playing the most. To me "Love Gun" is quintessential KISS and is probably one of the five signature essential songs. I played bass on the song. I was at a point where I liked going to Electric Lady recording demos on my own and coming up with the parts and the arrangements. With some songs it was clearly a matter of giving people parts to play because the vision I had was complete. A song was not only a song but it was an arrangement. So it was easier to go in the studio and say here's what the picture looked like. If I remember, no one was available to come in to play bass, which was all the better. The bass part just made sense.

CORKY STASIAK: On May 18 and 19 we did the lead vocals on "Love Gun" and on May 23 we recorded strings for a song on the album.

★ "HOOLIGAN" ★

PETER CRISS: "Hooligan" is an old '20's term for gangster, punk . . . and my grandmother always used to call me that! "You're nothin' but a hooligan, you're runnin' around with street gangs . . ." I'm still a street fighter.

STAN PENRIDGE: I happened to mention the word "hooligan" in a conversation. Peter and I would approach writing songs that way. We'd sit and talk and I'd be writing down lil' sayings or "Peterisms." Peter told me that his grandmother used to call him a hooligan. There was the first line of the song and a way to tell a story. We scribbled the rest out in a few minutes and recorded it. Those early tunes were all improvised around simple 1-4-5 changes or variations thereof. "Hooligan" was one that happened to make the album. The original demo for "Hooligan" was written and recorded at the Record Plant. It was part of two songs recorded that evening, the other being "Love Bite." I played all the guitars and bass and Peter played drums and sang. It was probably the first true collaboration between Peter and myself.

STAN PENRIDGE: "Hooligan," "Baby Driver," and "Dirty Livin'" became KISS tunes. They lost the roll of the rock but added an edge. That's the only way I can describe what they did to the demos that were presented. The spontaneity and fun seemed to have been replaced by crunch and hype. For the most part I always felt there was an element of overkill to everything involved with KISS at that point.

CORKY STASIAK: On May 12, we cut "Hooligan." Peter was writing the lyrics as we were recording. Those guys didn't have their homework done for the album, only because of the pressures of the road and touring all around the world. A lot of times groups would start recording with half ideas because they just didn't have the time to finish the songs. But it did turn out to be a great album. Eddie was not happy with the original chorus for "Hooligan" so Peter was writing the lyrics on the spot while we were recording. I came up with the line "I'm a hooligan, don't want to go to school again." I came up with that lyric, that's my big claim to fame [laughs].

★ "ALMOST HUMAN" ★

GENE SIMMONS: There was a book that I had started reading about the idea of lycanthropes. Werewolves were always a fascinating kind of Jekyll and Hyde idea, that you are a human being but only kind of. [Recites lyrics] "I'm almost human, can't help feeling strange, the moon is out, I think I'm gonna change." We brought in Jimmy Maelin, a longtime friend of ours who was one of the top percussionists. He was in a group on Paramount Records called Ambergris. It was like congas, and that's me on guitar. On other songs where you think it's Ace or Paul on guitar, it's me. "War Machine" and "Plaster Caster," that's me on guitar and bass.

★ "PLASTER CASTER" ★

GENE SIMMONS: "Plaster Caster" was written as an ode to groupies. The Plaster Casters were groupies out of Chicago. These girls had a very healthy hobby of taking plaster casts of various appendages and keeping them as mementos. That always fascinated me so I wrote a song about it. Groupies have had a major influence on my life. They've kept many a cold night's chill away. I love groupies and I like the concept of groupies. I think it's wonderful when women want to give of themselves to you. That's magic. They don't want to be taken out to dinner, they don't want jewels, they don't want anything. They just want to give you pleasure. In return, they just want a slice of fantasy, something that they can tell their friends about. "You know who I was with?" That's their reward. That's nice because you both enjoy yourself and the guy doesn't have to act like a servant. None of this "Let me take you out to dinner and pay your way." Guys ought to get hip to that.

CYNTHIA PLASTER CASTER: Initially when I heard about the song I was not thrilled because I had never intended to cast KISS. I felt that in writing the song Gene was sending out the message to the world that he had been cast or that I should do him. I wasn't that much of a KISS fan. Over the years, the song has grown on me, it's very catchy. I'm a sucker for catchy tunes. I've since met Gene and he said that he wrote the song not for the reasons that I had once believed, but in fact it was a fantasy of his.

CORKY STASIAK: On Friday, May 13, according to my diaries, we had a problem recording "Plaster Caster." That day the guys got measured for their new costumes of that era. I remember that Bill Aucoin brought in the original painting for the *Love Gun* album cover. They loved it. The next day we finished "Plaster Caster." We also sat around together and watched KISS on *Don Kirshner's Rock Concert.* Ace also did leads for "Tomorrow and Tonight."

★ "THEN SHE KISSED ME" ★

GENE SIMMONS: Paul walked in one day and said, "How about if we do this song?" And we started playing with it and recorded it. We also toyed with "Go Now," a song by the Moody Blues when Denny Laine was in the band. That's a great song. KISS used to perform that live right around the first album. We were thinking of recording that, but we thought lyrically that it didn't make sense. Here's our first album, gotta go.

PAUL STANLEY: I was a big fan of the song "Then She Kissed Me." One thing you'll never get from me is bullshit. There are songs that I think are monumental and we've written some great stuff. Some things in retrospect just didn't work. That's a great song and it needs to get redone like "I Want to Hold Your Hand" needs to get redone. It's a song you don't mess with.

CORKY STASIAK: I remember Paul saying we had to record a song by somebody else. They were thinking of doing "Jailhouse Rock" but decided upon "Then She Kissed Me." It was the last song we recorded for the album. We cut that on May 21.

ALIVE II

Release date: October 24, 1977
KISS / EDDIE KRAMER–producer / CORKY STASIAK–engineer / BOB KULICK–session lead guitarist
SEAN DELANEY–songwriter / DAVE CLARK–songwriter / DENNIS WOLOCH–album designer
CAROL KAYE–publicist, the Press Office Ltd.

PAUL STANLEY: *Alive II* is great. I'd give it four and a half stars. I think the live stuff on there is really, really good. It's kind of like saying to somebody if *Alive!* scored 100, then *Alive II*, I'd give a 95 to. The problem with it was KISS *Alive!* documented a complete concert. We couldn't do that on *Alive II* without repeating songs. So to avoid that we only used songs from the previous three albums. But of course we found ourselves short of material, hence the studio side. I love *Alive II*. I don't even call it a companion piece. It's just an extension from KISS *Alive!* The only difference between the two are the songs.

ACE FREHLEY: I thought *Alive II* was good. There was just something about your first live record that was kind of special. *Alive II* was just kind of like the sequel. It was a four.

GENE SIMMONS: As a live document it's pretty good. I don't think it's quite as good as *Alive!* We decided to put on new material. We just didn't think it was enough to do *Alive II*. We also thought it was another good bookend for a couple of years in the band. I'd give it three stars.

PETER CRISS: I'd give it five stars. I love live albums. It was more live than *Alive!* because we were much better as musicians, as entertainers. We had our shit together. We knew what we had to do. We knew our jobs. We were seasoned by then. We knew now that timing was important and that we couldn't get away with a lot of shit so we paid more attention to the music on it.

GENE SIMMONS: *Alive II* was another one of those big bumps in the road. The more successful we got, the more wacky Ace and Peter became. Management came to us and said, "You have to record a new live album." And that was a surprise to us.

BILL AUCOIN: *Alive!* did so well and now record sales were kind of waning a little bit so we thought, "How about doing *Alive II*?" The idea about not having to be in the studio with each other for all those hours certainly made sense to everyone. It was a natural.

EDDIE KRAMER: With me, KISS saw an English rock 'n' roll producer who loved their music and loved the challenge of making them sound great. The most challenging records I ever did were the ones I made with KISS. To make those guys sound good was tough because they had a very particular way of playing live that was just balls to the wall, all energy, jumping up and down and going crazy. And in the beginning, it was tough to make them sound very tight. Later on it became easier because they got better. Everybody put them down. They were the underdogs. Radio wouldn't play them. But they had all these fans who loved and adored them. I thought if I can make them sound really cool and give them some of the edge of some of the other bands I've worked with, like Zeppelin, then I've done my job.

GENE SIMMONS: We all said that we needed to make *Alive II* different from *Alive!* I got the idea of putting new studio songs on side four from a ZZ Top live album where half of it was live and the other half was new material. *Alive II* is okay. We knew more, we played a little bit better. Some of the songs we didn't do live, there were some afternoon recordings done at sound check with "Hard Luck Woman" and "Tomorrow and Tonight."

CORKY STASIAK: We recorded the basic tracks for the studio cuts on *Alive II* at the Capitol Theatre in Passaic, New Jersey. The guys were professional, they knew they had a job to do and nailed it. Their recording schedule was nuttier than ever, we had to work quickly. I think they were on a week break. I cut "Tomorrow and Tonight" and "Larger Than Life" on September 13, 1977. "Rockin' in the USA" and "Rocket Ride" were recorded on the 14th. "Any Way You Want It" was cut on the 15th and "All American Man" on the 16th.

EDDIE KRAMER: For the studio songs, we had to use other guitar players. The record had to go forward, if Ace wasn't available for whatever reason, it was important that we went ahead. The guy we used [Bob Kulick] was a good guitar player but he wasn't Ace. I think Anton [Fig] played drums on a couple of tracks. If my memory serves me correctly, for one track, Peter wasn't available for some reason and we needed to get the track done.

ACE FREHLEY: [laughing] I don't even remember what those songs were. I think I was out in the ozone somewhere.

BILL AUCOIN: Ace was in the ozone. Ace was kind of off partying. He was probably pissed off at one of them or something. You can't live with someone day and night without problems. It's like being married. Sooner or later you're gonna say, "Hey, screw you!"

PAUL STANLEY: There were times let's say when I don't know if Ace knew the back side of the guitar to the front and it was probably due to ingesting certain liquids.

GENE SIMMONS: As early as *Destroyer* and actually even earlier than that, alcohol and some other chemicals were starting to rule Ace's life and cloud his judgment. He wasn't on all of *Destroyer* either. He would not show up. He would call in sick or stay in bed for three days or whatever and you know we had to continue. So there were some solos that Ace did not play.

PETER CRISS: That really bothered me. It pissed the shit out of me. Something happened to his hand. I think he got in an accident. Something went wrong and he couldn't play. I wasn't as enthused with it. I may have just walked in, did my thing, and left.

BOB KULICK: I played on three of the four studio songs on *Alive II*, "All American Man," "Larger Than Life," and "Rockin' in the USA," where I played the solo and the rhythm guitars. I was just in a real good space for playing on their stuff at that time. Eddie Kramer got a really good guitar sound and I felt really comfortable. It was that period of time where Gene and Paul looked at me like I was their savior—whenever they needed anyone to plop some lead guitar on a record, it was "Let's call Bob." Paul called me and said that they were having some problems with Ace. He asked if I would come in to do some guitar stuff on the album, primarily solos. He told me that it would be kept on the QT, it would be a friend thing and I would get paid. And I said, "Of course, fine." Ace was in the lounge on the floor while I was doing solos. They ascertained that Ace was incapable of giving them what they needed in the time frame that they needed it. They had a deadline. So they brought in the guy who they knew could play, who they knew all along was the better player but they picked the guy who fit the band better imagewise. It was a no-brainer for them, it was like, "Get Bob." Stylistically what I did and what KISS did were the same thing so I knew exactly what they wanted. I played like me.

BOB KULICK: I knew that they were enthusiastic about my playing even though there were times when I'd play one note and Gene would say, "Stop." I'd say, "What did you stop the tape for?" "Oh, I didn't like that note." I said, "But you didn't know where I was going." And he said, "But that's not Ace." Then I'd play a solo, which Ace could never play even if he got somebody's brain transplant and a new set of fingers and he'd think it sounds like him. "You can't play that because Ace would never play that one note." But that's part of what being a musician is. "That's not right for you, how about this?" But in the end I always really liked whatever it was that we wound up with, even if it wasn't what I initially came up with or parts were left out or modified or parts were mixed down.

EDDIE KRAMER: I don't think *Alive II* is as great as the first live album. It's historical and hysterical. The first live album is the one that really established them and made them big. Anything subsequent to that is never going to be quite as good. It was a very competent second live record. I think it was done under a lot of pressure. I'm sure it was self-generated, "It's got to be better than the first live album." I'm sure the record company demanded it and the fans demanded it. I recorded an entire live record with the band in Japan at the Budokan, which was okay. It wasn't great. I don't think the performances were up to par and that's why it didn't come out.

EDDIE KRAMER: *Alive II* had much less in the way of fix-up than the *Alive!* album. There were some fixes, but not as much as the first live album.

DENNIS WOLOCH: What I remember most about the *Alive II* cover is we didn't have any new pictures. I was just going through our old files trying to find stuff that we could use. So that's why there wasn't one great big picture like on *Alive!*, one big shot. You never get a good band shot with four guys looking good. *Alive!* was posed to look live. Anyhow, I was looking around for another live band shot but there just wasn't one. It didn't exist. So I just took four little shots and put them on the cover with the logo. Sometimes as a designer you have to solve those problems.

CAROL KAYE: I remember coming into the office and someone said, "Carol, you're on the front page of the *Wall Street Journal*!" The article starts, "Carol Kaye is a publicist with a problem, she can't seem to squelch the rumors that KISS does not stand for Knights In Satan's Service." That was so off-the-wall. There was about a year of these real radical groups picketing KISS shows and telling people not to buy their records because their name stands for Knights In Satan's Service. To combat this false information, we sent out press releases, the band did interviews. It wasn't the worst thing to happen because KISS were a band that parents were really afraid to have their kids go and see.

★ "ALL AMERICAN MAN" ★

PAUL STANLEY: That was written real quickly. I wrote that in my dining room with Sean Delaney. I don't have any real connection to "All American Man." At that point I was struggling to come up with songs. I have to say that when I was having trouble writing sometimes I would have people come around [laughing] keeping me in one place until I came up with something.

BOB KULICK: I played lead guitar on that song. Paul's a really good rhythm guitar player when he puts his mind to it. I always thought he had a Keith Richards thing goin' on. To me, Paul had that sloppy yet precise kind of attack rhythm guitar vibe, which to me worked for all the stuff that he writes. All the stuff that he comes up with like "All American Man" fits the motif of his playing.

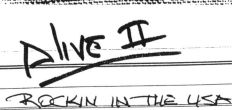

Alive II

ROCKIN IN THE USA

I'M FLYING IN A 747 · PASSIN' BY THE
PEARLEY GATES
I'M COMIN' REAL CLOSE TO HEAVEN · AND
MY GUITAR JUST CAN'T WAIT
IT JUST CAN'T WAIT

AND FRANCE REALLY HAD THEIR OWN CHANCE
YES THERE WAS PLENTY ROMANCE
I'VE BEEN TO ENGLAND TOO THERE WASN'T
MUCH TO DO
ONE THING I KNOW IS TRUE
WHAT I WOULD RATHER DO

[IS ROCKIN IN THE USA

WELL GERMANLAND WAS LOTS OF FUN
AND ROCK 'N ROLL HAS GOT ME ON THE RUN
DENMARK WAS GREAT · BUT I JUST CAN'T WAIT
ROCKIN' IN THE USA

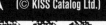

★ "ROCKIN' IN THE USA" ★

GENE SIMMONS: Everybody in the band hates it, especially Paul. He thinks it's schlock, just the *worst.* We go to do our makeup and often he starts singing it as a kind of "Boy, is that lame." We were on tour and I'm *very* patriotic about America. It made everything possible for me, and I always read my own comments and I come off sounding like one of these hard-hat guys. You know, "If you don't love America then get the fuck out." Ted Nugent said something that comes off very right-wing yet there's something emotional inside of me that said, "Yeah, that's right." And it's unkind what he said. It was, "If you don't speak English then get the fuck out of America." Now, that's not right. Yet on the other hand I'm thinking, I'm from another country and if this country is gonna give me everything and anything I ever wanted . . . Social Security, free libraries, free political thinking, I can tell the President to go fuck off, do anything I want to do. I will not disappear off the streets, then that's right. Learn English or get the fuck out. So, emotionally I think that's right.

★ "LARGER THAN LIFE" ★

GENE SIMMONS: I like the drums on "Larger Than Life." The drums were the impetus to going back to that kind of [John] Bonham sound on *Creatures of the Night.* I did an interview with a guy and he said, "What is it about you with girls?" I said, "Well, I'm not the best-looking guy in the world, I'm not the richest guy in the world, I'm not this or this or this . . . but I'll tell you what I've got, what I've got is larger than life." I heard myself say it and after the interview, I jotted it down on paper, both the imagery and the physical sort of pun. Physically and figuratively speaking. "Larger Than Life" just sort of happened very naturally. I picked up the guitar and there it was.

★ "ROCKET RIDE" ★

ACE FREHLEY: That's the first time I was satisfied with my vocal projection. I originally wrote the song for my solo album, but when we were putting *Alive II* together and decided to have a studio side with new songs, I gave it up for the album. That was the song that really gave me confidence that I could sing and really project a song. Sean and I wrote it at my house in Irvington [New York]. I had a studio in my attic. We got together one summer day, wrote it and did the demo in my attic.

SEAN DELANEY: "Rocket Ride" was written in Japan. I was taken over to Japan for only one reason and that was to write songs with the guys. They were all having a writer's block where all of a sudden you are incapable of writing songs. So for me to go to Japan that was the stipulation, that I would write songs with them. Ace got mad and went to Bill and said, "Well, he's over here for all of us, not just Gene and Paul!" So it was actually an appointment [laughs]. There was a time and a schedule. I went into his room and said, "Do you have any riffs?" And he said, "Oh yeah, there's this one but I don't think the guys in the band are capable of playing it." [laughs] Ace had that incredible guitar riff. He was playing the riff for "Rocket Ride" and I came out with the lyric and the melody.

★ "ANY WAY YOU WANT IT" ★

PAUL STANLEY: Everything that's been done should be left alone. Nobody should remake old films and nobody should remake old songs. You can't do them better than they were initially done. Spontaneity isn't something that you can re-create. Spontaneity is what it is because it's that initial burst of energy. And if you're trying to re-create it . . . I mean we've been guilty of it too. One of my favorite old songs was a Dave Clark Five song called "Any Way You Want It," which Gene and I just loved. We went in and did it on *Alive II* and it's good. But the difference between our version and the original version is the original version sounded like it was gonna fall apart any minute because there was so much energy in it and when we did it it was too studied. "Any Way You Want It" was chaos on the original. What we did was try to construct chaos and that doesn't work the same. When Dave Clark Five did it, it just sounded bombastic, like any minute it was gonna fall apart, which was part of what made it so great. When we did it it was crafted and I don't think that's the same.

DAVE CLARK: I like KISS's version of our song. I never looked at the DC5 as being heavy metal, but I suppose when you listen to that song and a few other DC5 songs they are quite heavy. Heavy in the sense of being loud. And what we managed to get on that record was very ballsy loud songs, which would jump out of the grooves without distorting. I later met Gene Simmons and he was very complimentary about the DC5 and "Any Way You Want It."

DOUBLE PLATINUM

Release date: April 24, 1978
KISS / SEAN DELANEY–producer / BILL AUCOIN–manager
CAROL KAYE–publicist, the Press Office Ltd.
DENNIS WOLOCH–album designer

PETER CRISS: God, *Double Platinum*, I guess I'd give it three stars because we didn't really participate a lot on it.

PAUL STANLEY: I'd give that two stars. It's okay. It's just a compilation where somebody went in and started rearranging songs that didn't need to be rearranged. Honestly, the band had nothing to do with that album. It was a time where someone might say, "Let's put out a compilation." We were riding such a wave of success that there were certain people in the camp that wanted to put out as much product as possible.

GENE SIMMONS: At the time, everybody thought the band was going to break up because Ace and Peter yet again were going through turmoil. Ace wanted to leave the band. Ace always felt that his talent wasn't appreciated by the band and the fans. He's always wanted to get up there and have the Ace Frehley Band to show people he was the writer and he was the star. When he first joined the band he refused to sing. He always said, "I just wanna be the guitar player." In a very real way KISS created a

Frankenstein. We created a guy who started to believe he should be leading his own band. I was also going off the deep end. I had met Cher and my whole life was turned upside down. All of a sudden I was seduced by a girl. She's a great person and we get along fine today. I needed somebody who didn't want to be with me because I was in a band. Someone who didn't want anything from me. Someone who had their own money and their own notoriety. It was someone who I could let my guard down with. I'm very happy I met her. At that point everybody was scattered.

ACE FREHLEY: Sean Delaney and Mike Stone did a lot of remixing of songs and we weren't there at the time. I think it could have been done better. Three stars.

PAUL STANLEY: "Strutter '78" was Neil Bogart's idea that we could get mileage out of "Strutter" if it was recut with more of a quote unquote disco feel. So we went into the studio and recut the song with Jimmy Ienner, who worked with a lot of cool people like Raspberries, Grand Funk, and Three Dog Night. Once in a while you do things to make your record company happy. I don't think we do anything anymore except have big records to make our record company happy. In the beginning, you tend to do things politically because they make sense to do. If you painted the *Mona Lisa* once I don't know why you have to do it twice. Not that "Strutter's" the *Mona Lisa*, but once something's been done there's no reason to do it again. They wanted us to do it, thought we could get some mileage out of it, so we went along with it. It was totally unnecessary.

ACE FREHLEY: I thought it was kind of a silly thing to do because I don't think the new version was that different. It was just extended solos and what-not.

PETER CRISS: I liked the original [version of "Strutter"]. But it was all right. It was a little bit more advanced and it was more disco.

BILL AUCOIN: Don't forget, we weren't a radio band for the most part. The only way we could keep our name out there was to keep putting out albums and touring. My philosophy was KISS weren't really profound in their writing ability. And other things got in the way. Once they started making money it was like a curse. We used to spend hours talking about what we would do, what was coming up next and planning ideas for the show, and that changed drastically when the money came into play. When you start having money in your pocket it changes your life. I remember the time Gene went and spent a fortune on a coat for Diana Ross and a couple of days later Paul bought a Tiffany lamp for forty or fifty thousand bucks. Years earlier Paul came in and made small talk with me at the office. I later found out he had wanted to borrow five bucks from me for cab fare home. I was listening to what he was saying and he saw the hole in my sweater. I leaned back in my chair and put my feet up on the desk and I had a hole in my shoe. And this was in the winter. And when he saw the hole in my shoe, he decided not to ask me for the five bucks.

SEAN DELANEY: KISS needed product because the solo albums was the next big thing that was coming out. It was going to take a period of time and they needed something to come out from KISS now. KISS always flooded the market, there was no slow-down on doing albums. We had finished Gene's solo album, the part in England. All of a sudden I get a phone call from Bill [Aucoin] and Neil Bogart. They want us to sequence together enough songs for an album called *Double Platinum*. They sent us the quarter-inch tapes for us to sequence together. Then we found something horrible. As we tried to put two songs back-to-back they would sound totally different. One would be really strong-sounding and one would sound totally weak. You couldn't put them back-to-back because of the drastic difference in the sound. We had to literally get the master tapes sent from New York to us in London. We were at Trident Studios, myself and the engineer, Mike Stone. KISS's receptionist was the courier. The tapes had to be hand-carried, these were the master tapes. So she was allowed to fly to London, deliver them to us, and go straight back to the airport and fly straight back. She wasn't even allowed to stay a weekend in London. Mike and I got these master tapes and we started listening to each one. Try to imagine being told over the phone after you've just gone several weeks of almost never leaving the studio that you have to do twenty-one titles. And they have to be done in nine days. Mike Stone and I almost had a nervous breakdown. But we did it within the time frame.

SEAN DELANEY: The idea was to make the songs sound better than the initial releases. I remember on "Hard Luck Woman" as we were going through and setting up the board we left the drums out and when they came in we said, "Man, that sounds so fuckin' great! We can segue that from here to there, it's great."

SEAN DELANEY: We found with each of the producers that had done a KISS album that they had done them totally different. For instance, Eddie Kramer recorded all of his drums in mono. You couldn't change anything on a Bob Ezrin tape because he recorded it that way. If there was echo and slap-back on something, it was recorded that way so it could never be changed. We had to come up with a sound that all the other stuff had to be brought up to. Bob Ezrin's was the tape we had to go and try to match. It's the difference between playing a CD today against a 45, and having them right next to each other, this big digital CD sound and then you're into the sound of a 45. That was the difference between the Bob Ezrin sound and the other producers.

CAROL KAYE: I had to be a very creative publicist and I was always thinking of ways to keep KISS in the press. I decided to send KISS's boots on tour. Those boots were in a museum and they toured around the world. KISS were so big [laughing] that their boots went on the road without them!

DENNIS WOLOCH: That album cover was a technical feat. We printed the cover on Mylar. We could have printed on foil paper, which would have held the emboss a lot better. My boss, Howard [Marks], insisted on Mylar, which is a plastic material. Unfortunately, Mylar has a memory so when you bend it, stretch it, and try to emboss it, eventually it's gonna go back to where it wants to go back to. It remembers that it's supposed to be flat, it has this memory. So consequently it doesn't hold a really high emboss. But the upside was it's the shiniest material around, very silvery. So that's why we did it with the Mylar. It was a technical feat. The printer got printing awards for that album.

PAUL STANLEY

Release date: September 18, 1978
KISS / BOB KULICK—lead guitarist / STEVE BUSLOWE—bass
DOUG KATSAROS—piano, omni string ensemble / RICHIE FONTANA—drums
DAVE WITTMAN—engineer / MIKEL JAPP—songwriter / CARMINE APPICE—drums
PEPPY CASTRO—background vocalist / CAROL KAYE—publicist, the Press Office Ltd.

PAUL STANLEY: If there was a sixth [star], it would get it. I think it's a really good album. I think the writing is really good. It's kind of like a diary because there was a lot of stuff going on at that point that I was writing about. I think the songs are real good. It's a very close-to-the-bone kind of album.

GENE SIMMONS: Paul's solo album was a lot closer to the KISS thing, but the solo record I enjoyed most was Ace's. I thought that had a lot more rock 'n' roll spirit and I liked the guitars on it. When Paul sticks to the harder-edged lyric, I like it more, but there's a lot of stuff on there that's "love this and love that," "Wouldn't You Like to Know Me?" "Hold Me, Touch Me" kind of stuff. When Paul starts to get romantic I turn off. But as a rock 'n' roller, you can't touch him. So as long as he stays hard it works for me. When he gets soft, "I miss you, I love you," I go, "You're spineless, get out!" Two stars.

ACE FREHLEY: I'll give Paul's a five. I thought Paul's was probably the second best of the solo albums.

PAUL STANLEY: I love the album. Let's just say that it needs a second chapter around now. It's great for what it was and it's great for a certain period but it's almost like you need book two. There certainly is that possibility. Ron Nevison was originally going to produce my solo album and at the last minute had to pull out because he was working with the Babys. He was running behind schedule so at that point he pulled out of the record.

PAUL STANLEY: I don't think it's a good idea to try and create a lot of different kinds of music at the same time. You have to decide on one and stick with it. I could've stayed with folk guitar but there are people who do a lot better than I do. That doesn't mean that because we don't record any folk music that it leaves my life. I can still sit in my room and get off playing acoustic guitar. That's what our solo albums were good for. It gave us a chance to let those kinds of ballads come to the front.

BOB KULICK: Paul's solo album was straight-ahead rock, which he's really good at. The songs had little twists because of Paul's varied influences. They were better played and better fleshed out by this group of players rather than a stiffer, more regimented approach that KISS may have brought to the table.

STEVE BUSLOWE: I remember on the first session in New York how impressed I was with Paul. He was playing his guitar through a Marshall amp, and to this day I have never heard anyone that could make it sound the way Paul did. Of course it was extremely loud, but Paul had such a majestic way of playing it that it almost sounded like an orchestra.

STEVE BUSLOWE: I did two sessions at Electric Lady Studios. The first was on February 22, 1978. The second was on the 25th. The first song we recorded was "Tonight You Belong to Me." It seems that we did the whole thing that night, overdubs, etc. I remember that Paul, Bob [Kulick], Richie [Fontana], and I wasted very little time learning the songs. It all came so easily. Paul was producing the sessions as well. I remember that he encouraged me to play more than I might normally have played. He listened to all of our ideas, and accepted many of them.

BOB KULICK: It was interesting because Gene wanted me to play on his solo record and I got caught in the middle between the two of them. After I was done with Paul's, Gene sent me a note saying, "I heard what you did on Paul's stuff and I think you played great, looking forward to you doing some stuff on my record and we'll be in touch soon." I spoke to Paul and he said, "I don't think it's right for you to do Gene's record because you left such a big stamp on my record." I understood what he was saying. When you have an artistic relationship with people sometimes you have to bend. It was a no-win situation. What was I supposed to do, go to Gene and tell him to go fuck himself? Or cause a problem between them or alienate one or the other? Gene understood immediately and said, "Look, Paul has a thing about you playing on my record so no big deal, next time." And that was the way it was left. There was a period of time when they thought I was the guitar god. I don't think it lasted very long [laughs]. Well, for what they were doing and for what I played on the stuff, it was perfect, it was right and it made sense. It was more aggressive and more melodic and flashier than Ace but still having the same vibe.

BOB KULICK: Most of the stuff on Paul's solo album was recorded live, which was great because it was always played like a band. We did half the record in New York and the other half in L.A. The part that we did in New York took no time at all. L.A. seemed interminable. It was just the difference in the intensity level of us being New Yorkers working in New York at a New York pace. "What time is it?" "Three A.M." No problem, we were still having fun. L.A. it was like, "What time do you want to start?" "Well I want to go to the pool and I might drive down to the beach to have lunch so maybe four or five o'clock." And then I get a call and it's like, "Let's say seven." And then I go in at seven and all of a sudden it's 11:30 and it's like, "Let's go out for a drink." We didn't get anything done. We were in the Jacuzzi [laughs]. There were girls hanging around. Guys were horny. Drummers were coming in and drummers were going out [laughs]. Paul always had an idea of what he wanted. He just played the song to us. We'd stumble around a couple of times and go out there and plug in. We'd work it up, find some parts, and see what anybody could come up with.

RICHIE FONTANA: Recording the songs for Paul's album went very smooth. He knew exactly what he wanted, plus me and all the other musicians, Bob Kulick [guitar] and Steve Buslowe [bass], were very much into the material that Paul had written for this project. It was great to see Paul stretch his creative muscles, writing songs that were of a more personal nature to himself. The four of us just got around in a circle at Electric Lady Studio A, had everything miked up, rehearsed the songs right there, and then recorded them on the spot. The basic tracks for the four songs that I played on were done in two sessions on two separate days. I like all of them; "Tonight You Belong to Me" is a great piece of work, "Ain't Quite Right" is just class all the way, "Move On" rocks, and "Wouldn't You Like to Know Me?" I love, because that sort of thing is right up my alley. I've always loved melodic tunes that have power, power pop à la Raspberries and Cheap Trick. This soon led to more session work. Shortly after, Paul was producing some tracks for a pop-rock duo, the Alessi Brothers, for which he called upon the same players, Bob Kulick, Steve Buslowe, and myself. Bruce Kulick was also part of that session clique that we had going for a while.

CAROL KAYE: I had the pleasure of accompanying Paul to the studio while he was recording the album at Electric Lady Studios. I remember Desmond Child and Rouge singing background vocals on the album. To me, it's still one of my favorite records of all time. Paul's solo record is quintessential rock 'n' roll. That album stands the test of time. It's powerful, emotional. "Hold Me, Touch Me" is a song that no one expected from Paul. It's the most sensitive, beautiful song. That's the kind of man Paul is, he's a sensitive, beautiful, amazing person. I think his solo album captured a time in Paul's life. It truly captured Paul's personality and soul.

CAROL KAYE: One the highlights of my career was working the KISS solo albums. This had never been done before. The anticipation was unbelievable building up to the release of the records. We put together a beautiful press kit. We had these plastic shopping bags made up with the images of each solo album on the bag. I sent the four solo albums in the shopping bag to the press and had them hand-delivered, which made it a special event. It made quite an impression on the press and we reaped a lot of coverage.

★ "TONIGHT YOU BELONG TO ME" ★

PAUL STANLEY: It was the lead-off track from my solo album. It's a song I remember writing about some-one whose name I'm not gonna mention 'cause it will make her real happy and maybe she shouldn't be at this point.

BOB KULICK: That feel of "Tonight You Belong to Me," there's the heart and soul of what Paul is. It was dramatic. It was big. It was heartfelt. It gave me chills. There were moments on that record that I felt were as good as Led Zeppelin. When we put those rhythm guitars on "Tonight You Belong to Me" [imitates the opening of song] we both looked at each other and said, "If that doesn't sound like the shit, what does?" He knew that. There was that period of time when we were best friends. We connected in a musical way. The guy respected everything I did. I respected everything he did.

★ "MOVE ON" ★

PAUL STANLEY: Musically, I was thinking along the lines of some of the Bad Company stuff, the swaggering machismo kind of songs about life. At that point I thought female vocals in the background would be great. I was good friends with Desmond Child and Rouge. They were one of the best live bands I ever saw in New York. Everybody took turns being the lead singer. Desmond was on keyboards. It was just a fabulous band. I have yet to hear any girls who could sing like them. I called them up and they all showed up a half-hour later. It was a gas because I was such a fan of theirs. I wanted to add that flavor to the album.

MIKEL JAPP: I played Paul an idea, which was the beginnings of "Move On." All of a sudden new energy was found and we were off again having fun and, yes, writing. He loved it and so did I. We penned at least half of the song by the end of that day at SIR.

★ "AIN'T QUITE RIGHT" ★

MIKEL JAPP: The first song Paul and I wrote together was an idea I had which became "Ain't Quite Right." We met at SIR rehearsal studios for the first time, plugged in our guitars, and I played him the idea. He loved it so we continued on having fun and writing. We basically finished "Ain't Quite Right" that day. We worked for many hours and we both felt really good and positive about the way it had taken shape, both the feel of the song and the lyric. I think Paul's solo album had great vocals, material, players, and production. And being the only writer on it with Paul, I was proud then as I am now of being a part of it.

PAUL STANLEY: I like that song a lot. Sonically, there are things on the album that are questionable. But the album is a really good reflection of who I was and where I was at at that point. I would have loved to have worked with a great producer on that album. Unfortunately, nobody that I wanted to work with was available. After having recorded what I thought were going to be demos and then trying to recut them, I realized the demos were going to be the album. When I started recording with a co-producer it wasn't what I hoped it to be and went back to doing it myself. I was hoping to do the album with Ron Nevison. He was doing the Babys. He was the type of producer that I wanted to work with.

STEVE BUSLOWE: Paul had asked me to replace a bass part that had been recorded by another bassist for the track "Ain't Quite Right." It had some tricky bass slides, that I had trouble capturing the way Paul wanted me to. I was very frustrated that I couldn't get it quite right and was very nervous. I remember that Paul came in and played the part on my bass exactly how he wanted it played. Although he could have played it himself, I felt that he did not want to humiliate me, and gave me the opportunity to get it myself. I eventually did play it close enough to what he wanted to hear. When I think of that experience, it warms my heart. Here's Paul Stanley, who could afford to hire the most expensive musicians in the world, and he had the patience to allow me to work through getting that part correctly. I shall not forget that session, as it proved to be another building block for me in becoming a good studio musician. I think it speaks volumes for Paul's character. A very classy guy, I thought.

PAUL STANLEY UNMASKED,
TOUR OF EUROPE, MAY 1976
(© KISS Catalog Ltd.)

★ "WOULDN'T YOU LIKE TO KNOW ME?" ★

PAUL STANLEY: The song had some of my little Raspberries licks, my Raspberries steals. It's also [Raspberries songs] "Tonight" and also a little of "Ecstasy." It's my Raspberries homage. The Raspberries were absolutely awesome. What they did, they did brilliantly. I saw the original Raspberries at Carnegie Hall. And then Eric [Carmen] was out with us with Mike McBride and Scott McCarl, the later Raspberries.

BOB KULICK: That was a cool tune. We did that song in five minutes. "Bam, there it is!" It was obvious, here's what it sounds like, here we go. I remember Paul had a bunch of guitars and every time I'd play a different guitar I'd play something different because the guitar felt different and it sounded different. It just inspired something different.

★ "TAKE ME AWAY (TOGETHER AS ONE)" ★

PAUL STANLEY: "Take Me Away (Together as One)" started with a verse that Mikel Japp had. Mikel had one of those great raspy, bluesy voices that we associate with the English blues scene. I came up with the chorus and the lyrics. It was more an arrangement piece, something that was more dynamic and symphonic. Sometimes some songs lend themselves to something that's almost aurally cinematic in scope. So it's like watching a movie in IMAX. I wanted something that had an epic feel.

MIKEL JAPP: I played and sang Paul a couple of the verses I had for "Take Me Away (Together As One)." I explained to him that it was about a girl I had met in South Africa while on tour when I was in the band Marmalade. He looked at me and said, "It's great but with the songs I already have plus what we've done today, I think I have enough for my album." I thought, "Fair enough," so we called it a day and finished off "Ain't Quite Right" and "Move On" over the phone, with me in L.A. and Paul in New York. Paul then demoed the songs in New York before actually cutting the record, and they sounded great. About two to three weeks later my phone rang and it was Paul. "Hi Mike, it's Paul. Remember that last idea you played me at SIR?" I replied, "Yes." Then he said, "I wanna do it and I think I've written a great bridge, the melody sticks in my head. Let's go over the chords." That's how "Take Me Away (Together As One)" was written.

STEVE BUSLOWE: "Take Me Away" was recorded at the Record Plant in Los Angeles during the first week of July of 1978. We spent that first week recording, having only completed "Take Me Away" at those sessions. It was certainly thrilling for me to play with Carmine [Appice], as I had been such a big fan of the Vanilla Fudge while growing up. However, I believe the chemistry of that band was not what it was in New York.

CARMINE APPICE: I was right in the middle of doing a lot of Rod Stewart stuff. We were touring a lot. I came in from Australia and I went right into the studio. I was really jet-lagged and out of it and played on five songs. They only used one of the songs that I played on, not because of my performance, just the fact of the song itself. It was all done in one day.

BOB KULICK: Carmine's flamboyant, over-the-top drum style got in the way of what Paul was doing, which was straight-ahead KISS rock 'n' roll. The drums were so loud, it was really painful even with headphones on. At the end of the tune, Carmine asked if he could cut loose and play all those big drum fills. He played everything but the kitchen sink. I'm listening to the fills after it's done and he's all over the place time-wise because he was showing off. After Carmine leaves, we're all wondering how we're going to overdub on this track because his timing was off. We could have recorded the song again in the time that it took to fix those drum fills. That was part of what went on with the recording in L.A. Everything took two, three times as long to do whereas the New York stuff was done very quickly. Paul thought they were demos at first. Demos? It sounds like a record! [laughs]

★ "IT'S ALRIGHT" ★

PAUL STANLEY: I recorded "It's Alright" in L.A. and did the vocal in England at Trident Studios. I mixed the album at Trident. "It's Alright" was a song that I thought was missing from the album, which was an uptempo, kick-ass rock 'n' roll song.

★ "HOLD ME, TOUCH ME (THINK OF ME WHEN WE'RE APART)" ★

PAUL STANLEY: Good songs come easily. The lyrics were real easy and then there were a couple of lines that I couldn't get and I just stayed in the studio until I had it done. But the song itself was written real quickly. I was real suspicious when I wrote it because it sounded so familiar, but I don't know what it sounds like. A good song should sound familiar. A good song should be something that you can sing after hearing half of it and it's one of those kind of songs. I love it. Hey, women love that kind of stuff and we gotta please the women. Without women we're in trouble. At some point a woman will probably do that song and have a hit with it. On "Hold Me, Touch Me," that's my favorite lead guitar work of all the things I've done.

GENE SIMMONS: I thought "Hold Me, Touch Me" was a real brave departure for Paul and a well-written song. Somebody could have a hit with that today.

DOUG KATSAROS: Paul said to me, "I have trouble writing ballads, I'm a rock 'n' roller." So I wrote him a little ballad and he said, "That's beautiful, Doug, but you've inspired me." He went home and came up with "Hold Me, Touch Me." I thought it was a beautiful song, right up there with "Beth." Paul was really happy he'd written a ballad. But he was so generous and marvelous enough to always make me feel as if I had been helpful to him. He said, "Thank you for writing a song to inspire me to write a great song." It's always about someone else with Paul. He is a gentleman, he's smart and he was always very good to the people he was with. I'm very proud of the caliber of work we did at the time and the caliber of a person he was. It was fun recording that song. It was done in an afternoon. He totally threw it in my hands and said, "Make the strings beautiful," and I did. We actually put seven tracks of strings on it.

PEPPY CASTRO: It was great working on Paul's solo album. Paul had a lot of fun and he really enjoyed himself. I sang on a bunch of songs. "Hold Me, Touch Me" rivaled anything that a classic songwriter would write. Paul was definitely going through his melodic phase where he really wanted to sing and not have to scream and sing over heavy rock tracks. He wanted to really be heard. Paul has honed his craft so much now, that he's not only a great writer but a great singer. He's been a major talent for the last twenty-five years. Paul never gets that credit but he's got a good consolation, a very big bank account [laughs]. Paul is so creative that there's not enough outlets for him to do what he would love to do. Paul's a musicologist. I was in a band called Balance with Bob Kulick. There was a song on our first album called "Falling in Love." Paul loved the song and asked me if he could sing backgrounds on it and he did. It's the most lush beautiful backgrounds. He's in there doing all these backgrounds on it with me.

★ "LOVE IN CHAINS" ★

PAUL STANLEY: Being in the studio doing my solo album, I basically had two bands. I had my New York band, which recorded a certain amount of songs, and I had the L.A. band, which was a different rhythm section, a different drummer, and a different bass player. On "Love in Chains" I used a different lead player, Steve Lacey. Bob [Kulick] wasn't available. Steve had a wild kind of ability that was not unlike what Bob was doing. I had Craig Krampf playing drums. Craig was in a band called the Robbs.

★ "GOODBYE" ★

PAUL STANLEY: We needed one more track on the album. Everybody showed up, Bob, Craig Krampf, Eric Nelson. Everyone showed up for a session and I said, "I don't have a song." [laughs] I told them, "Go have dinner and come back in an hour or two and I'll have something." And when they showed up I had written "Goodbye." Pressure was always a great way to write. Sometimes, I would book time in the studio without a song and then just work for a day or two before nonstop and write something. It was gonna be the last song on the album and I kind of wanted to sum everything up. It was about how things don't always turn out the way we want them to. Some relationships are not forever, they're only for now.

GENE SIMMONS

Release date: September 18, 1978
GENE SIMMONS / SEAN DELANEY—producer / BOB SEGER—background vocals
JOE PERRY—guitarist / JANIS IAN—vocalist / RICK NIELSEN—guitarist / RICHIE RANNO—guitarist
MITCH WEISSMAN—background vocals / ALLAN SCHWARTZBERG—drums
BILL LETTANG—demo session drummer / CAROL KAYE—publicist, the Press Office Ltd.

GENE SIMMONS: There were so many songs lying around that KISS will never do because people just wouldn't get who it is or they wouldn't trust the feeling behind it. By that point, I was totally seduced by power, fame, and wealth, and women especially. I started seeing Cher so I was lost completely. I've always been straight, never been high, but that doesn't mean that my senses weren't dulled by other things. One second you're picking your toenails and taking lint out of your belly button and the next second you're flying on the Concorde with Charlton Heston sitting next to you and it's like, "Hey, how you doin?" So, you completely lose sight of who you are and where you're going or what real things are about. So, in a lot of ways my solo record was probably a reflection of a completely disjointed guy who was just doing everything. I'd give it one star.

PAUL STANLEY: I think a danger with Gene sometimes is that he may get more involved with the packaging, or the impression something gives, than what's really there. A cast of thousands isn't gonna make much difference. I mean what have you got?

Forget about a list of thirty celebs. I think he may have gotten caught up in that presentation instead of really writing his best songs. I think he can write much better than the stuff on that album. If five is the best, I'd give that one a two.

ACE FREHLEY: I'll give Gene's a three.

GENE SIMMONS: I played guitar on that record, not bass. In fact a lot of the KISS records, the way things are done is that sometimes the instruments that you think are members of the band are not members of the band at all, or the member of the band that you think is playing the instrument. On "I Still Love You" from *Creatures of the Night*, that's Eric Carr playing bass, only because he honed in on a feel that maybe I didn't have. There are no ego things to worry about. "War Machine" is me on guitar and bass. So, none of those things are important. On my solo record, I played guitar because I thought it would be too simple just to play bass. There would be no challenge. So, I played guitar and picked a fine bass player, Neil Jason. I had the strangest collection of people appear on the record, but actually more people agreed to appear on the record than actually appeared due to lack of time. People from John Lennon to David Bowie to Jerry Lee Lewis agreed to appear on the record. But time limitation limited them. I never actually spoke with Paul McCartney, but got word back that he was interested and wanted to be on the album. The album had been done, but I left a little time [ten days] to record the guest spots. So, the people that wound up on it were the people that had the time. Everybody wanted to do it, it became the hot thing. Strange combinations of people, Bob Seger, Joe Perry, and Helen Reddy. I like that combination because it gets people angry. I'd rather get a reaction from people. I mean, I wanted the Bay City Rollers on it. I wanted people you respected and people you hated. To me to get a rise out of people is more important than to get apathy. If you think, "Yeah, he's okay," then I want to get someone you hated. At least it gets your emotions going. In fact I sent a crew to Radio City Music Hall to record the Radio City Rockettes tap-dance and we didn't get around to that. We sent a mobile truck out to the guy who owns Lassie, because I wanted Lassie on the record. I wanted Donny and Marie Osmond to sing on my record. I wanted Marie to sing a duet with me on "Living in Sin." Obviously her family wouldn't even hear of it. So, it could have been a much stranger record. I never heard from John Lennon personally, only through his secretary. Everybody was all over the country. It's difficult to get anybody down, but she said he wanted to do it.

BOB SEGER: I always felt a great debt of gratitude to Gene and told him I'd be happy to sing on his solo album. A lot of times when you're called up to do things like that you're not in town or you're really busy. Back then I was writing an album, recording an album, and touring. It was one after another for eight years solid. I was always busy. I happened to be in L.A. Gene asked and I said, "Sure, man." It was really easy. I said,

"What do you want me to do?" It was kind of fun because I'm used to telling everybody else what to do and it was fun to lend my chops out for change [laughs].

GENE SIMMONS: When I put together my solo record, I thought I could do anything I wanted to. I flew everybody to London, Cher, the kids, the dogs, bodyguards, and took over the Manor Studio in Oxford, England. I wanted all different kinds of people to appear on the record. I wanted to break down the walls of what was considered cool. What I noticed was real heavy rock 'n' roll fans talk heavy rock 'n' roll but when they listen to radio, they listen to everything. They'd listen to Abba and the Archies at the same time as they'd listen to Led Zeppelin. I was honest enough with myself to say I'm just like that. If I hear a B. J. Thomas song I like it. At the same time, I also liked the Monkees, and Deep Purple, and the Crazy World of Arthur Brown. Why are there these walls? Like if you like Led Zeppelin you're not supposed to like B. J. Thomas. So the notion of the record was to piss off KISS fans and push it in their faces to say that you're one-dimensional and I don't wanna be.

JOE PERRY: Over the years, I kind of felt like there was camaraderie between us [Aerosmith]. We would run into each other in New York and hang out in '76, '77, '78. They would come to the studio and hang out and go to parties. We got to be really good friends. Gene didn't drink or do drugs, but we hit it off. Gene and I and Rick Nielsen [Cheap Trick guitarist] would always go to this sushi restaurant in New York. Gene would be in a suit, Rick would look like Rick Nielsen, and I'd look like a rock star. We were on the road all the time. More often than not we'd run into each other in Chicago, New York, or L.A. It was while in L.A. that Gene asked me to play on his solo album. I was living at the Beverly Hills Hotel and he was staying at Cher's house. We went over to Cher's house. They were lying in bed, wearing their pajamas at eight at night, which was perfectly normal, because we just got out of bed. Gene played me about twenty songs. I listened to a few and heard some that sounded real good. I played on "Radioactive." I thought it was a good track, we had a good time doing it. He had a good idea of what he wanted. It was easy. It was one of the first times I was asked to play on someone else's album. I may have played on a couple of other songs too. I did it at Cherokee Studios. That's the first time I met Rick Nielsen. Gene was nice enough to send me a Gold record. Gene's a really nice guy, very businesslike. The thing about his solo album was if you read the credits of who plays on it, it's like a who's-who of Hollywood and rock 'n' roll. He was living with Cher at the time and he had Rin Tin Tin on the album. I think the upshot of doing it was I had heard of Cheap Trick through Jack Douglas because he had produced their record. I was sitting making use of the glass top of the pinball machine and Rick Nielsen walked in. I see this goofy-looking guy and it's hard to miss him. He's got Cheap Trick written on his fucking eyelids [laughs]. I had always wanted to meet him. He was slated to be in on the session.

I think there were four other guitar players besides me just scheduled for that day. When I listened to the track I had trouble discerning whether I even played on it but it was fun. I was flattered that Gene called me up to do it.

RICK NIELSEN: I felt completely flattered to get asked to play on his record 'cause he had his pick of anybody.

MITCH WEISSMAN: Gene told the press, "I tried to get Paul McCartney and John Lennon to sing background vocals but they couldn't do it so I got the next best thing," which was me and Joe Pecorino. We had both had been in *Beatlemania*. Joe and I went down to the studio and did backgrounds. I really liked the songs we sang on, they were so Beatle-esque. Those songs were really well written. Singing backgrounds on "See You Tonite," "Mr. Make Believe," and "Always Near You/Nowhere to Hide" was me, Joe, Gene, and Eric Troyer, who later sang on [John Lennon's] *Double Fantasy*. When we were doing the session I remember that [Beatles producer] George Martin was in the next room producing America. I was honored to see KISS perform "See You Tonite" on *Unplugged*. I was beaming at home seeing those guys do harmonies that Gene and I had come up with in the studio.

RICHIE RANNO: Back in '75, I was on the road with Starz. This was before we released our first album. Sean Delaney was with us and we were spending some extra time in Detroit, writing songs. One night I had this strange, vivid dream that Gene had done a solo album and I played on it. The cover was just his face, but it went from corner to corner on the album cover. It was odd for two reasons. First of all, KISS was only selling 50,000 to 100,000 copies of their albums and weren't really big yet, and, KISS was a real group, not the kind of band that you would expect solo albums from. I told Sean about the dream and that was that. Of course, three years later they really did make solo albums. At first, I wasn't included on Gene's album. I was busy doing preproduction for Starz's *Coliseum Rock* album at the time. When they were done mixing the album in England, Sean called me and said that they weren't happy with either of the solos that Joe Perry and Jeff Baxter put down on "Tunnel of Love." Gene had requested that Nils Lofgren be brought in, but Sean said, "I want Richie to do it. He'll know exactly what to do and lay it down right away." So, I got the call and went into Blue Rock Studios. Mike Stone was the engineer [Queen's engineer]. Gene and Sean were there and kind of coached me as I played along to the track. Gene said he wanted me to come up with a theme for the solo. I don't really know if I did that, but they all seemed pretty happy with it. Gene eventually gave me a Platinum album award for my wall.

SEAN DELANEY: I was really depressed when I found out I wasn't going to produce Peter's solo album. About two days later, I'm in my office and Gene comes in and says, "Sean, do you have time to talk?" And I said, "Sure." And he's got these albums underneath his arms. They're albums that I've produced, Piper, Billy Squier's band, and Toby Beau. Gene had listened to these albums thoroughly and had sixty questions. The questions were, "How did you do that?" He wanted me to technically tell him how I did it. It was almost like he was questioning whether it was Sean who did it or Mike Stone who did it. I say that in hindsight now. It was me that did it. Mike made it happen audio-wise, but I would sit there and go, "No, I want that note to sound like icicles." And we would sit there until it sounded like I wanted it to sound. So, then Gene asked me to produce his solo album and I said yes. The experience was pretty rabid. Gene had all these folk songs [laughs]. I'm not joking, I'm sitting there listening to this tape of material and it's all acoustic guitar and it's all just this side of the Beatles, things like "Mr. Make Believe." He must have had seventy songs like that. Gene and I started with all this preproduction. I called up all of my guys that I used on Peter's solo album, everyone from Elliot Randall to Allan Schwartzberg. I told Gene I wanted to record the album in a place that Mike Stone and I are familiar with. Gene says, "I want to have as many special guests on this as I can." So his job was to find special guests. Mine was the music. Here's the first problem. In Gene's and Paul's life the big argument in KISS, the big division, was between musicians and show personalities. Gene and Paul were show. When we first started working on characters and the theatricality of KISS, Gene and Paul took to it like ducks to water. They would do the show exactly the same way every single night. It was like lines from a script. Peter and Ace were musicians. In any band I've ever been in I can sit there and say, "This is in the key of E" and that's all you'd have to say. You hear the rhythm, the drummer would come in with the correct beat, the guitars would be messing around and you'd be jamming. Here's Gene, in no way, shape, or form, at the same level of musicianship as these guys. Gene didn't play bass on his solo album. I don't remember Gene playing guitar on the record. Gene could play rhythm guitar to write a song but he wasn't a guitar player. So why on earth when you have a guitar player of the caliber of a Skunk Baxter or Elliot Randall would you ever have him play?

SEAN DELANEY: I told Gene, "There's two ways you go with your solo album. One, you can make it like 'God of Thunder,' a whole album like that, the evil demon. Or you can do anything that you want." He really wanted to have this other side of him seen to the world. The rabid experience of working on Gene's solo album was when you clearly saw the top musicians being chastised by someone who did not have the ability to play. Gene didn't yell and push people. It was getting the arrangements for the songs. It literally came down to where I sang every note to everybody that played. There is an ongoing battle between live stage performers and studio musicians, between show biz and music. I got everybody over to England. I was using this place called the Manor. We got there one morning and Gene put up a schedule that said

"Breakfast at eight o'clock, in the studio at nine A.M." There were even breaks listed like you were running a manufacturing plant. I told him that these guys aren't even going to get up until one in the afternoon. Everybody just sort of let it go. So, Gene's there trying to run it like a business. At one point, we were all in the big dining hall—because we had a cordon bleu chef that cooked all of our meals there—Mike Stone stood up and verbally wasted Gene in front of everyone because of how he was treating everybody. I was just astonished [laughs]. He was saying stuff like, "You are a bastard, the quality of the musicians you have here, you don't even have a thought!" At that moment Gene changed. All of a sudden he became part of it and then it became a good project. But it was rabid up until then.

SEAN DELANEY: We actually almost had the Beatles reunited on the album. They were smart because we would have flat-out lied to them. If we had the Beatles on there we would have worked that until the cows came home three or four times. Gene was making calls. It was a yes from John, Paul, and George. The person who threw the wrench in was Ringo. I was going to have them sing on "Mr. Make Believe," "Always Near You/Nowhere to Hide," all the ones that sounded Beatley. We almost had them and Ringo said no. They said we might do it if you don't tell anyone we did it and we went, "Of course we won't" . . . the album would have went, "Gene Simmons and the Beatles."

SEAN DELANEY: It's a good record but it wasn't KISS. I don't think there's one cut on there that's bad. If you'd taken any one of those songs and made the whole album like that you'd have been better off calling it something like "Lenny Witz" and having a new band [laughs].

ALLAN SCHWARTZBERG: I had a fun time recording Gene's solo album. We did it at the Manor in England. Cher was there with her family. I liked the song "Radioactive," great production, great song. I picked that as a single back then and Cher really liked it too. I also enjoyed how the producer, Sean Delaney, really pushed the musical envelope on that album.

BILL LETTANG: Gene and I hit if off because of our love for monster movies. I played drums on demos for songs like "Radioactive," "Rotten to the Core," "Jellyroll," "See You Tonite," "Burning Up with Fever," "Man of 1,000 Faces," "See You in Your Dreams," and "True Confessions." I remember playing drums and doing handclaps on the "Radioactive" demo that's on the KISS box set.

SEAN DELANEY: I was so against KISS doing solo albums because I knew out of solo albums that this was competition. There would be winners and there would be losers and that would be the end of KISS. Once you put your hands on one of your band members and physically attack them it's over. Once you use somebody else to play it's over. I was out on the road with Starz or Toby Beau and I got summoned back to New York. I had to go to SIR studios in Manhattan because KISS was starting rehearsals for a tour and I walked in and Peter had just stood up, took his drumsticks and thrown them, hitting Gene dead in the head. There was a fight getting ready to blow out. I remember yelling at the top of my lungs, "When the fuck did this shit start!" I just took over and stopped it dead in the tracks.

SEAN DELANEY: It was my idea for the interlocking KISS posters to be included inside the solo albums. To get the entire poster you had to buy all four solo albums. My idea went even farther than the posters. I wanted to give $1 million away. There were four posters and if brought together in the middle it would say "winner." They would get $1 million, but that got stopped because of lottery. The other idea I came out with was, "Guys, do four solo albums, but have the members of the band back each of you on your album. KISS does Gene's album, it's Gene's songs and his voice. Everybody does Ace's album." But it didn't happen. By that time, Howard Marks had gotten to the guys. They were all taking the solo albums as the most serious thing they'd ever done in their lives.

★ "RADIOACTIVE" ★

GENE SIMMONS: There's a song called "Radioactive" on my solo album which Cher thinks is all right. It's about her. It's kind of a double entendre, basically a fancy word piece about this lady who's got a certain aura about her. I'd like to get closer but I can't because she won't let me. But I can't go away because I can't stay away from her. I've gotten to the point where I feel comfortable writing about boy-girl relationships, whereas before, the relationship would be, "Get on your knees and let me bite your head off."

SEAN DELANEY: On "Radioactive" there's something really strange. There's an actual old legend, you are not allowed to use the devil's triad in music. The devil's triad is a progression that you have to go through several times and then you will hit a tone thirteen times in a row. When this happens the human mind cannot resolve itself, it doesn't know where to go to resolve this music you've heard. In every song you ever hear it always resolves going into the chorus line or coming out of a verse. If you play the devil's triad and there's a person alone in a room they will start feeling anxious. And the anxiety will rise itself to the point where they will turn into a screaming maniac trying to get out of the room. In the beginning part of "Radioactive" that is the devil's triad but I resolve it. Janis Ian is playing the part of a nun and I'm playing the part of Satan in the song. I'm saying [speaks in demonic voice] "Sanctum! Sanctum!" Then I'm saying some foreign-sounding words which mean, "Their death, our death, my death in this ritual of the holy night."

BOB SEGER: I thought "Radioactive" was really great. I've still got the Platinum album Gene gave me. It's up on the wall in my studio.

JANIS IAN: I sang the part of a nun on the song "Radioactive." It was a difficult part, a lot of contrapuntal stuff. We were living next door to each other in New York and he was funny because he kept saying, "Hi, Janis, I'm Gene," and I would say, " Hi, Gene," and I would have no idea what he was talking about. One day he just stopped me in the elevator and said, "I'm Gene Simmons," and I said, " Well, how am I supposed to know without your makeup on?" So that was funny. Then my friend, Ron Frangipane, who arranged that for him, was discussing with Gene who should sing the part of the nun. My name came up and Gene got real excited. He was lovely. He did one of the coolest things. He sent me a Platinum record. I thought that was real neat, that's not ordinarily done. I think when you're in a band like KISS, you reach a point where you really want to prove that you do have some intelligence, and Gene's a great guy. It's so easy to get stereotyped. I think it must be really hard to be part of a band. Much harder than being a soloist, 'cause even working with a band I can see where you make compromises. You have to be a whole lot more open than you have to be with your own music.

★ "BURNING UP WITH FEVER" ★

GENE SIMMONS: "Burning Up with Fever" was a cross between the Jeff Beck song "Rock Me Baby" and the guitar scale that Leslie West used in "Mississippi Queen." Donna Summer came down to sing on the track.

★ "SEE YOU TONITE" ★

GENE SIMMONS: "See You Tonite" goes back to about '69. I was still at school and had been playing in a summer rock 'n' roll group. It was a version of Bullfrog Bheer with Steve Coronel. At that point, Steve and I were tossing around some ideas. One of them became "She" and the other "Goin' Blind," which was originally called "Little Lady." "See You Tonite" came very fast. It was one of those songs that wrote itself in a linear way, very stream-of-consciousness. Steve thought it was a song from *Beatles VI.* It does sound like one of those songs written by the Beatles in 1966. Those songs come easier for me than KISS songs. I have to be aware of where I'm going when I write a KISS song. It's almost like you don't want to drive down the highway with your eyes closed. I have to keep my eyes open so I don't veer off the road. A guy who's six foot two who looks like he blows up buildings doesn't feel right doing that kind of Beatles sounding material. The song doesn't really have a chorus. "See You Tonite," "Deuce," and even "Domino" don't really have a chorus as such. Those kind of songs are harder to write. The imagery for the song was Romeo and Juliet. It's about a guy outside who's wooing a girl. My reference point for that song was it came during a time when I wrote a batch of Beatles-sounding songs, "See You Tonite," Mr. Make Believe," "Nowhere to Hide."

CAROL KAYE: "See You Tonite" is an amazing song. Who expected that kind of song from Gene Simmons? The Beatles could have written that song. It was that good.

★ "TUNNEL OF LOVE" ★

SEAN DELANEY: On "Tunnel of Love" Gene was sitting there and I went out to Allan Schwartzberg and I was singing drum parts to him [imitates drum pattern]. I stayed with him until he got the beat. I did this kind of stuff on every song. You had to appease Gene without jeopardizing the musicianship.

★ "TRUE CONFESSIONS" ★

GENE SIMMONS: That song has more to do with what I need as a person from people who are trying to relate to me.

★ "LIVING IN SIN" ★

GENE SIMMONS: Howard Marks, our business manager, came up with the line, "Living in sin at the Holiday Inn." I thought it was a funny enough idea, the notion being you did the show and then you did the encores back at the hotel. I took the riff that I originally had for "Drive Me Wild," which eventually became "Rock and Roll All Nite" with Paul, and recycled it. That became the centerpiece of "Living in Sin." When I recorded it, Cher and her daughter, Chastity, were the girls in the background on the song calling on the telephone, giggling and saying "Which room are you in?"

★ "ALWAYS NEAR YOU/NOWHERE TO HIDE" ★

GENE SIMMONS: "Always Near You and Nowhere to Hide" were two things laying around that I could never finish. Then I remember reading an interview with Paul McCartney about how some of the Beatles songs were put together like "A Day in the Life," where there was a Lennon song and there was a McCartney song and neither could figure out how to finish it. So, I think it was Lennon who just stuck them together. All of a sudden "Woke up got out of bed . . ." and you have this different mood thing that happens. So it struck me that you don't have to finish an idea, that a song can really be a pastiche. Songs really didn't have to follow the A, B, A sort of format, verse, chorus, bridge, chorus, and solo. You could have pieces. That's where that idea came from.

★ "MAN OF 1,000 FACES" ★

GENE SIMMONS: "Man of 1,000 Faces" was written about Lon Chaney Sr., the guy who created the Phantom of the Opera, although in some ways it's also about me. I was working out my own issues about myself, coming from Israel and living in America. Dressing British, thinking Yiddish, being Jewish but having a very Anglo-Saxon name. Being onstage as the Demon and being offstage as the other guy. It's the dichotomy that is me. There's more than one Gene and somehow all of it makes up who I am. The question I ask myself is, "Who is the man of 1,000 faces?"

★ "MR. MAKE BELIEVE" ★

GENE SIMMONS: "Mr. Make Believe" is about all these fantasy figures people have had during different periods in their lives, from making believe you're someone else when you're in the sandbox to the time you're sitting in an office when you've grown up and daydreaming about being a swashbuckler or a model or whatever. Everybody has all these different people inside of them.

★ "SEE YOU IN YOUR DREAMS" ★

GENE SIMMONS: "See You in Your Dreams" was originally done as a demo where I played the guitars and the background singers were the Group with No Name, this band that I got a deal on Casablanca Records. Katey Sagal was in the band, we went out at that time. I liked the vibe and sound of the girls singing the chorus and a sloppier guitar played by me. It felt looser and more like Joe Cocker's *Mad Dogs and Englishmen* than a Stonesy, KISS feel. When KISS recorded it it became that sound we have. I thought it lost that quality. I didn't like the way we did it as a band, which was why I re-recorded it on my solo album. When I re-recorded it I tried to keep the same vibe. The same girls sang the background vocals. Rick Nielsen of Cheap Trick played the guitar solo. He did a very cool thing, one of the first melodies of his solo is "When You Wish upon a Star."

★ "WHEN YOU WISH UPON A STAR" ★

GENE SIMMONS: All the sights and sounds in America played a very important role in my development as a kid. When I went to see *Pinocchio* and I heard Jiminy Cricket at the end of the movie singing, "When You Wish upon a Star," I really thought he was singing to me. He was saying, "You, Gene, I'm talking to you. They all hear me but I'm speaking to you. When you wish upon a star all your dreams come true." I did that song for me. I knew everybody would say "Oh, that's nonsense." As a homage, I felt that I had to record that song in some way to pay back Jiminy Cricket because my dreams at that point had come true. I cried on the recording of the song. It hit me really hard, big lump in the throat. When I went into the sound booth and I was singing the song, all those original memories came back. In some ways it was a connection to the little boy. When no one's looking, even the big guys cry. It's an astonishing melody. The lyrics are truer than most religious lyrics because it doesn't ask anything from you. It just says "believe." It's not a song for kings, it's a song for the Everyman in all of us.

SEAN DELANEY: When he got to America, at his school they put a sign on him that said "If I look lost, point me in the right direction." The first English words that Gene ever learned were the words to Jiminy Cricket's "When You Wish . . ." and if you listen to Gene's version, you'll hear his voice crack, because at that point he was crying. I wouldn't let him re-record the vocal.

ACE FREHLEY

Release date: September 18, 1978

ACE FREHLEY / EDDIE KRAMER—producer / ANTON FIG—session drummer

CAROL ROSS—president of the Press Office Ltd. / CAROL KAYE—publicist, the Press Office Ltd.

ACE FREHLEY: I'd give it a five. Paul and Gene are partially responsible for me doing such a great record because right before we left to do that record they really kind of implied that to me. And when people tell me I can't do something I try my hardest to prove them wrong, which is what I did. It was kind of an awakening for me that whole recording experience. Working with Anton Fig and Eddie Kramer away from some of the negative vibes that sometimes encompassed a KISS record kind of opened my eyes. That's when I started thinking that maybe I would be better off away from those guys because a lot of times we didn't see eye-to-eye. There were definitely some conflicts there.

PAUL STANLEY: I would give Ace's solo album close to three because at least it was honest. It was surprising for Ace, because I didn't think he was going to do anything that good, to be honest with you. I was worried whether or not he was going to be able to even make an album. I thought that "Rip It Out" was very cool. When I heard that song I went, "All right, Ace!" Very cool. I said that sounds like a really good KISS song.

GENE SIMMONS: Ace's judgments have been clouded since the beginning and that's being kind. I clearly remember even when we were a band in the loft that I was saying, "Write! You can sing." When he wrote "Cold Gin," he was given full writing credit for the song when the truth is I contributed a bridge and that middle section and Paul arranged it. There was a lot of give instead of take in all of these situations and we tried to push Ace the same and he wouldn't do it. He said, "No, I don't want to sing this, you do it." I think it's easier for Ace to swallow the idea that in some ways he was held back because that emotionally is an easier pill for him to swallow. It's nonsense. The truth is when Ace wanted to leave the band we said, "Stay in the band and you can also have a solo career." You can have your cake and eat it too. I don't think he knew his left foot from his right at that point. I still think he's a little out there. Three stars.

ACE FREHLEY: Before I did my solo album, I was pretty dormant in the area of writing and singing. The solo album really brought me out of my shell and made me much more confident as a singer and guitarist.

EDDIE KRAMER: We did the album at the Colgate mansion in Connecticut. We mixed it at Plaza Sound. We cut some tracks there too. Anton's [Fig] brilliant. He's a great drummer. It was a lot of fun. That stands out. We did so much weird shit at that mansion.

KISS TOUR MANAGER, BILLY MILLER, AND ACE FREHLEY, JAPAN, MARCH 1977
(© KISS Catalog Ltd.)

It was haunted, people were scared to stay in the place. I have tons of photographs of that session actually. I have a photograph of Ace with a Halloween mask on singing background vocals with me singing the background parts next to him. I've got pictures of the room with all the amps. Each room had a different sound. We had like thirty amplifiers in a row. We'd go from one amp to the next sampling which is the best one. I mean combining different amps and speaker cabinets. It was great. We had a fucking great time. And the food was, Oh God! We had this company that was catering for us. I remember all the food and the wine. Man, we had a blast. Ate ourselves silly, we played great, recorded. It was killer [laughs].

PETER CRISS: I heard Ace's album when he came over and played it for me. I said to him, "New York Groove" is a hit. And he said, "Aw, get out of here." He didn't believe me but it was a hit. I used to love playing it on stage. It was a great song, it fit him.

EDDIE KRAMER: All three of the other guys' solo records went into the shitter and Ace's was the only one that sold because we had a great single with "New York Groove," which we found. My ex-brother-in-law, who's an engineer's assistant, and I were going through tapes and we found this song one day and gave it to Ace. We worked up the arrangement on it and man, that thing became a big hit.

BILL AUCOIN: The solo albums were centered around giving the guys a break from each other. It gave them independence. There was renewed energy and excitement. Everyone wanted to do their own thing. Even though they were all separate it was like a whole new KISS again. It was never meant for all of the solo albums to come out together. We thought we'd put one out at a time. They weren't getting along, they were starting to have that tear in the fabric.

CAROL KAYE: Ace's solo album is a great record. Because of the success of "New York Groove," Ace's solo album received the most attention. The album took everyone by surprise because it was so good. With Ace's reputation they weren't expecting such an accomplished record. Musically, it was a great leap forward. It surprised the press as well as KISS. "New York Groove" is being used now in a local commercial for the Marriott Hotel chain. It started running in New York after September 11 [recites lyrics], "I'm back, back in the New York groove."

CAROL ROSS: Doing publicity for the solo albums was the hardest thing to do. A good portion of the press would ask to interview Gene first and Paul second. We tried to give everybody equal time. I would go to the guitar magazines for Ace, the drum magazines for Peter so everybody would be covered. Many times management told me that they wanted Paul to do the interviews. When I would finally get the editors interested to talk to KISS they just wanted to talk to Gene. So there was a lot of strain and diplomacy that I had to use and also favors and finagling.

CAROL KAYE: When the solo albums were released, I arranged for *Trouser Press* to do a photo shoot with the KISS dolls for a major piece on the band. It appeared in the December 1978 issue. The article was called "The Aesthetics of KISS." I discussed a layout with the editor, Ira Robbins. Well, the end result was not what I expected and I was freaking out. The initial photos show the KISS dolls standing with four Barbie dolls. Then the photos start to degenerate into a real rock 'n' roll situation. With each succeeding photo, the Barbie dolls and KISS have less clothes on until they positioned the KISS dolls simulating sex acts with the now naked Barbie dolls. As a publicist we can't always control the end result. Gene thought it was hilarious. When they saw it and they laughed, I cannot tell you the sigh of relief I felt [laughs]. I was starting to pack my little bag [laughs]. I thought I was going to be fired [laughs].

★ "RIP IT OUT" ★

ACE FREHLEY: It's one of my favorite songs off the record. Recently I heard it and it sounded real good. It was a good track. My tracks, a lot of the time, I do them spontaneously. My live versions are usually a little more relaxed and free-flowing.

★ "FRACTURED MIRROR" ★

ACE FREHLEY: It's classic, it just came to me. It's weird. Most of the songs I write seem like they're being beamed down to me into my head by aliens or something. When I think about the three "Fractured Mirror" instrumentals I've done, I'd love to do some computer animation to those because they lend themselves to that.

PETER CRISS

Release date: September 18, 1978

PETER CRISS / VINI PONCIA—producer / STAN PENRIDGE—songwriter

SEAN DELANEY—songwriter / ALLAN SCHWARTZBERG—drums / BILL AUCOIN—manager

CAROL KAYE—publicist, the Press Office Ltd.

PETER CRISS: I'd give mine a five, not because it's mine or to be egotistic, but because I really worked hard. Stan and I wrote some great shit, Vini Poncia did a wonderful fucking job. I just got out of a car accident so all my fingers were broken. My ribs were broken. I got a concussion. I had to get plastic surgery. I played on everything, fucking A, with these iron braces on all my fingers and tape on all fingers. It was my baby. I'd give my baby a five. I worked on her, especially "Don't You Let Me Down" and "I Can't Stop the Rain." I had horns. I went all soul. I did "Tossin' and Turnin'." I thought that even my little autobiography song, "Hooked on Rock 'n' Roll," was brilliant. I wrote a song about my career. If you listen to the lyrics it's all about my drumming, when I started, how I went along. [recites lyrics] "I was vaccinated with a Victrola needle" . . . The whole thing is about my life. I thought the fans would love that. "You Matter to Me" is a great song even though I didn't write it. It's a cool song. It's got a great feel. [sings] "So you matter to me and that's why, that's why." It's got a cool poppy feel to it. I think it's a great tune. [On Paul's, Gene's, and Ace's solo albums] I'd give them all a five because I know each one of them put every bit of fucking energy into it. They all worked their balls off. They all wanted the best of what they were in their own habitat and their own world and realm. I give it a five out of a labor of love

ACE FREHLEY: I'll give Peter's a three.

PAUL STANLEY: I think Peter's record summed up a lot about what was a problem, ultimately, with the band. That album I just don't get. I can't give it any stars.

GENE SIMMONS: Zero. Out of all the records that we've ever done solo or as a group I think that one showed that the guy behind it didn't really have a clue. Not only about songwriting, but just about direction and who he is. Ironically enough Peter probably, although he really can't sing—he's tone deaf—the actual straight tone that comes out of his mouth is probably my favorite out of all of us, that whiskey voice, but he can't control it.

CAROL KAYE: Peter's solo album was totally unexpected. It was a departure from KISS and that confused a lot of the press.

PETER CRISS: It got to be, "Who's gonna have the best album? Who's gonna outsell whose album?" That's when that ego, that cancer, came in. I would be surrounded by people who would say, "You don't need those fucking jerks, listen to how good that song is." When we got back together we had to decide which songs from the solo albums we would play on tour and that caused nothing but major heartaches. I still think that although we were the only band to do it, [the idea] was still a mistake. Casablanca had to ship them all Platinum to keep us quiet. Nineteen seventy-eight was the downfall of the band. It was dangerous. We did that crazy movie. After the movie I got in a major car accident. I had a 928 Porsche and I almost got killed. I went through the window, broke my nose, my hands, broke some ribs, lost vision in my right eye, had plastic surgery. They kept it out of the papers, that's how powerful Casablanca Records was.

VINI PONCIA: It was a lot of fun doing the album. At the time we were making it, our focus was on Peter the singer. It was designed around Peter doing songs that were emotional, songs that he could relate to. He's got a good soulfulness about him and he's a good soul. What the album did foremost was give Peter a chance to get in touch with his roots. He was able to do some white R&B, and bluesy kind of things that he grew up with. He was able to show the world a different side to him. Peter's always had a bluesy side to him, even when he sang "Beth," there's always that blues, white R&B soul tinge to what he does, so Peter's album reflected that.

STAN PENRIDGE: During the time Lips was together, we recorded a number of my tunes for Kama Sutra Records. Those two early sessions included the original recordings of "Don't You Let Me Down," "Hooked on Rock 'n' Roll," "Baby Driver," "That's the Kind of Sugar Papa Likes," and "I'm Gonna Love You." The exception being that I was the lead vocalist at the time. The songs authored by Sean [Delaney] were recorded at Electric Lady in New York. They were very chaotic sessions. You have to give Vini and Bobby a lot of credit for being able to salvage those takes we used. The sessions in L.A. were tame in comparison. Peter and I lived together in L.A. During those twelve weeks, we were picked up and dropped off daily by Rosie Licata, Peter's bodyguard/driver/nursemaid, whatever. We kept normal eight-hour sessions daily, five days a week . . . basically because Vini was producing another album during that same period.

SEAN DELANEY: In the band, Peter Criss and I were best friends. I absolutely loved Peter's voice. I had been writing songs for Peter's solo album. He told me, "You're the only one who understands my voice. You are my Svengali." Then one day Peter comes back from this big meeting with Glyn Johns, the guy who produced Small Faces and

Rod Stewart, and he turned him down flat. The tape that Peter had of songs done by him and Stan Penridge was so bad. Peter comes back now and says to me, "Sean, would you produce my album?" I said, "Well, I can't. Gene asked me and I made an agreement with him." Peter gets all pissed off. Then I went to Gene and told him that Peter's having problems now because his demo tapes are pure shit and Glyn Johns just turned him down. Gene just didn't want any kind of publicity like that out there. I told him, if I get your permission I can go into the studio and do a demo tape of some of Peter's songs and that'll help him get a producer. Gene said, "Oh yes, yes!" Gene gives me permission to go in the studio and work with Peter. So I get my guys together and go into Electric Lady Studios. I have some of the most important musos in the studio sitting there and Peter's late! Finally, Pete gives me a call and says, "I'll be there in a couple of hours." I said, "Well, you just get your ass down here as quickly as possible." So I went out in the studio and started recording. These were my songs so I started recording them, "I Can't Stop the Rain," "Rock Me, Baby," and there were two others. So Peter gets there and I'm playing the stuff that we've done back to him. He says to these guys, "Fellas, I really want to thank you, I really appreciate you coming and doing this. And I want you to know that your work is going to be given to a real producer and they're going to really do it right." These guys are literally almost walking out of the studio. I'm running around trying to assuage their anger. I calm everybody back down. Part of "I Can't Stop the Rain" is my voice. With Peter and I, it was almost always a very intimate thing when we did vocals. He'd sit out there on a stool and I'd sit out there on a stool with him and he'd sing to me. We get through those songs and I'm getting ready to start mixing them and Peter and I get into a big argument. I tell him to go fuck himself. I said, "In fact, man, these are my songs, screw you!" I paid for the session and went about my business doing Gene's solo album. After the albums were all done, Gene's was the first one completed. I can't say under budget because there was no budget. Each of the guys on his solo albums was responsible for the bill on their solo albums. They weren't given a budget by Casablanca. Then one day I get a phone call at three o'clock in the morning from Howard Marks [Glickman/Marks company]. He wants to know the names of the musicians that were used on Peter's solo album. I said, "Why don't you call the producer? I don't know who they used." He then started listing off songs that I had done, the two that I had written, and another one called "Easy Thing," which I had totally redone. I said to Howard, "What do you mean my shit's on his solo album?" He said, "Well, Sean, let's put it this way. Do you want me to tell Neil Bogart that you are the one person stopping the solo albums from release, costing him millions of dollars? How do you think he's going to feel about your upcoming solo album now?" So I was blackmailed into releasing those songs. They used three of my songs. They used them because they couldn't do them any better.

ALLAN SCHWARTZBERG: We did those sessions at Electric Lady, there were a lot of drugs flying around. I remember Peter sat down on the floor by the drums while I played. He was real nice and seemed to like my playing. There was no negative vibe.

BILL AUCOIN: The solo albums got bungled a bit. The Handleman Group, which is the major record distributor, calls up Neil and orders a million units of each album! And Neil goes nuts. So he presses up another million and a quarter [laughs]. Now we have five and a quarter million records pressed up. When you walked into a record store, it looked like the entire store was KISS. That wasn't necessarily good because it never looked like they sold any of the solo albums. It never looked like the pile went any-where. And then I find out that Neil had pressed another million and a quarter because he thought, "Wow, if one company's gonna order so much." So there was so much product out there that it looked like a disaster. But they all went Platinum eventually.

★ "YOU MATTER TO ME" ★

VINI PONCIA: John Vastano was in a band that I produced called White Water. He was a very bluesy singer and songwriter. He was always writing those kind of white R&B songs and that's what Peter loved. John brought the song in and Michael Morgan and I designed it for Peter. Peter could sing that stuff well. He had that certain Rod Stewart/Joe Cocker gravel sound in his voice. He wasn't as good a singer as Rod Stewart or Joe Cocker, but he certainly had the emotional resonance.

DYNASTY

Release date: May 23, 1979
KISS / VINI PONCIA—producer / JAY MESSINA—engineer / DESMOND CHILD—songwriter
STAN PENRIDGE—songwriter / ANTON FIG—session drummer / BILL AUCOIN—manager
DENNIS WOLOCH—album designer

PAUL STANLEY: I like *Dynasty*. I like some of the songs more than the production. Too sanitized. We lost some edge, and we lost our balls on that and *Unmasked*. *Dynasty* was an album where Peter was going through a lot of problems. The band also was falling prey to vices, compulsions, and every kind of distraction. That album really is born out of that. The songs were better than most of the production on the album, but that was something we wholeheartedly went along with. We were groping and grasping for stability as a band. The album was going to be safer. Bill [Aucoin] thought we should appeal to a broader base audience. The first question is why and that never really got answered. The simple cure-all for being too aggressive musically is to kill the guitars and add a synthesizer [laughs]. Songs like "Magic Touch" and even "Sure Know Something" had a lot more grit to it that was ever out on the record.

But that being said, it gave us our biggest international hit ["I Was Made for Lovin' You"]. It was a transitional album. It was very much an album that reflected where were at that time. Two or three stars.

GENE SIMMONS: We'd sort of gone through another phase of a lot of different material and we thought we can't keep doing the same thing. Let's get some new blood in the band and see if we can push this a little further. By that point, year after year, we were the toy kings and the Gallup Poll toppers, favorite band and all that. We were doing massive stadium shows. So, we thought that it wasn't enough to just be a rock 'n' roll band, which is a big mistake actually. We decided to bring in a guy that would bring in a totally different point of view and that was our producer, Vini Poncia. Two stars.

PETER CRISS: A three. Things were really shaky. I demanded Vini Poncia produce the album or I'd quit. I think I made a real solid move, either he comes in or I go. Good album but not great. Bad vibes. I was getting ready to leave and that was sort of in the back of my mind.

ACE FREHLEY: I enjoyed working with Vini [Poncia]. The one thing I didn't like about that record was the departure from rock 'n' roll to the disco tune ["I Was Made for Lovin' You"]. I have to say that it was a hit and it was a good song, but I don't think it had anything to do with KISS other than Paul wrote it and we played on it. I'd give it three and half stars.

GENE SIMMONS: I think both the *Dynasty* and *Unmasked* albums were wrong albums to do because I think we lost our essence. At that point, we were playing baseball stadiums and we didn't think anything could go wrong and, of course, all the toys and things that came out and I think we lost touch. I think we lost the sense of what we were about. It was a guitar band and all of a sudden synthesizers started to appear on the record. So, they may be interesting diversions; tangents are interesting, but it's not what you should be doing all the time. I thought they were wrong records. There may have been a cut or two that I liked, but I thought for the most part that they were wrong things to do. We were doing things out of bravery. It's like, "I Was Made for Lovin' You" was a smash worldwide, but it wasn't KISS. It has nothing to do with our heart and our soul. Sometimes we will do something like that just to prove to people that we can do it.

PAUL STANLEY: He [Vini Poncia] was really from the old school, kind of like a '60s type of mentality. Vini's a good songwriter and a real song man. With those albums we wanted to take ourselves off the path a bit. It was real interesting. I wouldn't want to change it, but there's nothing I'd want to do again.

KISS UNMASKED IN THE STUDIO. LEFT TO RIGHT: PRODUCER VINI PONCIA, PAUL STANLEY, AND GENE SIMMONS SINGING BACKGROUND VOCALS, CIRCA 1979/80 (© KISS Catalog Ltd.)

VINI PONCIA: I've been in this business for over thirty years. I had a hit record when I was sixteen. I made hit records with every possible kind of people you can imagine, R&B, pop. From the generation that I come from you made all kinds of records. KISS knew I had had success with people like Ringo Starr.

ACE FREHLEY: Vini's a great producer. He may not have captured the essence of the band live, but we explored avenues with Vini. I was feeling more confident as a writer. Me and Vini [Poncia] got along well. He believed in me as a guitarist and writer. The success of my solo album made Paul and Gene take me more seriously. It also made them more nervous. They knew I was more cocky. After the success of my solo album I realized I didn't need them to be a rock star. I could have my own band. As far as I'm concerned, Gene Simmons is a good musician and a good songwriter, but in the year 2002 Gene uses the bass as a vehicle to be a businessman, promote KISS merchandise, get laid, and do a hundred other things. After the success of my solo album, I realized that I had the ability to be taken more seriously as a musician. Prior to that I used to be very frustrated with write-ups. Most of the time reviewers would talk about the show rather than the musicianship. I consider myself a musician first and a showman second, and that frustrated me. That's one of the reasons I originally left the group 'cause I wanted to prove to everybody that I could carry a band on my own, which I did.

JAY MESSINA: The point of doing a record like *Dynasty* was to get a little more musical, more commercial, and more vocal-oriented. That was what Vini [Poncia] brought to the table. The album didn't feel wrong, it was just a departure for them. It showed a different side of KISS. The band liked and respected Vini. I think they got off on the fact they were doing something a little more musical, getting a little more sophisticated with their harmonies. Gene, Paul, and Ace were pretty open to what Vini and I had to offer. Vini gave me a lot of free rein in terms of capturing sounds and coming up with effects.

VINI PONCIA: The whole idea of *Dynasty* was to show the business that this band could write better songs and make a better album than they had previously done from a songwriting standpoint. KISS had never ventured outside of what they'd written before. I didn't go into the KISS record saying I wanted to make a more poppy record. Stylistically, it's going to come out poppier because that's my background from my days working with Phil Spector. At that time, Paul, who has a lot of natural pop instincts, was exploring. It was 1979 and music was going away from rock 'n' roll. The disco era was just starting.

VINI PONCIA: We all had a great time making that album. It was new for Paul and Gene to be working in that format, putting a lot more emphasis on the hooks and rhythms, pulling the songs apart. They were never in a situation where there was such attention to detail. Gene, Paul, and Ace liked that whole process of pulling the song apart, building it up. They were learning how to be record producers. It was really me, Paul, and Gene involved with the basic tracks. Ace was there every day working on it, but he would go away while we did the vocals and did all the backgrounds. Gene and Paul were there every step of the way.

ANTON FIG: I played on Ace's solo record and he recommended that I play on *Dynasty* when Peter couldn't make it. He had broken his arm or something like that. It took about ten days to record all my drum tracks. The pressure was on and I was under the gun. But we worked real hard and everything went very smoothly. Also, I think *Dynasty* was the last session done at Electric Lady where they had the old console that Jimi Hendrix used. Paul, Gene, and Ace all played really strong with a lot of conviction. It was a real thrill. I remember Vini was very methodical. He used to have long lists of things, ideas and overdubs, and he'd scratch them off. I got paid $10,000 or $15,000 on *Dynasty*, and on *Unmasked* I got $20,000. Not bad for ten days' work.

BILL AUCOIN: Around the *Dynasty* period, the band felt they weren't being taken seriously as musicians. They were starting to get upset that they weren't recognized because they wore makeup. Rush could walk into a place and be recognized, Cheap Trick could be recognized, but they [KISS] couldn't. I think that really started to bother them. They wanted to be known, they wanted people to recognize them when they walked into restaurants or parties. They didn't want to be a kiddie band so they wanted me to cut the merchandising. And the only way this is all gonna happen is we take off the makeup. I was against all of those things and this was the beginning of a flap between the band and I.

BILL AUCOIN: They weren't selling records as much. We didn't get the number of people at shows. We weren't making money on the road, we were just paying our bills off. Everyone started working against me from another side. People get paid by the artists; whether it's business managers or lawyers, for the most part they are going to be yesmen. In my case, KISS's business managers, Howard [Marks] or Carl [Glickman], were yessing this group to death. Howard even worked against me to take over the group, which he admitted to people afterward, and he later achieved it. Money talks and he was on the money side. And also the lawyers; the lawyers would say yes to the group at any given time. I remember one day when our lawyer, Paul Marshall, was listening to the new tracks. He let Gene know which one he thought was the single. I almost went crazy. I would have sued their asses off today. I was just too young and naive. As I walked out of the lawyer's office, he handed me a letter stating that he was no longer my attorney and that they were now representing KISS. Today I would have said, "Screw you, if you do that I'm bringing you up on charges." I would have gone to the hilt. In those days, we were keeping everything together and there was plenty of money coming in. Everything seemed to be on an even keel and I didn't want to shake up everything. There's a lot of things along the way that had nothing to do with KISS or me. It had to do with people around us manipulating the situation because there was so much money. That's kind of sad for all of us when all we both wanted to do was to be successful and make it last as long as it could.

DENNIS WOLOCH: We used star photographer Francesco Scavullo for the shoot. We shot it at Francesco's studio off Third Avenue in New York. I had a layout in my head, it was their four heads together, kind of like what we did later with *Creatures of the Night* but a little different. I explained this to Francesco, but when we got there they just started moving around saying, "Look this way, look that way." My boss was butting in. Bill Aucoin had his two cents to throw in, and I sat by. Being the art director, I began to wonder: Why am I here? Finally, I went over to Francesco and the guys and told them what I wanted. They put their heads together, we looked at them. I said, "That's fine, Francesco, shoot that." He shot it and that was the cover. Paul was the most picky about his face. We would get shots where I felt all the four guys looked great and Paul wouldn't like how he looked. Or he would like his face but he wouldn't like his hair. So we'd have to take hair from another picture or partial hair and put it into another picture and his head from another shot. So it was kind of a jigsaw puzzle. For that cover, I think two guys are from one shot and Paul and somebody else are from another shot. And then Paul's photo had to be put together in two or three parts. We got our cover shot fairly early on in the day and we still had a few hours left in the day and the band wanted to get their money's worth. Somebody came up with the idea of putting the band in straitjackets. Somebody took a cab down to Bellevue Hospital, went down to the mental ward, and came back with four straitjackets. We put them up in the straitjackets, wrapped them up in some wire that was laying around the photo studio and took some shots this way too. The straitjacket shots turned out well. One of the shots was used for the poster that came inside the album. What we actually did was airbrush out the straitjackets and made it look like they were wearing black turtlenecks. But they were wearing straitjackets.

★ "I WAS MADE FOR LOVIN' YOU" ★

PAUL STANLEY: It was a very big song around the world. Disco was so big. I listened to that stuff and said, "This is a cinch to write." So it was kind of like a lark or a dare. I said, "I'll write one of those songs." So I just turned on a drum machine and just got [slaps out disco rhythm] that kind of thing coming out and wrote "I Was Made for Lovin' You." It's a real formula song. It was like, "Let's use everything on dance records, let's use all the sound effects." It was kind of like trying to make a point to ourselves that it's not that hard to have a hit if you're willing to really analyze something and pick it apart. We don't do that very often. Desmond Child was involved with that and so was Vini. Desmond is a really brilliant songwriter and great talent. He also has an amazing ability to get together with somebody and lock into what they're doing.

DESMOND CHILD: Writing with KISS is something that just happened by accident. The first song Paul and I ever wrote together was "I Was Made for Lovin' You." I was kind of pioneering a style of music, which was combining dance beats with rock music. That's what I was doing in Desmond Child And Rouge. I thought it would be very cool to try that with KISS. We were at SIR Studios and they had rented a big grand piano. I sat down and started playing the chords for the verse. Paul contributed the chorus and was writing along with me and then continued writing the song with Vini. I loved the record. Paul is a really great lyricist, he loves wordplay, inner rhyming and double entendres. His writing is direct and clever.

VINI PONCIA: When they brought "I Was Made for Lovin' You" to me, the verse had already been written. I wrote the chorus. I finished them in the tradition of the Brill Building. A lot of those things that sounded like pop influences in the songs were Paul's idea, like "Sure Know Something." The whole idea of *Dynasty* was to show the business that this band could write better songs and make a better album than they had previously done. Not that "Sure Know Something" is a better song than "Detroit Rock City" but at that time those songs were considered lesser songs from a songwriting standpoint. *Dynasty* was a great KISS album. If that album was a solo album for Paul Stanley or some of those songs like "Magic Touch," those are good songs by today's standards. We all had a great time making that album. They liked the whole process of pulling a song apart, building it up. I like *Dynasty* because it was the first step for everybody in that area. It was the first time that Paul and Gene got involved in something that smacked of such commercialism but still had a lot of good emotion. It came from the heart.

ANTON FIG: I pretty much played the way I wanted to play on the album. Vini did get pretty specific on "I Was Made for Lovin' You" because that was one of the few songs that we recorded with a click track. And we overdubbed the toms separately. I came up with the idea of the sort of gunshots in there. I got a lot of direction from Vini on that song.

GENE SIMMONS: I didn't play bass on "I Was Made for Lovin' You." But there are a lot of songs in our history where people think that the people who played the instruments actually played them. It's not true. On "Almost Human" I played guitar. I played guitar on "Plaster Caster," "See You in Your Dreams." I played keyboards on "Christine Sixteen." There were also other songs where Paul would stick in a bass part—who plays the instruments is not the point.

PETER CRISS: I could give you a million songs Gene didn't play bass on. You would not believe how many basses are done by Ace Frehley. It would blow your fucking mind. When you read my book you're gonna go, "He didn't play on that, he didn't play on that." You wouldn't believe all of the songs that Gene hasn't played bass on.

★ "2,000 MAN" ★

ACE FREHLEY: That's a Rolling Stones song. A friend at a recording studio where I used to do demos came up with the idea to cover that song. He said, "Try it." So I jammed on it one day. It's a spacey song with spacey lyrics so it fits my character. It's like the song was written for me. It's talking about computers and all that stuff.

VINI PONCIA: That was Ace's idea to cover that Stones song. It was a good version. Knowing that the album was going to be a little bit left or a little bit right, Ace was trying to keep the lifeline open between the old KISS fans. "2,000 Man" is real raw rock 'n' roll from the standpoint of how Ace feels and how he plays guitar.

★ "SURE KNOW SOMETHING" ★

PAUL STANLEY: It's a good song and it was fun. Vini and I wrote that and it was just real easy to write. That song's on the *Unplugged* album too. "Sure Know Something," in particular, was a perfect song to benefit from being stripped down. It's not unusual for the essence of something to get lost in the trappings and "Sure Know Something" was always fairly simple. To play it acoustically was only to show it off that much more. I still like it very much.

VINI PONCIA: "Sure Know Something" has always been my favorite song that I ever wrote with Paul. Every once in a while you write a song where the combination of lyric, chords, melody, and groove all comes together. That's a great groove song. Easy to play, great melody, and on the chorus Paul displays some of his Rod Stewart influence. In fact, Paul came up with the chorus. He would set the tone on which way he wanted a song to go. We would throw ideas back and forth. The end product would be the result of our collaboration. Paul could be screaming rock 'n' roll one day and he could be poppy the next day. Paul can come up with "Sure Know Something" where Ace would never write a song like that. His instincts were basic rock 'n' roll.

★ "DIRTY LIVIN' " ★

PETER CRISS: Stan Penridge and I wrote that in the early '70s, right after Chelsea broke up. That song was ahead of its time. I wrote it about living in New York and about drugs. I fought tooth and nail to keep it as close as possible to the demo. I had a tough time getting songs on albums, so did Ace. I was always fighting to get something in there. I would bring in five, six, seven songs but none of them were good enough. Then it got to be fights so bad that they'd have to at least give me one song. And if they did give me the song they'd have to touch it, do this, do that to it.

STAN PENRIDGE: "Dirty Livin'" was another song written during those Lips years. Vini Poncia, during the preproduction of Peter's solo album, *Out of Control,* had come to New York to do a number of demos with Peter and myself. He added a new storyline to the lyric but the music remained the same. Those demos were recorded at ODO Studios on 54th Street during the month of December 1979. I visited a few KISS recording sessions. Never did I see all the members in one room at the same time and working. Peter and I visited Vini while he was recording the rhythm track of "Dirty Livin'." Anton Fig played drums on most of that album. Peter and I were doing the *Out of Control* album at the time.

VINI PONCIA: "Dirty Livin' " was a song I co-wrote with Peter after working with him on his solo album. Peter said, "I've got to make some demos for the new KISS album, do you want to do them with me?" That was the one song out of all the Peter songs submitted that Gene and Paul liked and that would fit on a KISS album. That's the thing that got them thinking about using me as a producer on the album. It was strong and they liked it.

★ "CHARISMA" ★

GENE SIMMONS: "Charisma" came from something Howard Marks said in Beverly Hills when he was making fun of me. He saw how girls would always come up to me and that I would be comfortable talking about myself. He was doing me going, "What is my charisma? Is it my power? Is it my fame? Yeah, because I'm cool!" He was poking fun at me and I'm going, "No, Howard, that's *good!*" The beginning intro of "Charisma" is "Simple Type," musically, with a touch of my own riff in "Black Diamond."

★ "MAGIC TOUCH" ★

PAUL STANLEY: "Magic Touch" was a great song that unfortunately got mucked up when it was recorded, as did a lot of songs on *Dynasty* and *Unmasked.* "Magic Touch" was a song that was really powerful and really heavy and got kind of wimped out. Just the wrong vocal interpretation, wrong way of singing it. But I like the song a lot. Originally the chords for "Magic Touch" were much grander. It was ballsier. We were dealing with a more poppy approach to our songs in working with Vini. During *Unmasked* and *Dynasty* I was trying to find my voice as a singer. I certainly liked all the early stuff I did, but I wanted to go someplace else. I wanted to be able to sing what I heard in my head and I wasn't there yet. To do that song today would be a gas. I would love to sing it. Back then I was on a bike with training wheels.

★ "HARD TIMES" ★

ACE FREHLEY: "Hard Times" is one of my favorite songs that I've written because the lyrics talk about when I used to go to high school and cut classes. I went to high school for five years [laughs]. I was a sophomore for two years, one year I partied away [laughs] and I don't remember half the things I did.

★ "X-RAY EYES" ★

GENE SIMMONS: That song just happened. [sings some of song lyrics] "I can see right through your lies, because I've got X-ray eyes." In those days I was constantly in the studio doing demos. Even when I didn't have material, I forced myself to just go in there and see what happened.

★ "SAVE YOUR LOVE" ★

ACE FREHLEY: I was listening to "Save Your Love" the other day. When we were preparing for *Psycho Circus,* Gene would diligently write one song a day. He told me by the time we went into the studio he had a hundred songs. I can't just say I want to write a song. I have to be motivated whether it be something that happens or somebody says a line that triggers something in my brain that could be a good chorus or song title.

UNMASKED

Release date: May 29, 1980
KISS / VINI PONCIA–producer / JAY MESSINA–engineer / BILL AUCOIN–manager
ANTON FIG–session drummer / TOM HARPER–session bassist / BOB KULICK–songwriter
GERARD McMAHON–songwriter / PEPPY CASTRO–songwriter
VICTOR STABIN–album cover artist / DENNIS WOLOCH–graphic designer

PAUL STANLEY: *Unmasked?* I would give that one star. A song like "Tomorrow" is really a great song, but I think *Unmasked* is a pretty crappy album. It's wimpy. A lot of those songs started out sounding much ballsier, and much more rock 'n' rolly. Somehow they lost something on their way to vinyl. A lot of the early albums don't sound particularly good to my way of thinking, but there's a saying, "If it ain't broke, don't fix it." If something works you don't question it. Sonically, a lot of our stuff doesn't sound that great to me. There's songs on *Unmasked* that were really good songs that I thought were arranged and recorded in a kind of neutered and ball-less way. But again you don't fuck with the past. The concept of a lot of films where there's time travel involved is that if you go back in time you don't mess with anything because there's a chain reaction and it affects all kinds of things. That's how I feel about everything we've done. If you change one thing you change everything.

GENE SIMMONS: One star. I think a group and an album is always more than just songs. It's direction and attitude and if it was always just about songs then those K-Tel records would be the biggest things in the world because there's some good songs on there. By that point Peter Criss was in the Twilight Zone. He also started to have problems very early on. By *Unmasked*, it got so bad. and he was so out of touch with reality that we had to use Anton Fig for the whole album. There was not a track Peter played on.

ACE FREHLEY: I thought my songs were good. I don't think Paul and Gene were that thrilled with the stuff they did or the production of it. You have to realize at this point in time the band was going through a transition. Peter is leaving the group. Everybody was kind of doing their own thing. For instance, on my tunes I played the bass parts. [laughs] I wouldn't let Gene play. We were at that point where we really needed to be away from each other. I think Paul might have even played bass on some of his songs. For a lead guitar player, bass isn't really that hard to do. Gene was pretty good about it. He wasn't the kind of bass player that said, "I want to do it." I know Keith Richards plays a lot of bass on the Stones records. But Gene's a talented guy. I'd give the album three and half stars.

PAUL STANLEY: We were not functioning as a band. Peter didn't play on *Unmasked* or *Dynasty*. By *Unmasked* it was clear that that wasn't an ongoing workable situation. Certainly for the fans' benefit you would often paint a picture that wasn't true and at times that comes back to haunt you. People get the idea that you're that comic version of the Beatles where the four guys live in connecting houses or sleep in the same bed and do everything together. And that was absolutely never the case. Everybody didn't do an equal share of the work and everybody didn't have equal amounts of songs to bring to the party nor were the songs up to standard. We wanted to create something for the fans that was cheery and fit the picture that they had of us, sometimes covering up people's shortcomings. By the time of *Unmasked*, it was clear that [laughing] none of the tires were full, but one seemed real flat.

VINI PONCIA: The *Unmasked* album didn't have the kind of emotion as *Dynasty*. It didn't have that kind of reality and believability to it. It was like a character sketch of the other album, so it lacked the soulfulness of *Dynasty*. For me, the problem with the *Unmasked* album was it was a rush job. The *Dynasty* album was very well planned and thought out because it was a new venture. It was a new direction for KISS. With the success of *Dynasty*, I felt that we should have spent more time on *Unmasked*. Don't forget, with Neil Bogart, when you handed in a record, the album jackets were already made and at the factory [laughs]. So you finished it on Friday and it was out on Tuesday [laughs].

JAY MESSINA: *Destroyer* was really well produced and it still sounded raw and gusty, whereas *Dynasty* and *Unmasked* sounded a little too nice in terms of musicality over raw energy. Instead of turning up the amps to ten, maybe they were on nine for those records.

VINI PONCIA: Why did we do poppier songs on *Unmasked*? Well, those were the kind of songs that Paul was writing. It wasn't my idea to come in and change anything. They were taking advantage of my pop sensibilities in those areas and I was taking advantage of certain songwriting talents that Paul and Gene had in those areas. Paul and Gene have never done anything that they didn't want to do. They wanted to find out if they could work in that pop area and be effective.

ANTON FIG: I remember rehearsing for *Unmasked*. The rehearsals were largely like they were writing the songs and rearranging them. They weren't rehearsals for me to get to know them. They were pretty much working out the tunes as well. It took about a week or ten days in the studio to do the drums. There was some discussion of me joining KISS at one stage. But at that time I had a band called Spyder that was also managed by Bill Aucoin, our song "New Romance" was on the charts and the timing just didn't seem right.

TOM HARPER: The preproduction rehearsals were at a rehearsal place out in Queens. It was there that Vini and the band worked out the arrangements and selected the material that ended up on the album.

BILL AUCOIN: There were some great songs on those records. I think the problem with it is that the band was getting tired.

BILL AUCOIN: I thought they really wanted to be unmasked for that album. Paul and Gene especially had been talking about taking the makeup off for a while, but we talked them out of it.

DENNIS WOLOCH: The *Unmasked* cover was done by Victor Stabin, he had not done any music stuff at the time. He was a very good painter. I like the cover a lot, I didn't even mind the concept. I know it was kind of a bomb because it came out at a funny time where the music wasn't the best. I think as a cover, it worked great.

VICTOR STABIN: I was proud of the cover. Howard Marks Advertising Agency gave me the script and I came up with the visuals. Paul, Gene, and Ace came by my studio and they were real into what I was doing. Gene, with his comic book background, gave me some clever suggestions and smart input into the cover. I did the three panels that comprise the front cover in twenty-eight days. I worked with three people, day and night—Mark Samuels, Jose Rivero, and Sherry Schneider. I recently found out KISS sold the original *Unmasked* painting at their official auction for fourteen grand.

★ "IS THAT YOU?" ★

GERARD McMAHON: One of the great experiences in my songwriting career is having one of my first covers done by KISS. I remember coming home from a gig one night and on my answering machine was a message from Vini Poncia saying, "Check this shit out." It was a recording of KISS performing "Is That You?" I was inspired to write the song late one night on a Midwest tour, in the hotel bar in Duluth, Minnesota. After the gig, I was sitting at the bar, drinking a whiskey, and this girl came up to me, dressed in black leather with handcuffs at her waist and a whip in her back pocket! After contemplating the adventurous night that could lay ahead, I headed back to my room and wrote the lyric and music for "Is That You?" after my interesting meeting with the dominatrix.

★ "SHANDI" ★

PAUL STANLEY: "Shandi" was a big hit. I heard [Bruce] Springsteen's song "Sandy" on the radio and I liked something about the song, so that's where that song came from. It's not a steal at all. It couldn't have been "Sandy" because Bruce had a song out with that title. Vini came up with the name "Shandi." There was singer at that time named Shandi Cinnamon. It's a great song with a well-thought-out lyric. I'm real fond of the song. I'm my own worst critic. I'm not crazy about the recording of it, but as a song if I sit down and play it it's real good. That was recorded at a time where we were experimenting and also lost our way somewhat. The funniest thing about "Shandi" was being in the studio recording a KISS song for a KISS album and looking around me and seeing Tom Harper on the bass, Anton Fig on the drums, and Holly Knight on the keyboards.

TOM HARPER: I was Paul's guitar tech on the *Dynasty* tour in 1979. It was my first big tour. KISS had been in the Record Plant for a while laying down basic tracks for *Unmasked* with producer Vini Poncia. I remember being impressed with the song when they first played it in preproduction rehearsals out in Queens. I think that Vini was responsible for encouraging the guys to explore their songwriting talents more than they had in the past. "Shandi" was a departure from the songs that Paul had written previously for KISS. Vini was a very musical producer and a great singer-songwriter himself. Gene called one night to say that he was sick and wouldn't be in the following day. Vini reached into his bag and pulled out a cassette of the "Shandi" demo and said, "Learn this, you're playing tomorrow." The basic track was just the three of us: Paul, Anton Fig, and myself. (Paul later played the lead guitar part as well, I don't think Ace played at all on "Shandi.") I remember being a bit nervous about the situation, which was to be expected, but the guys made me feel pretty comfortable. I used my treasured 1963 Gibson Thunderbird bass on the track, and remember being really pleased with its sound that day. Gene came in the following week and heard the basic track with my bass part. He nodded and said, "Good, keep it." Gene later would refer to me as "the guy who played bass on 'Shandi' " whenever he saw me in public. I received a check for $500 for that session.

PAUL STANLEY: That song didn't necessarily sound like KISS. Vini's input at that point was taking us in a direction that we weren't comfortable with. But if everybody is honest about it, nobody protested very loudly because we were already beginning to lose sight of who we were. Everybody was more involved in their own world, friends, and indulgences to really care very much. Everybody can say what they want about *Dynasty* or *Unmasked* or Vini Ponica, but whatever protesting there was was so halfhearted. Everybody was more involved in their own stardom, wealth, and their notoriety than they were when KISS started.

VINI PONCIA: "Shandi" was really poppy [laughs]. That even made me nervous. It was funny because the late great Neil Bogart loved all that pop stuff that we were doing with KISS because he was always a singles-oriented guy. Neil swore that was a number one record. Had that song been a number one record, who knows what would have happened? He thought "Shandi" would be a great follow-up to "I Was Made for Lovin' You" and that the song would firmly establish KISS as hitmakers. But it was probably too far to the left and didn't sound enough like KISS. If Paul had an idea to write a song like "Shandi," we would sit down and write it. And it would be a good song because Paul's a very talented songwriter and so am I [laughs]. In retrospect, whether you like that song or whether it worked at that particular time, you can't say it's not a great song. I know Paul and I were excited about "Shandi," but I'm not sure the rest of the group were excited about it. If you're a band, you don't say to the record company, "Fuck that song." Ace may have felt that way about the song. It's like when "I Was Made for Lovin' You" became a Top 10 single, nobody was really complaining. But when it doesn't become a hit then it opens up the doors for criticism. Nothing succeeds like success.

★ "TALK TO ME" ★

ACE FREHLEY: "Talk to Me" was a semi-hit in Europe. I haven't played that song in a long time. It came together pretty quick. I used a special tuning on that song, either a G or D tuning, a tuning like Keith Richards would do. A lot of times if I pick up a guitar at a pawn shop or I get a new gadget and I plug my guitar into it, it will inspire me to come up with a song idea. I do that every now and then. I'll buy a guitar even if I'm not a hundred percent crazy about it, but I figure if I bring it home and play it something different will happen, it'll be a catalyst that will trigger a song. A lot of times I get song ideas just as I'm waking up when I'm in half a dream state and half awake. I think it's called the beta stage. Oddly enough, I get song ideas when I'm driving and I have to pull over to the side of the road and write it down.

★ "NAKED CITY" ★

GENE SIMMONS: Bob Kulick played me the riff for "Naked City." He said, "This is awful, we have to rewrite this." I said, "No, there's something here." It hit me at that point how New York City was really like that old TV show, *Naked City.* A lot of the lyrics [recites lyrics], "older women with younger men, looks like I'm in trouble again." It was just imagery of cities [recites lyrics], "lonely people and lovers at first sight." Everybody's got their own story, there are eight million stories in the Naked City.

BOB KULICK: I wrote most of the music, Gene wrote some lyrics, Peppy Castro contributed some music and melody stuff, and Vini contributed the bridge. Somebody should recut that song. To me KISS ruined "Naked City." The demo sounded like heavy KISS. They turned it into this pop song. Ace could never play the guitar phrase like I played it. Because I co-wrote the song, they really should have let me play on it. They compromised the song by having him play it.

PEPPY CASTRO: Every instinct that I would have for the song would get reinterpreted through Gene's vision of what's right for KISS. I think this album was their pop phase and was just a natural outgrowth of their career. They had taken so many slams from critics over the years for not being proficient as singers or players, which was all total bullshit. To know them and to see how talented they are outside of the genre as KISS is amazing. They're multitalented. The great thing about them is they never want to be an imitation of KISS so they keep reinventing the wheel for themselves.

★ "WHAT MAKES THE WORLD GO 'ROUND" ★

VINI PONCIA: That song had one of those sing-along R&B choruses, which was kind of fun. A lot of it was an opportunity for Paul to do in the studio things that he had never done before, those kind of background vocals, writing those kind of songs, making those kind of records. It was also a good flexing-of-the-muscles kind of experience because Paul is capable of writing a lot of that stuff really well. I think he can write more of those songs because he's melodic-oriented. The *Dynasty* and *Unmasked* albums gave KISS credibility as songwriters.

PAUL STANLEY: I was a friend of Vini Poncia, and I was also tapping what he was into. I think that's where that song came from. Vini was really good at what he did. I think we veered too much toward it.

★ "TOMORROW" ★

PAUL STANLEY: "Tomorrow" is cool. It originally didn't quite sound like that. It was much harder and had a lot of guitar. Vini Poncia's background was a little different, a little more polished, a little poppier. So, it came out a little different than it originally was supposed to be. It was a guitar song. We wound up with all these keyboards. It just kind of got diffused, distilled, diluted.

VINI PONCIA: Paul and I sat down in a room and threw ideas around. Usually he would come up with a couple of ideas or if I had an idea I would play it. In retrospect, maybe it didn't work in an album context for KISS because it alienated a lot of fans. But I think it was also a boost to their career.

★ "TWO SIDES OF THE COIN" ★

ACE FREHLEY: "Two Sides of the Coin" is a good song. There was some thought behind that, it's kind of poetic. At the time I think I wasn't getting along with my wife and was seeing someone else, two sides of the coin. Or it could have been two girlfriends, I don't know [laughs]. Maybe my wife wasn't very involved at all. We had a very open relationship.

★ "SHE'S SO EUROPEAN" ★

GENE SIMMONS: I just sat down and wrote a song about this imaginary girl I'd probably meet and did and often and repeatedly, in a manner in which she became accustomed to. It's about what an imaginary girl would be like in Europe. Ultimately, whenever you go out on tour you always think, "Gee, what are the girls going to be like this tour?" It's always about girls.

VINI PONCIA: Writing songs with Gene was different. He'd have an idea like "She's So European." There was no baring of his soul, it was strictly writing the best song you could. But it didn't necessarily have to mean anything.

★ "EASY AS IT SEEMS" ★

PAUL STANLEY: I was at my girlfriend's house and I woke up and I was singing this song. I was thinking of the Spinners. I never really saw "Easy as It Seems" as a song for us. But that's happened before. I'll come up with a song and have no intention of us doing it like "Hard Luck Woman." "Hard Luck Woman" wasn't meant for us, it was like a Rod Stewart kind of thing.

★ "TORPEDO GIRL" ★

ACE FREHLEY: I listened to that the other day and I was on the floor laughing. It was hysterical, that song is probably the funniest song I ever wrote. That was just one of those silly songs I decided to write. That and "Rocket Ride." I want my personality to come through on record. I don't take myself as seriously as Paul and Gene do. That's one of the things that I don't enjoy about them when I work with them is that a lot of times they take everything so fuckin' seriously as a heart attack. I keep telling them to lighten up. It's only fuckin' rock 'n' roll. When I'm offstage I'm running around at home with jeans and a T-shirt. I don't want to be recognized, I don't want to sign autographs, I just want to be me. I don't want people treating me any differently. I just want to be a normal person, work with computers, write music, and have fun.

VINI PONCIA: In writing a song like "Torpedo Girl," Ace wanted to make sure the rock element was maintained on the album. He was concerned about the album being too poppy. He always wanted to make sure the songs had enough edge to it. Ace has a good mind and he knows what he wants to do. It's not unusual to sit down with Ace and come up with something ironic or a little left of center like "Torpedo Girl." Working with Ace was very easy, it was very clearly defined what he wanted to do.

★ "YOU'RE ALL THAT I WANT" ★

GENE SIMMONS: I convinced Paul to demo that with me while we were out on the road in Middle America somewhere. Paul and I demoed that one up on the road and my demo kills the version that we ended up putting out. It sounds more like Free.

MUSIC FROM "THE ELDER"

Release date: November 16, 1981
KISS / BOB EZRIN–producer/songwriter / BILL AUCOIN–manager
ALLAN SCHWARTZBERG–session drummer / DENNIS WOLOCH–album designer

PAUL STANLEY: I would give *The Elder* [laughing] a big question mark. It might deserve stars if it was a different band's album. It's always interesting to me if somebody said, "Play the guitar and play those songs or you're dead," I'd probably be dead because I can't remember any of that music. It was real foreign to us. It was us pushing ourselves to do something different, but it was so foreign that I don't think that any of us really remember much of it. Once in a while we play some of that stuff, but we never make it past four or five bars into it. I think it's an odd album where we were trying to do something else and see where we were trying to go. And it's nice to know people are appreciating it. I scratch my head sometimes when I hear it. It's a little bizarre and it's okay, but I wouldn't want to do a sequel.

GENE SIMMONS: As a KISS record I'd give it a zero. As a bad Genesis record, I'd give it a two. There's just not enough songs on there and it's a bit pompous from the opening. I get a sense that the band was thinking, "Okay, here's our epic." But epics are determined by the people who listen to it, not the band who says, "Here's our epic." We were starting to lose touch. We actually did that one for the critics. You should never go for respect because on the day that critics and your mom like the same music that you do it's over. Right after *The Elder* we were so shocked into reality that we decided to do a very hard record.

ACE FREHLEY: Two stars. It would have been better if they hadn't cut out some of my solos. In retrospect, the band were getting further and further apart. Out goes Peter and in comes Eric Carr and they had brought in Ezrin, who I didn't think was right at this point in our career. My gut feeling was at this point in our career it was time to do a really heavy metal record and get back to basics and Paul and Gene didn't agree with me. They wanted to do a concept album with Ezrin and I was against the whole project. But I was outvoted. Here I am in one of the biggest groups in the world and I feel like my balls have been cut off because they could negate any of my votes because it was a two to one. Without Peter there to balance it off, Paul and Gene could run the group. When I realized that, I became very unhappy with the whole situation and I started abusing drugs even more and alcohol because I was really frustrated. I was in a Catch-22 situation. I have the original solos that were cut. I'd say 40 or 50 percent of the guitar solos and overdubs that I did were never used by Bob Ezrin. To this day I don't really understand why.

BOB EZRIN: I enlisted the aid of a number of people in the writing and recording of *Music from "The Elder."* I even brought Lou Reed in to write some lyrics for us. We auditioned and hired actors to read the dialogue. I contracted a specialist in medieval music to play the wind instruments that were used on the "Fanfare." We scored an orchestra for "A World Without Heroes." In short, we took the project very seriously, too seriously, as it turns out. The project ended up being KISS's least successful album and I can understand why. It was completely out of character for the band and probably not a very good idea to start with.

GENE SIMMONS: That record was interesting, but I don't think it had the soul of the band. I thought it was a tangent record. It was written after a short story that I wrote called "The Elder." Ultimately, it should be material that we can get up onstage, just plug in and play. That's the essence. The essence of the band is that the songs are not too flamboyant in their arrangements. I thought *The Elder* was an interesting exercise in creativity, no more, no less.

ACE FREHLEY: I think it's a good record. There was a problem between myself and Paul, Gene, and Bob Ezrin because a lot of the time I was recording in my home studio in Connecticut and they were recording up in Canada and some things got lost in the translation.

BOB EZRIN: It was an abomination. Gene had this story in mind, but the development of the story was very much a collaboration. The idea to make an album out of this story and make a stage show and all that other stuff was something he had to really be pushed into. The rest of the band had to be forced to go along with it. Nobody thought it was that good of an idea at the time. In retrospect they were right. Given the time and the band that we were working with, it was not the right vehicle. What we attempted to do was impossible for KISS of 1981. There are certain moments on it that are wonderful, certainly the theme of it, the concept of a young man against the world and all that stuff, is good. There's a couple of really good songs. "World Without Heroes" is a classic, but is it a KISS classic? That is the question. What I mean is that album done by KISS at that time was not the right thing. It was a bad time for all of us and we were different people then. I had a drug problem during the making of that record that really contributed a lot to my misjudgment. There were some great moments but I felt that I wasn't all there or I was all there but in a distorted form.

PAUL STANLEY: We were delusional, excited in the same way that somebody that's high was excited. You're lost in a haze [laughs]. I think we got caught up in the Emperor's new clothes. We got caught up in something that really had no place in our lives. But then again we were at a point, personally, individually and as a band, where we were becoming complacent and very comfortable with our success.

GENE SIMMONS: I blame me. I really believed in the vision. I always dabbled in Hollywood anyway. I wrote this short story and I wanted to make it into a film. Ezrin said it was a great idea for a concept record. So when he held up the mirror to my face, poor delusional Gene really bought it hook, line, and sinker. I'm going, "Yeah, I am great!" I take full blame for pushing it. I wanted credibility, which is very stupid really when you think about it. If you've got everything else, who cares? Ace wanted to rock out most. And when he couldn't get his way he simply didn't show up. He just stayed home and refused to come up. We had to send twenty-four-track tapes to Ace's home. We were trying desperately to hold the band together and Ace took the point of view rightfully or wrongfully that he didn't believe in it and he just wasn't going to show up.

PAUL STANLEY: *The Elder* is probably the biggest misstep of our whole musical career. It was everything that was wrong with us. It was pompous, contrived, self-important, and fat. It was mediocre. We were living in fancy houses. I think the band was losing sight of what made us what we are and how good and special that was. *The Elder* was wrong for so many different reasons. It was an important catastrophe [laughs]. Nobody here can take all the blame or be blameless. It's KISS, it's all of us. Bob came in and said, "Let's do a concept album." We believed that Bob could save us and get us back on track. Bill [Aucoin] also very much believed that this was a way to take us to another level and that we would impress the people who'd never been into us. And we thought the same thing. Like I said, we were delusional.

BILL AUCOIN: The record company was screaming for another album. They were tired. "Oh, do we have to go back in and do another album? We don't have the songs." I had a meeting and Bob said, "How about some sort of album that can tell a story?" For some reason because Bob's very bright we got into this mythological thing and it got way out of line. In truth, everyone was off the wall. There was no one who was going to fight it at that point because at least we were going to get the album done. It was a very strange time because it was all really loose. After that when the guys came to me and said, "Well look, this album didn't work and we want to take off our makeup." That was really the beginning of the end for me as well with them.

GENE SIMMONS: I do like the album. There's some songs I like. I think "Only You" is interesting. I would have liked to have sung "Odyssey." Initially I was going to sing it but at the last minute Paul sang it. I thought it could have been much more of a Beatle-esque kind of song, less operatic. That was written by a guy named Tony Powers. We started playing "I" and Eric [Carr] had just joined the band and he couldn't cop the feel so we had to use Allan Schwartzberg, who played on my solo album. Eric just couldn't play that feel and he was devastated.

ACE FREHLEY: I don't think *The Elder* was a bad record, I just don't think it sounded like a KISS record. It wasn't bad but to me it wasn't what KISS represents in my mind and that's why I found it offensive. The last time I played *The Elder* I was driving up to Milbrook Studios 'cause I was producing a group. I was listening to it and I got a speeding ticket [laughs]. So I took the tape out and threw it out the window and said "This is a bad-luck album for me all the way around!"

BOB EZRIN: There are a few pieces of music that we had cut in a session prior to the making of *The Elder*. We did four songs and then scrapped them. One of them was the "Carr Jam," which ended up on the *Revenge* album. There was another one called "Sentimental Fool." It was pretty weird stuff [laughs]. It just didn't seem to suit KISS.

ALLAN SCHWARTZBERG: I recorded drum overdubs for two songs on *The Elder* up at Ace's studio in Connecticut, "I" and "Odyssey." I remember it was a killer to overdub drums on one of the songs. After I was done, Bob [Ezrin] said, "Great, now double every single note you just played." [laughs] It took hours and hours to do. It bothers all studio musicians when we don't get credit on work that we do. But with KISS it's understandable, they chose not to credit me so the fans would think it was only their idols playing on the album.

DENNIS WOLOCH: It was a very different album for KISS so we had to do a concept album cover. I went shopping for chairs, tables, and props for about a week. The first thing I realized was that I needed a door. We got the layout done and I had it approved, mostly by Paul. It seemed to be his baby more than anybody else. That's Paul's hand on the cover incidentally. It wasn't his originally. We had somebody else's. He didn't like it. He hinted around pretty heavily that he had nice hands. And we took him down and shot his hands. I made the door that appears on the cover. I went out with a Polaroid camera and I walked around New York City looking at church doors because those are the most Gothic-looking doors. So, that particular one was based on a church on 86th Street and Park Avenue called the Park Avenue Methodist Church. I brought the photo to a model maker called Manhattan Modelworks and he made me a door. It's only a section of a door, it's about the same width of a door but it's only half the height. And he made that knocker too. The inner sleeve was shot on 18th Street in New York by a guy named David Spindel. I got that door and chairs at a place on 53rd Street called Newell Art Galleries, they have a lot of antiques and funky stuff in that place. For the problem that I was given, it's not a bad job for an album cover.

★ "FANFARE" ★

BOB EZRIN: "Fanfare" was a neoclassical piece that was supposed to set the fantasy-heroic atmosphere of the story of the Elder. To achieve an otherworldly effect, we decided to use medieval instruments such as the racket and krummhorn. They create an eerie and atmospheric sound that is never heard on rock records (maybe that's a good thing). In retrospect, it sounds a bit too serious and pretentious to me.

★ "JUST A BOY" ★

PAUL STANLEY: "Just a Boy" was just a mistake [laughs]. It was a great attempt to do something, but perhaps it fell short. We meant very well on *The Elder.* It was part of a debacle, just part of a big misstep, an attempt to do something that we shouldn't have been doing. Not because it's not valid, but because it really wasn't valid for us. When you have ability and talent as a writer what comes out can often have quality, it just may not be what's called for. It's a decent song, it just has nothing to do with KISS. It has its place in some sort of a show as opposed to a band's album. Singing that song was a picnic. That kind of singing was easy and was sometimes done because I was trying to find my voice at that point. Sometimes singing falsetto when I was still trying to learn to sing full voice was easy.

BOB EZRIN: Once we had decided upon the theme and storyline for *Music from "The Elder,"* the writing began. Paul came up to Canada to visit and write with me. He and I went into a little four-track studio in Aurora, Ontario, where we messed around for an afternoon and came up with an idea for a song called "Just a Boy." I think "Just a Boy" is a phenomenal song. It belongs on Broadway, but certainly not on a KISS record. We made a demo of it with Paul on guitar and bass and me thrashing away on drums and playing organ. The song was very dramatic and in retrospect, melodramatic. We were very proud of ourselves for having come up with the signature tune for the new concept album. Both of us have a very theatrical side and we slipped easily into writing what was more of a show tune than a rock song. We had a lot of fun demoing it—and it should probably have ended there. But, we brought it back to Gene, who agreed that it was "brilliant" and that we were on our way to writing our masterpiece.

★ "ODYSSEY" ★

PAUL STANLEY: It was a good song when I heard Tony Powers, the guy who wrote it, sing it because it was unique. And it was very much suited to him. Me singing it was just tragic.

BOB EZRIN: Tony Powers wrote "Odyssey" outright. That is weird. I fully understand the song, but I completely reject KISS doing it now that I look back on it. I don't know where we were coming from on that. Well, we tried . . .

★ "ONLY YOU" ★

GENE SIMMONS: We had an off-day in Cleveland and I went into the studio and played all the instruments myself, and pretty much wrote the song on the spot. It kept getting sidetracked because the first chord was a minor, and then it was finally recorded for *The Elder*. But Bob Ezrin changed it and added a middle from another one of my songs. And then the original version was then re-recorded by Doro Pesch, who liked my original demo.

★ "UNDER THE ROSE" ★

GENE SIMMONS: Even though some of the lyrics and melody are mine, Eric Carr wrote a lot of "Under the Rose." He came in with a melody idea, that central guitar riff in the song. Ezrin suggested a few things and rearranged it. But Eric had a lot to do with that. I came up with the title and most of the lyrics.

★ "DARK LIGHT" ★

ACE FREHLEY: "Dark Light" was originally called "Don't Run." Bob Ezrin and the other guys didn't feel my lyrics were strong enough so they brought in Lou Reed to rewrite the lyrics since everybody was happy with the musical track.

BOB EZRIN: I played bass on the song.

★ "A WORLD WITHOUT HEROES" ★

PAUL STANLEY: It started off with a song of mine called "Every Little Bit of Your Heart." From that song, we kept the verse and the feel. Bob [Ezrin] had a big hand in the rest of the music. Lou Reed wrote the lyrics to that. I remember him coming in and reading the lyrics to us. I played the guitar solo on that. It's a pretty expressive and emotive guitar solo. At that point Ace wasn't always around. Ace wouldn't come up to Toronto. It was not a good time for Ace in the band and there was work to be done. Ace didn't agree with the direction, rightly so, in retrospect. I believe our mistakes are as important to get us where we wind up as our successes. I don't regret any of it. It was just an eye-opener later on to listen to.

GENE SIMMONS: I'm never really a big fan of some of the lyrical stuff that Paul brings in. I tend to veer toward dark, here-comes-the-monster-from-my-ass kind of lyric, and Paul always thinks that's kind of cartoonish. We each try to push the other in the direction we think the other should go. I always loved the melody of "Every Little Bit of Your Heart." Once that didn't make it on a record, Paul just put it aside and went to work on something else. I wanted to revisit that. I liked the chordal pattern. I brought it to [Bob] Ezrin and started singing a different kind of a melody over that. Bob brought in Lou Reed. We barely knew Lou. Lou's a big fan of the record today. Lou was writing down certain phrases on a piece of paper and immediately "A World Without Heroes" jumped out at me. I said, "How about that?" And that was mostly Lou's contribution to the song. Then the lyric writing happened between Bob, myself, and Paul. The rest of it was mainly Bob and I writing a lyric and Paul's melody. That's why all four of us are credited on there.

BOB EZRIN: Everybody knows everybody in New York and KISS and Lou Reed were both part of the New York music scene. I had already done the *Berlin* album with Lou and I had brought him onto the Nils Lofgren album and other things. Lou was kind of intrigued with the concept of *The Elder* and he came up with a bunch of these lyrics and we worked by telephone on this. He came up with reams of lyrics and downloaded them over the telephone to me onto a little tape machine and then we started to mess around with them in Canada.

★ "THE OATH" ★

PAUL STANLEY: "The Oath" is token KISS, not real KISS. Compared to some of the other stuff on the album in terms of heaviness, it's "Purple Haze." It's okay. I have nothing good to say about any of *The Elder* stuff. As close as it got to hitting the bull's-eye, we weren't even in the firing range. Some of the riffs in "The Oath" got used later in "Keep Me Coming" and "I've Had Enough."

★ "MR. BLACKWELL" ★

GENE SIMMONS: Lou [Reed] flew up, I wrote the track, and he came up with some lyrical ideas. That was his contribution and then Ezrin and I finished the song. But musically, the track was me.

★ "ESCAPE FROM THE ISLAND" ★

ACE FREHLEY: I recorded that up in Montreal in Bob Ezrin's basement. I vividly remember me, Eric Carr, and Bob Ezrin jamming on that in the basement of his house. Bob was playing bass. We jammed on that for about a half an hour until we got it right.

★ "I" ★

GENE SIMMONS: I wrote "I" myself. It was written while we were putting together *The Elder* in Ace's studio because he refused to work anywhere else. So, while we were over at his house, we were trying to put together the album based on my story idea, *The Elder*. Bob [Ezrin] had a blackboard and he tried to plan the story line. He would figure out when we needed a song that would somehow define what the story was really about. So, I started to juggle around licks and lyrical ideas. "I" became semiautobiographical. [recites lyrics] "I don't need to get wasted, it only holds me down. I believe in me." That's been my motto. At the end of it, Bob added a few things, changed a few lyrics, but basically I wrote the song.

KILLERS

Release date: spring 1982
KISS / MICHAEL JAMES JACKSON–producer / BOB KULICK–session lead guitarist
ADAM MITCHELL–songwriter / MIKEL JAPP–songwriter

PAUL STANLEY: I'd give that one or two stars. It was us trying to regain our balance and sanity after doing *The Elder*. We were at an interesting point then. We were gearing up to do *Creatures*. The stuff that was on *Killers* was basically warm-up. It was us sitting around saying we want to be what KISS has always been and redirect ourselves to what made us in the first place. What comes easiest and is most comfortable is what we want to be. So those were kind of the first songs that we wrote.

BOB KULICK: At that time, it was getting way more difficult working with KISS because nothing seemed like it was good enough for them. It used to be everything I played they liked, but when I was playing on the new songs on *Killers*, it became "don't play this, don't play that." I think they were reaching that point where they were starting to second-guess themselves. It wasn't what feels good anymore, it was, "How does this stack up against the competition? How does this stack up against Eddie Van Halen and Randy Rhoads?" They were beginning to overanalyze everything. I was like, "Look, you're not that good of a band. Stop trying to compete with Van Halen and Ozzy. Compete on the level that you are, superheroes that play cool, simplistic stuff. Don't try to be something you're not." And of course every time they tried to be something they were not like *The Elder*, it just didn't work. I mean, be true to yourself and you're not going to fall on your face. Honestly, my attitude was I was tired that they couldn't recognize something that was good anymore. I said, "Wait a minute, I do this for a living, this is a good fuckin' solo." And they'd say, "Nah." It got really bad. It got to the point where I didn't really want to be there.

BOB KULICK: Michael [James Jackson] was like the referee on that album because Paul and Gene seemed to be having this tug-of-war about where the band should go. This was no different than they've ever been, it's just when they are in a production capacity it becomes draining. Michael was an objective person who didn't necessarily favor one or the other. We had fun with what we did but it seemed to me, and he may disagree with this, at the time I came in to play they were also auditioning guitar players at the same time. They had a lot of people in and out. I'm talking about people who came down in the middle of sessions [laughs] to audition. Steve Farris [Mr. Mister] who did the solo on *Creatures of the Night*. He came down in the middle of my doing guitar stuff 'cause they were checking him out. *Killers* and *Creatures* were done essentially at the same time. So they flew me out from New York to do the KISS *Killers* thing and then I came back to do some stuff on *Creatures*, but it wasn't even defined which was which [laughs]. That was at the time I noticed Vinnie Cusano hanging around. He was sitting in the studio one day and I remember asking Paul who was that and he said, "We're writing with him and he also plays guitar." And I said, "Well, is he good?" And he said, "Yeah, he's really good." And I said, "Then why don't you take him in the band?" And he said, "Well, we're not that sure about him." So I said, "I'll just hang until you figure out what you're going to do." I had suggested my brother, Bruce, at the time, saying that they get somebody who could be a permanent guy because at the time I had a record deal with CBS for a band called Balance. And it was frustrating for me because I would have really liked to have been turned loose on this stuff to see what I could come up with and not have to pretend that I was Ace or anybody else. On the *Killers* album there was a push to do or not do certain things. I played a little rhythm on the album too. But by and large it was mainly solos. From that album I thought "Nowhere to Run" was really great. It could have sounded better. I wish that that had had the sonics that *Creatures* had.

PAUL STANLEY: That album came out after *The Elder* and we were at a point where it was though *The Elder* did so badly that it was kind of like being knocked out by Mike Tyson. We spent a bit of time trying to get the cobwebs out of our heads and those were the first songs that we wrote. It was kind of like getting back on sure footing again.

GENE SIMMONS: *Killers* would get one star. It's okay. "Partners in Crime" was okay but "Nowhere to Run" is a better song. I like "Down on Your Knees" too.

MICHAEL JAMES JACKSON: When I first met KISS, I was completing production on a record for Jesse Colin Young, formerly of the Youngbloods. Going from Jesse Colin Young, one of the great icons of folk-rock, to KISS was no less than a quantum leap. I was somewhat of an oddity when I entered their world because I came from such a totally different place musically. I had primarily been focused on working with singer-songwriters and melodic bands, and had never really considered producing a band like KISS. We hooked up after *The Elder* record and at that point, musically, my impression was that they were pretty confused. KISS had previously enjoyed such a tremendous amount of success that when *The Elder* had not been met with equal enthusiasm, I think it was a big disappointment, most particularly for Gene. It also seemed that for a number of reasons KISS's career, in general, had stalled. At that time in music, most of the big rock 'n' roll bands were leaning toward more melodic songs. My response to their problem was to persuade them to break out of the old mold, one where they had relied much more on attitude and performance than on melody and songs. While no one had ever come close to emulating the amazing live theatrics of a KISS performance, it also seemed clear it was time to make a different kind of record. I suggested very strongly that they come to California and collaborate with some different writers to give them some alternate points of view. For some odd reason, which even startled me, they were very receptive to the idea. I also think they were anxious to explore other alternatives because it was clear that the old KISS formula just wasn't working.

MICHAEL JAMES JACKSON: The band had a contractual obligation to deliver a compilation record and that became the KISS *Killers* LP. When we had our first meeting in New York, one of the initial songs they played for me was "Nowhere to Run." The band seemed to think that it was just fine the way it was. Gene also didn't really think they needed a producer anyway, so he was promoting the idea that they should produce themselves. Paul had a far stronger and better sensibility that what they really needed was an outside opinion. Their career was at a turning point and there was no question they had to make a change. It was also an unusual experience to have flown cross-country on the red-eye to attend this meeting only to hear Gene so casually say that he didn't think they really needed a producer anyway. I remember I had a lot of comments about "Nowhere to Run." It had great potential. Once we began recording, we made the necessary changes and it was included on KISS's *Killers*. We also recorded several other new songs that came out of collaborations like "Down on Your Knees," "I'm a Legend Tonight," and "Partners in Crime." That was a truly great period of time. There was a tremendous effort, from all of us, to rebuild something, a determination to regain a real sense of who the band was, to restate what KISS was about and get that on tape. While still in the midst of *Killers*, we also began working on the *Creatures* LP at the same time. We were recording at the Record Plant in Los Angeles. The deadlines on both projects ultimately became so intense that at one point I was running two studios side by side at the same time, Paul in one, Gene in the other. Personally, I was very determined to help them get back to where they wanted to be. *Killers* was a good start, but I think it was *Creatures* that really made the point.

★ "I'M A LEGEND TONIGHT" ★

ADAM MITCHELL: "I'm a Legend Tonight" and "Partners in Crime" were both written at my house in the Hollywood Hills. I had a studio set up, a sixteen-track Tascam one-inch tape machine, plate echo, and one of Roger Linn's first drum machines. Paul and I or Gene and I would cut our demos there in my studio using the drum machine, a couple of guitars, and bass. "I'm a Legend Tonight" and "Partners in Crime" were amongst the first demos we cut. We also cut a demo of "Danger" in my studio around that time. I remember when we had finished it, Paul and I were really excited because the demo had turned out great. We both liked the demo more than the finished track.

PAUL STANLEY: I think it's pap. Certainly there's going to be some fan who goes, "How can you say that about a song that I like?" I've always done my best, but we can all look back at times when we were well intentioned and may not have delivered what we hoped to.

★ "DOWN ON YOUR KNEES" ★

PAUL STANLEY: I don't really remember much about how that song came about or how it was written. We were kind of grasping around trying to figure out what we were doing.

MIKEL JAPP: Bill Aucoin came and banged on my door one night and said, "I want you to call Paul at the hotel, so you guys can do some writing." I said okay. I called Paul, went to the hotel, and found him playing his guitar and recording an idea. It was late when I got to the hotel and by the time we'd finished talking, it was too late to get into writing. So I left him a tape of the beginnings of "Saint and Sinner" that Gene and I finished. And, as it turned out, the half-finished version of "Down on Your

Knees," which Bryan Adams and Paul completed. It's not public knowledge, but I played the meaty guitars on "Down on Your Knees."

★ "NOWHERE TO RUN" ★

PAUL STANLEY: "Nowhere to Run" was written about somebody I had met. We had a quick, torrid relationship and then she split and went back to somebody she was involved with. In some ways, writing the song was cathartic because what I couldn't say to her, I could put in a song if only for myself. It's like writing a letter that you don't have any intention of sending but you say what needs to be said and you get it off your chest.

BOB KULICK: Listen to that solo on "Nowhere to Run" and that huge overbend [of guitar notes], that was me being totally frustrated. "You want something fuckin'different, well, try this on." "Wow, what's that?" they said. "That's me being really pissed off is what that is." Same with "Partners in Crime." "Let me get a wang bar guitar out here. You can't decide on any notes I play that are good so let's do some effects with the whammy bar. Does that sound like Eddie Van Halen to you?" I could see the writing on the wall. They were searching for something that wasn't there.

★ "PARTNERS IN CRIME" ★

PAUL STANLEY: I hate it. It goes back to always doing your best. But your best isn't always as good as your best on any given day. Everything on *Killers* was confused. It was a good attempt at trying to shake off *The Elder* and the excesses of becoming lethargic, self-important rock stars.

CREATURES OF THE NIGHT

Release date: October 25, 1982
KISS / MICHAEL JAMES JACKSON—producer / DAVE WITTMAN—engineer
RICHARD BOSWORTH—assistant engineer / ADAM MITCHELL—songwriter
MIKEL JAPP—songwriter / JIMMY HASLIP—session bassist
DENNIS WOLOCH—album designer

GENE SIMMONS: *Creatures* was the band realizing that we better get back to who we are and not worry so much about what's around us. We paid attention to sonics, to what we were writing about. It's similar in a lot of ways to *Revenge* where the band was really unified in its approach and everybody had their feet planted firmly on the ground. *Creatures* was a reaction to *Killers* and the records that came before that. We started to record those four songs for *Killers* and it was Eric Carr who kept saying, "We gotta get heavy, we have to go back to being a rock 'n' roll band." *Creatures* sounds like KISS but it's a different band because we've got two brand-new members. Michael James Jackson produced that record. I'm the guy that gave him the "James" in the middle. Up until then he was Michael Jackson and you can't call yourself Michael

Jackson, what are you on crack? It was Michael James Jackson who brought in Bryan Adams to co-write some songs. He brought in a number of people to put a spin on it. Paul and I co-produced it. We had a lot to do with it. How the microphones were set up, the arrangements, the songs, so it was very much a group record. Four and a half stars.

PAUL STANLEY: I'd give five stars to *Creatures*, if for no other reason, it's got teeth. It's heavy, but not heavy in music, heavy in attitude and determination. It was an album where we were determined to free ourselves of any remnants of what we'd done on *The Elder*. *Creatures* was the album I wanted to take the makeup off for. Gene was very reluctant and scared. No guts, no glory. Sometimes you have to take a chance to find out what you're made of. I figured if we couldn't succeed without the makeup, we didn't deserve to be a band anyway. I thought the album was great. It really was us reclaiming our purpose. We'd become complacent, wealthy, and deluded. Listening to sycophantic friends. After *The Elder* we realized how much we'd taken for granted what we had. The album had a purpose. We clearly knew what we wanted to do as individuals and as a band.

MICHAEL JAMES JACKSON: Moving from *Killers* to *Creatures* was the true beginning of an effort to redefine KISS. For that reason, that's why the overall sound and songs on *Creatures* have a very powerful common thread that runs through all of it. Of all the records I did with the band, it's my personal favorite. I believe that it truly captured a sense of the band's character in a very authentic way.

MICHAEL JAMES JACKSON: The *Creatures* record was designed to be the kind of project that would give KISS's audience something to really believe in again. It accomplished this because it revalidated that KISS was still alive and doing better than ever before. There had also been a tremendous amount of talk about the band finally taking the makeup off. To many people it was viewed as the last card the band should play. But the truth of the matter is the rejuvenation of the band was really due to the quality of the music. Their writing had matured and grown so much that eventually it was very clear that KISS would not live or die on whether they wore the makeup or not, it would be on the quality of their records.

DAVE WITTMAN: I really thought that was a breakthrough album for them. The material seemed so much cooler than any KISS stuff before. This album showed diversity that had never been there before.

MICHAEL JAMES JACKSON: At the beginning of the record, before we even started recording, Gene and I went on a search-and-destroy mission all over Los Angeles to find a great drum room. I finally took him to Record One where we eventually cut the tracks. I used vintage microphones on the drums, and the room itself was also well covered with microphones. Niko Bolas, who engineered the tracks with us, also did a great job. The end result was excellent, and was later further enhanced by the fine work Bob Clearmountain did in the mix at the Power Station in New York.

MICHAEL JAMES JACKSON: Because Ace wasn't on the record, there were many other guitarists who auditioned. And there were several who actually played solos on the record. For example, on "I Still Love You," the guitarist doing the solo is Robben Ford, a hands-down tremendous technician. The guys were really blown away with Robben. Steve Farris, who was in Mr. Mister, played the solo on "Creatures of the Night." As I recall, we brought in about eight different guitarists and rejected about six of them. This was a long and tedious procress to find the right guy with the right feel. Bob Kulick also did a great job on a bunch of stuff. It was just such a crazy time in those days but we were all so driven to do something special, something that counted, something that would last. The technology was also exploding at that time. Bob Kulick played a great solo on "Danger" but we soon decided it was in the wrong key for Paul to sing. It was also a little slow. Using prototypes of new equipment that wasn't even available yet, and with the help of our engineer, Dave Wittman, we sampled the entire song, modulated it to a different key, sped it up, and were able to keep Kulick's solo from a track that had been played in a different key and at a different speed. At the time, this was all quite amazing. The guitar solos, in general, were a serious problem because it was clear Ace was most likely not going to be the one who played on the record.

VINNIE VINCENT: I was still very, very new to the situation. They were still auditioning tons of guitar players. The way they auditioned them was to have some of them come into the studio and play on some of the tracks. I think that was part of the audition process. At some given point, I was asked to play. Once I came in to play, the fact that we were writing really well together, I ended up finishing the record and eventually joined the group. I was this new kid off the block. Five of my songs were recorded for that album.

ADAM MITCHELL: I got involved with KISS because of their producer, Michael James Jackson. He knew my songs and suggested that after the misstep of *The Elder*, they should try to work with a couple of other songwriters. Gene came over to my house first and we wrote a couple of songs, which turned out well although didn't end up on the record. Paul liked them and so he came over and we hit it off. At one point he and I were going out with two models who were roommates. So if we weren't writing, singing, recording, or checking out guitars, we were going to movies and clubs. I remember being impressed by how not just famous they were, but incredibly famous. We couldn't stop at a stoplight in Paul's car without someone recognizing him.

VINNIE VINCENT: I met Ace once and he seemed like a really nice guy. We got on very well. It was a very short conversation. I don't think I've ever run into Ace again. I think I met him when I first joined the band. He wished me luck and said, "Have fun, good luck," and that's about it. What was hard for me [about replacing Ace] was taking the place of someone that fans really loved. It's a really hard thing to do to be the new person and to walk into someone's shoes, literally, that is loved by so many people. I did not want to take anyone's place. I was just there because I was asked to be there. I hoped that I could give the fans my best and hoped that they would be happy with me. It was a brand-new experience and it was very intense. It was also a lot of fun. We learned a lot, we had some great tours, great shows . . . Rio. The shows were a little tentative at first because I was still learning the show and it was pretty difficult. But then as we got to know each other and the tours went on, it got better and better.

JIMMY HASLIP: I had worked with KISS's producer, Michael James Jackson, on a prior session with Robben Ford, who also played on *Creatures of the Night.* Michael called me and said he wanted me to come down to the Record Plant and play bass on several songs for the new KISS record. I think the band was running into some scheduling problems and needed to finish up the tracks quickly. One of the songs I played on was "Danger." Gene was there with me in the studio and taught me the tunes. I felt fairly awkward about being there because he was the bass player. But Gene made me feel comfortable and liked what I did.

MICHAEL JAMES JACKSON: I brought Jimmy Haslip in because Gene was having problems laying down a bass part. It was more musically demanding for Gene so I brought in a seasoned player who could nail the part.

RICHARD BOSWORTH: While working with KISS on *Creatures of the Night*, Paul knew I had worked with some of the Southern California music mafia like Linda Ronstadt, Jackson Browne, and the Eagles. One day while we were cutting a track, he asked for a little more volume of his guitar in his headphones. So I turned it up a little bit. After listening to it Paul said, [laughing] "Richard, I'm in KISS, not the Eagles. When I say I need a little more guitar, I really need more guitar!" [laughs]

DENNIS WOLOCH: Actually, *Creatures* may be my favorite album cover of all I've done for KISS because it went from pure concept to finish without many people putting in their changes and two cents' worth. It was all done with a camera except for the glowing eyes, which we had to retouch. Of course now with computers these days you could do it very easily. In those days we had airbrushes.

★ "CREATURES OF THE NIGHT" ★

PAUL STANLEY: "Creatures of the Night" was very much a recapturing of our desire and our focus as a band and a reclaiming of what was important to us. We had become rich, fat, and lazy and became enamored with the idea of having our peers think we were smart and musical and really all the things that are poison to us. When we did *Creatures* it was that step of us declaring that we were back, not in terms of sales or anything else but back in terms of knowing what we were about and what was important to us. And there's actually a great sixteen-track demo of "Creatures of the Night" that is virtually identical to the master. It came about at Adam Mitchell's house. As soon as we were writing it we knew it would start the album. For me that's always important. Once that song's written, the rest is much easier. To me the first song sets the identity and tone for the album.

ADAM MITCHELL: After the *Creatures* album had been released, I was at home clicking through the TV channels and I see this guy on some religious channel waving the *Creatures* album and screaming at the top of his voice how this song was written by the devil. I thought, "No, dude, me and Paul wrote that in my kitchen." [laughs]

ADAM MITCHELL: "Creatures of the Night" and "Danger" were both written in my house and demoed in my studio at home in Hollywood. I always had a special place in my heart for the *Creatures* album because we had so much fun recording it. I sang some of the backgrounds on "Creatures of the Night" and "Danger." And I played that guitar riff that comes in halfway through and at the very end of "Creatures of the Night."

MICHAEL JAMES JACKSON: "Creatures of the Night" was co-written by Paul and Adam Mitchell, one of the writers I had introduced the band to. The song had such a great character to it that we knew early on it would be the title track of the album.

GENE SIMMONS: I didn't play bass on the song "Creatures of the Night." I remember some guy sitting there playing bass and I said, "Gee that sounds good, leave it."

★ "SAINT AND SINNER" ★

GENE SIMMONS: "Saint and Sinner" was written with Mikel Japp. I was introduced to him and we had started tossing around a couple of ideas. I remember that he came up with the initial chorus riff and then I added lyrics and melody.

MIKEL JAPP: When Gene and I wrote "Saint and Sinner," it went through many, many other working titles. We worked on that song at my house, Diana Ross's house, in between sessions at the Record Plant, and over the phone. It was a lot of fun. Gene and I always had fun, good conversations but always stayed focused on the job at hand, the song.

★ "KEEP ME COMIN'" ★

PAUL STANLEY: I love "Keep Me Comin'," it's got a Zeppelin groove. It was the last song cut for *Creatures*. It was cut in New York City at Media Sound. I think we were one song short. *Creatures* was very much our attempt to get back at being a loud, hard, for lack of a better term, metal band.

ADAM MITCHELL: "Keep Me Comin'" was written at Paul's apartment in New York. As we were sitting there I was looking in his awe at his amazing guitar collection. The title of the song was Paul's idea but we both shared the lyrics.

★ "ROCK AND ROLL HELL" ★

GENE SIMMONS: "Rock and Roll Hell" started off with Bryan Adams and Jim Vallance. I'd been introduced to them by our producer. At that point Bryan hadn't achieved major success except for a disco hit he had, "Let Me Take You Dancing." Most of the song was done. My contribution wasn't a lot, it may have been a bridge and a few lyrical changes. Mostly it was an Adams and Vallance song. Their names should have been at the top ahead of mine.

★ "DANGER" ★

PAUL STANLEY: "Danger" was like a sister song to "Creatures of the Night." It was written by me and Adam Mitchell. He was a race car driver and he was also in a band called the Paupers, a big band in Canada in the '60s. Adam and I wrote "Creatures" and "Danger" around the same time.

★ "I LOVE IT LOUD" ★

GENE SIMMONS: "I Love It Loud" was a song I started writing with Vinnie Vincent when I was living at Diana's [Ross] house in Beverly Hills. We were working on *Creatures of the Night* and I said, "I want to write something that sounds like "My Generation," something that says, "This is who I am and this is what I believe in." I started the chordal pattern. If you listen to what the guitars are doing it is in fact "My Generation" without being a rip-off. And the drum pattern I got off of an old drum pattern that Eric Carr did. It was a tape loop and I did a four-track demo of it. I came up with the idea of "I Love It Loud" and then Vinnie and I wrote the lyric. Some of the songs that people like, I like but they don't have the same impact on me. People seem to love "I Love It Loud" but when I was busy writing it, it was only another song. You never knew what it is that hits the jugular. It's hit-and-miss.

VINNIE VINCENT: "I Love It Loud" was the first song Gene and I wrote together. When we recorded that record I was still new to the band. That record was recorded at a studio in L.A. called Record One and it was a tiled room. The drums had an incredible echo in this room, the best drum sound I have ever heard. That was my favorite recording experience, because of the studio and the experimentation that went into that record. I was very new to the band at the time. It was a real thrill. For "I Love It Loud," Gene had a chant, which was used at the beginning of the song, and I wrote the lyrics. We had good interplay. We spoke the same language, we spoke the same attitude.

MICHAEL JAMES JACKSON: I had a particular technique and type of microphones that I used in getting drum sounds. I brought in a special drum kit that wasn't Eric's and used vintage mikes to create that big sound. A tremendous amount of work went into it capturing that drum sound. Gene was very determined to try and recapture the best of KISS. There was an attitude that really got captured on that record. "I Love It Loud" was pure Gene. I can't even remember how many people we threw into the room to record the backgrounds but it was a lot.

DAVE WITTMAN: I sang background vocals on "I Love It Loud." I was one of many. Gene was there and we grabbed a whole bunch of people. What I did was say, "Hey, let me sing, I wanna get on this record." So Gene said, "Get out there."

★ "I STILL LOVE YOU" ★

PAUL STANLEY: "I Still Love You" is less personal than some might believe. People might think it's about someone or a certain time in my life but there are songs that are written purely from inspiration or from a thought. Then there's other ones about certain people. I hate to say but when I wrote "I Still Love You" I was in a great relationship. It was more Vinnie [Vincent] and I loving Zeppelin and loving bands that could play something at a solo tempo that was powerful and majestic, big drums. And it could spotlight someone's vocal.

★ "KILLER" ★

GENE SIMMONS: "Killer" started off as a piece that Vinnie started writing by himself and I came in later and started changing it around adding some different lyrical point of views. But Vinnie was the initiator of that one.

VINNIE VINCENT: That's a good song. The band was already recording at the Record Plant in Los Angeles. We were writing this while the record was being recorded and I think I came up with the idea. Gene added some good stuff to it and the song just grew and became finished. We finished it in the studio.

MICHAEL JAMES JACKSON: That's a very Gene song. I was always very pleased with how this came out with the backward piano effect that went on the end.

★ "WAR MACHINE" ★

GENE SIMMONS: I had one of these toy synthesizer computers that only had five notes. I started playing with it and came up with the riff on the keyboard. If you try playing it on a guitar it's very awkward. Bryan Adams and Jim Vallance came up with the verse music. "War Machine" was Bryan's title. Bryan and I are friends now but initially upon meeting me he thought I was a prick. I remember while we were working at Record Plant, I would be busy in the parking lot with whatever girl would come to see me, and there was one moment where Bryan got in his rent-a-car and said, "Well, see you around." He kept going around the block and stopping, going, "What are you doing?" I was busy drilling the girl in her car and he would go around the block and keep stopping. I would keep saying to him, "Would you get the fuck out of here? Get out of here!"

LICK IT UP

Release date: September 23, 1983

KISS / MICHAEL JAMES JACKSON–producer / DANNY GOLDBERG–creative consultant

RICK DERRINGER–session guitarist / DENNIS WOLOCH–album designer

---

PAUL STANLEY: I'd give *Lick It Up* four stars. *Lick It Up* is a good album, *Creatures* is a great album. I'd always believed that *Lick It Up* was the proof that people hear with their eyes. The response to *Lick It Up* was four times the response to *Creatures* and I think that's purely because people were tired of the image of the band and couldn't hear past what they saw. It's a really good album but it's not in the same league as *Creatures of the Night*.

GENE SIMMONS: At that point in my life I'd moved on from Cher to Diana Ross so I went deeper into the Twilight Zone. I was gone. Every day of the week you'd be going to parties and meeting people who couldn't have cared less about rock 'n' roll. So everybody would be nudging you, *People* magazine and the cover of the tabloids, and it warps your sensibilities. So I'd give *Lick It Up* two stars. Although I thought at least we hadn't gone off into discoland again.

VINNIE VINCENT: We actually recorded demos of four or five songs of songs that later were re-recorded for that album. We recorded a version of "A Million to One."

MICHAEL JAMES JACKSON: *Lick It Up* was a very special record. As always with KISS, there were critical deadlines that needed to be met. To meet them, we simply did the same thing we always did, which was "whatever we had to." We worked from noon each day to two or three in the morning, six days a week. Our one day off became a blur that briefly passed between sessions. Toward the end of the record, because of the deadlines, we again wound up using two separate studios simultaneously just to get the work done. The difference this time was that it was New York City, and the studios were now in different parts of town, so going back and forth in cabs to get the work done was commonplace. But when you have the right people involved, all working under the incredible pressure that comes with difficult deadlines, it can often bring out the best in everyone and this experience was no exception. Neither Gene or Paul ever let go of their determination to do the best possible job. Always. *Lick It Up* had the advantage of being the first record the band had done without the makeup, so it was clear it would have a life of its own. As a record, I thought it easily stood on its own regardless of that event. The public's response and the amount of airplay the record received confirmed that.

MICHAEL JAMES JACKSON: Two songs that stand out to me are "Lick It Up" and "All Hell's Breakin' Loose." It was Paul's idea to rap out the lyrics on "All Hell's . . ." and it was a good one. Both of those tracks were very accessible for radio and departed somewhat from what KISS usually did.

MICHAEL JAMES JACKSON: There were just some things that Vinnie couldn't play. His sensibility was often too melodic for the band's style. Vinnie was always struggling to find his place within KISS, both musically and personally. His end goal, of course, was to please Paul and Gene. Given their musical differences, this was not an easy task. He hadn't really matured as an artist himself enough to grasp how to approach their style. Often he would play solos that may have showed off a flashy left hand with a million notes. But to produce a great feel, you really need an essential right-hand style, which he was lacking. It was a problem. As I recall, we brought Rick Derringer in to take a pass. Moments like this were difficult for Vinnie, but the attitude all of us maintained was that the quality of the record would always be the priority rather than anybody's ego.

PAUL STANLEY: The "Lick It Up" video was the first we did without makeup. At the end we're getting stuff squirted into our mouths, I think it was yogurt or yogurt and cottage cheese. It was their idea of postnuclear holocaust survival food.

VINNIE VINCENT: We did a lot of trial album covers for *Lick It Up*, a lot of different settings . . . without makeup.

DENNIS WOLOCH: It's the only album that I put together that I wasn't present at the photo shoot. I guess they didn't feel like they needed anybody.

DANNY GOLDBERG: I stayed friends with Gene and Paul. We reconnected on the *Lick It Up* album. I wanted to be their manager but they didn't want to call anyone their manager so they called me their creative consultant. I did a lot of what a manager would do on *Lick It Up* and *Animalize*. KISS were at a commercial low point. They were at their lowest point since they first started in terms of record sales and concert attendance. The makeup was now a cliché and was not press-worthy or exciting anymore. My recollection is that it was my idea for them to take off the makeup. Clearly it was something that they had thought about. Gene had teased it a little bit appearing in photos with Cher where he'd have a kerchief over his face. I pressed the issue. I remember sitting with their business manager, Howard Marks, and Gene and Paul, saying, "Guys, you have to do something dramatic. There's no chance of turning the clock back so you've gotta go forward." It didn't take much persuading. It was in the back of their mind that someday they were going to take the makeup off. They're smart guys. They could see the truth of what I was saying. Within a relatively short length of time they decided to do it. I think Paul, in particular, was excited about this. To me, Gene was the theatrical one, the genius behind some of the makeup whereas Paul coveted acceptance as a singer and to be part of the real rock 'n' roll world, not just a cartoon version of rock 'n' roll. It was liberating for Paul, he could be a regular rock singer. It absolutely worked. We did a press conference live on MTV where they took the makeup off. That was absolutely the right way to launch it. And I got Martin Kahane to do the "Lick It Up" video and he did a really good job. The video really brought the band back. And they really made a comeback. *Lick It Up* did double or triple what the previous album had done.

★ "EXCITER" ★

VINNIE VINCENT: That song was originally called "You." I said, "Let's call this 'Exciter.'" Unfortunately for me, there's two sides to the coin. There's a good time and a bad time with the albums I did for them. Yes, the albums I did with them were great KISS albums but unfortunately the guitar playing on those records has nothing to do with me. I think what KISS really wanted was more of an old-school player who wouldn't get in the way and sit in the corner and behave himself and do what he was told. Their love of guitar playing lies back in the past, and I love that too, but I'm a guitarist of today and tomorrow. I speak through my guitar, that's my voice and I am that guitar and that guitar is me. For someone else to be in control of what they do with that love of mine, when they fuck with that, it becomes broken into little pieces. It's not that beauty, that creation that it is.

RICK DERRINGER: I played on "Exciter." I did a couple of things with them. I've known them from the beginning and Gene and Paul are still good friends to this day. I'm happy that they asked me to play on that. In terms of direction, they probably said, "Just go crazy."

VINNIE VINCENT: I don't think Gene and Paul liked what I played on "Exciter" and I did. I loved it. I thought it was one of my best pieces, and for some reason, that angered me quite a bit. Because I wasn't told about it until after it was done. I liked what I played better than what ended up on that song. But I think Rick's a great guitar player.

★ "NOT FOR THE INNOCENT" ★

GENE SIMMONS: "Not for the Innocent" started off with a guitar lick that Vinnie brought me. I like the song a lot. There was this group called Hydra and their lead singer had no teeth. One of their records was called *No Rest for the Wicked.* I thought that was a bit cartoonish but there's something about the idea of starting off with something negative. I thought, "Let's write something like 'Do Not Feed the Animals.'" It's a very stern warning with a negative at the beginning and "Not for the Innocent" came out of that.

★ "LICK IT UP" ★

PAUL STANLEY: "Lick It Up" was written by Vinnie and I at my place in New York. Before we wrote I thought it was important to know what we were going for and to have a game plan. There were times we sat down and wrote whatever came to mind. I thought we needed a catchy phrase and a memorable hook. It took hours of throwing ideas around before we came up with "Lick It Up." The writing wasn't that difficult once we knew what we wanted to do.

VINNIE VINCENT: I remember saying to Paul, "I've got a great idea for a song," and I started singing it. I don't think it clicked with him. He didn't seem excited about it. I said to myself that I think this would be a great new single for the record. I had the title and the melody and I said to Gene, "I think I've got a winner here and I think you should hear it." When Gene heard it he said, "That sounds like a great idea, you should play it for Paul." I said, "I already did but I don't think it clicked with him." The next time I played it for Paul, this was like a week later, he didn't even realize he had dismissed it. He said, "Hey, Vinnie, we need a single. This record needs a single." So I said, "Listen, I have a great idea for a single," not even telling him I had come up with this thing a week ago and he had shot it down. I said, "What do you think of this?" [sings verse melody line in "Lick It Up"] And he goes, "God, that's a great idea." I said, "It's called 'Lick It Up,' what do you think of the title?" And he said, "That's great." We ended up working on it. And he came up with some great parts and together it just became "Lick It Up." Lots of times, songs, when you hear them, you may not be in the right frame of mind to hear something quickly but, another day, another time, another moon, you go, "Hey, that's great." So that's how "Lick It Up" began.

★ "YOUNG AND WASTED" ★

GENE SIMMONS: It was the title of an article in the *Soho Weekly News* that was all about being young and wasted for the social circle that revolved around the art houses and art galleries. I thought the phrase summed up an entire generation so much. Very much like Richard Hell's "The Blank Generation" summed up an attitude. Not to me, but there's certainly a segment of the population that prefers to be wasted than to be alive.

★ "GIMME MORE" ★

PAUL STANLEY: I remember we wanted a song that was really up-tempo and balls-out. I enjoyed writing with Vinnie. Vinnie was always interesting to write with both musically and lyrically because he would throw some really interesting lyrical points of view and things that might spur me on.

★ "ALL HELL'S BREAKIN' LOOSE" ★

PAUL STANLEY: Eric came in with this track that was in an open tuning. He was very proud of it. It was very Zeppelinish. Eric came up with the whole track and I went in and came up with the rap. Gene came up with the "All Hell's Breakin' Loose" chorus. Eric was a very sensitive guy and was completely destroyed at hearing what he believed was the ruination of his song. Eric hated it. I'm not quite sure what he heard over it in his mind. He enjoyed the fact that he had written a song for the album. Eric was always more frustrated by what he wasn't than thrilled with what he was. When something wouldn't get used or got altered he only saw a half-full glass. I just remember his jaw hitting the floor when he heard what had been done. I'm smiling as I say it because it was just so clearly off from what he heard, but the alternative would have been to do something that would have turned into mimicry of something else.

★ "A MILLION TO ONE" ★

PAUL STANLEY: I like that song. I wrote it with Vinnie. Sometimes a song may border on sappy, but it's what I was feeling at the time.

MICHAEL JAMES JACKSON: As a songwriter, Vinnie was prone to a more melodic style. Of the songs Vinnie contributed to *Lick It Up,* this one wound up having that strong melodic element to it. While it wasn't particularly in KISS's traditional style, in the end, the band still made it their own.

★ "FITS LIKE A GLOVE" ★

GENE SIMMONS: "Fits Like a Glove" started off with a guitar pattern that I had. Then Vinnie stuck in the middle. We played it a lot during the '80s. We never did it well enough live. We just couldn't pull it off. It was way too high for me to sing. My favorite part of the song is in the middle, the talking part [recites lyrics], "When I go through her, it's just like a hot knife through butter . . ." I love that kind of stuff.

★ "DANCE ALL OVER YOUR FACE" ★

GENE SIMMONS: I tried to rip off "Larger Than Life" with "Dance All Over Your Face." I don't think I succeeded. Sometimes when you do write something, if it strikes the right chord, you try to recapture it. Usually, you don't succeed.

★ "AND ON THE 8TH DAY" ★

GENE SIMMONS: Vinnie was a very talented guy. I'd come in with a line like, "On the 8th day God created rock 'n' roll" and we'd just sit down and toss it around. He was very, very fast with his ideas. Vinnie could also contribute with lyrics too. Those songs written for the *Lick It Up* album were done very fast.

ANIMALIZE

Release date: September 13, 1984

KISS / MICHAEL JAMES JACKSON–basic tracks producer

JEAN BEAUVOIR–bass, background vocals, songwriter / BRUCE KULICK–lead guitar

DESMOND CHILD–songwriter / MITCH WEISSMAN–songwriter

ALLAN SCHWARTZBERG–session drummer / DANNY GOLDBERG–creative consultant

DENNIS WOLOCH–album designer

PAUL STANLEY: I'd give *Animalize* four stars. It's a better album than *Lick It Up*. I think "Heaven's on Fire" is good enough on its own. I took over the reins on that record because I basically had no choice. That was the story of the '80s. In most cases I could either do something or it wouldn't get done. For *Animalize* Gene had basically taken a commitment to be in a film. He ran into the studio, knocked out all his tracks, and left. Then upon listening to the songs most of them were unusable. So I had to redo those tracks and also record the rest of the album. It was a bit overwhelming because I got left with a box of parts, some that needed to be junked and some that needed to be built. I was left on my own to do a KISS album. It was freeing but it was also overwhelming because everything was put in my lap and there was no choice but to get it done.

GENE SIMMONS: I liked *Animalize* a little more than *Lick It Up*. I'll give it an A for effort, but two stars because on *Animalize*, at least we were trying although again once the makeup came off I didn't know who I was. More and more I was starting to look like Phyllis Diller. During *Animalize*, I was there for the basic tracks. But at that point I had started working on my first movie, *Runaway*. Paul and I were working in separate studios. I put on my vocals and bass on most of the record and the rest of it was left for Paul to finish. We were going through another bump in the road. Paul was very upset with all my Hollywood stuff, with Cher and Diana [Ross], with the movies. He felt it was detracting from KISS. Perhaps he was right, but that's what I needed to do. For the time, I thought both *Animalize* and *Asylum* were decent records for what they tried to do, which was to basically keep KISS going. We had new members, we had taken off our makeup. Do you stay rock 'n' roll when everybody's going to the Yngwie [Malmsteen] school of playing as many notes as possible without caring about the notes? Don't stand still and hold a note and squeeze the life out of it when you can be just flying across the fretboard. It was the days of guitar acrobatics. So, the style of that record was kind of a hybrid of "Look at how many notes I can play" with some rock 'n' roll content.

DANNY GOLDBERG: *Animalize* came rather quickly after the *Lick It Up* album. Paul was really focused on writing a hit. "Heaven's on Fire" was one of the biggest songs that they had and got them up well over Platinum. That album completed the comeback. Their live business was a lot bigger.

MICHAEL JAMES JACKSON: *Animalize* was well positioned at that time to capitalize on the momentum of *Creatures of the Night* and *Lick It Up*. Caught in a schedule conflict with another project, I knew I would only be able to start the record but not finish it. Consequently, I worked with the band on the preproduction in New York, cut and edited the drum tracks together for the record, and once that was finished, unfortunately had to leave.

PAUL STANLEY: Working with Mark St. John on *Animalize* was a challenge. For all his ability, Mark could not play the same thing twice. We were used to having solos that were worked out and perhaps developed. When I was recording with Mark I found that there was no thread. To get something that followed a direction was very difficult. Sometimes there were notes or passages that didn't quite work so I would record little parts of my own and piece it together. Most of those solos were sung to Mark and worked very hard to get.

MARK ST. JOHN: I wasn't a KISS fan. I never had any of their albums. I was brought up on jazz and classical music. I was teaching at the time at a music store. I happened to get the audition for KISS and was asked to join. I didn't prepare at all for the audition. I had no idea what they sounded like. We played a country and western version of "Stairway to Heaven." Mostly we did a lot of talking. At first they didn't really want me in the band and I was gonna fly back to Hollywood. And then they said they wanted to hear me again in the morning. I was drunk the night before but I kind of pulled all the stops out and they hired me.

MARK ST. JOHN: The recording of the album went by really fast. We knocked it out in two weeks [author's note: his guitar work]. I've had a lot of training; I've had a lot of lessons. My approach with music is melody is most important. A lot of guitar players listen to other guitar players and they sound like other guitar players. I myself listen to different instruments, piano, saxophone, violin, and the way the intervals are stacked on the musical scale it comes out different so you don't sound like your next Van Halen, which is important to me 'cause you have to have an element of originality. At first, I got to play what I wanted to because Gene was doing his movie *Runaway*. Paul was in Bermuda with Lisa Hartman and Eric was in Florida. So me and the engineer were having a good time for about two weeks. Then they came back, heard it, and were disgusted with it because it was too much guitar going everywhere. So they erased everything and I was on kind of a leash after that. The rhythm tracks were already done by Paul. I just came in and doubled some of the parts, doing different inversions and voicings of the chords, and then played the lead. I'm happy that the band liked it and I'm happy that the fans liked it. It went Platinum in about two weeks and two or three albums before that, it took years to go Gold. It makes me feel good. I was frustrated a little bit, but it's all right.

MARK ST. JOHN: First of all, we barely knew each other. We'd only been together for six weeks. It was a lot of pressure for Paul because that was his first time at being a producer of a KISS record. It was as much pressure for me as it was for him. At the end of the sessions before Gene went off and did the movie, I played bass on a few songs. But before that Gene would be at the Hit Factory in New York and Paul would be at Right Track. They'd get on the phone and ask, "Can I use Mark?" "Can I use Mark?" So I'd be back and forth in a taxicab for two weeks, one studio to the other. Mitch Weissman played a little guitar and bass on the record, the guy who looks like Paul McCartney.

MARK ST. JOHN: Eric [Carr], God bless his soul, was a great drummer. Nice guy. We hung out together a lot. He showed me the ropes of how Gene and Paul were. He seemed frustrated a lot, he was being held back a lot. He wanted to sing live, he was always pushing for that. Gene the mogul . . . Gene is a hard person to characterize. He has so many different levels of intelligence. Music is just a small part of what he does. It's like an iceberg, the tip of the iceberg, but underneath is the big part. I think Paul runs the show as far as decision-making because when we did the album everything had to go through him for verification. He has a lot of responsibilities. I was close to all of them, but I'm the kid from Hollywood and they're all from New York. It was hard for me to adjust to their way of life.

ALLAN SCHWARTZBERG: I overdubbed drum fills on a few songs on the *Animalize* album. I think the songs needed that little kick and I think it helped.

MARK ST. JOHN: There are two songs on *Animalize* that I didn't play on. "Lonely Is the Hunter" and "Murder in High Heels." That's Bruce [Kulick] playing guitar, he's a very accomplished guitar player, very nice guy too. Gene was in one studio and Paul was in the other. They couldn't get me into both studios at the same time and the album had to be finished in a couple of days. Or maybe he did a better job, I'm not sure. I met Bruce for the first time when we were getting ready to go on tour in Europe. We were rehearsing at SIR Studios, he came in and I was just back from California after being diagnosed with arthritis. They had to take off in two weeks. They had seventeen concerts in the U.K. to fulfill and the pressure was on and they needed somebody to play. I had rheumatory arthritis. Before I joined the band I was playing violin concertos on the guitar, Paganini. When I got in the band, we were just playing two-chord diads and stuff. I think maybe it was the weather or the stress. Playing with a band, I'm a musician, I can do that. But it's dealing with the other twenty-two hours that is hard. It's their way or the highway with everything. I went to the best doctors in Beverly Hills and none of them really knew what was going on until I went to a rheumatologist and they said I had arthritis. It ran its course in about a year. What happened was my knuckles on my left hand, the three middle ones, were swollen up and my left kneecap and my Achilles tendon. So virtually I had to walk with a cane, I was always the last one in the limo and the last one on the airplane. It was a hard situation for both KISS and I. It was the biggest tour they were going to do in ten years. The album was their biggest and their guitar player was sick with arthritis. They'd call me every day from a different city to see if I was ready. But I still wasn't ready to do a full tour. But when they did come back to the U.S., I flew out and hung out with them for four or five weeks and watched Bruce play, even sat in a few times. I didn't even know if I was gonna play. It was sort of funny. I never rehearsed with the band. So they'd say, "You're gonna play tonight, Mark," and I'd go, "Okay." I didn't know what songs we were playing, I didn't know the arrangements, didn't know the key. I was just thrown out there in the lion's den in front of twelve thousand people. But it was all right. Then it was decided that we split our ways. It was hard for them. They couldn't continue with the two lead guitar players thing. They were telling the public lies that I was Bruce and Bruce was me type of thing. It was in the best interest for me to say goodbye. I left the band when they were in Terre Haute, Indiana. When I left, it was for medical reasons, it was amicable. They had to do what they had to do. If I kept on playing I probably wouldn't be playing now.

BRUCE KULICK: By *Animalize* Gene had moved out to California and was in full Hollywood mode. He was trying to break into that world and his attentions started to get split. Paul saw that and he just wanted to do the music. I think it did take its toll on Gene's songwriting. He didn't know who he was, the makeup came off and he still was a little confused, whereas Paul was this good-looking guy, chicks love him. He's doing his thing and Gene didn't mind. He knew he'd get his partner to pick up the slack. Paul may have resented it a bit but I think he also liked the responsibility. On *Animalize,* for example, it says "Produced by Paul Stanley."

JEAN BEAUVOIR: Watching Paul produce, he was very meticulous and clear in his vision of what he wanted to accomplish. Rock 'n' roll carries the illusion of people being fuck-ups. Paul never fell into that. I respected the fact that he could be so together and still maintain his rock star persona.

DENNIS WOLOCH: That's not my favorite album cover. The back cover was shot in a sand quarry out on Long Island in the early wee hours of the morning. It's not a bad cover but it could have been better. If I could do it again I probably would have done different things with those animal skins and I probably would have lit it differently. It's kind of flat. It's my fault, I didn't give the photographer enough direction.

★ "I'VE HAD ENOUGH (INTO THE FIRE)" ★

PAUL STANLEY: The song started with the guitar riff. Desmond started throwing out lyric ideas. Desmond will sit down, close his eyes, clench his fist, and shake his head back and forth and start singing great stuff. Very emotive, very descriptive, very thematic thoughts. And from there we got to the studio and the song was basically done. Eric Carr came in with the "Out of the cold, into the fire" part so it became an answer type chorus.

DESMOND CHILD: Paul and I wrote songs in all different ways. Usually it was me asking, "What kind of song do you want to write?" Then we'd just start and ideas would come and we'd let it happen.

★ "HEAVEN'S ON FIRE" ★

PAUL STANLEY: I was striving for simplicity. Desmond and I wrote that at his house. There were a lot of people who liked that song 'cause I've heard it since on a whole lot of albums with different titles. It was a track, in listening to it, where I did wonder if it was too simple. But I love it.

DESMOND CHILD: Paul taught me about the simplicity of creating the right chant like we did on "Heaven's on Fire." All the songs that Paul and I wrote together had simplicity, melody, and a kind of boldness. They're direct but they're clever.

MARK ST. JOHN: I remember doing the vocal tracking on that. We had to have all four of us in the studio singing one line and doubling it again and doubling it again until we had thirty or forty voices going. That was very interesting. I learned a lot about recording with those guys. I remember doing the video. I was in the hospital and a limo came up and pulled me out of the hospital. I put on my spandex and boots and did a twelve-hour shoot.

MITCH WEISSMAN: I was in the studio when KISS was recording *Animalize*. Paul's singing the vocal on "Heaven's on Fire" and he does one vocal take. He asked me, "How was that?" And I said, "It was pretty good." He said, "I think I can do it better, let me do another take." They run the tape back and Paul's doing his vocal exercises. He's doing that yodeling thing. They start rolling tape and he sang this vocal exercise one more time. As he finished it, the song kicks in and they kept it. It was one of those magical moments.

★ "BURN BITCH BURN" ★

GENE SIMMONS: [recites lyrics] "When love rears its head I wanna get on your case, I wanna put my log in your fireplace." The whole notion of sex is very silly for all the trouble we have to go through getting some nookie. It's so much ado about nothing. We all enjoy it and guys are willing to get in fights about it. And girls will do anything, torture us, lipstick and high heels to pique our interest.

★ "GET ALL YOU CAN TAKE" ★

MITCH WEISSMAN: Writing with Paul was a quieter process than writing with Gene. More introspective. We spoke about the basic idea for "Get All You Can Take." For that song there were about thirty verses, I kept writing verses after verse [laughs]. Then we edited it down. Paul took this jangly riff that I had and made it into a very bombastic, Led Zeppelin kind of tune. Then we wrote the stuff around it. We got stuck on the third line in the chorus. We called Gene at home and had a three-way conversation. Me in the bathroom, Paul in the living room, and Gene at home, and we're throwing lines at each other. I was surprised when Paul put in, "What fuckin' difference does it make?" I admired his ballsiness to say that.

MICHAEL JAMES JACKSON: The song had a cool Zeppelin groove. Although I was only involved in the cutting of the basic track for this song, I'd like to say that Paul is an extraordinary rhythm player. During the course of cutting tracks, I always relied on Paul for holding the groove down with the drums.

★ "LONELY IS THE HUNTER" ★

BRUCE KULICK: I went down to do a ghost guitar thing like my brother used to do with KISS. Paul was the only one there. He asked me if I had a guitar with a Floyd Rose on it, which I just did get. He played me some of the tracks, "Heaven's on Fire." He wanted to show me the vibe of the record. It went very quickly. It was a lot of fun, no stress at all. I did the solo on "Lonely Is the Hunter." I also played guitar on "Murder in High Heels," a couple of tag lines at the very end.

★ "UNDER THE GUN" ★

DESMOND CHILD: I think we started out with one of those chugga-chugga guitar licks. When we'd write I'd be at the piano and Paul would be playing guitar.

PAUL STANLEY: I'm a real tough critic of the songs I write. If it doesn't impress me, they aren't good enough. Ultimately you have to live with yourself and you have to live with what you do. I'm also tough on my singing. You can overdo it and go for something perfect and you lose the soul of it.

★ "THRILLS IN THE NIGHT" ★

JEAN BEAUVOIR: Paul and I became friends long before we wrote a song together. We had a common bond coming from such outrageous bands as KISS and the Plasmatics. We were opposites in a way. I was a black guy with a blond mohawk and him being who he was. But somehow we clicked as friends and creative partners. We both felt we had more to say than what people may have expected. "Thrills in the Night" was written very spontaneously while sitting on a couch in Paul's apartment. The music came quickly. We actually wrote the lyrics over the phone. It was very strange [laughs]. We would spend hours on the phone throwing lyrics back and forth. My playing bass on *Animalize* happened very casually. I had already played bass on a simple four-track demo of "Thrills in the Night" and we wanted to keep the same feel so I played bass on the actual recording.

GENE SIMMONS: It didn't bother me that Jean Beauvoir played some bass on the record. He had a much better feel for the tracks that he played on.

★ "WHILE THE CITY SLEEPS" ★

GENE SIMMONS: "While the City Sleeps" was written during the period when I got the acting bug and was working on the film *Runaway.* Paul was mostly caught in the studio trying to keep the ship afloat and I didn't put in anywhere near as much time as I should have. Mitch Weissman showed me a couple of chord changes. I used to read through *TV Guide* to get ideas for song titles and lyrical ideas. There was a movie called *While the City Sleeps,* a murder mystery from the '50s. The basic idea was there are people who only live at night. Garbage collectors only come out at night but also crooks, robbers, hookers, pimps. It's a different world.

★ "MURDER IN HIGH HEELS" ★

GENE SIMMONS: "Murder in High Heels" was the name of a paperback book in the '50s. They used to call it pulp. "Murder in High Heels" immediately sounded like a Raymond Chandler novel. Some detective with a cigarette over a dim light wondering about [adopts menacing voice], "She was a killer, a real killer. She was murder in high heels." I remember being attracted to that title. I always liked the song "Rice Pudding" by the Jeff Beck Group. There was a guitar figure in the song that was similar to "Open My Eyes" by the Nazz. I came up with a variation of that riff.

MITCH WEISSMAN: Gene was the sort of guy who would throw any idea against the wall and see if it would stick. For years, Gene's had a book where he collected phrases. One of the phrases was "Murder in High Heels." The two of us started strumming our guitars and we got into this funky groove. We'd walk around and throw out funky lyrics. Even some dumb lines were hysterical. Then the song came together.

ASYLUM

Release date: September 12, 1985
KISS / DESMOND CHILD—songwriter / JEAN BEAUVOIR—bass, background vocals, songwriter
DENNIS WOLOCH—album designer

PAUL STANLEY: Three stars. It was an attempt to follow up *Animalize,* but I don't think it was as good. Other than "Tears Are Falling" and a few other tracks, I think it was a reworking of past ideas.

GENE SIMMONS: Horrendous [album] cover. I probably feel the same way about that album as I do about *Animalize.* Two stars. In the same way that *Rock and Roll Over* and *Love Gun* were sister records. We were desperately trying to recapture who we were in the '70s but also didn't want to sound '70s, which was why we got a faster guitar player and tried to do some production stuff. But by the time *Revenge* came out, I thought we stopped playing games and let the material be what it is and not try to figure out what works and what doesn't.

BRUCE KULICK: *Asylum* was a chance for me to be there from the ground up. I don't remember much of the preproduction except doing some writing with Paul. But Paul and Gene produced the record and they would each have me working on stuff, I'd be working twenty-one days straight in the studio [laughs]. It drove me a little bit crazy but hey, I was the guitar player in KISS, why would I complain?

BRUCE KULICK: Writing with Paul and Gene is interesting. They're both very different and very difficult in their own way. Paul is always searching. If we're on it he's not sure and that drives me crazy. I had to sometimes tell Paul, "I think the song is there." Gene's more risky, he'll throw a hundred things at the wall and see what sticks. At times, I'd feel Gene and I had captured a song idea and then we'd lose the essence of a song because he'd be too experimental. Then again, it made me work harder too. Paul and Gene always compete. I think it's healthy. Gene and Paul are yin and yang, good cop, bad cop with each other. It is valuable for them. In some ways, the potential and the quality suffers because sometimes one gives in to the other when they shouldn't even be buying into that crap. They do compete and it makes them strive to be better.

DENNIS WOLOCH: The *Asylum* cover came about when Paul showed me an album cover he liked by a group called the Motels. They had a photo, which had paint on it. I took photos of them and I splashed a lot of paint around until somebody said, "That looks good." I think it's okay. It reminds me of an Andy Warhol thing.

★ "KING OF THE MOUNTAIN" ★

PAUL STANLEY: "King of the Mountain" is a fun track. But the '80s lacked a lot of depth for me. I just don't think that *Asylum* stands up to *Animalize*.

BRUCE KULICK: I had the vibe for the verse. I played it for Paul and we started fooling around with it, developing it. At that time, Paul came up with a lot of riff things that we turned into drum parts for Eric Carr. Then we got Desmond Child involved. I saw why Paul used him on "Heaven's on Fire" and why Bon Jovi got involved with him. The guy was very creative. We got busy right away. The song started to take shape and as soon as they had the concept of "King of the Mountain" it came together.

★ "ANY WAY YOU SLICE IT" ★

GENE SIMMONS: I was living at the time in Beverly Hills with Diana Ross. Across the street from her home lived Howard Rice, an engineer and a writer. He later wound up writing and producing a big hit for Patti LaBelle, "New Attitude." Howard showed me some of the chordal patterns, which I liked very much. I sat down and wrote the lyrics and melody very fast.

★ "WHO WANTS TO BE LONELY" ★

PAUL STANLEY: That was basically a groove and a riff. I think it's okay. A lot of those songs are reflective of a period where we explored and sometimes veered off of what our heart and soul was. Jean [Beauvoir] and I had reached a certain point where I thought someone else could tie up all of the loose ends and that was Desmond [Child]. Jean and I had written everything except for some of the lyrics in the chorus.

DESMOND CHILD: I love that one. Paul made friends with Jean Beauvoir and we wrote it with him. Paul wanted to do something that had a real R&B-ish rhythm.

JEAN BEAUVOIR: Going to see KISS perform a song that I was involved with in front of thousands of people was amazingly gratifying. I felt "Who Wants to Be Lonely" delivered an emotion that I still feel today when I hear it. It's very honest. It touches on the fear that so many people have about living a life of loneliness.

★ "TRIAL BY FIRE" ★

BRUCE KULICK: I gave Gene a demo for a song idea I had. It was really simple, it had an AC/DC feel. Gene responded to it right away. He originally had different words for it naming the song "Live Fast, Die Young" and then he changed it.

★ "I'M ALIVE" ★

BRUCE KULICK: Paul and I had the music for that. I remember showing Paul the verse, that fast riff. Before you knew it we had finished the music really quickly. Paul had a different lyric concept that later he wasn't happy with and that's when we brought in Desmond Child to write lyrics.

★ "LOVE'S A DEADLY WEAPON" ★

GENE SIMMONS: "Love's a Deadly Weapon" was a song that Paul wrote. We recorded four songs at Ace's home studio because he refused to come down to the city to record. This was around 1980. Mid-recording, we decided Bob Ezrin should produce our new record. Bob had the idea about a concept record. Bob latched on to a short story of mine called "The Elder" and so *The Elder* concept was born. Those songs we recorded at Ace's studio were pushed aside. When we started working on another studio record, I remembered parts of "Love's a Deadly Weapon." My songwriting style is if I like something I'll put it together Frankenstein style, a piece from here and a piece from here and create something new. I remember reading that the Beatles did it that way, with Lennon and McCartney sticking pieces of their own songs and brand-new songs would be born. That's what I did with "Love's a Deadly Weapon."

★ "TEARS ARE FALLING" ★

PAUL STANLEY: I was watching MTV and the Eurythmics were on doing "Would I Lie to You?" which reminded me of the beginning of Stevie Wonder's song "Uptight." I kind of took my interpretation of that riff and made it the basis of the song. I had also finished a relationship with a girlfriend and the song was pretty much about looking at somebody and knowing that it's over and that they're lying.

BRUCE KULICK: I remember Paul was really excited about the demo—he played it over the phone for me and I thought that it was gonna be cool. It's a simple song but very catchy. Paul played all the rhythms on that and then I came in and there was a nice meaty spot for a solo, almost an entire verse. I like those kind of challenges where you can develop a melody and just really create something that will lift a song. That's always my goal. And right away, I started to come up with some of the solo, the way it started off. I think it was Paul's suggestion to try some of it in harmony 'cause Paul was always very big on that. I made sure to stick in some flashy riffs. I was really pleased with the solo. It was the highlight for me, both the recording of it and the video we later did.

★ "SECRETLY CRUEL" ★

GENE SIMMONS: This is a story of an actual girl that I met. This was a girl who had pictures of me all over her wall and one almost life-size poster, that was sort of parallel to her bed. So it was lying on its side and there was a certain piece sticking out of the picture, a well-placed spot. When the lights went out you could let your imagination take over. So when nobody was looking, she was doing the nasty. I finally met this girl after seeing pictures and letters. The letters didn't lie, so the song was written after her. Her name shall be kept a secret to protect the innocent. In fact, she wasn't very innocent.

★ "RADAR FOR LOVE" ★

PAUL STANLEY: I'm proud of my roots and sometimes I let them show a little more. I'm not uncomfortable doing a song that clearly relates to another song, as long as it's not plagiarism. The song is a tip of the hat to Led Zeppelin.

DESMOND CHILD: I love all of the stuff we did. I think it's all classic. Paul is a really great lyricist, he loves wordplay, inner rhyming, and double entendres. His writing is direct and clever. All of that was very helpful to me in my writing with Aerosmith and Bon Jovi.

★ "UH! ALL NIGHT" ★

JEAN BEAUVOIR: "Uh! All Night" was based on a groove. I remember playing a bass riff and then Paul started to add a guitar riff. We would regularly jam in this way until we hit on something. With "Uh! All Night," we felt we had captured a moment. Desmond came in afterward and helped with the lyrics. He was very good at helping us deliver the essence of what we were trying to say in the best possible way. We were all single guys, running around and having fun with the opposite sex and the lyrics reflected that with a cleverness and a sense of humor. If people had to work all day, at least they could look forward to being able to "uh!" all night [laughs]. I played bass on the record. Gene and Paul liked the groove that I created on the demo and wanted to keep the same feeling.

DESMOND CHILD: I love that one. I don't think the title came first with that. It was the punch line. Paul and I always came up with songs, it was never a problem. Paul is very conscious of what KISS fans like and don't like. So the songs we wrote were always within the context of what a KISS song should sound like.

CRAZY NIGHTS

Release date: September 21, 1987
KISS / RON NEVISON—producer / DIANE WARREN—songwriter / ADAM MITCHELL—songwriter
MITCH WEISSMAN—songwriter / TOBY WRIGHT—assistant engineer
DENNIS WOLOCH—album designer

PAUL STANLEY: I'd give it three stars. I think it's a better album than it wound up sounding. I think it's a bit plastic-sounding. The material, and what it could have been, was better than what it turned out to be. It's not an album I'm in any way ashamed of though. I tried writing on keyboards especially with *Crazy Nights* 'cause I wanted to see how it would affect my writing.

GENE SIMMONS: *Crazy Nights* was one of my least favorite records of any of the ones that we've done. I thought it sounded thin. I thought we became a happy band although it sold a ton of records worldwide. If it was Paul, probably four stars, if it was me, two. It's much too happy. "Let's have a good time, I love you" makes me want to retch. I think the playing is okay and some of the songwriting's okay, but it's much too pop.

BRUCE KULICK: Ron Nevison produced that record and he was brought in as a song guy. He had a very strong track record in the '80s, especially with multi-Platinum artists. He also was good at getting the right song to radio. Paul was especially attracted to that concept and making that work. Although I felt Nevison left a really great song off that record, "Sword & Stone," which has been bootlegged. Desmond, Paul, and I wrote that song. Paul Dean of Loverboy covered it. It was also on the *Shocker* soundtrack. I had four co-writes on the album so I was very happy. Ron had a certain vision for the record which in some ways Gene was concerned about that it was a little bit too pop. What will happen when you work with a producer with a good track record is the record will be very cohesive. That was very clearly a rock-pop album for 1987. I think *Crazy Nights* is a very, very well done pop album for us. I liked that Nevison made sure that when I did a solo it took center stage.

RON NEVISON: I previously had worked on Led Zeppelin's *Physical Graffiti* and The Who's *Quadrophenia* as an engineer, that was all before 1975. I did the first three Bad Company records. So Paul [Stanley] was familiar with my work since the '70s. As a producer, I started to have success on CHR [contemporary hit radio] in those days with big hit singles. I had hits with the Babys, Dave Mason, Survivor. Then of course

Heart, I had two number one singles with them, big singles with Chicago and Ozzy Osbourne. Especially Heart and Ozzy. In 1987, by the time that KISS was ready to do an album, they were looking in my direction. Paul was writing with Desmond Child and he was looking for some hits too. They came up with a great ballad, "Reason to Live." I thought that song should have been a big single. And "Crazy Crazy Nights" was a big hit in England too. In America, the *Crazy Nights* album was a Platinum-plus record.

RON NEVISON: In those days you almost had to drag rock stars onto the pop charts. Being commercial was viewed as selling out. I was bringing outside tunes to bands like Heart and the Babys and having big success with that. Paul was savvy enough to be getting the kind of co-writers that would help him achieve. I thought that we had a couple of singles on the record. In hindsight, listening back I think I used a little bit too much synthesizer on the album. But I thought they had a fan base that was really fanatical and dedicated. I didn't want to piss them off, but I wanted to break new ground. I went with what was happening on pop radio for two or three of the songs. The synthesizer added a bigness to it. Only three or four of the songs have that. "Crazy Crazy Nights" has a synth in the chorus. In retrospect I would have mixed down the synthesizers a little bit more.

RON NEVISON: There was always Gene's brand of rock 'n' roll with KISS, which was different from Paul's brand of rock 'n' roll. Gene would send me twenty-five songs of which there would be three or four good ones. Paul would send me three or four songs and they were all good. Gene would send me everything and I'd weed through it. Paul would spare me that [laughs]. Gene would send me songs like "Burn Bitch Burn" [recites lyrics] "I wanna put my log in your fireplace." The two of them have a different brand of rock 'n' roll but it all works as KISS.

RON NEVISON: Gene wasn't the singer that Paul is. I don't think he's the lyricist that Paul is but he had something special, he had a distinction. There was no question in my mind, if I was going to have a pop hit with KISS then it would have to be with Paul. Paul was writing more of the catchy, commercial songs like "Crazy Crazy Nights." There was a bunch of really good songs like "My Way." "Turn on the Night" was a really cool song. I think "Crazy Crazy Nights" and "Reason to Live" were my favorites. They had a lot of great songs on that record. Paul was also writing with hit writers. Gene was writing with Eric and Bruce, and certainly they were good. It was great working with Bruce Kulick and Eric Carr, they were amazing. It was a truly great band.

RON NEVISON: It was an effortless record to make. I've worked with bands that had different writers and different lead singers. They're always trying to lobby me for their songs.

There was none of that with KISS. Gene wasn't terribly bothered that Paul had more songs on the record than he did. He accepted everything. You couldn't ask for more professional musicians. I mean, Eric Carr, what a drummer, God bless him. Bruce Kulick was a virtuoso, an amazing guitar player, he could do anything. And a great guy.

RON NEVISON: Maybe the record was too soft-sounding, maybe people expected KISS to rock more. Maybe that's my fault. It was a gamble to make them more pop. I had just had success with Ozzy a year before with "Shot in the Dark" from *The Ultimate Sin* album. I was on a roll a little bit and thought, "What the heck, it worked with everybody else." [laughs] I was confident in the songs. What I had going against me was the name KISS in terms of pop. They were listening, but they weren't getting it as KISS. It was a big hit in England because they don't have the bias there. In England, everything's cool. David Cassidy can be a star in England, they don't care that he's a TV star. This is KISS, they're not gonna be pop stars. That's what I was working against and I thought I could pull it off. So, in retrospect, if I had done another album with them it would have rocked more. Knowing what I know now I would have made an album version and I would have made singles versions that were mixed differently solely for pop radio. We just didn't do that then. I think the record turned out a little slick. If the record exploded with two big hit singles it might have done more damage than it even did being slick [laughs].

ADAM MITCHELL: The thing that stays with me about recording the whole *Crazy Nights* record was how good Bruce played in the studio. He always had great ideas and of course if someone else came up with one, no matter how difficult it was, Bruce would just whale on it right away like it was easy. I remember thinking if I went home and practiced for two hundred years I still wouldn't be that good.

ADAM MITCHELL: One of the reasons it was so much fun to be working with KISS is everyone in the band has a great sense of humor. Gene and Paul can both be very funny and Eric was absolutely hysterical. I don't remember any time, especially in the studio, when things ever got uptight or too serious. Each of the guys in the band really does contribute something special but when you have had the opportunity to see it from the inside, it really is true. Chemistry is what's made this band right from the beginning. Gene is a real fundamental, big-picture guy as you might expect, always concerned with how heavy it is. He really wants it to crunch all the time. Paul has great melody ideas. I remember how impressed I used to be at how fucking high he could sing and not blow his voice out. I mean touring, recording, demoing, he has as close to a bulletproof voice as I've ever seen.

TOBY WRIGHT: I had worked with KISS on the *Crazy Nights* album as Ron Nevison's assistant. That record was crazy. It was all about fuckin' 1987 guitars. Ron had just come off doing Ozzy. KISS were trying to ride on the wave. They did a fairly good job but it wasn't great.

DENNIS WOLOCH: Paul gave me that idea for the *Crazy Nights* album cover. He said, "I want you to try something with pictures in a broken mirror." I thought the idea sucked. I just thought it was a cliché but I couldn't talk him out of it. I had been given some poor ideas in the past that I had to take and make look good. I used Walter Wick, this great problem-solving photographer. If I tell him I want faces reflected in the mirror and it has to be a million pieces, he'll figure out a way to do it. And he did. We didn't have the band there. We had photos of the band reflected into a broken mirror that was on the ground. And we stood up on a great big mirror and shot straight down. The ones that I did initially had the mirror shattered in a billion pieces and their faces were reflected a billion times. Really sharp pieces and just jagged and dangerous-looking and I loved that. But Paul didn't like it because "Well, you can't see my face." And he made me make sure everybody's face size was equal so I had to go back and get equal pieces of broken glass and tilt them and reflect them so there was two thirds of Paul's face and two thirds of Gene's face.

★ "CRAZY CRAZY NIGHTS" ★

PAUL STANLEY: I was out one night with Adam [Mitchell], who I write with sometimes, and I said "Man, 'Crazy, Crazy Nights,' that's a great title," and he says, "Yeah." I went home and came up with the chorus and called him up. He came over in the morning and we wrote it. I get tired of people talking about anthems because if there is an attempt at writing an anthem then it's not really heartfelt. Then it's calculated. It seems everybody and their mother tries to write rock anthems right now. That's not what it's really about. Once in a while you'll be able to write one, but it's not because you try.

ADAM MITCHELL: We did the demos for "Crazy Crazy Nights" and "I'll Fight Hell to Hold You" at Electric Lady in New York. Both of the demos were great, especially "Crazy Crazy Nights" because we really had a lot more of the crowd singing in the background than ended up on the finished record. That was Ron Nevison's choice, not mine. On the demo, it sounded like the whole arena was singing along and I dug that. I always loved both those songs lyrically and of course "Crazy Crazy Nights" was a huge hit in the rest of the world, especially England.

★ "I'LL FIGHT HELL TO HOLD YOU" ★

PAUL STANLEY: It was real weird how that song happened. I came up with a riff. Bruce [Kulick] turned the riff into a song, and then the song got scrapped.

BRUCE KULICK: I know that Paul was tooling around with the big riff that's in the song but it had a totally different rhythm to it. We tried to work on it but never got anywhere with it. Then one day I approached the riff in a whole new manner and showed it to Paul and he liked it. Later that week I was speaking to Adam [Mitchell] and he said, "We worked on this great song, 'I'll Fight Hell to Hold You.'" And I went, "Oh really? What's it like?" And he described the song and how it has this riff. I said, "Oh cool, that's the thing I started with Paul."

★ "BANG BANG YOU" ★

PAUL STANLEY: Some of those tracks border just a little too close to kitsch for me. But it's a fun song. It works within its place in the '80s.

DESMOND CHILD: I love that one. Paul and I were always a fan of the Sonny Bono song "Bang Bang (My Baby Shot Me Down)." I think that song was definitely influenced by it.

★ "NO, NO, NO" ★

GENE SIMMONS: "No, No, No" is one of those car accidents. Bruce Kulick started fooling around with a lick. Whenever you plan something too much it tends to backfire. We tried to do something really fast because those fast songs were popular at the time. The lyrics came very fast. Most of the chordal changes came from Bruce. It's not one of my favorite songs. It has that "Who are you trying to impress" vibe in a musicality sense.

★ "HELL OR HIGH WATER" ★

GENE SIMMONS: That song started with Bruce Kulick. He came up with some chord patterns I liked a lot and the title was his idea too. I wrote the lyrics and melody, [recites lyrics] "Here I am all alone, been two days since you been gone."

★ "MY WAY" ★

PAUL STANLEY: That's just something I came up with on the keyboards. Since I don't know how to play the keyboards it was kind of interesting. I think that songs like "My Way" are in unnecessary high keys. I was so fascinated with my own range [laughs] that it really became more of a challenge to me to see how high I could sing. There's times where if I sang any higher dogs would run into the street. I like the songs on *Crazy Nights,* I just don't think sonically they're everything they could have been.

★ "WHEN YOUR WALLS COME DOWN" ★

BRUCE KULICK: I remember having a couple of verses, kind of Van Halen–like bouncy things. Paul liked it. We sat down and worked on it. I wasn't around when he finished the song with Adam Mitchell.

★ "REASON TO LIVE" ★

PAUL STANLEY: I wanted to have a ballad on the record but ballads are real touchy because when you do a ballad you have to make sure you're not wimping out. Because you write a ballad or because you write a song about relationships, that doesn't mean you have to write about being miserable and not being able to live without somebody. So we felt real good about it.

DESMOND CHILD: That song was mostly my concoction. It was more of a keyboard kind of song. Paul's contribution were lyrics. He wrote stuff on it but that was more my style than KISS's style.

★ "GOOD GIRL GONE BAD" ★

GENE SIMMONS: The record company [Mercury Records] president at the time was Davitt Sigerson, who had produced the Bangles. I was living at Shannon's [Tweed] apartment. Davitt and I sat and tossed ideas around. We wrote the lyrics together, but the melody and the chordal structure came from me. I had lost my way at that time. I thought we had become a pop band. "Crazy Crazy Nights" was a big hit in Europe but I never liked it. Even the record I didn't like. We just became what we looked like in the videos. Silly. Not as good as Bon Jovi, not as good as Poison. They were better versions of what we did. Better-looking guys, younger and thinner, who wrote better songs in that pop vein. When you're in the eye of the hurricane you're not aware of what's going on outside. While we were doing it we thought that's what you're supposed to be doing. There were very few options. We couldn't out-Motörhead Motörhead. We weren't as classic as Led Zeppelin. We couldn't really do the classic version of KISS without Ace and Peter. So we did the best we could with what we had.

★ "TURN ON THE NIGHT" ★

DIANE WARREN: I hadn't had a lot of hits at the time but Paul had a lot of belief in me. Paul has a good pop sensibility. Paul's a song guy. He's a good writer and he appreciates good songs. I had a lot of fun writing "Turn on the Night" with him. I thought it would have been a bigger hit than it turned out to be.

PAUL STANLEY: I'd known Diane before she ever became Diane Warren in capital letters [laughs]. When I was writing songs for *Crazy Nights* I very much wanted to write a song with her. Diane came up with the title and then we wrote it. She was a very big part of writing that song.

★ "THIEF IN THE NIGHT" ★

GENE SIMMONS: Mitch Weissman, the Paul McCartney look-alike in *Beatlemania,* showed me a chordal piece. I liked it and suggested a few changes. The song was originally written for Wendy O. Williams. She later recorded it.

MITCH WEISSMAN: "Thief in the Night" was a musical idea I had totally finished. Then Gene and I wrote the lyrics. Gene had the title and a lyrical idea, very much a film noir tone. It's like a mystery novel kind of song.

SMASHES, THRASHES AND HITS

Release date: November 14, 1988

KISS / DESMOND CHILD—songwriter

GENE SIMMONS: The *Smashes, Thrashes and Hits* stuff was remixed but nothing was re-recorded. I don't like the two new songs, "Let's Put the X in Sex" and "Rock Hard." But it's interesting when you do stuff your perspective isn't always clear. When we were doing it we said, "Gee, this rocks!" When you're a kid and you keep hearing these phrases will it stand the test of time you don't know what that stuff means. But in retrospect now you see that is the real gauge. Is it gonna work ten years from now? For a new fan I'd probably give it a higher rating. For the new fan, three stars, for the old fan, one or two.

PAUL STANLEY: *Double Platinum* came out ten years before it. We spent a lot of time remixing, remastering, making sure that all the songs were everything they could be. The whole idea was to polish things up and remix, but never to change anything. Having Eric [Carr] sing "Beth" was a natural. Eric's a great singer. The two new songs were written three days before we went into the studio. I think the new songs written for that blow. I think they really suck. But I think besides that, it's a really great album. Five stars.

BRUCE KULICK: That was another greatest hits compilation. Having Eric Carr sing "Beth" was torture for him. A knife at Peter was thrown for sure!

★ "LET'S PUT THE X IN SEX" ★

PAUL STANLEY: "X in Sex" wound up being a second-rate version of "Addicted to Love" by Robert Palmer. Working at that point with Desmond [Child] and Diane [Warren], who were both brilliant writers, I think we crossed a dangerous line into kitsch.

BRUCE KULICK: I was disappointed in the song because it was like flavor of whatever was going on in the music scene then. We rehearsed that and the other new song, "(You Make Me) Rock Hard," and cut them fairly quickly in New York. Gene didn't have much participation. It was another time where Gene let Paul do something because Gene was too busy with something else. It's funny, when we used to do "X in Sex" on the [KISS] convention tour, people would go nuts. Musically speaking, the song was very derivative of things that were going on in the late '80s.

★ "(YOU MAKE ME) ROCK HARD" ★

DESMOND CHILD: Paul and I wrote that with Diane Warren. I like that one. It was more of a joke in a way. We were saying, "Isn't that sexual inneundo obvious, you make me rock hard?"

PAUL STANLEY: I don't like it at all. It's just too contrived and kitschy. I don't even know quite honestly who played on that track. It wasn't one of our finer moments. It was really the height of us being overly aware of what other people were doing.

BRUCE KULICK: Paul was copying what was popular at the time. It's not a song to be proud of.

HOT IN THE SHADE

Release date: October 17, 1989
KISS / VINI PONCIA—songwriter/production assistance / LARRY MAZER—manager
ADAM MITCHELL—songwriter / TOMMY THAYER—songwriter

PAUL STANLEY: That was a good first step toward getting back home, not re-creating what we had done before, but reasserting ourselves, redefining ourselves. That's what we had to do with *Hot in the Shade*. We had to look and say, "Is there anything we are doing or is there anything that's come along in the last fifteen years that is unnecessary baggage? Let's get rid of it and make sure the basis of what we are doing is rock 'n' roll and guitars, because that's why we started this and let's not ever forget it." *Hot in the Shade* is an album that really goes back to what people think of as vintage KISS. It's much closer to that than some of the more recent stuff.

GENE SIMMONS: *Hot in the Shade* was a nice attempt. The songwriting was not up to par for me. I was busy making movies, but slowly but surely realizing that you can't do it all. Since we didn't have the time to work out the material, all of us separately were doing twenty-four-track demos and then sometimes playing on each other's demos. Whatever started to happen happened naturally. The demos started to sound good and it became the album. I'd give it two stars.

BRUCE KULICK: *Hot in the Shade* was my least favorite KISS album. There was nobody cracking the whip and everything was a compromise and ultimately the music suffered, although I think "Forever" is a big shining diamond on that record. We started off doing demos on twenty-four-track. It wasn't that expensive because we weren't in a studio that was that fancy. It wound up where we said, "Let's just overdub on the demos." I don't really like doing that, but I understand the process. We wound up working on the stuff and adding things and replacing things. I think we should have used an outside producer to come in and say, "You don't need fifteen songs and you guys don't have a clear direction here." Eric Carr was very unhappy during that record. There's even a song or two that have a drum machine instead of him playing drums and that bothered him. I think it was one of Gene's songs. And I didn't have the guts to say what I wanted to say. I wasn't really that pleased with the record although there were a couple of really shining moments.

BRUCE KULICK: With Gene and Paul producing the albums, they thought that no one knows KISS better than us. They felt we know our market and it seems very hard to be able to break beyond our market. That was very, very clear. It's like, we can spend a million dollars on this but we'll still only sell x. If we spend a half a million dollars on this and we do it our way, we'll still sell x. Is that ultimately the right way to do it? I'm not gonna judge. Do I feel that the music and the band suffered? To a certain extent and it's not because neither one of them are really talented or capable of doing a good job. But you compromise more because they have to deal with each other about it. And hence on *Psycho Circus* they brought in a producer. There was no way they were gonna have the stress of that without a [Bruce] Fairbairn.

LARRY MAZER: We put the tour together and came up with the stage show, the Sphinx from the album cover. It was one of the greatest live shows they've ever done including the reunion tour. We put together the tour and then we had a meeting about opening acts. Ace Frehley had a record out and I thought it might be really cool and help sell tickets even more if we had Ace as a support act. Paul and Gene were up for it and Ace turned it down.

LARRY MAZER: In thirty years of management, it was the most fun I ever had managing an act. Every day I would laugh. They were the best clients I ever had on a creative level. Where I had problems was the whole money thing where with Gene everything was money, money, money. To me, I always had the policy, cool first and money second. Every single thing was about money, which I had a problem with. To hire a manager after you've been in the business for twenty years, to have some guy come in and give you some really left-field ideas such as putting the makeup back on in the "Rise to It" video, doing a club tour, which is how we launched the *Revenge* record. A lot of artists—Pat Benatar, Cheap Trick, Peter Frampton—fought me on a lot of things that I wanted to do. There's not one idea in the years that I worked with KISS that I brought to the table where they said no. Not one.

★ "RISE TO IT" ★

PAUL STANLEY: *Hot in the Shade* is closer to our roots. The beginning to "Rise to It" is kind of showing where all that stuff started, which is slide guitar and blues. Real blues, not what the English were doing fifteen years ago, but where they got their stuff from. I wrote that with Bob Halligan. Bob very much had the basis for that song. It fit well. It felt authentic. It was fun to do that little bottleneck thing at the beginning of it.

BRUCE KULICK: I thought "Rise to It" was a strong song for that era. It was bluesy and catchy. It was another tongue-in-cheek title, of course. But the "Rise to It" video with Gene and Paul putting on the makeup again really confused me.

LARRY MAZER: After "Forever" we came with another rock track, "Rise to It." Ever since I'd gotten involved with KISS, promoters had approached me about convincing the band to put the makeup back on. Promoters would call me out of the blue and say, "What would it take to put the makeup back on?" KISS had been doing steady concert business but not over-the-top concert business. We talked about it, but I didn't believe in KISS putting the makeup back on. I said to them, "To me that's the endgame," which years later became the endgame [laughs]. To me when you do that you say, "Now this is the end." Once you do that you don't go backward. I always fought it, but there were obviously people out there that were curious for it. And since there's a whole new generation of kids who never experienced KISS that way, I thought, "Why don't we come up with something that harks back to that?" That's how we came up with the concept for the "Rise to It" video where Paul and Gene put on the makeup again. Paul and Gene were totally into it; it wasn't a heavy sell job. The concept was to create this flashback scenario where they were in makeup and were talking in the video about if in the future they could ever go without makeup. In the video Gene says, "Nah, it'll never happen," and Paul goes, "Sure it could, we're still KISS." It was a great video shoot. We had a lot of press coverage for it. The song didn't do that well. I went back to all these people and went, "See, at the end of the day, nobody really cares about these guys in makeup, because that video wasn't a real big video and the song wasn't a real big rock song." So it said to me that that period was over.

★ "BETRAYED" ★

GENE SIMMONS: "Betrayed" started off as a riff. It was originally kind of sexual. Then I remember reading a story about this guy who felt that life had owed him a favor and that he always felt things never went his way. Hopefully it's an up song. Things aren't so bad, at least you're not crucified. Everybody feels at some point that life has betrayed them.

TOMMY THAYER: I sat down with Gene and we worked on riffs, hummed melodies, and then Gene wrote the lyrics. I remember working out the chorus melody [sings], "Betrayed." I worked with Gene before, he had produced two Black 'N' Blue albums. We had done a significant amount of writing on those so it was comfortable to be around him. We did the demos at Fortress Studios in Hollywood. I remember Gene and I and Eric Carr cutting those tunes, "Betrayed" and "The Street Giveth and the Street Taketh Away." Eric was a great drummer. I really enjoyed playing with him, that's a real fond memory because he was one of my favorite people.

★ "HIDE YOUR HEART" ★

PAUL STANLEY: I got together with Holly Knight. The music came real quickly and then Holly came up with the chorus and the melody. Then I went back to New York and Desmond Child helped with the lyrics and part of the melody. It's real funny. The three of us wrote it together, but we were never all together. It's easy to write songs like that. That's just about life in New York and that's about things that happen to all of us. Maybe we all don't get shot, but getting into situations when two people are involved in love and relationships. When you start fooling around with people's pride and their heart, all kind of devastating things can happen.

DESMOND CHILD: "Hide Your Heart" and "Heaven's on Fire" are my favorite songs that I wrote with Paul. Paul had originally started the song and it was called "Bite Down Hard." We wrote it with Holly Knight, who also had a song with the same title so we changed it to "Hide Your Heart."

LARRY MAZER: I got hired after *Hot in the Shade* was done. The first single and video "Hide Your Heart" was already set for release. It was a very strong song. The problem was at the exact same time there were several other covers of the song that came out simultaneously, one by Ace Frehley, one by a girl named Robin Beck, and one by Molly Hatchet. That diluted the song a bit.

★ "PRISONER OF LOVE" ★

BRUCE KULICK: Gene turned "Prisoner of Love" into a shuffle and it wasn't. It was very frustrating for me. I had a really cool Def Leppardy plucking guitar thing, like "Domino" but slower. It had a great groove to it. I remember Gene pulled into the garage of the condo where I was living in his Rolls-Royce and said, "Bruce, I think we need to change this into a shuffle." And I was like [makes pained expression], "Oh no." In some ways I felt it did work, but I was already happy with the song.

★ "READ MY BODY" ★

PAUL STANLEY: Bob [Halligan] is a real good writer. "Read My Body" is a venture into rap. I'm never going to compete with Ice-T or Public Enemy or Tone Loc, but it's a cool song, good chorus.

★ "LOVE'S A SLAP IN THE FACE" ★

GENE SIMMONS: "Love's a Slap in the Face" is my philosophy about love. When you're hit by love it's like a sledgehammer hitting you, your horns come out and you just don't care what anybody says, the primal urge is there. There was an old song performed by the Crystals that Phil Spector produced, "He Hit Me (It Felt Like a Kiss)." And it was that sort of imagery I was going for.

★ "FOREVER" ★

PAUL STANLEY: You can trust your gut a lot of times. If it feels right in your gut, it's right. "Forever" was started and not finished because we couldn't quite figure out how to wrap it up. Michael [Bolton] split and since I started the song with him, you don't want to finish something without somebody. I was sitting with Vini Poncia and I just picked up a guitar and he said, "What do you have for the record so far?" I played him on an acoustic guitar just the verse and the chorus. He said, "You're there." We all knew it was a pretty good song. Friends are one thing, collaborating songwriters are another. I think you become friends as you are writing. If nothing else you have a friendship based on writing together. Writing songs together is almost religious. It's real cool because you are tapping into a part of each other that a lot of people don't know. You are showing each other a part of your perspective and outlook that a lot of other people don't get to see. You're sharing something real special. It is if nothing else the basis of a friendship.

BRUCE KULICK: My solo on that was originally done on electric guitar where I played the melody real sweet. It's very easy sometimes when you're in the control room to go "You know what, maybe we don't need that, maybe you can try a different approach." As soon as Paul started talking about a Led Zeppelin acoustic kind of guitar solo I said, "Okay, I get you, this is totally the other way." By the time he ran out to go get the track I was already in there laying down ideas and literally had the solo 95 percent there. It's an important song, people play it at weddings.

LARRY MAZER: I felt that "Forever" was a very strong song that had crossover potential. KISS hadn't really had Top 40 success since "I Was Made for Lovin' You." I wanted a song that could move a lot of units. We did a beautiful video with Mark Rezyka. The song was a smash at rock radio and then we crossed it over to Top 40 and it went to number eight on the *Billboard* charts. It was their first Top 10 single in many years. The success of "Forever" revitalized ticket sales for the *Hot in the Shade* tour. We had set up a tour right after "Hide Your Heart" came out and promoters were just not that enthused about it. So we pulled back and decided to wait to tour. I booked the tour after "Forever" was a hit and the tour did incredible.

★ "SILVER SPOON" ★

PAUL STANLEY: In the song I sing, "I always knew I would be somebody." And that's true. I always kept in my head that I would be somebody. I never felt like everybody else. I was fueled by the belief that I could make it. I'm a guy that is lucky that I pay the rent and everything is taken care of by playing the guitar. That's what I always wanted to do. I have my freedom. I can do things my way. I don't have to answer to anybody.

VINI PONCIA: "Silver Spoon" was our version of the type of rock-pop song Bon Jovi was doing at that time. Paul wanted to establish himself in the circle of successful songwriters at that time, people like Desmond Child, Holly Knight, Diane Warren. He felt he was as good as them. He wanted people to know he could write a really good rock song with a quality lyric and not just writing songs about fucking. From "Silver Spoon" to "Sure Know Something," what was good about the songs I wrote with Paul is that it was quality work. Good lyrics, strong melodies.

★ "CADILLAC DREAMS" ★

GENE SIMMONS: "Cadillac Dreams" was that pop, New York, R&B-flavored thing, which depending upon your taste may or may not have hit the mark. "Cadillac Dreams" was never recorded well by KISS. My demo is much better. Vini Poncia came to me with that title. When he was growing up in New York City, the sign of success in New York was a Cadillac. If there was an old ghetto building but a Cadillac in front of it that meant the people inside that building had made it. Cadillacs in those days went for $7,000. If your yearly income was $7,000, then that was a lot of money. "Cadillac Dreams" was about "Am I gonna make it?", the American Dream. But the track never worked. I wrote that with Vini Poncia. The songwriting style of the band tried to take in new influences. Clearly *Destroyer* sounded different because Bob Ezrin was around. When Vini Poncia was around the songwriting changed. We were open to bringing in different aesthetics. Yet it was always with Ezrin somehow that the band felt like a better version of KISS. I thought *Creatures of the Night* was good and Michael James Jackson was involved with that. But I think it had more to do with Paul and I just sort of forcing our way through it. Ace wasn't there to either torture us or keep us grounded in that original rock 'n' roll style. Peter was gone so we tended to get heavier and go off the deep end.

VINI PONCIA: I think the best song I ever wrote with Gene was "Cadillac Dreams." That was a song about a kid growing up who had Cadillac dreams. That song touched on how Gene felt, coming to America and living the dream. It resonated closer to something that he could relate to rather than writing a song like "She's So European."

★ "KING OF HEARTS" ★

VINI PONCIA: At that time, we were competing with all the Bon Jovi songs. Those were the kind of songs that set the template for what was going on at the time in rock 'n' roll. Paul loved the Bon Jovi stuff, he loved "Living on a Prayer." We felt that was the direction that the big rock 'n' roll bands were going in and if you wanted to compete radio-wise you were going to have write songs that were in the same vein. And "King of Hearts" is like that.

BRUCE KULICK: Vini [Poncia] started writing with Paul. I was a little concerned when Vini got involved with the songwriting, thinking he doesn't bring with him a vintage KISS sound. When I hear [Bob] Ezrin's name, I get happy. Most of *Hot in the Shade* were demos that became the record. I think it was a very compromised album. I don't have fond thoughts about many of those songs. Paul's intro was clever, but as a song it didn't do it for me. Paul was growing out of that Bon Jovi/'80s thing, but not really landing in the right era anyway. I think he was groping to find a direction. Most of the *Hot in the Shade* songs I don't feel happy about.

★ "THE STREET GIVETH AND THE STREET TAKETH AWAY" ★

TOMMY THAYER: I came in with the main guitar riff that's in the chorus. I started working with Gene on this riff. I remember going up to Gene's house, sitting around his dining room table working on this tune. I think we put together most of the music first and then Gene started working on the lyrics. He called me a few days later and he was really excited because he thought he had come up with some real significant lyrics that he was proud of. He compared them to be Mick Jagger type lyrics talking about the street. That's the thing I liked about the songs on the *Hot in the Shade* album, they weren't just the tits-and-ass rock 'n' roll songs, which I like too. The songs spoke more about life experiences.

★ "YOU LOVE ME TO HATE YOU" ★

DESMOND CHILD: Paul and I wrote it at the Sunset Marquis. I had written "I Hate Myself for Loving You" for Joan Jett. It's the same words, just rescrambled.

★ "SOMEWHERE BETWEEN HEAVEN AND HELL" ★

GENE SIMMONS: Vini Poncia and I sat down and wrote four or five songs. One of them was "Somewhere Between Heaven and Hell." That's Vini's title. We didn't feel Vini should produce *Hot in the Shade*. Although he did a fine job with *Dynasty* and *Unmasked,* it was a different kind of KISS. More poppy, more danceable, more R&B. We thought we'd lost a lot of the personality of who we were. The demo of the song is much better than the record, much heavier.

★ "LITTLE CAESAR" ★

GENE SIMMONS: The song had a Marvin Gaye title, "Ain't That Peculiar," although it was a different song. I said, "You can't call it that. Tell me some of your nicknames." Eric [Carr] said, "They used to call me Little Caesar when I was a kid." I go, "Guess what, that's the name of the song."

ADAM MITCHELL: Working with Eric [Carr] was always great. Eric was one of the funniest people I've ever known. It was impossible to be around him for more than two minutes at a time without cracking up. He was into Monty Python and all kinds of crazy voices and just really had a funny view of the world. And what a great drummer he was. His drum solo was my favorite part of KISS's live show. I worked with Eric on "Little Caesar." Eric had a lot of musical sides to him that people may not know about. He could get down and be real funky and you can hear some of that on "Little Caesar." One time during recording in New York we went out to an Italian restaurant and we ate way too much garlic. It hit us about two hours later when we were in the middle of doing vocals. Man, we stunk up the joint and singing across a mike from each other was brutal.

★ "BOOMERANG" ★

BRUCE KULICK: I think I was high when I wrote it. I had this fancy, fast riff and thought, "Whoa, this is cool." It was like AC/DC on speed. That song was definitely not to Paul's liking. He was against that kind of stuff. I thought that fast double-bass-drum thing fit for that era. Gene really liked it. Lyrically, Gene had the concept of a song about a girl that keeps coming back to him like a boomerang. As much as Paul hated it, we needed an up-tempo song for the album.

REVENGE

Release date: May 19, 1992
KISS / BOB EZRIN–producer/songwriter / LARRY MAZER–manager
VINNIE VINCENT–songwriter / DICK WAGNER–session guitarist

GENE SIMMONS: Four and a half stars. *Revenge* is probably the most satisfying record I've worked on since *Creatures*. It's one of KISS's better records because Bob Ezrin was involved. I'm not a guy that tosses around lots of easy praise. Bob is about as good as they come in terms of being a coach. He's really terrific that way. It's Bob Ezrin who brought all that stuff out from us. I am the one who pushed the idea of letting Bob produce one song first ["God Gave Rock 'n' Roll to You II"] because *The Elder* was not a good experience. Bob was not healthy. Even though there are a few songs on that album that I like, it was clearly a faulty record and Bob wasn't at his best. And before he started working with us I wanted to make sure that Bob is happening. I think "God Gave Rock 'n' Roll to You II" is one of the best things we've ever done.

PAUL STANLEY: Five stars. When you stop wasting time on things that aren't really worth your while, it's no coincidence that you suddenly come up with songs that are. I think a lot of it is that everybody realized how good it is to be in this band. But that there's also a big responsibility to being in this band, and that there's no time to jerk around. If you want to go off and do other things that's okay, but it leaves you less quality time to be doing what's supposedly the most important thing. I think everyone in the band had become very focused. I don't think it came about because of anything, except everybody realized that it was possible for Bruce Kulick to play better. It was possible for us to write better songs. It was possible to do all kinds of things. Eric Singer did some tremendous playing and also changed the chemistry somewhat of the band so it all felt right.

PAUL STANLEY: Bob [Ezrin] did an album that arguably is one of the best we've done and he also did the worst. He did two very important albums for us, one that helped us rise to the top, and [laughing] one that helped us crawl our way to the bottom. When we were talking about working with Bob, it was important for us to find out who Bob is now, because we were sure who KISS was. So we got together with Bob and the initial meetings were real good. First, we had to clear the air and make sure everybody understood the feelings about *The Elder*. Truthfully, the only profanity that ever got spoken in the studio [this time] was the word "Elder." When that was spoken everyone got nauseous. It was good that Bob was very much in agreement, then it was just a matter of us figuring out what it was gonna take to make a great album. We started by spending about three months writing, then getting together and throwing most of it away. You're on this perpetual treadmill. We went back to work, writing and going through it all over, and over, and over. Turning out a good album is easy. Turning out a great album is real difficult.

PAUL STANLEY: You have to check yourself to make sure that you're not writing "Son of Strutter," or something like that, and at the same time you don't want to deny who you are. And maybe what happened with *Revenge* was that we didn't deny who we are. We embraced it, but at the same time made sure we weren't just re-creating it.

BOB EZRIN: We were all lamenting about the loss of innocence that rock music had seemed to have gone through. We were looking back nostalgically at early KISS and AC/DC saying that this was the style of rock music that the audience was in most desperate need of. And also it was the style we most enjoyed playing, real bare-boned tough-ass rock music. What we did was go in with the intention of writing that sort of stuff. It was almost like stepping back in time from the minute we started working on the *Revenge* project. We reverted to our old roles, started telling the old jokes again, teasing each other in the old way, and reliving a lot of the moments we had shared in New York. It was very much like a family reunion. As well as having worked together we were very good friends and we kind of lost each other along the way and *The Elder* didn't help. In fact, for years after *The Elder*, Paul was really angry with me. And I can't say I blame him. I had been angry with myself for years after that period of my life, which was terrible. I had gone through a divorce, I had drug problems, I was just not a well person. We came back together, all three of us healthy and well directed, and it worked.

VINNIE VINCENT: I ran into Gene and Paul in A&M studios and we talked about some things. It was good to see them again, I hadn't seen them in a long time. Shortly after, I got a call from Gene asking if I would like to write for the *Revenge* record. I thought it was a great idea. "Unholy" came out great. "I Just Wanna" I liked a lot.

BRUCE KULICK: Gene got really focused for the *Revenge* album and wrote some great stuff. When we got to *Revenge* there were some songs where Paul might have only added one guitar later or didn't play at all. Ezrin made sure he got as much of Paul as he could. He played on "Domino." As a guitar player Paul's got a great feel, especially for KISS music. I liked working with Paul more so than Gene on solos. Gene would sometimes come up with something out of left field, but Paul was very clear about his ideas. But lots of times he'd let me go for it and then we'd fine-tune it, like the "Forever" acoustic solo. The *Carnival of Souls* record was a little more skewed where I might have played all the rhythms. Not on every song. On *Animalize*, I'm pretty sure Paul played all of the rhythm guitars. There's a couple other songs on *Asylum* that were Jean Beauvoir co-writes that there's a good chance that Paul possibly played all of the rhythms. There were even some songs where Gene would play rhythm guitar. Like on *Hot in the Shade*, Gene played rhythm guitar on "Cadillac Dreams" because I didn't like it. I said, "You've got a better feel for this, you should play it." "Little Caesar" is a song where I played all of the guitars and Eric played bass. It got handed around a lot.

PAUL STANLEY: I remember that Bob was incredibly hard on Bruce, which was a really good thing. Bruce would come in with solos and Bob would go, "These just aren't good enough." I think it shook Bruce up and made him forsake a lot of the technical frills he might have relied upon and gone more for primal emotion. A lot of that stuff was uncharacteristic for him but certainly is by far his best work.

BRUCE KULICK: Before *Revenge* we went through these pop kind of albums. We were just doing a lot of '80s rock. And all of a sudden we get Bob Ezrin involved and suddenly the riffs are getting a little tougher. Look at "Tough Love," look at "Unholy," which went through a million changes. Then all of a sudden we had a discussion about the lead guitar and it was like "You gotta kick ass." I said, "Okay." I'll just crank it up, take out a couple of distortion pedals, get the wah-wah going again, and really just get nasty. There was brutal honesty on that album, there was no compromise. It allowed something to happen that couldn't happen on *Hot in the Shade*. Ezrin will absolutely rip out your asshole, he doesn't care who you are. I gotta admit he's a little easier on Paul than he is on Gene. There's a terrific track of a song that never made it on *Revenge*. It was called "Do You Wanna Touch Me Now." Paul wrote it with the guy from Skid Row. Great track, we cut it, it has a solo but it never made it. I think Paul is closer friends with Ezrin than Gene is with Ezrin. When I say he wasn't as hard on Paul, he still didn't allow anything to get by. But with Gene he could really say, "That blows, forget it." With Paul it'd be like, "I don't think this is working." So you see there's a little different approach.

BRUCE KULICK: We cut half the record and took time off to write more to make sure we had great songs. Every KISS album should be approached the way *Revenge* was. The planets aligned on that record. It was a very hard record for everyone. Hard for Eric Carr, it was weird about "Who was gonna play drums?" But one thing was that everyone was gonna be brutal to each other and make a great record. I remember walking out of mixing *Revenge* going, "I can't believe that I'm involved with an album that I'm 99 percent absolutely thrilled over."

BRUCE KULICK: As a team player I always understood my role in KISS. Especially when I first joined the band I wouldn't want to tell these guys who were already successful what to do. Ultimately I began to voice my opinions the longer I was in the band. On a creative level, I remember having a couple of breakthroughs with Gene and Paul telling them I'm just trying to follow my instincts, I'm not trying to make a power play. I said, "I know that you guys have been fucked over by various other guitar players." But I did have to play the game in the sense that if Gene and I and Eric Carr wrote "No, No, No," even if it's not the greatest song in the world, at least there was an up-tempo song for the record. By the time we got to *Revenge* everyone took off the gloves and said what they had to say. We were really brutal and honest with each other. We wanted to make a difference. It had nothing to do with Eric [Carr] being ill. I think we saw we really had a chance to grab a moment. The *Hot in the Shade* tour proved a lot so let's make a difference and test the water with Ezrin, who was like a brutal schoolteacher. Fortunately everyone had their right foot forward even though it was a very tumultuous time with Eric getting sick. Where *Hot in the Shade* was a compromise of demos between Gene and Paul, which is not the way to do a great record, and *Crazy Nights* was totally Nevison's trip, with *Revenge* all the elements combined together to create magic. That's why I'll always rave about *Revenge*.

ERIC SINGER: I feel blessed and I don't take it lightly. I am the only person to ever become a member of KISS who was truly a KISS fan from the beginning. I was totally into KISS since day one. My first involvement with KISS was doing demos with Paul for the *Hot in the Shade* album. Because Eric Carr lived in New York, Paul called me up and asked me to play on a couple of demos. I had a good relationship working with Paul. I played drums on his solo tour. It became a natural progression for me to be in KISS. One thing I've noticed with bands like KISS is that you're used to working with the same people for a number of years and a lot of it's about a comfort zone. We know technically that a lot of musicians can come in and play the guitar parts or the drum parts for most bands. But it's really about how you fit into a band chemistry-wise.

ERIC SINGER: The first thing I did in the studio with KISS was "God Gave Rock 'n' Roll to You." That was a way for them to see how the chemistry and vibe worked again with Bob Ezrin. I was on tour with Alice Cooper while they were working on *Revenge*. They tried working with a couple of other studio drummers, Aynsley Dunbar was one of them, but it didn't work out with them. I had literally come home from the airport, walked into my apartment, and Paul Stanley was leaving a message on my answering machine. I picked up the phone and Paul said, "We need you to help us out on the recording of our new record." The original intention was for me to only play on half of the tracks and then have another drummer come in and do the remainder. I went right up to Gene's house and I was given a tape of some of the material to learn. That same night I went into a rehearsal room with Bruce and he started showing me some of the songs. We rehearsed three or four days and then we went into the studio and cut the tracks for half the songs. Ezrin said, "You should just have Eric play on the whole record because obviously the chemistry seems to be working." They knew I had to go on tour with Alice Cooper. Ezrin said they'd work on overdubbing on these songs and when I came back we'd finish recording the rest of the *Revenge* record.

LARRY MAZER: *Hot in the Shade* was a successful record, it sold about 600,000 to 700,000 records. It was a very successful tour. Then we sat down and I made what I call the "Mazer Proclamation," which was, "Now we have to take this to the next level." This is really where the competitiveness between Gene and Paul came out and this is where I had my work cut out for me. But I still got my way in the end. Since "I Love It Loud," which was the last single released from their final makeup album, *Creatures of the Night,* Gene had never had a song released as a single in the nonmakeup era. Never. I said, "Listen, we have to bring back the Prince of Darkness. That's what the real KISS fans want." When I had my very first interview to be their manager, I said to them, "If I'm going to do this, here's what has to happen. Gene, no more Simmons Records, no more managing Liza Minnelli, and no more sticking your tongue out onstage because to me people don't care about that anymore. With makeup it's one thing but without the makeup you look like an old man. There's no point to it." They agreed to all of it. When it came time to do *Revenge,* I said, "Now we've got to take this to the next level. We've gotta bring back the Prince of Darkness. Gene Simmons has got to come back and be a member of KISS." He admitted it in interviews that he had totally lost the path because he had stars in his eyes. During that period, Gene would say his ego and his desire to get into movies and records really took him away from the band, which is how Paul seized power at that point. Gene almost became a sideman in KISS. So then I said, "Gene, you've got to write some great songs." If you listen to the songs he wrote on *Hot in the Shade, Animalize,* or *Asylum,* they really were garbage. He played me the demos for "Unholy" and "Domino," which I loved. The next step was we had to make a real great-sounding record. I had a lot of complaints about *Hot in the Shade,* which they produced themselves because they wanted to save a lot of money. They had a huge deal with Mercury but the more money they could put in their pockets is all they cared about. So *Hot in the Shade* they produced by themselves. I thought for the most part it sounded very average. There were three good songs and twelve pieces of crap. The three songs were the singles we released. I said, "Look, we have to make *Destroyer,* Part Two. Every single song has to be great. And we've got to get a sound that's contemporary." They had done "God Gave Rock 'n' Roll to You II" with Bob Ezrin. I said, "We have to get Ezrin to do the whole album. We've gotta recapture the *Destroyer* vibe." We had a meeting with Ezrin in L.A. and he agreed to do it. We went in and did the record. Next to *Destroyer,* and *Love Gun,* I think it's the best KISS album song for song that they ever released.

LARRY MAZER: I told the guys, "Look, we have to start with a Gene track and it's got to be a metal radio track. It doesn't even matter if it gets played ever on AOR rock stations. We need a metal radio hit to really set the pace." Gene had changed his image. He grew his hair long. He had that goatee. He was starting to wear really heavy metal outfits onstage. He looked like the Prince of Darkness. I said we have to start with "Unholy." Then I said, "Then I wanna follow it up with 'Domino.'" That's when I could tell that Paul really had a problem. Although Paul never said it, I could tell it bothered him because he had always been the front man. Gene's the one who really expressed it to me saying, "We have to go with a Paul song second." I said, "Why? Let's drive it home." He goes, "No, we have to keep the peace." We picked what I thought was the heaviest Paul song on the album, "I Just Wanna." When we finished the European tour we went back to England and did both videos with a guy named Nick Morris, who had done a bunch of Cinderella videos. We did those videos and we went with "Unholy," which became a big metal radio song. To me it was a real evil video, it really brought back the image of the evil-guy Gene Simmons. Then we came with "I Just Wanna." In retrospect, I should have really fought tooth and nail. To drive it all home, everybody says to this day that we should have gone with "Domino" as the second single, which we should have. But again I thought "I Just Wanna" was a little stronger. It wasn't the typical pop KISS Paul Stanley song. The video was kind of edgy. "I Just Wanna" came out and it did decently at rock radio. Then it came time for the third single and we went with "Domino." The song became a real crowd-pleaser. At that point the record was selling less than *Hot in the Shade*. It went Gold, but it wasn't really kicking. I am shocked to this day that *Revenge* is not a Platinum record. I told the guys, "Let's go with the ballad"—"Every Time I Look at You"—which I thought was just as strong as "Forever." Did a great video with Mark Rezyka. The expense of promoting a Top 40 record is so expensive that I think Mercury internally took the position of "We spent enough money. We think the album is played out. We're not going to spend another couple of hundred thousand." They just didn't get behind it, which I think is a total shame. I think the song is a smash. We were all pissed off, which started the problem of the relationship between the band and Mercury. Also, at the same time I was going through the exact same problems with Cinderella in that the label had changed presidents and there wasn't the "Let's bring it home" attitude like there was with the previous president. And I think it really affected Cinderella on *Heartbreak Station* and it affected KISS on *Revenge*. The label just didn't go the extra mile and it's a shame.

LARRY MAZER: I always try to find unique ways to launch records. I try to find event launches, which you can only do with big bands. I said, "Look, let's do something nobody's ever done before. Let's go do a club tour." So I booked thirteen clubs from San Francisco to New York including the Trocadero in Philly and the Troubadour in L.A.

LARRY MAZER: Eric Carr got sick and he was not gonna get better. I don't think anyone knew he was going to die so soon. The band had to move forward. They used him in the "God Gave Rock 'n' Roll to You II" video out of respect. We sat for hours at Gene's house talking about the situation. They were heartbroken. I said, "We've gotta move forward." The momentum from *Hot in the Shade* was so strong that I felt we've got to get back in there with a new record, a new tour. It was obvious that Eric would not have the stamina to do a tour. The decision was made, which management was clearly a part of, to replace him. I'm sure people will look at it as cold-hearted but the fact of the matter was he was very ill. Everybody feels bad. I feel bad to this day but a decision was made which was not done in any malicious or mean-spirited mentality. Unfortunately Eric was not going to make it and KISS had to carry on. I know they have been criticized over the years for being insensitive. This is one time where I have to say that this was a very hard decision, but it was a decision that absolutely had to be made. Paul and Gene can in no way, shape, or form ever be treated as bad guys on that decision.

ERIC SINGER: It was an unusual time because I wasn't really a member of KISS. Everybody knew that Eric Carr was very sick. I think they were thinking if Eric wasn't better by the time they went on tour, they'd have another drummer fill in on the tour. I basically took the attitude that I was doing the album as a session player but I also realized if Eric's condition would unfortunately worsen, there's probably a good chance they'd ask me to play drums for them. The earth doesn't stop spinning if one of us dies as horrible as it is. I don't mean that in any kind of cavalier way. It's just the reality of life. KISS has been one of these bands that are survivalists. Even if it looks like they're drowning, somehow they're able to stick a straw out of the water and still keep breathing. That's the way I look at it. Sometimes bands have to make tough choices.

ERIC SINGER: I think *Revenge* is a well-produced, well-written, and well-executed record. Had that record come out a couple of years earlier I think it would have been a really big record. That was one of the few times that critics and fans both liked a KISS record and embraced it. The critics were actually giving KISS props at the time. I think there was also a hint of the old KISS about our look at the time because everyone was wearing black and more leather. It was a streamlined, tougher look. I think it's the best Gene's ever looked, in or out of makeup.

LARRY MAZER: We did the tour, which had the Statue of Liberty centerpiece. The tour didn't do as well as *Hot in the Shade*. I think bands like KISS were being affected by the whole grunge, Nirvana thing. It affected Cinderella, it affected Poison, and it affected KISS even though we had made a heavier record. The tour did well but it didn't make what *Hot in the Shade* made.

LARRY MAZER: We were trying to come up with a cover. I wanted something very progressive. My hero for album covers is Storm Thorgerson, he did all the Pink Floyd and Led Zeppelin album covers. I knew he would be impossible to get and would never do a band like KISS. Hugh Syme was the American Storm Thorgerson. He did covers for Rush, Megadeth. We flew him to L.A. and the idea was we wanted something heavy. So the idea was to get the side of a battleship with bullet holes shot in it and the holes were bleeding. And that was the *Revenge* cover. The band loved it. To this day, I think it's a great, classy-looking cover.

★ "UNHOLY" ★

GENE SIMMONS: I got the idea for "Unholy" from a song that Adam Mitchell wrote that Doro Pesch recorded called "Unholy Love." I just loved the word "unholy." I came up with most of "Unholy" including the title. I finished the demo originally and came back with the "Unholy" chorus. Vinnie stuck in some of the lyrics. He twisted the song inside out. Vinnie and I wrote the lyric together.

★ "TAKE IT OFF" ★

PAUL STANLEY: I wanted to write a song for the strip clubs, a song that would be great for the dancers to take off their clothes. "Lick It Up" had been used in strip clubs. It wasn't intentional. I thought, let me write something that is a celebration of strip clubs and these amazing-looking women strutting around. It was more my homage to the hardworking women in the strip clubs.

ERIC SINGER: That's the only song I didn't play on the record. It was getting late in the day and I cut the track. I knew my drum work wasn't great. I was leaving the next day on a European tour with Alice Cooper, Ezrin felt it could be better and so Kevin Valentine came in and played drums on "Take It Off."

★ "TOUGH LOVE" ★

BRUCE KULICK: We had a rough time deciding what key to do "Tough Love." Since I wrote the main riff in the song, I said to Gene, "Do you wanna learn this?" And Bob Ezrin said, "Why don't you play it for now." And I did. And then he used me on a couple of other songs like that. I played bass on "Every Time I Look at You." I also played bass on "Forever" from *Hot in the Shade* and maybe one or two other Paul songs from that album. I do a damn good imitation of Gene. But Gene is a real great bass player, very creative. But if the bass wound up in my hand I was doing my version of Gene, using certain phrases and the attack. I don't think Gene cares about any accolades about his actual musicianship, which is unfortunate because I think he's always been extremely creative on the bass, although he does have to work at it. He cares much more about a lot of other things.

★ "SPIT" ★

GENE SIMMONS: I came up with the title "Spit," which came from the term "swapping spit." Then started tossing around the idea, "It don't mean spit to me." It's another way of saying "shit." I was writing with Scott Van Zen. I told him, "I have an idea for 'Spit' and I want to rip off an old Fleetwood Mac song called 'Green Manalishi.'" There's a guitar lick that starts off at the beginning and everything stops while the singer sings. So I ripped off old lyrics I had for a song called "Mongoloid Man." [recites lyrics] "I got no manners and I'm not too clean, I know what I like if you know what I mean." Scott sat in front of me with the guitar and I'd sing out the riffs. Those were all horn lines. When I think in terms of guitar or bass riffs they're horn lines.

BRUCE KULICK: Putting in a bit of the "Star-Spangled Banner" in the solo of "Spit" was me thinking how everything had to be really extreme and wild for the *Revenge* album. Since there was that stop in the song it felt right to do it.

★ "GOD GAVE ROCK 'N' ROLL TO YOU II" ★

BOB EZRIN: For "God Gave Rock 'n' Roll to You," we were both creating a song for a very cool film [*Bill & Ted's Bogus Adventure*] and also experimenting with being back together as a team. Gene and Paul and I took up exactly where we had left off in New York—like family more than friends—and were enjoying working together right off the bat. Eric Carr was battling his terrible illness and could not play on the record, though he did come in to sing backup vocals. Eric Singer was brought in to take his place and this was the first thing he did with KISS. He was very nervous at first but soon fit right in. He is a wonderful drummer and a gentle and kind soul. We were instantly comfortable with him and soon made the decision that this unit—Eric, Bruce, Paul, Gene, and I—would go on to make another KISS album together. The most poignant part of this session was when Eric Carr arrived. He was visibly weakened by his ordeal, but in very good spirits. He showed off the scar on his chest and referred to himself jokingly as "the dead guy." His pure, high voice was an important part of the breakdown section of the tune. It gave it a special humanity and I cannot hear this section without envisioning his face tilted upward toward the mike, filled with joy at being alive and in the studio again. It was the last time I would see him.

PAUL STANLEY: We were asked by Interscope Records if we would do that song. The truth about that song is nobody has any recollection about the original version except for the chorus. If you listen to Argent's version, I don't know what the hell the song was about, they're singing about flowers, trees, and snakes. We told the label that we'd do it but we'd have to rewrite it. It's a track I'm very very proud of.

★ "DOMINO" ★

GENE SIMMONS: "Domino" happened very fast. I sat down and wrote it almost linear. "Domino" sounds like a cross between ZZ Top and something else. I had the title first. I came up with the chordal patterns and then scatted some melodies and then wrote the lyric last after the track was done. I didn't have time to demo the song so I brought in Silent Rage, the guys that were on my record label, and I showed them the arrangement, told them what the parts would be, and let them record it. In fact, the version that is on the box set is Silent Rage's version, which is very close to KISS's recorded version.

★ "HEART OF CHROME" ★

BRUCE KULICK: "Heart of Chrome" is a great track. Gene and I were kicking around a song called "Chrome Heart." Our track didn't get off the ground and all of a sudden Paul came in with "Heart of Chrome." On *Revenge,* the stakes were higher and we were more openly brutal with each other about everything. The gloves were off.

PAUL STANLEY: The original "Chrome Heart" was a Jim Steinman song and that's where that title came from. It just twisted around nicely into "Heart of Chrome" as opposed to "Heart of Stone." It's a track that I'm real proud of. I like the arrangement and the parts. Anything that's on *Revenge* has Bob Ezrin's stamp all over it.

VINNIE VINCENT: I left during the writing of "Heart of Chrome" so I wasn't there at the finishing stage. I think that song could have come out a lot better.

★ "THOU SHALT NOT" ★

GENE SIMMONS: I sat down with Mark Damon from Silent Rage and said, "Let's write a song like Humble Pie's 'I Don't Need No Doctor.'" It has three chords, A, C, D, which is also the chords to the Montrose song "Rock Candy." We fooled around with the time signature. I suggested a few chordal things and then sat down and wrote the lyric. I got the title when somebody told me they'd seen a girl group that really sucked and they were called Thou Shalt Not. I immediately said, "What a great name for girl group but especially what a great song title." Once I had the song title, the song wrote itself. I've always had a very combative view of holier-than-thou figures whether they're political or religious. Priests always shake their finger in your face and say you shouldn't do this or that. My first question is, "Who died and made you king?" So the notion of this priest hypothetically talking to me [recites lyrics], "Kindly reconsider the sins of your past, I said, 'Mister you can kindly kiss my ass.'" I'm the arbiter of my own taste. I don't need to check in with anybody to see if it's okay if I enjoy life. "Thou Shalt Not" is a nice middle-finger gesture to somebody with a collar who thinks that he is my judge and jury.

★ "EVERY TIME I LOOK AT YOU" ★

PAUL STANLEY: I love writing ballads. I love writing memorable tunes. I come from playing an acoustic guitar. For me, it's always about the simplicity of the song rather than the production. "Every Time I Look at You" is a great song. I still sit around in my house sometimes and play it for somebody. It was clearly the right song at the wrong time. When the record company didn't really give it what it needed, and when it didn't meet with the response that I had hoped for, I realized that there are a lot of things in life that are beyond our control and that's one of them [laughs].

DICK WAGNER: I played a solo on the song. I was out in Los Angeles and KISS were recording. Bob [Ezrin] called me in to play on it. I think Bruce had tried to play on it but didn't come up with anything that was good enough or more appropriate.

★ "PARALYZED" ★

GENE SIMMONS: Bob Ezrin and I wrote that together. Most of it was mine. Bob came up with the title and some of the melody. Bob was steering me, "Try that." I prefer the demo over the album version. It sounds more the way I sound like on "Domino," low voice, more matter-of-fact, spit-it-out-of-your-mouth kind of stuff. Bob brought down a black rapper to rap on it. He actually sat down and wrote a rap in the middle of the song and Bob tried to get 'em to rap in the middle of the song and do this guy's lyrics. It never worked out.

★ "I JUST WANNA" ★

PAUL STANLEY: The song's similarity to part of "Summertime Blues" was not conscious but was organically part of the song. It could have easily been "Black Dog," or "Green Manalishi" by Fleetwood Mac. It was just the idea of having a vocal and a guitar part that answer each other. I love the song. I love the "wake up baby, don't you sleep" breakdown in "I Just Wanna." But I love almost everything on *Revenge*. It was great to be in the studio with Bob [Ezrin].

BRUCE KULICK: As soon as I heard it I thought they took the vibe of a Who song [the cover of Eddie Cochran's "Summertime Blues"] and turned it into a really cool *Revenge* song. I liked the play on words in the chorus. It sounds like Paul is gonna say "Fuck" but he doesn't. That was really clever. Everything on *Revenge* was a step up from *Hot in the Shade*.

★ "CARR JAM 1981" ★

GENE SIMMONS: Eric, bless him, was one of these weird guys, even though he played drums, he taught himself how to play guitar. Within six months he was fooling around with it. He would walk in with these tracks with him playing bass, drums, and humming melodies. He put in a lot more work than Ace at the time. This was written around *The Elder*. It was one of those bits and pieces that was never finished. It was left as is. Bruce added some guitar and we included it on *Revenge* as a tribute to Eric.

BRUCE KULICK: I heard "Breakout," which was on Ace's solo record. That's what "Carr Jam" became. Eric and Ace jammed on that and later it became a song. It was a little eerie doing that track. It was also one of the first things I recorded after Eric's funeral. I enjoyed the fact that I got to rip a bit and it showcased Eric's drum work.

ALIVE III

Release date: May 18, 1993
KISS / EDDIE KRAMER–producer / LARRY MAZER–manager

PAUL STANLEY: I'd give it three stars. I'm very proud of it. Does it capture the magic of the first two? Gee, I don't think *Godfather III* does but if you saw *Godfather III* you'd say it's a good film. If you see it next to the other two it's got mighty strong company. On *Alive III* I think the songs were played very, very well, I think the performance is great, and I think the spirit on that album is fabulous.

GENE SIMMONS: Three stars. *Alive III* was with a different lineup. It's clear to me there's better musicianship, we're singing better and the songs have a better feel. But there's no denying that rock 'n' roll is this kind of primitive music that often is loved more for its primitiveness, not for how well the songs are played. I like *Alive III* but I know it doesn't have that kind of primitive innocence that *Alive!* has.

LARRY MAZER: I told them partially through the *Revenge* tour that it was time for another live album. It had been fifteen years since *Alive II*. I said, "We have all this new material. Let's do *Alive III*." We brought out Eddie Kramer, who had done the first two live albums. We had Mark Rezyka direct what became *KISS Konfidential* and filmed and recorded *Alive III*. The record went Gold. Nobody cared, which blew me away. I guess I misread what people wanted. To me it was time for *Alive III*. We launched it by doing a nationwide record-signing tour.

ERIC SINGER: *Alive!* is always going to be the album by which all KISS records will be judged. That record stands on its own, you can't top it. Looking back on *Alive III*, some of it's cool, some of it I don't like. I tend to approach the songs differently now. I tend to play them now much more simplistic and more straightforward.

ERIC SINGER: They tried to do everything like they did the two prior live albums, working with Eddie Kramer, recording in Detroit, Cleveland, and Indianapolis. I don't think the shows were recorded that well. It could have sounded a lot better if it was recorded differently.

EDDIE KRAMER: I think it was Paul's idea to keep the historical aspect of our relationship together. I was honored, and very pleased to do it. It was recorded in Cleveland, Indianapolis, and Detroit. KISS had a huge backlog of material, which I hadn't worked on. They wanted to do a live record and go back and try and recapture some of that earlier stuff that we had done together. They were very much in charge of what they wanted to do on that record. There was a lot of fixing to make things just right. I would have been quite content to leave some of the mistakes in. It's not a question of honesty, it's a question of personal preference. I would have preferred to have been left alone to do my thing, fix up a couple of notes here and there and let me mix it instead of trying to make it something that it wasn't designed to be. It's too perfect. A live record is supposed to be a live record. I thought some of the overdubs were unnecessary, quite frankly. It's a decent record. I would have preferred it to have been more spontaneous.

EDDIE KRAMER: From the early days to now, Paul has emerged as the strongest musical leader and I think the whole band of course over the last fifteen to twenty years have improved as musicians. They're very good musicians today. I think Paul had a kind of a sensitivity that Gene, Ace, and Peter didn't have. My relationship with the band is a great one. I still love them in spite of all the craziness. That's probably why I still love them [laughs].

BRUCE KULICK: I love Eddie Kramer but I gotta admit there were a lot of problems with the audience track and there were problems with how he recorded certain things.

Again, Paul and Gene were pretty critical about the live tracks. I can say one thing for sure, the drums, most of the bass, some of the rhythm guitars, some vocal things were from the actual performances. And then a lot of the stuff was just created in the studio. I was along for the ride and I was not gonna make a stink of it. Not with Eddie Kramer either. Eddie is a good friend of theirs and a very well respected guy. I wasn't gonna say, "What are you nuts?" They wanted to make it right. I gotta admit anything that I redid I did it in one take as if I were doing it live. I remember I had to repair the first note in "Forever," you know the low D note, I just dropped that in. When it came to me I tried to do as little as possible without fighting them. I know that Paul had to do some of the raps again because they weren't down right. He obviously did some vocals again. You can tell that.

ERIC SINGER: For the record, the whole *Frampton Comes Alive!* album was done in the studio. Most people don't know that. Most people don't care, it's still a great record. On *Alive III*, the drums are completely live. The overdubbing was done if you hit a bad chord or a vocal line was sung badly. In my opinion, if you're going to put out a live record you should record as many shows as possible and take the best versions of each song. Let them have the mistakes on it. I have some bootlegs of KISS shows in '92 when we first went out on the club tour that sound better than *Alive III*. I like how the bootlegs sound. I think they sound raw and it's the real deal.

MTV UNPLUGGED
Release date: March 12, 1996
KISS / DANNY GOLDBERG—president of Mercury Records

PAUL STANLEY: I'd give the *Unplugged* album three stars. I'm very pleased with it. The point on that album was not really to prove anything to anybody or win converts. It really was us, maybe for ourselves, showing how good those songs are. We did them during the KISS conventions. So many of those songs were written on acoustic guitars, they were written in a much more simple fashion than they're played. The philosophy has always been, if it doesn't sound good on one guitar it's a shitty song [laughs]. "Sure Know Something" is one of my favorite songs on that album. *Unplugged* was the perfect place to showcase our songs.

ACE FREHLEY: I only worked on a few songs. It was pretty cool. I had fun playing "Beth" acoustically. Eric [Singer] and me have become very close friends. I don't like to rate my own work because I never think I'm playing well enough. All I can tell you is my favorite KISS song is "Deuce." My least favorite is "I Was Made for Lovin' You" [laughs].

GENE SIMMONS: I'd give it three and a half stars. I quite like that album. Why? Again, language is limiting and music is an emotional connection, it either connects with you or it doesn't.

PETER CRISS: I'd give it a four. Although I didn't play on many songs, they really got this acoustically pretty good. That night was a magic moment for me. I knew immediately when Ace and I walked out that this is it, this is really the shit. And I felt real cocky and I felt scared but I felt at home. It was like, this is the way it really should be every night of my life. It was wonderful.

ERIC SINGER: That was one of the coolest things I got to do in the band. It finally showed people that without the makeup and smoke and mirrors that we actually could play half decent and we could sing half decent. MTV heard about the buzz from the KISS conventions and they came out to one of the conventions in Detroit to check it out and then they decided they wanted to do something.

BRUCE KULICK: The *Unplugged* show made them break bread and make amends with Ace and Peter, which was a long time coming, especially because Ace and Peter certainly weren't having the kind of success that they'd like to. And even if KISS was considered to be coasting along with Eric and I, it was still very profitable compared to where they were at. They were at a point where they should all talk. I wasn't really privy to all the behind-the-scenes stuff. I know that everybody worked very hard to make the *Unplugged* show an event. And it was, it was really special. The rehearsals were a little odd but everybody went out of their way to make everyone feel comfortable. The actual show was great. Knowing that I was gonna be on MTV and millions of people would see this made me very nervous, but I was also confident that I would play well. But I'm a real perfectionist, so I really wanted to play my heart out. The whole thing about the *Unplugged* thing was to show that KISS wasn't about flash bombs and volume and pyro and loud amps, the four of us could play. And there's these great classic songs. We were picking real interesting material too. The majority of that *Unplugged* performance is with Eric and I in the band. I think we really kicked ass on those songs, they came out great. All of us really wanted to make the show different. With us playing acoustically at the KISS conventions, I learned more KISS songs from being at the conventions than being in KISS all those other years. And that's 'cause kids would scream out titles and I'd watch Paul and Gene struggle through it and I could follow along because I'm quick that way. Next thing I know I'm going, "That's great, we should do that. We should do something from your solo album, Paul." I loved that we could finally do a Beatley kind of thing with Gene's song, "See You Tonite" and that we could do "World Without Heroes" and let Paul take the solo. That's when the version of KISS that I was in really worked as a band. And what happens is when you all contribute and the forum is open for everybody to say their peace and bring up ideas, everybody benefits, especially the fans. I saw Gene and Paul go for it at the conventions, trying any KISS song fans would request. It was pretty funny. These are two guys that didn't do drugs, so it wouldn't be that hard for them to suddenly do "Love Theme from Kiss" [laughs]. And I'd be like, "What's that?"

ERIC SINGER: It was a really cool experience. I think the show went off well. During sound check, we sounded great, much better than the actual performance. Gene seemed real nervous to me because rehearsals with the four original guys were a bit shaky and rough all week. I think Peter and Ace rose to the occasion and did a good job. From my own personal point of view, being a KISS fan since the '70s, getting to play with all the four original guys on the show was a very cool experience.

DANNY GOLDBERG: When I got to Mercury KISS had already taped the *Unplugged* show. Alex Coletti, who worked at MTV, loved them. Alex talked MTV into doing a KISS *Unplugged*. When it came time to get the rights to put it out as a record, we had resistance from them. They thought it was the wrong image for *Unplugged*. As the years go by, KISS goes in and out of fashion and it was a moment when they were out of fashion. I had to call Tom Freston at MTV and grovel. I said, "I just got this new job, don't do this to me," and he said okay. They let us put the record out and it did okay. It was like a rerun of the *Lick It Up* period, but in reverse. It had been played out again. It was time to put the makeup back on. It doesn't take a genius to think of this. I certainly advocated it. I strongly urged it on the theory that this was the only thing that was gonna make any difference. I wasn't surprised at how successful it was. Having worked with them and followed the way these things go in the culture, I was pretty sure that this was an idea that was gonna work and it did. The passage of time leans so much in KISS's favor because it now gave them this legendary status. The *Psycho Circus* record did not do great. The catalogue did better and we sold some records. The big, big success came in the live show. Other than the Rolling Stones, probably the most famous touring band is KISS.

DANNY GOLDBERG: I had our label hire Ken Sunshine. He's a PR guy for Barbra Streisand and Leonardo DiCaprio. He has a sense of making news as opposed to getting a record reviewed or a photo in *Rolling Stone*. We wanted to try and do something dramatic. It was his idea to do KISS reunion tour press conference on the *Intrepid* aircraft carrier.

YOU WANTED THE BEST, YOU GOT THE BEST!!

Release date: June 25, 1996

KISS

PAUL STANLEY: There's a lot of stuff we recorded from concerts including ones that weren't used on the first live album. We recorded some shows leading up to that. Actually, I was in the studio putting that album together. It was really cool to find some tracks that nobody's heard and that stood up. "Room Service" is the best of all of them and "Two Timer." It's all cool stuff. That's just kind of like a sampler. The purpose of that album is for some of the new fans perhaps who don't have the entire history or the entire catalogue. If you haven't had the whole meal, here's a little taste of each course. I'd have to listen to it again and let you know how many stars I'd give it.

GENE SIMMONS: Three stars. Record companies have an interesting point of view, which doesn't always jibe with fans. Fans always say, "Look, I've been here for thirty years, what do I need another greatest hits record for?" Well, because you're not a record company and because there are new fans every year. I personally buy greatest hits albums by the Temptations and Sweet even though there's been ten of them released. These people that aren't necessarily fans don't want every record, they just want a selection of stuff. The truth is most fans come and go. You always try and stick on extra stuff, you always try and give people bang for the buck. Three of the songs are from a show in Wildwood. "Two Timer" used to go into "Let Me Know" and that's the way it is on the record. Later on we did "Let Me Know" with that riff that wound up on the end of "She." Originally, we stuck that on when we did it in clubs . . . after the a cappella version came that riff. We moved that around and stuck it on the end of "She."

PETER CRISS: I thought it good we put something out, as we didn't have anything to put out at the time of the reunion tour. Paul and Gene sort of came up with that idea. Of course I'm gonna give it a five [laughs] because a lot of that stuff was cool. Again, it was a really good idea and it worked and I got a Gold record for it. It was a fun thing.

CARNIVAL OF SOULS

Release date: October 28, 1997

KISS / TOBY WRIGHT—co-producer / CURT CUOMO—songwriter / TOMMY THAYER—songwriter

GENE SIMMONS: We basically said, "Let's make believe this is a brand-new band." At that point we never saw a hope of getting back together with Ace and Peter. So we went, "Forget about all the rules, forget KISS, forget everything. Let's try to make a home for Eric and Bruce." To me it was a very brave record and I have no regrets.

PAUL STANLEY: I was dead-set against doing that kind of an album, but there are times in the band where somebody acquiesces or gives in based upon somebody else feeling strongly about something. That album was Gene believing that's what we should do. I never believed that the world needs a second-rate Soundgarden, Metallica, or Alice in Chains. It was a very labored attempt at doing something that I think was a big misstep. Two stars.

BRUCE KULICK: *Revenge* was a great approach for a record but that still had a lot of classic KISS elements in it and that was 'cause of Bob Ezrin. He was involved a little in the beginning of that record. And KISS was always looking at what was going on around us and realized that some of the bands that were doing really well that they liked and that were influenced also by KISS—Soundgarden and Alice in Chains— were like *Revenge* but even heavier. All of a sudden we wanted to be heavier. I remember Paul coming in with some songs that were very pop and Ezrin said, "Nope, that's not the right direction." Paul came up with some Pink Floyd kind of things, it was weird. Gene clearly had some fresh ideas of what would become "I Walk Alone" and "Childhood's End." We were fooling around with these things at least a year and a half before we actually recorded the album. I got very hungry about it, saying, "If you want riffs, I'm gonna sit in my studio and record a hundred heavy riffs." So I started fooling around with drumbeats and riffs. I used drop D tuning, which opened up a whole vibe for us. I was familiar with that tuning from Led Zeppelin. "I Walk Alone" is tuned to that Zeppelin kind of tuning. It wasn't super-intentional to be like this or that, you had Zeppelin and Black Sabbath doing stuff like that. But all of a sudden we concentrated on a lot of very dark stuff. It was odder of course for Paul, but he jumped into it. Toby [Wright], our producer, was there to give it a vibe. Toby was around since the *Crazy Nights* days working with Nevison. Again, Paul always put it that he was there for a vibe. Toby's not Ezrin and is not Nevison but he clearly was able to help us continue with that vibe, which I'm not sure was the right thing. I do like a lot of the record although there's parts of it that I felt could have even been better. I like some of my demos better. Paul and I worked really hard on the demos and it was not a record that I walked out saying I was 99 percent happy with it. I played bass on quite a few of the Paul songs, "Jungle," "Rain," "It Never Goes Away," and "I Will Be There." I really wanted Gene to play as much bass as he would.

TOBY WRIGHT: KISS sought me out as somebody who was not afraid to take chances and maybe put a different kind of a sound together. Someone who was not afraid to break the boundaries. They were looking for someone who was hot at the time. I think Gene had it in his mind with this grunge thing, "We have to get into this darker music." So that's why he hired me most likely because of my Alice in Chains experiences and bringing the dark music to the table. They didn't want to write a happy KISS record. At the time, the dark, grungy thing was happening. Gene and Paul and I did have discussions about the direction of the album when we listened to the demos. I gave them comments about what I thought. I'm a very honest human being. I'm not going to tell them that things are great if they're not. I'll find an eloquent, creative, and nice constructive way to say that, "Hey, this might need a little help." The sound that I was putting out then was a little different especially for KISS. At that point, I'd done three or four Alice in Chains records, maybe a Wallflowers record.

TOBY WRIGHT: Gene had wanted to change the direction of the band and be more modern. This was before they went on their reunion tour. KISS weren't really doing that well at that point in the public eye. The musical image world was Nirvana and the grunge thing, which was pretty big. Gene and I had discussions where he said, "I want to be like Billy Corgan!" [Smashing Pumpkins] We had a little disagreement and I told him no. "You don't want to be like Billy Corgan, you are a legend unto yourself. It would be really nice if you were true to yourself. You can take your own path of what you want to do, you don't have to follow Billy Corgan because he's on the top of the charts." My point to him was, "Let's be creative and be ourselves." And he said, "Well, how 'bout if the fans don't like it?" And I said, "You can't help what people like" [laughs] and he knows that. I just took their ideas and basically crafted modern sounds around them. They were looking for something a little darker, a little edgier, more angry.

TOBY WRIGHT: KISS was a little leery about pushing the boundaries of their sound. They wanted to be back on top so Gene was making an attempt at being modern. Paul was more about the good songs. He's a complete pro. True to his form, he'll sing whatever you want him to sing, try whatever you want him to try if it's within him. Sometimes I got Paul to sing a little harder.

TOBY WRIGHT: That record was mostly the Bruce and Toby show. Paul always played his own guitars and sang all his parts and Gene played his bass and sang his songs. Mostly for all the guitar work and the direction of the guitars, which at that point was dictating a sound as far as song structure, how you orchestrate your guitars. It's a pretty thick, layered record. That was mine and Bruce's concept in terms of how the guitars would sound.

BRUCE KULICK: On the *Carnival of Souls* album we stretched the boundaries on that album. What I tell people is, "If you love the record, great!" Then you can tell me I really contributed to it. But if you hate the record don't blame me just because I had more co-writes on the album and sang a song. In some ways "I Walk Alone" was more KISS-like than a lot of the rest of the record. I thought it was weird that people would say that *Carnival of Souls* was like my solo album. Listen to *Audio Dog* and you'll see it's not my solo record.

ERIC SINGER: Many times we have emotional attachments to records. Sometimes you just have to remove yourself from that and look at things subjectively. It's obvious that the record is well played. It was KISS in a weird time trying to take some chances. Obviously we were all listening to Alice in Chains, Soundgarden, and STP. If it was a record by any other band I would say it's a pretty cool record. But I listen to it and go, "That's not KISS." It's a lot of rock, but no roll. I give the band credit for taking a chance and trying to do something different. To me it's the modern version of *The Elder* fifteen years later [laughs]. It was going off the beaten path and taking a left-hand turn and realizing when they got down that road that it wasn't leading us to where we needed to be going. So you turn around and you get back on the main road. KISS went back to their roots and eventually back to the makeup.

ERIC SINGER: No matter what anyone wants to think, at the end of the day, it's about songs. It doesn't matter who plays them or who writes them, it's about if a song is good or not. Gene used to say to me, "I don't care if a fucking plumber wrote it, a good song's a good song." It's about the team, not the individuals, the sum is greater than the parts.

CURT CUOMO: This was the first KISS album that I worked on. I call it their "dark" album. It was not as popular with the KISS Army. But I think it's a real cool record that wasn't afraid to dive into some core issues in the dark corners of our psyches.

TOBY WRIGHT: It didn't come out for a while because KISS did the makeup tour. The record eventually got leaked. I know it was on the Internet. It was one of the biggest bootlegged records before the record company put it out. Right around the end of the sessions we knew it was a possibility that KISS would go on a makeup tour. They started talking about it at the end of the record. It wasn't like a personal conversation, "Hey, should we?" It was more of announcing to the room, whoever was in there, "Hey, we might do this makeup thing. Wouldn't that be funny?" I said, "No, man, that's the wrong move, don't do it" [laughs] 'cause I knew it would cost Bruce and Eric their jobs [laughs]. I remember asking Gene, "So is this record going to come out or is it going to be on hold?" He told me it was going to come out and they were doing a KISS tour and maybe incorporate some of those songs but that never happened. The album did eventually come out years later.

BRUCE KULICK: That album was destined to be like *The Elder II* because of the reunion tour. The record company just destroyed any chance that record had. They buried it by not pushing it.

BRUCE KULICK: It was while we were mixing the record that Gene and Paul told us they were going to do the reunion tour with Ace and Peter. I always felt it would happen sometime. I realized this could be the end of my days with the band, but at least they were being up-front as to how they were handling it. It kind of bothered me when the record was not released for a long time. Then it got bootlegged and that really bothered me. Eric [Singer] and I used to get into conversations about if a KISS reunion would happen. I knew it would happen and Eric didn't believe it would ever happen.

ERIC SINGER: We were doing the *Carnival of Souls* record and two days before we finished it, Gene and Paul decided to have a meeting and they just said, "We're doing a makeup tour with Ace and Peter." And that was it. For me, I knew it was the beginning of the end.

TOBY WRIGHT: In hindsight, I think artistically the record is a little unfocused. Sonically, it's excellent; musically, it is what it is. If you like it, you like it and if you don't, you don't. I wish I had taken more time to work on some songs, but I do remember it being kinda quick. "Okay, these are our songs, go!" We didn't have a lot of time to stand there and look at the songs and go, "Are these our best songs?" Gene always has deadlines. So he was like, "Get these songs done and then we're going on tour." [laughs] I'm very proud of the record. It's definitely a different record for KISS. I'm proud that the one that I did is different in a lot of ways. It was kind of underground. It's not a standard KISS record.

TOMMY THAYER: I was around for those sessions. It's a little known fact, but we videotaped the recording of the whole record too, from start to finish. There's hours of footage. That's something that's never been done, maybe someday people will see that. There's also a little bit of recording studio footage of the *Psycho Circus* sessions.

★ "HATE" ★

BRUCE KULICK: Gene presented it at rehearsal to me and Eric. We loved the riff and jumped on it right away. I contributed a bridge riff at rehearsal. Toby took that one over the top. Toby's a really talented guy, but he really wanted to make a statement with KISS. I have rough mixes of *Carnival of Souls* that would have gone over better with the KISS fans. They sounded more straight-ahead.

★ "RAIN" ★

TOBY WRIGHT: That song came out of the Curt Cuomo writing sessions. It sounded amazing and still does today [laughs].

BRUCE KULICK: I was experimenting with something in a 7/4 time signature. I was working a lot with detuned strings, where the low strings are tuned down. I had the beat and that riff and I remember playing it for Curt Cuomo and Paul. Paul told me he liked it. We arranged it and he came up with a melody. Ultimately, Toby mixed it very bizarrely, gating all the guitars and made it sound very bizarre, but it's a cool track.

CURT CUOMO: I love this riff Bruce came up with. It was a dark, heavy-footed, odd-timed monster and it just took off from there. It was great working on melodies with Paul because he has such a powerful voice. He has great range and also has the ability to sing dynamically.

★ "MASTER & SLAVE" ★

BRUCE KULICK: I actually wrote the bridge/chorus for that, that whole vibe. We really worked hard on the song because if you think about it, it only had two parts, riff and the bridge. Gene helped arrange that song even though he didn't help write it. It might have been his suggestion to have the verses come down to nothing, just bass. Since the song was very repetitive in some ways, dynamics would help make it more interesting. And there's a hell of a scream from Paul on it too.

CURT CUOMO: I remember writing a busy riff-like melody and showing it to Paul and Bruce. It got slightly altered to become the main driving force of the song and the rest took off from there.

★ "CHILDHOOD'S END" ★

GENE SIMMONS: *Childhood's End* was an Arthur C. Clarke novel about the last stages of evolution when we become spirit entities. We leave the body and become energy sources and these elemental beings help us on our journey. Like birth and death, it's a turbulent transition and human beings tend to fight any change. I always loved the notion of childhood's end, now it's time to be grown-up. "Childhood's End" was not about an actual person. It was just a sort of rock 'n' roll nihilism. Rock 'n' roll guys killing themselves off was a very romantic notion. I wondered what it would be like to be the friend of a guy who you grew up with and becomes a rock star and [recites lyrics] "I read in the *New York Times* that you passed away, you blew your mind, but you were always my friend . . ."

BRUCE KULICK: One of the reasons I had nine co-writes on the album was I would not let go of a thing. I was in their face all the time and they were glad for it. I was contributing a lot and I had ideas. I remember Gene going to a demo studio and he wanted to review all the tapes of the stuff that he'd written. I said, "I wanna be there." And he said, "No problem." So I show up and he's playing the idea for the chorus of "Childhood's End." And I go, "That's really good." Later on he plays me the verses of that song. It hit me that the two fit together. So in essence I didn't write the chorus, but I was involved a bit on some of the things that we did in the verses but the point was these things worked together. And all of sudden we had this very strong song.

TOMMY THAYER: The chorus changes and melody was something that I brought in to Gene two or three years prior. Then they were working on *Carnival of Souls* and Gene pulled that out. For the rest of the song, the verses and stuff, he worked with Bruce Kulick.

GENE SIMMONS: Everybody in the band hated the idea of having kids sing on it. They said it was hokey. It's funny, when Ezrin wanted to do it it wasn't hokey. But I loved to hear kids singing along especially if it's got that kind of innocence.

TOBY WRIGHT: We went 'round and 'round about concepts. I usually speak to my artists about, "What's your concept on your record?" When we got to Gene's concept on that song, he couldn't really explain it to me. But then we got into the studio and it became this whole involved story. He wanted kids on it, and playgrounds, just taking you back, just a kind of a vibey song with a good beat and a lot of aural scenery in it.

★ "I WILL BE THERE" ★

PAUL STANLEY: I wrote the music on a very strange instrument that had been given to me as a present, it was something between a dulcimer and a peculiar guitar. I think it only had three or four strings on it. I made up a tuning for it and based the song around it. Bruce and I put on acoustic guitars, some Indian drums, some tablas and things like that. Lyrically, it was an easy song to write once I focused on what it was about, which was the bond between me and my son.

BRUCE KULICK: Paul is a rock star, period. But having a kid really makes you come down to earth. He wanted to write something for his son, Evan. I think it was cool that if he was gonna write a love song, now there was truly something that he had a lot of feelings about, which was his own flesh and blood. I remember when Paul and Curt were working on this acoustic twelve-string kind of thing. I had some ideas for the bridge.

CURT CUOMO: During another writing session with Paul, he picked up a very strange, stringed instrument. I'm not sure what it was. He started playing it and magical sounds started to happen and this beautiful, moody song was born. This song was written for his son, Evan. Of course, the song can apply to any of us. It's a great song with a universal theme.

TOBY WRIGHT: It was a very personal song. I was asking for emotion from them. I was of the opinion that listeners can hear everything you mean and feel when you're singing a song. That really had it right from the beginning. Paul felt that so hard. It was just undeniable. It had to be on the record.

★ "JUNGLE" ★

BRUCE KULICK: I knew that when we had the vibe for "Jungle" we had a really strong track. I remember playing the demo to Michael James Jackson, the producer that worked on *Lick It Up,* and he said, "That's really terrific." And sure enough, we had a big radio hit with it. I was really proud that we did something unique that was also accessible.

CURT CUOMO: Bruce came up with a killer riff. I remember thinking that the riff was busy and that a juxtaposition melody would be perfect to put over it—long, haunting notes. That's how the verses began. I remember working on the lyrics late into the night at Paul's. It was well worth the effort as this was released as the single for the album and would go on to win the 1997 *Metal Edge* Reader's Choice Poll as "Song of the Year." It was one of my favorite collaborations between Paul, Bruce, and myself.

TOBY WRIGHT: "Jungle" is an amazing song. If you listen to that song on a huge system, we put some amazing things on it, 808s and tablas. Eight-oh-eights are a big boom that comes out of pickup trucks when you're annoyed in Orange County somewhere [laughs]. You've heard the cars go by with their big old boomy systems and the whole car vibrates, it's one of those kind of sounds. There's a whole bunch of long 808s, djembes, an African drum, and tablas, which is like a talking drum [imitates sound]. On "Jungle," Justin Walden programmed a few percussion loops using those things. I physically played some loops in the studio on that stuff.

★ "IN MY HEAD" ★

GENE SIMMONS: "In My Head" was written during a period where Scott Van Zen and I were tossing around lots of ideas. Scott would sit there and I would hum guitar parts. Or sometimes he would come in and by accident I heard something that was backward [imitates backward guitar part], which was the backward intro. I immediately said, "What the hell is that? I like that a lot." So the backward intro wound up being the tag of "In My Head." I wrote a lyric, which I wasn't entirely happy with, so I tossed it to Jaimie St. James and he fine-tuned the lyric.

★ "IT NEVER GOES AWAY" ★

BRUCE KULICK: "It Never Goes Away" was one of the first dark riffs Paul presented that Curt [Cuomo] and I got a handle on. I remember slowing it down. Paul had a lot of that song done already, but it just didn't feel right. I used to call the song "Black Sabbath" because it was dark and dirgey. It's really trippy. I play a twelve-string guitar solo on it.

CURT CUOMO: It's a great commentary on how we feel like we never get enough of what we really *don't* need. It's about how that constant search for power and "things" never ends. On the surface it can seem like a negative song but in reality the song serves as an observation and provides insight, which can lead to positive change.

★ "SEDUCTION OF THE INNOCENT" ★

GENE SIMMONS: "Seduction of the Innocent" comes from a book written by Dr. Fredric Wertham. It was the reason why the Comics Code authority came into being. He was a very Moral Majority conservative type. The notion of the book was that comic books were evil. They were teaching our kids the wrong things. Batman was gay because he had Robin, his ward, a young boy living with him, and that was suspicious. A rich man with a young ward who's not married. And Wonder Woman was a dyke. All these notions about superheroes. "Why are these grown men walking around in costumes and tights?" He was against the violence in comic books. There was a comic book company called EC who went out of business because of government pressure. They were also responsible for *Mad* magazine, which did survive. They created a Comics Code authority which was a self-policed group of comic book people who made sure the comic books were never too extreme so it didn't offend. I always loved the title "Seduction of the Innocent," which was astonishing in its range, scope, and depth. I started hearing more and more about Catholic priests molesting children; this was years ago. It seemed apropos to write a song about that. When Scott Van Zen was around I started humming a few things to him saying, "What would happen if you tried to play like the jazz guitarist Wes Montgomery?" He had the style of hitting two notes at the same time, and always octaves. So, it sounded like two guitars were playing. I thought back to my childhood when I had a song called "My Girl Gave Me Chocolate Ice Cream," which was a very simple song based on one chord. In the middle of the song, I couldn't think of anything to do, so I kept strumming a G chord and hummed a Middle Eastern melody because I come from the Middle East. I tried that melody in "Seduction of the Innocent" and the song then wrote itself. [recites lyrics] "Like a vulture circling overhead . . ." These were the most heinous crimes. It was a very important song for me, in some ways it was a song unrealized from my childhood. I was fourteen when I wrote that and finally to hear that melody was great.

★ "I CONFESS" ★

GENE SIMMONS: I met this guy, Ken Tamplin, who's a born-again religious guy. We tossed some ideas around and I told him about an old Montgomery Clift film I had seen called *I Confess,* about a priest who had committed a crime. The notion was if you're sitting in a confessional confessing, who does the priest who listens to all the confessions confess to? I thought, forget the priest stuff, let's make this more about my own notion of myself, who am I? Can I be completely clean? [recites lyrics] "When I look inside the mirror, it's my face that's looking back at me. My father, all he left me was his name." All those sort of up-front ideas. The song was about me being completely up-front so there's no hidden skeletons in my closet about girls, about who I am, where I come from, what I believe in, all of it.

★ "IN THE MIRROR" ★

BRUCE KULICK: Another cool Hendrix-sounding riff. Paul responded to it well. It had this dreamy kind of B section to it with a tricky 5/4 time signature.

CURT CUOMO: Another song that I love conceptually. It's about taking a good, honest look at yourself. It's kind of like a "get real" song. It asks the question, "Who are you and do you like what you see when you look in the mirror?"

★ "I WALK ALONE" ★

BRUCE KULICK: We couldn't get a total handle on "I Walk Alone." I kept experimenting with it and started developing backward chord progressions and sections. Then all of a sudden I gave a different piece to Gene that the melody would have worked in it and he noticed that and the song came into shape.

PSYCHO CIRCUS

Release date: September 22, 1998
KISS / BRUCE FAIRBAIRN–producer / MIKE PLOTNIKOFF–engineer
CURT CUOMO–songwriter / DANNY GOLDBERG–president of Mercury Records

PAUL STANLEY: I think it's a spectacular album. *Psycho Circus* is right up with anything that I consider our best. There may be parts of it that I'm not that fond of. But as far as the overall album and my contribution to it, I'm very pleased with it. Bob [Ezrin] and I will sometimes talk about, if only he could have been involved. That would have been just awesome. I'd give that album four stars. My complaint with that album is some of the left-field stuff was Bruce Fairbairn's focus and Bruce Fairbairn's folly. Bruce was a wonderful guy, but he didn't have a clue what KISS was all about. For whatever reason he had his nose up Gene's butt too much. It was unfortunate because when I would bring in songs, either he was underwhelmed or he would say, "That's great," and then try to change them into something completely different. I think there are a lot of elements of that album that went drastically wrong. I fought tooth and nail to keep the integrity of that album.

GENE SIMMONS: I like some of the songs a lot, "Psycho Circus," "Within," and "You Wanted the Best." There are enough tunes on it to say the band accomplished something. I think it's one of the better records. Look, I've bought Rolling Stones records all my life, and the earlier ones are better than the later ones. I don't know what to tell you. It's something about the spirit. Some of the tunes on *Psycho Circus* could have been found on earlier KISS records. Three stars.

ACE FREHLEY: Three stars. I think it was a good album. One of the things probably that isn't cool about the album is the fact that Peter and I didn't really play on the record. I would have loved to have played on the whole thing. After we had finished the tour, we had taken some time off. They [Paul and Gene] had started working on a lot of the songs and I didn't even fly out until the songs had already been recorded. I was still working at home on some of my solo stuff. That's one of the things that I think is lacking on the record, that me and Peter weren't involved on a lot of the tracks.

MIKE PLOTNIKOFF: The reason Ace and Peter didn't play much on the *Psycho Circus* album is because of a decision Bruce [Fairbairn] made. Even though Gene and Paul wanted it to be the original band on the record, when Bruce heard Ace and Peter play in preproduction, he thought to make the kind of record he wanted to make, Ace and Peter wouldn't cut it as players. Kevin Valentine played drums on all the songs except for "Into the Void." He was an amazing drummer. Gene, Paul, and Kevin would lay down all the basic tracks. Ace played on "Into the Void" and he did a couple of guitar solos as well, probably two others.

BRUCE FAIRBAIRN: Up until the point I started working with the band I was a passive KISS fan. I was a fan because they were so outrageous. I was into a few of their tunes. As a producer, KISS weren't known for their songwriting and the musicality of the songs although they had some great songs that came out from time to time. They were known more for their stage show and as a live band. I had *Destroyer*, that was the one I really enjoyed the most. But now I'm a die-hard fan, I've got the disease.

BRUCE FAIRBAIRN: I was really excited about doing a KISS record because they're a legendary band. I tried to immerse myself in the KISS world before we went in and did the record. The guys were right on the same page as I was in terms of how I like to make a record. You adapt to the different characters in the band, everybody has a different style of working. If you're a good producer you understand that early in the game and you work with it so that they're comfortable. After all, you're making a KISS record, you're not making a Bruce Fairbairn record with KISS playing.

BRUCE FAIRBAIRN: Gene and Paul took a great attitude. They said, "This is your record, Fairbairn, you can hang yourself with it or you can make a great record. We're not gonna get in the way unless it looks like it's going south at 120 miles an hour and we're headed for the ditch." They were very supportive in all aspects of the production. I had the sense that Gene especially knew what I was gonna do before I did it. As a producer himself, he had confidence in what I was doing to the point where he could relax and think about other things, writing, and singing. There were times when Gene and Paul would put suggestions on the table. Paul and Gene were very knowledgeable. They had really good ideas. I'd come in sometimes and Gene would be sitting at the control desk and the speakers would be fuckin' flying off the wall. He'd be sitting there pushing faders and just having a great time, totally in a trance. It was great. After he was done, he would say, "Aw I needed that, that was great." [laughs]

BRUCE FAIRBAIRN: We didn't want to make a concept album where everything had to relate to the concept. But we did consciously look at this and go "Welcome to the show." Then the first song is "Within." Once you're here and you've come through the door we're gonna take you on this trip. Once you get past "Within" it becomes a little looser in terms of presentation of songs, they're just stories. But then at the end, you've been on this journey and lyrically ask a few questions, "Did you fly without wings? Did you hear? Did you see?" So, there was a bit of a closure to the record, lyrically more than musically although it's a spacious kind of tune ["Journey of 1,000 Years"]. We could have made an older-sounding KISS record or we could have made a real slick 1999 record. None of those would have worked. We had to find the right spot and choose the songs accordingly.

BRUCE FAIRBAIRN: There were a couple situations with the record with overdubs where it could have kept going on and on and got bigger and bigger. "Journey of 1,000 Years" is one of those kind of songs which you could produce until the day you die. Part of the job I have as a producer is knowing when to pull the plug and say, "Listen, we're done, if we put more parts on this song it's just gonna go downhill."

MIKE PLOTNIKOFF: Paul and Gene are both great singers. They were very professional, they'd nail a vocal pretty much the first time. They were good at what they did. Paul played most of the rhythm guitars on the record. He's a great rhythm guitar player. He also played some lead guitar. Tommy Thayer played on the record. He's an amazing player. Because he's such a huge KISS fan, Tommy copped Ace's style. He plays like Ace. I'm sure Tommy had some guitar on most every track.

MIKE PLOTNIKOFF: We recorded nineteen songs for the record, ten made it. Some songs were slated for B sides. Most of the songs that didn't make it on the record were Gene's songs and there were some real good ones, "I Wanna Rule the World" and "I Am Yours." They're very Beatle-esque, more ballad-oriented songs. Some other Gene songs were "Rear View," "Sweet and Dirty," and "Carnival of Souls." There's also a Paul song that didn't make the record, "Body and Soul." Gene had enough songs left over for a double record. Bruce had to walk a fine line when he chose what songs to record. He had to make sure it was even, there had to be the same number of Gene and Paul songs on the record.

BRUCE FAIRBAIRN: Gene had three or four cassette tapes of tunes. Paul, on the other hand, only had a few snippets of ideas. Ace had three or four things that he'd been working on. Peter had a few things too. Paul is a pressure writer. His best stuff is done when his back's up against the wall and he comes up with songs like "Psycho Circus." With Ace it's about going through the songs he's got. He loves everything because he's the Ace. A lot of it's really good in a different context. But you really have to try and find the right Ace songs for the record that really show him off.

ACE FREHLEY: When I write songs I don't really think that much about them. I don't really ponder lyrics. Sometimes I might not write a song for a month or two. Gene Simmons told me he submitted a hundred songs for *Psycho Circus* and they used four. To me that's insanity. If I start something and I don't think it's going anywhere I'm not gonna waste my time and finish it. To me it appears Gene doesn't know the difference between a good and a bad song because if you write a hundred songs and not know which one's better than the other doesn't make sense to me.

MIKE PLOTNIKOFF: Gene and Paul were pretty serious guys trying to get the record done. We had a good time working on it, there was really no tension. Paul would only come in when he had to do his parts. Gene was the only one who was there all the time, first one in the studio and last one to leave. It seemed Gene and Paul got along well with Bruce. They had a good relationship. In terms of making decisions, from my perspective, Bruce sided with Gene all the time and not with Paul. Paul made comments when Bruce wasn't around indicating that he wasn't happy with Bruce's production decisions.

MIKE PLOTNIKOFF: Ace was sitting next to me putting down a solo on one of Paul's songs. I was looking away from him at the tape remote where I was punching in to record. Bruce was behind Ace and Paul was sitting on the couch. I kept punching in to record trying to get the right solo. Then a little while later I did it again and nothing happened. I got worried that I'd accidentally erased something on the track. But what really happened was Ace fell asleep in the middle of doing a guitar solo [laughs]. Bruce had to slap him in the back to wake him up [laughs]. And then soon afterward he nailed it.

MIKE PLOTNIKOFF: I know that Bruce [Fairbairn] really enjoyed working with KISS. He really liked and respected Gene, and Paul too. Bruce mentioned to me that he was surprised how many songs they'd written before we started the record. And how fast they could come up with new material. He'd be like, "I need a new song," and the next day Gene or Paul bring another new song in and it would be usable. He was impressed with their songwriting.

BRUCE FAIRBAIRN: Records are kind of like snapshots, you expose one period in a band's musical development. I look at *Psycho Circus* as being a really legitimate snapshot of where the band was musically at that point in time.

DANNY GOLDBERG: I thought *Psycho Circus* was a really good record but we didn't do that great with it. It's a totally different business. With a tour oftentimes you're selling nostalgia. People want to hear "Rock and Roll All Nite," they want to see Gene Simmons breathe fire. They want to see Paul jump around. They want to say they saw KISS. But there's twenty-five, thirty albums you can buy with all those songs on them. To sell a new record you need a hit song. It's that simple. They didn't have hit songs on that album, they had really good songs but none turned out to be hits. So if people were interested in KISS they were more likely to buy an old record. Same thing with the Rolling Stones. The recent records by the Rolling Stones haven't done real well but their tours do amazingly well. Same exact situation.

★ "PSYCHO CIRCUS" ★

PAUL STANLEY: The hardest part for me in writing for an album is writing the first song, coming to grips with it thematically and finding out the direction for the album. Not surprisingly the first song written is the song that winds up as the first song on the album. It becomes the signature piece. "Psycho Circus" was me wanting to create the power and atmosphere that I thought *Destroyer* had. When I went in to do the demo I called Bob Ezrin and asked him if he would go in with me because Bob had originally been slated to produce that album. We very, very much wanted him to do it. We were very disappointed when he couldn't because of his time commitments. I called him and asked him if he would help with the demo and he couldn't. While I was in the studio working, most of the time all I was thinking was, "What would Bob do?" [laughs] When I finished it and played it in my car to Bob, he had this big smile on his face. When it was done I said to him, "All I was trying to figure out is what you would have done." He smiled and said, "You did it."

CURT CUOMO: As often as I would go to Paul's to write, Paul would come to my house and write and record in my home studio. We'd get together quite often and have great creative sessions. One time I was in the kitchen making coffee and Paul was in the other room playing. He was experimenting with different riffs on the guitar and suddenly one riff in particular grabbed my attention. I immediately started to hear a melody over it. So I ran into the studio and began singing over the riff. The chorus to "Psycho Circus" was born. It was very exciting to see it go all the way to number one on the *Billboard* Mainstream Rock charts and get a Grammy nomination for Best Rock Performance. It was also exciting to see the album, *Psycho Circus,* go Gold in just five weeks. Paul gave a superb vocal performance on that song.

BRUCE FAIRBAIRN: I remember getting in Paul's car and listening to the demo of that. We didn't have an opener for the record. He said, "Check this out, this is it." He put it up on ten, and we both sat there and looked at each other and started to laugh because that was it.

★ "WITHIN" ★

GENE SIMMONS: I came up with that while I was working at a little eight-track recording studio. The song was written while fooling around on bass. Lyrically, the song idea came from a George Harrison track, "Within You, Without You." I was never really into the spirituality of stuff. But I sat down to try and write something very cerebral, the meaning to which I can't tell you to this day. But it felt right.

BRUCE FAIRBAIRN: My favorite song on the record is "Within." It always grabbed me. It's a very thought-provoking lyric. I like the groove in it, it's really heavy. That weird heavy guitar sound that comes in, it was so exciting when we brought that sound into the studio.

MIKE PLOTNIKOFF: Gene brought in a demo of "Within." We ended up taking that backward stuff on his demo and adding it into the recording.

★ "I PLEDGE ALLEGIANCE TO THE STATE OF ROCK & ROLL" ★

PAUL STANLEY: I started the idea for that at Curt Cuomo's house and then worked on it. I couldn't find a finishing direction for it. I ultimately went over to see Holly Knight and she really zeroed in on it. "Pledge Allegiance" is a great song. All I can say is my songs on that album are great. And that may be a matter of opinion but I can also say when some of my songs aren't. The songs that are on that album are everything that I would want them to be.

MIKE PLOTNIKOFF: Bruce was back home in Vancouver when we recorded "Pledge Allegiance." It was Paul and myself.

★ "INTO THE VOID" ★

ACE FREHLEY: I thought that song was one of the strongest songs I presented first to the band. I wrote it with my friend Karl Cochran, who played bass for me on my last solo tour. He came up with the riff and basically I just added the arrangement, changed some chords, and wrote the bridge, wrote all the lyrics. Once I presented the song to the band and we decided we were going to track it, Paul helped me arrange it so it would breathe a little more. He said, "Let's open it up and let one measure drone, let it breathe a little." He also came up with that high guitar part which goes though the chorus. I think it's a real good hook.

PETER CRISS: I remember going over to Ace's house on a Sunday morning. He called me up to fuck around with him on it. I really got off on that. Out of all the songs I really took to it. Ace was like, "Hey, man, you didn't get a tune on the album, come on over, let's fuck around with my tune 'cause I just love the way you play drums." And that was a real compliment.

MIKE PLOTNIKOFF: It was hard to get a good song out of Ace. We were almost finished doing overdubs and Bruce had to keep bugging Ace to hear songs. The first three songs Ace played Bruce were horrible. I had to leave the room because I started laughing [laughs]. But then eventually Ace delivered a good song with "Into the Void." Paul and Gene helped him with the track. I was the biggest KISS fan growing up. "Into the Void" is one of my favorite songs on the record because they all played on it, they put it down live. Somebody said that "Into the Void" was one of the first times on any of their records that KISS laid down all the tracks in the studio together. We took some time off so they'd be able to rehearse. It was actually really cool to see. It didn't take that long to nail it. We spent the day on it doing the bed tracks and then the overdubs followed. Everybody was excited, they all got along great. They were really happy it was all going down. Then to work with them in the studio and to do "Into the Void," where they were all in the studio, was great. You could tell Peter had lost a lot of his chops. He just needed to practice a bit but he still had the ability. Ace's playing was a little rough. I like Ace's style as a guitar player. Sometimes it would take him a few takes to nail a solo. Technically he's not the greatest player but as far as feel and putting good ideas down he was great. If we had to cut the album with only the four original members of KISS it would have taken us a year.

BRUCE FAIRBAIRN: The reason we grabbed that song from Ace is it had that KISS vibe.

★ "WE ARE ONE" ★

GENE SIMMONS: I always have the band on my mind when writing songs. It's really tough to write pivotal, signpost songs that say, "This is KISS." I like the idea of "all for one, one for all." Then I came up with the line "we are one." I couldn't apply it so much to the band because the track sounded Beatle-esque. I got Silent Rage to demo the original song, and I sang on it. I preferred my original version to the version that KISS cut. Ours was ploddier and more arranged. I had visions of the Coca-Cola commercial [sings "I'd Like to Teach the World to Sing"] and all these people from different races singing. [recites lyrics] "Everywhere I go, everyone I see, I see my face looking back at me. You are me, I am you" kind of notion.

BRUCE FAIRBAIRN: "We Are One" is a side of Gene's writing that nobody really hears. Gene has songs like that which are really melodic and creative but they never see the light of day on a KISS record. I told him, "I'd like to see a different side of the Demon, you're always doing this kind of stuff [imitates demonic sound]. What if you took a chance and gave KISS fans a little bit of a glimpse of those other type of songs that you write as well." We decided we'd do that with "We Are One" to show people the other side of him. It's very much a song to the fans and a song for all of them together.

★ "YOU WANTED THE BEST" ★

GENE SIMMONS: "You Wanted the Best" was originally called "Just Give Me Love." The drum opening for the song was taken from Chubby Checker's "Let's Twist Again." That was one of the first records I bought. I was a Chubby Checker fan. I became a Twist champion. So I gave the song to Bruce Fairbairn and rewrote the chorus to "You Wanted the Best." It felt like one of those band songs that I'm fond of. The verse deals with the infighting over the years in the band. What I wanted to do was have the original guys in the band sing the verses back and forth, line by line. A lot more than what was done on the record. Just like Sonny and Cher.

BRUCE FAIRBAIRN: The guys all had to come in and do these lines like they were pissed off at each other. And going to Peter, you have to sound pissed off, and he went, "Oh, I can do that, no problem, check this out!"

★ "RAISE YOUR GLASSES" ★

PAUL STANLEY: "Raise Your Glasses" came together really easily for me. The only thing I was having a real problem with was nailing down the lyrics for the verse in particular. Holly [Knight] understood it real quickly and she was a real help.

BRUCE FAIRBAIRN: We first thought that "Raise Your Glasses" was too clichéd a title. We went through all kinds of different possibilities, but we always came back to "Raise Your Glasses" because it's one of those sentiments. It could be a bar, here's to you. It's a toast and a celebration.

★ "I FINALLY FOUND MY WAY" ★

PAUL STANLEY: I wrote it with Bob Ezrin. Bob came down and we were saying that Peter needed a really great ballad to sing on the record. So we went into the studio and wrote it. For me, it was just a matter of writing a song that would be great for Peter's voice. He's got an unmistakable voice. It was really written for him. When he sings it, somebody is going to hear it and immediately it's the voice of the guy who sang "Beth," so it better be good.

MIKE PLOTNIKOFF: Bob Ezrin was in the studio playing a Fender Rhodes keyboard on "I Finally Found My Way," a song he wrote with Paul. With these two powerhouse producers in the same studio I could sense there was a tension in the room. Perhaps because Bob had produced some of KISS's best records and I think Bruce [Fairbairn] felt concerned, "Is Bob going to critique what I'm doing?" Paul sang harmony on the bridge to support Peter's voice because sometimes he had a hard time singing in tune. It took a while to get a good vocal from Peter. That was a bit of work. But we finally did get a great vocal out of him. He has a great voice though, that smoky voice. He was really enthusiastic and wanted to sing it. Everybody thought that this song was gonna be the follow-up to "Beth." That's how it was viewed in the studio.

BRUCE FAIRBAIRN: The way Peter took that lyric and made it so personal, the way he sang it, I was almost in tears sometimes just listening to him sing and coming to grips with that song. It was a very special moment for me.

★ "DREAMIN'" ★

PAUL STANLEY: I wrote "Dreamin'" with Bruce [Kulick]. I came up with the idea for "Dreamin'" when we were cutting the twenty-four-track demos and Bruce was there helping me out. He's such a great friend and a great musician. I can't play everything myself and it's much easier to have somebody as good as him helping out. The pieces for "Dreamin'" were basically coming together in the studio while I was doing demos. It was like a jigsaw puzzle where there were key pieces missing to connect everything. There were just chordal connections that weren't there because it was written so spontaneously and so quickly. And Bruce was there and he came up with the missing pieces and the glue. So that was what he did. Then I went off and wrote the lyrics and the melody.

★ "JOURNEY OF 1,000 YEARS" ★

GENE SIMMONS: Floyd Mutrux and I were developing a KISS motion picture. He came up with the phrase "It's the journey of a thousand years," which I thought had that kind of "We're off to see the Wizard on the Yellow Brick Road" feel. The film didn't come to pass but I always remembered that line. When I was writing for *Psycho Circus* I came up with these chordal patterns that I liked and stuck in the chorus melody and chords of an old song I'd written called "You're My Reason for Living." It was a song never recorded by KISS, it was considered too Beatle-esque. I took those chords and rewrote the lyrics.

BRUCE FAIRBAIRN: Recording the strings and having them play the guitar theme from "Psycho Circus," if anybody can pull it off it's KISS. Anyone else trying to pull off that kind of a reprise wouldn't be accepted because it's too corny. We realized if we did it right it would be very believable. That was quite exciting seeing all those string players doing that theme. It was Paul's melody from "Psycho Circus" that we were bringing back into the context of one of Gene's songs. It was a great thing.

★ ACKNOWLEDGMENTS ★★★★★★

David Leaf and Ken Sharp wish to thank the following individuals for their friendship, encouragement, and support:

John Ackler, Denny Anderson, Diana Aronson, Peter Arquette, Bill Baker, Matt Beighley, Scott Bergstein, Rodney Bingenheimer, John Bionelli, Joseph Bongiovi, Gary Borress, Mike Brandvold/KISSONLINE, Jim "The Bull" Bullotta, Chris Camiolo, Gilda Caserta, Michael Corby, Dave Cunningham, Eva Easton, John Ford, Mark Ford, Barb Gilbert, Jay Gilbert, Julian Gill, Curt Gooch, Ken Gullic, Geoff Hanson, Matt Hautau/Signatures, Louis Hirshorn, Jeremy Holiday, Jay Jacobs, Brooke Jarden, Tom Jermann, Carol Kaye, Elliot Kendall, the KISS Army, Mike Kobayashi, Harvey Kubernik, Bob Laird, David Lang, Robbie Leff, Greg Loescher, Janet Macoska, Melissa Madden, Dennis Martin, Dan Matovina, Bill May, Brian McEvoy, Doc McGhee, Joe Merante, Peter Oreckinto, Ken Patrick, Mark Perkins, Brian Rademacher, Mike Rinaldi, Bruce Roper, Steven Rosen, Ritchie Rubini, Jack Sawyers, Cody Schneiders, Dale Sherman, J. R. Smalling, David Snowden, Daniel Soiseth, Trina Jane Stasiak, Tom Stewart, Dave Streicher, Jeff Suhs, Tim Sullivan, Jeff Tamarkin, Tommy Thayer, Todd Trombetta, Jaan Uhelszki, Jacques van Gool, Joop van Pelt, Kathleen Wagner, Tim Wargo, Chris White/KISS Asylum, and Michael Wolf.

Big thanks to our agent, Mike Harriot, for his tireless belief in our project and to our editor, Dan Ambrosio, for taking this project all the way.

Ken would also like to offer special thanks to Terri Sharp for her support and for keeping the faith.

Ken wishes to thank his family for never telling him to turn his KISS music down:

My mother, Carol Sharp, Jim Sharp, Margie Sharp, Carol Paula Sharp, Larry Sharp, and my lovable basset hound, Herman.

Ken offers a concert arena alight with Bic lighters to those individuals who graciously consented to be interviewed for this project: Ian Anderson, Giuseppe Andrews, Mark Anthony, Carmine Appice, Rod Argent, Bill Aucoin, Kevin Bacon, Joseph Barbera, Jean Beauvoir, Joyce Bogart, Jim Bonfanti, Jon Bon Jovi, Richard Bosworth, Ron Boutwell, Don Brewer, Joel Brodsky, Michael Bruce, Steve Buslowe, Jonathan Cain,

Captain & Tennille, Eric Carmen, Peppy Castro, Paul Chavarria, Desmond Child, Dave Clark, Maria Contessa, Alice Cooper, Steve Coronel, Stan Cornyn, Fin Costello, Jayne County, Peter Criss, Curt Cuomo, Roger Daltrey, Dave Davies, Paul Dean, James DeBello, Sean Delaney, Rick Derringer, Buck Dharma, Frank Dimino, Mike Dirnt, Carl V. Dupré, John Entwistle, Bob Ezrin, Bruce Fairbairn, John Fannon, Anton Fig, Richie Fontana, Kim Fowley, Peter Frampton, Ace Frehley, Ian Gillan, Steve Gerber, Danny Goldberg, Bob Gruen, Rob Halford, William Hanna, Tom Harper, Larry Harris, John Harte, Jimmy Haslip, Dave Hill, Dave Hlubeck, Noddy Holder, Steve Howe, Mark Hudson, Ian Hunter, Janis Ian, Michael James Jackson, Mikel Japp, Ron Johnsen, John Paul Jones, Doug Katsaros, Carol Kaye, Kenny Kerner, Eddie Kramer, Lenny Kravitz, Robby Krieger, Harvey Kubernik, Bob Kulick, Bruce Kulick, Jim Lea, Geddy Lee, Stan Lee, Ron Leejack, Julian Lennon, Bill Lettang, Alex Lifeson, Barry Mann, Ray Manzarek, Brian May, Larry Mazer, Gerard McMahon, Jay Messina, Brett Michaels, Billy Miller, Adam Mitchell, Lee Neaves, Ron Nevison, Rick Nielsen, Ted Nugent, John Oates, Ozzy Osbourne, Brooke Ostrander, Stan Penridge, Joe Perry, Cynthia Plaster Caster, Mike Plotnikoff, Vini Poncia, Don Powell, Dee Dee Ramone, Joey Ramone, Johnny Ramone, Marky Ramone, Richie Ranno, Bruce Redoute, Adam Rifkin, Paul Rodgers, Al Ross, Carol Ross, Mark St. John, Hank Schmel, Allan Schwartzberg, Norman Seeff, Bob Seger, George Sewitt, Kim Simmonds, Gene Simmons, Eric Singer, Nikki Sixx, Neil Smith, Rick Springfield, Billy Squier, Victor Stabin, Paul Stanley, Ringo Starr, Corky Stasiak, Tim Sullivan, Sylvain Sylvain, Tommy Thayer, Pete Townshend, Stephanie Tudor, Jaan Uhelszki, Kathy Valentine, Frankie Valli, Vinnie Vincent, Dick Wagner, Diane Warren, Mitch Weissman, Tom Werman, Paul Westerberg, Brad Whitford, Brian Wilson, Nancy Wilson, Richie Wise, Dave Wittman, Dennis Woloch, Roy Wood, Angus Young, James Young, and Tony Zarrella.

And lastly to KISS—Paul Stanley, Gene Simmons, Ace Frehley, and Peter Criss—our eternal gratitude for sharing their memories . . .